D1620779

International Macroeconomic Dynamics

International Macroeconomic Dynamics

Stephen J. Turnovsky

The MIT Press
Cambridge, Massachusetts
London, England

Second printing, 1999

© 1997 Massachusetts Institute of Technology

All rights reserved. No part of this book may be reproduced in any form by any electronic or mechanical means (including photocopying, recording, or information storage and retrieval) without permission in writing from the publisher.

This book was set in Times New Roman on the Monotype "Prism Plus" PostScript Imagesetter by Asco Trade Typesetting Ltd., Hong Kong.

Printed and bound in the United States of America.

Library of Congress Cataloging-in-Publication Data

Turnovsky, Stephen J.
  International macroeconomic dynamics / Stephen J. Turnovsky.
    p. cm.
  Includes bibliographical references and index.
  ISBN 0-262-20111-9 (alk. paper)
  1. International economic relations—Econometric models.
2. Macroeconomics—Econometric models. 3. International finance—Econometric models. I. Title.
HF1359.T88   1997
337—dc21   97-22966
                                                                     CIP

Contents

	Preface	ix
1	**Introduction and Overview**	1
	1.1 Some General Background	1
	1.2 Scope of the Book	4
	1.3 Equilibrium and the Representative Agent Model	6
	1.4 Outline of the Book	8
I	**SMALL OPEN ECONOMY**	15
2	**The Basic One-Good Monetary Model**	17
	2.1 Basic Monetary Model	17
	2.2 Optimal Government Policies: A General Characterization	29
	2.3 Optimal Monetary Growth	31
	2.4 Optimal Monetary-Fiscal Package	35
	2.5 Sluggish Adjustment in Basic Monetary Model	36
	2.6 Upward-Sloping Supply Curve of Debt	42
	2.7 Some Final Comments	47
	Appendix: Saddlepoint Behavior	49
3	**One-Sector Models of Capital Accumulation**	55
	3.1 Introduction	55
	3.2 One-Good Model of Physical Capital Accumulation	57
	3.3 Two-Good Model of Physical Capital Accumulation	77
	3.4 The Laursen-Metzler Effect	83
	3.5 Tariffs	86
	3.6 Some Final Comments	93
	Appendix: Formal Solutions for Temporary Disturbances	94
4	**Two-Sector Models**	101
	4.1 The Dependent Economy Model: Some Background	102
	4.2 The Two-Sector Dependent Economy	105
	4.3 Analysis of Structural Shocks	115
	4.4 Traded Investment in the Dependent Economy Model	121
	4.5 Traded versus Nontraded Capital in the Dependent Economy Model	123
	4.6 Dependent Economy Model with Traded and Nontraded Capital	125
	4.7 Structural Shocks with Two Types of Capital	134
	4.8 Generalizations of Production Technology	142
	Appendix	146

5	**Capital Accumulation and Long-Run Growth**	151
	5.1 Introduction	151
	5.2 One-Good Model of Endogenous Growth	158
	5.3 Equilibrium in One-Good Model	164
	5.4 Utility-Enhancing Government Expenditure	169
	5.5 Some Extensions to One-Good Model	176
	5.6 Two-Sector Model of Endogenous Growth	182
	5.7 Determination of Equilibrium in Two-Sector Model	185
	5.8 Applications of the Two-Sector Model	197
	5.9 Some Final Comments	203
II	**TWO-COUNTRY MODELS**	207
6	**Fiscal Policy in a Two-Country World Economy**	209
	6.1 Fiscal Policy Shocks	210
	6.2 Two-Country Macroeconomic Structure	213
	6.3 Viability of Alternative Tax Regimes	217
	6.4 Macroeconomic Equilibrium	220
	6.5 Transmission of Tax Shocks under a Source-Based Taxation Regime	225
	6.6 Government Consumption Expenditure and Endogenous Labor Supply	231
	6.7 Macroeconomic Equilibrium in Expanded Model	234
	6.8 Government Expenditure under Alternative Forms of Tax Financing	237
	6.9 Welfare Effects	246
	6.10 Conclusions	249
7	**Relative Price Adjustments in Two-Country Models**	253
	7.1 Adjustment Costs in a Two-Country World	254
	7.2 Macroeconomic Equilibrium	257
	7.3 A Two-Good, Two-Country World	261
	7.4 Equilibrium Dynamics in a Two-Good, Two-Country World	267
8	**Strategic Behavior in the World Economy**	279
	8.1 Strategic Behavior in International Economics: Some Background	279
	8.2 A Simple Two-Country Model with Two Types of Government Expenditure	283
	8.3 Noncooperative Strategic Behavior	297
	8.4 Noncooperative Behavior and Bimatrix Games	301

	8.5	Cooperative Equilibrium	305
	8.6	Strategic Behavior in a Two-Good Model	307
	8.7	A Simple Dynamic Game Theory Formulation	314
	8.8	Some Final Remarks	318

III STOCHASTIC GROWTH MODELS — 323

9 Stochastic Growth in a Small Open Economy — 325

9.1	Introduction	325
9.2	Some Basic Results from Continuous-Time Stochastic Calculus	327
9.3	Stochastic Small Open Economy	333
9.4	Macroeconomic Equilibrium	339
9.5	Equilibrium Solutions	343
9.6	Stochastic Terms of Trade Shocks	347
9.7	Terms of Trade Shocks and Growth	350
9.8	Terms of Trade Shocks and the External Account	354
9.9	Terms of Trade Shocks and Welfare	356
9.10	Effects of Income Taxes	357
9.11	Optimal Tax Policy	361
9.12	Optimal Integrated Fiscal Policy	363
	Appendix	367

10 A Stochastic Monetary Growth Model and Financial Policy — 373

10.1	Introduction	373
10.2	The Analytical Framework	376
10.3	Macroeconomic Equilibrium	386
10.4	Equilibrium Properties	396
10.5	Risk and the Equilibrium Growth Rate	402
10.6	Applications to Issues in International Finance	406
10.7	Government Finance Policy and Welfare	411
10.8	The Optimal Target Interest Rate	413
10.9	Alternative Financial Rules	416
10.10	Optimal Debt Policy	418
10.11	Some Final Comments	420

11 Stochastic Growth in the World Economy — 425

11.1	Introduction	425
11.2	Two-Country Stochastic World Economy	426
11.3	Equilibrium in the World Economy	430

11.4	Effects of Risky Investment on Growth and Welfare	437
11.5	Effects of Production Risk on the World Economy	439
11.6	Effects of Government Expenditure	444
11.7	Export Instability, Growth, and Investment	446
11.8	Contemporaneous Responses to Current Shocks and Real Business Cycle Models	448
11.9	Nontraded Consumption and the Real Exchange Rate	455
11.10	Distortionary Taxes and Growth	459
11.11	Some Final Comments	460
References		463
Index		481

Preface

One of the most significant developments in macroeconomics during recent years has been the increasingly central role played by international transactions in both goods and assets. Economists working in small open economies have always been acutely aware that the international environment is critical to the understanding of how these economies operate and the macroeconomic policy options they face. But it is now generally accepted that large economies like the United States, which have traditionally viewed themselves as more or less closed, also operate in a global environment, and that this must be recognized when studying the macroeconomic policies of such economies, as well.

Changes in the methods of macroeconomic analysis have been mirrored in the analytical development of international macroeconomics. Thus the IS-LM framework of the 1960s, the asset accumulation models of the 1970s, the rational expectations models of the mid-1970s to the mid-1980s, and the more recent representative agent models all have their counterparts in the study of international macroeconomics. During this evolutionary process, models have increased in rigor; logical consistency and rationality have been increasingly emphasized. As part of this development, the need to provide macro models with firm microeconomic foundations—meaning that they should be derived from some form of intertemporal optimization—has become the dominant focus since the 1980s. Many variants of such models exist, and although they continue to dominate current research in macroeconomics theory, they receive their share of criticism. The usefulness of the representative agent framework has certainly come into question, and no doubt it, too, will be superseded over time.

The evolution of general macrodynamic models is the theme of my book, *Methods of Macroeconomic Dynamics*, published in 1995 by The MIT Press. Most of that book is devoted to the development of rational expectations and the representative agent model, the latter in both a deterministic and a continuous-time stochastic framework. International aspects are dispersed throughout the book, but mainly as illustrative examples, and not with the intention of providing a systematic treatment of international macroeconomic dynamics per se. But, given the growing interest in the subject, such a focus is desirable.

The objective of this book is to provide a systematic treatment of the representative agent model in an international economy, in both a deterministic and a stochastic context. By focusing on this particular paradigm, the book is not intended to be a comprehensive treatment of the entire field of international macroeconomics and finance. Instead, it is intended to provide an in-depth coverage of a series of important macroeconomic dynamic models as applied to the international economy. As in my 1995 book, the emphasis is very much on the development of the analytical models themselves. While the models are applied to a range of important issues, the issues chosen frequently are only illustrative, and the reader is invited to view the analysis as a blueprint for other applications.

My interests in international macroeconomics date back to the period I spent at the Australian National University during the 1970s. Australia is a good example of a country in which international considerations play a central role in the teaching, research, and practice of macroeconomics. Since that time I have regularly taught graduate courses in international macroeconomics at the University of Illinois and, more recently, at the University of Washington. These courses have evolved over time with the field, and during more recent years they have been based on the material of this book. In addition, over the past several years I have had the opportunity to teach short graduate level topics courses on various aspects of international macroeconomics; these, too, have helped shape this book. The first of these short courses was in 1989 as part of the "Network Quantitative Economics" program organized by a consortium of Dutch universities and taught that year at the University of Leiden. Subsequent courses were taught at Palm Cove, Australia, in September 1993; the Winter School, Delhi School of Economics, in December 1995; the Bank of Portugal, in April 1996, and the Institute of Advanced Studies, Vienna, in September 1996.

As will be evident from reading the volume, much of the material is drawn from my own research efforts since the later 1980s. It therefore represents a somewhat personalized approach to the subject. At the same time, I have always tried to direct my work toward issues that most economists would regard as being central to international macroeconomics, so I like to view the focus as very much in the mainstream. In all cases, where the exposition has been drawn from previous material, it has been extensively revised, adapted, updated, sometimes generalized, and modified in order to present a coherent, unified approach to the subject. Thus, the book can be viewed as being a research monograph, though with the emphasis on unity and exposition, it is to be hoped that it may serve as a textbook for a second-year graduate course in international macroeconomics, particularly one in which the focus is on the development and analysis of dynamic models.

Chapter 2 is based in part on "Optimal Monetary Growth Accommodating Fiscal Policy in a Small Open Economy, *Journal of International Money and Finance* 6 (1987). The first part of Chapter 4 is drawn from "Investment in a Two-Sector Dependent Economy," *Journal of Japanese and International Economies* 9 (1995), written with Partha Sen; the latter part of that chapter is adapted from "The Dependent Economy Model with Traded and Nontraded Capital," *Review of International Economics*, 2 (1994) written with Philip L. Brock. The one-sector model of Chapter 5 is adapted from "Fiscal Policy, Growth and Macroeconomic Performance in a Small Open Economy," *Journal of International Economics* 40 (1996). The two-sector model is drawn from "Endogenous Growth in a Dependent Economy with Traded and Nontraded Capital," *Review of International Economics* 4 (1996).

The basic model in Chapter 6 is adapted from "The International Transmission of Tax Policies in a Dynamic World Economy," *Review of International Economics* 1 (1992), and the analysis of government expenditure shocks is adapted from "International Effects of Government Expenditure in Interdependent Economies," *Canadian Journal of Economics* 30 (1997), both written with Marcelo Bianconi. The analysis of strategic policy in Chapter 8 draws upon an unpublished manuscript written with Bianconi.

The analysis of terms of trade shocks in Chapter 9 is drawn from "The Impact of Terms of Trade Shocks on a Small Open Economy," *Journal of International Money and Finance* 12 (1993). The analysis of tax policy is an extension of the first part of "Capital Income and Risk-Taking in a Small Open Economy," *Journal of Public Economics*, written with Patrick Asea. The material in Chapter 10 is adapted from my paper with Earl Grinols, "Optimal Government Finance Policy and Exchange Rate Management in a Stochastically Growing Open Economy," *Journal of International Money and Finance* 15 (1996).

I wish to reiterate, however, that, being free of the constraints imposed by limitations of journal space, the exposition here tends to be more leisurely, with more attention being paid to ensure that sufficient details and intuition are included, so as to make the discussion as comprehensible as possible. Also, in many cases, the analysis has been modified in substantive ways.

Much of my work has been done with colleagues and former students, and it is a pleasure to acknowledge their contributions, either directly, in the joint works noted above, or indirectly, as discussed elsewhere in this volume. In this regard, I wish to express my gratitude to Patrick Asea, Arthur Benavie, Marcelo Bianconi, Philip Brock, William Brock, Max Corden, Walter Fisher, Earl Grinols, and Partha Sen. I am also grateful to Marcelo Bianconi, Philip Brock, Michael Devereux, Theo Eicher, Charles Engel, Walter Fisher, Ken Kletzer, Vasco d'Orey, Søren Nielsen, and Partha Sen for comments on specific parts of the manuscript at various stages, or on the underlying research. Comments by graduate students in international macroeconomics at the University of Washington, who were exposed to parts of the material in draft form, as well as by participants in the short courses abroad, were helpful. I wish to thank Duk Joon Ahn and Santanu Chatterjee for proofreading the manuscript, and Christian Murray for preparing the index. I am grateful to Terry Vaughn, Victoria Richardson, and Melissa Vaughn of The MIT Press for their efficient handling of this project and to the anonymous reviewers for their helpful comments. Finally, as in the past, I am grateful to my wife, Michelle, for her patience and support.

1 Introduction and Overview

1.1 Some General Background

International macroeconomics has become an area of intensive research activity since the early 1960s. For many years, macroeconomics as taught and studied, particularly in the United States, dealt almost exclusively with a closed economy. International aspects were neglected, or at best treated in passing. Recently there has been a pronounced shift in this view, and international transactions are now treated as a much more integral part of the macroeconomic system. It is increasingly recognized that one cannot fully understand domestic macroeconomic relationships without considering the global economy within which each country operates. This realization has stimulated research activity in the area of international macroeconomics.

Several considerations have led to the growing interest in international macroeconomics. One is the increased integration of world financial markets. Another is the increased appreciation of the interdependence that exists between fiscal deficits, on the one hand, and trade deficits, on the other. For given levels of national savings and investment, an increase in a country's fiscal deficit must be matched by an equivalent increase in its trade deficit. A third reason for the increased awareness of the international dimensions of macroeconomics may be attributed to changing political structures and economic relationships between countries, the most significant of which is the development of the European Union. The specific issues at the forefront of policy discussions and the resulting attention that they have received from researchers have changed over time. The international macroeconomic models of the 1970s were motivated primarily by monetary issues and the transmission of monetary shocks in a world of increasingly flexible exchange rates and integrated financial markets. By contrast, the 1980s saw a decided switch in interest toward fiscal issues. There is no doubt that this could, to a large degree, be attributed to the growing U.S. government deficit and its implications for the U.S. trade deficit, and the repercussions for those of its trading partners. More recently, with the development of the European monetary union, issues such as exchange rate target zones and the harmonization of tax regimes have become widely discussed.

The analytical methods employed by economists to address issues in international macroeconomics have changed dramatically over the years. An important milestone in the development of the subject was the work by Mundell (1962) and Fleming (1962). The so-called Mundell-Fleming model, pioneered by these authors and pursued by others, was a static one, in effect being an extension of the standard IS-LM model to an open economy.

The subsequent evolution of international macroeconomics paralleled the corresponding developments in the macroeconomics of a closed economy. The 1970s saw the development of macrodynamic models that emphasized the process of asset accumulation as being the key source of dynamics. In the closed economy the assets were of domestic origin, consisting of domestic money, government bonds, and physical capital. In the open economy foreign assets were a further source of wealth accumulation. The dynamics of this type of system were emphasized, for both the closed economy and the open economy, in Turnovsky (1977), where I referred to them as representing the *intrinsic dynamics* of the macroeconomic system. By that I meant that they were an integral part of a consistent macroeconomic system stemming directly from the relationships linking stocks and flows in the economy. These relationships necessarily impose a dynamic structure on the economy, even if all the underlying behavioral relationships are static, because the accumulation of wealth causes these behavioral relationships to shift over time. These dynamics were backward looking, in the sense that the economy, whether closed or open, was assumed to evolve gradually from some given initial state defined by its initial endowment of assets.

In the mid-1970s two major developments heavily influenced the subsequent development of international macroeconomics. The first was the seminal paper by Dornbusch (1976) dealing with the issue of "exchange rate overshooting." That model contrasted the dynamics of exchange rates, which were free to respond instantaneously to clear financial markets, on the one hand, with the adjustment of output price, which was constrained to move gradually to clear the commodity market, on the other hand. This combination of assumptions imposed the burden of short-run equilibrating adjustments on the exchange rate. In particular, a sustained monetary expansion was shown to cause the short-run response of the exchange rate to overshoot its long-run adjustment. This phenomenon of overshooting, showing how domestic monetary policy could induce instability in the economy's exchange rate, was a very strong proposition. It led to an industry of papers addressing its robustness with respect to alternative models. The Dornbusch model itself abstracted from asset accumulation dynamics; subsequent authors combined the exchange rate and price dynamics of the original model with the accumulation of financial assets (see, e.g., Dornbusch and Fischer 1980).

The second major development in the mid-1970s was the impact of rational expectations on macroeconomics in general, and on international macroeconomics in particular. The key methodological innovation here was the observation that while certain economic variables were *backward looking*, others embodied expectations about the future and were *forward looking*. This view fundamentally changed the way macroeconomic dynamics were carried out. Instead of starting from some given initial state, macrodynamics were determined by a combination of backward-looking and forward-looking dynamics, reflecting the fact that some economic variables are tied to the past, whereas others are looking to the future. This distinction was embodied in macrodynamics by treating some variables as "jump variables," meaning that they can respond instantaneously to new information as it becomes available, and other variables as "sluggish variables," meaning that their evolution is constrained to continuous adjustments over time. In the case of the Dornbusch model, the exchange rate was treated as an example of the former, and the price level was an example of the latter. In other contexts, the capital stock is naturally treated as being sluggish, while prices often serve the role of jump variables.

Rational expectations are typically associated with saddlepoint behavior, in which the dynamics of the system involves stable as well as unstable elements. In order for a dynamic system to have a unique, stable equilibrium path, the number of jump variables has to equal the number of unstable roots (see Blanchard and Kahn 1980; Buiter 1984). Thus the existence of jump variables has become an important part of the determination of a well-defined dynamic equilibrium solution.

A second strand of the rational expectations literature was the development of linear stochastic models. These were basically extensions of the new classical rational expectations models to the open economy. This proved to be a particularly fertile application of this framework because the underlying assumptions concerning market efficiency and information were particularly appropriate insofar as the foreign exchange market was concerned. This stochastic approach provided a convenient framework for categorizing disturbances according to whether they were temporary or permanent, anticipated or unanticipated, all of which are factors determining how they will impact on the economy.

The rational expectations methodology dominated macroeconomic dynamics from around 1975 to 1985. One criticism leveled at it was the view that while the models assumed rational behavior in the sense of expectations not being systematically wrong, the rest of the model in which the expectations were embedded typically was arbitrarily specified. Critics argued that a good macro model should be based on sound microeconomic foundations, and that involved deriving the behavioral relationships of the macro model from the intertemporal optimization of micro agents. This has led to the so-called representative agent model, which has become the dominant macro paradigm. This has been true for both general macroeconomics and international macroeconomics.

Most of the literature employing the representative agent framework is deterministic. Stochastic intertemporal optimization is difficult and often very formal. One approach that many researchers have found to be fruitful is the method of continuous-time stochastic calculus. This has played a prominent role in the theory of finance, and in particular in international finance; it has been less used in macroeconomic dynamics, although that is gradually changing. A brief review of this literature is provided by Malliaris and Brock (1982) and Turnovsky (1995). The main problem with the method is that it is tractable only under restrictive conditions and for specific functional forms. But when it is tractable, it offers tremendous insight and, in my experience, is more transparent than the corresponding discrete time methods. Under the assumption that the underlying stochastic processes are Brownian motions, it naturally leads to an equilibrium in which the means and variances of the relevant variables are jointly determined. This has the advantage of being able to integrate issues in finance, which are of relevance to macroeconomics, and international macroeconomics, in a meaningful way. Questions such as the determinants of the foreign-exchange risk premium and the effect of risk on key macroeconomic indicators of performance, such as growth and inflation, can now be addressed in a tractable and enlightening way.

1.2 Scope of the Book

In Turnovsky (1995) I attempt to provide a general overview of the evolution in the methods of macroeconomic dynamics. Most of that book is devoted to a closed economy, though examples applying the various methods to an international economy are provided. However, that book does not attempt to present a systematic treatment of the application of the methods of macrodynamics to an international context. Yet much of the interest in macroeconomics these days pertains to the open economy and to the international aspects. Interest in the international aspects of macroeconomics has traditionally been strong in Europe, Latin America, Asia, and Australasia, where the proportion of GDP devoted to international activities has always been high. With the globalization of the world economy, it is becoming increasingly important in the United States.

The objective of this book is to provide a systematic treatment of the representative agent model in an international economy, in both deterministic and stochastic contexts. But by focusing on this particular paradigm, the book is not intended to be a comprehensive treatment of the entire field of international macroeconomics and finance. It does not deal with the earlier models, such as the Mundell-Fleming, sticky price Dornbusch, or new classical models. Nor does it discuss empirical or institutional issues pertaining to international finance. Exchange rate determination is dealt with as part of the macroeconomic equilibrium process, rather than as a detailed topic in its own right. Exchange rate policy and exchange market intervention are given only passing treatment in the development of the stochastic monetary growth model of Chapter 10. While the accumulation of foreign debt is a central part of the macrodynamic system we develop, for the most part this is treated from the standpoint of an advanced economy having unlimited access to a perfect world capital market. Issues related to sovereign debt and Third World problems are not addressed in detail; they are only touched upon in two places where the implications of an upward-sloping supply curve of debt, which such economies are likely to face, are addressed. There is a growing number of excellent books providing a more general overview of recent developments in international macroeconomics and finance. Among them, Obstfeld and Rogoff (1996) is notable for its exhaustive coverage of almost the entire field. Frenkel and Razin (1987), and its revision Frenkel, Razin, and Yuen (1996), consider a narrower range of topics, focusing mainly on fiscal policy and growth; in this respect their coverage is closer to that of the present volume. They differ by discussing a wider range of models, including earlier models, but not considering the intertemporal and stochastic aspects in the depth that we pursue them here. Finally, Agénor and Montiel (1996) provide a comprehensive treatment of macroeconomics from the standpoint of a developing economy.

In focusing on the intertemporal optimizing representative agent model, like Turnovsky (1995) the emphasis is on familiarizing the reader with the tools necessary to analyze such models. To accomplish this, the book develops a sequence of models of increasing complexity that deal with a variety of issues that are important to international macroeconomics. The focus is very much on the formulation and rigorous analysis of these models. The book begins with an extensive discussion of models of a small open economy. It then extends this framework to address issues relevant to a two-country world economy, and finally develops a series of stochastic models that are applied to both small and large economies. We wish to stress that what is being provided is a blueprint, a framework for analyzing a wide range of policy questions. The policies analyzed are selective and chosen to illustrate the workings of the models in various contexts.

There is one methodological matter that arises in the modeling of dynamic economic systems, and that is the choice of discrete versus continuous time. The merits of each has been long debated and is discussed in Turnovsky (1977). The preference in this book is for continuous-time formulation, mainly because we find it to be more tractable and often more transparent. But to some degree this choice is a question of taste.

1.3 Equilibrium and the Representative Agent Model

Two important concepts in the development of the representative agent model are the notions of *perfect foresight* and a *perfect foresight equilibrium*. The former is the deterministic analog of Muth's (1961) rational expectations hypothesis, the assumption that prediction errors are purely random. This assumption is maintained throughout the book, and its merits have been discussed in Turnovsky (1995, Chapter 3). The latter is defined as follows. The economy is assumed to consist of a large number of identical agents, comprising the households and firms in the economy. These agents make their choices to maximize their respective objective functions; utility maximization for households, profit maximization for firms. In some cases it is possible, without loss of generality, to consolidate the households and firms into a single agent. In any event, carrying out their maximizations yields a set of demand and supply functions for output, labor, and the various assets in the economy, in terms of market prices and asset returns, that the private agents take as given. A perfect foresight equilibrium is then defined as a situation in which the planned demands for output, labor, and the various securities in the economy equal the corresponding supplies; in addition, all anticipated variables are correctly forecast. There are no forecast errors. The perfect foresight equilibrium thus focuses on these equilibrium quantities and imposes conditions ensuring that such an equilibrium always exists.

The representative agent framework has many desirable features (in addition to its tractability), and for this reason has become the standard tool for modern macroeconomic dynamics. First, it is based on rational behavior, embodying forward-looking agents so that the full intertemporal dimensions of the economic environment, both inherited from the past and looking into the future, impact on the evolution of the economy. In particular, the intertemporal budget constraints confronting the private and public sectors in the economy are brought to the fore. Second, by being based on utility maximization, it provides a natural framework for analyzing the welfare implications of macroeconomic policy shocks or other structural changes, which many would argue are of ultimate concern. A third and related advantage is that an equilibrium based on rational behavior serves as a natural benchmark from which deviations in such behavior can be measured. But despite its almost uniform adoption as the current standard macroeconomic paradigm, it is viewed much more critically by economic theorists (see, e.g., Kirman 1992).

The conventional assumption made in macroeconomic theory is that there are many identical agents, whose behavior is summarized by that of the "representative agent." Under certain conditions, such as homothetic utility functions and linearity, aggregation may well be possible and the representative agent may indeed be a reliable representation of the individuals (see, e.g., Lewbel 1989). But such an ideal situation is not generally the case, and Kirman has articulated the difficulties that may arise when they are not met. He illustrates this with a simple example in which, even though the representative agent makes the same choices as the aggregate of choices of the individuals in the economy, the preferences of that agent may be quite opposite to those of the individuals he represents. That being the case, it is a poor indicator for welfare analysis.

A second line of criticism centers on the empirical evidence supporting the representative agent approach. This is frequently done through the estimation of Euler equations, derived as first-order optimality conditions, and are the stochastic analog of the arbitrage relationships that feature prominently throughout this volume. These conditions are frequently rejected by the data. As Kirman discusses, this raises the question of what is being rejected. Is it the particular relationship that is being tested, or the representation of the economy by a single optimizing agent? He argues that one should be focusing on heterogeneous agents, and that some of the paradoxes identified in the data may be the result of the special framework and may be resolved by extending the economy to different agents with different preferences. The same observation has been made by others (see, e.g., Summers 1991; Lippi 1988).

Do these criticisms mean that we should abandon the representative agent model? Kirman seems to suggest that we should, although that view seems extreme. There are several points in support of the representative agent model. First, it is important to have a tightly structured framework to serve as a benchmark and to avoid, or at least reduce, the arbitrariness of the earlier macroeconomic models. For this purpose, the representative agent model is the best available at the present time, although the extent to which it succeeds in eliminating the arbitrariness associated with macroeconomic modeling should be kept in perspective. A good deal of arbitrariness still remains, which is inevitable in any theorizing. The nature of the objective function, the range of decision variables, the specification of the constraints, and the market structure are often taken for granted, yet all are typically subject to choice. Second, few could deny that by emphasizing the importance of intertemporal budget constraints, the representative agent model has enhanced our understanding of intertemporal issues in macroeconomics. Furthermore, while simple examples can be constructed in which the preferences of the aggregate might misrepresent those of diverse agents, it has not been established that this is a significant problem in the analysis of macroeconomic shocks. Simulation analysis by McKibbin (1991) using large econometric models based on intertemporal optimization of representative agents supports this general view. He finds the differences in the aggregate response to macroeconomic disturbances between (1) having a single representative agent and (2) aggregating over the responses of a number of individual agents from a disaggregated version of the model, to be rather small.

Any model as widely employed as the representative agent model has become, begins to take on a life of its own and to be accepted almost as an axiom. It is therefore important in using the model to be aware of its limitations. Despite the criticisms that have been made, we feel that the representative agent model provides a useful framework that offers a lot of insight. But it should be viewed as just a step in the continuing development and understanding of macroeconomic dynamics. Over time, models are superseded; indeed, the extension to heterogeneous agents seems like a promising avenue for future research.

1.4 Outline of the Book

Part I, which consists of Chapters 2 through 5, develops a series of dynamic models for a small open economy. Chapter 2 begins with a basic one-good monetary model of a small open economy in which labor is the only factor of production and all prices are flexible. This serves as a natural starting point, being typical of earlier monetary models, such as Dornbusch and Fischer (1980). Not surprisingly, in the absence of any sluggishness, the dynamics of this basic model degenerate and the equilibrium it yields is always in steady state. While this may be disappointing from the viewpoint of generating macroeconomic dynamics, it is advantageous in that it enables one to study optimal policy making in a simple, tractable way. Thus we are able to relate optimal policy to such standard propositions as the Friedman (1969) optimal monetary rule and the trade-off between income tax and inflation introduced by Phelps (1973), both of which were developed in a static framework. In order to derive nondegenerate dynamics, some source of sluggishness must be added to the model. Various sources of sluggishness, such as an endogenous rate of time preference, brokerage costs associated with holding foreign assets, and having overlapping generations are discussed briefly. But the source of sluggishness most stressed, discussed in the latter part of the chapter, is the situation where the economy faces an upward-sloping supply curve of debt. This as an important extension of the basic model because it not only gets away from some of the awkward consequences associated with assuming a perfect world capital market and a fixed rate of time preference, but also is quite realistic, particularly for developing economies. It is also gradually getting more attention in the literature.

Chapter 3 introduces the most important source of sluggishness, the accumulation of physical capital and its associated adjustment costs. This provides the basic framework upon which subsequent chapters build. The first part of the chapter begins with a one-good model and develops its analytical structure in detail. An increase in government expenditure is used to illustrate the macroeconomic dynamic adjustments generated by permanent and temporary policy shocks, showing how the latter have permanent effects. This is a striking feature, and one that stems from the restrictions necessary in order for a finite steady-state equilibrium to exist in a world of perfect capital mobility. But the one-good model is obviously limited, and in the latter part of the chapter we extend the model—still assuming one productive sector—to include an imported consumption good. This immediately introduces a relative price (real exchange rate), enabling us to address some of the basic issues in international economics having to do with terms of trade shocks and tariffs. Much of this literature has been developed in a static trade context, and important insights are obtained by analyzing it in an intertemporal macroeconomic context.

International trading activities affect different parts of the economy differently. These cannot be adequately captured in a one-sector framework, and it is therefore important to extend the analysis to a multisector framework. This is undertaken in Chapter 4. It begins by developing the dependent economy model, which has served as one of the basic workhorse models in studying issues such as the real exchange rate. Despite its long history, this model has only rather recently been extended to incorporate capital accumulation. An important issue here concerns the tradability or nontradability of capital, and this issue is dealt with at length. The analysis begins by introducing each form of capital separately, analyzing various forms of demand and supply shocks in this framework. It then goes on to develop a more general model that incorporates both forms of capital simultaneously, showing how the production characteristics of nontraded capital are more important for the *internal* dynamics of the economy, while those of traded capital become relevant in determining the *external* dynamics. The latter part of the chapter briefly discusses some variants of the production technology, including costly intersectoral adjustment costs; the role of sector-specific factors of production, which also has a long history in international economics and has recently been incorporated into the intertemporal capital accumulation framework; and the extension to three production sectors.

Economic growth is one of the most fundamental issues in macroeconomics and has a long history. After a fifteen-year hiatus it has again become an area of intensive research activity, with the development of endogenous growth models. The recent work in growth theory has been very wide-ranging, and we do not attempt to provide a comprehensive treatment. That is a huge subject in itself with extensive treatments available (see Grossman and Helpman 1991; Barro and Sala-i-Martin 1995). Rather, Chapter 5 restricts its focus to so-called investment-based growth models that, by imposing restrictions on technology and preferences, yield growth equilibria that are analogous to the stationary equilibria of the capital accumulation models in earlier chapters. But unlike the Ramsey-type growth models, in which the long-run growth rate is fixed by demographic characteristics, these models have the property that fiscal policy is able to influence the long-run equilibrium growth rate. The first part of this chapter develops an endogenous growth analog to the one-sector model of capital accumulation of Chapter 3. This has the characteristic that production and consumption in the economy are always on their respective balanced growth paths; there are no transitional dynamics. Issues pertaining to tax policy and optimal fiscal policy are analyzed. A number of extensions are discussed, including the introduction of traded and nontraded capital, thereby introducing transitional dynamics. This is therefore an endogenous growth analog of the two-sector dependent economy model of Chapter 4. An attractive feature of considering a small open economy is that it becomes possible to solve explicitly for the transitional dynamics, at least to a linear approximation.

Part II is devoted to two-country models and consists of Chapters 6 through 8. Chapter 6 extends the basic one-good model of capital accumulation of Chapter 3 to two symmetric economies producing the same good. The first part develops a model in which labor supply is fixed and analyzes the international transmission of tax shocks. It emphasizes the viability of alternative tax regimes, an issue that has been addressed by several authors, most notably Frenkel, Razin, and Sadka (1991). The model is then extended to endogenize the labor supply. This is important because the shock we shall study is government consumption expenditure, in which the endogeneity of labor supply plays a crucial role in generating the dynamics. We use the model to analyze the effects of government expenditure on activity and economic welfare both in the domestic economy and abroad. The analysis emphasizes the importance of the mode of government financing in determining these effects, and we compare the effects of an expansion in expenditure under (1) lump-sum tax financing; (2) capital income tax financing; and (3) wage income tax financing. Both the domestic effects and the transmission abroad are seen to be sensitive to what one assumes about how the expenditure is being financed.

The analysis of Chapter 6 emphasizes the role of foreign asset accumulation as the source of the international transmission of shocks. It is based on several important assumptions: (1) while the total stock of capital at any instant of time is fixed in the world economy, the existing stocks can be instantaneously and costlessly shuffled between the economies at any point of time; (2) agents have equal, unrestricted access to the assets of both economies; (3) the existence of a single traded good. These are obviously restrictive assumptions and are modified in the two models developed in Chapter 7. In the first of these, capital accumulation involves adjustment costs, as it did in the models of the small open economy. The introduction of such costs implies that the initial response of the world economy to an unanticipated shock is a jump in the shadow value of capital, rather than an instantaneous reshuffling of the stocks. In addition, the adjustment costs associated with capital (its shadow value) become a critical part of the dynamics of the world economy. The second model relaxes assumptions (2) and (3). Each country specializes in the production of a (different) single good, and the representative agent is now permitted to hold only domestic capital and traded bonds. The adjustment of relative prices, absent in the one-good model, becomes critical in the dynamics of the world economy.

Once it is recognized that policy in one country has spillovers abroad, the potential for strategic behavior by policy makers is introduced. This has long been recognized in discussions of the optimal tariff and commercial policy, but the more general macrodynamic consequences have only rather recently begun to receive attention. An introduction to these issues is provided in Chapter 8, where we focus on fiscal policy. Since the spillovers are sensitive to the nature of the government expenditure—whether it is on a consumption good or on a production good—the chapter begins by comparing the transmission and dynamics associated with both types of government expenditure. They are markedly different, and the contrast between them is brought out most sharply in the case where the labor supply is fixed. Various types of strategic behavior are discussed. We begin with noncooperative games, where each policy maker acts like a Nash player, taking the decisions of his rival as given when making his own decisions. Several such games, corresponding to alternative assumptions regarding the form of government expenditure and the mode of financing, are considered. The choice of financing and the corresponding combination of actions give rise to what is known as a bimatrix game, and we can analyze the optimal mode of financing as being to determine the Nash equilibrium outcome of such a game. Other topics discussed include cooperative behavior and the gains from cooperation; the chapter concludes with a brief introduction to some key solution concepts from dynamic game theory.

Part III, consisting of Chapters 9 through 11, develops a series of continuous-time stochastic models. The models are all linear, having a stable stochastic growth rate, so that Part III can be viewed as the development of stochastic endogenous growth models of the international economy. In this regard the models build on Chapters 5 and 6, although some of the issues they address were studied in the absence of risk in Chapters 2 and 3.

Chapter 9 reviews the basic methods of continuous-time stochastic calculus. These methods are not familiar to most advanced students and generally are not included in basic graduate courses. Thus it is convenient to begin with a brief summary of the basic techniques that will be used. They are very attractive and, when tractable, provide considerable insight. The next two parts of the chapter use these methods to derive the equilibrium of a simple model of a stochastically growing economy, using it to address two important issues. The first, the analysis of terms of trade shocks, enables us to extend the discussion of issues related to the Laursen-Metzler effect, introduced in Chapter 3, to a stochastic context. The second application of the model is the analysis of tax shocks in a stochastically growing economy. This is important because the viability issues stressed in a deterministic context evaporate once risk is introduced. The effects of tax shocks on portfolio adjustment, growth, and economic welfare are analyzed. Issues relating to optimal fiscal policy in a stochastic economy and the relationship to optimal fiscal policy in the absence of risk, as discussed in Chapter 5, are also considered.

Chapter 10 applies the stochastic optimizing techniques to develop a mean-variance equilibrium model for a stochastic small open economy augmented by the inclusion of a monetary sector. The model is then used to focus on three general issues. First, it examines the effects of means and variances of the policy shocks and other structural changes on the equilibrium, and in particular on the equilibrium growth rate. Next, it addresses several topics in international finance, including the determination of the foreign exchange risk premium and capital asset pricing relationships. The third major question that the model addresses is monetary policy, in particular, optimal exchange rate management. This issue received a lot of attention in the 1980s, using a very different framework; the current approach, based on intertemporal stochastic optimization in a growing economy, offers interesting new perspectives.

The final chapter develops a two-country stochastic model to analyze issues pertaining to growth and capital accumulation in the world economy, then uses the model to address a range of questions. The first is the role of international risk sharing in influencing growth and welfare, an issue addressed in a similar type of model by Obstfeld (1994). The second issue is the response of the stochastic equilibrium to changes in its stochastic structure, in particular the effects of productivity risk, as measured by the variances of the productivity shocks, on growth and welfare. This focus on the structural effects of risk contrasts with that of the real business cycle literature, which directs its attention to the short-run stochastic comovements (correlations) between certain key variables. Since our model is similar in dimension to that typically employed by real business cycle theorists, the latter part of the chapter considers some of the correlations between contemporaneous shocks, thereby relating our framework to that approach.

I SMALL OPEN ECONOMY

2 The Basic One-Good Monetary Model

This chapter begins with what is a natural extension of a simple, but standard, monetary model of the 1970s. It consists of a single traded good produced by a single factor of production, labor, and two assets, domestic money and traded bonds. The main point to emerge from this initial analysis is that in the absence of any sluggishness, the dynamics in this simple model degenerate. That is, the economy must always be in steady-state equilibrium. The degeneracy of the dynamics imposes constraints on the options available to the policy maker. Appropriate accommodation by some policy instrument, either fiscal or monetary, is required to ensure that the equilibrium is sustainable, given the aggregate budget constraint facing the economy.

The characteristics of the equilibrium, such as the level of employment and trade balance, depend upon the chosen policy parameters and method of accommodation. This naturally leads into questions of optimal policy making, and the representative agent optimizing framework we shall develop provides a convenient framework in which to address these issues. Thus, for example, the optimal rate of monetary growth depends critically upon what the accommodating fiscal policy variable is chosen to be. Moreover, the fact that the equilibrium requires some fiscal accommodation leads naturally to a second issue, the determination of optimal fiscal policy in conjunction with the optimal rate of monetary growth. One advantage of the absence of dynamics is that these issues become particularly tractable to analyze and are addressed in Sections 2.2–2.4.

Thus some form of sluggish behavior is crucial to introducing dynamics into this economy. There are several ways that this can be accomplished. Some of these, discussed in Section 2.5, include (1) the introduction of a variable rate of time preference; (2) the introduction of transactions costs in the foreign bond market; (3) the introduction of overlapping generations of agents. But the form of sluggishness most emphasized is that of an upward-sloping supply curve of debt. A small model embodying this assumption is developed in Section 2.6. The discussion illustrates how the functional form one specifies for this relationship is important in determining the extent to which it generates dynamics in response to specific shocks. Finally, much of the analysis throughout this volume involves saddlepoint behavior. The Appendix summarizes some of the basic results necessary to employ these methods.

2.1 Basic Monetary Model

We begin by specifying a monetary model of a small open economy operating in a world of ongoing inflation. The economy consists of three types of agents: consumers, firms, and the government. All consumers and firms are assumed to be identical, enabling us to focus on the representative individual in each group. Agents are assumed to have perfect foresight.

Structure of Economy

The environment we consider is characteristic of those assumed in the standard monetary models of the 1970s (see, e.g., Dornbusch and Fischer 1980). The domestic economy produces and consumes a single traded good, the foreign price of which is given in the world market. In the absence of any impediments to trade, purchasing power parity (*PPP*) is assumed to hold; expressed in percentage change terms, it is described by

$$p = q + e, \tag{2.1a}$$

where

p = rate of inflation of the good in terms of domestic currency,

q = rate of inflation of the good in terms of foreign currency, assumed to be exogenously given to the small economy,

e = rate of exchange depreciation of domestic currency.

This equation asserts that under free trade the rate of inflation in the domestic economy must equal the exogenously given world rate of inflation, plus the rate of depreciation of the domestic currency.

We assume that domestic residents holds two assets. The first is domestic money, which is not held by foreigners. Second, we assume that there is a traded world bond, with uncovered interest parity (*UIP*) holding at all times. Thus,

$$i = i^* + \varepsilon, \tag{2.1b}$$

where

i = domestic nominal interest rate,

i^* = foreign nominal interest rate, assumed to be exogenously given,

ε = expected rate of exchange depreciation.

Under the assumption of perfect foresight, the expected rate of exchange depreciation, ε, equals the actual rate of exchange depreciation, e.

The assumptions we have made of *PPP* and *UIP* are standard benchmarks in the international macroeconomic literature. We do not pretend that they are good assumptions empirically. They generally are not.[1] They do, however, serve as a natural starting point from which the analysis can be extended.

The representative consumer is assumed to choose his level of consumption, labor supply, real money balances, and holdings of the traded bond by solving the following intertemporal optimization problem:[2]

$$\text{Maximize} \int_0^\infty U(c, l, m, g) e^{-\beta t} dt \quad U_c > 0, U_l < 0, U_g > 0, \quad (2.2a)$$

subject to the budget constraint, expressed in real terms as

$$c + \dot{m} + \dot{b} = (1 - \tau)(wl + \Pi) + (i^* - q)b - (q + e)m - T, \quad (2.2b)$$

and initial conditions

$$m(0) = \frac{M_0}{P(0)}, \quad b(0) = \frac{E(0)B_0}{P(0)} = \frac{B_0}{Q_0}, \quad (2.2c)$$

where

c = real consumption,
g = real government expenditure,
m = real money balances; M = nominal money balances,
b = real stock of traded bonds; B = nominal stock of traded bonds,
l = supply of labor,
w = real wage rate,
Π = real profit, paid out to consumers,
β = rate of time preference, taken to be constant,
P = domestic price level,
Q = foreign price level,
E = nominal exchange rate,
τ = rate of (distortionary) income tax,
T = real lump-sum taxes.

The utility function is assumed to be concave in its four arguments, c, g, l, and m. Consumers are assumed to derive positive marginal utility from the consumption of both private and public goods, but negative marginal utility from providing labor services. We shall assume that for given values of c, g, and l, the marginal utility of money balances satisfies

$$\text{sgn}(U_m) = \text{sgn}(m^* - m),$$

so that m^* defines the corresponding satiation level of real money balances, as in Friedman (1969). For real money holdings less than these satiation balances, the marginal utility of holding money is positive; for money holdings in excess of the satiation balances, the holding costs outweigh the benefits and the net marginal utility of holding money balances becomes negative.

The introduction of money as an argument in the utility function requires comment. It is intended to capture, if only imperfectly, the three key roles of money in the economy: (1) its role as a store of wealth; (2) its role as the medium of exchange; and (3) its role as a unit of account. Within the infinite horizon model two approaches have been adopted to incorporate the role of money. The first is to incorporate its role as a medium of exchange through the so-called cash-in-advance constraint, originally proposed by Clower (1967). The basic idea here is to formulate the role that money plays in carrying out transactions, through the explicit introduction of a "transactions technology." One difficulty with this approach is that the introduction of the various constraints, embodying the role played by money in transactions, can very quickly become intractable. Accordingly, a shorthand alternative to this, originally due to Sidrauski (1967b), is to introduce money directly into the utility function. By facilitating transactions, money is assumed to yield a direct utility to the representative agent that is not associated with other assets such as bonds, which yield only an indirect utility through the income they generate and the consumption goods they enable the agent to purchase.[3]

But the introduction of money into the utility function has often been the subject of criticism by monetary economists, who have argued that one should model the process of transactions explicitly. Recently, however, this criticism appears to have been muted, at least in part because of an important paper by Feenstra (1986), who studied the relationship between these two approaches. He showed that under certain regularity conditions, the maximization problem with money modeled by means of a cash-in-advance constraint may be equivalent to a maximization problem with money in the utility function. Thus the procedure of introducing money directly into the utility function seems to be generally viewed as being an acceptable approximation, and accordingly is the formulation that we shall adopt.

The agent's budget constraint (2.2b) is expressed in real flow terms. At each instant of time the representative household is assumed to acquire resources from a variety of sources. Households supply labor to firms, which they own, at a real wage, w. As owners, they receive profit, Π, with this total factor income being taxed at the rate τ. In addition they hold traded bonds, denominated in foreign currency and paying a nominal interest rate i^* and domestic money balances, the real rates of return on which, given the assumptions of PPP and UIP, are $(i^* - q)$ and $-p = -(q + e)$, respectively. The real interest rate $i^* - q$ is assumed to be positive, and for notational simplicity only, interest income is assumed to be untaxed. Finally, households are subject to lump-sum taxation, T.

In determining his optimal plans for c, l, m, and b the representative consumer is assumed to take g, e, q, Π, w, i^*, E, Q, and P as given. The initial conditions relate to the initial stocks of real bonds and money held by consumers. By definition, these are the corresponding initial nominal stocks, assumed to be accumulated gradually, divided by the initial price level. In the case of the real money stock, this is endogenously determined through an appropriate initial jump in the nominal exchange rate. By contrast, given that foreign prices are assumed to evolve continuously, the initial real stock of traded bonds is predetermined.

To solve the consumer's optimization problem we set up the Hamiltonian

$$H \equiv e^{-\beta t} U(c, l, m, g) + \lambda e^{-\beta t} \{(1 - \tau)(wl + \Pi) + (i^* - q)b - (q + e)m - T - c - \dot{m} - \dot{b}\}, \tag{2.3}$$

where $\lambda(t)$ is the costate variable associated with the agent's budget constraint (2.2b) and represents the marginal utility of wealth, measured in terms of the traded good. The resulting optimality conditions for the agent are described by the following:

$$U_c(c, l, m, g) = \lambda \tag{2.4a}$$

$$U_l(c, l, m, g) = -(1 - \tau)w\lambda \tag{2.4b}$$

$$U_m(c, l, m, g) = (i^* + e)\lambda \tag{2.4c}$$

$$\dot{\lambda} = \lambda[\beta - (i^* - q)]. \tag{2.4d}$$

The first two equations are straightforward static efficiency conditions. Equation (2.4a) asserts that for the consumer to be in equilibrium, the marginal utility of consumption must equal the marginal utility of wealth. Equation (2.4b) requires that the marginal utility of an additional unit of leisure must equal the marginal utility of the consumption forgone, priced at the opportunity cost of a unit of leisure—namely, the after-tax real wage rate. The ratio of these two quantities is a standard marginal rate of substitution relationship linking the ratio of marginal utilities to their relative price, the after-tax real wage.

The remaining two equations are dynamic efficiency conditions relating the returns on assets. To see this, rewrite (2.4c) as

$$\frac{U_m(c, l, m, g)}{\lambda} - p = i^* + e - p = i^* - q. \tag{2.4c'}$$

This equation asserts that the real rate of return on money, which equals the utility from the consumption of money services plus its real return as an income earning asset $(-p)$ must equal the real return on holding traded bonds. In the absence of direct utility benefits, money would be dominated by bonds and would not be held in equilibrium.

Equation (2.4d), rewritten as the arbitrage relationship

$$\beta - \frac{\dot{\lambda}}{\lambda} = i^* - q, \qquad (2.4d')$$

is one of the most fundamental relationships in intertemporal macroeconomics. It asserts that in equilibrium the (equal) rates of return on the two assets in the economy, money and traded bonds, must equal the rate of return on consumption, defined by the left-hand side of (2.4d').

Equation (2.4d') can be derived in a more intuitive way by considering the agent's consumption at two adjacent points in time. Suppose that at time t he decides to decrease consumption by an amount dc; to invest the savings for a short period of time, dt, until time $t + dt$; and then to consume the proceeds. At all other points of time, consumption and asset holdings remain unchanged. The reduction in consumption at time t leads to a utility loss at that time of $U_c(t)\, dc$. With the rate of return on savings being $(i^* - q)$, consumption at time $t + dt$ can be increased to $[1 + (i^* - q)\, dt]\, dc$, the marginal utility of which at time t is discounted to $U_c(t + dt)[1 + (i^* - q)\, dt]e^{-\beta dt}dc$. If the agent is optimizing, the impact of this switch in consumption on intertemporal utility must be zero; that is,

$$U_c(t)\, dc = U_c(t + dt)[1 + (i^* - q)\, dt]e^{-\beta dt}dc.$$

Noting that for small dt, $e^{-\beta dt} \cong 1 - \beta\, dt$, and $U_c(t + dt) \cong U_c(t) + \dot{U}_c(t)\, dt$, this equality can be approximated by

$$U_c(t)\, dc \cong [U_c(t) + \dot{U}_c(t)\, dt][1 + (i^* - q)\, dt][1 - \beta\, dt]\, dc.$$

Expanding the right-hand side and dividing by dc enables us to write the equation in the form

$$\{(\dot{U}_c(t) + U_c[(i^* - q) - \beta]) + o(dt)/dt\}dt = 0,$$

where $o(dt)$ denotes terms of order smaller than dt. Dividing by dt and using the property $\lim_{t \to \infty}(o(dt)/dt) = 0$, we find that as $dt \to 0$, this converges to $\beta - (\dot{U}_c/U_c) = i^* - q$, which is (2.4d'). This relationship will play a prominent role throughout this volume.

Many intertemporal macro models assume that the supply of labor is fixed, and abstract from money, in which case $U_c = U_c(c)$. Differentiating this expression with respect to t, $\dot{\lambda}/\lambda = U_{cc}\dot{c}/U_c$, enabling the intertemporal arbitrage condition (2.4d') to be expressed as

$$\frac{\dot{c}}{c} = -\frac{1}{\eta(c)}[(i^* - q) - \beta], \qquad (2.4d'')$$

where $\eta(c) \equiv U_{cc}c/U_c < 0$ is the elasticity of the marginal utility of consumption with respect to consumption. The quantity η reflects the curvature of the utility function, and for the frequently used logarithmic function, $\eta = -1$. Equation (2.4d'') is known as the Keynes-Ramsey rule and asserts that consumption will be increasing or decreasing over time according to whether the rate of interest is greater or less than the rate of time preference. In the former case, the agent is relatively patient and finds it optimal to reduce consumption in the short run, allowing it to increase over time.

The elasticity η plays a prominent role in macroeconomic dynamics and has been used to measure two distinct characteristics. In a continuous-time deterministic context, such as the present, $-1/\eta$ can be shown to equal the instantaneous elasticity of substitution of consumption over time (see, e.g., Blanchard and Fischer 1989, p. 40). At the same time $-\eta$ also measures the degree of relative risk aversion in a stochastic context (see Part III). The constant elasticity utility function c^γ/γ has the property that both measures are characterized by the same parameter γ. This need not be the case, and a more general utility function that separates out these concepts is used by Obstfeld (1994).[4]

The relationship (2.4d') differs in one important respect from the corresponding condition in the closed economy. With the rate of time preference β and the real interest rate $i^* - q$ both being exogenously given constants from the standpoint of the small open economy, in order for (2.4d') to imply a finite interior steady-state value for the marginal utility λ, we require $\beta = i^* - q$. That is, the rate of time preference must equal the given world real interest rate. But this further implies that $\dot{\lambda} = 0$ for all t, so that the marginal utility of wealth is in fact constant for all time, that is, $\lambda = \bar{\lambda}$. As we will see throughout this volume, this has important consequences for the dynamics. But the choice of constant is not arbitrary; it is endogenously determined as part of the equilibrium. In the case that the labor is supplied inelastically, the constancy of λ implies the constancy of consumption over time; in other words, there is complete "consumption smoothing."

The assumption that the rate of time preference in the small economy equals the given world rate of interest is a standard one in general equilibrium models of a small open economy based on intertemporal optimization. While it is strong and has been the source of criticism of the representative agent model as applied to the small open economy, this assumption is required if an interior equilibrium is to be attained when β and $i^* - q$ are both given constants. One justification is that a small open economy, facing a perfect world capital market, must constrain its rate of time preference by the investment opportunities available to it, and that these opportunities are ultimately determined by the exogenously given rate of return in the world capital market. If that were not the case, the domestic agent would end up either in infinite debt or in infinite credit to the rest of the world, and that would not represent a viable interior equilibrium. The economy would cease to be small.

How acceptable this assumption is depends in part upon the specific shock one is analyzing. For demand and productivity shocks, which typically leave both β and $i^* - q$ unchanged, it is adequate. However, it would be unsatisfactory if one wishes to analyze independent changes in either β or i^*, which would break the assumed equality between them. In this case, one alternative has been to allow the rate of time preferences to be variable. This approach was first adopted by Obstfeld (1981), who endogenizes the consumer rate of time preference through the introduction of Uzawa (1968) preferences, though this, too, is subject to its own criticisms, as we shall note in Section 2.5.

In addition to the optimality conditions set out in (2.4a)–(2.4d), the transversality conditions

$$\lim_{t \to \infty} \lambda m e^{-\beta t} = \lim_{t \to \infty} \lambda b e^{-\beta t} = 0 \tag{2.4e}$$

must be met, thereby ruling out explosive behavior. These equations assert that as long as the agent assigns some positive marginal value to the asset, the present discounted value of its stock at the end of the planning horizon must be reduced to zero. Otherwise, the agent would be wasting what would be a valuable asset. The significance of transversality conditions in ensuring that the intertemporal budget constraints facing both households and the government is met is discussed at length by Turnovsky (1995).

In the absence of physical capital, the firm's optimization problem is simple. It is to hire labor so as to maximize real profit

$$\Pi = F(l) - wl \quad F' > 0, F'' < 0, \tag{2.5}$$

where the production function $F(l)$ has the property of positive but diminishing marginal physical product of labor. The optimality condition equates the marginal product of labor to the real wage:

$$F'(l) = w. \tag{2.6}$$

The final agent, the government, operates in accordance with its flow budget constraint, expressed in real terms as

$$\dot{m} + \dot{a} = g + (i^* - q)a - (q + e)m - \tau(wl + \Pi) - T, \tag{2.7}$$

where $a = A/P =$ real stock of traded bonds issued by the domestic government, and $A =$ nominal stock of bonds. This equation asserts that the real government deficit, which equals its expenditures plus the real interest owing on its debt, less the revenues raised through inflation (the inflation tax), income tax, and lump-sum taxation, must be financed either by issuing more bonds or by printing more money.

Subtracting (2.7) from (2.2b) and noting (2.3), the sectoral budget constraints imply

$$\dot{n} = F(l) - c - g + (i^* - q)n, \tag{2.8}$$

where $n \equiv b - a$ is the net stock of traded bonds (i.e., the net credit) of the domestic economy. That is, the rate of change of net credit of the domestic economy (the rate of accumulation of traded bonds) equals the balance of payments on current account, which in turn equals the balance of trade plus the real interest earned on foreign bond holdings. With a single traded commodity, the balance of trade is simply the excess of domestic production over domestic absorption by the domestic private and government sectors. There is nothing to rule out $n < 0$, in which case the country is a debtor, rather than a creditor, nation. In fact, in our discussion in Section 2.6, it is more natural to focus on a debtor rather than a creditor economy.

To complete the description of the economy, government policy needs to be specified. In general, the government has five policy instruments available to it: M, A, τ, T, and g, any four of which can be chosen independently. While in general these can vary quite arbitrarily over time (though subject to the government's intertemporal budget constraint), one can show that for the perfect foresight equilibrium of the present model, the optimal policies turn out to be stationary over time.[5] Thus we can, without loss of generality, restrict ourselves to constant time-invariant policies at the outset. Specifically, we shall assume that the government allows the domestic nominal money supply to grow at a fixed rate—ϕ, say. The rate of real monetary growth is therefore

$$\dot{m} = (\phi - q - e)m, \tag{2.9a}$$

with the corresponding rate of change of real domestic government bonds being

$$\dot{a} = g + (i^* - q)a - \tau(wl + \Pi) - \phi m - T. \tag{2.9b}$$

Macroeconomic Equilibrium

The macroeconomic equilibrium considered is one where all agents optimize, all markets clear, and there is perfect foresight, so that all expectations are realized. Combining the optimality conditions (2.4a)–(2.4d) of consumers with that of firms, (2.6), together with the definition of profit, (2.5), the accumulation equations (2.2b) and (2.7), policy specification (2.9a), and the current account relationship (2.8), the macroeconomic equilibrium is described by the set of relationships

$$U_c(c, l, m, g) = \bar{\lambda} \tag{2.10a}$$

$$U_l(c, l, m, g) = -F'(l)\bar{\lambda} \tag{2.10b}$$

$$U_m(c, l, m, g) = (i^* + e)\bar{\lambda} \tag{2.10c}$$

$$\dot{m} = (\phi - q - e)m \tag{2.10d}$$

$$\dot{b} = (1 - \tau)F(l) - c + (i^* - q)b - \phi m - T \tag{2.10e}$$

$$\dot{n} = F(l) - c - g + (i^* - q)n, \tag{2.10f}$$

together with the transversality conditions.

The dynamics of this macroeconomic equilibrium degenerate. This can be seen most clearly by considering the case where the utility function is additively separable in m, though it extends to the general case as well.[6] With the shadow value of wealth remaining constant over time, the marginal conditions (2.10a) and (2.10b) imply that both c and l must remain constant over time. Extreme consumption smoothing is optimal. Next, (2.10c) can be solved for the rate of exchange depreciation as a function $e = e(m)$, with $e'(m) < 0$. Substituting this into (2.10d) yields the differential equation in m:

$$\dot{m} = (\phi - q - e(m))m.$$

This is an unstable equation and yields a finite steady-state stock of real money balances if and only if[7]

$$\phi = q + e(m), \tag{2.11}$$

which implies that both m and e remain constant over time. With c and l being constant, the equation (2.10e) describing the accumulation of bonds by the private sector can easily be solved. Integrating this equation, the solution for the consumer's holdings of real bonds is

$$b(t) = e^{(i^*-q)t}\left[b_0 + \frac{(1-\tau)F(l) - c - T - \phi m}{i^* - q}(1 - e^{-(i^*-q)t})\right],$$

where b_0 is the initially given real stock of bonds held by domestic residents. For the transversality condition in (2.4e) to hold, we require

$$b_0 + \frac{(1-\tau)F(l) - c - T - \phi m}{i^* - q} = 0. \tag{2.10e'}$$

This equation represents the agent's intertemporal budget constraint in a stationary equilibrium. It asserts that his initial stock of bonds plus the constant flow of net savings—after-tax income from current production less consumption, the lump-sum tax, and inflation tax—capitalized at the real interest rate $i^* - q$, must sum to zero.

One further requirement we impose on the economy is its intertemporal budget constraint, ruling out the possibility that the country can run up indefinite credit or debt with the rest of the world. This is expressed by the condition

$$\lim_{t \to \infty} n(t) e^{-(i^* - q)t} = 0. \tag{2.12}$$

Solving the accumulation equation (2.10f) for $n(t)$ and substituting into (2.12), this reduces to the condition

$$(b_0 - a_0) + \frac{F(l) - c - g}{i^* - q} = 0, \tag{2.10f'}$$

where, from the definition of n, $b_0 - a_0 \equiv n_0$. This equation asserts that in equilibrium the economy must run a trade balance that precisely finances the interest it earns (or owes) on its initial net stock of foreign assets.

Thus the perfect foresight equilibrium reduces to the following five equations:

$$U_c(c, l, m, g) = \bar{\lambda} \tag{2.13a}$$

$$U_l(c, l, m, g) = -F'(l)\bar{\lambda}(1 - \tau) \tag{2.13b}$$

$$U_m(c, l, m, g) = (i^* + \phi - q)\bar{\lambda} \tag{2.13c}$$

$$(1 - \tau)F(l) - c - T - \phi m + b_0(i^* - q) = 0 \tag{2.13d}$$

$$F(l) - c - g + (i^* - q)(b_0 - a_0) = 0. \tag{2.13e}$$

As these equations indicate, there are no dynamics. There is no accumulation of foreign bonds, and the economy is always in steady state.[8] Basically, what happens is that any shock to the system generates an instantaneous jump in the nominal exchange rate, E, causing real money balances to jump to ensure that (2.11) holds, with all other variables responding immediately to maintain equilibrium (2.13). The fundamental point is that there is no sluggishness in the system. Nothing prevents it from fully adjusting to any shock instantaneously. Sluggish adjustment can be introduced in various ways, and alternative approaches will be discussed in Sections 2.5 and 2.6. With the initial stock of bonds held, b_0 being predetermined by past savings, and a_0 being the initial stock of government bonds outstanding, these five equations determine the stationary solutions for c, l, m, $\bar{\lambda}$, and *one* of the policy instruments: ϕ, T, τ, or g. In other words, three of the policy parameters can be specified arbitrarily, with the remaining one accommodating so as to sustain the equilibrium.

Finally, we have already mentioned the intertemporal government budget constraint. This is obtained by subtracting the private sector's intertemporal budget constraint, (2.10e′), from the national intertemporal budget constraint (2.10f′). Combining these two equations leads to the relationship

$$a_0 + \frac{g - \tau F(l) - \phi m - T}{i^* - q} = 0.$$

This asserts that the (constant) current government budget deficit, capitalized at the real interest rate, $i^* - q$, plus its initial debt, must sum to zero.

Despite the rigor with which the underlying equilibrium is derived, it is not very interesting, at least insofar as dynamics are concerned. We can analyze the effects of various shocks on the equilibrium, under alternative modes of accommodation. But in view of the lack of dynamics, this is of limited interest, and such exercises are postponed to later models having nondegenerate dynamics.

The macroeconomic equilibrium (2.13) highlights two key points with respect to monetary policy in this rational intertemporal framework. First, if the utility function is additively separable in c, l, on the one hand, and m, on the other, the equilibrium levels of consumption, employment, and output are determined jointly through the marginal conditions (2.13a) and (2.13b), together with the national resource constraint (2.13e), and are therefore independent of the monetary growth rate. In this case, money is said to be *superneutral* (see Sidrauski 1967a, 1967b). Monetary policy therefore impacts on the real part of the system only through the interaction of the real money stock with the marginal rate of substitution between consumption and labor. Second, the fact that some form of taxation must accommodate to any chosen monetary growth rate in order to sustain the equilibrium, emphasizes the constraints that exist between monetary and fiscal policy. The stationarity of the equilibrium in the present simple model merely serves to simplify the nature of these constraints.

In the next three sections we shall devote our attention to the determination and characterization of optimal government policy, for which the lack of dynamics has the virtue of analytical tractability. We shall focus on the case where the rate of monetary growth, ϕ, is always chosen to optimize welfare, and consider the two cases where the necessary accommodation is undertaken by a lump-sum tax, T, on the one hand, and a distortionary tax, τ, on the other. We shall refer to this as *fiscal* accommodation.

Other forms of fiscal accommodation are possible. For example, the policy maker may set the income tax rate and spend the resulting revenues, thus treating government expenditure as the accommodating variable. This case is not discussed; instead, we will focus on the optimal determination of g (along with ϕ) in Section 2.4. An alternative means of sustaining equilibrium is for the monetary authorities to set the appropriate initial values of a_0 and b_0 through an initial open market operation with domestic residents. But this is equivalent to accommodation by means of lump-sum taxation and is a manifestation of the Ricardian equivalence property characteristic of infinitely lived intertemporal utility-maximizing representative agent models of this kind.

Yet a further possibility, though one not considered here, is to reverse the choice of policy instruments; that is, for the policy maker to set the distortionary tax arbitrarily and for the accommodation to be accomplished through an endogenous adjustment in the monetary growth rate. But the key point to observe is that the viability of the perfect foresight equilibrium with perfect capital mobility requires an accommodation of some sort on the part of the domestic policy maker in order to sustain the equilibrium. Monetary policy and fiscal policy cannot be set entirely independently. This is necessary in order to rule out the possibility that would otherwise exist for the small economy to borrow indefinitely from abroad. This possibility does not exist either with imperfect capital mobility or in a closed economy, and in such cases this accommodation is not required (see, e.g., Turnovsky and Brock 1980; Turnovsky 1985).

2.2 Optimal Government Policies: A General Characterization

We now consider the general conditions characterizing the optimal choice of government policy in this small open economy. We assume that the domestic government is benevolent and seeks to determine policies that maximize the intertemporal welfare function of the representative agent, (2.1a), subject to the equilibrium constraints set out in (2.13). Since everything is stationary, this optimization can be accomplished by maximizing the instantaneous utility function, subject to this static set of constraints.

The problem can be formulated by expressing the optimized consumer utility as an indirect utility function in terms of government policy variables and then optimizing with respect to the latter. Alternatively, it can be stated in terms of maximizing the following Lagrangian expression:

$$L \equiv U(c,l,m,g) + v_1[\bar{\lambda} - U_c(c,l,m,g)] - v_2[U_l(c,l,m,g) + F'(l)(1-\tau)\bar{\lambda}]$$
$$- v_3[U_m(c,l,m,g) - (i^* + \phi - q)\bar{\lambda}]$$
$$+ v_4[(1-\tau)F(l) + (i^* - q)b_0 - T - \phi m - c]$$
$$+ v_5[F(l) + (i^* - q)(b_0 - a_0) - c - g], \qquad (2.14)$$

where the constraints in (2.14) correspond to the equilibrium conditions (2.13). We present the optimality conditions in two parts: the first pertains to the decision variables of the private sector—c, l, m, $\bar{\lambda}$—and the second relates to the policy variables, although in general only a subset of the latter will be optimized.

The optimality conditions are shown below.

Private Sector Variables

$$\frac{\partial L}{\partial c} \equiv U_c - v_1 U_{cc} - v_2 U_{lc} - v_3 U_{mc} - v_4 - v_5 = 0 \qquad (2.15a)$$

$$\frac{\partial L}{\partial l} \equiv U_l - v_1 U_{cl} - v_2[F''(1-\tau)\bar{\lambda} + U_{ll}] - v_3 U_{ml} + v_4(1-\tau)F' + v_5 F' = 0 \qquad (2.15b)$$

$$\frac{\partial L}{\partial m} \equiv U_m - v_1 U_{cm} - v_2 U_{lm} - v_3 U_{mm} - \phi v_4 = 0 \qquad (2.15c)$$

$$\frac{\partial L}{\partial \bar{\lambda}} \equiv v_1 - v_2 F'(1-\tau) + v_3(i^* + \phi - q) = 0. \qquad (2.15d)$$

Policy Variables

Some subset of

$$\frac{\partial L}{\partial \phi} \equiv v_3 \bar{\lambda} - m v_4 = 0 \qquad (2.16a)$$

$$\frac{\partial L}{\partial T} \equiv v_4 = 0 \qquad (2.16b)$$

$$\frac{\partial L}{\partial \tau} \equiv v_2 F' \bar{\lambda} - v_4 F = 0 \qquad (2.16c)$$

$$\frac{\partial L}{\partial g} \equiv U_g - v_1 U_{cg} - v_2 U_{lg} - v_3 U_{mg} - v_5 = 0. \qquad (2.16d)$$

In addition, the underlying equilibrium constraints (2.13a)–(2.13e) must hold.

2.3 Optimal Monetary Growth

We now use the general characteristics contained in (2.15)–(2.16) to determine the optimal rate of monetary growth, showing how it varies under the alternative choices with respect to the accommodating fiscal instrument.

The question of the optimal monetary growth rate has been discussed at length in the literature from a variety of perspectives. Early authors such as Bailey (1956) and Friedman (1971) have analyzed the question from the viewpoint of the maximization of government revenue from the inflation tax and have shown how the optimal monetary growth rate depends upon the interest elasticity of the demand for money. Tobin (1968) focused on the consumption-maximizing monetary growth rate and showed that this involves driving the economy to the golden rule capital-labor ratio. Most significant is the work that originated with Bailey (1956) and Friedman (1969), which examines the optimal growth of money within a utility-maximizing framework.[9] The most important proposition to emerge from this last approach is the Friedman "full liquidity rule," which concludes that the optimal rate of monetary growth is to contract the money supply at a rate equal to the rate of consumer time preference. Such a rule drives the nominal interest rate to zero.

This literature has been restricted to a closed economy, so that the present analysis can be viewed as an extension of this analysis to a small open economy (see Turnovsky 1987). In this respect, under the assumptions of *PPP* the choice of monetary growth rate is equivalent to the choice of the equilibrium rate of exchange rate depreciation, or rate of exchange rate crawl. The crawling peg system has often been advocated as an attractive regime in that it combines stability with flexibility. On the one hand, steady adjustments in the exchange rate minimize fluctuations, yet at the same time the crawling peg may allow individual countries to pursue independent monetary policies. Different rates of exchange rate depreciation have different welfare implications for an open economy, just as differential rates of monetary growth do for a closed economy. Some years ago, Mathieson (1976) addressed the question of the optimal exchange rate crawl from the perspective of consumption maximization under the assumptions of *PPP* and *UIP*, using a model based on arbitrarily specified behavioral relationships.[10] Our analysis can be viewed as addressing this issue by using a natural framework for this type of welfare analysis.

Accommodation through Lump-Sum Taxation

We begin with the case where the domestic government chooses to maintain the equilibrium by levying an appropriate lump-sum tax, T. In this case, the relevant optimal policy conditions are (2.16a) and (2.16b), which together yield

$$v_4 = 0,$$

$$v_3 \bar{\lambda} = 0.$$

The second equation implies two possibilities. First, if $\bar{\lambda} = 0$, then (2.13a)–(2.13c) imply $U_c = U_l = U_m = 0$, yielding constant optimal values of $\hat{c}$, $\hat{l}$, and $\hat{m}$. But with a_0 and b_0 assumed to be given, the optimal values $\hat{c}$ and $\hat{l}$ are in general inconsistent with the national budget constraint (2.13e).

Thus consider instead $v_3 = 0$. The equilibrium now reduces to

$$(U_c F' + U_l) - v_1(U_{cc}F' + U_{cl}) - v_2(U_{lc}F' + U_{ll} + F''(1-\tau)U_c) = 0 \quad (2.17a)$$

$$v_1 - v_2 F'(1-\tau) = 0 \quad (2.17b)$$

$$U_m - v_1 U_{cm} - v_2 U_{lm} = 0 \quad (2.17c)$$

$$F'(1-\tau)U_c + U_l = 0 \quad (2.17d)$$

$$U_m - (i^* + \phi - q)U_c = 0 \quad (2.17e)$$

$$(1-\tau)F(l) - c - T - \phi m + b_0(i^* - q) = 0 \quad (2.17f)$$

$$F(l) - c - g + (i^* - q)(b_0 - a_0) = 0. \quad (2.17g)$$

Equations (2.17a)–(2.17d) and (2.17g) determine the optimal values for c, l, m, v_1, and v_2. Given these values (2.17e) determines the optimal rate of monetary growth, and (2.17f) determines the lump-sum tax, T, necessary to sustain the equilibrium.

The expression for the optimal rate of monetary growth contained in the solution is virtually identical to that derived by Turnovsky and Brock (1980) for a closed economy. In particular, solving (2.17a), (2.17b), and (2.17d) for v_1 and v_2 yields

$$v_1 = \frac{\tau(1-\tau)(F')^2 U_c}{\Delta} \quad (2.18a)$$

$$v_2 = \frac{\tau F' U_c}{\Delta}, \quad (2.18b)$$

where

$$\Delta \equiv F'(1-\tau)[U_{cc}F' + U_{cl}] + U_{cl}F' + U_{ll} + F''(1-\tau)U_c.$$

Given the concavity of U in c and l, and that of F in l, a sufficient condition for $\Delta < 0$ is that $U_{cl} < 0$; that is, the marginal utility of consumption must increase with leisure (decline with work effort). This assumption is plausible and shall be maintained. Substituting these expressions for v_1 and v_2 into (2.17c) and using (2.17e), the optimal rate of monetary growth is given by

$$\hat{\phi} = \frac{\tau F' U_c}{\Delta} \frac{\partial}{\partial m}\left(\frac{U_l}{U_c}\right) - (i^* - q). \tag{2.19}$$

From this relationship we observe that the optimal rate of monetary growth is identical to the Friedman full liquidity rule,

$$\hat{\phi} = -(i^* - q) \quad \text{or equivalently} \quad i \equiv i^* + e = 0,$$

if and only if either (1) $\tau = 0$ or (2) the marginal rate of substitution of consumption for labor is independent of the real stock of money balances. In the former case there is no income tax to distort the consumption-leisure choice; in the latter case, the utility function is additively separable in m, which therefore leaves the choice between consumption and leisure unaffected.

If, for example, $\partial(U_l/U_c)/\partial m < 0$, reducing the real money balances, m, below their satiation level, m^*, will increase the marginal rate of substitution of labor for consumption; workers will be willing to supply more labor, output will increase, and the utility from consumption will rise correspondingly. The opposite is true if $\partial(U_l/U_c)/\partial m > 0$. In effect, the optimal policy calls for a balancing of the direct utility of money, on the one hand, with its indirect effects resulting from its interaction with consumption and leisure, on the other. Turnovsky and Brock (1980) have referred to (2.19) as describing a "distorted" Friedman liquidity rule. Using the steady-state relationship, $\phi = q + e$, (2.19) translates immediately into an equivalent relationship describing the optimal crawling peg, $\hat{e}$:

$$\hat{e} = \frac{\tau F' U_c}{\Delta} \frac{\partial}{\partial m}\left(\frac{U_l}{U_c}\right) - i^*. \tag{2.19'}$$

Accommodation through Distortionary Income Tax

We now determine the optimal monetary growth rate under the assumption that the stabilization authorities maintain equilibrium by adjusting the income tax rate, τ, rather than through lump-sum taxation. This leads to an optimal policy in which the distortions due to the income tax are traded off against the distortions due to the inflation tax. This issue was first discussed in the context of a closed economy by Phelps (1973). Using (2.16c), the equilibrium conditions are summarized by

$$(U_c F' + U_l) - v_1(U_{cc} F' + U_{cl}) - v_2(U_{lc} F' + U_{ll} + F''(1-\tau)U_c)$$
$$- v_3(U_{mc} F' + U_{ml}) - v_4 \tau F' = 0 \qquad (2.20a)$$

$$U_m - v_1 U_{cm} - v_2 U_{lm} - v_3 U_{mm} - \phi v_4 = 0 \qquad (2.20b)$$

$$v_1 - v_2 F'(1-\tau) + v_3(i^* + \phi - q) = 0 \qquad (2.20c)$$

$$v_3 \bar{\lambda} - m v_4 = 0 \qquad (2.20d)$$

$$v_2 F' \bar{\lambda} - v_4 F = 0, \qquad (2.20e)$$

together with the constraints (2.13a)–(2.13e).

To establish the trade-off, it is convenient to assume that utility is additively separable in m when under lump-sum taxation, the Friedman full liquidity rule, $\phi = -(i^* - q)$, is obtained. The critical relationship is (2.20b), which with $U_{cm} = U_{lm} = 0$ simplifies to

$$U_m - v_3 U_{mm} - \phi v_4 = 0. \qquad (2.20b')$$

Solving (2.20) and (2.13) for v_3 and v_4, we find

$$v_3 = \frac{\tau(F')^2 U_c m}{\Omega},$$

$$v_4 = \frac{\tau(F')^2 U_c^2}{\Omega} = \frac{U_c v_3}{m},$$

where

$$\Omega \equiv F'[F(1-\tau) - m(i^* + \phi - q)][U_{cc} F' + U_{cl}]$$
$$+ FF' U_{cl} + F U_{ll} + [FF''(1-\tau) + \tau(F')^2] U_c.$$

Under mild restrictions $\Omega < 0$, in which case $v_3 < 0$ and $v_4 < 0$.[11] Thus, (2.20) and (2.13) together imply

$$(i^* + \phi - q)(U_c - v_4) = v_3 U_{mm} - v_4(i^* - q)), \qquad (2.21)$$

which, given the signs of v_3, v_4, U_c, and U_{mm}, implies $\phi > -(i^* - q)$.

In other words, the optimal rate of monetary growth (contraction) falls short of the Friedman full liquidity rule $\phi = -(i^* - q)$. The reason for this can be seen by subtracting (2.13e) from (2.13d) and writing the steady-state domestic government budget constraint in the form

$$\phi m + T + \tau F(l) = g + (i^* - q)a_0.$$

The Friedman full liquidity rule implies a constant rate of monetary contraction, yielding an inflation subsidy rather than an inflation tax. This means that additional revenue must be raised through the income tax. But this will reduce the employment of labor, and therefore the level of output and consumption, thereby increasing the distortions caused by this form of taxation. In effect, the optimal monetary growth requires a balancing of the distortions caused by the required adjustment in τ on the utility level from real activity against the cost ϕ imposes on liquidity. In the process of achieving this balance, only partial adjustment to the Friedman rule is achieved. This conclusion is essentially an extension of the Phelps result to a small open economy.

2.4 Optimal Monetary-Fiscal Package

Until now we have assumed that government expenditure remains fixed. We now consider the situation where the government chooses its optimal expenditure level, g, in conjunction with the monetary growth rate, ϕ.

We assume that the accommodation required to sustain steady-state equilibrium is carried out through lump-sum taxation, in which case the optimality conditions consist of simply appending the marginal condition (2.16d) to the set (2.17a)–(2.17g). Having previously established that $v_3 = v_4 = 0$ (by virtue of the accommodating lump-sum tax, T), the marginal condition (2.16d) reduces to

$$U_g - v_1 U_{cg} - v_2 U_{lg} - v_5 = 0. \tag{2.16d'}$$

Combining this equation with (2.15a), v_5 may be eliminated to yield

$$U_g - U_c - v_1(U_{cg} - U_{cc}) - v_2(U_{lg} - U_{lc}) = 0. \tag{2.16d''}$$

We have also established above that with accommodating lump-sum taxation, v_1 and v_2 are given by (2.18a) and (2.18b). Substituting these expressions into (2.16d''), the optimality condition for government expenditure is given by

$$U_g = U_c \left[1 + \frac{\tau(1-\tau)(F')^2}{\Delta}(U_{cg} - U_{cc}) + \frac{\tau F'}{\Delta}(U_{lg} - U_{lc}) \right]. \tag{2.22}$$

Using (2.17d), this can be written in the equivalent form

$$U_g = U_c \left(1 + \frac{\tau F' U_c}{\Delta} \left[\frac{d}{dg}\left(\frac{U_l}{U_c}\right) - \frac{d}{dc}\left(\frac{U_l}{U_c}\right) \right] \right). \tag{2.23}$$

In essence, this condition equates the marginal utility of government expenditure to an adjusted marginal utility of private consumption. The adjustment reflects the distortions on the work-leisure decision due to the presence of the nonzero income tax rate, τ.[12]

The expression for the optimal monetary growth rate is still given by (2.19). The only difference is that in general, the optimal choice of g will impact on the marginal rate of substitution between consumption and labor. If the utility function is additively separable in g, then this expression is independent of g and the optimal monetary growth rate is invariant with respect to the chosen level of government expenditure.

Finally, suppose that the government chooses the optimal tax rate, τ, in conjunction with the rate of monetary growth, ϕ, and its level of expenditure, g. In this case, (2.16c) must be added to the above optimality conditions (2.17a)–(2.17g) and (2.16d'). With $v_4 = 0$, (2.16c) now implies $v_2 = 0$, which from (2.17b) in turn yields $v_1 = 0$. From (2.18a) and (2.18b) we further obtain $\tau = 0$, and the optimality conditions for this overall policy optimization reduce to

$$\tau = 0 \tag{2.24a}$$

$$\phi = -(i^* - q) \tag{2.24b}$$

$$U_c F' + U_l = 0 \tag{2.24c}$$

$$U_m = 0 \tag{2.24d}$$

$$U_g = U_c \tag{2.24e}$$

$$F(l) - c - \phi m + b_0(i^* - q) = T \tag{2.24f}$$

$$F(l) - c - g + (i^* - q)(b_0 - a_0) = 0. \tag{2.24g}$$

This describes an optimal integrated macroeconomic policy package in which the income tax rate is set to zero, thereby eliminating this source of distortion. As a consequence, the optimal condition for government expenditure simply reduces to equating its marginal utility to that of private goods. Moreover, with $\tau = 0$, the optimal monetary growth rate should now be set at the Friedman full liquidity rule, $\phi = -(i^* - q)$. The corresponding optimal levels of $\hat{c}$, $\hat{l}$, $\hat{m}$, and $\hat{g}$ are jointly determined by the marginal conditions (2.24c)–(2.24e), together with the national budget constraint (2.24g). Finally, the required lump-sum taxation, necessary to sustain this equilibrium, is determined residually by the private sector's budget constraint, (2.24f).

2.5 Sluggish Adjustment in Basic Monetary Model

As we have emphasized throughout the discussion, the system is continuously in steady-state equilibrium. In order to generate dynamics, some sluggishness needs to be introduced into the system. This can be done in various ways. In this section, we consider three alternative ways of introducing sluggishness and thereby restoring dynamics in this simple monetary model. A fourth way, through the introduction of an upward-sloping supply curve of debt, will be discussed in some detail in Section 2.6.

A key feature of the model giving rise to the degeneracy of the dynamics is the condition

$$\beta = i^* - q. \tag{2.25}$$

Thus, within the context of a simple a model such as this, sluggishness can be conveniently introduced by modifying the assumptions relating to time preference and capital mobility, insofar as they impact on this relationship. These will be discussed briefly.

Endogenous Rate of Time Discount

The earliest monetary models restored nondegenerate dynamics to this model by, in effect, modifying this relationship. Obstfeld (1981) does so by endogenizing the consumer rate of time preference β, through the introduction of Uzawa (1968) preferences. Obstfeld considers an economy in which labor is supplied inelastically and the agent seeks to maximize the intertemporal utility function

$$V = \int_0^\infty U(c,m) e^{-B(t)} dt, \tag{2.26a}$$

where instantaneous utility is of the additively separable form $U(c,m) \equiv u(c) + v(m)$, in consumption and real money balances, and the discount factor at time t is defined to be

$$B(t) = \int_0^t \beta(s)\, ds, \quad \beta(s) = \beta[U(c(s), m(s))]. \tag{2.26b}$$

The instantaneous rate of time preference is thus a function of the level of utility at time t. The marginal utility of wealth is no longer constant over time, and the condition

$$\beta[U(c,m)] = i^* - q$$

now holds only in steady-state equilibrium. In effect, the exogenously given world real interest rate $i^* - q$ now determines the equilibrium level of instantaneous utility, which will equate the domestic rate of time preference to the world real interest rate. By assuming that the function β is positive and satisfies

$$\beta'(U) > 0, \quad \beta''(U) > 0, \quad \beta(U) - U\beta'(U) > 0, \tag{2.26c}$$

one can show that the dynamics will have a saddlepoint property, thereby giving rise to nondegenerate dynamics.

The agent's optimization problem is to maximize (2.26a), subject to (2.26b) and the asset accumulation equation

$$c + \dot{m} + \dot{b} = \bar{F} + (i^* - q)b - (q + e)m - T, \tag{2.26d}$$

where $\bar{F} \equiv F(\bar{l})$ and the bar denotes the fact that output is fixed, and the distortionary tax rate is set to zero. For convenience we have consolidated the household and the firm.

As Obstfeld discusses, the solution to the problem is simplified by changing variables from real time, t, "to psychological time," $B(t)$, using the fact implied by (2.26b) that

$$dB(t) = \beta[U(c(t), m(t)] \, dt. \tag{2.26b'}$$

With this change of variable, the agent's problem may be expressed as choosing c, m, and b to maximize

$$\int_0^\infty \frac{U(c, m)}{\beta[U(c, m)]} e^{-B} dB, \tag{2.27a}$$

subject to

$$\frac{dm}{dB} + \frac{db}{dB} = \frac{\bar{F} - c + (i^* - q)b - (q + e)m - T}{\beta[U(c, m)]}, \tag{2.27b}$$

where variables are now taken to be a function of B rather than of t.

The corresponding optimality conditions can now be shown to be

$$\left\{1 - \frac{\beta'}{\beta}[U + \lambda(\bar{F} + (i^* - q)b - (q + e)m - T)]\right\} U_c = \lambda \tag{2.28a}$$

$$U_m = U_c(i^* + e) \tag{2.28b}$$

$$\frac{d\lambda}{dB} = \lambda\left(\frac{\beta - (i^* - q)}{\beta}\right), \tag{2.28c}$$

where λ is the Lagrange multiplier associated with the accumulation equation (2.27b). Using (2.26b'), the time derivative of λ is given by

$$\dot{\lambda} = \lambda\{\beta[U(c, m)] - (i^* - q)\}. \tag{2.28c'}$$

This is analogous to (2.4d), the difference being that the rate of time discount evolves over time with c and m.

As long as $\beta' \neq 0$, the solution for c implied by (2.28) is of the form $c = c(m, b, \lambda)$. Taking this in conjunction with (1) (2.28b), (2) the monetary growth rule (2.9a), (3) the accumulation equation (2.10e) and current account relationship (2.10f), and (4) (2.28c′), the equilibrium dynamics of the system can be described by the third-order autonomous system of the form

$$\dot{\lambda} = x_1(\lambda, m, n)$$
$$\dot{m} = x_2(\lambda, m, n) \qquad (2.29)$$
$$\dot{n} = x_3(\lambda, m, n).$$

Under the assumptions (2.26c), the linearized system can be shown to have one stable and two unstable eigenvalues. With the initial exchange rate assumed to be endogenously determined, this implies that the initial real stock of money balances is also endogenously determined. In addition, the shadow value is free to undergo an initial jump in response to new information. Thus, with the system having two unstable eigenvalues accompanied by two "jump variables," we know that the dynamic system (2.29) exhibits well-behaved saddlepath dynamics, giving rise to a unique stable adjustment path.[13] (For a detailed discussion of saddlepoint dynamics with economic applications, see Turnovsky 1995, Chapter 6). A brief summary of some of the most relevant analytical methods is provided in the Appendix to this chapter.

The problem with this approach is that the rationale for the restrictions on the function β are not particularly compelling and have been subject to criticism. In particular, the requirement that the rate of time discount β must increase with the level of utility, and therefore with consumption, is not particularly appealing. It implies that as agents become richer and increase their consumption levels, their preference for current consumption over future consumption increases, whereas intuitively one would expect the opposite to be more likely. For this reason we do not pursue this model in further detail. Instead, the methods of saddlepoint dynamics will be discussed in greater detail in connection with the models to be developed below.

A closely related specification of preference structures is recursive preferences. These were first proposed by Epstein and Hynes (1983), and have been used by several authors in the context of modeling international capital accumulation (see, e.g., Devereux and Shi 1991). They are specified as follows. We define C to be the consumption path, where $c(t)$ is the rate of consumption at time t. The utility associated with the consumption path is defined to be

$$U(C) = -\int_0^\infty e^{-\int_0^t u(c(s))ds} dt, \qquad (2.30)$$

where the instantaneous utility function $u(c)$ has the usual properties of positive but diminishing marginal utility. The parallels between (2.30) and (2.26a) and (2.26b) are clear and give rise to the same general characteristics as those obtained in Obstfeld's model.

Costs of Holding Foreign Bonds

Turnovsky (1985) adopts a somewhat different approach to relaxing the relationship (2.25). He introduces nontraded bonds, which are imperfect substitutes for traded bonds. He does so by introducing quadratic costs on holding foreign bonds, thus introducing a term of the form $\alpha b^2/2$ into the representative agent's budget constraint. This can be justified in two ways. First, it is a convenient way of capturing, within a certainty equivalent framework, the imperfect substitutability between domestic and foreign bonds. In a stochastic model, such as the one we shall develop in Part III, the cost parameter will be a function of the degree of exchange risk and the degree of risk aversion of the domestic investors. Second, one might argue that the acquisition of foreign assets involves transaction costs that are substantially higher than those incurred when purchasing domestic bonds. Information is harder to obtain, and there are brokerage fees associated with obtaining the foreign exchange necessary to purchase the foreign assets.[14]

The key effect of introducing this cost term is that equation (2.25) is now modified to the pair of equations

$$\beta - \frac{\dot{\lambda}}{\lambda} = i - (q + e) \tag{2.31a}$$

$$b = \frac{1}{\alpha}(i^* + e - i), \tag{2.31b}$$

where i denotes the (endogenously determined) domestic nominal interest rate, so that the right-hand side of (2.31a) is now the endogenously determined domestic real interest rate. Given this interest rate, the second equation determines a net demand for foreign bonds as dependent upon the uncovered interest risk differential. Observe that as costs tend to zero ($\alpha \to 0$), these two equations collapse to (2.25).

This procedure can also be shown to give rise to a saddlepoint property, though it suffers from two drawbacks. First, while the demand function for foreign bonds is perfectly plausible and has been used in the literature (see, e.g., Driskill and McCafferty 1980), the fact is that this formulation represents a shortcut. It is clearly preferable to model imperfect capital mobility (or imperfect substitutability) within an explicit stochastic framework, something that we undertake in Part III. Second, dynamic responses to shocks may, or may not, degenerate, depending upon the shocks and the precise formulation of these costs. In fact, this procedure tends to highlight the arbitrariness that still remains, even when the model is grounded in intertemporal optimization.

To illustrate this point, suppose that the cost parameter, α, is assumed to vary inversely with the stock of wealth (as it would if the agent is assumed to have constant relative risk aversion). The equilibrium relationship (2.31b) is then modified to

$$\frac{b}{W} = \frac{1}{\alpha'}(i^* + e - i), \qquad (2.31b')$$

where W denotes the agent's wealth. The modified relationship indicates that under this alternative assumption it is the proportion of traded bonds in the agent's portfolio, rather than their absolute quantity, that depends upon the uncovered risk differential. While the system can still be shown to be characterized by saddlepoint behavior, replacing (2.31b) with (2.31b') can be shown to yield very different implications for the dynamic adjustment of the system in response to demand shocks, for example.

Overlapping Generations Model

The model we have been discussing is that of a representative agent who lives forever. Needless to say, this is an abstraction, since economies are populated with individuals who live and die, so that the agents alive at any moment in time are continually changing. An alternative way of introducing nondegenerate dynamics is through some form of the overlapping generations model. This model was first introduced by Samuelson (1958) and Diamond (1965). Early formulations were based on a two-period time horizon and introduced two generations each period—the young who work and the old who consume—with each generation living for two periods. In the next period the young become old, the old die, and a new generation of young is born. The economy replicates itself in this manner over time, possibly growing in population. Overlapping generations models of small open economies have been developed by Buiter (1981), Dornbusch (1985), Persson (1985), and Persson and Svensson (1985). Applications to two-country world models include those of Persson (1985), Buiter (1987), and Frenkel, Razin, and Yuen (1996).

The fact that agents are continually changing means that we do not require $\beta = i^* - q$ in order to rule out an unstable adjustment path for consumption, as we have been discussing. Even though each individual's consumption may rise or fall over his individual lifetime [as implied by (2.4d″)], after two periods he dies and is replaced by an identical member of the next generation. It is therefore possible for the aggregate consumption of the economy to remain constant, and for nondegenerate dynamics to obtain, even if $\beta \neq i^* - q$.

The traditional overlapping generations model is based on a two-period time horizon. Blanchard (1985) introduced the finite life aspect into a continuous-time infinite horizon framework, closer to that of the representative agent framework we have been developing, by introducing the assumption of an uncertain lifetime. This is done by assuming that throughout his life each individual faces a constant probability of death. While this specific assumption is restrictive, it has the important advantage of restoring nondegenerate dynamics while preserving analytical tractability. For specific forms of the utility function—for example, if it is logarithmic—an aggregate consumption function of the form

$$\dot{c} = (i^* - q - \beta)c - \xi(m + b) \tag{2.32}$$

is obtained. This equation replaces the condition (2.25) and, as long as the coefficient on wealth, ξ, is nonzero, will again give rise to a third-order system of the generic form (2.29), and which in general will yield saddlepoint behavior. The coefficient, ξ, is shown by Blanchard to depend upon the agent's fixed probability of death. In the case where this is zero, the agent becomes infinitely lived, $\xi \to 0$, and (2.32) reduces to the condition $\beta = i^* - q$. The same form of equilibrium can be obtained by assuming a growing population of overlapping infinitely lived households, as in Weil (1989).[15]

2.6 Upward-Sloping Supply Curve of Debt

The prevalent assumption that the economy is free to borrow or lend as much as it wants at the given world interest rate in a perfect world capital market is a strong one. While it is convenient and may be a reasonable assumption for developed economies with highly integrated capital markets, it is less realistic for small developing economies. Experience with external borrowing in such economies has shown that debt repayments are not always made on time. Long gestation lags in investment projects have led to difficulties in meeting repayment commitments in some cases (see Kharas 1984; Kharas and Shishido 1987). International capital markets are likely to react to their perception of a country's ability to repay, with lenders requiring a risk premium on the rate at which they are willing to lend to such economies, and in some cases imposing credit ceilings on such borrowers.[16]

We incorporate this idea by assuming that the small economy faces an upward-sloping supply schedule for debt that embodies the risk premium associated with lending to a sovereign borrower. We will show that the effect of such a constraint on borrowing acts as a form of sluggishness, thereby restoring a nondegenerate dynamic adjustment (in most cases) to the system.

In its simplest form the upward-sloping supply schedule for debt facing the economy is expressed by assuming that the interest rate, $i(z)$, on foreign debt, z, is

$$i(z) = i^* + \omega(z); \quad \omega' > 0, \tag{2.33}$$

where i^* is the given interest rate prevailing internationally and $\omega(z)$ is the country-specific risk premium that increases with the stock of debt issued by the nation. By specifying (2.33) we are viewing the imperfection of the bond market from the standpoint of the borrowing nation. This seems more natural in the sense that it is the debtor nation that in reality is the source of risk. But recognizing that $z = -b$, the stock of net credit, one can formulate the analysis symmetrically in terms of a downward-sloping supply of credit.

Equation (2.33) specifies that the cost of debt increases with the *absolute* level of foreign debt. This formulation was originally introduced by Bardhan (1967), who simply postulated it (as we are doing) as a constraint facing the debtor nation. It was first derived as a continuous function from a formal intertemporal optimizing model of international lending with sovereign risk by Kletzer (1984), building on earlier work by Eaton and Gersovitz (1981), whose specific analysis yielded a steplike function. The relationship was utilized by Obstfeld (1982) in his intertemporal optimizing representative agent analysis of terms of trade shocks, and more recently by Bhandari, Haque, and Turnovsky (1990) and Fisher (1995). Other authors, such as Sachs (1984), Sachs and Cohen (1982), and Cooper and Sachs (1985), have shown how a country, by adopting growth-oriented policies, can shift the upward-sloping supply function outward, so that at each level of debt a lower risk premium is charged. These effects can be incorporated by assuming that the risk premium depends upon the level of debt *relative* to some measure of earning capacity, and therefore to debt-servicing capacity, such as output. Thus, for example, one can plausibly modify (2.33) to

$$i(z) = i^* + \omega(z/f(l)); \quad \omega' > 0. \tag{2.33'}$$

This specification is more convenient if one wishes to incorporate an upward-sloping supply curve of debt in a model of ongoing growth. An example of such a model is provided by van der Ploeg (1996); see also Section 5.5.[17]

We shall also assume a form of risk-adjusted interest parity. That is, the domestic interest rate prevailing within the small economy is equal to

$i(z)$, the rate at which the country can borrow from abroad. Under this assumption (2.33) [or (2.33′)] also represents the interest rate at which the domestic government can borrow from its residents.

Macroeconomic Equilibrium

To simplify the analysis, and thus highlight the role of the imperfect debt market, we abstract from money, so that the only asset is foreign debt, and also abstract from distortionary taxes. Firms and households are consolidated into a single agent. We will also assume the absolute form of the debt supply function, (2.33), although we will also briefly consider the relative form (2.33′) below.

The representative agent's optimization problem is now expressed as

$$\text{Maximize} \quad \int_0^\infty U(c,l,g)e^{-\beta t}dt \quad U_c > 0, U_l < 0, U_g > 0, \quad (2.34a)$$

subject to the budget constraint

$$\dot{z} = c + i(z)z + T - F(l) \quad (2.34b)$$

and initial condition

$$z(0) = z_0. \quad (2.34c)$$

All variables are as defined in Section 2.2; the only additional restriction is that $U_{cl} < 0$, to reflect the plausible assumption that the marginal utility of consumption increases with leisure. The flow constraint (2.34b), expressed from the standpoint of a debtor, asserts that to the extent that the agent's consumption, outstanding interest payments, plus lump-sum tax payments exceed his flow of output, he will increase his stock of debt.

It is important to emphasize that in performing his optimization, the representative agent takes the interest rate as given. The borrowing rate facing the debtor nation, as reflected in its upward-sloping supply curve of debt, is a function of the economy's *aggregate* debt, which the representative agent, in making his decisions, assumes he is unable to influence. With this in mind, the optimality conditions are

$$U_c(c,l,g) = \lambda \quad (2.35a)$$

$$U_l(c,l,g) = -F'(l)\lambda \quad (2.35b)$$

$$\dot{\lambda} = \lambda[\beta - i(z)], \quad (2.35c)$$

together with the transversality condition

$$\lim_{t \to \infty} z\lambda e^{-\beta t} = 0, \quad (2.35d)$$

where λ is the marginal utility of wealth, which for a borrower is the marginal utility of reducing debt. Solving (2.35a) and (2.35b) yields the solutions

$$c = c(\lambda, g) \tag{2.36a}$$

$$l = l(\lambda, g), \tag{2.36b}$$

where $c_\lambda < 0$, $l_\lambda > 0$, implying that an increase in the marginal utility of wealth induces the agent to increase his work effort and reduce consumption.

For simplicity we assume that the government maintains a balanced budget, so that $g = T$. Substituting (2.36a) and (2.36b) into the accumulation equation (2.34b), the evolution of the economy is described by the pair of equations

$$\dot{z} = c(\lambda, g) + i(z)z + g - F(l(\lambda, g)) \tag{2.37a}$$

$$\dot{\lambda} = \lambda[\beta - i(z)]. \tag{2.37b}$$

Linearizing this pair of equations about the steady state, we obtain

$$\begin{pmatrix} \dot{z} \\ \dot{\lambda} \end{pmatrix} = \begin{pmatrix} i + i'\tilde{z} & c_\lambda - F'l_\lambda \\ -\tilde{\lambda}i' & 0 \end{pmatrix} \begin{pmatrix} z - \tilde{z} \\ \lambda - \tilde{\lambda} \end{pmatrix}, \tag{2.38}$$

where $\tilde{z}$ and $\tilde{\lambda}$ denote steady-state values and all the elements of the matrix in (2.38) are evaluated at steady state. The determinant of the matrix is $D \equiv \tilde{\lambda}i'(c_\lambda - F'l_\lambda) < 0$, so that the long-run equilibrium is a saddlepoint with eigenvalues $\mu_1 < 0$, $\mu_2 > 0$. We assume that the stock of debt is accumulated gradually, while its shadow value can respond instantaneously.

Starting from an initial stock of debt, z_0, the stable dynamic time paths followed by debt and its shadow value are

$$z(t) = \tilde{z} + (z_0 - \tilde{z})e^{\mu_1 t} \tag{2.39a}$$

$$\lambda(t) - \tilde{\lambda} = -\frac{\tilde{\lambda}i'}{\mu_1}(z(t) - \tilde{z}). \tag{2.39b}$$

Equation (2.39b) describes the stable arm of the saddlepath. It is positively sloped, reflecting the fact that the shadow value of wealth increases with the stock of debt (decreases with wealth).

Steady State

The steady state of the economy is reached when debt accumulation ceases and the shadow value of wealth is constant. Setting $\dot{z} = \dot{\lambda} = 0$ in (2.37a) and (2.37b), we see that $\tilde{z}$ and $\tilde{\lambda}$ are determined by

$$F(l(\tilde{\lambda},g)) = c(\tilde{\lambda},g) + i(\tilde{z})\tilde{z} + g \qquad (2.40a)$$

$$i(\tilde{z}) = \beta. \qquad (2.40b)$$

Equation (2.40b) shows how the steady-state stock of debt, $\tilde{z}$, is determined so that the domestic interest rate just equals the given domestic rate of time preference. When $\tilde{z}$ has been obtained, the marginal utility of wealth, $\tilde{\lambda}$, is then determined so that the labor supply and the consumption it induces will ensure that the economy produces sufficient output to cover its private and public consumption, plus the servicing of its debt.

Dynamic Adjustments to Policy Shocks

It is evident from a consideration of (2.39) together with (2.40) that only shocks that cause a change in $\tilde{z}$ will generate dynamic responses in the economy. Thus, for example, an increase in government expenditure leaves $\tilde{z}$ unchanged. Its only effect is to cause an appropriate adjustment in $\tilde{\lambda}$, such that the immediate response in c and l is to accommodate the increase in g, while maintaining the current account balance of the economy. The same applies to any other form of demand shock.

By contrast, an increase in the world interest rate, i^*, shifts the supply schedule of debt up, resulting in a decrease in the long-run stock of debt, $\tilde{z}$. This causes the shadow value of wealth to increase on impact, inducing agents to supply more labor and to reduce consumption. This causes debt to decline over time. As this occurs, the marginal utility of wealth declines, inducing the agent to increase consumption. In the long run the borrowing rate is restored to its original level as determined in (2.40b), and the long-run reduction in debt servicing costs, associated with the reduced debt, enables consumption to be increased in the long run. We will not spell out the dynamics in further detail, since we will be doing so in subsequent chapters with respect to other types of shocks. A careful analysis of the dynamics generated in response to this particular shock is provided by Fisher (1995).

Alternative Supply of Debt Function

To illustrate how the dynamics depends upon the form of the supply of debt function assumed, we briefly consider the specification of debt costs in the relative form (2.33′). The dynamics can be shown again to be a saddlepoint, analogous to (2.39). Steady state is now described by the pair of equations:

$$F(l(\tilde{\lambda},g)) = c(\tilde{\lambda},g) + i(\tilde{z}/F[l(\tilde{\lambda},g)])\tilde{z} + g \qquad (2.41a)$$

$$i(\tilde{z}/F[l(\tilde{\lambda},g)]) = \beta. \qquad (2.41b)$$

The main point we want to make is that when the cost of debt depends upon the economy's level of output, it is clear that a demand disturbance, such as a change in government expenditure, will have an impact on the long-run stock of debt and will thereby generate a dynamic response. Thus, for example, an increase in g will affect the marginal utility of wealth, thereby influencing the supply of labor, the level of output, and therefore the economy's supply of debt function.

For example, in the case where the utility function is additively separable in g, (2.41a) and (2.41b) simplify to

$$F(l(\tilde{\lambda})) = c(\tilde{\lambda}) + i(\tilde{z}/F[l(\tilde{\lambda})])\tilde{z} + g \qquad (2.41a')$$

$$i(\tilde{z}/F[l(\tilde{\lambda})]) = \beta. \qquad (2.41b')$$

The taxes necessary to finance an increase in g will lower the agent's wealth, thereby raising his marginal utility of wealth, inducing an increase in the labor supply, and thereby increasing output and the long-run level of debt that the country can finance. The fact that debt is accumulated only gradually implies that change in the long-run debt induces a dynamic adjustment.

2.7 Some Final Comments

This chapter has presented a first pass at developing a macroeconomic model of a small open economy in which all behavioral relationships are derived from the intertemporal optimization of representative agents. From the standpoint of deriving a dynamic equilibrium it is disappointing, since for the most part the equilibrium is always in steady state. On the other hand, this aspect is also a virtue, since it renders the analysis of optimal government policy quite tractable. We are readily able to characterize the optimal rate of monetary growth (or exchange rate depreciation) and determine how this interacts with fiscal accommodation and optimal fiscal policy.

We conclude by commenting on three aspects of the analysis. First, the assumption of a single traded good and *PPP* is not a cause of the breakdown of the dynamics. If this assumption is relaxed, in the absence of sluggishness the perfect foresight equilibrium will still require the economy to be in continuous steady-state equilibrium, with some accommodation by the fiscal authorities. With two goods, an appropriate relative price for the two goods needs to be established; this is accomplished by a once-and-for-all jump analogous to that undertaken by the exchange rate. The second point is that temporary policy shocks will generate transitory dynamics. In the short run, the temporary implementation of some policy shock will take the system away from equilibrium, and after the policy ceases, the system will gradually return to its initial equilibrium. An example of this in the context of a simple monetary model is provided by Obstfeld (1983). We will also discuss temporary shocks in the context of the real model of capital accumulation, which we shall develop in Chapter 3.

The third concerns the contrast between the representative agent model and the overlapping generations model, which naturally raises the question of the choice between them. The representative agent framework is probably the main paradigm in modern macroeconomic dynamics, and we shall focus on it entirely throughout this book. It is a useful device for analyzing many important issues in macroeconomic dynamics, but it cannot address all. For example, it is limited in its ability to analyze important generational questions associated with debt. For this purpose the overlapping generations model is better suited.

But while the overlapping generations framework is important and yields many insights, we have two main reasons for not pursuing it. The first is a practical one. The framework is rather different from the representative agent, and if the model is to be introduced, it needs to be done carefully and completely. To pursue both models in parallel would consume a lot of space and would crowd out other topics that we wish to discuss and that are also important. Besides, excellent discussions of the overlapping generations model in an international context are available elsewhere (see, e.g., Obstfeld and Rogoff 1996; Frenkel, Razin, and Yuen 1996). Second, the basic two-period overlapping generations model is itself restrictive. The time unit of a generation (say thirty years) is somewhat awkward from the standpoint of serving as a time unit relevant for macroeconomic policy making. In addition, the basic two-period model is a polar one that assumes each generation is completely selfish, caring only about itself and not about subsequent generations. This is an unrealistic assumption, since bequests are obviously an important fact of life. Alternative specifications of overlapping generations models assume that each generation cares not only about its own welfare over the two periods of its life, but also about the utility of its immediate descendants. Provided that the agent discounts this utility at his rate of time discount, this leads to an objective function in which the agent maximizes the discounted utility of the consumption of all future generations, not just that of his immediate descendants.[18] This objective function turns out to be identical to that optimized by a single infinitely lived representative agent. In this case, the overlapping generations model and the representative agent model converge. Bearing this in mind, the representative agent model is not as restrictive as it may at first appear.

Appendix: Saddlepoint Behavior

Any second-order scalar differential equation can be represented by a pair of first-order differential equations and vice versa. Turnovsky (1995, Appendix to Chapter 6) provides a general treatment of the dynamics and solutions for such a pair of first-order linear differential equations. It represents the dynamic evolution of a pair of variables, $x(t)$ and $y(t)$, that are driven by arbitrary forcing functions, $f_1(t)$ and $f_2(t)$. Given an arbitrary time profile for the forcing functions $f_1(t)$ and $f_2(t)$, one can derive the corresponding solutions for $x(t)$ and $y(t)$. In general, the solutions may turn out to be quite cumbersome, depending upon the nature of the functions $f_i(t)$. This Appendix briefly reviews the main characteristics of the dynamics in the case where they are described by saddlepoint behavior.

In many economic applications, the forcing functions $f_i(t)$ take the form of once-and-for-all shifts from one constant level to the other. This is the case, for example, with respect to most of the changes to be introduced in later chapters. These shifts may occur either at some initial time 0, in which case they are unannounced; or they may be announced (at time 0, say) to take place at some time T in the future. The latter may represent some expansion that is to take place in the future, or they may represent the restoration of some policy change to its original level after a temporary change that initially took place at time 0. The formal solutions to these types of changes are the same. The response of the system to such one-time shifts is relatively easy to establish, and we now demonstrate this in the case where the dynamics are described by a saddlepoint.

Consider a linear system represented by the pair of dynamic equations

$$\dot{x}(t) = a_{11}x(t) + a_{12}y(t) + \bar{f}_1 \tag{2.A.1a}$$

$$\dot{y}(t) = a_{21}x(t) + a_{22}y(t) + \bar{f}_2, \tag{2.A.1b}$$

where $\bar{f}_1$ and $\bar{f}_2$ represent constant values of some forcing function. The specific economic context is irrelevant at this point. The corresponding initial steady-state equilibrium solutions for x and y, denoted by $\bar{x}_1$ and $\bar{y}_1$ say, are obtained by solving the pair of equations

$$a_{11}\bar{x}_1 + a_{12}\bar{y}_1 + \bar{f}_1 = 0 \tag{2.A.2a}$$

$$a_{21}\bar{x}_1 + a_{22}\bar{y}_1 + \bar{f}_2 = 0. \tag{2.A.2b}$$

Subtracting (2.A.2) from (2.A.1), the dynamics can be written in the form

$$\begin{bmatrix} \dot{x} \\ \dot{y} \end{bmatrix} = \begin{bmatrix} a_{11} & a_{12} \\ a_{21} & a_{22} \end{bmatrix} \begin{bmatrix} x - \bar{x}_1 \\ y - \bar{y}_1 \end{bmatrix}. \tag{2.A.3}$$

Suppose that at time 0 it is announced that $\bar{f}_1$ and $\bar{f}_2$ are to increase, at time $T \geq 0$, to $\bar{\bar{f}}_1$ and $\bar{\bar{f}}_2$, respectively. The new steady states after the shifts have occurred are obtained from

$$a_{11}\bar{\bar{x}}_2 + a_{12}\bar{\bar{y}}_2 + \bar{\bar{f}}_1 = 0 \tag{2.A.4a}$$

$$a_{21}\bar{\bar{x}}_2 + a_{22}\bar{\bar{y}}_2 + \bar{\bar{f}}_2 = 0, \tag{2.A.4b}$$

with the dynamics after the shift being specified by

$$\begin{bmatrix} \dot{x} \\ \dot{y} \end{bmatrix} = \begin{bmatrix} a_{11} & a_{12} \\ a_{21} & a_{22} \end{bmatrix} \begin{bmatrix} x - \bar{\bar{x}}_2 \\ y - \bar{\bar{y}}_2 \end{bmatrix}. \tag{2.A.5}$$

In comparing (2.A.3) with (2.A.5), it is seen that the equilibrium of the system shifts at time T, when the shift in the forcing functions $\bar{f}_i$ occurs. The solutions for $x(t)$ and $y(t)$ are obtained by solving the differential equations (2.A.3) and (2.A.5), and linking them appropriately at time T. The arbitrary constants in the solutions are determined by imposing a combination of (1) initial conditions; (2) terminal conditions; (3) continuity of the solutions at time T.

As long as the shifts are *additive*, so that the coefficients a_{ij} remain unchanged between the two regimes, the eigenvalues μ_1 and μ_2, say, of (2.A.3) and (2.A.5) are identical. For simplicity, and without loss of generality, we shall assume that they are real. The fact that the dynamics are described by a saddlepoint means that the product

$$\mu_1 \mu_2 = a_{11}a_{22} - a_{12}a_{21} < 0.$$

We shall assume $\mu_1 < 0$, $\mu_2 > 0$. In order to ensure stability, one of the variables, say $y(t)$, must be a jump variable, while the other, $x(t)$, is assumed to evolve continuously at all times.

Over the period $0 < t \leq T$, before the shifts in $\bar{f}_i$ occur, the solutions for $x(t)$ and $y(t)$ are of the form

$$x = \bar{x}_1 + A_1 e^{\mu_1 t} + A_2 e^{\mu_2 t} \tag{2.A.6a}$$

$$y = \bar{y}_1 + \left(\frac{\mu_1 - a_{11}}{a_{12}}\right) A_1 e^{\mu_1 t} + \left(\frac{\mu_2 - a_{11}}{a_{12}}\right) A_2 e^{\mu_2 t}. \tag{2.A6b}$$

Note that since μ_i are eigenvalues,

$$\frac{\mu_i - a_{11}}{a_{12}} = \frac{a_{21}}{\mu_i - a_{22}} \qquad i = 1, 2,$$

in which case, (2.A.6b) can be rewritten equivalently as

$$y = \bar{y}_1 + \left(\frac{a_{21}}{\mu_1 - a_{22}}\right) A_1 e^{\mu_1 t} + \left(\frac{a_{21}}{\mu_2 - a_{22}}\right) A_2 e^{\mu_2 t}. \tag{2.A.6b'}$$

Likewise, for the period $t \geq T$, after the shifts have occurred, the solutions for $x(t)$ and $y(t)$ are

$$x = \bar{x}_2 + A'_1 e^{\mu_1 t} + A'_2 e^{\mu_2 t} \tag{2.A.7a}$$

$$y = \bar{y}_2 + \left(\frac{\mu_1 - a_{11}}{a_{12}}\right) A'_1 e^{\mu_1 t} + \left(\frac{\mu_2 - a_{11}}{a_{12}}\right) A'_2 e^{\mu_2 t}. \tag{2.A.7b}$$

The key difference is in the shift in the steady-state equilibria. Completing the solutions involves the determination of the arbitrary constants A_1, A_2, A'_1, and A'_2.

Before turning to the solutions, we wish to characterize the general dynamic behavior described by a system such as (2.A.6) or (2.A.7). These equations characterize saddlepoint behavior and embody a combination of stable and unstable behavior, due to the simultaneous occurrence of both an exploding and an imploding exponential. The resulting dynamics depend upon the constants. We shall focus on (2.A.7), though identical comments apply to (2.A.6).

Suppose $A'_2 = 0$. In this case (2.A.7a) and (2.A.7b) reduce to

$$x = \bar{x}_2 + A'_1 e^{\mu_1 t} \tag{2.A.7a'}$$

$$y = \bar{y}_2 + \left(\frac{\mu_1 - a_{11}}{a_{12}}\right) A'_1 e^{\mu_1 t}. \tag{2.A.7b'}$$

With $\mu_1 < 0$, these two equations describe stable adjustment paths along which x and y converge exponentially to their respective steady-state equilibrium values. Eliminating $A'_1 e^{\mu_1 t}$ from these equations yields

$$(y - \bar{y}_2) = \left(\frac{\mu_1 - a_{11}}{a_{12}}\right)(x - \bar{x}_2). \tag{2.A.8}$$

This is a linear locus in $y - x$ space and describes the stable arm of the saddlepoint. That is, along this locus the system is converging to its steady state. The slope of (2.A.8) depends upon the signs and magnitudes of the coefficients a_{ij}. Examples will be given in subsequent chapters. Using the fact that λ_1 is an eigenvalue, (2.A.8) may be written equivalently as

$$(y - \bar{y}_2) = \left(\frac{a_{21}}{\mu_1 - a_{22}}\right)(x - \bar{x}_2). \tag{2.A.8'}$$

The reason for noting these alternative ways of describing the stable path is that, depending upon the signs of the coefficients a_{ij}, either (2.A.8) or (2.A.8') may prove to be more convenient in terms of indicating the slope of the locus they describe.

At the other extreme, consider $A_1' = 0$. In this case (2.A.7a) and (2.A.7b) reduce to

$$x = \bar{x}_2 + A_2' e^{\mu_2 t} \tag{2.A.7a''}$$

$$y = \bar{y}_2 + \left(\frac{\mu_2 - a_{11}}{a_{12}}\right) A_2' e^{\mu_2 t}. \tag{2.A.7b''}$$

With $\mu_2 > 0$, these two equations describe unstable adjustment paths along which x and y diverge exponentially from their respective steady-state equilibrium values. Eliminating $A_2' e^{\mu_2 t}$ from these equations yields

$$(y - \bar{y}_2) = \left(\frac{\mu_2 - a_{11}}{a_{12}}\right)(x - \bar{x}_2). \tag{2.A.9}$$

This is a linear locus in $y - x$ space and describes the unstable arm of the saddlepoint. That is, along this locus the system is diverging. Since μ_2 is also an eigenvalue, (2.A.9) may be written equivalently as

$$(y - \bar{y}_2) = \left(\frac{a_{21}}{\mu_2 - a_{12}}\right)(x - \bar{x}_2). \tag{2.A.9'}$$

Again, (2.A.9') may or may not be more illuminating than (2.A.9) in indicating the slope of the unstable arm.

As long as $A_1' \neq 0$, $A_2' \neq 0$ (2.A.7) will give a combination of both types of behavior, arching around the equilibrium point. Initially it will be attracted toward the stable arm, although eventually it will diverge away from it toward the unstable arm, because the unstable root ultimately dominates. This behavior can be characterized in the phase diagram describing the motion. Since this depends upon the signs of the coefficients a_{ij} describing the dynamics, we postpone illustrating such a system until Chapter 3, when a specific example is developed in detail.

We return now to the determination of the arbitrary constants A_1, A_2, A_1' and A_2'. We begin by imposing the condition that the solution be bounded. As we have seen, this is usually a consequence of the transversality conditions. In order for $x(t)$ and $y(t)$, not to diverge as $t \to \infty$, it is clear that after time T, when (2.A.7) is in operation, the system must lie on the stable locus pertinent to that regime. That is, we require $A_2' = 0$, in which case, after time T, $x(t)$ and $y(t)$ must follow the stable paths described by (2.A.7a') and (2.A.7b'), so that they lie on the stable arm (2.A.8) or, equivalently, (2.A.8').

The remaining constants are obtained by imposing an initial condition on the sluggish variable $x(t)$ and continuity at time T of both variables. This latter condition precludes jumps that are foreseen. These are ruled out because they would imply anticipated infinite rates of return at the instant of the jump, a condition that would violate the arbitrage conditions. Thus, assuming $x(0) = \bar{x}_1$, say, (2.A.6a) implies

$$A_1 + A_2 = 0. \tag{2.A.10a}$$

The condition that the solutions be continuous at time T means that the solutions for $x(t)$ and $y(t)$ obtained from (2.A.3) and (2.A.5) should coincide at that time. Hence,

$$(A_1 - A_1')e^{\mu_1 T} + A_2 e^{\mu_2 T} = d\bar{x} \tag{2.A.10b}$$

$$\left(\frac{\mu_1 - a_{11}}{a_{12}}\right)(A_1 - A_1')e^{\mu_1 T} + \left(\frac{\mu_2 - a_{11}}{a_{12}}\right)A_2 e^{\mu_2 T} = d\bar{y}, \tag{2.A.10c}$$

where $d\bar{x}$ and $d\bar{y}$ represent the shifts in the steady states obtained from (2.A.2) and (2.A.4). Given these shifts, the constants A_1, A_2, and A_1' can be determined. Substituting these into (2.A.7) and (2.A.7′) yields the solutions before and after time T.

The essential feature of these solutions is that the dynamics involve *three* phases. The announcement at time 0, say, of a shift to occur at time T in the future generates an immediate response in the jump variable. Setting $t = 0$ in (2.A.6b) and using (2.A.10a), the initial response is given by

$$y(0) - \bar{y}_1 = \left(\frac{\mu_2 - \mu_1}{a_{12}}\right)A_2,$$

where A_2 is obtained from (2.A.10b) and (2.A.10c). It can be shown that the size of the initial jump is inversely proportional to the lead time T. After the initial jump, the system follows the unstable locus (2.A.6) until time T, when the announced policy is implemented. At that time, the system reaches the stable locus (2.A.8), which it then follows into the new equilibrium. In the case where $T = 0$ and the shift is unannounced, the system jumps instantaneously to the new stable locus (2.A.8).

Notes

1. There is an extensive literature empirically testing the *PPP* and the *UIP* relationships. *PPP* has been tested both in absolute form and in relative form over varying time periods. In general, both relationships perform poorly, although the *PPP* relationship does better over the long run than in the short run. Its performance also varies over different time periods. A comprehensive review of much of the earlier empirical literature is contained in Levich (1985). A more recent survey of the empirical evidence relating to *PPP* is provided by Froot and Rogoff (1995). Recent evidence on *UIP* has been surveyed Lewis (1995).

2. Throughout this book, where no ambiguity can arise we shall adopt the convention of letting primes denote total derivatives and appropriate subscripts denote partial derivatives. Time derivatives will be denoted by dots above the variables concerned. Thus, we shall let

$$f'(x) \equiv \frac{df}{dx}; \quad f_i(x_1,\ldots,x_n) \equiv \frac{\partial f}{\partial x_i}; \quad f_{ij}(x_1,\ldots,x_n) \equiv \frac{\partial^2 f}{\partial x_i \partial x_j} \text{ etc.}; \quad \dot{x} \equiv \frac{dx}{dt}.$$

A bar above a letter is used to denote either a stationary equilibrium value in a dynamic system, or the fact that the variable to which it is applied is fixed exogenously. The intended meaning should be clear from the particular context.

3. One advantage of introducing money in the utility function over the cash-in-advance constraint is that it is consistent with a range of alternative velocities of circulation of money, whereas the latter is much more rigid in this regard.

4. This involves the use of a recursive utility function, specified by a difference equation.

5. This is demonstrated formally by Turnovsky (1987).

6. The utility function is of the form $U(c,l) + V(m)$, implying that $U_c = U_c(c,l)$, $U_l = U_l(c,l)$, $U_m = V'(m)$.

7. This condition is stronger than the transversality condition on money contained in (2.4e). That is, it is sufficient, but not necessary, for that condition to hold.

8. The monetary model developed by Hodrick (1982) also lacks any source of sluggishness, so that it, too, requires the system always to be in steady-state equilibrium.

9. The optimal rate of monetary growth has continued to attract the attention of economists (see Kimbrough 1986; Abel 1987; Guidotti and Vegh 1993; Correia and Teles 1996). Kimbrough (1991) discusses the issue in an open economy.

10. See also Clarke and Kingston (1979); Mantel and Martirena-Mantel (1982).

11. One set of conditions that suffices to ensure $\Omega < 0$ is:

$$U_{cl} < 0; \quad FF''(1-\tau) + \tau(F')^2 \leq 0; \quad F(1-\tau) - m[i^* + \phi - q] > 0.$$

For the Cobb-Douglas production function, $F(l) = l^\varepsilon$, the second condition reduces to $\varepsilon + \tau \leq 1$. The third condition can be written as $v > i/(1-\tau)$, where $i = i^* + \phi - q$ is the domestic interest rate, and $v \equiv F/m$ is the velocity of circulation of money. For plausible parameters both conditions will be met.

12. Condition (2.23), equating the marginal utility of government expenditure to the tax-adjusted marginal utility of consumption, is analogous to conditions (8.10) derived in Chapter 8, where the distortion from the income tax is reflected in the net asset position of the economy.

13. In general, a dynamic system embodying rational expectations will have a unique equilibrium if the number of jump variables equals the number of unstable roots (see Blanchard and Kahn 1980).

14. An anecdotal piece of evidence supporting this assumption is that brokerage fees associated with mutual funds purchasing foreign stocks are substantially higher than those specializing in domestic assets.

15. Other ways to generate dynamics in this model also exist. One is through the introduction of nominal price or wage rigidities (see van de Klundert and van der Ploeg 1989 for an example of such an analysis). Another alternative is to assume that utility depends upon both the current and habitual level of consumption, as originally proposed by Ryder and Heal (1973). Mansoorian (1993) develops such an analysis for a fixed output (pure endowment) economy and shows how it generates a saddlepoint equilibrium in the habitual level of consumption and its shadow value.

16. See, e.g., Eaton and Gersovitz (1980, 1981), Sachs (1984), and Cooper and Sachs (1985). See Lewis (1995) for a more recent discussion of the empirical literature on the risk premium.

17. For extensive surveys of issues relating to debt and growing economies, see Cohen (1994) and Kletzer (1987, 1994).

18. One further requirement is that negative intergenerational transfers cannot be ruled out.

3 One-Sector Models of Capital Accumulation

3.1 Introduction

The most important source of sluggishness introduced in the recent intertemporal optimizing models of the international economy is the accumulation of physical capital, which in general is assumed to be associated with convex adjustment costs. This chapter is devoted to developing the one-sector model along these lines. There is a substantial recent literature using this framework, and the models have generally been real; see, for instance, Frenkel and Razin (1987), Frenkel, Razin, and Yuen (1996), Buiter (1987), Sen and Turnovsky (1989a, 1989b, 1990), Turnovsky and Sen (1991), Brock (1988), Engel and Kletzer (1990), Gavin (1991), and Sen (1994). We, too, shall follow this tradition and accordingly drop money and nominal prices. As we will see, the framework is very adaptable, and the same structure can be applied to the analysis of a variety of disturbances and policy shocks. In addition, the one-sector model lends itself to extensions in many directions, some of which will be pursued in subsequent chapters.

We begin by retaining the one-good model, in which the representative agent produces and consumes a single traded commodity. The key source of sluggishness is through the adjustment costs associated with capital accumulation, as a result of which investment behavior is generated by a Tobin-q function.[1] Using this framework, we will find that the equilibrium has nondegenerate dynamics. The model is sufficiently tractable to enable us to characterize the dynamic adjustment of the economy in detail and to highlight the critical role played by the accumulation of capital in this process. In particular, the evolution of the current account is seen to mirror that of capital.

To illustrate the model we will analyze the effects of a change in government expenditure on the single traded good. Two types of policy changes are analyzed: an *unanticipated permanent* and an *unanticipated temporary* expansion. A striking feature of the latter is that a *temporary* fiscal (or other) shock has a *permanent* effect on the economy. The reason for this is that, as we will demonstrate below, the steady state corresponding to a sustained policy depends in part upon the initial conditions of the economy at the time this policy is introduced. The adjustment that occurs during a temporary policy change will have an important bearing on the initial conditions in existence at the time the temporary policy is permanently revoked.

The fact that the steady state may depend upon initial conditions in models with infinitely lived maximizing agents, having a constant rate of time discount, and facing perfect capital markets (assumptions being made here) has been discussed by Giavazzi and Wyplosz (1984). However, its significance for the implications of temporary shocks was not immediately apparent, although it has been investigated in a number of papers by Sen and Turnovsky (1989a, 1989b, 1990). Yet this is an important issue, especially in light of the recent interest in hysteresis and the random walk behavior of real variables such as output and employment (see Blanchard and Summers 1986; Lindbeck and Snower 1987). The present framework is a plausible one for generating this type of behavior, at least in a small open economy.

In characterizing the dynamic adjustment path generated by this fiscal disturbance, the analysis identifies several channels through which a fiscal shock is transmitted to the rest of the economy. First, there is the usual direct impact effect. This is simply the channel whereby an expansion in government expenditure on the traded good impinges directly on the trade balance. Second, a fiscal expansion induces a short-run change in the price of capital (the Tobin q), which in turn determines the transitional adjustment in the capital stock over time. The model is forward-looking, and as a consequence, the short-run adjustment depends upon the long-run response of the capital stock. Third, a fiscal expansion generates a wealth effect, just as it does in a closed economy. However, in contrast to the closed economy, with access to a perfect world capital market, this effect remains constant over time. Moreover, because the economy accumulates wealth while a temporary policy is in effect, thereby determining the initial conditions in existence when the policy ceases, this wealth effect provides the channel whereby the temporary policy has a permanent effect. It is the essential source of the hysteresis generated by the model.

While the one-good model is illuminating in terms of clarifying the dynamics, it is limited in terms of the policy issues it is capable of addressing. Some of the most important involve the real exchange rate, both its direct effect on the evolution of the economy and the role that it plays in the dynamic adjustment. To address these issues it is necessary to extend the model to include a second good and sometimes two or more sectors. Section 3.3 therefore embarks on this by extending the model to deal with a situation where the agent consumes two commodities, a domestically produced good and an imported good. This immediately raises the possibility that government expenditure may be devoted to either or both of these goods. This is not pursued here, since it has been analyzed in detail in Turnovsky (1995, Chapter 12). Rather, we address two issues pertaining directly to the real exchange rate. Section 3.4 analyzes the Laursen-Metzler proposition regarding the effects of terms of trade (real exchange rate) shocks on the level of output and welfare of the economy. This proposition, originally developed within a static equilibrium framework, has been analyzed within an intertemporal macroeconomic framework by authors such as Svensson and Razin (1983), Persson and Svensson (1985), Matsuyama (1988), Sen and Turnovsky (1989a), and Sen (1994). The second issue, discussed in Section 3.5, is an analysis of tariffs. This, too, has traditionally been considered within the context of a static trade model, although more recently several authors have analyzed it by using the type of intertemporal framework to be developed in this chapter (see, e.g., Edwards 1987; Sen and Turnovsky 1989b; Fender and Yip 1989; Engel and Kletzer 1990; Gavin 1991).

3.2 One-Good Model of Physical Capital Accumulation

The Macroeconomic Framework

For present purposes, the household and production sectors may be consolidated. The representative agent accumulates capital (k) for rental at its competitively determined rental rate and supplies labor (l) at its competitive wage. The agent produces output, z, using a neoclassical production function having positive, but diminishing, marginal physical productivity in the two factors of production; that is,

$$z = F(k, l); \quad F_k > 0, F_l > 0, F_{kk} < 0, F_{ll} < 0.$$

For simplicity, capital is assumed not to depreciate; the introduction of capital that depreciates at a constant exponential rate is straightforward, and adds little in this case. In addition, F is assumed to be linearly homogeneous in the private factors, capital and labor, implying that $F_{kk}F_{ll} - F_{kl}^2 = 0; F_{kl} > 0.$[2]

A critical feature of the model is the assumption that investment involves installation costs. Expenditure on a given increase in capital, $\dot{k} = I$, involves adjustment costs specified by the function

$$I + \psi(I) \equiv C(I) \qquad \psi \geq 0, \tag{3.1}$$

where the addition of I units of capital requires the use of $\psi(I)$ units of output. The function $\psi(I)$ is specified to be a nonnegative, convex function of the rate of investment. The convexity of the cost of adjustment component implies $C' \geq 0; C'' > 0$. By choice of units we may set

$$\psi(0) = 0; \quad \psi'(0) = 0; \quad \text{that is,} \quad C(0) = 0; \quad C'(0) = 1,$$

so that the total cost of zero investment is zero and the marginal cost of the initial installation is unity.

The cost of adjustment function has played a prominent role in recent macrodynamic models, both for the closed economy and in an international context, and many variants of its specification can be found in the literature. It therefore merits further comment. First, the assumption of nonnegativity implies that disinvestment at the rate $I < 0$ involves positive dismantling costs also represented by ψ. Second, the assumption that ψ depends upon the level of investment is made largely for convenience and is assumed in much of the literature, including the early contributions by Eisner and Strotz (1963), Lucas (1967), and Gould (1968). By contrast, the adjustment cost function is sometimes specified in the form

$$I + \psi(I,k) = \left(\frac{I}{k} + \psi\left(\frac{I}{k}, 1\right)\right)k \equiv C\left(\frac{I}{k}\right)k \quad \psi \geq 0, \tag{3.1'}$$

where the function $\psi(I, k)$ is specified to be a nonnegative, linearly homogeneous, convex function of the rate of investment and the capital stock. The homogeneity of the installation cost function ensures that the market value of the capital stock is invariant with respect to changes in the scale of the economy.[3] As we will see in Chapter 5, the homogeneity assumption is necessary in order to sustain an equilibrium of ongoing growth in the presence of adjustment costs. But outside this context, little is lost by retaining the simpler assumption, (3.1). Third, in models that include the depreciation of existing capital (taken to be zero here), the question arises of whether ψ should be specified to be a function of gross or net investment. Both specifications can be found in the literature, the latter being closer to the treatment here.[4] Further discussion of the cost of adjustment function is provided by Hayashi (1982).

At the same time, we should point out that the cost of adjustment approach is not without its critics. For example, Kydland and Prescott (1982) argue that when an adjustment cost function having plausible values of the adjustment cost parameter (at least for the absolute rather than the proportionate form of the cost function) is introduced into a small macro model, the implied covariance properties of that model are grossly at variance with the U.S. data over the postwar period. Thus the approach should be accepted with some caution insofar as its empirical relevance is concerned.

The rest of the model remains as set out in Chapter 2, with the representative agent able to accumulate net foreign bonds (b) that pay an exogenously given world interest rate (r^*). Assuming that all taxation is lump-sum, the agent's instantaneous budget constraint is

$$\dot{b} = F(k,l) - C(I) - c + r^*b - T, \tag{3.2a}$$

where r^* denotes the foreign interest, which is now *real*. In addition, the rate of capital accumulation and investment are related by the constraint

$$\dot{k} = I. \tag{3.2b}$$

The agent's decisions are to choose his consumption level, c; labor supply l; rate of investment, I; and rates of asset accumulation, $\dot{k}$ and $\dot{b}$, to maximize

$$\int_0^\infty [U(c,l) + W(g)]e^{-\beta t}dt \qquad U_c > 0, U_l < 0 \quad W_g > 0. \tag{3.2c}$$

The optimization is subject to the constraints (3.2a) and (3.2b) and to the given initial stocks $k(0) = k_0$ and $b(0) = b_0$. For simplicity, the instantaneous utility function is assumed to be additively separable in consumption and labor, on the one hand, and public expenditure, on the other. We also assume that the utility function is concave and that the marginal utility of consumption increases with leisure, meaning that $U_{cl} < 0$.

The discounted Lagrangian for this optimization is expressed by

$$H \equiv e^{-\beta t}[U(c,l) + W(g)] + \lambda e^{-\beta t}[F(k,l) - C(I) - c + r^*b - T - \dot{b}]$$
$$+ q^*e^{-\beta t}[I - \dot{k}], \tag{3.3}$$

where λ is the shadow value of wealth in the form of internationally traded bonds and q^* is the shadow value of the agent's capital stock. Exposition of the model is simplified by using the shadow value of wealth as numeraire. Consequently, $q \equiv q^*/\lambda$ can be interpreted as being the market price of capital in terms of the (unitary) price of foreign bonds.[5]

The optimality conditions for this problem with respect to c, l, and I are, respectively:

$$U_c(c,l) = \lambda \tag{3.4a}$$

$$U_l(c,l) = -\lambda F_l(k,l) \tag{3.4b}$$

$$C'(I) = q. \tag{3.4c}$$

The first two equations are analogous to (2.4a) and (2.4b), while (3.4c) equates the marginal cost of investment to the market price of capital. With a nonhomogeneous cost of adjustment function, the Tobin q determines the absolute level of investment.

Since we are assuming that the rate of time preference is fixed, for reasons discussed in Section 2.2 we require $\beta = r^*$, implying that the marginal utility of wealth remains constant at $\lambda = \bar{\lambda}$. In addition, the market value of capital evolves in accordance with

$$\frac{F_k(k,l)}{q} + \frac{\dot{q}}{q} = r^*. \tag{3.4d}$$

Equation (3.4d) is an arbitrage relationship equating the rate of return on domestic capital to the rate of return on the traded bond. The former consists of two components—the dividend yield (the marginal physical product divided by the price of a unit of capital) and the rate of capital gain. The latter is equal to the world interest rate.

Finally, in order to ensure that the private agent satisfies his intertemporal budget constraint, the transversality conditions must hold:

$$\lim_{t \to \infty} \lambda b e^{-r^*t} = \lim_{t \to \infty} qke^{-r^*t} = 0. \tag{3.4e}$$

Turning to the domestic government, its flow constraint, expressed in terms of new output, is described by the equation

$$\dot{a} = g + r^*a - T, \tag{3.5}$$

where a is the stock of (traded) bonds issued by the domestic government. This equation is analogous to (2.7) and requires no further comment.

Subtracting (3.5) from (3.2a), and recalling the definition of national credit, $n \equiv b - a$, yields the national budget constraint:

$$\dot{n} = F(k,l) - c - g - C(I) + r^*n, \tag{3.6}$$

which has the same interpretation as (2.8). To rule out the possibility that the country can run up infinite debt or credit with the rest of the world, we impose the following intertemporal budget constraint:

$$\lim_{t \to \infty} ne^{-r^*t} = 0. \tag{3.7a}$$

This relationship, together with the transversality condition (3.4e), imposes a corresponding intertemporal budget constraint on the domestic government:

$$\lim_{t \to \infty} ae^{-r^*t} = 0. \tag{3.7b}$$

The complete macroeconomic equilibrium can now be described as follows. First, the consumer optimality conditions (3.4a) and (3.4b), with $\lambda = \bar{\lambda}$, may be solved for consumption and employment as follows:

$$c = c(\bar{\lambda}, k) \quad c_{\bar{\lambda}} < 0, c_k < 0 \tag{3.8a}$$

$$l = l(\bar{\lambda}, k) \quad l_{\bar{\lambda}} > 0, l_k > 0. \tag{3.8b}$$

The formal expressions for the partial derivatives of these functions are obtained by taking the differentials of (3.4a) and (3.4b).[6] Intuitively, an increase in the marginal utility of wealth, $\bar{\lambda}$ (which is constant and is determined by the steady state), shifts the consumption-leisure trade-off against consumption and in favor of labor. An increase in k raises the real wage, thereby leading to a substitution of work for consumption. It is evident from (3.4a) that the dependence of consumption upon capital, and therefore its time dependence, arises because of the assumption that $U_{cl} \neq 0$, and the assumption that employment is variable. If, instead, employment is fixed, then consumption depends only upon $\bar{\lambda}$ and therefore also remains constant over time.

Equation (3.4c) equates the net marginal cost of capital to the shadow price of capital, q. This relationship may be immediately solved to yield

$$I = I(q) \quad I' > 0 \tag{3.8c}$$

and is a "Tobin q" theory of investment. Given the choice of units, $C'(0) = 1$, it follows that $\dot{k} \gtreqless 0$ according to whether $q \gtreqless 1$. In the case where the cost of adjustment is expressed relative to the stock of capital, as in (3.1'), this equation determines the ratio I/K.

Note that the short-run equilibrium does not depend directly upon government expenditure, although it does do so indirectly through the impact of the latter on $\bar{\lambda}$ and q. This is a consequence of the assumed additive separability of the agent's utility function in private and public consumption.

The evolution of the system is determined by substituting the short-run equilibrium into the dynamic equations and ensuring that the transversality conditions are met. It is readily apparent that in fact the dynamics can be determined sequentially. Equations (3.2b) and (3.4d) can be reduced to a pair of autonomous differential equations in the capital stock k and its shadow value q, and these constitute the core of the dynamics that determine the path of real activity in the economy.

Having determined the core dynamics, equation (3.6) then yields the dynamics of the net credit of the domestic economy. This equation may in turn be reduced to an autonomous differential equation in n, after substituting the solutions for q and k. The same applies to the government budget constraint (3.5).

Equilibrium Dynamics

Consider first equations (3.2b) and (3.4d) rewritten as

$$\dot{k} = I(q) \tag{3.9a}$$

$$\dot{q} = r^* q - F_k[k, l(\bar{\lambda}, k)]. \tag{3.9b}$$

Linearizing this pair of equations about the steady state yields

$$\begin{pmatrix} \dot{k} \\ \dot{q} \end{pmatrix} = \begin{pmatrix} 0 & 1/C'' \\ -[F_{kk} + F_{kl}l_k] & r^* \end{pmatrix} \begin{pmatrix} k - \tilde{k} \\ q - \tilde{q} \end{pmatrix}, \qquad (3.10)$$

where $\tilde{k}$ and $\tilde{q}$ denote steady-state values of k and q. Note that in steady state $I = 0$ and $C' = 1$. The determinant of the matrix of coefficients in (3.10) is

$$D \equiv (1/C'')[F_{kk} + F_{kl}(\partial l/\partial k)],$$

which, evaluating $\partial l/\partial k$, can be shown to imply

$$D = (1/C'')F_{kk}\left[\frac{U_{cc}U_{ll} - U_{cl}^2}{\Gamma}\right] < 0,$$

where $\Gamma \equiv U_{cc}U_{ll} - U_{cl}^2 + \bar{\lambda}F_{ll}U_{cc} > 0$. This implies that the long-run equilibrium is a saddlepoint with eigenvalues $\mu_1 < 0$, and $\mu_2 > 0$. Whereas the capital stock always evolves continuously, the shadow price of capital q may jump instantaneously in response to new information; that is, k_0 is predetermined, while $q(0)$ is freely determined.

Starting from an initial capital stock, k_0, the stable dynamic time paths followed by k and q are

$$k = \tilde{k} + (k_0 - \tilde{k})e^{\mu_1 t} \qquad (3.11\text{a})$$

$$q = \tilde{q} + \mu_1 C''(k - \tilde{k}). \qquad (3.11\text{b})$$

Being an eigenvalue of the matrix in (3.10), μ_1 is a solution to the quadratic equation

$$\mu_1 C'' = [F_{kk} + F_{kl}l_k]/(r^* - \mu_1).$$

It is evident from (3.11) that the convexity of the adjustment cost function is an important component of the dynamics. In the absence of such costs, q adjusts instantaneously to its steady-state equilibrium value $\tilde{q}$ (shown below to equal unity). Capital adjusts immediately to its steady-state level, with no new investment; see (3.4d) and (3.19d). This instantaneous adjustment is possible because the small economy facing a perfect world capital market and having no adjustment costs can purchase as much capital as it desires from the world market. It is not constrained by its own productive capacities, as a closed economy would be.

To complete the discussion of the dynamics, we must consider the two budget constraints: the domestic government budget constraint (3.5) and the national budget constraint (3.6). First, solving the former and invoking the terminal condition (3.7b) leads to the intertemporal government budget constraint

$$a_0 + \int_0^\infty [g(t) - T(t)]e^{-r^*t}dt = 0, \qquad (3.12)$$

where a_0 is the initial stock of bonds issued by the domestic government. This equation is standard. If the domestic government has an initial stock of debt outstanding, then it cannot run a deficit in each period. At some point it must run a surplus to pay off the interest on the debt. With lump-sum tax financing, the time path for $T(t)$ must be chosen to satisfy (3.12) in order for the government to be intertemporally solvent, and we shall assume this to be the case.

The national budget constraint (3.6), together with (3.7a), can be similarly solved to yield the intertemporal national budget constraint

$$n_0 + \int_0^\infty [F(k,l) - c - C(I) - g]e^{-r^*t}dt = 0, \qquad (3.13)$$

where n_0 is the initial stock of foreign bonds held by the domestic economy. If the country starts out as a net creditor to the rest of the world ($n_0 > 0$), it cannot run a trade surplus indefinitely; at some point it must run a trade deficit order for (3.13) to be met. The opposite holds true for a debtor nation.

However, (3.13) differs in a fundamental way from (3.12), in that given the time path for government purchases, there is nothing the government can choose to ensure that (3.13) is satisfied. Output and consumption are determined by market forces. In fact, this intertemporal constraint imposes an additional constraint on the evolution of the economy, determining the stable adjustment of the current account.

To see this, we substitute for c and l from (3.4a) and (3.4b) into (3.6) to yield

$$\dot{n} = F[k, l(\bar{\lambda}, k)] - c(\bar{\lambda}, k) - C(I) - g + r^*n. \qquad (3.14)$$

Linearizing this equation around steady state yields

$$\dot{n} = (F_k + F_l l_k - c_k)(k - \tilde{k}) - I'(q - \tilde{q}) + r^*(n - \tilde{n}),$$

where we are using the fact that $C'(0) = 1$ at the steady state when $I = 0$. Using (3.11a) and (3.11b), this equation may be written as

$$\dot{n} = \Omega(k_0 - \tilde{k})e^{\mu_1 t} + r^*(n - \tilde{n}), \qquad (3.15)$$

where

$$\Omega \equiv F_k + F_l l_k - c_k - \mu_1 > 0.$$

Assuming that the economy starts out with an initial stock of traded bonds $n(0) = n_0$, the solution to (3.15) is

$$n(t) = \tilde{n} + \frac{\Omega}{\mu_1 - r^*}(k_0 - \tilde{k})e^{\mu_1 t} + \left[n_0 - \tilde{n} - \frac{\Omega}{\mu_1 - r^*}(k_0 - \tilde{k})\right]e^{r^* t}.$$

Invoking the transversality condition (3.7a) implies

$$n_0 = \tilde{n} + \frac{\Omega}{\mu_1 - r^*}(k_0 - \tilde{k}), \tag{3.16}$$

so that the solution for $n(t)$ consistent with long-run solvency is

$$n(t) = \tilde{n} + \frac{\Omega}{\mu_1 - r^*}(k_0 - \tilde{k})e^{\mu_1 t}. \tag{3.17}$$

Equation (3.16) is a linear approximation to the national intertemporal budget constraint (3.13) that corresponds to the stable path followed by capital, while (3.17) describes the relationship between the accumulation of capital and the accumulation of traded bonds during the transition, if this condition is to be met. Differentiating this latter relationship with respect to t, we obtain

$$\dot{n}(t) = \frac{\Omega}{\mu_1 - r^*}\dot{k}(t), \tag{3.18}$$

where in the absence of any distortionary taxes, we can show that

$$\frac{\Omega}{r^* - \mu_1} > 1,$$

so that a unit increase in the rate of capital accumulation leads to a greater than unit decrease in the net credit position of the domestic economy.[7] The definition of Ω given in (3.15) emphasizes that capital exercises two channels of influence on the country's trade balance. First, an increase in k raises output both directly, and indirectly by raising the real wage and inducing the agent to substitute labor for consumption. In addition, an increase in k lowers the shadow value of capital, q, thereby reducing investment and the economy's rate of absorption. Both of these effects improve the country's balance of trade.

Savings, Investment, and the Current Account

The equilibrium dynamics we have been discussing include a number of important relationships between savings, consumption, investment, and the accumulation of foreign assets. It is important that these be drawn out more explicitly. Central to this discussion is the role of "consumption smoothing," which is a key feature of any macroeconomic model based on intertemporal optimization. In principle, it is possible to combine the optimality conditions of the representative agent with this intertemporal budget constraint to derive the consumption function in terms of the entire future time path of income. Explicit solutions of this form can easily be obtained when the underlying utility function is logarithmic or isoelastic (see, e.g., Turnovsky 1995, Chapter 9; Obstfeld and Rogoff 1996, Chapter 2). This is precisely a statement of the standard permanent income or life cycle hypotheses of consumption. In the present general equilibrium context, this life cycle behavior is represented by the solution

$$c = c(\bar{\lambda}, k). \tag{3.8a}$$

The fact that consumption depends upon the marginal utility of wealth, which depends upon long-run factors and is constant through time, implies that consumption changes only gradually over time in response to the evolving capital stock. If the utility function is additively separable in consumption and labor, it follows further from (3.4a) that $c = c(\bar{\lambda})$, and is in fact independent of the accumulating capital stock, so that consumption remains constant over time.

The ability to borrow and lend abroad plays an important role in bringing about consumption smoothing. This can be seen by substituting (3.8a) and (3.8b) into (3.6) to yield

$$\dot{n} = F(k, l(\bar{\lambda}, k)) - c(\bar{\lambda}, k) - g - C(I(q)) + r^* n. \tag{3.6'}$$

Suppose, for example, that there is a temporary shock in output. Since it is temporary, there is little response in the marginal utility of wealth, $\bar{\lambda}$, which is determined by long-run equilibrium conditions. There may be a some adjustment in q, which also is a forward-looking variable, but tends to discount temporary shocks (see the discussion below). Thus, while the output shock may lead to a small increase in the rate of investment, it is met primarily by an accumulation of foreign bonds. Rather than raising consumption, which they wish to keep relatively constant over time, the agents choose to invest their windfall income abroad. Similarly, rather than reducing consumption in response to a temporary increase in government spending, and the lower income that that entails, the agents choose to finance their stable flow by reducing their holdings of foreign assets, or even borrowing from abroad.

This contrasts somewhat with the corresponding behavior in a closed economy. The current account relationship (3.6') is now replaced by the domestic product market clearing condition:

$$F(k, l(\lambda, k)) - c(\lambda, k) - g - C(I(q)) = 0.$$

In this case, the marginal utility of wealth is no longer constant through time, but is free to respond instantaneously to unexpected shocks (see Turnovsky 1995, Chapter 9). A temporary shock in output will now require some response in consumption, in order for goods market equilibrium to prevail. How this shock is shared between an increase in consumption and an increase in investment will depend in part upon the costs of investment, as measured by the convexity of the investment function.

National nonhuman wealth of the economy, W, is defined by $W = qK + n$. Differentiating this relationship, and using the fact that savings, S, equals the rate of wealth accumulation, yields

$$S = \dot{W} = \dot{q}k + q\dot{k} + \dot{n}$$

and enables us to bring out the relationship between savings and investment along the transitional path in this small open economy. Using equations (3.11) and (3.18), we obtain

$$S = \left(\mu_1 C''k + q + \left[\frac{\Omega}{\mu_1 - r^*}\right]\right)\dot{k}.$$

Suppose the economy is on a path of positively accumulating capital. While the accumulation of physical capital is associated with positive savings, this is offset by the decline in the value of capital along the path. In addition, (3.18) implies that in the neighborhood of steady-state equilibrium, the rate of capital accumulation ($\dot{k} > 0$) along a stable adjustment path is associated with a more than offsetting decumulation of foreign credit ($\dot{n} < -\dot{k} < 0$), so that the net effect is that positive investment is associated with negative savings. This inverse relationship may become a positive one away from equilibrium, where capital grows more rapidly and the economy has a larger q. It is also more complex in the two-good model of Section 3.3, where the negative relationship between the accumulation of capital and the decumulation of foreign bonds is less clear-cut.

In any event, the above discussion suggests that the relationship between savings and investment in an open economy with high capital is at best a weak one. Feldstein and Horioka (1980) empirically investigated the relationship between these two variables by regressing the investment:output ratio on the savings:output ratio of sixteen OECD countries over the period 1960–74. Their expectations were that given high capital mobility, these two variables would be weakly related, with any divergence between them being accommodated by lending or borrowing abroad, as our model has suggested. Instead, they found a strongly positive correlation, with a regression coefficient quite close to unity. They interpreted this as evidence against the high mobility of capital, which gave rise to what has become known as the Feldstein-Horioka puzzle.

The resolution of this puzzle has generated extensive research activity, and a number of potential explanations of the Feldstein-Horioka results have seen suggested (see Obstfeld and Rogoff 1996, Chapter 3). These explanations tend to be of three types. The first says that persistent technology or productivity shocks correlated across time and across countries generate comovements in savings and investment. The second explanation relies on balance of payments policy reactions by national governments. A third type of explanation relies on various types of market imperfections. In Chapter 11 we shall look at the correlations between investment and savings implied by a stochastic model and show how the implications of that model are in fact consistent with the Feldstein-Horioka findings. That approach has been pursued in detail by Grinols (1996).

Steady State

The steady state of the economy is obtained when $\dot{k} = \dot{q} = \dot{n} = 0$ and is given by the following set of relationships:

$$U_c(\tilde{c}, \tilde{l}) = \bar{\lambda} \tag{3.19a}$$

$$U_l(\tilde{c}, \tilde{l}) = -F_l(\tilde{k}, \tilde{l})\bar{\lambda} \tag{3.19b}$$

$$\tilde{q} = 1 \tag{3.19c}$$

$$F_k(\tilde{k}, \tilde{l}) = r^* \tag{3.19d}$$

$$F(\tilde{k}, \tilde{l}) - \tilde{c} - g + r^*\tilde{n} = 0 \tag{3.19e}$$

$$n_0 = \tilde{n} + \frac{\Omega}{\mu_1 - r^*}(k_0 - \tilde{k}). \tag{3.19f}$$

These equations jointly determine the steady-state equilibrium solutions for $\tilde{c}, \tilde{k}, \tilde{l}, \tilde{q}, \tilde{n}$, and $\bar{\lambda}$.

Several aspects of this steady-state merit comment. First, the steady-state value of q is unity, consistent with the Tobin q theory of investment. Second, the steady-state marginal physical product of capital is equated to the exogenously given foreign interest rate, thereby determining the domestic capital:labor ratio in precisely the same ways it is determined by the rate of time discount in a closed economy. Third, (3.19e) implies that in steady-state equilibrium, the current account balance must be zero. The interest earned on the nation's net holdings of foreign assets must just finance its trade balance; a net creditor country can finance a trade deficit and vice versa. Equation (3.19f) describes the equilibrium relationship between the accumulation of capital over time and the accumulation of traded bonds consistent with the nation's intertemporal budget constraint. The quantity $n_0 + [\Omega k_0/(r^* - \mu_1)]$ measures the initial present value of total resources available to the economy and can be termed national wealth. This can be broken down into initial nonhuman wealth, $n_0 + k_0$ (assuming $q(0) = 1$), plus the present value of resources generated by the accumulation of capital starting from the initial capital stock, k_0. It is through this relationship that the steady state depends upon the initial stocks of assets k_0, and n_0, as a result of which *temporary* policy (or other) shocks have *permanent* effects. Finally, we should recall that this steady state is sustainable only as long as the government maintains a feasible debt and taxing policy consistent with its intertemporal budget constraint (3.12).

Long-Run Effects of a Fiscal Expansion

Since the analysis is based on the assumption of perfect foresight, the transitional adjustment is determined in part by the expectations of the long-run steady state. It is therefore convenient to begin with a consideration of the long-run equilibrium effects of an increase in government expenditure. Differentiating the equilibrium system (3.19) with respect to g, these effects can be summarized by the following expressions:[8]

$$\frac{d(\widetilde{k/l})}{dg} = 0 \tag{3.20a}$$

$$\frac{1}{\tilde{k}}\frac{d\tilde{k}}{dg} = \frac{1}{\tilde{l}}\frac{d\tilde{l}}{dg} = \frac{1}{\tilde{z}}\frac{d\tilde{z}}{dg} = \frac{(F_{kk}/l)[U_{lc} + F_l U_{cc}]}{D} > 0 \tag{3.20b}$$

$$\frac{d\tilde{c}}{dg} = -\frac{F_{kk}[U_{lc}F_l + U_{ll}]}{D} < 0 \tag{3.20c}$$

$$\frac{d\tilde{\lambda}}{dg} = -\frac{F_{kk}[U_{cc}U_{ll} - U_{lc}^2]}{D} > 0 \tag{3.20d}$$

$$\frac{d\tilde{n}}{dg} = -\left(\frac{\Omega}{r^* - \mu_1}\right)\frac{d\tilde{k}}{dg} < 0, \tag{3.20e}$$

where

$$D \equiv (U_{lc} + F_l U_{cc})[F_l F_{kk} + F_{kl} r^* (\Omega/(r^* - \mu_1) - 1)] + F_{kk}(U_{ll} + F_l U_{lc}) > 0.$$

These results are straightforward to interpret. Since the world interest rate r^* remains fixed, and the production function is homogeneous of degree one, the marginal physical product condition (3.19d) implies that the long-run capital:labor ratio is constant, independent of g. Capital and labor therefore change in the same proportions, so that the marginal physical product of labor, and hence the real wage rate, also remain constant. Because government expenditure is not directly productive and does not affect the marginal productivities of capital and labor, an increase in g, with its accompanying increase in taxes over time, leads to a fall in private wealth and consumption, and consequently to a less than proportional increase in output; $d\tilde{z}/dg < 1$. The marginal utility of wealth therefore rises, inducing agents to increase their supply of labor. During the transition to the new steady state, the increase in labor supply raises the marginal physical product of capital above its (unchanged) long-run equilibrium value, thereby encouraging capital accumulation until the capital:labor ratio is restored to its original fixed equilibrium level, determined by the world interest rate. At the same time, the increase in the steady-state stock of capital leads to a decline in the steady-state stock of traded bonds held by the domestic economy.

These responses are much as in the closed economy (see Turnovsky 1995, Chapter 9). There we identified the effect that we have been discussing as a pure (negative) *wealth effect* of the expansion in government expenditure. In addition, to the extent that g interacts directly with private behavior, as it will if it enters nonadditively in the agent's utility function or production function, this will give rise to a second effect through its direct impact on the behavior of the private agent. It is straightforward to extend the present analysis to deal with these cases, and some consideration of them will be presented in our discussion of the international transmission of fiscal shocks in chapters 6 and 8.

Transitional Dynamics

As discussed above, the dynamics of k and q are described by a saddle-point in $k - q$ space. The nature of the dynamics can be conveniently understood by consideration of the associated phase diagram. This is illustrated in Figure 3.1 and is constructed as follows.

First, the horizontal locus AA denoted by $q = 1$ corresponds to the value of q at which investment ceases, so that $\dot{k} = 0$. Next, the locus BB describes the combination of the capital stock and its price at which the dividend on investing in capital, F_k/q, just equals the return on the foreign bond, so that the price of capital remains constant. This has the negative slope

$$\left(\frac{dq}{dk}\right)_{\dot{q}=0} = \frac{F_{kk} + F_{kl}l_k}{r^*} < 0.$$

Since an increase in k decreases the marginal physical product of capital (even after allowing for its positive effect on employment), q must decline

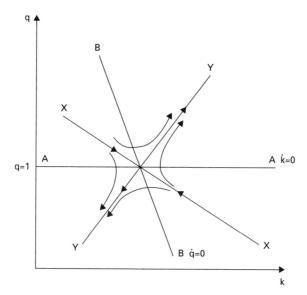

Figure 3.1
Phase diagram

in order to maintain the rate of return equal to the fixed world interest rate.

The locus XX described by

$$q - 1 = \mu_1 C''(k - \tilde{k}) = \left(\frac{F_{kk} + F_{kl}l_k}{r^* - \mu_1}\right)(k - \tilde{k}) \tag{3.21a}$$

is the stable arm of the saddlepoint passing through the equilibrium point $(\tilde{k}, \tilde{q})$. Along this line, both k and q follow adjustment paths,

$$\dot{k} = \mu_1(k - \tilde{k}); \quad \dot{q} = \mu_1(q - \tilde{q}),$$

which imply a stable adjustment of the system to its equilibrium. It is negatively sloped, but flatter than the locus $(dq/dk)_{\dot{q}=0}$.

Likewise, the locus YY, described by

$$q - 1 = \mu_2 C''(k - \tilde{k}) = \left(\frac{F_{kk} + F_{kl}l_k}{r^* - \mu_2}\right)(k - \tilde{k}), \tag{3.21b}$$

is the stable arm of the saddlepoint passing through the equilibrium point $(\tilde{k}, \tilde{q})$. Along this line, k and q follow adjustment paths,

$$\dot{k} = \mu_2(k - \tilde{k}); \quad \dot{q} = \mu_2(q - \tilde{q}),$$

which describe unstable adjustment of the system away from its equilibrium. This is a positively sloped locus.

Everywhere above the line AA is associated with an increasing capital stock (i.e., $\dot{k} > 0$) and everywhere below it with a decreasing capital stock. Likewise, everywhere to the right of BB is associated with an increasing price of capital, and everywhere to the left of it the price of capital is decreasing. This implies the directions of motion indicated by the arrows. All these loci initially approach the equilibrium before ultimately veering away. Note that when they cross the AA locus, the direction of motion is vertical (there is no motion in the k direction), and when they cross the BB motion, the dynamics must be horizontal because at that point the price of capital is unchanging.

Permanent Increase in Government Expenditure

As long as no future change is anticipated, the economy must lie on the stable locus XX. With k_0 being predetermined, the initial jump in $q(0)$, following an unanticipated permanent increase in g is [see (3.11b)]

$$\frac{dq(0)}{dg} = -\mu_1 C'' \frac{d\tilde{k}}{dg} > 0. \tag{3.22}$$

The perfectly anticipated long-run increase in the capital stock thus gives rise to a short-run increase in the shadow price $q(0)$.

The dynamics following an unanticipated permanent increase in g is illustrated in figures 3.2A and 3.2B. Part A describes the adjustment in q and k, while Part B describes the evolution of the stock of traded bonds. Suppose that the economy starts in steady-state equilibrium at the point P on the stable arm XX and that there is a permanent increase in g. The new steady state is at the point Q, with a higher equilibrium stock of capital $\tilde{k}$, and an unchanged shadow value of capital $\tilde{q} = 1$. In the short run, q jumps from P to A on the new stable locus $X'X'$. From (3.4c), it is seen that the increase in q has an immediate expansionary effect on investment, and capital begins to accumulate.

From (3.8a) and (3.8b), the initial responses of employment and consumption are given by

$$\frac{dl(0)}{dg} = \frac{\partial l}{\partial \bar{\lambda}} \frac{\partial \bar{\lambda}}{\partial g} > 0 \tag{3.23a}$$

$$\frac{dc(0)}{dg} = \frac{\partial c}{\partial \bar{\lambda}} \frac{\partial \bar{\lambda}}{\partial g} < 0. \tag{3.23b}$$

These operate entirely through the induced jump in the marginal utility of wealth, $\bar{\lambda}$. The increase in the constant marginal utility of wealth resulting from an increase in government expenditure leads to an immediate shift from consumption to labor. Differentiating (3.8) at steady state and

Chapter 3

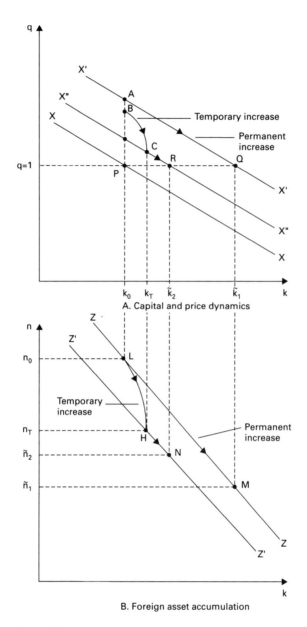

Figure 3.2
Increase in government expenditure

comparing with (3.23), we obtain

$$\frac{d\tilde{l}}{dg} = \frac{\partial l}{\partial \bar{\lambda}}\frac{\partial \bar{\lambda}}{\partial g} + \frac{\partial l}{\partial k}\frac{\partial \tilde{k}}{\partial g} > \frac{dl(0)}{dg} > 0$$

$$\frac{d\tilde{c}}{dg} = \frac{\partial c}{\partial \bar{\lambda}}\frac{\partial \bar{\lambda}}{\partial g} + \frac{\partial c}{\partial k}\frac{\partial \tilde{k}}{\partial g} < \frac{dc(0)}{dg} < 0.$$

Thus, a permanent increase in g has the same qualitative effect on employment and consumption in the short run as it does in the steady state, though the initial adjustments toward the new equilibrium are only partial. The increase in capital that occurs along the transitional adjustment path reinforces the substitution to labor from consumption generated by the wealth effect in the short run.

The endogeneity of labor is critical to these adjustments. To see this, consider the steady-state relationships (3.19) and assume instead that employment is fixed, so that the optimality condition (3.19b) is no longer applicable. The marginal productivity condition (3.19d) now implies that the equilibrium stock of capital (rather than the capital:labor ratio) is determined exogenously by r^* and is independent of g. It therefore follows from (3.11a) and (3.11b) that the capital stock and the shadow price of investment remain constant at all points of time. Output is therefore unchanged. There are no dynamics, and all that happens is that the fiscal expansion leads to a once-and-for-all decline in private consumption c.[9]

Part B of Figure 3.2 illustrates the relationship between n and k, which, combining (3.11a) and (3.17), is

$$n(t) - \tilde{n} = \frac{\Omega}{\mu_1 - r^*}(k(t) - \tilde{k}).$$

This is a negatively sloped line, denoted by ZZ. Since $d\tilde{n}/dg = (\Omega/(\mu_1 - r^*))(d\tilde{k}/dg)$, this line remains fixed. The movement along A to Q in Figure 3.2A corresponds to a movement along LM in Figure 3.2B. From this figure, we see that an increase in government expenditure on the traded good leads to an immediate decumulation of foreign bonds. Despite the fact that the increase in g stimulates employment, and therefore output, while reducing consumption, this is more than offset by the direct claim on output of the government, plus the stimulus to investment. Over time, as the capital stock is accumulated and output increases while investment declines, the rate of decline of the stock of foreign bonds is reduced.

Temporary Increase in Government Expenditure

We now consider the dynamic adjustment to a temporary increase in g. In analyzing such a temporary policy, care must be taken to specify its nature precisely. Specifically, we assume that at time 0, say, the government increases its expenditure, which it maintains at the higher level until time $T > 0$, say, when it is restored to its original level. We assume that agents understand at the outset (time 0) that the change is only for the duration of the period $(0, T)$, so that at time T, when the expenditure is cut back, this action has been fully anticipated and there is no surprise. The only new piece of information occurs at time 0, when the temporary increase is put into effect; this is the only time at which the shadow value of wealth undergoes a discrete jump. The fiscal expansion can thus be characterized as being a priori temporary. This is in contrast to a situation where what is initially considered to be a permanent increase at time 0 in fact turns out to be only temporary when, at time T, say, agents learn that government expenditure is being reduced to its initial level. This type of fiscal expansion can be characterized as being ex post temporary. There are two instances when new information is acquired—at time 0 and at time T—and each of these is associated with a jump in the shadow value of wealth, giving rise to a different transitional adjustment path.

The formal solutions underlying this analysis are presented in the Appendix. The transitional adjustment is as follows. As soon as the increase in g occurs, the stable arm XX will shift up instantaneously (and temporarily) to $X'X'$ while the shadow price q increases to the point B, which lies below $X'X'$, at which point the initial rate of capital accumulation is moderated. The same is true for employment. As is the case for a permanent expansion, the increase in (r^*q) is less than the increase in the marginal physical product of capital, resulting from the additional employment, so that q begins to fall; see (3.4d). Moreover, the accumulation of capital is accompanied by a decumulation of traded bonds. Hence, immediately following the initial jump, q and k follow the path BC in Figure 3.2A., while k and n follow the corresponding path LH in Figure 3.2B. At time T, when the level of government expenditure is restored to its original level, the stock of capital and traded bonds will have reached a point such as H in Figure 3.2B. The accumulated stocks of these assets, denoted by k_T and n_T, will now serve as initial conditions for the dynamics beyond T, when g reverts permanently to its original level. As noted in discussing equation (3.19), these stocks will therefore in part determine the new steady-state equilibrium. With no information being received at time T (since the temporary nature of the fiscal expansion was announced at the outset) and no further jumps, the stable locus relevant for subsequent adjustments in q and k beyond time T is the locus $X''X''$, parallel to XX, which passes through the point $k = k_T$. Likewise, the relevant locus linking the accumulation of capital and traded bonds is now $Z'Z'$.

After time T, q and k follow the stable locus CR in Figure 3.2A to the new steady-state equilibrium at R, while k and n correspondingly follow the locus HN in Figure 3.2B to the new equilibrium point N. One can establish formally that $X''X''$ lies above the original locus XX, while $Z'Z'$ lies below ZZ, as these curves have been drawn. In the new steady state, the shadow value q reverts to 1, but with a higher stock of capital and a lower stock of traded bonds than originally. The striking feature of the adjustment is that the *temporary* increase in government expenditure leads to a *permanent* increase in the stock of capital, accompanied by a lower stock of traded bonds. This is because during the transitional adjustment period, during which the fiscal expansion is in effect, the accumulation of capital and bonds will influence subsequent initial conditions, which in turn affect the subsequent steady state.

As the figures are drawn, C lies above R and H lies above N, respectively. The complete adjustment paths BCR and LHN are therefore monotonic. We are unable to rule out the possibility of C lying below R and H lying above N, in which case the accumulation of capital and decumulation of bonds would be reversed at some point during the transition. In any event, the temporary increase in the relative price of domestic goods generates an initial current account deficit, which continues as long as capital is being accumulated.

To understand the intuition behind this result further, it is useful to define the quantity

$$V(t) \equiv n(t) - \frac{\Omega}{\mu_1 - r^*} k(t),$$

which represents a linear approximation to the present value of total resources available to the economy—national wealth, say—starting from the stock of assets $[k(t), n(t)]$ at time t. Using this notion, $V(0)$ is the national wealth starting from the initial endowment at time 0. From (3.11a), (3.16), and (3.17), the equation $V(t) = V_0$ describes the comovement of n and k along the stable adjustment path. It corresponds to a movement along the locus ZZ in Figure 3.2B and represents how the initial endowment constrains the final equilibrium.

Similarly

$$V_T \equiv n_T - \frac{\Omega}{\mu_1 - r^*} k_T$$

serves as the initial value of wealth conditioning the movement for the period after time T, when the temporary fiscal expansion ceases. The economy will converge to its original level after the removal of a temporary policy if and only if $V_T \neq V_0$, which is therefore a necessary and sufficient condition for a temporary shock to have only a permanent effect. In general, however, $V_T \neq V_0$ following a temporary shock, and this is the case here. This is because during the period $(0, T)$, while the temporary shock is in effect, the economy will follow an unstable path taking it off the locus ZZ at time T. It will revert to a new stable path only after time T, when the temporary shock has been permanently removed. Typically, the wealth effects generated while a policy is temporarily in effect will permanently change the present value of resources available to the economy after the shock is removed. This will cause the capital stock to return to some point other than where it began, thereby giving rise to a permanent effect.

Some Further Applications of One-Good Model

The model we have presented in this section is a generic model of a single-good, small open economy, accumulating assets and facing a perfect world capital market. Before proceeding further, other areas of application should be noted.

For example, Sen and Turnovsky (1990) use this model to study the effects of an investment tax credit (ITC) on the dynamics of a small open economy. These authors focus particular attention on the case of a temporary ITC, since this has often been introduced as a temporary measure to stimulate investment. The contrast between the temporary and the permanent policy is particularly striking in that case. While an important feature of the present analysis is that a temporary expenditure increase has a permanent effect, it is in the same direction as the permanent effect. By contrast, in the case of the ITC, the permanent effect of the temporary policy is in the opposite direction; that is, while a permanent ITC will raise the long-run capital stock, a temporary ITC will ultimately result in a long-run contraction in the capital stock. The intuition for this unexpected result is that a temporary ITC has a strong positive impact on investment, stronger than if it were permanent (see Abel 1982). Thus, while the ITC is in effect, the country accumulates capital rapidly. As a consequence, the higher level of national wealth at the time the temporary ITC is removed (the new initial condition for the subsequent adjustment) encourages more consumption and less investment thereafter. The result is that capital decumulates more than if the initial accumulation of wealth had not occurred.

The one-sector model has been used extensively to study other issues pertaining to capital income tax issues; see, for instance, Bovenberg (1986, 1994), Sinn (1987), Frenkel and Razin (1987), Frenkel, Razin, and Yuen (1996), Frenkel, Razin, and Sadka (1991), Nielsen and Sørensen (1991). Issues of optimal taxation in small open economies have been studied by

Sørensen (1990), Frenkel, Razin, and Yuen (1996), and Correia (1996). Correia shows how the well-known result that the optimal tax on capital will converge to zero in steady state, originally obtained by Judd (1985) and Chamley (1986) for a closed economy, extends to a small open economy. Issues pertaining to both capital income taxation and optimal tax policy will be taken up at various stages in subsequent chapters: Chapter 5 in the context of a growth model; chapters 6 and 7 in a two-country framework; Chapter 9 in a stochastic growth context.

3.3 Two-Good Model of Physical Capital Accumulation

We now extend the model to include two consumption goods, one of which is produced domestically and the other of which is imported. The country remains specialized in the production of the domestically produced good, though part of the output will now be exported in exchange for the import good. We shall construct the model on the assumption that the economy can be characterized as being a "semi-small" open economy, meaning that while it is small in the international asset market and in the market of its import good, it is able to influence the price of its export good. However, the Laursen-Metzler effect pertains to a small economy, which takes its terms of trade as given; when it comes to discussing that issue in Section 3.4, we shall specialize the economy to that case.

Macroeconomic Framework

The basic model remains as set out in Section 3.2. The main difference is the introduction of the imported consumption good and the tariff that is levied on it. Domestic private consumption of the domestic good is now denoted by x, and domestic consumption of the imported consumption good is y. Government purchases are analogously denoted by g_x and g_y. While the price of the import good is taken as given, the economy is large enough in the production of the domestic good to affect its relative price and, therefore, the nation's terms of trade.

Equation (3.24a) describes the representative agent's instantaneous budget constraint, expressed in terms of units of foreign output:

$$\dot{b} = \frac{1}{\sigma}[F(k,l) - C(I) - x - \tau\sigma y + \sigma r^* b - T], \tag{3.24a}$$

where

σ = relative price of the foreign good in terms of the domestic good (the real exchange rate),

τ = 1 plus the tariff rate,

and all other variables are as defined previously. The only difference from (3.2a) arises from the import good together with the tariff. Capital accumulation incurs adjustment costs as set out in (3.1), and the rate of capital accumulation and investment continue to be related by (3.2b), where for simplicity we continue to abstract from the depreciation of capital.

The agent's decisions are to choose his consumption levels, x and y; labor supply, l; the rate of investment, I; and the rates of asset accumulation, $\dot{k}$ and $\dot{b}$, to maximize the intertemporal utility function, now specified as

$$\int_0^\infty [U(x,y) + V(l) + W(g_x, g_y)]e^{-\beta t}dt$$
$$U_x > 0, U_y > 0 \quad V' < 0, \quad W_{g_x} > 0, W_{g_y} > 0. \tag{3.24b}$$

The optimization is subject to the constraints (3.24a) and (3.2b) and the given initial stocks $k(0) = k_0$ and $b(0) = b_0$. For simplicity, the instantaneous utility function is assumed to be additively separable in the private consumption goods x and y, labor l, and the public expenditures g_x and g_y. We also assume that the utility function is concave and that the two private goods are Edgeworth complementary, meaning that $U_{xy} > 0$.

The optimization proceeds precisely as before. Analogous to (3.4), we obtain the first-order optimality conditions:

$$U_x(x,y) = \frac{\lambda}{\sigma} \tag{3.25a}$$

$$U_y(x,y) = \tau\lambda \tag{3.25b}$$

$$V'(l) = -\frac{\lambda}{\sigma} F_l(k,l) \tag{3.25c}$$

$$C'(I) = q. \tag{3.25d}$$

The main difference arises with the appearance of equation (3.25b), which is the optimality condition with respect to the imported consumption good, the relevant price of which for the domestic agent is its tariff-adjusted relative price, $\tau\sigma$. In addition, these optimality conditions reflect the assumed additive separability of the utility function in employment.

Since we are assuming a perfect capital market, we continue to require the condition $\beta = r^*$, so that the marginal utility of wealth remains constant at $\lambda = \bar{\lambda}$. In addition, the market value of capital evolves in accordance with

$$\dot{q} = \left(r^* + \frac{\dot{\sigma}}{\sigma}\right)q - F_k(k,l). \tag{3.25e}$$

Given the assumption of interest rate parity, the domestic (real) interest rate $r(t)$ is related to the world interest rate by

$$r(t) = r^* + \frac{\dot{\sigma}}{\sigma}. \tag{3.26}$$

Equation (3.25e) is therefore an arbitrage condition equating the rate of return on capital $(F_k + \dot{q})/q$ to the domestic interest rate $r(t)$. Finally, the transversality conditions (3.4e) must hold.

With the presence of the import good and the tariff imposed on private imports, the domestic government flow constraint, expressed in terms of the foreign good, is described by the equation

$$\dot{a} = \frac{1}{\sigma}[g_x + \sigma g_y + \sigma r^* a + (\tau - 1)\sigma y - T], \tag{3.27}$$

where $(\tau - 1)y$ is the tariff revenue collected by the government from the private sector's imports.

Analogous to (3.6), the national budget constraint, expressed in terms of the foreign good, is

$$\dot{n} = \frac{1}{\sigma}[F(k, l) - (x + g_x) - \sigma(y + g_y) - C(I) + \sigma r^* n]. \tag{3.28}$$

Furthermore, the corresponding intertemporal budget constraints (3.7a) and (3.7b) must hold.

In addition to these optimality conditions and accumulation equations, there is one further equilibrium condition to be met: the domestic output market must clear. This is described by

$$F(k, l) = x + Z(\sigma) + C(I) + g_x, \tag{3.29}$$

where $Z(\sigma)$ is the amount of the domestic good exported, with $Z'(\sigma) > 0$. Since we are not trying to explain behavior in the foreign economy (assumed to be large), we simply postulate that the quantity of exports increases as the domestic real exchange rate depreciates (i.e., as σ increases).

The static equations (3.25a)–(3.25d) and (3.29) may be solved for x, y, l, I, and the relative price, σ, in terms of $\bar{\lambda}$, k, q, and g_x as follows:

$$x = x(\bar{\lambda}, k, q, \tau, g_x) \quad x_{\bar{\lambda}} < 0, x_k > 0, x_q < 0, x_\tau < 0, x_{g_x} < 0 \tag{3.30a}$$

$$y = y(\bar{\lambda}, k, q, \tau, g_x) \quad y_{\bar{\lambda}} < 0, y_k > 0, y_q < 0, y_\tau < 0, y_{g_x} < 0 \tag{3.30b}$$

$$l = l(\bar{\lambda}, k, q, \tau, g_x) \quad l_{\bar{\lambda}} \gtrless 0, l_k \gtrless 0, l_q > 0, l_\tau < 0, l_{g_x} > 0 \tag{3.30c}$$

$$\sigma = \sigma(\bar{\lambda}, k, q, \tau, g_x) \quad \sigma_{\bar{\lambda}} > 0, \sigma_k > 0, \sigma_q < 0, \sigma_\tau > 0, \sigma_{g_x} < 0 \tag{3.30d}$$

$$I = I(q) \quad I' > 0, \tag{3.30e}$$

The explicit expressions for the partial derivatives can be obtained by taking the differentials of (3.25a)–(3.25d) and (3.29) and solving. The following intuitive explanation can be given.

I. An increase in the marginal utility of wealth induces domestic consumers to reduce consumption of both goods and to increase their savings and labor supply. Since the economy is large in the market for the domestic good, this reduction in the demand for that good causes its relative price to fall; that is, σ rises, thereby stimulating exports. The overall effect on the demand for domestic output depends upon whether this exceeds the reduction in x. If it does, then domestic output and (given k) employment both rise; if not, both fall.

II. An increase in the stock of capital raises output and the real wage. The higher domestic output stimulates the consumption of x, though by a lesser amount, and the relative price σ rises. With the two private goods being Edgeworth complementary ($U_{xy} > 0$), the increase in the consumption of the domestic good increases the demand for the imported good as well. While the rise in the real wage rate tends to decrease V', thereby stimulating employment, the rise in σ has the opposite effect and the net effect on employment depends upon which influence dominates.

III. An increase in q stimulates investment. This increases the demand for the domestic good and its relative price rises; that is, σ falls. This in turn raises the marginal utility of the domestic good, implying that the consumption of x must fall; and with $U_{xy} > 0$, y falls as well. On balance, the increase in investment exceeds the fall in demand stemming from the reduction in x and lower exports, so that domestic output and employment rise.

IV. An increase in the tariff rate reduces the demand for the import good; and with $U_{xy} > 0$, y falls as well. This lowers the relative price of the domestic good, thereby reducing domestic output and employment.

V. An increase in government expenditure on domestic output raises the demand for that good, thereby raising its relative price (lowering σ). Employment and domestic output are therefore stimulated. However, the increased output, together with the reduced exports stemming from the fall in σ, is smaller than the increase in demand generated by the additional government expenditure, so that x must fall in order for domestic goods market equilibrium to prevail. With $U_{xy} > 0$, the reduced demand for the domestic good spills over to the import good.

Two aspects of these short-run effects should be noted. First, there are some differences from the corresponding short-run responses in (3.8a) and (3.8b). For example, the negative effect of an increase in capital on consumption in the one-good model stems from the previous assumption $U_{cl} < 0$. By contrast, the positive effect of capital on consumption in the two-good analysis is a combination of the additive separability of utility in labor, the assumed Edgeworth complementarity of the two consumption goods, and the adjustment of the relative price. Likewise, the relative price adjustment plays a role in the effect of capital on short-run employment.

The responses to changes in the tariff or the government expenditure g_x measure only the partial effects of these policy changes. In addition, either policy generates jumps in the marginal utility of wealth and the shadow value of capital, thereby inducing further responses. The complete short-run responses consist of a combination of these effects. Finally, we may note that given the additive separability of the utility function in private and public goods, the short-run equilibrium does not depend directly upon g_y. However, government expenditure on the imported good has an indirect effect through its impact on $\bar{\lambda}$ and q.

The evolution of the system is determined by substituting the short-run equilibrium into the dynamic equations and ensuring that the transversality conditions are met. As in the one-good model, the dynamics can be determined sequentially. The dynamic equations determining k are $\dot{q}$ (3.9a) and (3.25e), but a minor complication is introduced due to the fact that $\dot{\sigma}/\sigma$ appears in the latter equation. A linear approximation to this effect on the dynamics can be taken into account by first differentiating (3.30d) with respect to t—

$$\dot{\sigma} = \sigma_k \dot{k} + \sigma_q \dot{q} \qquad \sigma_k > 0, \sigma_q < 0, \tag{3.30d'}$$

which describes the rate of change of the real exchange rate in terms of the rate of accumulation of capital and its shadow value—and then substituting this equation, together with (3.30c) and (3.30d), into (3.25e).

Using the domestic goods market clearing condition, (3.29), the current account (3.28) may be expressed in terms of exports minus imports plus the interest service account:

$$\dot{n} = \frac{1}{\sigma}[Z(\sigma) - \sigma(y + g_y) + \sigma r^* n]. \tag{3.28'}$$

This equation may in turn be reduced to an autonomous differential equation in n, after substituting the solutions for q and k. The same applies to the government budget constraint (3.27).

Equilibrium Dynamics

The linearized equilibrium dynamics now become[10]

$$\begin{pmatrix} \dot{k} \\ \dot{q} \end{pmatrix} = \begin{pmatrix} 0 & 1/C'' \\ -\rho[F_{kk} + F_{kl}l_k] & r^* \end{pmatrix} \begin{pmatrix} k - \tilde{k} \\ q - \tilde{q} \end{pmatrix}, \tag{3.31}$$

where

$$\rho \equiv \frac{\sigma}{(\sigma - q\sigma_q)} > 0,$$

and are virtually identical in structure to (3.10). The linearized dynamics of k and q are therefore qualitatively identical to those of the one-good economy, so that (3.11a) and (3.11b) continue to apply.[11]

The nature of the intertemporal government and national budget constraints (3.12) and (3.13) remain as before, the only difference being the inclusion of the traded consumption good, where appropriate. Thus, these two relationships, expressed in terms of the foreign good, are modified to

$$a_0 + \int_0^\infty \left\{ \left(\frac{g_x}{\sigma}\right) + g_y - (\tau - 1)y - \left(\frac{T}{\sigma}\right) \right\} e^{-r^* t} dt = 0 \qquad (3.12')$$

$$n_0 + \int_0^\infty \left\{ \frac{1}{\sigma}[F - x - g_x - C(I)] - (y + g_y) \right\} e^{-r^* t} dt = 0. \qquad (3.13')$$

Using (3.29), (3.13') can be expressed more compactly as

$$n_0 + \left\{ \frac{Z(\sigma)}{\sigma} - (y + g_y) \right\} e^{-r^* t} dt = 0.$$

The linearized solution to this equation is now heavily influenced by the role of relative prices. To see this, we consider (3.28') in the form

$$\dot{n} = \frac{Z[\sigma(\bar{\lambda}, k, q, g_x)]}{\sigma(\bar{\lambda}, k, q, g_x)} - [y(\bar{\lambda}, k, q, g_x) + g_y] + r^* n. \qquad (3.32)$$

Linearizing and following the procedures set out in Section 3.2, we again obtain (3.16) and (3.17), where now

$$\Omega = \frac{1}{\bar{\sigma}}[\xi(\sigma_k + \sigma_q \mu_1 C'') - \sigma(y_k + y_q \mu_1 C'')]$$

and $\xi \equiv Z' - Z/\sigma$. In comparison to (3.15), this definition of Ω reflects the role of the relative price adjustment on the current account.[12] An increase in k raises the relative price σ, both directly and through the accompanying fall in q, as seen in (3.21b). What this does to the trade balance depends upon ξ. From the above definition of ξ, $\xi > 0$ if and only if the relative price elasticity of the foreign demand for exports exceeds unity. At the same time, the increase in k increases imports both directly and again indirectly through the fall in q, and this reduces the trade balance. While either case is possible, we shall assume that the relative price effect dominates, so that $\Omega > 0$, as in the one-good model.

Steady State

The steady state of the economy now consists of the following set of relationships:

$$U_x(\tilde{x}, \tilde{y}) = \frac{\bar{\lambda}}{\tilde{\sigma}} \tag{3.33a}$$

$$U_y(\tilde{x}, \tilde{y}) = \tau\bar{\lambda} \tag{3.33b}$$

$$V'(\tilde{l}) = -F_l(\tilde{k}, \tilde{l})\frac{\bar{\lambda}}{\tilde{\sigma}} \tag{3.33c}$$

$$\tilde{q} = 1 \tag{3.33d}$$

$$F_k(\tilde{k}, \tilde{l}) = r^* \tag{3.33e}$$

$$F(\tilde{k}, \tilde{l}) = \tilde{x} + Z(\tilde{\sigma}) + g_x \tag{3.33f}$$

$$Z(\tilde{\sigma}) + \tilde{\sigma}r^*\tilde{n} = \tilde{\sigma}(\tilde{y} + g_y) \tag{3.33g}$$

$$n_0 = \tilde{n} + \frac{\Omega}{\mu_1 - r^*}(k_0 - \tilde{k}). \tag{3.33h}$$

These equations jointly determine the steady-state equilibrium solutions for $\tilde{x}$, $\tilde{y}$, $\tilde{k}$, $\tilde{l}$, $\tilde{q}$, $\tilde{\sigma}$, $\tilde{n}$, and $\bar{\lambda}$, with government policy ensuring that the intertemporal government budget constraint is met. The parallels between (3.33) and the corresponding conditions in the one-good economy, (3.19), are clear.

This completes the description of the two-good model. We can now use it to address issues pertaining to terms of trade shocks and the impact of tariffs.

3.4 The Laursen-Metzler Effect

The effect of a deterioration in the terms of trade faced by a small open economy has been the subject of some controversy since the early 1950s, when Laursen and Metzler (1950) and Harberger (1950) developed what has become known in the international trade literature as the Laursen-Metzler effect. This predicted that a worsening of the terms of trade lowers real income, thereby reducing savings and, given the level of investment, leading to a deterioration of the current account balance.

This proposition has recently been the subject of considerable scrutiny within a neoclassical framework. The focus has shifted away from the static Keynesian savings and investment functions, and toward an analysis based on intertemporal optimization. The appraisal was initiated by Obstfeld (1982) and has been further pursued within a variety of related frameworks by a number of authors. Svensson and Razin (1983), Persson and Svensson (1985), Bean (1986), Sen and Turnovsky (1989a), Sen (1994), and Karayalcin (1995) analyze the effects of terms of trade shocks in a range of deterministic models. Stockman and Svensson (1987) and Backus (1993) do so within a stochastic real business cycles framework, while Stulz (1988) and Turnovsky (1993) analyze terms of trade shocks in a stochastic growth context. These latter contributions will be considered in Part III.

One conclusion to emerge from this literature is that the validity or otherwise of the Laursen-Metzler proposition depends critically upon the assumption and specifications of the model. For example, Obstfeld (1982) considers a model that abstracts from capital accumulation and assumes that the rate of time preference is taken to be a function of the level of utility, as set out in Section 2.5. He finds that in such an economy a deterioration in a small country's terms of trade leads it to save more and to run a current account surplus, thereby contradicting the Laursen-Metzler proposition. The intuition is as follows. As will be recalled from Section 2.5, this form of utility function requires that in the long run the level of instantaneous utility must be such that the rate of time preference equals the world real interest rate. With the latter remaining unchanged, the long-run utility level must ultimately remain unchanged as well. A deterioration in the country's terms of trade requires that its level of expenditure, measured in terms of the domestic good, must increase to maintain the original level of utility. Since the current account must eventually be in balance, and since the level of output measured in terms of the domestic good is assumed to be fixed, the additional expenditure necessary to restore utility must be financed by the interest earned on holding a higher long-run stock of foreign bonds. The accumulation of these bonds during the transition implies an initial current account surplus.

On the other hand, one can show that if in this model the rate of time preference is taken to be constant, a permanent terms of trade shock causes the economy to jump immediately to its new steady state; there is no effect on the current account. This type of instantaneous adjustment was the essence of the model presented in Chapter 2; the presence of a second consumption good has no impact on that aspect of behavior. By contrast, temporary and anticipated future terms of trade shocks still give rise to nondegenerate current account dynamics due to intertemporal consumption smoothing and price speculation. For example, Obstfeld (1983) shows how a temporary deterioration in the terms of trade leads to a current account deficit for the duration of the adverse movement in the terms of trade. Eventually the current account moves into surplus when the terms of trade shock ceases and the economy returns to its initial long-run equilibrium level.

Using a two-period framework, Svensson and Razin (1983) demonstrate that a priori, the effects of a rise in the price of importables is ambiguous. Extending their model to an infinite horizon, they show how if the discount rate is increasing in utility, then the Obstfeld results are confirmed. But it should be recalled that the assumption on the discount rate necessary to give this result is a controversial one, as discussed in Section 2.5.

Persson and Svensson (1985) analyze the effect of a terms of trade shock within an overlapping generations framework. They demonstrate how the effect depends critically upon whether the shock is temporary or permanent, on the one hand, and whether it is anticipated or unanticipated, on the other. The response of the economy is very different, depending upon the duration of the shock and when the news of the shock is received.

With a minor modification, the two-good model developed in Section 3.3 can easily be adapted to study the effects of terms of trade shocks in an economy accumulating capital. This literature relates to a small open economy, in which the terms of trade (relative price) are taken as exogenously given, whereas in our model σ is endogenously determined. This modification is easily accomplished by noting that the economy is small in the world market for both the domestically produced good and the import good. We can thus assume that σ is given exogenously on the world market, in which case the domestic product market equilibrium condition, (3.29), in which this relative price was previously determined, is no longer relevant. The model therefore simplifies substantially, reducing to a mild extension of the one-good model analyzed in detail in Section 3.2.

Sen and Turnovsky (1989a) use the present framework to analyze the effects of (1) an unanticipated permanent, (2) an unanticipated temporary, and (3) a future anticipated shock in the terms of trade. The main result they establish is that in all cases, the short-run dynamics of the economy depends critically upon the long-run response of the capital stock to the deterioration in the terms of trade. This deterioration in turn is shown to consist of a negative substitution effect together with a positive income effect. The resulting behavior depends upon which effect dominates, and neither possibility can be ruled out a priori.

In the case that Sen and Turnovsky argue is more plausible—where the substitution effect dominates—they show how, irrespective of whether the terms of trade deterioration is permanent or temporary, anticipated or unanticipated, the current account goes into surplus when the news of the shock arrives. This is contrary to the Laursen-Metzler proposition and is the consequence of a fall in investment. By contrast, in the case where the income effect dominates, the news of such a shock generates an investment boom, driving the current account into deficit. While in this case the Laursen-Metzler effect on the current account is vindicated, the action is coming primarily from the investment side of the model rather than from the savings, as they had originally argued.

The fact that everything is driven by the long-run capital stock is clear from the structure of the model as laid out in sections 3.2. and 3.3. To calculate the effect of a terms of trade shock on the evolution of the economy, one begins with the steady-state equilibrium as laid out in (3.33) and calculates the effects of a change in σ. The substitution effect originates from the effect of σ on the marginal rate of substitution conditions implicit in (3.33a)–(3.33c). The source of the income effect can be seen by writing the equilibrium current account condition in the form

$$F(\tilde{k}, \tilde{l}) = (\tilde{x} + g_x) + \sigma(\tilde{y} + g_y - r^*\tilde{n}) \tag{3.34}$$

and observing that to the extent $\tilde{y} + g_y > r^*\tilde{n}$, a deterioration in the terms of trade (increase in σ) reduces real income.

Intuitively, a deterioration in the terms of trade causes a substitution away from the import good and toward the domestic good. Given the assumption that goods are complementary in utility ($U_{xy} > 0$), these two adjustments lead to a decline in the marginal utility of consumption, and therefore in the equilibrium marginal utility of wealth, $\bar{\lambda}$. This induces workers to supply less labor, thereby lowering the marginal physical product of capital, and eventually the stock of capital. The income effect works in reverse. With $\tilde{y} + g_y > r^*\tilde{n}$, an increase in σ lowers real income—which, with x and y being normal goods, reduces their consumption. The lower income raises the marginal utility of wealth, $\bar{\lambda}$, causing workers to supply more labor and raising the productivity of capital and the incentives to increase the capital stock. The net effect on the equilibrium capital stock is determined by which of these two effects dominates; once that is established, the dynamics can be analyzed along the lines set out in Section 3.2. This is pursued in detail by Sen and Turnovsky (1989a) for a range of terms of trade shocks.

3.5 Tariffs

A related issue that has engaged the attention of international economists concerns the macroeconomic consequences of tariffs. Much of the formal analysis of the theory of tariffs has been conducted in the context of traditional static Heckscher-Ohlin pure trade models, although there has always been some interest in its macroeconomic consequences. Discredited after the 1930s, tariffs have returned to play a more central role in policy discussions. After a slow start, a substantial literature analyzing the role of tariffs has evolved. This literature has addressed two issues that are at the forefront of policy discussions: the effects of commercial policies in general, and of tariffs in particular, on employment, on the one hand, and the effects on the current account and trade balance, on the other.

The modern theoretical literature analyzing the macroeconomic consequences of tariffs originated with Mundell (1961), who established the proposition that a tariff is contractionary. The essential steps of his argument were that a tariff will raise the terms of trade, thereby increasing savings, reducing aggregate demand, and necessitating a fall in aggregate supply in order for the goods market to clear. Though the result was based on a very simple model, relying on the Laursen-Metzler effect just discussed, subsequent work by Chan (1978) and Krugman (1982) suggested that the result is in fact quite robust with respect to various extensions of the basic *IS-LM* model. Krugman also demonstrated that by reducing income more than expenditure, the tariff will lead to a deterioration of the current account balance.

The basic Mundell model is static. The first analysis of tariffs in a macrodynamic setting was by Eichengreen (1981), who, using a currency substitution model, emphasized the intertemporal trade-offs involved in a tariff. Whereas the contractionary effects suggested by Mundell were found to hold in the long run, the short-run effects of the tariff were likely to be expansionary due to the protection granted to the domestic economy. This, however, is gradually reversed over time through savings and the current account surplus.

The Eichengreen model is a dynamic portfolio balance model in which the underlying behavioral relationships are postulated arbitrarily. There is a growing literature analyzing the role of tariffs within the intertemporal optimizing representative agent framework. Some of this is within the one-sector model being developed here (see, e.g., Sen and Turnovsky 1989b). However, the introduction of tariffs has important consequences for the allocation of resources across sectors, so that much of the recent literature employs some kind of multisector framework (see, e.g., van Wijnbergen 1987; Engel and Kletzer 1990; Turnovsky 1991; Gavin 1991; Brock and Turnovsky 1993).

Some of the multisector issues will be discussed in Chapter 4 when we introduce two-sector models. Here we shall indicate how the two-good model of Section 3.3 can be used to address some of the intertemporal aspects of the aggregate effects of tariffs. This topic has been addressed in

Table 3.1
Long-run effects of increase in tariff

1. Capital-labor ratio:

$$\frac{d(\widetilde{k/l})}{d\tau} = 0$$

2. Capital, employment, and output:

$$\frac{1}{k}\frac{d\tilde{k}}{d\tau} = \frac{1}{l}\frac{d\tilde{l}}{d\tau} = \frac{1}{z}\frac{d\tilde{z}}{d\tau} = -\frac{\bar{\lambda}F_l}{\sigma l D}[-U_{xx}\sigma Z' + \xi U_{xy}] < 0$$

3. Relative price (real exchange rate):

$$\frac{d\tilde{\sigma}}{d\tau} = \frac{\bar{\lambda}}{\sigma D}\left\{V''\sigma + \frac{\sigma}{l}FF_l U_{xx} + \psi U_{xy}F_l\right\} < 0$$

4. Consumption of domestic good:

$$\frac{d\tilde{x}}{d\tau} = -\frac{\bar{\lambda}}{D}\left\{U_{xy}\frac{F_l}{\sigma}\left(\frac{F\xi}{l} + Z'\psi\right) + V''Z'\right\} \gtrless 0$$

5. Consumption of imported good:

$$\frac{d\tilde{y}}{d\tau} = \frac{\bar{\lambda}}{D}\left\{U_{xx}\frac{F_l}{\sigma}\left(\frac{F\xi}{l} + Z'\psi\right) + V''\frac{\xi}{\sigma}\right\} \gtrless 0$$

6. Marginal utility:

$$\frac{d\tilde{\lambda}}{d\tau} = \frac{\bar{\lambda}}{D}\left[V''\left(-\sigma Z'U_{xx} + \frac{\bar{\lambda}}{\sigma} + \xi U_{xy}\right) + \frac{\bar{\lambda}F_l}{\sigma^2}\left(\sigma F\frac{U_{xx}}{l} + \psi U_{xy}\right)\right] < 0$$

7. Net foreign assets:

$$\frac{d\tilde{n}}{d\tau} = -\frac{\Omega}{r^* - \mu_1}\left(\frac{d\tilde{k}}{d\tau}\right) > 0$$

where

$$\psi \equiv -\frac{\sigma r^*\Omega}{r^* - \mu_1}\left(\frac{\tilde{k}}{l}\right) < 0; \quad \xi \equiv Z' - Z/\sigma > 0; \quad \Delta \equiv U_{xx}U_{yy} - U_{xy}^2 > 0$$

$$D \equiv -V''[U_{xy}Z' + \tau(\bar{\lambda}/\sigma) - \tau Z'U_{xx}\sigma] - V''\xi[\tau U_{xy} - (1/\sigma)U_{yy}]$$
$$- F_l\psi U_{xy}\tau(\bar{\lambda}/\sigma^2) - F_l(F/l)U_{xx}\tau(\bar{\lambda}/\sigma) + \Delta(F_l/\sigma)[(F_l\xi/l) + \psi Z'] > 0$$

detail, using this model, by Sen and Turnovsky (1989b), so again we shall focus on a few aspects.

The starting point is the steady-state equilibrium (3.33). The long-run effects of an increase in the tariff rate, summarized in Table 3.1, are obtained by taking the differentials of these relationships. These results are based on the conventional assumption in the analysis of tariffs: that the revenues collected by the tariffs are redistributed back to the agents in lump-sum form.

Since the world interest rate is assumed to be fixed, the marginal product condition (3.33e) implies that the capital-labor ratio remains constant and independent of τ. Capital and labor therefore change in the same proportions; both in fact decline in response to the tariff. Intuitively, the imposition of a tax in the form of a tariff on the imported consumption good leads to an initial substitution away from that good and toward the other goods favored by consumers: the domestic good and leisure. With $U_{xy} > 0$ this lowers the marginal utility of consumption, and therefore the equilibrium marginal utility of wealth, $\bar{\lambda}$. Consumers are willing to supply less labor, making capital less productive, so that the long-run capital stock, employment, and therefore output, decline. The long-run effects of the tariff are therefore contractionary, consistent with the long-run analysis of Eichengreen (1981). The decline in domestic output raises the relative price of the domestic good; that is, σ falls. On the other hand, the relative price of the good y facing the consumer, $\tau\sigma$, is higher than before. The decline in the stock of capital leads to a long-run increase in the stock of traded bonds held by the economy. The net effect on the two consumption goods is ambiguous, reflecting the offsetting influences of the wealth and substitution effects.

Rewriting (3.33g) in the form

$$Z(\tilde{\sigma}) - \tilde{\sigma}(\tilde{y} + g_y) = -r^*\tilde{\sigma}\tilde{n}, \tag{3.35}$$

we see that the imposition of the tariff certainly causes the steady-state trade balance, when measured in terms of foreign output $(-r^*\tilde{n})$, to fall. When measured in terms of domestic currency, however, it will also fall as long as the country is a debtor nation $(\tilde{n} < 0)$; for a creditor nation it may either rise or fall, depending upon the size of the relative price effect.

The overall impact of the tariff on the domestic consumption of the two goods is unclear. While the substitution effect is away from y in favor of x, the income effect is ambiguous. One effect of the reduction in domestic output resulting from the higher tariff is to reduce domestic income. But at the same time, the reduction in the relative price serves to raise income as measured in terms of domestic goods. The net effect depends upon which dominates.

The dynamic response of the economy to the tariff is illustrated in Figure 3.3. Due to the contractionary effect of the tariff, this is essentially the mirror image of Figure 3.2, which relates to the expansionary effect of an increase in government expenditure. The figure is constructed in an identical manner. In order to ensure that the economy lies on the stable locus, XX, (3.11a) and (3.11b) (or equivalently (3.21a)), a permanent increase in the tariff rate must give rise to the following jump in its initial shadow value $q(0)$:

$$\frac{dq(0)}{d\tau} = -\mu_1 C'' \frac{d\tilde{k}}{d\tau} < 0. \tag{3.36}$$

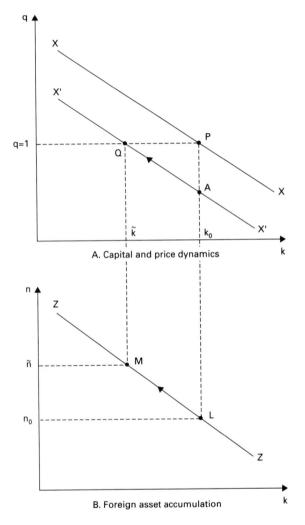

Figure 3.3
Increase in tariff

The long-run decline in the capital stock thus gives rise to a short-run decrease in the shadow price $q(0)$, causing the rate of investment to decline.

The initial responses of other key variables include

$$\frac{dl(0)}{d\tau} = \frac{\partial l}{\partial \tau} + \frac{\partial l}{\partial \bar{\lambda}}\frac{\partial \bar{\lambda}}{\partial \tau} + \frac{\partial l}{\partial q}\frac{\partial q(0)}{\partial \tau} < 0 \qquad (3.37a)$$

$$\frac{d\sigma(0)}{d\tau} = \frac{\partial \sigma}{\partial \tau} + \frac{\partial \sigma}{\partial \bar{\lambda}}\frac{\partial \bar{\lambda}}{\partial \tau} + \frac{\partial \sigma}{\partial q}\frac{\partial q(0)}{\partial \tau} \qquad (3.37b)$$

$$\frac{dx(0)}{d\tau} = \frac{\partial x}{\partial \tau} + \frac{\partial x}{\partial \bar{\lambda}}\frac{\partial \bar{\lambda}}{\partial \tau} + \frac{\partial x}{\partial q}\frac{\partial q(0)}{\partial \tau} \tag{3.37c}$$

$$\frac{dy(0)}{d\tau} = \frac{\partial y}{\partial \tau} + \frac{\partial y}{\partial \bar{\lambda}}\frac{\partial \bar{\lambda}}{\partial \tau} + \frac{\partial y}{\partial q}\frac{\partial q(0)}{\partial \tau}, \tag{3.37d}$$

which consist of two channels of influence. First, there are the direct or "implementation" effects, consisting of the partial derivatives such as $\partial l/\partial \tau$. Second, there are the indirect effects, or "news" effects, which operate through induced jumps in $\bar{\lambda}$ and q. These may or may not work in the same direction as one another, or as the direct effect.

In the case of employment, for example, the direct effect of the higher tariff is contractionary. This is accentuated by the fact that it generates a short-run reduction in the shadow price of investment. At the same time, the fall in the marginal utility of wealth has a further impact on employment, though for reasons noted in Section 3.3, the direction is not entirely clear. However, one can establish that on balance the contractionary effects dominate, so that the imposition of the tariff reduces employment and output in the short run. There are various ways to see why this must be so. One way is to consider (3.25e) on impact. We have already seen that the immediate effect of the tariff is to cause q to drop instantaneously. Since q is unchanged in the steady state, after this initial fall it immediately starts to rise, basically for the reason opposite to that relevant to Figure 3.2 in the one-good model, while k starts to fall; that is, $dq(0) < 0$, $d\dot{q}(0) > 0$, $d\dot{k}(0) < 0$. It then follows from (3.30d') that $d\dot{\sigma}(0) < 0$, so that interest rate parity implies an instantaneous fall in the interest rate-; that is, $dr(0) < 0$. Given these responses, the only way for the arbitrage condition (3.25e) to hold is for the marginal product of capital to fall instantaneously. With the stock of capital being predetermined, this occurs through a fall in employment.

The initial response of the relative price (real exchange rate) is in general unclear. The direct effect, together with the induced reduction in the shadow price of capital, causes it to rise; the fall in the marginal utility of wealth causes it to fall. The fact that $\dot{q} > 0$, $\dot{k} < 0$ at all points on the stable locus implies that σ falls steadily over time, [see (3.30d')], so that there is continuous real exchange rate appreciation, leading ultimately to a lower relative price σ. The fact that $\dot{\sigma} < 0$ also means that the initial reduction in the domestic real interest rate persists along the transitional path until equilibrium is restored, when it returns to the given world rate.

The initial reductions in q and $\bar{\lambda}$ serve to stimulate consumption. In the case of the import good, this is offset by the negative effect of the higher tariff. This is also true in the case of the domestic good, as long as $U_{xy} > 0$.

If the utility function is additively separable in the two consumption goods, then in this latter case only the indirect effects occur; the tariff on the import good stimulates the short-run consumption of the domestic good.

The dynamic responses to the tariff depend critically upon two aspects of the model: (1) the endogeneity of employment and (2) the endogeneity of the relative price. The first plays exactly the same role as it does with respect to government expenditure discussed in the one-good model. If employment is fixed, only shocks in the production function generate dynamics. Regarding the role of the relative price, suppose that the economy is sufficiently small for to be fixed exogenously, as in the discussion of the Laursen-Metzler effect. It is then seen from the optimality conditions (3.33a) and (3.33b) that consumptions x and y are determined by the constant values of $\bar{\lambda}$, τ, and σ and are therefore constant over time; there is consumption smoothing. On the other hand, employment, being a function of the capital stock, does evolve over time as capital is decumulated. In order to restore dynamics to the consumption levels x and y, the assumption of additive separability of utility in goods and labor made in this analysis must be dropped. In that case, x and y will depend upon the dynamics of k in the same way as does employment.

The final aspect concerns the effect of the tariff on the current account. Under the assumption $\Omega > 0$, we see that the net effect of the decrease in capital is to create a current account surplus. With n being predetermined, the trade balance, as measured in terms of the foreign good, also increases. In terms of the domestic good, it will rise if the relative price σ increases; it may fall if σ falls sufficiently. Over time, the initial accumulation of foreign bonds is reversed. This occurs through the fall in σ and k, which causes the trade balance to decline over time.

The effects of the tariff on the trade balance have often been emphasized; indeed, they provided one of the early rationales for tariffs by Robinson (1937), as a means of stimulating domestic employment. The present analysis highlights the intertemporal dimension of these benefits. Whereas the balance of trade may improve in the short run, as Robinson suggested, (3.35) suggests that in the long run it will almost certainly deteriorate.

Sen and Turnovsky (1989b) also discuss the effects of a temporary tariff and an expected future tariff increase. These are not pursued here. Instead, there is one main conclusion we wish to highlight with respect to the effects of tariffs. That is that the introduction (or increase) of a tariff is contractionary, both in the short run and in the long run. In particular, employment is reduced both in the short run and in the long run, so that there no significant intertemporal trade-off, as obtained by Eichengreen (1981). The fall in the long-run capital stock causes an immediate reduction in the rate of investment, which in turn leads to a current account surplus. While this response of the current account is in accordance with much (but not all) of the traditional macroeconomic literature on tariffs, the mechanism by which it is achieved, the decumulation of capital, is different. Also, the fact that the decline in capital stock is accompanied by an accumulation of foreign bonds means that the saving effects of the tariff are unclear, depending upon which influence dominates. This ambiguity of savings is, however, very different from those obtained in other models. For example, the absence of capital in the Edwards (1987) model means that the ambiguity in the response of the current account to a tariff translates directly to a corresponding ambiguity in the behavior of savings.

3.6 Some Final Comments

In concluding this analysis, we should remind ourselves that it is based on the assumption that the country can borrow or lend as much as it wants at the fixed world real interest rate. Bhandari, Haque, and Turnovsky (1990) have incorporated the upward-sloping supply curve of debt introduced in Section 2.6 into a model of physical capital accumulation. With this formulation, the recursive dynamic structure associated with a perfectly elastic supply of debt breaks down. This is because the marginal cost of capital facing firms, and therefore determining their investment decisions, is dependent upon the outstanding stock of national debt. Conditions in the international capital market therefore become important in determining the growth of capital in the domestic economy. Bhandari, Haque, and Turnovsky show analytically how this causes the dynamics involving (1) the stock of capital k, (2) the marginal utility of wealth λ, (3) the shadow value of wealth q, and (4) the stock of national debt z (or credit $n = -z$) to become interdependent. Formal analytical solutions become harder, although not impossible, to derive. The system involves two "jump" variables, λ and q, and two "sluggish" variables, k and n. Under reasonable conditions one can show that the dynamics has two stable and two unstable roots, giving rise to a saddlepoint. The stable dynamics in response to a permanent shock is no longer linear, though one can characterize the asymptotic adjustment path, using the dominant eigenvalue method of Calvo (1987). Bhandari, Haque, and Turnovsky were able to conduct a fairly explicit analysis of the dynamic adjustment of the system in response to a variety of conventional disturbances. It is felt that this offers a promising formulation to address a number of pertinent issues pertaining to policy making in developing economies, such as questions relating to the taxation of capital and trade liberalization.

Appendix: Formal Solutions for Temporary Disturbances

Suppose that the economy starts off from steady state at time 0 with government expenditure initially set at the level g_0, and with the corresponding stocks of physical capital k_0 and foreign assets n_0. At time 0, government expenditure is changed to g_1, where it remains until time T, when it is changed back permanently to its original level, g_0. Because of the shift nature of these changes, it is convenient to consider the dynamics over two periods: (1) the period $(0, T)$, when the temporary policy is in effect, and (2) the period after T, when the policy is permanently removed.

We begin by considering the steady state that *would* prevail if g_1, the temporary level of expenditure, *were* to continue indefinitely. From equations (3.19) this is given by the set of equations

$$U_c(\tilde{c}_1, \tilde{l}_1) = \tilde{\lambda}_1 \tag{3.A.1a}$$

$$U_l(\tilde{c}_1, \tilde{l}_1) = -F_l(\tilde{k}_l, \tilde{l}_1)\tilde{\lambda}_1 \tag{3.A.1b}$$

$$\tilde{q}_1 = 1 \tag{3.A.1c}$$

$$F_k(\tilde{k}_1, \tilde{l}_1) = r^* \tag{3.A.1d}$$

$$F(\tilde{k}_1, \tilde{l}_1) - \tilde{c}_1 - g_1 = r^*\tilde{n}_1 \tag{3.A.1e}$$

$$\tilde{n}_1 - n_0 = \frac{\Omega_1}{\mu_1 - r^*}(\tilde{k}_1 - k_0), \tag{3.A.1f}$$

where, as in the text, $\mu_1 < 0$ is the stable eigenvalue and now $\Omega_1 \equiv F_k + F_l l_k - c_k - \mu_1 > 0$. Tildes denote steady states, and the subscript 1 denotes the first regime (i.e., when the temporary policy is in effect). These equations may be solved for $\tilde{k}_1$ and $\tilde{n}_1$, in particular, in the form

$$\tilde{k}_1 = \gamma(k_0, n_0, g_1) \tag{3.A.2a}$$

$$\tilde{n}_1 = \delta(k_0, n_0, g_1). \tag{3.A.2b}$$

Using this notation, the assumption that k_0 and n_0 are initial steady states implies

$$k_0 = \gamma(k_0, n_0, g_0) \tag{3.A.3a}$$

$$n_0 = \delta(k_0, n_0, g_0). \tag{3.A.3b}$$

One-Sector Models of Capital Accumulation

The partial derivatives of the functions γ and δ can be obtained by taking the differentials of the system (3.A.1). In particular, we may establish

$$\frac{\partial \gamma}{\partial k_0} \equiv \gamma_k = \frac{\Omega_1}{r^* - \mu_1} \gamma_n \tag{3.A.4a}$$

$$\frac{\partial \gamma}{\partial n_0} \equiv \gamma_n = \frac{r^* F_{kl}}{D} [U_{lc} + F_l U_{cc}] < 0 \tag{3.A.4b}$$

$$\frac{\partial \gamma}{\partial g_0} \equiv \gamma_g = -\frac{F_{kl}}{D} [U_{lc} + F_l U_{cc}] > 0 \tag{3.A.4c}$$

$$\frac{\partial \delta}{\partial k_0} \equiv \delta_k = -\frac{\Omega_1}{r^* - \mu_1} [\gamma_k - 1] \tag{3.A.4d}$$

$$\frac{\partial \delta}{\partial n_0} \equiv \delta_n = 1 - \gamma_k \tag{3.A.4e}$$

$$\frac{\partial \delta}{\partial g_0} \equiv \delta_g = -\frac{\Omega_1}{r^* - \mu_1} \gamma_g < 0, \tag{3.A.4f}$$

where $D > 0$ is defined below equations (3.20).

The dynamic adjustments of the state variables, k, q, and n over the initial phase $(0, T)$ are given by the equations

$$k(t) = \tilde{k}_1 + A_1 e^{\mu_1 t} + A_2 e^{\mu_2 t} \tag{3.A.5a}$$

$$q(t) = \tilde{q}_1 + A_1 \mu_1 C'' e^{\mu_1 t} + A_2 \mu_2 C'' e^{\mu_2 t} \tag{3.A.5b}$$

$$n(t) = \tilde{n}_1 + \left[n_0 - \tilde{n}_1 - \frac{A_1 \Omega_1}{\mu_1 - r^*} - \frac{A_2 \Omega_2}{\mu_2 - r^*} \right] e^{r^* t} + \frac{A_1 \Omega_1}{\mu_1 - r^*} e^{\mu_1 t}$$

$$+ \frac{A_2 \Omega_2}{\mu_2 - r^*} e^{\mu_2 t}, \tag{3.A.5c}$$

where $\mu_2 > 0$ is the unstable eigenvalue, $\Omega_2 \equiv F_k + F_l l_k - c_k - \mu_2$, and the constants A_1 and A_2 are yet to be determined. Observe that equations (3.A.5a)–(3.A.5c) describe the time paths that in the absence of a future disturbance would be ultimately unbounded.

For the period after time T, when the temporary policy is removed, the steady state is now determined by the set of equations

$$U_c(\tilde{c}_2, \tilde{l}_2) = \bar{\lambda}_2 \tag{3.A.6a}$$

$$U_l(\tilde{c}_2, \tilde{l}_2) = -F_l(\tilde{k}_2, \tilde{l}_2) \bar{\lambda}_2 \tag{3.A.6b}$$

$$\tilde{q}_2 = 1 \tag{3.A.6c}$$

$$F_k(\tilde{k}_2, \tilde{l}_2) = r^* \tag{3.A.6d}$$

$$F(\tilde{k}_2, \tilde{l}_2) - \tilde{c}_2 - g_0 = r^*\tilde{n}_2 \tag{3.A.6e}$$

$$\tilde{n}_2 - n_T = \frac{\Omega_1}{\mu_1 - r^*}(\tilde{k}_2 - k_T), \tag{3.A.6f}$$

where the subscript denotes the second regime, and k_T and n_T denote the stocks of k and n at time T, the instant government expenditure is restored to its original level. Solving these equations for $\tilde{k}_2$ and $\tilde{n}_2$ yields the solutions

$$\tilde{k}_2 = \gamma(k_T, n_T, g_0) \tag{3.A.7a}$$

$$\tilde{n}_2 = \delta(k_T, n_T, g_0), \tag{3.A.7b}$$

where the functions γ and δ are of the form in (3.A.2).

In order for the transversality conditions to be met, the dynamics over this latter period must be stable and are given by

$$k(t) = \tilde{k}_2 + A_1' e^{\mu_1 t} \tag{3.A.8a}$$

$$q(t) = \tilde{q}_2 + A_1' \mu_1 C'' e^{\mu_1 t} \tag{3.A.8b}$$

$$n(t) = \tilde{n}_2 + \frac{A_1' \Omega_1}{\mu_1 - r^*} e^{\mu_1 t}, \tag{3.A.8c}$$

where A_1' is yet to be determined.

The constants A_1, A_2, and A_1' are determined by (1) an initial condition on k_0 and (2) continuity conditions on k and q at time T. The latter rules out anticipated jumps in the price of capital and an associated infinite rate of return at that instant. Thus, setting $t = 0$ in (2.A.4a) and equating the solutions for (3.A.5a) and (3.A.8a), and (3.A.5b) and (3.A.8b) at time T yields

$$A_1 + A_2 = -(\tilde{k}_1 - k_0) \tag{3.A.9a}$$

$$A_1 e^{\mu_1 T} + A_2 e^{\mu_2 T} - A_1' e^{\mu_1 T} = (\tilde{k}_2 - \tilde{k}_1) \tag{3.A.9b}$$

$$A_1 \mu_1 C'' e^{\mu_1 T} + A_2 \mu_1 C'' e^{\mu_2 T} - A_1' \mu_1 C'' e^{\mu_1 T} = (\tilde{q}_2 - \tilde{q}_1). \tag{3.A.9c}$$

In order to evaluate these constants, we must first determine the changes in the relevant steady-state equilibrium. First, equations (3.A.1c) and (3.A.6c) immediately imply

$$\tilde{q}_2 - \tilde{q}_1 = 0. \tag{3.A.10a}$$

Second, (3.A.2a) and (3.A.3a), together with (3.A.4), imply

$$\tilde{k}_1 - k_0 = \gamma_g \, dg, \tag{3.A.10b}$$

where $dg \equiv g_1 - g_0$. The evaluation of $\tilde{k}_2 - \tilde{k}_1$ is more complicated. From (3.A.7a), (3.A.2a), and (3.A.4), we obtain

$$\tilde{k}_2 - \tilde{k}_1 = \gamma_n \left[\frac{\Omega_1}{r^* - \mu_1} (k_T - k_0) + (n_T - n_0) \right] - \gamma_g \, dg.$$

Using equations (3.A.5a) and (3.A.5c) to determine k_T, n_T and (3.A.1f), this last equation may be rewritten as

$$\tilde{k}_2 - \tilde{k}_1 = \gamma_n \left[A_2 e^{\mu_2 T} \left(\frac{\Omega_2}{\mu_2 - r^*} - \frac{\Omega_1}{\mu_1 - r^*} \right) \right.$$

$$\left. + \left(n_0 - \tilde{n}_1 - \frac{A_1 \Omega_1}{\mu_1 - r^*} - \frac{A_2 \Omega_2}{\mu_2 - r^*} \right) e^{r^* T} \right] - \gamma_g \, dg.$$

Noting further that

$$\tilde{n}_1 - n_0 = \frac{\Omega_1}{\mu_1 - r^*} \gamma_g \, dg,$$

we obtain

$$\tilde{k}_2 - \tilde{k}_1 = \gamma_n \left(\frac{\Omega_2}{\mu_2 - r^*} - \frac{\Omega_1}{\mu_1 - r^*} \right) A_2 e^{\mu_2 T} - \gamma_n \left(\frac{A_1 \Omega_1}{\mu_1 - r^*} + \frac{A_2 \Omega_2}{\mu_2 - r^*} \right) e^{r^* T}$$

$$- \gamma_g \left(1 + \frac{\gamma_n \Omega_1}{\mu_1 - r^*} e^{r^* T} \right) dg. \qquad (3.A.10c)$$

Substituting (3.A.10a)–(3.A.10c) into (3.A.9a)–(3.A.9c), we can solve for the constants A_1, A_2, and A_1'. In particular, we may establish

$$A_1 = -\gamma_g \, dg - A_2,$$

$$A_2 = (\gamma_g \mu_1 + (1/C'')) \frac{dg}{D'},$$

where

$$D' \equiv (\mu_2 - \mu_1) e^{\mu_2 t} + \mu_1 \gamma_n \left[\frac{\Omega_1}{\mu_1 - r^*} - \frac{\Omega_2}{\mu_2 - r^*} \right] [e^{r^* t} - e^{\mu_2 t}] > 0.$$

In evaluating this expression for D', we are using the result, immediate from (3.10), that $\mu_2 = r^* - \mu_1 > r^*$.

Having thus obtained the solutions for k, q, and n, the following relationships may be further established:

$$\tilde{q}_1 - \mu_1 C'' \tilde{k}_1 > q_T - \mu_1 C'' k_T > q_0 - \mu_1 C'' k_0,$$

$$n_0 + \frac{\Omega_1}{r^* - \mu_1} k_0 > n_T + \frac{\Omega_1}{r^* - \mu_1} k_T$$

The first of these implies that both $X''X''$ and $X'X'$ lie above XX, with $X''X''$ lying in between, as drawn in Figure 3.2A. The second implies that the line $Z'Z'$ lies below ZZ, as drawn in Figure 3.2B. The shapes of the paths BC and LH can also be established from the solutions for k, q, and n.

Note that in order for the consumer optimality conditions to hold, λ must be constant at all times other than at time 0, but including at time T. It therefore jumps instantaneously at time 0 to its new steady state value $\bar{\lambda}_2$. It can be shown that a temporary increase in g implies a permanent reduction in $\bar{\lambda}_2$.

Notes

1. This approach to investment is also adopted by Buiter (1987). His analysis of the small open economy is based on numerical simulations. The present model is investigated entirely analytically. For further applications of the cost of adjustment approach to investment to the analysis of alternative macro disturbances in open economies, see, for instance, Matsuyama (1987); Brock (1988); Sen and Turnovsky (1989a, 1989b).

2. Linear homogeneity in capital and labor implies the following relationships:

$$F_{kk}F_{ll} = F_{kl}^2; \quad F_{kk}F_l - F_{kl}F_k = F_{kk}(z/l); \quad F_{kl}F_l - F_{ll}F_k = F_{kl}(z/l),$$

where z denotes output.

3. See Hayashi (1982). In his discussion he draws the difference between the average q and the marginal q and shows how the relationship between them depends upon the linear homogeneity of the installation cost function.

4. See, e.g., Abel and Blanchard (1983, p. 377).

5. This can be shown formally by setting up the decentralized version of the optimization problem and using the equilibrium condition equating the ratio of the shadow value of capital to that of bonds to their relative market price.

6. The formal expressions are as follows:

$$c_\lambda = (U_{ll} + \bar{\lambda}F_{ll} + F_l U_{cl})/\Psi < 0; \quad c_k = \bar{\lambda}F_{lk}U_{cl}/\Psi < 0;$$

$$l_\lambda = -(U_{cl} + F_l U_{cc})/\Psi > 0; \quad l_k = -\bar{\lambda}F_{lk}U_{cc}/\Psi > 0,$$

where $\Psi \equiv (U_{ll} + \bar{\lambda}F_{ll})U_{cc} - U_{cl}^2 > 0$.

7. To show $\Omega/(r^* - \mu_1) > 1$ in the neighborhood of steady state, we observe that at steady state, where, $F_k = r^*$, $\Omega = r^* - \mu_1 + F_l l_k - c_k > r^* - \mu_1$.

8. Note that these expressions ignore the change in $(\Omega/(\mu_1 - r^*))$ associated with the variation in g. This is because this change is multiplied by the quantity $(k_0 - \tilde{k})$. For a small variation in g this term is small relative to the other terms and to a linear approximation can be neglected.

9. Actually, it is the assumption of endogeneity of employment in conjunction with infinitely lived agents that is critical. This is so because it gives rise to short-run dynamics that are driven by long-run changes in the capital stock alone; see equations (3.11) and (3.19). This may be compared with Buiter's (1987) model, for example, where employment is fixed but consumers have finite lives. In this case, the long-run capital stock is also independent of everything other than the foreign interest rate, and is therefore independent of domestic fiscal policy. However, in contrast to the present analysis, temporary changes in the capital stock may still occur. This is due to the fact that the short-run dynamics are also driven by long-run changes in other forms of financial wealth that may be generated by changes in domestic fiscal policy.

10. Note that the (2-2) element r^* in the matrix (3.31) is obtained as follows. In general, following the procedure discussed, it is equal to $\rho[r^* + (\sigma_k/C''\sigma) - F_{kl}l_q]$. Evaluating the derivatives σ_k and l_q, and noting the steady-state conditions given in (3.33), this expression evaluated at steady state reduces to r^*.

11. There is a marginal difference due to the fact the eigenvalue, μ_1, is now a function of ρ.

12. It is also possible to derive an equivalent expression for Ω, more parallel to (3.15), if one solves the bond accumulation equation in the form (3.28). However, this form turns out to be more complex and is not pursued.

4 Two-Sector Models

The one-sector production model, although it is an essential analytical tool of aggregate economics, is of course limited as a framework for analyzing the full impact of policy shocks and structural changes in an international environment. Not only is the one-sector framework restrictive as a description of production conditions in any economy, but it also fails to capture one of the key characteristics of an international economy, the fact that international trading activities affect different parts of the economy differently. In an international economy some parts specialize in exports or export-related activities; others, in imports or import-related activities; and still others, such as service industries, operate more or less independently of the international environment. The differential impacts on these various sectors was a central issue in the debate over the Dutch disease and the discovery of oil in northern Europe, as well as in assessing the effects of mineral discoveries in Australia. In either case, the discovery of the resource led to a change in the country's terms of trade, and this in turn had an effect on both the country's traditional export sectors and its import-competing sectors. Or, to take another example, a tariff imposed on a country's imports, by changing the country's terms of trade, will have consequences elsewhere in the economy. To capture these relative price effects, one needs to augment the basic model to introduce a second sector, or perhaps even more. This can be done in various ways, and alternative models will be discussed in this chapter.

We will begin by developing the two-sector dependent economy of a small open economy. The original model basically employed the traditional static Heckscher-Ohlin production structure, in which the economy is incompletely specialized in the production of two goods using two factors of production, capital and labor. The basic model was concerned with a static allocation of these resources, and our objective is to embed these decisions within a dynamic process of capital accumulation. We will then use the model to analyze two types of shocks: demand shocks (government expenditure shocks) and supply shocks (productivity shocks).[1] As we will discuss in Sections 4.1 and 4.5, the tradability of investment goods is an issue that has generated substantial debate in this literature. This question will be addressed in detail. The initial model, to be developed in Sections 4.2–4.4, focuses on polar cases where investment goods are assumed to be either all nontraded (Sections 4.2–4.3) or all traded (Section 4.4). In Sections 4.6–4.7 we extend the model to include both types of capital goods simultaneously. Section 4.8 considers some modifications to the basic Heckscher-Ohlin two-good model. These include (1) the introduction of costs of adjustment associated with the intersectoral mobility of factors; (2) the addition of another fixed factor of production, specific to one sector or another (the specific factors technology); and (3) a brief extension to include three sectors of production.

4.1 The Dependent Economy Model: Some Background

The study of nontraded goods in the adjustment of the balance of payments has a long history. The earliest analysis of nontraded goods in a macroeconomic setting appears to be that of Cairnes (1859); Taussig (1917, 1920), Graham (1922), and Ohlin (1929) provided other early treatments.[2] Modern analytical treatments of nontraded goods in a macroeconomic setting can be traced to the Australian school of Salter (1959), Swan (1960), Corden (1960), Pearce (1961), and McDougall (1965), to which should be added the important work of Diaz Alejandro (1965) in a Latin American context. In the United States, the papers by Balassa (1964) and Samuelson (1964) singled out the role of productivity differences in the traded goods industries across countries as the primary long-run reason for differences in relative nontraded goods prices.[3] The first published use of the term "dependent economy" was by Salter (1959), to describe an economy that was a price taker on world markets but also produced nontraded goods for domestic use. The term is still very much in use even though nontraded goods account for a substantial share of GDP of large OECD countries, which can hardly be described as being dependent.

The dependent economy model has become a basic workhorse of international macroeconomics. By distinguishing between traded and nontraded goods, it provides a convenient general equilibrium framework for analyzing the behavior of the real exchange rate in both a static and a dynamic context, though the early models of the 1960s were purely static.[4] Whereas Balassa and Samuelson focused on the *supply-side* determinants of the relative price of nontraded goods, the Australian school's analysis focused on the *demand-side* determinants of the relative price of nontradables, taking the supply side of the economy as given.[5]

During the 1970s the incorporation of investment into the dependent economy model by Fischer and Frenkel (1972, 1974) and Bruno (1976) began a process of extending the short-run character of the model to a longer-run treatment of the determination of the relative price of nontradables, the capital stock, and the current account in a small open economy. These early models were open economy extensions of the standard portfolio balance macrodynamic models of that period. However, a decade or so later several authors had begun to incorporate capital formation into an intertemporal optimizing framework (see, e.g., Razin 1984;

Murphy 1986; Brock 1988; Obstfeld 1989). This development, while being of considerable importance for policy analysis, is also of interest to those who want to relate this literature to the standard two-sector optimal growth model, and to earlier open economy extensions that were based on the Heckscher-Ohlin technology (see, e.g., Fischer and Frenkel 1972; Bazdarich 1978; and Matsuyama 1988).

Once the distinction between traded and nontraded goods is introduced, how investment is to be classified becomes important. Intuitively, investment can reasonably be classified into either category. Capital goods, taking the form of infrastructure and construction, are presumably nontraded; investment goods in the form of machinery or inventories obviously are potentially tradable. Different treatments of investment, reflecting these different possibilities, can be found in the literature. For example, Obstfeld (1989), while allowing for capital to be instantaneously movable between sectors, assumes that only the traded good is used for investment. He therefore allows the capital stock to be instantaneously augmented at any point in time by an exchange of traded financial assets for capital. Brock (1988) also treats capital as being traded, though the investment process requires nontraded investment involving convex costs of adjustment, thereby constraining the rate of investment at any point in time to remain finite, as in the model of Chapter 3. By contrast, early authors such as Frenkel and Fischer (1972), and more recently Marion (1984), Murphy (1986), Turnovsky (1991), van Wincoop (1993), Turnovsky and Sen (1995), and Brock (1996), analyze models in which investment is treated as being nontraded.

There is a wide divergence among these papers in terms of (1) the types of disturbances they consider; (2) the time horizon of the analysis; and (3) the specifics of the production structure they adopt. Marion (1984) analyzes oil shocks, while Murphy (1986) discusses productivity shocks; both are both restricted to two-period time horizons. Transversality conditions, which play a central role in the present analysis, are much less significant in these two-period models. Turnovsky (1991) and van Wincoop (1993) both incorporate nontraded investment into a fully intertemporal three-sector framework. Turnovsky is concerned with analyzing the sectoral impacts of tariffs, while van Wincoop discusses the analogous implications of a resource discovery, modeling it as a transfer of income from abroad. Brock (1996) also considers this shock, his particular focus being on analyzing its impact on the current account. In an earlier unpublished version of this paper, he considers alternative production structures, rather than just the pure Heckscher-Ohlin technology.

In this chapter, we analyze the process of capital accumulation in a two-sector model of a small open economy producing nontraded as well as traded goods. Initially, most of our attention is devoted to the case where capital is nontraded. However, the case of traded capital is briefly discussed, with the purpose of trying to draw out the similarities, as well as the differences, between these two specifications of the investment process. In the absence of any installation costs, it is immediately seen that if traded goods are used for investment, then the instantaneous adjustment of the capital stock obtains.

On the other hand, if the capital accumulation is in the form of the nontraded good, then even in the absence of adjustment costs associated with investment, nondegenerate dynamics are obtained. The rate of investment remains finite due to the fact that the supply of nontraded goods is subject to increasing marginal costs. These increasing marginal costs in the case of *nontraded* investment play the same role as do adjustment costs in the case of *traded* investment. The dynamics are shown be have a saddlepoint structure, irrespective of the relative capital intensities of the two sectors. This is in contrast to the early model, with fixed terms of trade, in which the dynamics were shown to be unstable if the sector producing the investment good is relatively capital intensive.[6]

But the most interesting aspect of the dynamics is that its nature turns out to depend critically upon the relative capital intensities of the two sectors. If the traded good is the more capital intensive, the adjustment of the relative price of the nontraded to the traded good to any unanticipated permanent shock occurs immediately. The subsequent accumulation or decumulation of capital in response to such a shock takes place with no concurrent change in the relative price. By contrast, if the nontraded sector is the more capital intensive, then any initial adjustment in the relative price is only partial. The transitional adjustment in the capital stock is accompanied by a change in the relative price.

The emphasis of the analysis on nontraded investment turns out to be much more general than may at first appear. A recent paper by Brock and Turnovsky (1994) has begun to integrate both traded and nontraded investment into a single unified framework, a task that previously had been generally considered intractable. One of their important conclusions is that the fundamental dynamic characteristics of this integrated model are determined exclusively by the relative sectoral intensities in *nontraded* capital. This implies that as long as the economy utilizes *some* nontraded capital in production, the exclusion of traded investment involves no essential loss of generality, at least insofar as the fundamental dynamic structural characteristics are concerned. The accumulation of traded capital does play a critical role in the determination of the current account, but as in the one-sector model of Chapter 3, these dynamics are derivative.

4.2 The Two-Sector Dependent Economy

Economic Structure

Consider a small economy inhabited by a single infinitely lived representative agent who is endowed with a fixed supply of labor (normalized to be one unit), which he sells at the competitive wage, and who accumulates capital, K, for rental at the competitively determined rental rate. The agent produces a traded good, T (taken to be the numeraire), using a quantity of capital, K_T, and labor, L_T, by means of a neoclassical production function, $F(K_T, L_T)$. That is, both capital and labor are assumed to have positive, but diminishing, marginal physical products and to be subject to constant returns to scale. He also produces a nontraded good, N, using a quantity of capital, K_N, and labor, L_N, by means of a second production function, $H(K_N, L_N)$, having the same neoclassical properties. Until Section 4.4, we assume that the traded good is used for consumption only; the nontraded good may be used for either consumption or investment.

The agent also accumulates net foreign bonds, b, that pay an exogenously given world interest rate, r. Equation (4.1a) describes the agent's instantaneous budget constraint,

$$\dot{b} = F(K_T, L_T) + pH(K_N, L_N) - C_T - pC_N - pI - T_L + rb, \qquad (4.1a)$$

where C_T and C_N are the agent's consumption of the traded and the nontraded good, respectively; p is the relative price of the nontraded to the traded good; I denotes investment; and T_L denotes lump-sum taxes. In this framework, p is sometimes referred to as the real exchange rate; an increase in p—that is, a rise in the relative price of nontraded goods—measures a real appreciation. This measure of the real exchange rate is not identical to that in Chapter 3, where it was measured by the relative price of imports to the domestically produced traded good.[7]

We assume that the capital stock does not depreciate, implying the standard capital accumulation constraint:

$$\dot{K} = I. \qquad (4.1b)$$

As formulated, (4.1b) permits negative investment. The usual interpretation of this is that the agent is permitted to consume his capital stock or to sell it in the market for new output. Alternatively, one can incorporate negative net investment, while constraining gross investment to be nonnegative, by allowing capital to depreciate. This is done in the model we shall introduce in Section 4.6, but no significant loss is incurred by adopting the simpler formulation. The allocation of labor and capital between the two sectors is constrained by

$$L_T + L_N = 1 \tag{4.1c}$$

$$K_T + K_N = K. \tag{4.1d}$$

The agent's decisions are to choose his consumption levels, C_T and C_N; labor allocation decisions, L_T and L_N; the rate of investment, I; the rate of accumulation of traded bonds, b, and the capital allocation decisions, K_T and K_N, to maximize the intertemporal utility function

$$\int_0^\infty U(C_T, C_N)e^{-\beta t}dt, \tag{4.2}$$

subject to the constraints (4.1a)–(4.1d) and given initial stocks $K(0) = K_0$ and $b(0) = b_0$. The instantaneous utility function is assumed to be concave and the two consumption goods are assumed to be normal, in the sense that the demand for either is an increasing function of wealth (decreasing function of the marginal utility of wealth). The agent's rate of time preference is β and is taken to be constant.

This intertemporal optimization problem is analogous to those set out in Chapter 3. It is straightforward to show that the optimality conditions are

$$U_T(C_T, C_N) = \lambda \tag{4.3a}$$

$$U_N(C_T, C_N) = \lambda p \tag{4.3b}$$

$$F_K(K_T, L_T) = pH_K(K_N, L_N) \tag{4.3c}$$

$$F_L(K_T, L_T) = pH_L(K_N, L_N) \equiv w \tag{4.3d}$$

$$\frac{\dot{\lambda}}{\lambda} = \beta - r \tag{4.3e}$$

$$\frac{\dot{p}}{p} + H_K(K_N, L_N) = r, \tag{4.3f}$$

together with the transversality conditions

$$\lim_{t \to \infty} \lambda b e^{-\beta t} = \lim_{t \to \infty} \lambda p K e^{-\beta t} = 0, \tag{4.3g}$$

where λ, the Lagrange multiplier associated with the budget constraint (4.1a), is the shadow value of wealth, measured in terms of traded bonds.

As in previous chapters, the fact that the small open economy can trade in a perfectly competitive world bond market implies that in order to obtain a well-defined, finite steady-state value for the marginal utility, λ, and therefore for consumption, we require $\beta = r$, a condition that we continue to impose, implying that the marginal utility remains constant over all time; that is, $\lambda = \bar{\lambda}$.

The optimality conditions (4.3) are analogous to those obtained in Chapter 3. Equations (4.3a) and (4.3b) are the usual conditions equating the marginal utility of consumption to the shadow value of wealth, appropriately measured in terms of the numeraire. Equations (4.3c) and (4.3d) determine the sectoral allocation decisions by equating the marginal physical products of the two factors in the two sectors. These conditions are based on the assumptions that both factors are perfectly mobile across the two sectors. Equations (4.3e) and (4.3f) are arbitrage conditions. The latter equates the instantaneous rate of return on nontraded capital, which consists of its marginal physical product plus capital gain (in terms of the numeraire), to the rate of return on the traded bond.

The other agent in the economy is the government, which plays a simple role. It simply raises lump-sum taxes to finance its expenditures on the traded and the nontraded good, G_T and G_N, respectively, in accordance with

$$G_T + pG_N = T_L. \tag{4.4}$$

For simplicity, we assume that government spending yields no utility, so that it represents a pure drain on the economy.

Macroeconomic Equilibrium

For analytical purposes it is convenient to work in terms of sectoral capital-labor ratios, enabling us to exploit the linear homogeneity of the production functions. Thus, defining

$$k_i \equiv K_i/L_i$$

to be the capital:labor ratio in sector i, $i = T, N$, the corresponding production functions can be expressed in intensive form as

$$f(k_T) \equiv F(K_T, L_T)/L_T; \quad h(k_N) \equiv H(K_N, L_N)/L_N,$$

enabling the macroeconomic equilibrium to be summarized by the following set of relationships:

$$U_T(C_T, C_N) = \bar{\lambda} \tag{4.5a}$$

$$U_N(C_T, C_N) = \bar{\lambda}p \tag{4.5b}$$

$$f'(k_T) = ph'(k_N) \tag{4.5c}$$

$$f(k_T) - k_T f'(k_T) = p[h(k_N) - k_N h'(k_N)] \tag{4.5d}$$

$$L_T k_T + L_N k_N = K \tag{4.5e}$$

$$\dot{p} = p[r - h'(k_N)] \tag{4.6a}$$

$$\dot{K} = L_N h(k_N) - C_N - G_N \tag{4.6b}$$

$$\dot{b} = L_T f(k_T) - C_T - G_T + rb. \tag{4.6c}$$

Equations (4.5a)–(4.5d) and (4.6a) correspond to (4.3a)–(4.3d) and (4.3f), respectively; (4.5e) describes the capital allocation relationship in sectoral per capita terms. Equation (4.6b) specifies market clearing in the nontraded goods market. Any output in excess of domestic private or government consumption is accumulated as (nontraded) capital. Equation (4.6c) describes the economy's current account. The rate of accumulation of traded bonds equals the excess of the domestic supply of the traded good over domestic consumption of that good, plus the interest earned on the outstanding stock of foreign bonds.[8]

The set of equations (4.5a)–(4.5e) defines the following short-run equilibrium. First, the marginal utility conditions (4.5a) and (4.5b) may be solved for the consumption levels of the two goods, C_T and C_N in the form

$$C_T = C_T(\bar{\lambda}, p) \tag{4.7a}$$

$$C_N = C_N(\bar{\lambda}, p), \tag{4.7b}$$

where[9]

$$\frac{\partial C_T}{\partial \bar{\lambda}} < 0; \quad \frac{\partial C_T}{\partial p} \gtreqless 0; \quad \frac{\partial C_N}{\partial \bar{\lambda}} < 0; \quad \frac{\partial C_N}{\partial p} < 0.$$

Second, from the production block (4.5c)–(4.5e), and (4.1c) we may derive

$$k_T = k_T(p) \tag{4.8a}$$

$$k_N = k_N(p) \tag{4.8b}$$

$$L_T = L_T(K, p); \quad L_N = L_N(K, p), \tag{4.8c}$$

where

$$k'_T = \frac{h}{f''(k_N - k_T)}; \quad k'_N = \frac{f}{p^2 h''(k_N - k_T)}$$

$$\frac{\partial L_T}{\partial K} = \frac{1}{k_T - k_N}; \quad \frac{\partial L_T}{\partial p} = \left[\frac{L_N f}{p^2 h''} + \frac{L_T h}{f''}\right] \frac{1}{(k_T - k_N)^2} < 0;$$

$$\frac{\partial L_N}{\partial K} = \frac{1}{k_N - k_T}; \quad \frac{\partial L_N}{\partial p} = -\left[\frac{L_N f}{p^2 h''} + \frac{L_T h}{f''}\right] \frac{1}{(k_T - k_N)^2} > 0.$$

Substituting (4.8a)–(4.8c) into the production functions, we can solve for traded and nontraded output in the form

$$Y_T = Y_T(K, p) \tag{4.8d}$$

$$Y_N = Y_N(K, p), \tag{4.8e}$$

where

$$\frac{\partial Y_T}{\partial K} = \frac{f}{k_T - k_N}; \quad \frac{\partial Y_N}{\partial K} = \frac{h}{k_N - k_T}$$

$$\frac{\partial Y_T}{\partial p} = \left[\frac{L_T p h^2}{f''} + \frac{L_N f^2}{p^2 h''}\right] \frac{1}{(k_T - k_N)^2} < 0;$$

$$\frac{\partial Y_N}{\partial p} = -\left[\frac{L_T p h^2}{f''} + \frac{L_N f^2}{p^2 h''}\right] \frac{1}{p(k_T - k_N)^2} > 0.$$

Using these expressions, together with (4.5c) and (4.5d), we can establish the following relationships, use of which is made below in the derivation of the foreign asset accumulation relationship:

$$\frac{\partial Y_T}{\partial K} + p \frac{\partial Y_N}{\partial K} = \frac{f - ph}{k_T - k_N} = f' \tag{4.9a}$$

$$\frac{\partial Y_T}{\partial p} + p \frac{\partial Y_N}{\partial p} = 0. \tag{4.9b}$$

As is well known from two-sector trade models, the signs in (4.8a)–(4.8c) depend upon sectoral capital intensities. For example, a rise in the relative price of the nontraded good p will attract resources from the traded to the nontraded sector, causing the output of that sector to rise at the expense of traded output [see (4.8d) and (4.8e)]. If the nontraded sector is more capital intensive, capital increases in relative scarcity, causing the wage:rental ratio to fall and inducing the substitution of labor for capital in both sectors.

Equations (4.6a)–(4.6c) describe the dynamics and can be solved recursively as follows. First, substituting the solutions for C_T, C_N, k_T, k_N, and L_T into (4.6a) and (4.6b) leads to two equations describing the dynamics of the evolution of capital, K, and the real exchange rate, p. Next, by substituting the solutions obtained for K and p into (4.6c), one can obtain the evolution of the economy's claims against the rest of the world.

Equilibrium Dynamics

Performing the substitution into (4.6a) and (4.6b), and linearizing about steady state (denoted by tildes), the dynamics of *K and p* can be approximated by

$$\begin{pmatrix} \dot{p} \\ \dot{K} \end{pmatrix} = \begin{pmatrix} a_{11} & 0 \\ a_{21} & a_{22} \end{pmatrix} \begin{pmatrix} p - \tilde{p} \\ K - \tilde{K} \end{pmatrix}, \tag{4.10}$$

where

$$a_{11} \equiv -\frac{f}{p(k_N - k_T)} = \frac{h}{k_T - k_N} + r; \quad a_{21} \equiv \frac{\partial Y_N}{\partial p} - \frac{\partial C_N}{\partial p} > 0,$$

$$a_{22} \equiv \frac{h}{k_N - k_T} = \frac{\partial Y_N}{\partial K}.$$

Since $a_{11}a_{22} = -fh/p(k_T - k_N)^2 < 0$, the dynamics are always a saddle-point, irrespective of the relative capital intensities k_T and k_N. We shall denote the eigenvalues by $\mu_1 < 0$ and $\mu_2 > 0$. While the capital stock always evolves gradually, the relative price p may jump in response to new information. The stable solution is of the form

$$K(t) = \tilde{K} + (K_0 - \tilde{K})e^{\mu_1 t} \tag{4.11a}$$

$$p(t) - \tilde{p} = -\left(\frac{a_{22} - \mu_1}{a_{21}}\right)(K(t) - \tilde{K}). \tag{4.11b}$$

The dynamic behavior of the economy depends crucially upon the relative sectoral capital intensities, and the two cases, $k_T > k_N$ and $k_N > k_T$, need to be considered separately.

Case (I) $k_T > k_N$ This assumption asserts that the capital intensity of the traded good sector exceeds that of the nontraded good sector. It implies that $\mu_1 = a_{22} < 0$, $\mu_2 = a_{11} > 0$, so that the stable path (4.11a) and (4.11b) is

$$K(t) = \tilde{K} + (K_0 - \tilde{K})e^{a_{22}t} \tag{4.11a'}$$

$$p(t) = \tilde{p}. \tag{4.11b'}$$

In this case, the relative price of the nontraded good remains constant at its steady-state level during the dynamic evolution of the economy. The phase diagram for this case is illustrated in Figure 4.1A. The locus of points along which $\dot{p} = 0$ is illustrated by the horizontal line LL, while the $\dot{K} = 0$ locus, illustrated by MM, has a positive slope given by $d\tilde{p}/d\tilde{K} = -a_{22}/a_{21}$

Case (II) $k_N > k_T$ The contrary case, where the nontraded sector is more capital intensive, yields $\mu_1 = a_{11} < 0$, $\mu_2 = a_{22} > 0$, and the stable adjustment path now becomes

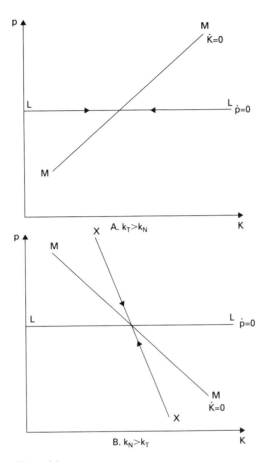

Figure 4.1
Phase diagram

$$K(t) = \tilde{K} + (K_0 - \tilde{K})e^{a_{11}t} \tag{4.11a''}$$

$$p(t) - \tilde{p} = -\left(\frac{a_{22} - a_{11}}{a_{21}}\right)(K(t) - \tilde{K}). \tag{4.11b''}$$

The stable arm is now negatively sloped. In this case, a shock (such as an increase in demand) that leaves the steady-state real exchange rate $\tilde{p}$ unchanged, causes a rise in p in the short run, (i.e., a real appreciation), so that resources can move to the nontraded sector and enable capital accumulation to take place. During the transition, an accumulation of capital is accompanied by a declining relative price of the nontraded good. This phase diagram is illustrated in Figure 4.1B. The locus of points along which $\dot{p} = 0$ remains the horizontal line LL, while the $\dot{K} = 0$

locus, *MM*, now has a negative slope, though less steep than the stable locus, *XX*.

The striking feature of the stable transitional adjustment paths described by (4.11a′) and (4.11b′) and (4.11a″) and (4.11b″) is the qualitative dependence of the behavior of the relative price p on the relative capital intensities of the two sectors. In part, this is because p is also playing the role of an asset price. The fact that in the case where $k_T > k_N$, p remains unchanged during the transition can be seen by considering the arbitrage relationship (4.6a) in the form

$$\frac{\dot{p}}{p} + h'(k_N) = r.$$

Suppose that instead of remaining fixed over time, p were to increase. Then as p increases, k_N increases, so that the marginal physical product $h'(k_N)$ declines.[10] In order to ensure that the rate of return on capital equals the exogenously given return on bonds, this requires $\dot{p} > 0$, that is, a further increase in p—clearly an unstable path. The same applies if p were to decrease over time. An unchanging relative price is the only possibility consistent with stability. On the other hand, if $k_N > k_T$, then an increasing p is associated with $\dot{p} < 0$—clearly a stable adjustment process.

Foreign Asset Accumulation, Investment, and Savings

To determine the accumulation of foreign bonds, we consider (4.6c) expressed in terms of p and K as follows:

$$\dot{b} = Y_T(K,p) - C_T(\tilde{\lambda},p) - G_T + rb, \tag{4.6c′}$$

and apply the procedure discussed in Chapter 3. This involves linearizing this equation, substituting for (4.11a) and (4.11b), and invoking the transversality condition (4.3g). Thus we may write

$$\dot{b} = \left[\frac{\partial Y_T}{\partial K} + \left(\frac{\partial Y_T}{\partial p} - \frac{\partial C_T}{\partial p}\right)\left(\frac{dp}{dK}\right)_{xx}\right](K - \tilde{K}) + r(b - \tilde{b}), \tag{4.12}$$

where

$$\left(\frac{dp}{dK}\right)_{xx} = -\left(\frac{a_{22} - \mu_1}{a_{21}}\right) = -\frac{\partial Y_N/\partial K - \mu_1}{\partial Y_N/\partial p - \partial C_N/\partial p} \leq 0$$

is the slope along the stable saddlepath. We have shown that this locus may be either flat or negatively sloped, depending upon the relative sectoral intensities. Adding and subtracting the term $p\partial C_N/\partial p$, (4.12) can be written as

$$\dot{b} = \left[\frac{\partial Y_T}{\partial K} + \left(\frac{\partial Y_T}{\partial p} + p\frac{\partial C_N}{\partial p}\right)\left(\frac{dp}{dK}\right)_{xx} - \frac{\partial C}{\partial p}\left(\frac{dp}{dK}\right)_{xx}\right](K - \tilde{K}) + r(b - \tilde{b}),$$

where $\partial C/\partial p \equiv \partial C_T/\partial p + p\partial C_N/\partial p < 0$ (recall note 9). Next, noting (1) the definition of $(dp/dK)_{xx}$, (2) the relationships (4.9a) and (4.9b), and (3) that in the neighborhood of steady state, $f'(k_T) = \tilde{p}r$, this expression simplifies to

$$\dot{b} = -\left[(\mu_1 - r)\tilde{p} + \frac{\partial C}{\partial p}\left(\frac{dp}{dK}\right)_{xx}\right](K - \tilde{K}) + r(b - \tilde{b}).$$

Starting from an initial stock of traded bonds, b_0, the solution to this equation is

$$b(t) = \tilde{b} - \left[\tilde{p} + \left(\frac{1}{\mu_1 - r}\right)\frac{\partial C}{\partial p}\left(\frac{dp}{dK}\right)_{xx}\right](K_0 - \tilde{K})e^{\mu_1 t}$$

$$+ \left[b_0 - \tilde{b} + \left(\tilde{p} + \left(\frac{1}{\mu_1 - r}\right)\frac{\partial C}{\partial p}\left(\frac{dp}{dK}\right)_{xx}\right)(K_0 - \tilde{K})\right]e^{rt}.$$

Applying the intertemporal solvency condition, the second term in this equation must equal zero, implying that the net foreign assets at time t are given by

$$b(t) = \tilde{b} - \left[\tilde{p} + \left(\frac{1}{\mu_1 - r}\right)\frac{\partial C}{\partial p}\left(\frac{dp}{dK}\right)_{xx}\right](K(t) - \tilde{K}) \tag{4.13a}$$

with

$$b_0 - \tilde{b} = -\left(\tilde{p} + \left(\frac{1}{\mu_1 - r}\right)\frac{\partial C}{\partial p}\left(\frac{dp}{dK}\right)_{xx}\right)(K_0 - \tilde{K}) \tag{4.13b}$$

This is of the same form as in Chapter 3, where now

$$\frac{\Omega}{\mu_1 - r} = -\left(\tilde{p} + \left(\frac{1}{\mu_1 - r}\right)\frac{\partial C}{\partial p}\left(\frac{dp}{dK}\right)_{xx}\right).$$

We see that the instantaneous effect on the current account of an increase in the capital stock may operate through two channels, both directly, and indirectly through the real exchange rate p.

If $k_T > k_N$, so that p remains fixed over time, only the first effect is operative. This reflects the purchase price of capital. In this case (4.13a) reduces to

$$\dot{b}(t) = -\tilde{p}\dot{K}(t).$$

An increase in K lowers $\dot{K}$ while increasing the rate of output in the traded sector and increasing the current account balance. A decumulating capital stock is therefore accompanied by an accumulating stock of foreign bonds. Moreover, since $\dot{b}(t) = -\tilde{p}\dot{K}(t)$, these flows are exactly offsetting, so that with p fixed over time, this implies a zero net rate of savings. There is no correlation between the rate of investment and savings.

If $k_N > k_T$, in addition to this effect, which still generates a negative relationship between $\dot{K}$ and $\dot{b}$, the second term reflects the capitalized value of savings along the transition path toward the steady state,

$$-\left(\frac{1}{\mu_1 - r}\right)\left(\frac{\partial C}{\partial p}\right)\left(\frac{dp}{dK}\right)_{xx} > 0,$$

in response to the high, but falling, relative price of nontradable goods that now accompanies the accumulation of physical capital. The decline in the relative price of nontradables along the saddlepath lowers consumption unambiguously and improves the current account by raising the consumption real interest rate.[11] But unless the savings response is large, the current account will still be negatively correlated with the accumulation of capital.

Finally, (4.13b) describes the economy's intertemporal solvency condition. It is in effect a linear approximation to the economy's intertemporal budget constraint, which corresponds to the linear approximation to the adjustment paths described by (4.11a), (4.11b), and (4.13a).

Steady State

The steady-state equilibrium of the economy, reached when $\dot{K} = \dot{p} = \dot{b} = 0$, implies

$$\frac{f'(\tilde{k}_T)}{\tilde{p}} = h'(\tilde{k}_N) = r \tag{4.14a}$$

$$(1 - \tilde{L}_T)h(\tilde{k}_N) - \tilde{C}_N - G_N = 0 \tag{4.14b}$$

$$\tilde{L}_T f(\tilde{k}_T) - \tilde{C}_T - G_T + r\tilde{b} = 0, \tag{4.14c}$$

where tildes denote steady-state values. Equation (4.14a) asserts that the values of the long-run marginal physical product of capital in the traded and nontraded sectors must equal the exogenously given world interest rate. The second equation requires that the output of the nontraded sector equal total consumption demand, and the third equation requires that the long-run current account balance must be zero.

The steady-state equilibrium can be determined in the following simple way. First, equations (4.5c) and (4.5d), which hold at each instant of time, together with (4.14a), jointly determine the steady-state sectoral capital intensities, $\tilde{k}_T$ and $\tilde{k}_N$ and the relative price, $\tilde{p}$. These quantities, being determined by production conditions, depend only upon supply shocks; they are therefore independent of any form of demand disturbance. Second, equations (4.7a) and (4.7b) determine long-run consumption levels, $\tilde{C}_T$ and $\tilde{C}_N$, as functions of $\bar{\lambda}$ and $\tilde{p}$. Third, substituting these expressions, together with the intertemporal solvency condition (4.13b), into the sectoral capital allocation condition (4.5e) and the equilibrium conditions (4.14b) and (4.14c) yields:

$$\tilde{L}_T \tilde{k}_T + (1 - \tilde{L}_T)\tilde{k}_N = \tilde{K} \tag{4.15a}$$

$$(1 - \tilde{L}_T)h(\tilde{k}_N) - \tilde{C}_N(\bar{\lambda}, \tilde{p}) - G_N = 0 \tag{4.15b}$$

$$\tilde{L}_T f(\tilde{k}_T) - \tilde{C}_T(\bar{\lambda}, \tilde{p}) - G_T + r\left[b_0 + \frac{\Omega}{r - \mu_1}(K_0 - \tilde{K})\right] = 0, \tag{4.15c}$$

which jointly determine $\tilde{L}_T$, $\tilde{K}$ and $\bar{\lambda}$. The equilibrium stock of bonds, and consumption can then be immediately derived.

At this point, two additional observations merit comment. First, equation (4.15c) highlights the fact that the steady-state equilibrium depends upon the initial stocks of assets K_0 and b_0. This dependence upon initial conditions is a consequence of the constant marginal utility and raises the potential for temporary shocks to have permanent effects. These can be analyzed along the lines outlined in Chapter 3; an example of this is provided by Brock (1996). Second, it is worth recalling that Ω depends upon the relative capital intensities in the two sectors.

4.3 Analysis of Structural Shocks

In this section we analyze the response of the model to both demand shocks and supply shocks, emphasizing the differences to which they give rise.

Demand Shocks

The demand shocks we shall consider take the form of permanent increases in government expenditures, directed toward the traded and the nontraded good, respectively. G_N can be thought of as generating two demand effects, a direct one and an indirect one through the wealth effect, $\bar{\lambda}$. This contrasts with G_T, which generates only the latter. It is equivalent to a transfer in the Brock (1996) model. The qualitative long-run effects of these policies are summarized in Table 4.1 and are straightforward. Neither form of fiscal expansion has any long-run impact on the relative price, $\tilde{p}$, or on sectoral capital intensities, $\tilde{k}_T$ and $\tilde{k}_N$, which are determined by production conditions alone.

Table 4.1
Long-run effects of permanent demand shocks

	Traded good	Nontraded good
$\tilde{k}_T$	0	0
$\tilde{k}_N$	0	0
$\tilde{p}$	0	0
$\tilde{L}_T$	+	−
$\tilde{K}$	$sgn(k_T - k_N)$	$sgn(k_N - k_T)$
$\tilde{b}$	$sgn[(k_N - k_T)\Omega]$	$sgn[(k_T - k_N)\Omega]$
$\tilde{\lambda}$	+	−
$\tilde{C}_T$	−	−
$\tilde{C}_N$	−	−

Government Expenditure on Traded Goods

An increase in G_T, say, raises the demand for traded goods. With the sectoral capital intensities remaining fixed, the additional output necessary to maintain equilibrium is produced by attracting labor from the nontraded sector, the output of which therefore declines. A further consequence of the sectoral capital intensities' remaining fixed is that the effect of the fiscal expansion on the long-run aggregate capital stock depends upon whether labor is moving from a relatively less, to a relatively more, capital-intensive sector. If it is, $\tilde{K}$ will rise; if not, $\tilde{K}$ will fall. The implications for the long-run stock of foreign bonds in turn depend upon the relationship between the rates of asset accumulation, described by Ω. With the balanced government budget, the increase in G_T implies a reduction in private wealth and an increase in its constant shadow value. This leads to a reduction in the private consumption of both goods, with the reduction in C_N matching the reduction in the output of the nontraded good.

Government Expenditure on Nontraded Good

Essentially a parallel argument applies with respect to an increase in government expenditure on the nontraded good, G_N. The major point worth noting is that the reversal of the employment effect is obviously reflected in the adjustment of the long-run capital stock and holdings of foreign bonds.

The dynamic adjustment paths are illustrated in Figure 4.2 and depend critically upon the relative sectoral capital intensities. If $k_T > k_N$, an increase in G_T, say, will lead to a gradual accumulation of capital, accompanied by a gradual decumulation of foreign bonds. With the long-run relative price (real exchange rate) remaining unchanged, and no

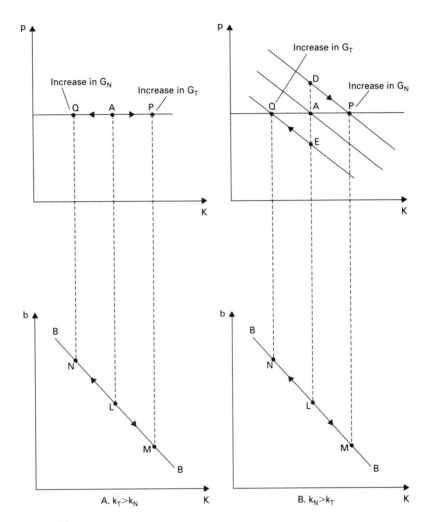

Figure 4.2
Demand shocks

transitional dynamic adjustment, p remains fixed throughout. So do the sectoral capital:labor ratios. The adjustment for K and p is the locus AP in the upper panel of Figure 4.2A, with the corresponding decumulation of bonds being represented by the path LM in the lower panel. In the absence of any instantaneous response in p, the adjustment of labor occurs gradually, as resources are attracted to the traded sector. The adjustment in response to an increase in G_N is just the reverse, as illustrated in the figure.

With the reversal of capital intensities, $k_N > k_T$, an increase in government expenditure on the traded good will lead to an initial real depreciation in the exchange rate; that is, $p(0)$ will drop. This causes an immediate shifting of resources away from the nontraded to the traded sector. With $k_N > k_T$, capital increases in relative abundance, the wage:rental ratio rises, firms substitute capital for labor, and the capital:labor ratio in both sectors increases. The drop in the relative price p causes an immediate shift of labor to the traded sector. Output of the nontraded sector immediately falls and investment begins to decline. Along the adjustment path the capital stock declines steadily, while the relative price is gradually restored to its original level. This is because the initial increase in k_N reduces the marginal physical product $h'(k_N)$, requiring a continuous rise in p in order for the rates of return on the assets to be equalized. In other words. the relative price, p, performs the twin functions of (1) equilibrating the goods market and (2) serving as an asset price. The adjustment in p and K is illustrated by the initial jump AE, followed by the continuous adjustment EQ, in the upper panel of Figure 4.2B. The corresponding path for bonds is illustrated in the lower panel by LN, and is drawn as negatively sloped, although now a positive slope is possible if the savings resulting along the transitional path are sufficiently large. Again, the dynamic response to an increase in G_N is just the mirror image.

Supply Shocks

We turn now to supply shocks, which are assumed to take the form of multiplicative shifts in the production functions of the two sectors.

Productivity Increase in Traded Sector

Consider first the production function in the traded goods sector, expressed in intensive form as $uf(k_T)$, with a proportional shift being parameterized by $du > 0$. Such a shift increases the level of output by increasing the marginal product of each factor proportionately. It is therefore a representation of a Hicks-neutral technological improvement. Since the steady-state capital intensity in the nontraded sector, $\tilde{k}_N$, is determined by conditions in that sector alone, it is independent of the shift du. There is therefore no change in $\tilde{k}_N$. It follows from the equilibrium conditions (4.5c) and (4.5d) that a proportional shift such as this leads to proportional adjustments in the capital:labor ratio in all sectors. In this case, $\tilde{k}_T$ remains unchanged as well. On the production side, all that happens is that the relative price of the nontraded good rises, in order to maintain equality among rates of return; that is,

$$\frac{d\tilde{k}_T}{du} = \frac{d\tilde{k}_N}{du} = 0; \quad \frac{d\tilde{p}}{du} > 0. \tag{4.16}$$

Two-Sector Models

Table 4.2
Long-run effects of permanent supply shocks

	Traded sector		Nontraded sector		
	Wealth effect	Relative price effect	Wealth effect	Relative price effect	Sectoral capital intensity effects
$\tilde{k}_T$	0	na	+	na	na
$\tilde{k}_N$	0	na	+	na	na
$\tilde{p}$	+	na	−	na	na
$\tilde{L}_T$	+	+	+	−	?
$\tilde{K}$	$sgn(k_N - k_T)$	$sgn(k_T - k_N)$	$sgn(k_T - k_N)$	$sgn(k_N - k_T)$	?
$\tilde{b}$	$sgn[(k_T - k_N)\Omega]$	$sgn[(k_N - k_T)\Omega]$	$sgn[(k_N - k_T)\Omega]$	$sgn[(k_T - k_N)\Omega]$	?
$\tilde{\lambda}$	−	?	−	?	?
$\tilde{C}_T$	+	?	−	?	?
$\tilde{C}_N$	+	−	−	+	?

na = not applicable.

From the steady-state relationships summarized in (4.15a)–(4.15c), one can determine the rest of the long-run responses. In contrast to the demand shocks, the rise in the relative price $\tilde{p}$ introduces further effects that counter the direct effects of the productivity shift du. The qualitative responses to the direct and relative price effects are summarized in the first two columns of Table 4.2.

One immediate effect of an increase in productivity in the traded sector is to increase the flow of output from the resources available to the economy. The economy's wealth increases, leading to a decrease in the shadow value of wealth, $\tilde{\lambda}$. In the absence of any change in the relative price, this wealth effect will increase the consumption of both traded and nontraded goods. With the productivity of labor and the capital:labor ratio in the nontraded sector remaining fixed, this additional output is obtained by causing labor to shift from the traded to the nontraded sector. But the concurrent rise in the relative price $\tilde{p}$ has an offsetting effect. It tends to reduce the demand for the nontraded good, and therefore the equilibrium output of the nontraded sector. The net effect upon the output of that sector, and upon the allocation of labor that determines it, depends upon whether or not the wealth effect dominates the relative price effect. In the special case of a homogeneous utility function, with the initial stock of foreign bonds being zero and there being no government expenditure, one can show that the relative size of these two effects can be parameterized simply in terms of the elasticity of substitution in consumption, $\eta \equiv U_N U_T / U U_{NT}$. If $\eta > 1$, the relative price effect dominates; the net demand for, and supply of, nontraded goods decline; and labor shifts from the nontraded to the traded goods sector—that is, $\tilde{L}_T$ rises. If $\eta < 1$,

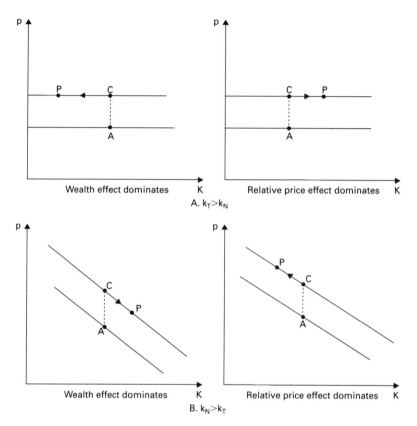

Figure 4.3
Traded sector productivity shock

the reverse is true. With the steady-state sectoral capital:labor ratios remaining fixed, the response of the aggregate capital stock depends upon (1) the net effect on the allocation of labor (i.e., $\tilde{L}_T$) and (2) whether the movement of labor entails a move from a relatively more, to a relatively less, capital-intensive sector. Once the adjustment in $\tilde{K}$ is determined, the net effect of the equilibrium stock of bonds follows.

Phase diagrams summarizing the adjustments in K and p are provided in Figure. 4.3. There are four possible scenarios, depending upon whether (1) $k_T \gtrless k_N$ and (2) the relative price effect dominates the demand effect. Corresponding to these paths, there are adjustment paths relating b to K, in accordance with (4.13a). However, these are not drawn.

In the case where $k_T > k_N$, the relative price immediately increases by its full amount. The capital stock steadily decreases or increases, with no further adjustment in p, depending upon whether the direct effect or the relative price effect of the productivity shock is the dominant one. The dynamics are represented by Figure 4.3A. But if the relative sectoral capital intensities are reversed, the relative price p does undergo transitional dynamics (Figure 4.3B). If the direct effect of the productivity shock dominates, it actually overshoots its long-run response on impact; p declines over time—that is, the real exchange rate depreciates as the capital stock is being accumulated. But in the other case, where the relative price effect prevails, the initial response in p is partial; it continues to rise while the capital stock decumulates.

Productivity Increase in Nontraded Sector

The long-run responses to a productivity shock in the nontraded sector are reported in the last three columns of Table 4.2. In contrast to a shock in the traded sector, a shift in the production function $vh(k_N)$, $dv > 0$, raises the marginal product of capital in the nontraded sector above the world interest rate. This leads to an increase in the capital intensity in that sector, $\tilde{k}_N$, and, given the proportionality of the shock, in the traded sector, $\tilde{k}_T$, as well. This in turn causes a decline in the marginal product $f'(\tilde{k}_T)$ and requires a decrease in the relative price $\tilde{p}$, in order for the arbitrage condition (4.14a) to be maintained. Thus,

$$\frac{d\tilde{k}_T}{dv} = \frac{d\tilde{k}_N}{dv} > 0; \quad \frac{d\tilde{p}}{dv} < 0. \tag{4.17}$$

The productivity shock in the traded sector impacts on the remainder of the steady state through (1) the wealth effect, (2) the relative price effect, and (3) adjustments stemming from changes in the sectoral capital intensities. The wealth effects are essentially analogous to those associated with the productivity shock in the traded sector. The only substantive difference is that it now attracts labor to the traded sector. The response of the equilibrium stocks of capital and traded bonds to this effect follow as before. The relative price effects are directly opposite to those arising from an analogous shock in the traded sector. However, the impacts resulting from the induced changes in the sectoral capital intensities are not straightforward. Many different patterns of response may result, and these cannot be determined without imposing further specific restrictions. Finally, the dynamic adjustment paths for K and p are illustrated in Figure 4.4. Again there are four scenarios, corresponding to whether $k_T \gtreqless k_N$ and whether K rises or falls in the long run.

4.4 Traded Investment in the Dependent Economy Model

We now briefly outline the consequences of assuming that the investment good is traded. The static equilibrium conditions (4.5a)–(4.5e) remain

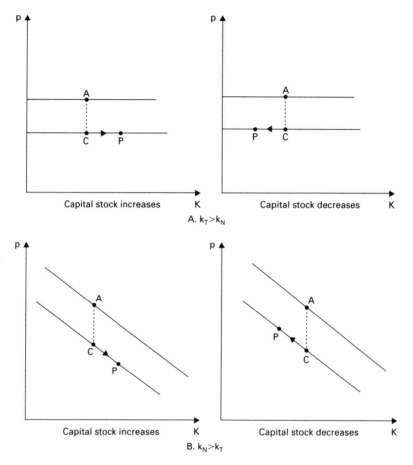

Figure 4.4
Nontraded sector productivity shock

unchanged. Equations (4.6a)–(4.6c), however, are modified as follows. First, the arbitrage condition (4.6a) becomes

$$f'(k_T) = r. \tag{4.6a''}$$

Second, with the nontraded good being a pure consumption good, the nontraded market equilibrium condition is

$$(1 - L_T)h(k_N) = C_N + G_N. \tag{4.6b'}$$

And third, the accumulation of traded bonds is described by

$$\dot{b} = L_T f(k_T) - C_T - G_T - \dot{K} + rb. \tag{4.6c''}$$

Equations (4.5a)–(4.5e), (4.6a'), and (4.6b'), which are now all static, determine solutions for k_T, k_N, L_T, C_T, C_N, p, and K, all of which remain constant over time. In particular, $\dot{K} \equiv 0$. The solution to the accumulation equation, consistent with the transversality condition (4.3g), is

$$rb_0 + L_T f(k_T) = C_T + G_T. \tag{4.18}$$

The system is therefore always in steady-state equilibrium. If a shock requires a change in K, then that is achieved by a one-time swap of traded bonds B for capital (see, e.g., Obstfeld 1989).

Nondegenerate dynamics are introduced by imposing convex costs of adjustment on investment, as in Chapter 3. This leads to a saddlepath, in terms of the capital stock and its shadow value, having a negatively sloped stable arm. The dynamics of the system are almost identical to that obtained in Section 4.2, in the case where the nontraded good is the more capital intensive (see McKenzie 1982), except that in this case it applies whether $k_T \gtreqless k_N$. The steady state consists of (4.5a)–(4.5e), (4.6a′), (4.14b), (4.14c), and the intertemporal budget constraint (4.13b), which reflects the accumulation of assets along the transitional path. The structure is therefore virtually identical to that discussed in Section 4.3. Demand shocks have the precisely the same long-run effects as before. But in contrast with the case where capital is nontraded, demand shocks will now generate transitory effects on the relative price and sectoral capital intensities, irrespective of whether $k_T \gtreqless k_N$. The only other difference is that with the equilibrium sectoral capital intensities being determined by (4.6a′), rather than (4.14a), $\tilde{k}_T$ and $\tilde{k}_N$ now depend upon the productivity shocks in the traded, rather than in the nontraded, sector.

4.5 Traded versus Nontraded Capital in the Dependent Economy Model

As we have already observed, the treatment of investment expenditure in intertemporal optimizing models of the dependent economy has been more problematical than the treatment of consumption. Whereas investment in a closed economy model requires the production of capital goods, investment in the dependent economy model requires either internationally traded capital (such as equipment) or domestically produced nontraded capital (such as structures).

Models that specify *investment goods to be traded*—such as Bruno (1982), Razin (1984), Engel and Kletzer (1989), and Ostry (1991)—have been criticized for the narrowness of that assumption. For example, in commenting on Bruno (1982), Svensson (1982, p. 225) pointed out that "Another necessary assumption for the simple investment theory and the given long-run price of nontraded goods [in Bruno's model] is that investment consists of traded goods only." Models with traded investment and traded installation costs, such as Bruno and Sachs (1982), are a variant of the class of models with traded investment.

Similarly, models specifying *investment goods* to be *nontraded*—such as Fischer and Frenkel (1974), Marion (1984), van Wijnbergen (1985), Murphy (1986), Turnovsky (1991), and van Wincoop (1993)—have also been criticized for the lack of realism of that assumption. For example, in discussing their own model, Fischer and Frenkel (1972, p. 213) wrote, "...it is usually assumed that there is no trade in capital goods and that additions to the capital stock consist only of domestic output of investment goods. This assumption has little but convenience to recommend it."

For any particular specification of investment goods, a further assumption that the *traded sector* is relatively *capital intensive*—such as that made in Fischer and Frenkel (1974), Dornbusch (1980), Obstfeld and Stockman (1985), Brock (1988), and Murphy (1989)—can be (and has been) criticized as much as the opposite assumption made by Bruno (1982) that the *nontraded sector* is *capital intensive*. Referring to a paper by Neary and Purvis (1982) that assumed a labor-intensive nontraded sector, Flemming (1982, p. 256) wrote, "The least acceptable restriction [of the model] is the exclusion of capital from any role in the production of nontradable services. These include extremely capital-intensive public utilities (electricity generation and transport) as well as housing, so that empirically it is quite probable that the tradable goods sector is *less* capital intensive" (emphasis in the original). In a comment on Bruno's (1982) model, Svensson (1982, p. 225) emphasized "the two crucial assumptions that traded goods production is oil dependent and that nontraded goods are relatively capital intensive. It is obvious that some of the effects mentioned above [in the paper] may change signs if either of these assumptions is changed."

It is clear from these comments that no one assumption has gained uniform acceptance. That being the case, it is desirable to extend the model to encompass both traded and nontraded capital simultaneously, and thereby accommodate the wishes of all. Brock and Turnovsky (1994) set out to do that by introducing investment expenditure into the dependent economy model in a way that they argue can satisfactorily answer many of the long-standing questions regarding the dependence of the model's results on the specificity of its investment and capital intensity assumptions. Their model includes both traded and nontraded investment expenditure, so that the production structure uses three factors (nontraded capital, traded capital, and labor) in two sectors (traded and nontraded). The model is, we believe, an attractive one, and it is identical to the model presented, but not solved, in the Appendix to Bruno (1976).[12] In addition to providing answers to questions concerning the dependence of the model's results on the choice of capital good and sectoral capital intensities, it is able to examine a previously unasked question regarding the dependence of the model's results on the complementarity or substitutability of traded and nontraded capital in the production structure. Sections 4.6 and 4.7 are devoted to an analysis of this model.

4.6 Dependent Economy Model with Traded and Nontraded Capital

The model is a direct generalization of the one studied in sections 4.2–4.5; thus our discussion can be brief, focusing primarily on the differences in the formulation of the model. Unless otherwise stated, variables are as defined in the previous analysis.

The Economic Structure

The key difference is that the agent now accumulates two kinds of capital for rental at the competitively determined rental rate. One type of capital good is nontraded, and we shall identify this good as *structures* (S). The other capital good is tradable, and we shall refer to this good as *equipment* (E). We assume that structures depreciate at the rate δ_S and that equipment depreciates at the rate δ_E. Thus investment expenditure on structures (I_S) and investment expenditure on equipment (I_E) are related to their respective stocks, S and E, by the accumulation equations

$$\dot{S} = I_S - \delta_S S \tag{4.19a}$$

$$\dot{E} = I_E - \delta_E E. \tag{4.19b}$$

The agent produces a tradable good (Y_T, taken to be the numeraire), using structures (S_T), equipment (E_T), and labor (L_T), by means of a linearly homogeneous neoclassical production function, which we write in intensive form as

$$Y_T = F(S_T, E_T, L_T) \equiv f(s_T, e_T) L_T,$$

where

$$s_T \equiv \frac{S_T}{L_T}, \quad e_T \equiv \frac{E_T}{L_T}.$$

The agent also produces a nontraded good (Y_N), using structures (S_N), equipment (E_N), and labor (L_N), by means of a second linearly homogeneous production function:

$$Y_N = H(S_N, E_N, L_N) \equiv h(s_N, e_N) L_N,$$

where

$$s_N \equiv \frac{S_N}{L_N}, \quad e_N \equiv \frac{E_N}{L_N}.$$

The relative price of nontraded goods (p) is taken as exogenously given by the agent and is determined by market-clearing conditions in the economy. All three factors of production are mobile across the traded and nontraded sectors, with the sectoral allocations being constrained by

$$L_T + L_N = 1 \tag{4.20a}$$

$$S_T + S_N = S \tag{4.20b}$$

$$E_T + E_N = E. \tag{4.20c}$$

In addition to accumulating the two types of capital, the agent receives an exogenously given flow of transfer income (τ) from the rest of the world and accumulates net foreign bonds (b) that pay an exogenously given world interest rate (r). Thus the agent's instantaneous budget constraint is described by

$$\dot{b} = \tau + f(s_T, e_T)L_T + ph(s_N, e_N)L_N + rb - C_T - pC_N - I_E - pI_S, \tag{4.21}$$

where the price of the traded investment good (equipment) is normalized to equal the unitary price of the tradable consumption good. This flow constraint also embodies the assumption that there is no domestic government.

The agent's decisions are to choose consumption levels (C_T, C_N), labor allocation decisions (L_T, L_N), capital allocation decisions (S_T, S_N, E_T, E_N), rates of investment (I_S, I_E), and the rate of accumulation of bonds ($\dot{b}$) to maximize the intertemporal utility function

$$\int_0^\infty U(C_T, C_N)e^{-\beta t}dt, \tag{4.22}$$

subject to the constraints (4.19)–(4.21); the initial stocks of assets S_0, E_0, b_0; and the fixed stock of labor.

The optimality conditions are now modified to

$$U_T(C_T, C_N) = \bar{\lambda} \tag{4.23a}$$

$$U_N(C_T, C_N) = \bar{\lambda}p \tag{4.23b}$$

$$f_s(s_T, e_T) = ph_s(s_N, e_N) \equiv r_S \tag{4.23c}$$

$$f_e(s_T, e_T) = ph_e(s_N, e_N) \equiv r_E \tag{4.23d}$$

$$f(s_T, e_T) - s_T f_s(s_T, e_T) - e_T f_e(s_T, e_T)$$
$$= p[h(s_N, e_N) - s_N h_s(s_N, e_N) - e_N h_e(s_N, e_N)] = w \tag{4.23e}$$
$$r_S = p(r + \delta_S) - \dot{p} \tag{4.23f}$$
$$r_E = r + \delta_E, \tag{4.23g}$$

where r_S is the rental rate on structures, r_E is the rental rate on equipment, and w is the real wage rate, all measured in terms of the numeraire. In addition, the transversality conditions

$$\lim_{t \to \infty} \lambda b e^{-\beta t} = \lim_{t \to \infty} \lambda p S e^{-\beta t} = \lim_{t \to \infty} \lambda E e^{-\beta t} = 0 \tag{4.23h}$$

ensure that the agent's intertemporal budget constraint is met.

The only substantive difference from the previous optimality conditions is that equations (4.23c)–(4.23e) now equate the marginal returns to the three factors of production—structures, equipment, and labor, respectively—across the two sectors. In addition, (4.23f) and (4.23g) now describe two arbitrage conditions, one for each form of capital. Observe that (4.23g) shows that the equilibrium rental rate on the traded capital equipment, also measured in terms of the numeraire, is fixed by the world interest rate and the rate of depreciation on equipment.

Macroeconomic Equilibrium

The macroeconomic equilibrium consists of equations (4.23a)–(4.23e) and (4.23g), together with

$$S = L_T s_T + (1 - L_T) s_N \tag{4.24a}$$
$$E = L_T e_T + (1 - L_T) e_N \tag{4.24b}$$
$$\dot{p} = p[(r + \delta_S) - h_s(s_N, e_N)] \tag{4.25a}$$
$$\dot{S} = (1 - L_T) h(s_N, e_N) - C_N - \delta_S S \tag{4.25b}$$
$$\dot{b} = L_T f(s_T, e_T) - C_T - I_E + rb + \tau. \tag{4.25c}$$

Equations (4.24a) and (4.24b) describe the sectoral allocation relationships (4.20a)–(4.20c), normalized per unit of labor. Equation (4.25a) rewrites the arbitrage condition (4.23f), combining it with (4.23c). Equation (4.25b) specifies equilibrium in the nontraded goods market. Any output in excess of consumption and depreciation of structures is accumulated as capital to be used as structures. Equation (4.25c) describes the economy's current account. The rate of accumulation of traded bonds equals the excess of the domestic output of the traded good over domestic consumption and investment expenditure, plus the interest earned on net foreign assets and the amount of the exogenous transfers from abroad.

The static equations (4.23a)–(4.23e) and (4.23g) define a short-run equilibrium that may be solved recursively as follows. First, the marginal utility conditions (4.23a) and (4.23b) may be solved for C_T and C_N, in the form (4.7a) and (4.7b) and having precisely the same properties. Second, the production block, (4.23c)–(4.23e) and (4.23g), may be solved for the sectoral intensities

$$s_T = s_T(p); \quad e_T = e_T(p); \quad s_N = s_N(p); \quad e_N = e_N(p). \tag{4.26a}$$

Expressions for the derivatives appearing (4.26a) are reported in the Appendix. They depend upon two sets of factors. As in the standard two-sector trade model, they depend upon the relative sectoral intensities of production in the nontraded capital good, structures. But, in addition, they depend upon the complementarity or substitutability of structures and equipment in production.

From the equations in (4.26a), we can immediately derive the short-run solutions for the rental rate on structures, r_S, and the wage rate, w, as follows:

$$r_S = r_S(p) \qquad w = w(p). \tag{4.26b}$$

Also, the equation for the sectoral allocation of structures (4.24a) allows us to express the sectoral allocation of labor (L_T) in the form

$$L_T = \frac{S - s_N(p)}{s_T(p) - s_N(p)} \equiv L_T(p, S). \tag{4.26c}$$

It follows immediately from (4.26c) that an increase in S, with p held constant, will shift employment to the tradable from the nontraded sector if and only if that sector is relatively intensive in structures.

Having obtained the sectoral allocation of labor, it is straightforward to solve for both the domestic output of the two goods (Y_T, Y_N) and the stock of equipment (E) as follows:

$$Y_T = L_T(p, S) f(s_T(p), e_T(p)) \equiv Y_T(p, S) \tag{4.26d}$$

$$Y_N = (1 - L_T(p, S)) h(s_N(p), e_N(p)) \equiv Y_N(p, S) \tag{4.26e}$$

$$E = L_T(p, S) e_T(p) + (1 - L_T(p, S)) e_N(p) \equiv E(p, S). \tag{4.26f}$$

The partial derivatives of the functions appearing in (4.26b)–(4.26f) are provided in the Appendix.

Equations (4.25a)–(4.25c) describe the dynamics and can be solved as follows. First, substituting the solutions for C_T, C_N, s_T, s_N, e_T, e_N, and

L_T into (4.25a) and (4.25b) leads to two equations describing the evolution of the relative price of nontraded goods (p) and the stock of structures (S). Next, substituting the solutions obtained for S and p into (4.25c), one can derive the evolution of the economy's current account.

Equilibrium Dynamics: Structures and Relative Prices

Performing the substitution into (4.25a) and (4.25b) and linearizing around steady-state values (denoted by tildes), the dynamics of p and S can be approximated by

$$\begin{pmatrix} \dot{p} \\ \dot{S} \end{pmatrix} = \begin{pmatrix} a_{11} & 0 \\ a_{21} & a_{22} \end{pmatrix} \begin{pmatrix} p - \tilde{p} \\ S - \tilde{S} \end{pmatrix}, \qquad (4.27)$$

where we can establish

$$a_{11} \equiv -\frac{dr_S(p)}{dp} + r + \delta_S = \frac{h}{s_T - s_N} + r + \delta_S$$

$$a_{21} \equiv \frac{\partial Y_N}{\partial p} - \frac{\partial C_N}{\partial p} > 0 \quad a_{22} \equiv \frac{\partial Y_N}{\partial S} - \delta_S = \frac{dr_S}{dp} - \delta_S = \frac{h}{s_N - s_T} - \delta_S.$$

The dynamic structure is seen to parallel that of (4.10), with structures now playing the role previously played by nontraded capital. Some minor differences arise due to there now being three rather than two factors of production, and with both types of capital allowed to depreciate. From these expressions one can verify that $a_{11}a_{22} < 0$, implying that the dynamics are always a saddlepoint having eigenvalues we shall denote by $\mu_1 < 0, \mu_2 > 0$.[13] In general, the stable solution is of the form

$$S = \tilde{S} + (S_0 - \tilde{S})e^{\mu_1 t} \qquad (4.28a)$$

$$p = \tilde{p} - \left(\frac{a_{22} - \mu_1}{a_{21}}\right)(S - \tilde{S}). \qquad (4.28b)$$

The stable eigenvalue, and therefore the nature of the dynamic evolution of the economy, depends critically upon the relative intensities of the two sectors in the nontraded investment good, structures. The two cases, $s_T > s_N$ and $s_N > s_T$, give rise to a flat and a negatively sloped saddlepath, respectively, identical to (4.11b′) and (4.11b″), respectively.

There are three key features of the dynamics of the model that we wish to highlight at this juncture. The first is that the simultaneous introduction of both traded and nontraded investment goods into the dependent economy model is relatively simple. The qualitative characteristics of the dynamic paths determining the internal behavior of the economy are essentially the same as those obtained where all investment is assumed to be nontraded, as in sections 4.2–4.5. The second key observation is that the dynamic response of the relative price of nontraded goods depends critically upon the relative sectoral intensities of the nontraded investment good, structures. This is because p is playing the role of an asset price as well as of the relative price of nontraded consumption. Finally, the speed of adjustment of the economy (μ_1) is driven by variables that dictate the rate at which the economy can produce structures. The speed of adjustment varies positively with average labor productivity in the nontraded sector, $h = H(S_N, E_N, L_N)/L_N$, since the nontraded sector produces structures. The speed of adjustment varies negatively with the absolute difference in sectoral structure intensities, $|s_T - s_N|$, since the opportunity cost of shifting structures to the production of nontraded investment rises with the size of the gap in sectoral structure intensities.

Equilibrium Dynamics: Equipment

The solution (4.26f) for E in conjunction with (4.28a) and (4.28b) enables us to determine the adjustment path followed by the stock of equipment as structures are accumulated. This path can be expressed in linearized form about its steady state, $\tilde{E}$, as follows:

$$E(t) = \tilde{E} + \left[\frac{\partial E}{\partial S} + \frac{\partial E}{\partial p}\left(\frac{dp}{dS}\right)_{xx}\right][S(t) - \tilde{S}], \tag{4.29}$$

where

$$\left(\frac{dp}{dS}\right)_{xx} = \frac{\mu_1 - a_{22}}{a_{21}}$$

is the slope of the stable saddlepath. This slope is equal to zero if $s_T > s_N$ and is negative if $s_T < s_N$. From equation (4.26f) we can establish that

$$\frac{\partial E}{\partial S} = \frac{e_T - e_N}{s_T - s_N}.^{14}$$

In addition, we will define equipment and structures to be substitutes in production if

$$\frac{\partial E}{\partial S} < 0$$

and to be complements in production if

$$\frac{\partial E}{\partial S} > 0.$$

Thus, in the case of the flat saddlepath, we see that an accumulating stock of structures will be accompanied by an accumulating stock of equipment if and only if the two capital goods are complements in production. With $s_T > s_N$, this will be so if and only if $e_T > e_N$.

In the case where the saddlepath is negatively sloped, the adjustment in the stock of equipment responds, in addition, to the decline in the relative price of nontraded goods, which now occurs along the saddlepath and is reflected in the term

$$\frac{\partial E}{\partial p}\left(\frac{dp}{dS}\right)_{xx}.^{15}$$

This latter term is in general ambiguous and depends upon the sectoral intensities of the two sectors in the two types of capital. For any given set of equipment intensities, this relative price effect can be shown to be opposite in sign to the direct effect associated with the accumulation of structures,

$$\frac{\partial E}{\partial S}.^{16}$$

Thus, in the case where the nontraded sector is structures intensive, any pattern of comovements in the two types of capital is plausible.[17]

Equilibrium Dynamics: The Current Account

To determine the accumulation of foreign bonds, we consider (4.25c) expressed in terms of p and S, in a form analogous to (4.6c'), as follows:

$$\dot{b} = Y_T(p, S) - C_T(\bar{\lambda}, p) - I_E(p, S) + rb + \tau. \tag{4.30}$$

By linearizing (4.30), substituting (4.28a) and (4.28b), and following precisely the same procedure as in Section 4.3, the stable adjustment of the stock of foreign assets consistent with intertemporal solvency can be shown to be

$$b(t) - \tilde{b} = -\left[\tilde{p} + \frac{e_T - e_N}{s_T - s_N} + \frac{1}{\mu_1 - r}\frac{\partial C}{\partial p}\left(\frac{dp}{dS}\right)_{xx} + \frac{\partial E}{\partial p}\left(\frac{dp}{dS}\right)_{xx}\right](S(t) - \tilde{S}) \tag{4.31a}$$

with

$$b_0 - \tilde{b} = -\left[\tilde{p} + \frac{e_T - e_N}{s_T - s_N} + \frac{1}{\mu_1 - r}\frac{\partial C}{\partial p}\left(\frac{dp}{dS}\right)_{xx} + \frac{\partial E}{\partial p}\left(\frac{dp}{dS}\right)_{xx}\right](S_0 - \tilde{S}), \tag{4.31b}$$

where now

$$\frac{\Omega}{\mu_1 - r} \equiv -\left[\tilde{p} + \frac{e_T - e_N}{s_T - s_N} + \left(\frac{1}{\mu_1 - r}\right)\frac{\partial C}{\partial p}\left(\frac{dp}{dS}\right)_{xx} + \frac{\partial E}{\partial p}\left(\frac{dp}{dS}\right)_{xx}\right].$$

Details of this derivation are provided in the Appendix. As in the case where there is only nontraded capital, the expression Ω describes the instantaneous effect of an increase in the stock of structures on the current account. This may operate through two channels: directly, and indirectly through the relative price of nontradables.

If the tradables sector is relatively intensive in its use of structures ($s_T > s_N$), so that the relative price of nontraded goods remains fixed over time at $\tilde{p}$, only the direct effect on the current account is operative. In this case, one can show that

$$\frac{\Omega}{\mu_1 - r} = -\left[\tilde{p} + \frac{e_T - e_N}{s_T - s_N}\right] = -\left[\tilde{p} + \frac{\partial E}{\partial S}\right],$$

so that the current account is

$$\dot{b} = -\left[\tilde{p} + \frac{e_T - e_N}{s_T - s_N}\right]\dot{S}. \tag{4.32}$$

Thus it is evident that the sign of the current account will depend on the complementarity of equipment and structures in production. Equation (4.32) indicates that if the relative intensities of equipment usage are the same across the two sectors, then the current account will solely reflect the cost of acquiring new structures; that is, $\dot{b} = -\tilde{p}\dot{S}$. When equipment intensities differ across the two sectors, the current account response to an increase in structures will be magnified if equipment and structures are complements. The current account response will be dampened (and may be reversed in sign) if equipment and structures are substitutes in production, since the economy will sell excess equipment in exchange for bonds.

If the nontradables sector is relatively structure intensive ($s_N > s_T$), the relative price of nontraded goods will change along the saddlepath. In this case, it is seen that in comparison with (4.32), there are now two additional effects, reflecting the adjustment in prices that now occurs along the transitional path. The first is the capitalized value of savings along the transition path toward the steady state,

$$-\left(\frac{1}{\mu_1 - r}\right)\left(\frac{\partial C}{\partial p}\right)\left(\frac{dp}{dS}\right)_{xx} > 0.$$

This effect was also present in (4.13). The second additional term,

$$-\frac{\partial E}{\partial p}\left(\frac{dp}{dS}\right)_{xx},$$

is new and reflects the effect of the traded investment. It captures the change in the stock of equipment that accompanies the decline in the relative price of nontraded goods along the saddlepath. For any given values of equipment intensities (e_T, e_N), this term will be negative if the traded sector is equipment intensive, thereby amplifying the deterioration of the current account arising from the investment in structures.

Equation (4.31a) demonstrates that the current account bears no simple relationship to the rate of accumulation of structures in the economy when the nontraded sector is structures intensive. The direct effect of purchases of structures will tend to deteriorate the current account. That effect will be amplified by the accrual of capital losses on structures during the transition and will be dampened by the reduction in consumption. Further ambiguity is introduced by the fact, noted above, that the accumulation of structures may be accompanied by an increasing or decreasing stock of equipment, depending upon the relative magnitudes of the direct effect and the relative price effect, which tend to be offsetting.

Steady-State Equilibrium

The steady-state equilibrium, reached when $\dot{p} = \dot{S} = \dot{E} = \dot{b} = 0$, implies the relationships

$$\frac{f_s(\tilde{s}_T, \tilde{e}_T)}{\tilde{p}} = h_s(\tilde{s}_N, \tilde{e}_N) = r + \delta_S \tag{4.33a}$$

$$(1 - \tilde{L}_T)h(\tilde{s}_N, \tilde{e}_N) - \tilde{C}_N - \delta_S \tilde{S} = 0 \tag{4.33b}$$

$$\tilde{L}_T f(\tilde{s}_T, \tilde{e}_T) - \tilde{C}_T - \delta_E \tilde{E} + r\tilde{b} + \tau = 0, \tag{4.33c}$$

where tildes denote steady-state values. These equations are analogous to (4.14a)–(4.14c). Equation (4.33a) asserts that the long-run values of the marginal product of structures in the two sectors must equal the long-run rental rate, which, expressed in terms of the traded good, is fixed at $r + \delta_s$. The second equation requires that the output of the nontraded sector equal private consumption demand plus depreciation of existing structures, and the third equation states that the long-run current account balance must be zero.

The steady-state equilibrium can be determined as follows. First, equations (4.7a) and (4.7b) determine long-run consumption levels, $\tilde{C}_T$ and $\tilde{C}_N$, as functions of the shadow value of wealth $(\tilde{\lambda})$ and the relative price of nontraded goods $(\tilde{p})$. Second, equations (4.23c), (4.23d), and (4.33a) jointly determine the steady-state sectoral intensities of structures, $\tilde{s}_T, \tilde{s}_N$, and equipment, $\tilde{e}_T, \tilde{e}_N$, and the relative price of nontraded goods, $\tilde{p}$. These equilibrium quantities are determined by production conditions alone, including foreign financial shocks insofar as they impact on r.

They are independent of any disturbance impinging elsewhere in the economy, including the exogenous income flow from abroad (τ). Third, having determined the sectoral capital intensities and the relative price of nontraded goods, equations (4.24a), (4.24b), (4.33b), and (4.33c), together with the intertemporal solvency condition (4.23h), jointly determine the equilibrium stock of structures ($\tilde{S}$), the equilibrium stock of equipment ($\tilde{E}$), the steady-state labor allocation ($\tilde{L}_T$), and the constant marginal utility of wealth ($\bar{\lambda}$):

$$\tilde{S} = \tilde{L}_T \tilde{s}_T + (1 - \tilde{L}_T)\tilde{s}_N \tag{4.34a}$$

$$\tilde{E} = \tilde{L}_T \tilde{e}_T + (1 - \tilde{L}_T)\tilde{e}_N \tag{4.34b}$$

$$(1 - \tilde{L}_T)h(s_N(\tilde{p}), e_N(p)) - C_N(\bar{\lambda}, \tilde{p}) - \delta_S \tilde{S} = 0 \tag{4.34c}$$

$$\tilde{L}_T f(s_T(\tilde{p}), e_T(\tilde{p})) - C_T(\bar{\lambda}, \tilde{p}) - \delta_E \tilde{E} + r\left[b_0 - \frac{\Omega}{\mu_1 - r}(S_0 - \tilde{S})\right] + \tau = 0. \tag{4.34d}$$

From the equilibrium quantities determined by (4.34a)–(4.34d), the equilibrium stock of bonds, consumption, and sectoral outputs can be derived.

Two further points should be noted. First, from (4.34d) it is clear that the steady-state equilibrium depends upon the initial stocks of structures, S_0, and traded bonds, b_0. This dependence upon initial conditions is a consequence of the assumption $\beta = r$ and raises the potential for temporary shocks to have permanent effects, as discussed in Chapter 3. Second, the expression Ω, which describes the relationship between the accumulation of structures and the stock of traded bonds, depends upon the relative sectoral intensities of the two types of capital.

4.7 Structural Shocks with Two Types of Capital

Permanent Increase in Foreign Transfers

To illustrate the behavior of the model, we shall consider one of the oldest and most important problems in the literature on the balance of payments, the adjustment of the economy to a permanent increase in the flow of transfer income (τ). The debate on the economic consequences of a financial transfer from one country to another originated with the reparations imposed on Germany at the end of World War I. A central issue in that discussion was the question of whether or not the payment of reparations imposed a secondary burden on the paying country by causing a deterioration in its terms of trade.

The long-run effects of an increase in transfers are reported in the Appendix and can be summarized as follows. As already noted, the long-run sectoral intensities of structures $(\tilde{s}_T, \tilde{s}_N)$ and equipment $(\tilde{e}_T, \tilde{e}_N)$, and the relative price of nontraded goods $(\tilde{p})$, all remain unchanged. An increase in transfers (τ) raises the long-run wealth of the economy, lowering its shadow value $(\tilde{\lambda})$. With the relative price remaining constant, and both goods being normal, the long-run consumption of both traded and nontraded goods must rise. In particular, the increase in demand for nontraded consumption requires the output of the nontraded good to rise; this rise is accomplished by attracting labor from the traded sector, whose output therefore declines. With the sectoral intensities of the two types of capital remaining unchanged, the effect of the increase in the flow of transfer income on the two types of capital depends upon whether labor is moving from a relatively less to a relatively more intensive sector in that type of capital. Specifically, an increase in τ will raise the long-run stock of structures $(\tilde{S})$ if and only if the nontraded sector is relatively intensive in its use of structures $(s_N > s_T)$. Likewise, an increase in transfer income will raise the long-run stock of equipment $\tilde{E}$ (imported from abroad) if and only if the nontraded sector is relatively equipment intensive $(e_N > e_T)$. What happens to the long-run stock of foreign bonds depends upon the response of the long-run stock of structures and how this response translates into the accumulation of assets, as described by Ω.

The dynamic adjustment paths, illustrated in figures 4.5 and 4.6, depend critically upon the relative intensities of the two sectors in the nontraded investment good, structures. Consider first the case where the traded sector is relatively structures intensive $(s_T > s_N)$. An increase in τ will lead to a gradual decline in the stock of structures. With the long-run relative price remaining unchanged, and with no transitional adjustment, p remains fixed throughout the transition. The adjustment path for S and p is therefore depicted by the horizontal locus AP in the middle panel of Figure 4.5. Moreover, the constancy of p along this path implies that sectoral structures and equipment intensities must remain fixed throughout the transition. The corresponding adjustment in the stock of equipment is illustrated in the upper panel. In the absence of any instantaneous jump in the relative price $\tilde{p}$, the adjustment of labor occurs gradually, as resources are attracted to the nontraded sector. Whether or not this gradual adjustment in labor toward the nontraded sector leads to an increasing or decreasing stock of equipment depends upon the long-run response of $\tilde{E}$, as determined by the relative sectoral intensities $e_T - e_N$. Alternative adjustment paths for the stock of equipment illustrated in the upper panel correspond to the two cases where equipment and structures are substitutes and complements, respectively, in production. In the former

136 Chapter 4

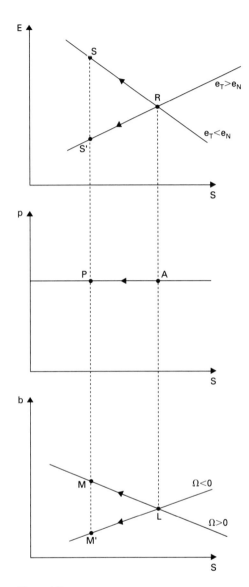

Figure 4.5
Adjustment of economy to increase in τ: $s_T > s_N$

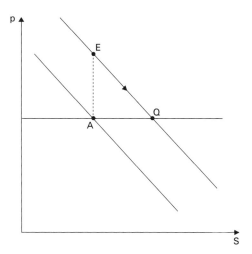

Figure 4.6
Adjustment of economy to increase in τ: $s_N > s_T$

case, $(e_T < e_N)$, equipment accumulates along the negatively sloped path *RS*; in the latter case $(e_T > e_N)$, the stock of equipment declines with structures along the positively sloped line *RS'*. Alternative time paths for the corresponding accumulation of bonds are presented in the lower panel. From (4.32) we see that—provided equipment and structures are complements or at most weak substitutes, so that $\Omega > 0$—the decline in structures will be accompanied by a current account surplus and bonds will accumulate along the negatively sloped locus *LM*. While we view this as the more likely scenario, the alternative case of an accompanying current account deficit is illustrated by the positively sloped locus *LM'*.

Suppose now that the relative structural intensities of the two sectors are reversed $(s_N > s_T)$. In this case, the decline in $\bar{\lambda}$, resulting from the increase in τ, generates an instantaneous increase in the demand for both consumption goods. In particular, with the stock of nontraded goods being fixed instantaneously, this will tend to raise their relative price, so that $p(0)$ will immediately rise. The increase in $p(0)$ causes an immediate shifting of resources away from the traded to the nontraded sector. With $s_N > s_T$, structures increase in relative scarcity, the ratio of the wage rate to the rental rate on structures tends to fall, and firms substitute labor for structures. While the structures:labor ratio falls in the traded sector, its net response in the nontraded sector depends to some degree upon whether equipment is a complement or a substitute for structures in the production of nontradables. Under plausible conditions, one would expect s_N to decline as well, but the opposite cannot be ruled out. The rise in the relative price of nontradables tends to cause an immediate shift of labor to the nontraded sector. Output of that sector immediately increases, and then the rate of nontraded investment begins to rise. Along the adjustment path, the stock of structures increases steadily, while the relative price of nontradables gradually returns to its initial equilibrium level. This type of adjustment takes place because the shift of resources to the nontradable sector resulting from the higher price raises the marginal physical product of structures in that sector, requiring a continuous decline in p in order for the rates of return on the assets to be equalized. The adjustment in p and S is illustrated in Figure 4.6 by the initial jump in AE, followed by the continuous adjustment along the saddlepath EQ. Because of the wider range of potential adjustments in E and b that are now possible, time paths for these variables are not illustrated. We should note, however, that the initial jump in $p(0)$ that now occurs will lead to an initial jump in the stock of equipment, with the direction of this jump depending upon the sectoral intensities of the two sectors in the two types of capital.

Welfare Effects

Thus far we have described the economy's adjustment to an increase in the flow of transfer income from abroad. What is of ultimate concern is the impact on economic welfare. In considering this aspect, the criterion will be taken to be the welfare of the representative agent, and we will consider both the time path of the level of instantaneous utility and the overall accumulated welfare over the agent's infinite planning horizon.

The instantaneous level of utility of the representative agent at time t, $Z(t)$, is specified to be

$$Z(t) = U(C_T(t), C_N(t)), \tag{4.35}$$

with the overall level of utility over the agent's infinite planning horizon being the discounted value of (4.35),

$$W = \int_0^\infty U(C_T, C_N) e^{-rt}\, dt = \int_0^\infty Z(t) e^{-rt}\, dt, \tag{4.36}$$

where, as before, the agent's discount rate β is assumed to equal the world interest rate r. The effects of τ on $Z(t)$ and W will be analyzed when C_T and C_N follow the paths described by (4.7a) and (4.7b), and S and p evolve in accordance with (4.28a) and (4.28b). The cases where $s_T > s_N$ and $s_N > s_T$ will be treated separately.

Traded Sector Relatively Intensive in Structures

This case is straightforward. As noted previously, the consumption of both goods is always at their respective steady-state levels, and therefore constant over time. Thus

$$Z(t) = \tilde{Z} = U(\tilde{C}_T, \tilde{C}_N) \quad \text{for all } t,$$

implying that

$$W = \frac{U(\tilde{C}_T, \tilde{C}_N)}{r}. \tag{4.37}$$

Since an increase in the transfer of income from abroad raises steady-state consumption of both goods, it follows immediately that welfare improves uniformly at all points of time.

Nontraded Sector Relatively Intensive in Structures

Writing

$$Z(t) = U(C_T(\bar{\lambda}, p(t)), C_N(\bar{\lambda}, p(t))), \tag{4.38}$$

we see that $Z(t)$ changes over time as p evolves along its transitional path. Differentiating (4.38) and noting (4.23a) and (4.23b), the following impacts on instantaneous welfare can be derived:

$$\frac{dZ(0)}{d\tau} = \bar{\lambda}\left[\frac{\partial C_T}{\partial \bar{\lambda}} + p\frac{\partial C_N}{\partial \bar{\lambda}}\right]\frac{\partial \bar{\lambda}}{\partial \tau} + \bar{\lambda}\left[\frac{\partial C_T}{\partial p} + p\frac{\partial C_N}{\partial p}\right]\frac{\partial p(0)}{\partial \tau} \tag{4.39a}$$

$$\dot{Z}(t) = \bar{\lambda}\left[\frac{\partial C_T}{\partial p} + p\frac{\partial C_N}{\partial p}\right]\dot{p}(t) > 0 \tag{4.39b}$$

$$\frac{d\tilde{Z}}{d\tau} = \bar{\lambda}\left[\frac{\partial C_T}{\partial \bar{\lambda}} + p\frac{\partial C_N}{\partial \bar{\lambda}}\right]\frac{\partial \bar{\lambda}}{\partial \tau} > 0, \tag{4.39c}$$

where

$$\frac{\partial C_T}{\partial p} + p\frac{\partial C_N}{\partial p} = \bar{\lambda}\frac{\partial C_N}{\partial \bar{\lambda}} < 0.$$

In the short run, an increase in the rate of income flow from abroad has two effects on the level of instantaneous welfare, $Z(0)$. The first is a positive wealth effect that is permanent and raises the level of consumption of both goods, and is therefore welfare-improving. However, the positive wealth effect is offset by an expenditure reduction effect, given by the second term in (4.39a). The initial increase in the relative price $p(0)$ induces more saving and less total consumption, thereby deteriorating welfare. On balance, without imposing further restrictions, one cannot say unambiguously which effect will dominate.[18] With the wealth effect constant over time, instantaneous welfare $Z(t)$ rises over time as the price of the nontraded good declines to its initial level, and the expenditure reduction effect is mitigated. In steady state, only the positive wealth effect prevails, and steady-state utility increases unambiguously.

A linear approximation to the overall level of welfare, represented by equation (4.36), can be obtained by observing that along the equilibrium path, $Z(t)$ can be approximated by

$$Z(t) \approx \tilde{Z} + (Z(0) - \tilde{Z})e^{\mu_1 t}. \tag{4.40}$$

Substituting (4.40) into (4.36), and integrating, yields

$$W \approx \frac{\tilde{Z}}{r} + \frac{Z(0) - \tilde{Z}}{r - \mu_1}. \tag{4.41}$$

The first term of (4.41) is the capitalized value of instantaneous welfare, $Z(t)$, evaluated at the steady state. It is the level of welfare that would obtain if the steady state were attained instantaneously. The remaining term reflects the adjustment to this, due to the fact that the steady state is reached only gradually along the transitional path. Differentiating (4.41) with respect to τ yields

$$\frac{dW}{d\tau} = \frac{1}{r - \mu_1}\left(\frac{dZ(0)}{d\tau} - \frac{\mu_1}{r}\frac{d\tilde{Z}}{d\tau}\right). \tag{4.42}$$

Substituting from (4.39a) and (4.39c), and with some manipulation, one can establish that $dW/d\tau > 0$, unambiguously. Thus, we conclude that even though an increase in transfer income from abroad may have a temporarily adverse effect on domestic utility, overall it will be welfare-improving, as one would expect.

Long-Run Relative Price Adjustment

Our objective in sections 4.6 and 4.7 has been primarily to integrate both nontraded and traded investment goods into the dynamic dependent economy model, and to show how the resulting system is both tractable and intuitive. To illustrate the behavior of this system, we have chosen a relatively simple shock to analyze—namely, the impact of a foreign transfer—though we hasten to add that this is an important shock with a long history in balance of payments analysis. From an analytical viewpoint, the significant feature of this disturbance is that it generates no long-run adjustment in the relative price of nontraded to traded goods, though there may be some short-run transitional price adjustment, depending upon the relative intensities of the nontraded and traded sectors in nontraded capital (structures). Furthermore, the relative traded capital (equipment) intensity of the two sectors plays no role in any transitional price adjustment that may occur; the relative intensity is, however, important in determining the evolution of the current account.

This limited role played by relative price adjustment applies with respect to any disturbance that does not impact directly on production decisions. The dynamics that we have been discussing would therefore characterize other disturbances, such as a change in tastes or in government expenditure policy. This is a consequence of the recursive structure of the steady-state equilibrium, outlined in Section 4.6. As noted in that discussion, the long-run relative price, $\tilde{p}$, and sectoral capital intensities, $\tilde{s}_T, \tilde{s}_N, \tilde{e}_T$ and $\tilde{e}_N$, are determined by production conditions alone. They will therefore respond to any shocks that impinge on production decisions, such as (1) differential tax and incentive treatments associated with different types of investment; (2) productivity shocks; (3) foreign financial shocks; (4) a change in the relative price of equipment to traded consumption. In particular, there is growing interest in studying the differential impact of taxes and subsidies on investment in equipment and structures (see e.g., Auerbach and Hines 1987). Most of the work in this area is being carried out in the context of a closed economy, and the framework developed by Auerbach and Hines is a natural one for addressing the international ramifications of this important policy issue.

We do not pursue a detailed analysis of these types of shocks, since any long-run change in the relative price of nontraded capital increases the possible range of outcomes for both the accumulation of structures and the behavior of the current account, relative to the corresponding outcomes associated with a transfer. But to illustrate the important role played by the long-run relative price adjustment to such shocks, we briefly discuss the case of an increase in the relative price of equipment to traded consumption, a relative price that De Long and Summers (1991) find to be empirically important in explaining economic growth. Denoting this price (which previously was normalized at unity) by p_E, one can establish that[19]

$$\frac{\partial \tilde{p}}{\partial p_E} = \frac{\partial E/\partial S}{(dr_S/dp) - r - \delta_S} = \frac{((e_T - e_N)/(s_T - s_N))}{(dr_S/dp) - r - \delta_S}, \quad (4.43)$$

where from (4.27) $(dr_S/dp) - r - \delta_S = \mu_1 - r < 0$ if the traded sector is structures intensive $(s_T > s_N)$, and $(dr_S/dp) - r - \delta_S = -\mu_1 > 0$ if the sectoral intensities in structures are reversed.

A consequence of the long-run adjustment in $\tilde{p}$ and in the corresponding sectoral intensities $\tilde{s}_T, \tilde{s}_N, \tilde{e}_T$, and $\tilde{e}_N$ is that a change in the relative price p_E impacts on the remainder of the steady state in three ways. First there is a wealth effect, analogous to the effect of the change in τ. In addition, there will be two other effects: a relative price effect resulting from the change in the long-run relative price $\tilde{p}$, and a further effect stemming from the accompanying changes in the sectoral capital intensities. These all impact on the long-run stock of structures in ways that are not straightforward and will themselves depend upon existing sectoral capital intensities. Given the various potential responses in $\tilde{p}$, it is evident that in the long run, $\tilde{S}$ and $\tilde{p}$ may rise together, fall together, or move in opposite directions.

But despite the potential ambiguities in these long-run responses, the transitional dynamics remain essentially as discussed previously and as illustrated in figures 4.4 and 4.5. Specifically, whether or not the relative price adjusts instantaneously to its new long-run equilibrium—irrespective of whether this adjustment involves a rise or a fall—depends solely upon the relative intensities of the two sectors in structures, just as it did before. If the traded sector is structures intensive, the adjustment is instantaneous; if the relative intensities are reversed, there will be an initial jump in the relative price, followed by a transitional adjustment to its new equilibrium.

4.8 Generalizations of Production Technology

Both models we have considered are based on the traditional Heckscher-Ohlin technology. This has the feature that at any instant of time the aggregate stocks of capital and labor are fixed, though both are freely mobile across sectors. The Heckscher-Ohlin analysis focuses on the static allocation decision, and the essential feature of our dynamic analysis has been to embed this allocation decision within the dynamic process of capital accumulation. We have seen that to incorporate both traded and nontraded capital simultaneously into one model is not as difficult as had previously been thought. Thus one can include both types of capital and thereby avoid the criticisms leveled at arbitrarily assuming that capital is either traded or nontraded, or choosing the traded sector rather than the nontraded sector as being relatively capital intensive. Observe, also, that once nontraded capital is introduced, adjustment costs on traded capital are no longer required in order to ensure that the dynamics is nondegenerate. Of course, one may wish to introduce such costs as a realistic aspect of the investment process, but if they are introduced, they generate an extra "layer" of dynamics, thereby augmenting the dynamics of the resulting equilibrium system.

We conclude this discussion of the two-sector model by discussing several variants of it that move it away from the pure Heckscher-Ohlin technology. We shall briefly consider three issues: (1) adjustment costs associated with intersectoral capital mobility; (2) an additional factor of production and the "sector-specific" production technology; (3) extension to three sectors.

Intersectoral Adjustment Costs

Few economists would argue with the proposition that shifting capital across sectors is costly. Capital that is in place for the production of, say, machines for export is unlikely to be appropriate for the production of a nontraded service industry, like banking. To move capital from one sector to another will involve its dismantling and the reconfiguration of the resources it embodies in a form appropriate to its new use. The argument that labor is perfectly mobile across sectors is probably less objectionable, although the movement from one sector to another is likely to involve retraining and the acquisition of new skills. These intersectoral adjustment costs are ignored in the Heckscher-Ohlin framework and in our analysis of this chapter.

Mussa (1978) recognized this process of "structural adjustment" and introduced the distinction between labor, which was assumed to be instantaneously mobile across sectors, and capital, which could be moved only gradually and at a cost. More recently, Gavin (1990) introduced these elements into the type of two-sector dependent economy model we have been developing in this chapter. The key feature of his analysis is the idea, introduced by Mussa, that capital cannot be instantaneously shifted between sectors. Rather, he introduces a perfectly competitive "retrofit sector" that purchases capital from sector i, say at price q_i, retrofits it, using some increasing cost technology, and sells it to sector j at a price q_j. Gavin assumes that moving capital between sectors requires labor.

Thus, for example, the profit, π_R, earned by the representative firm in the retrofit sector from moving capital from, say, the nontraded to the traded sector is

$$\pi_R = (q_T - q_N)I_T - wL_R(I_T),$$

where I_T is the volume of capital being moved and $wL_R(I_T)$ is the cost of retrofitting the capital that is being moved across the sectors. Gavin incorporates this cost into the representative agent's intertemporal utility-maximizing decision. One of the sectoral labor allocation decisions is now how much time to allocate to the process of retrofitting. Gavin uses his model to analyze the effects of an exogenous terms of trade shock on the dynamic adjustment. He has provided an interesting analysis that is applicable to a variety of issues.

Sector-Specific Factors

A limiting case of no intersectoral factor mobility is the "specific-factors" model due to R. W. Jones (1971) and Neary (1978). According to this technology, the two production functions for the traded and nontraded sector are, say, $F(Q, L_T)$ and $H(K, L_N)$, where Q denotes land and is used only in the production of the traded good, while capital, K, is now used only in the production of the nontraded good. The rationale for this specification is a developing economy in which the traded good is an agricultural good. Labor is still perfectly mobile across the two sectors.

The main modification to our analysis is that the optimal sectoral allocation conditions (4.3c) and (4.3d) are modified to the labor allocation decision

$$F_L(Q, L_T) = pH_L(K, L_N). \tag{4.3d'}$$

This, coupled with $L_T + L_N = 1$, implies that the rate of return on capital, expressed in terms of tradables, $r^K \equiv F_K(Q, L_T)$, is now a function of the capital stock, as well as of the relative price of nontradables:

$$r^K(K, p), \quad \text{with } r^K_K < 0; r^K_p > 0,$$

reflecting the decreasing marginal productivity of capital and of labor in producing the traded good.

The effect of this is that the locus $\dot{p} = 0$, which is now described by the condition

$$r^K(\tilde{K}, \tilde{p}) = \tilde{p}r,$$

is illustrated by an upward-sloping curve (not illustrated) in the phase diagram Figure 4.1

In an earlier version of his 1996 paper, Brock generalized the production structure by considering production functions of the form $F(Q, K_T, L_T)$ and $H(K_N, L_N)$. In this formulation capital is still perfectly mobile, but now land is specific to the production of tradable goods. As he discusses, once one introduces capital in both sectors, the range of factor intensities rankings is increased and alternative patterns of dynamic behavior are admitted.[20]

For example, labor may be used intensively in the nontraded sector, land used intensively in the traded sector, and capital may be a middle factor. In that case, R. W. Jones and Easton (1983) have shown that when capital and labor are sufficiently good substitutes, so that a rise in the real wage causes a strong economywide substitution toward capital, the rental on capital will unambiguously rise with an increase in the relative price of nontradables. In such a case, the economy's dynamics will remain qualitatively similar to those of the specific factors model. On the other hand, if capital and land are good substitutes, so that a rise in the rental rate on land produces a strong economywide substitution toward capital, then capital's rental rate will fall with a rise in the relative price of nontradables, although proportionately less than the fall in the rental rate on land. In that case the $\dot{p} = 0$ locus will become downward sloping.

The specific factors model has seen fewer dynamic applications than the dependent economy model based on the Heckscher-Ohlin technology. One application of the model is by Brock and Turnovsky (1993), who take a small open economy version, in which the relative price of nontradables is given exogenously. The two sectors are now identified as being an export sector and an import-competing sector, respectively, and the model is used to analyze the effects of tariffs in such an economy. In contrast to the analysis of Chapter 3, which found a tariff to be contractionary, Brock and Turnovsky find a uniform tariff on consumption and imported investment goods to be expansionary. Starting from free trade, the imposition of a small uniform tariff shifts labor into the import-competing sector, thereby raising the marginal product of capital and thus encouraging the accumulation of capital. By contrast, a tariff imposed on the investment good alone is contractionary. The framework lends itself to issues relating to tariff reform, and given the orientation of the model to developing economies, it is applicable to other macrodynamic issues arising in that context.

Three-Sector Model

The possible range of dynamic behavior increases when one extends the dependent economy model from two to three production sectors. Such models have been developed by Turnovsky (1991) in his analysis of tariffs and by van Wincoop (1993) in his analysis of the Dutch disease problem, analyzed in the form of the transfer of resources. Both Turnovsky and van Wincoop treat investment as being nontradable. Whereas Turnovsky considers a domestically produced consumption good together with an import-competing consumption good, van Wincoop breaks down consumption goods into tradable and nontradable goods. In either case, there are now two relative prices that are endogenously determined: the relative price of investment and the relative price of the domestically produced consumption, both expressed in terms of the tradable good as numeraire.

With three sectors, there are now three sectoral capital intensities that become relevant: k_M, the capital intensity of the import-competing consumption sector; k_X, the capital intensity of the traded consumption sector; and k_I, the capital intensity of the nontraded investment sector. This complicates the nature of the saddlepath in $p - K$ space. Analogous to our previous analysis, the saddlepath will be flat if $k_M > k_I$. However, if $k_I > k_M$, it will be negatively sloped—as before, if $k_X > k_I$—but it will now be positively sloped if $k_I > k_X$.

Being a demand shock, a tariff has no long-run effect on any of the three sectoral capital intensities. The long-run effect of a tariff therefore depends solely upon its effects on the employment of labor in each sector. While a higher tariff will protect the import-competing industry, leading to additional labor being employed in that industry, it will also lead to a decline in the relative price of import-competing goods in terms of the export good, leading to a reduction in the demand for the export good and causing a decline in that industry. The effect of this shift on the aggregate capital stock depends upon whether labor is moving from a relatively less to a relatively more capital-intensive industry. If it is, then given that the sectoral capital intensity remains fixed, the aggregate capital stock will be raised; otherwise, the aggregate capital stock will decline.

Both the two-sector models and the three-sector models emphasize the importance of the preexisting sectoral capital intensities in determining the nature of the dynamic adjustment path followed by the economy after some previously unanticipated shock. The responses we have been describing throughout this chapter are all based on the assumption that the relative magnitudes of the sectoral capital intensities remain unchanged throughout the adjustment, so that, strictly speaking, the changes must be infinitesimally small. But it is entirely possible that for larger changes, the economy will move from one configuration of relative sectoral capital intensities to another. Under perfect foresight, this needs to be taken into account at the outset. The potential for such structural shifts has important implications for the dynamic evolution of the economy and promises to be an interesting avenue for future research.

Appendix

In this Appendix we present some of the short-run and long-run comparative static results for the model with both traded and nontraded capital, together with the derivation of the current account dynamnics.

A.1 Properties of Short-Run Solutions

Production:

Differentiating the production block (4.23c)–(4.23e), we obtain

$$\begin{pmatrix} f_{ss} & f_{se} & -ph_{ss} & -ph_{se} \\ f_{es} & f_{ee} & 0 & 0 \\ 0 & 0 & ph_{es} & ph_{ee} \\ \begin{bmatrix} -s_T f_{ss} \\ -e_T f_{es} \end{bmatrix} & \begin{bmatrix} -s_T f_{se} \\ -e_T f_{ee} \end{bmatrix} & \begin{bmatrix} ps_N h_{ss} \\ +pe_N h_{es} \end{bmatrix} & \begin{bmatrix} ps_N h_{se} \\ +pe_N h_{ee} \end{bmatrix} \end{pmatrix} \begin{pmatrix} ds_T \\ de_T \\ ds_N \\ de_N \end{pmatrix}$$

$$= \begin{pmatrix} h_s dp \\ 0 \\ h_e dp \\ [h - s_N h_s - e_N h_e] dp \end{pmatrix},$$

from which the following derivatives are derived:

$$\frac{ds_T}{dp} = -\frac{hf_{ee}}{F(s_T - s_N)}; \quad \frac{de_T}{dp} = \frac{hf_{es}}{F(s_T - s_N)} \quad (4.A.1a)$$

$$\frac{ds_N}{dp} = \frac{1}{pH(s_T - s_N)}(-[h - (s_N - s_T)h_s]h_{ee} - (s_N - s_T)h_{se}h_e)$$

$$\frac{de_N}{dp} = \frac{1}{pH(s_T - s_N)}([h - (s_N - s_T)h_s]h_{es} + (s_N - s_T)h_{ss}h_e), \quad (4.A.1b)$$

where $F \equiv f_{ss}f_{ee} - f_{es}^2 > 0$, and $H \equiv h_{ss}h_{ee} - h_{es}^2 > 0$.

Rentals and Wages

The short-run effects of p on r_S and w are

$$\frac{dr_S}{dp} = f_{ss}\frac{ds_T}{dp} + f_{se}\frac{de_T}{dp} = \frac{h}{s_N - s_T} \quad (4.A.2a)$$

$$\frac{dw}{dp} = \frac{s_T}{s_T - s_N}. \quad (4.A.2b)$$

Sectoral Labor Allocations

The short-run effects on sectoral labor allocations are

$$\frac{\partial L_T}{\partial S} = \frac{1}{s_T - s_N} \quad (4.A.3a)$$

$$\frac{\partial L_T}{\partial p} = -\frac{1}{s_T - s_N}\left(L_T\frac{ds_T}{dp} + (1 - L_T)\frac{ds_N}{dp}\right), \quad (4.A.3b)$$

where ds_T/dp and ds_N/dp are obtained from (4.A.1a) and (4.A.1b), respectively.

Output and Equipment

The short-run effects on output and equipment are

$$\frac{\partial Y_T}{\partial s} = f\frac{\partial L_T}{\partial s} = \frac{f}{s_T - s_N} \quad (4.A.4a)$$

$$\frac{\partial Y_T}{\partial p} = f\frac{\partial L_T}{\partial p} + L_T\left(f_s\frac{ds_T}{dp} + f_e\frac{de_T}{dp}\right) \quad (4.A.4b)$$

$$\frac{\partial Y_N}{\partial S} = -h\frac{\partial L_T}{\partial S} = -\frac{h}{s_T - s_N} \quad (4.A.5a)$$

$$\frac{\partial Y_N}{\partial p} = -h\frac{\partial L_T}{\partial p} + (1 - L_T)\left(h_s\frac{ds_N}{dp} + h_e\frac{de_N}{dp}\right) \quad (4.A.5b)$$

148 Chapter 4

$$\frac{\partial E}{\partial S} = (e_T - e_N)\frac{\partial L_T}{\partial S} \qquad (4.A.6a)$$

$$\frac{\partial E}{\partial p} = (e_T - e_N)\frac{\partial L_T}{\partial p} + L_T\frac{de_T}{dp} + (1 - L_T)\frac{de_N}{dp}. \qquad (4.A.6b)$$

A.2 Derivation of Current Account Dynamics

Linearizing the current account relationship (4.30) yields

$$\dot{b} = \left[\frac{\partial Y_T}{\partial S} - \frac{\partial I_E}{\partial S} + \left(\frac{\partial Y_T}{\partial p} - \frac{\partial C_T}{\partial p} - \frac{\partial I_E}{\partial p}\right)\left(\frac{dp}{dS}\right)_{xx}\right](S - \tilde{S}) + r(b - \tilde{b}). \qquad (4.A.7)$$

Recalling (4.19a) and (4.25b), together with the definition of Y_N, we have

$$\frac{\partial Y_N}{\partial S} = \frac{\partial I_S}{\partial S}; \quad \frac{\partial Y_N}{\partial p} = \frac{\partial C_N}{\partial p} + \frac{\partial I_S}{\partial p},$$

enabling us to write (4.A.7) in the form

$$\dot{b} = \left[\left(\frac{\partial Y_T}{\partial S} + p\frac{\partial Y_N}{\partial S} - \frac{\partial I_E}{\partial S} - p\frac{\partial I_S}{\partial S}\right)\right.$$
$$+ \left.\left(\frac{\partial Y_T}{\partial p} + p\frac{\partial Y_N}{\partial p} - \frac{\partial C_T}{\partial p} - p\frac{\partial C_N}{\partial p} - \frac{\partial I_E}{\partial p} - p\frac{\partial I_E}{\partial S}\right)\left(\frac{dp}{dS}\right)_{xx}\right](S - \tilde{S})$$
$$+ r(b - \tilde{b}). \qquad (4.A.8)$$

Using the following relationship, obtained from the above short-run solutions,

$$\frac{\partial Y_T}{\partial S} + p\frac{\partial Y_N}{\partial S} = r_S + (r + \delta_E)\frac{\partial E}{\partial S}; \quad \frac{\partial Y_T}{\partial p} + p\frac{\partial Y_N}{\partial p} = (r + \delta_E)\frac{\partial E}{\partial p}$$

$$\frac{\partial I_E}{\partial S} + \frac{\partial I_E}{\partial p}\left(\frac{dp}{dS}\right)_{xx} = (\mu_1 + \delta_E)\left(\frac{\partial E}{\partial S} + \frac{\partial E}{\partial p}\left(\frac{dp}{dS}\right)_{xx}\right);$$

$$\frac{\partial I_S}{\partial S} + \frac{\partial I_S}{\partial p}\left(\frac{dp}{dS}\right)_{xx} = \mu_1 + \delta_S.$$

Substituting into (4.A.8), while noting (4.23f), leads to

$$\dot{b} = \left[(r - \mu_1)\left(\tilde{p} + \frac{\partial E}{\partial S} + \frac{\partial E}{\partial p}\left(\frac{dp}{dS}\right)_{xx}\right) - \frac{\partial C}{\partial p}\left(\frac{dp}{dS}\right)_{xx}\right](S - \tilde{S}) + r(b - \tilde{b}), \qquad (4.A.9)$$

solving which and imposing the intertemporal solvency condition leads to (4.31) of the text.

A.3 Long-Run Effects of Permanent Increase in Flow of Transfers

As noted in the text, the steady-state equilibrium values $\tilde{s}_T$, $\tilde{s}_N$, $\tilde{e}_T$, $\tilde{e}_N$, and $\tilde{p}$ are all independent of τ. Taking the differential of (4.34a)–(4.34d) yields

$$\begin{pmatrix} 1 & 0 & 0 & (s_N - s_T) \\ 0 & 1 & 0 & (e_N - e_T) \\ -\delta_S & 0 & -\partial C_N/\partial \bar{\lambda} & -h \\ (r/(\mu_1 - r))\Omega & -\delta_E & -\partial C_T/\partial \bar{\lambda} & f \end{pmatrix} \begin{pmatrix} d\tilde{S} \\ d\tilde{E} \\ d\bar{\lambda} \\ d\tilde{L}_T \end{pmatrix} = \begin{pmatrix} 0 \\ 0 \\ 0 \\ -d\tau \end{pmatrix}. \tag{4.A.10}$$

From (4.A.10) the partial derivatives

$$\frac{\partial \tilde{S}}{\partial \tau} = (s_T - s_N)\frac{\partial C_N/\partial \bar{\lambda}}{\Delta} \tag{4.A.11a}$$

$$\frac{\partial \tilde{E}}{\partial \tau} = (e_T - e_N)\frac{\partial C_N/\partial \bar{\lambda}}{\Delta} \tag{4.A.11b}$$

$$\frac{\partial \bar{\lambda}}{\partial \tau} = -\frac{h}{\Delta} < 0 \tag{4.A.11c}$$

$$\frac{\partial \tilde{L}_T}{\partial \tau} = \frac{\partial C_N/\partial \bar{\lambda}}{\Delta} < 0 \tag{4.A.11d}$$

are obtained; the determinant, $\Delta > 0$, is required for stability to obtain.

Notes

1. This analysis draws on Turnovsky and Sen (1995). Brock (1996) employs a similar model to analyze the response to transfers. This shock is discussed in the more general model that includes both traded and nontraded capital.

2. Cairnes (1859) analyzed the changes in the structure of Australian production, volume of trade, and the relative price of home goods following the discovery of gold in 1852. Graham (1922) employed data from the U.S. greenback period to test empirically Taussig's (1917) theory of relative price changes under a floating exchange rate regime. Taussig (1920) and Ohlin (1929) independently analyzed the role of nontraded goods in the macroeconomic adjustment process put into motion by the payment of reparations by Germany after World War I.

3. The two-sector model is also similar in structure to the Scandinavian model of inflation due to Aukrust (1977) and others. This model analyzes inflation in a small open economy that consists of an exposed (traded) sector and a sheltered (nontraded) sector. A clear exposition of this approach is provided by Frisch (1983).

4. See, e.g., McDougall (1965); Neary and Purvis (1982).

5. A testimony to the long-run importance of the dependent economy model is the special issue of the *Review of International Economics* in 1994; see Asea and Corden (1994). For some recent empirical studies examining the behavior of the relative price of nontraded goods, see Asea and Mendoza (1994); De Gregorio, Giovannini, and Krueger (1994).

6. See Fischer and Frenkel (1972).

7. Many definitions of the real exchange rate can be found in the literature. For an extensive discussion of this issue, see Obstfeld and Rogoff (1996, Chapter 4).

8. Since the domestic government is assumed to maintain a continuously balanced budget, there is no government debt and therefore national bond holdings (n) and private bond holdings coincide; that is, $n \equiv b$.

9. Taking the differentials of (4.7a) and (4.7b) yields the following partial derivatives (analogous to those in note 6 of Chapter 3: $\partial C_T/\partial \bar{\lambda} = [U_{NN} - pU_{TN}]/D < 0$; $\partial C_T/\partial p = -\bar{\lambda} U_{TN}/D$; $\partial C_N/\partial \bar{\lambda} = [pU_{TT} - U_{NT}]/D < 0$; $\partial C_N/\partial p = \bar{\lambda} U_{TT}/D < 0$, where $D \equiv U_{TT}U_{NN} - U_{TN}^2 > 0$. The derivatives with respect to $\bar{\lambda}$ reflect the assumption of normal goods.

10. Recall that

$$k'_N = f/p^2 h''(k_N - k_T) < 0 \quad \text{for } k_N > k_T.$$

11. See Dornbusch (1983) for a more detailed discussion of this effect in a model without capital.

12. Bruno (1976, p. 575) appeared to have considered the model unsolvable algebraically, stating: "[f]ull analytical characterizations for general models are hard to obtain."

13. To derive this, we evaluate $a_{11}a_{22}$ as given in (4.27) at steady-state equilibrium, invoking the appropriate steady-state conditions on the rates of return. These are complicated slightly by the presence of the terms involving the depreciation rate of nontraded capital.

14. More specifically, the expression for $\partial E/\partial S$ is obtained by combining (4.A.3a) and (4.A.6a) of the Appendix.

15. Following (4.26f), the stock of equipment can be written as $E = L_T e_T(p) + (1 - L_T)e_N(p)$, so that $\partial E/\partial p = (e_T - e_N)\partial L_T/\partial p + L_T de_T/dp + (1 - L_T)de_N/dp$. The expression for $\partial E/\partial p$ is obtained by utilizing expressions (4.A.1a), (4.A.1b), and (4.A.3b) of the Appendix. For any given equipment intensities, the sign of $\partial E/\partial p$ will depend on the relative equipment intensities.

16. To see this, for given equipment intensities, note 15 implies $\partial E/\partial p = (e_T - e_N)\partial L_T/\partial p$. Combining (4.A.3a) with (4.A.6a) of the Appendix implies $\partial E/\partial S = (e_T - e_N)/(s_T - s_N)$. Under the sectoral intensity assumption $s_T < s_N$, $\partial E/\partial p$ is immediately seen to be of opposite sign to $\partial E/\partial S$.

17. The fact that the covariation between the savings rate, investment, and the current account balance depends upon the sectoral capital intensities is also emphasized by Murphy (1986) in his two-period analysis of productivity shocks.

18. This will depend upon the relative magnitudes of the adjustments in $\bar{\lambda}$ and $p(0)$. A sufficient condition for the former to prevail, and for the increase in τ to be unambiguously welfare-improving in the short run, is that

$$\frac{\partial Y_N}{\partial p} \frac{p}{Y_N} + \frac{\partial C_N}{\partial \bar{\lambda}} \frac{\bar{\lambda}}{C_N} > 0.$$

This condition suffices to ensure that the price elasticity of supply of the nontraded good is sufficiently large to moderate the price rise in that good, thereby ensuring that the positive wealth effect dominates.

19. To establish (4.43), we must first introduce p_E into the basic equilibrium conditions (4.23), in which case $r_s = r_s(p, p_E)$. Having amended the model in this way, (4.43) is obtained by using essentially the same procedures as followed in the text in analyzing τ.

20. The specific factors model was introduced into a dynamic trade model by Eaton (1987).

5 Capital Accumulation and Long-Run Growth

5.1 Introduction

Economic growth is arguably the issue of primary concern to economic policy makers. Economic growth statistics are among the most widely publicized measures of economic performance and are always discussed with interest. Intertemporal models of capital accumulation along the lines of those developed in Chapters 3 and 4 are not well suited to addressing issues pertaining to long-run growth. This is because the equilibria they yield are ultimately stationary. Thus, while they emphasize the central activities of economic growth, savings and investment, the process of asset accumulation they describe is only a transitional one, in that ultimately the capital stock, and the associated productive capacity of the economy, will approach some new stationary level. But at the same time, empirical data suggest that the time for substantial convergence may in fact be long, being of the order of generations (see, e.g., Barro and Sala-i-Martin 1995, chapters 11 and 12). Transitional paths are therefore important, and macroeconomic policy may still be of practical significance insofar as growth is concerned for extensive periods of time. In short, the choice of the appropriate model depends upon the purpose to which it is being put and the time horizon one considers to be relevant.

Some Background

Long-run growth can be incorporated into the stationary intertemporal model by the introduction of a growing population coupled with a more efficient labor force; in fact this was the source of long-run growth in the traditional neoclassical growth pioneered by Solow (1956) and Swan (1956). The direct consequence of this approach is that long-run growth in these models is ultimately tied to demographic factors, such as the growth rate of population, the structure of the labor force, and its productivity growth (technological change), all of which were typically taken to be exogenously determined. Hence, the only policies that could contribute to long-run growth were those that would increase the growth of population and manpower training programs aimed at increasing the efficiency of the labor force. Conventional macroeconomic policy had no influence on long-run growth performance.

Growth theory has evolved into a voluminous literature in two distinct generations of models. The Solow-Swan model was the inspiration for a first generation of growth models during the 1960s, which for reasons just noted were associated with exogenous sources of long-run growth. These models are now sometimes referred to as being *exogenous growth models*. Research interest in these models tapered off around 1970, as economists turned their attention to other issues perceived as being of more immediate significance, such as inflation, unemployment, and oil shocks, and the design of macroeconomic policy to deal with them. Beginning with the seminal work of Romer (1986), there has been a resurgence of interest in economic growth theory, giving rise to a second generation of growth models. This revival of activity has been motivated by several issues, which include (1) an attempt to explain aspects of the data not discussed by the neoclassical model; (2) a more satisfactory explanation of international differences in economic growth rates; (3) a more central role for the accumulation of knowledge; and (4) a larger role for the instruments of macroeconomic policy in explaining the growth process (see Romer 1994). These new models seek to explain the long-run growth rate as an endogenous equilibrium outcome of the behavior of rational optimizing agents that reflect the structural characteristics of the economy, such as technology and preferences, as well as macroeconomic policy. For this reason they have become known as *endogenous growth models.*

The new growth theory is far-ranging. It has been analyzed in both closed and open economies. In fact, one of its characteristics is that it has more of an international orientation (see, e.g., Grossman and Helpman 1991). This may be a reflection of the increased importance of the international aspects of macroeconomics in general. In comparison with the first generation of growth models, the newer literature places a greater emphasis on empirical issues and the reconciliation of the theory with the empirical evidence. In this respect the most widely debated issue concerns the so-called convergence hypothesis. The question here is whether or not countries have a tendency to converge to a common per capita level of income. According to the Solow model, countries with similar technologies should converge to similar long-run levels of per capita income. Thus, to the extent that countries start from different initial income levels, one would expect poorer countries to catch up to richer countries. The notion of convergence is somewhat loose, and more precise notions have been proposed, depending upon the structural similarity or lack thereof, of the countries being compared (see Galor 1996). Evidence by Mankiw, Romer, and Weil (1992) suggesting that poorer countries having low initial income levels tend to grow faster than richer countries has been viewed as supporting the neoclassical growth model. It is thus advanced as evidence in favor of conditional convergence, meaning that the convergence is dependent upon the structural parameters of the economies being identical, with the exception of initial conditions. On the other hand, Quah (1996) provides evidence against conditional convergence but in support of a weaker form of convergence, known as club convergence, meaning that countries having the same structural characteristics and similar initial conditions converge to similar levels of per capita income;

that is, poor countries and rich countries converge to low and high income levels, respectively.

But new growth theory is also associated with important theoretical advances, and one can identify two main strands of theoretical literature that emphasize different sources of economic growth. One class of models, closest to the neoclassical growth model, emphasizes the *accumulation of private capital* as the fundamental source of economic growth. These models are basically extensions of the type of one- and two-sector models developed in Chapters 3 and 4. They differ in a fundamental way from the neoclassical growth model in that they do not require exogenous elements, such as a growing population, in order to generate an equilibrium of ongoing growth. Rather, the equilibrium growth is internally generated, though in order to achieve that, certain restrictions relating to homogeneity must be imposed on the economic framework. Some of these restrictions have a knife-edge character and have been the source of criticism (see, e.g., Solow 1994). The first, and most important, is that production must generally take place subject to constant returns to scale in the factors that are being accumulated.[1] But homogeneity must be preserved in other parts of the system as well. For example, the utility function must generate a consumption level that grows with the economy.

In the simplest such model, in which the only factor of production is capital, constant returns to scale imply that the production function must be linear in physical capital, being of the functional form $Y = AK$. For obvious reasons, this technology has become known as an "AK model." As a matter of historical record, explanation of growth as an endogenous process in a one-sector model is not new. In fact, it dates back to Harrod (1939). The equilibrium growth rate characterizing the AK model is essentially of the Harrod type, the only difference being that consumption (or savings) behavior is derived as part of an intertemporal optimization, rather than being posited directly. These one-sector models assume (often only implicitly) a broad interpretation of capital, taking it to include both human and nonhuman capital (see Rebelo 1991). A direct extension of this basic model is two-sector investment-based growth models, originally due to Lucas (1988), that disaggregate private capital into human and nonhuman capital (see also Mulligan and Sala-i-Martin 1993; Bond, Wang, and Yip 1996).

A second class of models emphasizes the endogenous development of knowledge, or research and development, as the engine of growth. The basic contribution here is that of Romer (1990), who develops a two-sector model of a closed economy, where new knowledge produced in one sector is used as an input in the production of final output. The knowledge sector has been extended in various directions by a number of authors (see, e.g., Aghion and Howitt 1992; and, more recently, Eicher 1996). A related class of models deals with innovation and the diffusion of knowledge across countries; a comprehensive discussion is provided by Barro and Sala-i-Martin (1995, Chapter 8).

One is beginning to see a merging of the old and new growth theories. The new growth models are often characterized by having what is known as scale effects, meaning that variations in the size or scale of the economy —as measured by, say, population—affect the size of the long-run growth rate. For example, the Romer (1990) model of research and development implies that a doubling of the population devoted to research will double the growth rate. Whether the AK model is associated with scale effects depends upon whether there are production externalities that are linked to the size of the economy (see Barro and Sala-i-Martin 1995). By contrast, the neoclassical Solow model has the property that the equilibrium growth rate is independent of the scale (size) of the economy; it is therefore not subject to such scale effects. Empirical evidence does not support the existence of scale effects. For example, C. Jones (1995a) finds that variations in the level of research employment have exerted no influence on the long-run growth rates of the OECD economies. Backus, Kehoe, and Kehoe (1992) find no conclusive empirical evidence of any relationship between U.S. GDP growth and measures of scale. These empirical observations are beginning to stimulate interest in the development of nonscale models. Such models are hybrids in the sense that they share some of the characteristics of the neoclassical model, yet their equilibrium is derived from intertemporal optimization, as in the new growth models. C. Jones (1995b) has proposed a specific model, in which the steady-state growth rate is determined by the growth rate of population, in conjunction with certain production elasticities, in his case pertaining to the knowledge-producing sector.

Scope of This Chapter

It is obviously beyond the scope of this chapter to present a detailed discussion of growth theory. That is a specialized topic in itself, and for that the reader should refer to Grossman and Helpman (1991) and Barro and Sala-i-Martin (1995), who provide extensive treatments of the subject. But given the broad nature of the subject, it is important to make clear how our discussion relates to this overall scheme.

The purpose of this chapter is a restricted one. It is to extend the macrodynamic models of Chapters 3 and 4 to a growing open economy, in which the equilibrium growth rate is the endogenous outcome of rational behavior. In these models the dynamics are generated by investment behavior and are responsive to the instruments of macroeconomic and trade policy. We will therefore restrict ourselves to the class of AK models, which is well suited for this purpose. Indeed, AK models have been extensively used to analyze the effects of fiscal policy on growth performance (see, e.g., Barro 1990; King and Rebelo 1990; L. E. Jones and Manuelli 1990; Rebelo 1991; L. E. Jones, Manuelli, and Rossi 1993; and Turnovsky 1996d). Most of these endogenous growth models have been developed for a closed economy, although some applications to an open economy are beginning to develop (see Razin and Yuen 1992, 1996; Rebelo 1992; van der Ploeg 1996; Mino 1996; Turnovsky 1996a, 1996b).

We should acknowledge, however, that the empirical evidence pertaining to the ability of fiscal policy to influence long-run growth rates is mixed. If one takes the evidence on nonscale growth models seriously, and accepts that the long-run growth rate is determined as suggested by C. Jones (1995b), the scope for fiscal policy is limited, although less so than in the Solow model. Indeed, empirical evidence by Easterly and Rebelo (1993) and Stokey and Rebelo (1995) suggests that the effects of tax rates on long-run growth rates are insignificant, or weak at best. Stokey and Rebelo argue that their findings provide evidence against those models, such as AK models, that predict large growth effects from taxation. For the predictions of these models to be consistent with their evidence, these growth effects would have to be largely offset by changes in other determinants of the long-run growth rate. But other studies, such as Grier and Tullock (1989), Barro (1991), and Barro and Lee (1994), obtain negative relationships between growth and government consumption expenditure; Barro and Lee also find that government expenditure on education has a positive effect on growth. Taken together, we do not view the empirical evidence as necessarily contradicting the ability of fiscal policy to influence the growth rate. It may well be the case that a higher income tax has a significant negative effect on the growth rate, but that this is roughly offset by a significant positive growth effect of the productive government expenditure it may be financing, thus having a small overall net effect. Indeed, the welfare-maximizing rate of taxation in the simple Barro (1990) model of productive government expenditure coincides with the growth-maximizing tax rate, so that if the tax rate is in fact close to being optimal, there should be little effect on the growth rate, precisely as the empirical evidence seems to suggest. But to understand this relationship, it is important to develop a model in which the various components of fiscal policy are introduced explicitly, and their separate and possibly conflicting effects on the growth rate are analyzed. It is in this vein that we view the AK model as providing an instructive framework for analyzing fiscal policy on growth.

Our restriction to AK models also serves a secondary purpose, as a transition to the stochastic models to be developed in Part III. Those models will enable us to address all kinds of important issues, particularly pertaining to tax policy under risk, without imposing the arbitrage restrictions often necessary to obtain interior solutions in deterministic models; we shall discuss them in Chapter 6. But the drawback is that these stochastic models are tractable only if the technology is of a restrictive type, namely, of the AK form. Consequently, the present analysis also serves as a background for our future work and provides a convenient benchmark model against which the effects of risk can be compared.

We begin our discussion by developing a one-good model analogous to that derived in Chapter 3. A key feature of the model is that the accumulation of capital involves convex adjustment costs. As we have seen in previous chapters, this is a standard feature of models of capital accumulation in small open economies having tradable capital and facing a perfect world capital market, being necessary for such models to give rise to nondegenerate dynamics. It is, however, less common in endogenous growth models, which typically treat the accumulation of capital as determined residually (see, e.g., Rebelo 1991; Barro 1990). In order to sustain an equilibrium with ongoing growth, these adjustment costs must be of the homogeneous form proposed in Section 3.2.

The introduction of adjustment costs in the endogenous growth context turns out to have several important implications. First, they may preclude the existence of a steady-state equilibrium growth path. Second, whereas in the closed economy single-sector model the steady state is one in which all assets grow at the same constant rate, in the small open economy with convex adjustment costs and unrestricted access to a perfect world capital market, investment and savings will in general converge to *different* steady-state growth rates. The growth rate of capital is tied to parameters describing investment opportunities, while the steady-state rate of wealth accumulation is determined in part by preferences and in part by the rate of return on the world asset. This difference in the two growth rates implies a transitional dynamic adjustment path for the accumulation of foreign assets, before it ultimately converges to the larger of these two steady-state growth rates. In equilibrium the long-run growth rate of domestic capital and the overall rate of asset accumulation do not coincide; this is significant because these two growth rates will be shown to respond very differently to certain fiscal instruments. But it is important to be aware that this equilibrium is a consequence of the assumption that the economy has access to a perfect world capital market, enabling it to trade bonds paying a fixed world interest rate. As we will show in Section 5.5, the two growth rates are driven to equality when the economy is confronted with an imperfect bond market, in the form of an upward-sloping supply curve of debt.

There is a third reason why the introduction of convex adjustment costs in investment is important. In equilibrium, the after-tax rates of return on the two assets available to the economy, traded bonds and capital, must be equal. Given the linear technology, the marginal physical product of capital is also constant, so that the equality between these two after-tax rates of return in general constrains the feasible choice of tax rates (see, e.g., Slemrod 1988; Frenkel, Razin, and Sadka 1991; Turnovsky and Bianconi 1992). By contrast, the presence of adjustment costs introduces a variable shadow value of capital (the Tobin q), which equilibrates the rates of return on these two assets, for any arbitrarily specified tax rates.

The model is illustrated by analyzing tax policy under a variety of assumptions. In performing such exercises, it is important to specify how the proceeds of the tax revenues are disposed. It is traditional, when discussing distortionary taxes, to assume that tax revenues are rebated in lump-sum fashion, thereby enabling us to separate out the pure distortionary effects of the tax from any expenditure effects. We, too, shall consider this as a benchmark. But it is more plausible to assume that the tax revenues are applied to government expenditure that has an impact on the behavior and welfare of the private sector. Thus, in general, the revenue and expenditure decisions of the fiscal authority are interdependent, and this interdependence is important. How taxes should be set depends upon both the disposition of the resulting revenue and the effect of this disposition on the decisions of the private agents in the economy. We shall also consider the case where government expenditure is utility-enhancing, interacting with private consumption in the welfare of private agents in the economy.

After indicating some extensions to this basic one-good model, in the latter part of this chapter we adapt the two-sector dependent economy model of Chapter 4 to one having a steady endogenous growth. In this case the AK characteristic requires the two production functions to be linearly homogeneous in the two types of capital, traded and nontraded, used to produce the two output goods. While two-sector endogenous growth models have in general proved to be intractable in terms of obtaining closed-form solutions, for a small economy facing a fixed world interest rate, such analytical solutions are much more easily obtained. Our analysis thus has the advantage of not only expositing how one may solve such a model, but also of providing a two-sector growth framework that, like the traditional dependent economy model, is applicable to a variety of issues.

5.2 One-Good Model of Endogenous Growth

Consider a small open economy populated by a representative agent who consumes and produces a single traded commodity. Domestic output, Y, of this commodity is determined by the domestic capital stock, K, using a simple linear technology $Y = \alpha K$, $\alpha > 0$. The agent consumes this good at the rate C, yielding utility over an infinite time horizon represented by the intertemporal isoelastic utility function

$$\Omega \equiv \int_0^\infty \frac{1}{\gamma} C^\gamma e^{-\beta t} dt; \quad -\infty < \gamma < 1. \tag{5.1a}$$

The exponent γ is related to the intertemporal elasticity of substitution s by $s = 1/(1-\gamma)$, with $\gamma = 0$ being equivalent to a logarithmic utility function.[2] The labor supply is fixed inelastically.

The agent also accumulates physical capital, with expenditure on a given increase in the capital stock, I, involving adjustment costs (installation costs) that we incorporate in the quadratic (convex) function

$$\Phi(I, K) = I + h \frac{I^2}{2K} = I \left(1 + \frac{h}{2} \frac{I}{K}\right). \tag{5.1b}$$

The linear homogeneity of this function is necessary if a steady-state equilibrium having ongoing growth is to be sustained.

In addition, the agent accumulates net foreign bonds, b, that pay an exogenously given world interest rate, r. We shall assume that income from physical capital is taxed at the rate τ_k, income from bonds is taxed at the rate τ_b, and consumption is taxed at the rate τ_c. Initially, we shall assume that revenues from all taxes are rebated to the agent as lump-sum transfers T.[3] Thus the agent's instantaneous budget constraint is described by

$$\dot{b} = \alpha(1-\tau_k)K + r(1-\tau_b)b - (1+\tau_c)C - I\left(1 + \frac{h}{2}\frac{I}{K}\right) + T, \tag{5.1c}$$

where we have substituted for the cost function $\Phi(I, K)$. For simplicity we assume that the capital stock does not depreciate, so that the agent also faces the physical capital accumulation constraint

$$\dot{K} = I. \tag{5.1d}$$

The agent's decisions are to choose his consumption level, C, his rate of investment, I, and his rate of asset accumulation so as to maximize the intertemporal utility function (5.1a), subject to the accumulation equations (5.1c) and (5.1d).[4] The present-value Hamiltonian for this optimization is

$$H \equiv \frac{1}{\gamma}C^{\gamma}e^{-\beta t} + \lambda e^{-\beta t}\left[\alpha(1-\tau_k)K + r(1-\tau_b)b - (1+\tau_c)C - I\left(1 + \frac{h}{2}\frac{I}{K}\right)\right.$$
$$\left. + T - \dot{b}\right] + q'e^{-\beta t}[I - \dot{K}], \tag{5.2}$$

where λ is the shadow value (marginal utility) of wealth in the form of internationally traded bonds and q' is the shadow value of the agent's capital stock. As before, analysis of the model is simplified by using the shadow value of wealth as numeraire. Consequently, $q \equiv q'/\lambda$ is defined to be the market value of capital in terms of the (unitary) price of foreign bonds.

The optimality conditions with respect to C and I are, respectively,

$$C^{\gamma-1} = \lambda(1+\tau_c) \tag{5.3a}$$

$$1 + h\frac{I}{K} = q. \tag{5.3b}$$

The first condition equates the marginal utility of consumption to the (consumption) tax-adjusted shadow value of wealth; (5.3b) equates the marginal cost of an additional unit of investment, inclusive of the marginal installation cost hI/K, to the market value of capital. The latter equation may be immediately solved to yield the following expression for the rate of capital accumulation,

$$\frac{I}{K} = \frac{\dot{K}}{K} = \frac{q-1}{h} \equiv \phi, \tag{5.4}$$

so that starting from an initial level K_0, the stock of capital at time t is $K(t) = K_0 e^{\int_0^t \phi(s)ds}$.

Applying the standard optimality conditions with respect to b and K (while in the latter case noting the relationship $q \equiv q'/\lambda$) implies the arbitrage relationships

$$\beta - \frac{\dot{\lambda}}{\lambda} = r(1-\tau_b) \tag{5.5a}$$

$$\frac{\alpha}{q}(1-\tau_k) + \frac{\dot{q}}{q} + \frac{(q-1)^2}{2hq} = r(1-\tau_b). \tag{5.5b}$$

Equation (5.5a) is the Keynes-Ramsey consumption rule, equating the marginal return on consumption to the after-tax rate of return on holding a foreign bond. With β, r, and τ_b all being constants, it implies a constant growth rate of the marginal utility, λ. In contrast to the stationary model of previous chapters, in which, in order to ensure a finite steady-state equilibrium, we had to set $\lambda = \bar{\lambda}$ for all t, the equilibrium is now consistent with a constant growth in λ. Implicitly, in most of our discussion we assume that $b > 0$, so that the agent is a net lender abroad and is taxed on his foreign income earnings. However, nothing rules out the possibility that $b < 0$, in which case the agent is a net borrower; indeed, in Section 5.5 this case is discussed in the situation where the economy faces an upward-sloping supply curve of debt, so that τ_b is a subsidy rather than a tax.

Likewise, (5.5b) equates the after-tax rate of return on domestic capital to the after-tax rate of return on the traded bond. The former consists of three components. The first is the after-tax output per unit of installed capital (valued at the relative price q); the second is the rate of capital gain; the third, which is less familiar, is equal to $(qI - \Phi)/qK$. This measures the rate of return arising from the difference in the valuation of the new capital, qI, and the value of the resources its utilizes, Φ, per unit of installed capital. Seen another way, this third component reflects the fact that an additional source of benefits of higher capital stock is to reduce the installation costs (which depend upon I/K) associated with new investment.

Equation (5.5b) also emphasizes the importance of adjustment costs and the associated market price in equilibrating the rates of return. In the absence of such costs ($h \to 0, q \to 1$), (5.5b) reduces to $\alpha(1 - \tau_k) = r(1 - \tau_b)$. Since α and r are given constants, this condition imposes a fixed constraint on the two tax rates when capital is freely adjustable; in this case they cannot be set independently.

Finally, to ensure that the agent's intertemporal budget constraint is met, the following transversality conditions must be imposed:

$$\lim_{t \to \infty} \lambda b e^{-\beta t} = 0; \quad \lim_{t \to \infty} q' K e^{-\beta t} = 0. \tag{5.5c}$$

To determine the macroeconomic equilibrium, we first take the time differential of (5.3a), to yield

$$(1 - \gamma)\frac{\dot{C}}{C} = -\frac{\dot{\lambda}}{\lambda}.$$

We then combine this equation with (5.5a) to find that the equilibrium implies the constant consumption growth rate

$$\frac{\dot{C}}{C} = \frac{r(1 - \tau_b) - \beta}{1 - \gamma} \equiv \psi. \tag{5.6}$$

An immediate consequence of (5.6) is that the equilibrium growth rate of domestic consumption varies inversely with the tax on foreign bond income, but is independent of all other tax rates. Equation (5.6) implies that the level of consumption at time t is

$$C(t) = C(0)e^{\psi t}, \tag{5.7}$$

where the initial level of consumption $C(0)$ is yet to be determined.

The critical determinant of the growth rate of capital is the relative price of installed capital, q, the path of which is determined by the arbitrage condition (5.5b). This needs to be analyzed further. To do so, we rewrite (5.5b) as the following nonlinear differential equation with constant coefficients:

$$\dot{q} = [r(1-\tau_b)q - \alpha(1-\tau_k)] - \frac{(q-1)^2}{2h} \equiv H(q). \tag{5.8}$$

For the capital stock domiciled in the economy ultimately to follow a path of steady growth (or decline), the stationary solution to this equation attained when $\dot{q} = 0$ must have (at least) one *real* solution. Setting $\dot{q} = 0$ in (5.8) implies that the steady-state value of q, $\tilde{q}$ say, must be a solution to the quadratic equation

$$\alpha(1-\tau_k) + \frac{(q-1)^2}{2h} = rq(1-\tau_b). \tag{5.9}$$

A necessary and sufficient condition for the capital stock ultimately to converge to a steady growth path is that this equation have real roots; this will be so if and only if

$$\alpha(1-\tau_k) \leq r(1-\tau_b)\left[1 + \frac{hr(1-\tau_b)}{2}\right]. \tag{5.10}$$

The smaller the adjustment costs $h > 0$, the smaller the marginal physical product of capital α must be, in order for a balanced growth path for capital to exist. This is because there is a trade-off between the first and third components of the rates of return to capital given by the left-hand side of (5.5b). The smaller the adjustment cost h, the greater the returns to capital due to valuation differences between installed capital and the embodied resources, and the greater the incentives to transform new output to capital. If for a given h, α is sufficiently large to reverse (5.10), the returns to capital dominate the returns to bonds, irrespective of the price of capital, so that no long-run balanced equilibrium can exist where the returns on the two assets are brought into equality.

Figure 5.1 illustrates the phase diagram for the differential equation (5.8) in the case where (5.10) holds, so that a steady asymptotic growth path for capital does indeed exist. In this case, the real solutions to the

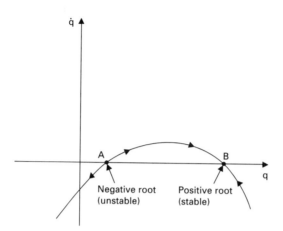

Figure 5.1
Phase diagram

quadratic equation (5.9) are

$$q_1 = [1 + hr(1 - \tau_b)] - \sqrt{[1 + hr(1 - \tau_b)]^2 - [1 + 2h\alpha(1 - \tau_k)]} \quad (5.11a)$$

$$q_2 = [1 + hr(1 - \tau_b)] + \sqrt{[1 + hr(1 - \tau_b)]^2 - [1 + 2h\alpha(1 - \tau_k)]}, \quad (5.11b)$$

indicating the potential existence of two steady equilibrium growth rates for capital.

Two cases can be identified:

Case I $r(1 - \tau_b) > \alpha(1 - \tau_k)$, which implies $q_2 > 1 > q_1 > 0$

Case II $r(1 - \tau_b) < \alpha(1 - \tau_k)$, which implies $q_2 > q_1 > 1$.

In either case it is seen from the phase diagram that the equilibrium point A, which corresponds to the smaller equilibrium value, q_1, is an unstable equilibrium, whereas B, which corresponds to the larger value, q_2, is locally stable. That is, if the system starts off with an initial value of q, lying to the right of point A, it will converge to B. Likewise, if it starts to the right of B, it will return to B. However, any time path for q that converges to B is inconsistent with the transversality condition (5.5c). To see this, observe that

$$\lim_{t \to \infty} q' K e^{-\beta t} = \lim_{t \to \infty} q \lambda K e^{-\beta t}.$$

Solving equations (5.4) and (5.5a) implies

$$K(t) = K_0 e^{\int_0^t \phi(s) ds}; \quad \lambda(t) = \lambda(0) e^{(\beta - r(1 - \tau_b))t},$$

where K_0 is the given initial stock of domestic capital and $\lambda(0)$ is the endogenously determined initial marginal utility, so that

$$\lim_{t \to \infty} q' K e^{-\beta t} = \lim_{t \to \infty} q\lambda(0) K_0 e^{\left\{\int_0^t ([q(s)-1]/h) ds\right\} - r(1-\tau_b) t}. \quad (5.12)$$

Substituting the larger root, q_2, from (5.11b) into this expression, it is seen that this limit diverges, thereby violating the transversality condition on the capital stock. Likewise, substituting the smaller root, q_1, from (5.11a), the transversality condition is shown to hold.[5] The behavior of q can thus be summarized by

Proposition 5.1 *The only solution for q that is consistent with the transversality condition is that q always be at the (unstable) steady-state solution q_1, given by the negative root to (5.8). Consequently, there are no transitional dynamics in the market price of capital q.* In response to any shock, q immediately jumps to its new equilibrium value. Correspondingly, domestically domiciled capital is always on its steady growth path, growing at the rate $\phi = (q_1 - 1)/h$.

In Case I, where $r(1 - \tau_b) > \alpha(1 - \tau_k)$, $q_1 < 1$ and the equilibrium is one of a steadily declining capital stock. In Case II, $r(1 - \tau_b)[1 + (hr(1 - \tau_b)/2)] > \alpha(1 - \tau_k) > r(1 - \tau_b)$; thus $q_1 > 1$ and the equilibrium is one of a steady growth in capital.

The domestic government is assumed to maintain a continuously balanced budget. Throughout this section we assume that all tax revenues are rebated back to the private sector, in accordance with

$$T = \alpha \tau_k K + r \tau_b b + \tau_c C. \quad (5.13)$$

Substituting this into the consumer's flow budget constraint (5.1c) implies that the net rate of accumulation of traded bonds by the private sector, the current account balance, is described by

$$\dot{b} = rb + \alpha K - C - I(1 + (h/2)(I/K)). \quad (5.14)$$

Substituting the expressions for I and $K(t)$ from (5.4) and $C(t)$ from (5.7) into (5.14), this accumulation equation can be written in the form

$$\dot{b} = rb + \vartheta K_0 e^{\phi t} - C(0) e^{\psi t}, \quad (5.15)$$

where ϕ and ψ are as defined in (5.4) and (5.6), respectively, and

$$\vartheta \equiv \alpha - \frac{(q^2 - 1)}{2h} = q(r - \phi) + [\alpha \tau_k - qr\tau_b]. \quad (5.16)$$

The q appearing in (5.16) is the negative root q_1, reported in (5.11a), though for notational convenience, the subscript 1 will henceforth be omitted.

The final step is to solve (5.15), which describes the accumulation of traded bonds. Starting from a given initial stock b_0, the stock of traded bonds at time t is given by

$$b(t) = \left(b_0 + \frac{\vartheta K_0}{r - \phi} - \frac{C(0)}{r - \psi}\right)e^{rt} - \frac{\vartheta K_0}{r - \phi}e^{\phi t} + \frac{C(0)}{r - \psi}e^{\psi t}. \tag{5.17}$$

To ensure national intertemporal solvency, the transversality condition

$$\lim_{t \to \infty} \lambda b e^{-\beta t} = 0 = \lim_{t \to \infty} \lambda(0) b e^{-r(1-\tau_b)t} = 0$$

must be satisfied. This will hold if and only if

$$r(1 - \tau_b) - \phi > 0 \tag{5.18a}$$

$$r(1 - \tau_b) - \psi > 0 \tag{5.18b}$$

$$C(0) = (r - \psi)\left(b_0 + \frac{\vartheta K_0}{r - \phi}\right). \tag{5.18c}$$

Condition (5.18a) is ensured by the solution q_1, while (5.18b) imposes an upper bound on the rate of growth of consumption. This latter condition reduces to $\beta > \gamma r(1 - \tau_b)$ and is certainly met in the case of a logarithmic utility function. The third condition determines the feasible initial level of consumption, and if this condition is imposed, the equilibrium stock of traded bonds follows the path

$$b(t) = \left(b_0 + \frac{\vartheta K_0}{r - \phi}\right)e^{\psi t} - \left(\frac{\vartheta K_0}{r - \phi}\right)e^{\phi t}. \tag{5.19}$$

5.3 Equilibrium in One-Good Model

Equations (5.4), (5.7), and (5.19), together with the solution for q and the initial condition (5.18c), comprise a closed-form solution describing the evolution of the small open economy starting from given initial stocks of traded bonds b_0 and capital stock K_0. One additional variable of importance is domestic wealth, $W(t) = b(t) + qK(t)$, which can be expressed as

$$W(t) = (b_0 + qK_0)e^{\psi t} + \frac{(\alpha \tau_k - qr\tau_b)}{r - \phi}K_0[e^{\psi t} - e^{\phi t}]. \tag{5.20}$$

A key quantity in the above solution is $(\vartheta/(r - \phi))$. From the definition appearing in (5.16), this equals $[q + (\alpha \tau_k - qr\tau_b)/(r - \phi)]$ and represents the tax-adjusted price of capital. Thus we shall define $W_T(t) \equiv b(t) + (\vartheta/(r - \phi))K(t)$ to be tax-adjusted wealth. Consequently, equation (5.18c) indicates that the initial consumption $C(0)$ is proportional to the initial tax-adjusted wealth $W_T(0)$. Furthermore, combining (5.4) and (5.19), we see that $W_T(t) = W_T(0)e^{\psi t}$, so that with consumption growing at the same rate, consumption is proportional to the tax-adjusted wealth at all points of time.

The following additional general characteristics of this equilibrium can be observed.

First, consumption and tax-adjusted wealth, on the one hand, and physical capital, on the other, are always on their steady-state growth paths, growing at the rates ψ and ϕ, respectively. The former is driven by the difference between the after-tax rate of return on foreign bonds and the domestic rate of time preference. The latter is driven by q, which is determined by the technological conditions in the domestic economy, as represented by the marginal physical product of capital α, and adjustment costs h, relative to the return on foreign assets. For the simple linear production function, the rate of growth of capital also determines the equilibrium growth of domestic output $\dot{Y}/Y$.

Thus an important feature of this equilibrium is that it can sustain differential growth rates of consumption and domestic output. This is a consequence of the economy being small and open. It is in sharp contrast to a closed economy in which, constrained by the growth of its own resources, all real variables, including consumption and output, would ultimately have to grow at the same rate. In order to sustain such an equilibrium, we shall assume that the country is small enough to maintain a growth rate unrelated to that in the rest of the world. Ultimately, this requirement imposes a constraint on the growth rate of the domestic economy. If it grows faster than does the rest of the world, at some point it will cease to be small. While we do not attempt to resolve this issue here, we noted earlier that the convergence of international growth rates has been an area of intensive research activity (see, e.g., Mankiw, Romer, and Weil 1992; Barro and Sala-i-Martin 1992a; Razin and Yuen 1992, 1996; Quah 1996; Galor 1996).

Second, holdings of traded bonds are subject to transitional dynamics, in the sense that their growth rate $\dot{b}/b$ varies through time. Asymptotically the growth rate converges to max $[\psi, \phi]$; what it will be depends critically upon the size of the consumer rate of time preference relative to the rates of return on investment opportunities. In the case of the logarithmic utility function ($\gamma = 0$),

$$sgn(\phi - \psi) = sgn\left(\beta - \frac{1}{h}\sqrt{[1 + hr(1 - \tau_b)]^2 - [1 + 2h\alpha(1 - \tau_k)]}\right). \quad (5.21)$$

Suppose that domestic agents are sufficiently patient (i.e., β is sufficiently small) so that both expressions in (5.21) are negative. Thus $\psi > \phi$, and in the long run, domestic consumption will grow at a faster rate than does the domestic capital stock or domestic output. Being patient, the agents choose to consume a small fraction of their tax-adjusted wealth. This enables them to accumulate foreign assets, running up a current account surplus and generating a positively growing stock of foreign assets. It is the income from these assets that enables the small economy to sustain a long-run growth rate of consumption in excess of the growth rate of domestic productive capacity. The opposite applies if $\psi < \phi$. In the long run, the country accumulates an ever increasing foreign *debt* [see (5.19)] and is unable to maintain a consumption growth rate equal to that of domestic output.[6]

Third, with all taxes being fully rebated, the equilibrium is completely neutral with respect to the consumption tax, which has no effect on any aspect of the economic performance. In this circumstance, the consumption tax acts like a pure lump-sum tax. This is because the labor supply is assumed to be fixed so that we are excluding a possible labor-leisure choice, which in general causes the consumption tax to have real effects.

Taxes and Growth

With the neutrality of consumption taxes, we can focus on the two forms of capital taxation. Differentiating the solution for q_1, together with the definition of the growth rate of capital, we obtain

$$\frac{dq}{d\tau_b} = \frac{qr}{r(1-\tau_b) - \phi} > 0 \tag{5.22a}$$

$$\frac{dq}{d\tau_k} = -\frac{\alpha}{r(1-\tau_b) - \phi} < 0. \tag{5.22b}$$

An increase in the tax on bond income lowers the rate of return on bonds, thereby inducing investors to switch their portfolios to capital, raising the price of capital, and inducing growth in capital. By contrast, an increase in the tax on capital income induces the opposite response.

At the same time, an increase in the tax on bonds induces agents to switch from savings to consumption, increasing the ratio of consumption to tax-adjusted wealth. This slows the rate of growth of consumption. On the other hand, the growth rate (but not the level) of consumption is independent of the tax on capital income.

Taxes and Welfare

A key issue concerns the effects of tax changes on the level of welfare of the representative agent when consumption follows its optimal path—namely, the expression

$$\Omega = \int_0^\infty \frac{1}{\gamma}[C(0)e^{\psi t}]^\gamma e^{-\beta t}dt = \frac{[C(0)]^\gamma}{\gamma(\beta - \gamma\psi)}. \tag{5.23}$$

Consider first a change in the tax on capital τ_k. Its effect on the initial level of utility, $(1/\gamma)[C(0)]^\gamma$, is given by $[C(0)]^{\gamma-1}(\partial C(0)/\partial \tau_k)$. Starting from an initial situation of zero taxes,

$$\frac{\partial C(0)}{\partial \tau_k} = (r - \psi)\left[\frac{\partial q}{\partial \tau_k} + \frac{\alpha}{r - \phi}\right] = 0, \tag{5.24}$$

leaving initial welfare unaffected. It then follows from (5.23) that the capital income tax has no effect on the time profile of utility, leaving total overall discounted welfare unchanged as well.

A tax on bond income has two effects on welfare. Starting from an initial zero tax equilibrium, its impact on initial consumption is

$$\frac{\partial C(0)}{\partial \tau_b} = \frac{r}{1-\gamma}\left[b_0 + \frac{\vartheta K_0}{r - \phi}\right] + (r - \psi)\left[\frac{\partial q}{\partial \tau_b} - \frac{qr}{r - \phi}\right]. \tag{5.25}$$

The first component reflects the fact that the higher tax on bond income raises the fraction of tax-adjusted wealth that is consumed and this is welfare-improving. The second component is the effect on the tax-adjusted price of capital and, like the capital income tax, this is zero. Thus, in the short run, a higher tax on bond income raises consumption and is therefore welfare-improving. However, its effect on the growth rate of consumption is negative, so that the short-run gains come at the expense of longer-run losses. Indeed, it is straightforward to establish that the net effects on the discounted utility measure (5.23) are exactly off-setting, so that starting from zero taxes, the imposition of a tax on bond income (with appropriate rebating) has no effect on overall intertemporal welfare. All it does is redistribute the time path of consumer welfare.

This result should not be surprising. It is familiar from static trade theory that starting from a zero tax, the imposition of a positive tax by a small open economy, with revenues fully rebated, has no effect on economic welfare. Raising a preexisting tax, however, is in general welfare-deteriorating. The effect of introducing a bond income tax on the time profile of welfare, raising it in the short run while lowering it by an equivalent amount over time, is less familiar, though analogous to the result obtained by Brock and Turnovsky (1993) in the case of the introduction of a uniform tariff in the specific factors model of Section 4.8.

Wasted Tax Revenues

An alternative assumption for separating tax effects from expenditure effects—introduced, for instance, by Rebelo (1991)—is to assume that the tax revenues, instead of being rebated, are wasted on useless government expenditure that has no effect on the behavior of the private sector or the resources available to it. The components of the equilibrium determined by the optimality conditions characterizing the behavior of the representative agent remain unchanged. In particular, the equilibrium value of q and the growth of capital ϕ remain as described in Proposition 5.1. The equilibrium growth rate of consumption ψ, which is determined by $\dot{\lambda}/\lambda$, also remains unchanged, as defined in (5.6). Because the tax revenues are no longer rebated, what change are the level of consumption and the measure of wealth to which it is tied. Specifically, one can show that now the evolution of wealth and that of consumption are related by

$$\dot{W} = r(1 - \tau_b)W - (1 + \tau_c)C(0)e^{\psi t}.$$

The solution to this equation, together with the transversality condition, implies that the equilibrium consumption:wealth ratio is now the constant

$$\frac{C(t)}{W(t)} = \frac{\beta - \gamma\psi}{1 + \tau_c}, \tag{5.26}$$

and wealth grows at the same steady rate as consumption.

Tax rates impact on the various growth rates in much the same way as before. The tax on foreign bond income raises q, and thus the growth rate of capital and domestic output, while it lowers the growth rate of total wealth and consumption. The tax on capital lowers the growth rate of capital but has no effect on the growth rates of consumption and wealth. The lack of impact on the growth of wealth is different from (5.20), which implied that with rebating, the capital tax will influence the transitional path of wealth.

The consumption tax has no effect on any growth rate and nor does it affect wealth. However, it does lower the consumption:wealth ratio, and therefore the level of consumption at all points of time. In the absence of rebating, this is unambiguously welfare-deteriorating. A tax on capital income leaves the consumption:wealth ratio unchanged. But by reducing the price of capital, q, it reduces wealth, thereby lowering consumption at all points of time. And it, too, is unambiguously welfare-deteriorating.

The tax on foreign bond income is less clear. By increasing q, it raises wealth while at the same time reducing the consumption:wealth ratio; this may result in either a higher or a lower level of consumption in the short run. But by reducing the growth rate of consumption, it always induces long-term losses. The foreign bond tax will always be ultimately welfare-deteriorating if $\psi > \phi$ when the domestic economy is a net creditor. However, if $\phi > \psi$, so that the economy is ultimately a net debtor, then such a tax may become welfare-enhancing. The reason is that without rebating, in this case it represents a subsidy rather than a tax.

5.4 Utility-Enhancing Government Expenditure

Thus far we have focused on the taxation side of the government budget. But most tax revenues are used to finance government expenditures, and we turn to the case where these interact with private consumption in the welfare of private agents, thereby impacting on their private decisions. Utility of the representative agent is now assumed to be described by

$$\Omega \equiv \int_0^\infty \frac{1}{\gamma}(CG^\eta)^\gamma e^{-\beta t} dt \quad \eta > 0; -\infty < \gamma < 1; \eta\gamma < 1; 1 > \gamma(1+\eta), \tag{5.27a}$$

where η measures the impact of public consumption on the welfare of the private agent. We assume that both private consumption and government expenditure, G, yield positive marginal utility, so that $\eta > 0$. The additional constraints on the coefficients appearing in (5.27a) are implied by the assumption that the utility function is concave in its two arguments.

In order for an equilibrium with steady ongoing growth to be sustained, the level of government expenditure must be tied to some index of growth in the economy. One natural measure is to assume that the government sets its expenditure as a fixed proportion of output—$G = g_k \alpha K$, $0 < g_k < 1$—so that government expenditure grows with the capital stock. While this specification is widely adopted in closed economy endogenous growth models, it turns out to be *infeasible* in the present context. The reason is that in order for a steady, balanced growth equilibrium to prevail, the ratio of private consumption to government consumption must ultimately remain constant. If G is proportional to K, then in the long run, private consumption must grow at the same rate as domestic capital. But, as we have seen (and it continues to apply in the present context), with the small open economy facing a fixed world interest rate, the growth rates of K and C are independent constants (see [5.4] and [5.6]), so that the ratio C/K *cannot remain constant* over time.[7] This policy is feasible in a closed economy because the domestic interest rate, which would determine the consumption growth rate, would now adjust endogenously to bring the two growth rates to equality. The same phenomenon reconciles the two growth rates in the case where the economy faces an upward-sloping supply curve of debt, discussed in Section 5.5.

Two government expenditure policy rules that are feasible from the standpoint of maintaining a long-run balanced growth equilibrium are

$G = g_c C,$

$G = g_w W.$

Since in a balanced growth equilibrium, the ratio of public to private consumption should remain constant, the first policy rule requires the constancy to be maintained at all times. The second policy rule ties government expenditure to overall domestic wealth rather than to the capital stock alone. Other policies, such as indexing government expenditure to GNP (but not domestic output), may also be feasible. In addition, determining government expenditure residually, equal to the total revenue raised, is also consistent with maintaining a steady growth path (see, e.g., Rebelo 1991).

These two policies have different implications for optimal tax policy, as long as the parameters g_c and g_w are set arbitrarily, though they converge when these expenditure ratios themselves are chosen optimally. Both these policies have been discussed elsewhere (see Turnovsky 1996a), and only the latter will be considered here. In our discussion we shall deal initially with the first-best optimum of the centrally planned economy, free to control resources directly, and then determine the configuration of taxes that will enable this equilibrium to be replicated in a decentralized economy. We shall also consider the case where the parameter g_w is set arbitrarily, as well as where it is set optimally along with the tax rates.

First-Best Optimum

Assume initially that the policy maker determines government expenditure in accordance with the rule $G = g_w W$, setting g_w at an arbitrary constant level. His optimization problem is to choose C, K, and b to maximize (5.27a), subject to the capital accumulation equation (5.1d) and the economywide resource constraint

$$\dot{b} = \alpha K + rb - C - I\left(1 + \frac{h}{2}\frac{I}{K}\right) - g_w[b + qK]. \tag{5.27b}$$

The most important modification to the solution involves the arbitrage conditions, equating the rates of return on consumption, foreign bonds, domestic capital, which now become

$$\beta - \frac{\dot{\lambda}}{\lambda} = r - g_w + \eta\mu = \frac{\alpha}{q} + \frac{(q-1)^2}{2hq} + \frac{\dot{q}}{q} - g_w + \eta\mu, \tag{5.28}$$

where $\mu \equiv C/W$. These equations are analogous to (5.5a) and (5.5b), though an important difference is that the returns to both bonds and capital now include two additional components, $-g_w + \eta\mu$. The first of these reflects the fact that with G tied to wealth, a unit increase in either asset leads the government to increase its claim on current output, thereby reducing the rate of return to private agents. Offsetting this, however, is the additional utility rate of return $\eta\mu$. This reflects the fact that if $\eta > 0$, the increase in total government expenditure raises the consumption benefits to the private agent.

Following the procedure of Section 5.2, the first-best equilibrium is obtained. The time path of K remains as specified by (5.4), where q is now the negative root of the quadratic equation

$$\alpha + \frac{(q-1)^2}{2h} = qr. \tag{5.29}$$

Thus the behavior of investment, being determined by production conditions, is independent of government expenditure policy. Consumption and wealth now grow at the common rate

$$\frac{\dot{C}}{C} = \frac{\dot{W}}{W} = \psi \equiv \frac{(r - g_w)(1 + \eta) - \beta}{(1 + \eta)(1 - \gamma)}, \tag{5.30}$$

and the consumption:wealth ratio equals

$$\frac{C}{W} = \frac{\beta - \gamma(r - g_w)(1 + \eta)}{(1 + \eta)(1 - \gamma)}. \tag{5.31}$$

For reasons identical to those presented previously, there can be no transitional dynamics in q if the transversality condition of the stock of capital is to be met. In addition, the transversality condition on wealth is imposed in deriving (5.31). These remarks also apply to the derivation of the decentralized equilibrium, provided below.

Observe that an increase in government expenditure will have an adverse effect on the overall rate of wealth accumulation in the economy. Even though an increase in government expenditure may reduce private consumption (if $\gamma < 0$), this is more than offset by the direct claim on total resources by the increase in G, causing a net reduction in the overall accumulation of assets by the private sector. With the rate of capital accumulation remaining unaffected, the reduction in the rate of wealth accumulation takes the form of a reduction in the rate of accumulation of foreign bonds; that is, the country runs a current account deficit.

If, in addition, the government chooses g_w optimally in conjunction with C and K, it is straightforward to show that the additional optimality condition must hold,

$$\frac{\partial U}{\partial G} = \frac{\partial U}{\partial C}.$$

The optimal choice of g_w in the centrally planned economy thus requires $\tilde{g}_w = \eta(C/W)$, which, combined with (5.31), yields

$$\tilde{g}_w = \left(\frac{\eta}{1+\eta}\right)\left[\frac{\beta - \gamma r(1+\eta)}{1 - \gamma(1+\eta)}\right]. \tag{5.32}$$

Substituting this into (5.30) and (5.31) leads to the first-best consumption and wealth growth rates, and associated consumption:wealth ratio, corresponding to the second policy rule. In other words, (5.30), (5.31), and (5.32) characterize the overall optimal consumption and wealth growth rates, and the associated consumption:wealth ratio, respectively. Furthermore, precisely the same overall optimum emerges if one optimizes directly with respect to G—that is, without postulating any specific form of expenditure rule.

Decentralized Economy

We turn now to the decentralized economy populated by a large number of identical representative agents. The typical agent's formal optimization problem in such an economy is to choose C, K, and b to maximize his intertemporal utility function (5.27a), subject to his wealth accumulation equation, which now becomes

$$\dot{b} = \alpha(1-\tau_k)K + r(1-\tau_b)b - (1+\tau_c)C - I\left(I + \frac{h}{2}\frac{I}{K}\right). \tag{5.27b'}$$

There is no lump-sum rebating of tax revenues; instead, these revenues are devoted to financing government expenditure. We maintain the present assumption that the government sets its aggregate expenditure in proportion to aggregate wealth. However, even though in the aggregate an increase in wealth leads to an increase in the provision of public services, the representative agent, in making his individual accumulation decision, assumes that he has a negligible impact on total wealth, and therefore ignores this aggregate linkage between private savings and public expenditures. This difference in the perception of the world between the central planner and the individual is the source of an externality generated by government expenditure and plays an important role in the determination of the optimal tax rates.

The assumption that the private agent fails to recognize the linkage between aggregate wealth and government expenditure when making his own individual consumption decision is a plausible one. An alternative polar case is the possibility that the agent recognizes such linkages perfectly. In this case his behavior is analogous to that of a central planner, and the externalities associated with government expenditure central to the present discussion do not arise.

Performing the optimization, the decentralized equilibrium is as follows.[8] The growth of capital remains specified as in (5.4), where q is given by the negative root of (5.9). However, the consumption growth rate is now modified to

$$\frac{\dot{C}}{C} = \frac{r(1 - \tau_b) - \beta}{1 - \gamma(1 + \eta)}. \tag{5.30'}$$

Government budget balance is expressed as

$$\alpha \tau_k K + r\tau_b b + \tau_c C = g_w W, \tag{5.33}$$

implying that if government expenditure, g_w, is assumed to be fixed, then only two of the three tax rates τ_k, τ_b, and τ_c can be chosen independently. Substituting this relationship into the agent's accumulation equation (5.27b') leads to the economywide resource constraint (5.27b). Recalling the expression for I and solution for q, this equation can be expressed in terms of the rate of accumulation of wealth as

$$\dot{W} = (r - g_w)W + (\alpha\tau_k - qr\tau_b)K - C. \tag{5.34}$$

Substituting further for K, this equation can be solved for $W(t)$ in a form analogous to that of (5.20), leading ultimately to a solution for C in expressed in terms of both W and K. Properties of this solution can then be discussed.

But instead of pursuing this aspect, we shall consider the determination of tax rates that will enable this decentralized equilibrium to replicate the first-best outcome. To do this, recall that in the first-best equilibrium the C/W ratio is constant, given by (5.31). In order for the decentralized equilibrium to have this same characteristic, the evolution of W, given in (5.34), must become independent of K, which grows at its own independent rate determined by (5.4). Thus, a first condition to be met is that

$$\alpha\tau_k = qr\tau_b, \tag{5.35}$$

so that (5.34) simplifies to $\dot{W} = (r - g_w)W - C$. Solving this equation, while recalling (5.30) and (5.5c), the optimal consumption:wealth ratio in the decentralized economy is

$$\frac{C}{W} = \frac{\beta - r(1 - \tau_b) + (r - g_w)[1 - \gamma(1 + \eta)]}{1 - \gamma(1 + \eta)}. \tag{5.31'}$$

Equation (5.35) is a key relationship between the two income tax rates and may be interpreted as a "tax neutrality" condition. It ensures that the allocation of the agent's portfolio between capital and bonds is independent of the two tax rates. This can be seen directly by substituting (5.35) into the arbitrage condition for the decentralized economy, (5.9), which then reduces to the corresponding relationship (5.29) for the centralized economy. This in turn ensures that the market price of capital q in the decentralized economy coincides with that in the centrally planned economy, thereby implying that the growth rate of capital replicates that of the first-best optimum.

Comparing (5.31) and (5.31′), the consumption:wealth ratio in this decentralized economy will mimic that of the first-best optimum if and only if

$$\frac{\beta - r(1-\tau_b) + (r-g_w)[1-\gamma(1+\eta)]}{1-\gamma(1+\eta)} = \frac{\beta - \gamma(r-g_w)(1+\eta)}{(1-\gamma)(1+\eta)}, \quad (5.36)$$

a condition that will also ensure the replication of the respective growth paths of consumption and wealth.[9] Rewriting (5.36), while noting the definition of the optimal ratio of government expenditure to wealth, $\tilde{g}_w$, in (5.32), and noting the tax neutrality condition (5.35), enables the solutions for the optimal taxes on traded bond income and capital to be written in the following convenient form:

$$\hat{\tau}_b = \frac{1}{r}\left[\frac{1-\gamma(1+\eta)}{1-\gamma}\right][g_w - \tilde{g}_w] \quad (5.37a)$$

$$\hat{\tau}_k = \frac{q}{\alpha}\left[\frac{1-\gamma(1+\eta)}{1-\gamma}\right][g_w - \tilde{g}_w]. \quad (5.37b)$$

Substituting for these expressions into the government budget constraint, (5.33), the corresponding solution for the optimal consumption tax is

$$\hat{\tau}_c = \frac{1}{(C/W)}\left\{\tilde{g}_w + \left(\frac{\gamma\beta}{1-\gamma}\right)(g_w - \tilde{g}_w)\right\}. \quad (5.38)$$

From (5.37a) and (5.37b) we see that optimal taxation in general involves taxing or subsidizing the income of both assets, depending upon whether g_w is above or below its socially optimal level $\tilde{g}_w$. The taxes on the two types of income are required to correct for externalities generated by this form of government expenditure policy and its interaction with financial markets in an economy with ongoing growth.[10] These distortions are absent if g_w is at its optimum $\tilde{g}_w$, in which case it becomes optimal to set $\hat{\tau}_b = \hat{\tau}_k = 0$, together with $\hat{\tau}_c = \eta$. The same overall optimum is obtained if, instead of tying expenditure to wealth, the government follows the expenditure rule $G = g_c C$ and chooses g_c optimally along with the tax rates (see Turnovsky 1996a).

In general, any arbitrary increase in government expenditure g_w will involve adjustments in all three tax rates, with the fraction $[1-\gamma(1+\eta)]/(1-\gamma)$ of the required increase in revenue being raised through income taxes and the balance $\eta\gamma/(1-\gamma)$ being financed by the consumption tax. In the case of a logarithmic utility function ($\gamma = 0$), the total amount of revenue raised by the consumption tax is $\hat{\tau}_c(C/W) = (\eta\rho/(1+\eta))$ and is *independent* of government expenditure. Thus any incremental increase in government expenditure should be *fully financed* by increases in the taxes on capital and bond income; that is, $d\tau_b = dg_w/r$; $d\tau_k = qdg_w/\alpha$. If $\gamma < 0$, the revenue raised by the income taxes exceeds the increase in expenditure. This is a consequence of the fact that an increase in the tax on asset income—$d\tau$, say—has both a negative income and a positive substitution effect on consumption. The former is equal to $-\alpha d\tau$ and measures the loss of resources to the private sector. The latter, measured by $\alpha d\tau/(1-\gamma)$, reflects the fact that the increase in the tax reduces the return on the asset, thereby inducing a switch to more consumption.[11] The net effect on the equilibrium consumption:wealth ratio is given by $\alpha\gamma d\tau/(1-\gamma)$. Thus, if $\gamma < 0$, the negative income effect prevails and consumption is reduced, declining by an amount sufficient to reduce the revenues raised by the consumption tax.

The intuition behind this optimal tax structure can be best understood by comparing the *social* and *private* returns to savings in the presence of government expenditure. It suffices to restrict our attention to bonds. The social return to saving in the form of bonds is defined in (5.28) as $r_s \equiv r - g_w + \eta\tilde{\mu}$, where $\tilde{\mu}$ denotes the equilibrium consumption:wealth ratio (corresponding to an arbitrarily set g_w) in the centrally planned economy. As noted before, this includes the impact on utility, due to the fact that as long as $\eta > 0$, the increase in aggregate government expenditure generated by the increase in wealth (bonds) raises the consumption benefits to the private agent, although this is offset by the government's claim on resources, g_w. By combining (5.31) and (5.32), the social rate of return to savings in the form of bonds can be written as

$$r_s = r + \left[\frac{1 - \gamma(1+\eta)}{1-\gamma}\right](\tilde{g}_w - g_w). \tag{5.39}$$

The key observation is that the deviation of the social return to investing in a bond from its market return, r, depends upon whether the value of the resources utilized by the induced government expenditure is greater than or less than the utility gains they yield, and this in turn depends upon whether government expenditure is less than or greater than its social optimum.

By contrast, the private return to bonds in the decentralized economy is simply the after-tax rate of return,

$$r_p \equiv r(1 - \tau_b). \tag{5.40}$$

This excludes any utility effects because the private agent operating in a decentralized economy treats the impact of his own rate of wealth accumulation on aggregate government expenditure as negligible. The nature of the optimal tax structure can now be easily understood by comparing (5.39) and (5.40).

We begin with the case where $\eta = 0$, so that government expenditure generates no direct consumption benefits. In this case $r_s = r - g_w$ and government expenditure has a negative spillover to asset markets. The social and private rates of return to bonds are equalized by setting the tax rate on bonds at $r\hat{\tau}_b = g_w$. Similarly, setting the tax on capital at $\alpha\hat{\tau}_k/q = g_w$, the total tax collected from these two income sources is precisely g_w, which is therefore self-financing, and permits the consumption tax $\hat{\tau}_c = 0$. Since government expenditure yields no spillover benefits to consumption, there is no need to change the relative price of the two consumption goods. Instead, since public expenditure is tied directly to the accumulation of wealth, it should be fully financed by taxing the income generated by the alternative forms of wealth in a neutral way—that is, satisfying (5.35).

However, if $\eta > 0$, there is a consumption externality generated by government expenditure requiring the implementation of a consumption tax. By failing to recognize the linkage between aggregate wealth and government expenditure, the agent does not take into account the impact of government expenditure on private consumption. Whether these externalities are positive or negative depends upon whether $g_w \gtreqless \tilde{g}_w$.

Suppose $\tilde{g}_w > g_w$, so that government expenditure is below its social optimum. Equation (5.39) implies that the utility returns from an extra unit of government expenditure exceed the resource costs, so that the social return to an additional bond exceeds the market return r. From (5.40) it is apparent that in order to achieve this social optimum in the decentralized economy, private savings must be stimulated through a subsidy; that is, $\hat{\tau}_b < 0$, $\hat{\tau}_k < 0$. In this case the government expenditure will need to be financed by a positive consumption tax that is also sufficient to finance the subsidy to savings. By contrast, if g_w is above its social optimum, the social return to savings is less than the market return and income should be taxed in order to attain the social optimum. Finally, if $g_w = \tilde{g}_w$, the market return to savings equals the social return and the externality disappears. The tax rate on asset income in the decentralized economy should be zero, and the government expenditure fully financed by a consumption tax.

5.5 Some Extensions to One-Good Model

There are several directions in which this one-sector model can be extended, and in this section some of these are briefly discussed.

Productive Government Expenditure

The government expenditure introduced in Section 5.4 is assumed to be on a social good that enhances utility. Equally plausible, and in many cases more relevant, is government expenditure on some form of infrastructure that enhances the productive capacity of the economy. Such models have been developed for a closed economy, in which investment is residually determined, by Barro (1990) and Turnovsky (1996d). To sustain an equilibrium with ongoing growth, the production function must be linearly homogeneous in, say, capital and government expenditure. In addition, once the adjustment costs of investment are recognized, a second productive role for government expenditure is naturally introduced. It now becomes plausible to suggest that the same features of government expenditure that enhance the productivity of the existing capital stock will also reduce the costs associated with investment and thereby facilitate the accumulation of the flow of new capital. This issue is addressed by Turnovsky (1996c), who shows how adjustment costs, and the ability of the government to influence them through its expenditures, have a significant bearing on the overall efficacy of fiscal policy. It is straightforward and useful to address these types of issues in an open economy.

Government versus Private Capital

Once one introduces productive government expenditure as an argument of the production function, the issue arises whether it is more appropriate to treat it as a flow or as a stock. Barro (1990) and Turnovsky (1996c) treat it as a flow, analogous to government expenditure on consumption. But several authors have argued that if what one has in mind is infrastructure such as roads and bridges, what one really has in mind is a stock of government capital. The introduction of such a stock means that the model involves two capital stocks, private and public capital. Futagami, Morita, and Shibata (1993) have developed a paper along these lines for a closed economy, and Turnovsky (1997) has constructed an analogous model for an open economy, in which investment entails costs of adjustment. The main analytical difference is that such a model introduces transitional dynamics. That is, the economy is not always on a balanced growth path, as it was in the one-sector model outlined in sections 5.2 and 5.3; instead, it will ultimately converge to such a path. In many respects this model behaves in a way similar to the two-sector model of traded and nontraded capital that we discuss in sections 5.6–5.8. It represents an important direction in which the basic model can be extended.

Congestion

The public good introduced in Section 5.4 is a pure public good in the sense that its use by one individual does not detract from its availability for others. An important feature of most public expenditures is that they are subject to congestion. As Barro and Sala-i-Martin (1992b) have argued, most public services are characterized by some degree of congestion; there are few pure public goods. It is straightforward to parameterize the degree of congestion. This is important because the degree of congestion is to some extent the outcome of a policy decision and, once determined, the degree of congestion turns out to be a critical determinant of optimal tax policy.

There are various ways that congestion can be modeled. One procedure, proposed by Barro and Sala-i-Martin (1992b) and used by Turnovsky (1996c), is to assume that the level of services, G_s, derived by the agent from government expenditure, is represented by

$$G_s = G(k/K)^\sigma \quad 0 \leq \sigma \leq 1, \tag{5.41}$$

where G denotes aggregate government expenditure and K denotes the aggregate capital stock, and k denotes the firm's individual capital stock. This equation implies that in order for the level of public services, G_s, available to the individual firm to remain constant over time, given its individual capital stock, k, the growth rate of G must be related to that of K in accordance with $\dot{G}/G = \sigma \dot{K}/K$ so that σ parameterizes the degree of congestion associated with the public good. The case $\sigma = 0$ corresponds to a nonrival, nonexcludable public good that is equally available to each firm, independent of the size of the economy; there is no congestion. Public expenditures such as education, medical services, and research and development that increase the efficiency of the labor force, and therefore the productivity of private capital, may be characterized as being of this type. At the other extreme, if $\sigma = 1$, then only if G increases in direct proportion to the aggregate capital stock, K, does the level of the public service available to the individual firm remain fixed. We can describe this case as being one of *proportional* congestion, meaning that the congestion grows in direct proportion to the size of the economy. Road services and infrastructure that play a productive role in facilitating the distribution of the firm's output may serve as examples of public goods subject to this type of congestion. In between, $0 < \sigma < 1$ describes partial congestion, where G can increase at a slower rate than does k and still maintain a fixed level of public services to the agent. The case $\sigma > 1$ can be interpreted as describing an extreme situation where the congestion of the public good is faster than the growth of the economy. There is in fact substantial empirical evidence supporting this case (see J. H. Y. Edwards 1990). One of the key properties of this type of specification is that the greater the congestion, the more the optimal tax moves away from a lump-sum tax toward an income tax (see Barro and Sala-i-Martin 1992b; Turnovsky 1996d).

Upward-Sloping Supply Curve of Debt

As we discussed in Chapter 2, the assumption that the economy is free to borrow or lend as much as it wants at the given world interest rate in a perfect world capital market is a strong one. While it is convenient and may be a reasonable assumption for developed economies having access to highly integrated capital markets, it is less realistic for developing economies. The dynamics change dramatically when the economy faces an upward-sloping supply curve of debt, having more of the characteristics of a closed economy. In order to sustain a macroeconomic equilibrium with ongoing growth, the debt supply function must be of the homogeneous form specified in Chapter 2. In the present context, this can be most conveniently specified by

$$r(Z/K) = r^* + v(Z/K); \quad v' > 0, \tag{5.42}$$

where $Z \equiv -b$ denotes the stock of debt.

To illustrate the role of the upward-sloping supply curve of debt, we return to the specification of Section 5.2, where we consider the impact of distortionary taxes, the revenues of which are rebated. The representative agent's optimization problem is now to maximize the constant elasticity utility function (5.1a), subject to the capital accumulation equation (5.1d) and the flow budget constraint

$$\dot{Z} = (1+\tau_c)C + I\left[1 + \frac{h}{2}\frac{I}{K}\right] - (1-\tau_k)\alpha K + (1-\tau_b)r\left(\frac{Z}{K}\right)Z - T. \tag{5.43}$$

The constraint (5.43), expressed from the standpoint of a debtor, asserts that to the extent that the agent's consumption, outstanding interest payments, investment expenses, and tax obligations exceed his output, he will increase his stock of debt.

It is important to emphasize that in performing his optimization, the representative agent takes the interest rate as given. The interest rate facing the debtor nation, as reflected in its upward-sloping supply curve of debt, is a function of the economy's *aggregate* debt, which the representative agent, in making his decisions, assumes he is unable to influence. With this in mind, the optimality conditions are

$$C^{\gamma-1} = \lambda(1 + \tau_c) \tag{5.44a}$$

$$\frac{\dot{K}}{K} = \frac{I}{K} = \frac{q-1}{h} = \phi, \tag{5.44b}$$

together with the arbitrage conditions

$$\beta - \frac{\dot{\lambda}}{\lambda} = (1 - \tau_b)r\left(\frac{Z}{K}\right) \tag{5.44c}$$

$$(1 - \tau_k)\frac{\alpha}{q} + \frac{\dot{q}}{q} + \frac{(q-1)^2}{2hq} = (1 - \tau_b)r\left(\frac{Z}{K}\right). \tag{5.44d}$$

These equations are analogous to (5.3a), (5.4), (5.5a), and (5.5b) in the basic model, but now the interest rate is endogenously determined as a function of the nation's debt:capital ratio Z/K. This changes the dynamics fundamentally.

As in Section 5.2, the government rebates all revenues in accordance with (5.13), now modified to

$$T + r\tau_b Z = \alpha \tau_k K + \tau_c C. \tag{5.13'}$$

The only difference is that with τ_b being applied to debt, as long as $Z > 0$, it is a subsidy and an expense, rather than a source of revenue. Combining (5.43) with (5.13') implies that the economy's net rate of accumulation of debt, its current account deficit, is described by

$$\dot{Z} = C + I\left[1 + \frac{h}{2}\frac{I}{K}\right] - \alpha K + r\left(\frac{Z}{K}\right)Z. \tag{5.43'}$$

To derive the macrodynamic equilibrium, we need to express it in terms of stationary variables. For this purpose, it is convenient to express it in terms of c, z, and q, where we define

$$c \equiv \frac{C}{K}; \quad z \equiv \frac{Z}{K} \tag{5.45}$$

as the consumption and debt per unit of capital. Differentiating these two equations, we have

$$\frac{\dot{c}}{c} = \frac{\dot{C}}{C} - \frac{\dot{K}}{K}; \quad \frac{\dot{z}}{z} = \frac{\dot{Z}}{Z} - \frac{\dot{K}}{K}. \tag{5.46}$$

Taking the time derivative of (5.44a), and combining it with (5.44b), (5.44c), and (5.45), we obtain

$$\dot{c} = c\left(\frac{1}{1 - \gamma}((1 - \tau_b)r(z) - \beta) - \frac{q-1}{h}\right). \tag{5.47a}$$

Next, dividing the current account relationship by Z, and using (5.44b) and (5.46), we obtain

$$\dot{z} = c + \left(\frac{q^2-1}{2h}\right) - \left(\frac{q-1}{h}\right)z - \alpha + r(z)z. \tag{5.47b}$$

Finally, we may rewrite (5.44d) in the form

$$\dot{q} = (1-\tau_b)r(z)q - (1-\tau_k)\alpha - \frac{(q-1)^2}{2h}. \tag{5.47c}$$

The set of equations (5.47a)–(5.47c) determines the evolution of c, z, and q. In contrast with the basic model, it will involve transitional dynamics, in a fashion similar to the two-sector model, to be developed below.

The steady-state growth path will be obtained when $\dot{c} = \dot{z} = \dot{q} = 0$, so that the corresponding steady-state values of c, z, and q, denoted by tildes, are determined by

$$\frac{1}{1-\gamma}((1-\tau_b)r(\tilde{z}) - \beta) = \frac{\tilde{q}-1}{h} \tag{5.48a}$$

$$\tilde{c} + \left(\frac{\tilde{q}^2-1}{2h}\right) - \left(\frac{\tilde{q}-1}{h}\right)\tilde{z} - \alpha + r(\tilde{z})\tilde{z} = 0 \tag{5.48b}$$

$$(1-\tau_k)\frac{\alpha}{\tilde{q}} + \frac{(\tilde{q}-1)^2}{2h\tilde{q}} = (1-\tau_b)r(\tilde{z}). \tag{5.48c}$$

The key difference from the basic model is that the constancy of the consumption:capital ratio forces consumption and output to grow at the same long-run equilibrium rate. In effect, the economy incurs a level of debt to capital such that these two growth rates are brought into equality.

This model responds very differently to policy shocks from the model developed in Section 5.2, in that any such disturbance will generate transitional dynamics before ultimately converging to the equilibrium described by (5.48). Linearizing the dynamic system (5.47a)–(5.47c) around the steady state (5.48a)–(5.48c), the local dynamics are described by

$$\begin{pmatrix} \dot{c} \\ \dot{z} \\ \dot{q} \end{pmatrix} = \begin{pmatrix} 0 & \frac{\tilde{c}}{1-\gamma}r'(\tilde{z})(1-\tau_b) & -\frac{\tilde{c}}{h} \\ 1 & [r(\tilde{z}) + r'(\tilde{z})\tilde{z}] - \left(\frac{\tilde{q}-1}{h}\right) & \left(\frac{\tilde{q}-\tilde{z}}{h}\right) \\ 0 & r'(\tilde{z})(1-\tau_b)\tilde{q} & (1-\tau_b)r(\tilde{z}) - \left(\frac{\tilde{q}-1}{h}\right) \end{pmatrix}$$

$$\times \begin{pmatrix} c-\tilde{c} \\ z-\tilde{z} \\ q-\tilde{q} \end{pmatrix}. \tag{5.49}$$

Recalling (5.18a), the determinant of the matrix of coefficients in (5.49) is negative, while the trace is positive. This implies that this system has two positive (unstable) and one negative (stable) eigenvalues.[12] Since consumption, c, and the price of capital, q, can jump instantaneously, whereas the stock of debt, z, is constrained to adjust continuously, the number of unstable roots to this equation equals the number of jump variables, so that starting from an initial stock of debt, z_0, the system has a unique stable transitional adjustment path, taking it into the steady state described by (5.48).

Combining (5.48a) and (5.48c) leads to

$$(1 - \tau_k)\frac{\alpha}{\tilde{q}} + \frac{(\tilde{q} - 1)^2}{2h\tilde{q}} = \beta + (1 - \gamma)\left(\frac{\tilde{q} - 1}{h}\right).$$

From this equation we show that an increase in the tax on capital will reduce the (common) equilibrium growth rate in the economy, while an increase in the tax on bonds will leave the equilibrium growth rate unaffected. Instead, an increase in τ_b, which is a subsidy on debt, will encourage the accumulation of higher debt such that its after-tax cost just equals the (unchanged) equilibrium rate of return on capital. This response is very different from that described in Section 5.2, where with a perfect world bond market a higher tax on bonds would raise the equilibrium growth rate of capital but reduce the growth rate of consumption and wealth.

5.6 Two-Sector Model of Endogenous Growth

We now expand the model to include nontraded as well as traded investment goods and thereby extend the dependent economy model of Chapter 4 to an endogenous growth context. While two-sector endogenous growth models have in general proved to be intractable, for a small economy facing a fixed world interest rate they become much more tractable. The version of the model we shall consider is the general one that includes both traded and nontraded capital goods. This development turns out to be important for two distinct reasons. First, understanding the ongoing growth process of the dependent economy model is of interest in its own right. But second, and of greater significance, if we identify *traded* capital as being *physical* capital, and *nontraded* capital as being *human* capital—a reasonable characterization—this model is formally equivalent to the two-sector model of physical and human capital pioneered by Lucas (1988).[13] Under the conditions characterizing a small open economy facing a perfect capital market, we are able to derive a closed-form solution for the transitional dynamic adjustment paths. This is in contrast to the existing two-sector growth literature, which either restricts itself to balanced growth paths (Lucas 1988; Devereux and Love 1994) or analyzes the transitional dynamics, using numerical simulation methods (Mulligan and Sala-i-Martin 1993; Pecorino 1993; Devereux and Love 1994).[14]

As before, the model is based on a single infinitely lived representative agent. The agent accumulates two types of capital for rental at the competitively determined rental rate. The first is physical capital, K, which is traded, and the second is human capital, H, which is nontraded. Neither of these capital goods is subject to depreciation.[15] For expositional simplicity, there is no government.

These two forms of capital are used by the agent to produce a tradable good, Y_T, taken to be the numeraire, by means of a linearly homogeneous production function,

$$Y_T = aK_T^\alpha H_T^{(1-\alpha)}; \quad 0 < \alpha < 1, \tag{5.50a}$$

where K_T and H_T denote the allocation of the respective capital goods to the production of the traded good. The agent also produces a nontraded good, Y_N, using the analogous production function

$$Y_N = cK_N^\delta H_N^{(1-\delta)}; \quad 0 < \delta < 1. \tag{5.50b}$$

The production setup is analogous to that in Chapter 4, the only difference —and it is a key one—being that the two production functions are linearly homogeneous in the two reproducible factors, K and H. This is critical for an equilibrium with steady growth to exist. The relative price of nontraded goods, p, is taken as exogenously given by the agent, though it is determined by market-clearing conditions in the economy. Both forms of capital are costlessly and instantaneously mobile across the two sectors, with the sectoral allocations being constrained by

$$K_T + K_N = K \tag{5.51a}$$

$$H_T + H_N = H. \tag{5.51b}$$

The accumulation of traded capital, $\dot{K} = I$, involves adjustment costs, represented by (5.1b).[16] With both production functions having constant returns to scale, and the small economy having access to a perfect world bond market, these adjustment costs are necessary in order to avoid imposing constraints on the technological parameters to ensure that the arbitrage conditions equating rates of return are met.[17]

In addition to accumulating the two types of capital, the agent accumulates net foreign bonds, b, that pay an exogenously given world interest rate, r. Thus the agent's instantaneous budget constraint is specified by

$$\dot{b} = aK_T^\alpha H_T^{1-\alpha} + pcK_N^\delta H_N^{1-\delta} + rb - C_T - pC_N - I\left(1 + \frac{h}{2}\frac{I}{K}\right) - p\dot{H}, \tag{5.52}$$

where C_T and C_N are the agent's consumption of the traded and nontraded goods. This is analogous to equation (4.21).

The agent's optimization decision is to choose the rate of consumption (C_T, C_N), capital allocation decisions (K_T, K_N, H_T, H_N), and rates of capital accumulation, I and $\dot{H}$, to maximize the intertemporal isoelastic utility function

$$\Omega \equiv \int_0^\infty \frac{1}{\gamma}(C_T^\theta C_N^{1-\theta})^\gamma e^{-\beta t} dt, \tag{5.53}$$

subject to the constraints (5.1d), (5.51), and (5.52), and the initial stocks of assets K_0, H_0, and b_0.

The following optimality conditions with respect to C_T, C_N, K_T, K_N, H_T, H_N, and I obtain

$$\theta C_T^{\theta\gamma-1} C_N^{\gamma(1-\theta)} = \lambda \tag{5.54a}$$

$$(1-\theta) C_T^{\theta\gamma} C_N^{\gamma(1-\theta)-1} = \lambda p \tag{5.54b}$$

$$a\alpha K_T^{\alpha-1} H_T^{1-\alpha} = pc\delta K_N^{\delta-1} H_N^{1-\delta} \equiv r_k \tag{5.54c}$$

$$a(1-\alpha) K_T^\alpha H_T^{-\alpha} = pc(1-\delta) K_N^\delta H_N^{-\delta} \equiv r_h \tag{5.54d}$$

$$1 + h\frac{I}{K} = q, \tag{5.54e}$$

where the shadow values, λ and q, are as defined previously. The first two are the usual intertemporal envelope conditions relating the marginal utility of the two consumption goods to the shadow value of wealth. Equations (5.54c) and (5.54d) equate the marginal returns to traded and nontraded capital across the two sectors. The quantities r_k and r_h define the marginal physical products of traded and nontraded capital, respectively, measured in terms of the numeraire good (traded output). Equation (5.54e) is identical to (5.4), so that starting from an initial level of K_0, the stock of capital at time t is

$$K(t) = K_0 e^{\int_0^t \phi(s) ds}.$$

The standard optimality conditions with respect to traded bond b, and the two forms of capital, K and H, leads to the arbitrage conditions

$$\beta - \frac{\dot{\lambda}}{\lambda} = r \qquad (5.55a)$$

$$\frac{r_k}{q} + \frac{\dot{q}}{q} + \frac{(q-1)^2}{2hq} = r \qquad (5.55b)$$

$$\frac{r_h}{p} + \frac{\dot{p}}{p} = r. \qquad (5.55c)$$

Equations (5.55a) and (5.55b) correspond to (5.5a) and (5.5b), respectively. Likewise, (5.55c) equates the total rate of return on nontraded capital, which consists of its marginal physical product plus its rate of capital gain, to the rate of return on the traded bond. Finally, the following transversality conditions must be imposed:

$$\lim_{t \to \infty} \lambda b e^{-\beta t} = 0; \quad \lim_{t \to \infty} q' K e^{-\beta t} = 0; \quad \lim_{t \to \infty} \lambda p H e^{-\beta t} = 0. \qquad (5.55d)$$

5.7 Determination of Equilibrium in Two-Sector Model

We define aggregate consumption C, expressed in terms of the traded good as numeraire, by

$$C \equiv C_T + pC_N.$$

This definition, together with the optimality conditions (5.54a) and (5.54b), implies that consumptions of the two goods are

$$C_T = \theta C; \quad pC_N = (1-\theta)C, \qquad (5.56)$$

leading to

$$\frac{\dot{C}_T}{C_T} = \frac{\dot{C}}{C}; \quad \frac{\dot{p}}{p} + \frac{\dot{C}_N}{C_N} = \frac{\dot{C}}{C}. \qquad (5.57)$$

Taking the time derivative of (5.54a) and combining it with (5.57) and (5.55a) implies that aggregate consumption grows at the rate

$$\frac{\dot{C}}{C} = \frac{r - \beta - \gamma(1-\theta)(\dot{p}/p)}{1 - \gamma} \equiv \psi(t), \qquad (5.58)$$

where at this point the rate of inflation of the relative price, $\dot{p}/p$, is yet to be determined. This corresponds to (5.6) in the one-good model.

The strategy in deriving the macroeconomic equilibrium involves three stages, the first of which determines the static allocation of existing resources, while the latter two determine the dynamics. In the first stage we express the sectoral capital intensities and marginal physical products of capital in terms of the relative price of nontraded to traded goods, as well as the absolute levels of the allocation of capital in terms of the gradually evolving aggregate stocks K and H. As is characteristic of two-factor, two-sector growth models, the dynamics of the system decouples, and in the second stage we solve for the price dynamics. Having determined the behavior of prices, the third stage then solves for the equilibrium rates of accumulation of the aggregate stocks of assets, K, H, and b.

Static Allocation Conditions

Let $\omega \equiv K_T/H_T$ denote the traded:nontraded (i.e., physical:human) capital ratio in the traded sector. Dividing (5.54c) by (5.54d) yields

$$\frac{K_N}{H_N} = \left(\frac{1-\alpha}{1-\delta}\right)\left(\frac{\delta}{\alpha}\right)\omega, \tag{5.59}$$

implying that the capital intensities in the two sectors move proportionately. Substituting (5.59) into the first equation of (5.54c) implies

$$\omega = mp^{(1/(\alpha-\delta))} \quad \text{where} \quad m \equiv \left[\left(\frac{\delta}{\alpha}\right)^\delta \left(\frac{1-\delta}{1-\alpha}\right)^{1-\delta}\frac{c}{a}\right]^{1/(\alpha-\delta)}. \tag{5.60a}$$

This equation, together with (5.59), yields simple relationships between the sectoral capital intensities and the relative price of nontraded to traded output. Combined with (5.54c) and (5.54d), these in turn lead to the following expressions for the marginal physical products of the two types of capital:

$$r_k(p) = a\alpha\omega^{\alpha-1} = a\alpha m^{\alpha-1} p^{(\alpha-1)/(\alpha-\delta)} \tag{5.60b}$$

$$r_h(p) = a(1-\alpha)\omega^\alpha = a(1-\alpha)m^\alpha p^{\alpha/(\alpha-\delta)}. \tag{5.60c}$$

Equation (5.59) and the sectoral allocation relationships (5.51a) and (5.51b) lead to the following expressions for the levels of the capital stocks instantaneously employed in the two sectors:

$$H_T = \frac{\delta(1-\alpha)\omega H - \alpha(1-\delta)K}{\omega(\delta-\alpha)}; \quad K_T = \frac{\delta(1-\alpha)\omega H - \alpha(1-\delta)K}{(\delta-\alpha)} \tag{5.61a}$$

$$H_N = \frac{\alpha(1-\delta)[K-\omega H]}{\omega(\delta-\alpha)}; \quad K_N = \frac{\delta(1-\alpha)[K-\omega H]}{(\delta-\alpha)}, \tag{5.61b}$$

which in turn can be expressed in terms of the relative price p by substituting from (5.60a). The effects, summarized in (5.61), depend upon the relative sectoral capital intensity $\delta - \alpha$. Intuitively, an increase in K, say, will raise the aggregate K/H ratio, attracting resources toward the sector that is relatively intensive in traded capital. Assuming $\alpha > \delta$, this is the traded sector. Thus K_T and H_T will rise. If H is held fixed, the additional nontraded capital used in the traded sector must be attracted from the nontraded sector, so that H_N declines. This lowers the marginal physical product of traded capital in the nontraded sector and induces a shift in traded capital away from that sector as well; that is, K_N declines.

In order for the sectoral capital allocations K_i and H_i to be nonnegative, the sectoral and aggregate capital intensities must satisfy the following conditions:

If $\delta > \alpha$: $\quad \dfrac{r_h}{r_k}\left(\dfrac{\delta}{1-\delta}\right) \equiv \dfrac{K_N}{H_N} > \dfrac{K}{H} > \dfrac{K_T}{H_N} \equiv \dfrac{r_h}{r_k}\left(\dfrac{\alpha}{1-\alpha}\right)$

If $\delta < \alpha$: $\quad \dfrac{r_h}{r_k}\left(\dfrac{\delta}{1-\delta}\right) \equiv \dfrac{K_N}{H_N} < \dfrac{K}{H} < \dfrac{K_T}{H_N} \equiv \dfrac{r_h}{r_k}\left(\dfrac{\alpha}{1-\alpha}\right).$

(5.62)

These inequalities define a cone within which the aggregate K/H ratio must lie for a feasible equilibrium to obtain.[18]

Price Dynamics

By observing the expressions for r_k and r_h given in (5.60b) and (5.60c), in conjunction with the arbitrage conditions on the two types of capital (5.55b) and (5.55c), it is seen that the dynamics of the relative price, p, and of the price of (installed) traded capital, q, proceed independently of the aggregate stocks of capital, being determined by the pair of equations

$$\dot{p} = rp - a(1-\alpha)m^\alpha p^{\alpha/(\alpha-\delta)} \tag{5.63a}$$

$$\dot{q} = rq - \frac{(q-1)^2}{2h} - a\alpha m^{\alpha-1} p^{(\alpha-1)/(\alpha-\delta)}. \tag{5.63b}$$

This pair of equations is itself recursive; the relative price of the two goods evolves autonomously in accordance with (5.63a), and in turn determines the evolution of the market price of installed traded capital.

Equations (5.63a) and (5.63b) emphasize the importance of adjustment costs and the associated price of capital in equilibrating the rates of return. In the absence of such costs $(h \to 0, q \to 1)$, and (5.63b) reduces to a static equation determining p. This will be consistent with (5.63a) if and only if the technological parameters are appropriately tied to the foreign rate of interest.[19]

The critical determinant of the growth of traded capital is the market price of installed capital q, the price of which is determined by the solution to the pair of differential equations (5.63a) and (5.63b). In order for the traded capital stock domiciled in the economy ultimately to follow a path of steady growth or decline, the stationary solution to this pair of equations, attained when $\dot{p} = \dot{q} = 0$, must have (at least) one *real* solution. Thus, the steady-state relative price of nontraded goods $\tilde{p}$ must be either 0, which we shall rule out, or

$$\tilde{p} = \left[\frac{r}{a(1-\alpha)m^\alpha}\right]^{(\alpha-\delta)/\delta}, \tag{5.64a}$$

so that the steady-state real rate of return on nontraded capital $r_h(\tilde{p})/\tilde{p}$ just matches the return on traded bonds, r. The corresponding steady-state value of q, $\tilde{q}$, is the solution to the quadratic equation

$$r_k(\tilde{p}) + \frac{(\tilde{q}-1)^2}{2h} = r\tilde{q}. \tag{5.64b}$$

A necessary and sufficient condition for the stock of traded capital ultimately to converge to a steady growth path is that this equation have real roots; this will be so if and only if

$$r_k(\tilde{p}) \leq r\left[1 + \frac{hr}{2}\right]. \tag{5.65}$$

This equation is analogous to (5.10) and has a similar interpretation.

Figures 5.2 and 5.3 illustrate the phase diagram for the price dynamics (5.63a) and (5.63b) in the case that (5.65) holds, so that a steady-state growth path for traded capital does exist. Figure 5.2 corresponds to $\delta > \alpha$, so that the nontraded sector is relatively intensive in traded capital, while Figure 5.3 assumes $\alpha > \delta$, so that the relative sectoral intensities in the two types of capital are reversed.[20] With (5.64b) having real roots, the potential arises for two steady-state equilibrium growth rates for traded capital to exist, just as it does for the one-good model, and, as before, the transversality conditions enable one to be eliminated.

Consider first Figure 5.2, which corresponds to $\delta > \alpha$. From the phase diagram it is seen that the equilibrium point B, which corresponds to the smaller equilibrium value, q_1, is an unstable node, while A, which corresponds to the larger equilibrium value, q_2, is a saddlepoint, with the vertical locus XY being the stable saddlepath. Thus, if the system starts from any point other than B on XY, it will converge to A; otherwise, it will diverge and there will be no steady growth path. But any time path for q that converges to A violates the transversality condition for traded capital (5.55d), which needs to be met.[21] The only solution for q that is consistent with the transversality condition and the attainment of a steady growth path for traded capital is the unstable equilibrium point B.

Figure 5.3, which corresponds to $\alpha > \delta$, is analogous. In this case, the equilibrium point B, which corresponds to the smaller equilibrium, q_1, is

Capital Accumulation and Long-Run Growth

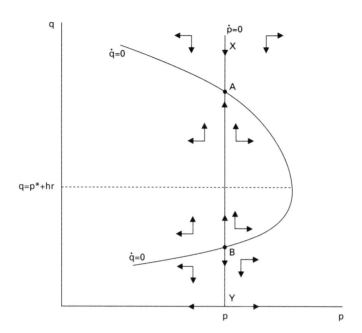

Figure 5.2
Phase diagram: $\delta > \alpha$

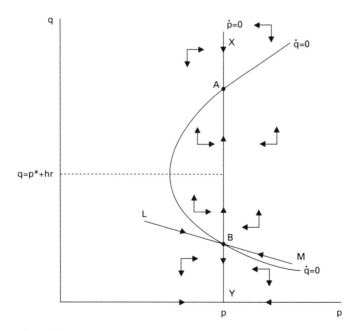

Figure 5.3
Phase diagram: $\alpha > \delta$

a saddlepoint, with the stable saddlepath being the negatively sloped locus *LM*. The equilibrium point *A*, which corresponds to the larger equilibrium value, q_2, is now a locally stable node. But, as in Figure 5.2, any time path for *q* that converges to A violates the transversality condition for traded capital.[22] Thus, in this case the only solutions for *p* and *q* that are consistent with both the transversality condition and the attainment of a steady growth path for traded capital lie on the stable saddlepath *LM*.

The behavior of prices can thus be summarized as follows:

Proposition 5.2 (1) If $\delta > \alpha$ so that the nontraded sector is relatively intensive in traded capital, the only solutions for *p* and *q* that are consistent with the transversality condition on traded capital are $p = \tilde{p}$, given by (5.64a), and $q = q_1$, the (unstable) steady-state solution given by the negative root to (5.64b). In this case there are *no transitional dynamics in either the relative price of nontraded to traded goods or the market price of capital*. In response to any shock, these prices immediately jump to their respective new steady-state values.

(2) If $\alpha > \delta$ so that the traded sector is relatively intensive in traded capital, the only solutions for *p* and *q* that are consistent with the transversality condition on traded capital are that *p* and *q* lie on the stable saddlepath *LM*, ultimately converging to $p = \tilde{p}$, given by (5.64a), and $q = q_1$, the (unstable) steady-state solution given by the negative root to (5.64b). In this case, a shock to the economy *will generate transitional adjustment paths in both p and q*.

The significant feature of Proposition 5.2 is that it indicates that the dynamic behavior of asset prices, $p(t)$ and $q(t)$, is intimately tied to the production structure of the economy, as reflected by the relative sectoral capital intensities. Many would argue that (2) is the more plausible of these two cases; that is, the tradable sector—manufacturing goods, say—is relatively intensive in tradable capital, such as equipment.[23] In this case, one would expect a shock to the economy to lead to a jump in asset prices, followed by a smooth transition. The stable eigenvalue of the linearized approximation to the dynamic system represented by (5.63a) and (5.63b) is $\delta r/(\delta - \alpha) < 0$, in which case the formal solution to the local dynamics is as follows:

$$p(t) - \tilde{p} = [p(0) - \tilde{p}]e^{\delta rt/(\delta - \alpha)} \tag{5.66a}$$

$$q(t) - \tilde{q} = \left[\frac{\left(\frac{1-\alpha}{\delta-\alpha}\right)\frac{r_k(\tilde{p})}{\tilde{p}}}{\frac{(1+hr)-\tilde{q}}{h} - \frac{\delta r}{\delta-\alpha}} \right] (p(t) - \tilde{p}). \tag{5.66b}$$

The equilibrium market price of traded capital, $\tilde{q}$, appearing in (5.66b), is the negative root q_1 to (5.64b), though for convenience, the subscript 1 is omitted.[24] From the solution, we see that $1 + hr > \tilde{q}$, so that with $\alpha > \delta$, (5.66b) is a negatively sloped locus (being a linear approximation to LM in Figure 5.3). Accordingly, the two asset prices move in opposite directions during this phase of the transition. Both prices are forward-looking variables so that their respective initial values, $p(0)$ and $q(0)$, will be determined to satisfy the transversality condition on nontraded (human) wealth; see (5.78).

The behavior of the sectoral capital intensities ω and K_N/H_N, and the real marginal physical products $r_k(p)$ and $r_h(p)$ will mirror that of p. Thus if $\delta > \alpha$, they, too, will remain constant throughout at their respective steady-state values—$\tilde{\omega}$, $\tilde{r}_k$, and $\tilde{r}_h$—while if the sectoral intensity is reversed, they will vary through time in response to the evolution of the relative price p.

As is standard in the two-good, two-sector, two-factor model, the steady-state relative price, and all factors that depend upon it, are determined solely by production conditions; they are therefore independent of any source of demand shock. The latter, however, will generate transitional responses in these variables when $\alpha > \delta$. We should also observe that the relative sectoral capital intensity plays precisely the same role in determining the nature of the price dynamics as it does in the Brock-Turnovsky (1994) Ramsey-type analysis, discussed in Chapter 4.

Asset Dynamics

To derive the dynamics of asset accumulation, it is useful to begin with the following relationships that express the equilibrium sectoral outputs in terms of the aggregate stocks of capital, K and H. These are derived from the production functions by utilizing the optimality conditions (5.54c) and (5.54d), together with (5.60b) and (5.60c), and reflect the equilibrium sectoral adjustments in K_T, H_T, and so on, as determined in (5.61a) and (5.61b):

$$Y_T = \left(\frac{1}{\delta - \alpha}\right)[-r_k(1-\delta)K + r_h\delta H];$$
$$Y_N = \frac{1}{p}\left(\frac{1}{\delta - \alpha}\right)[r_k(1-\alpha)K - r_h\alpha H]. \tag{5.67}$$

An increase in the aggregate stock of traded capital, K, will attract resources to the sector that is relatively intensive in traded capital. If $\alpha > \delta$, that sector is the traded sector, the output of which increases at the expense of the nontraded sector.

Define aggregate wealth in terms of the traded good as numeraire, as

$$W = qK + pH + b. \tag{5.68}$$

Differentiating this expression with respect to t and noting (1) the accumulation equations (5.1d) and (5.52); (2) the definitions of the production functions (5.50a) and (5.50b), in conjunction with (5.67); (3) the definition of aggregate consumption C; (4) the optimality condition for investment (5.4); and (5) the arbitrage conditions (5.55b) and (5.55c) leads to the following relationship describing the rate of aggregate wealth accumulation:

$$\dot{W}(t) = rW(t) - C(t). \tag{5.69}$$

The form of this wealth accumulation relationship is standard. The only difference here is that C evolves in accordance with (5.58), which depends upon $(\dot{p}/p)$, and which in turn depends upon the relative sectoral capital intensities. Indeed, the entire profile of asset accumulation depends upon whether $\delta \gtreqless \alpha$. Both cases will be discussed in turn.

$\delta > \alpha$: Nontraded Sector Relatively Intensive in Traded Capital

In this case p remains at its steady-state level $\tilde{p}$; $\dot{p} \equiv 0$ so that consumption grows at the steady rate (see (5.58)):

$$\frac{\dot{C}}{C} = \frac{r-\beta}{1-\gamma} \equiv \tilde{\psi}; \quad \text{that is } C(t) = C(0)e^{\tilde{\psi}t}. \tag{5.70}$$

Substituting this into (5.69) and solving, while invoking the transversality conditions (5.55d), imposes the restriction $r > \tilde{\psi}$ and implies the constant equilibrium consumption:wealth ratio

$$\frac{C}{W} = r - \tilde{\psi} = \frac{\beta - \gamma r}{1-\gamma}. \tag{5.71}$$

Aggregate wealth therefore grows at the same rate as consumption, with both variables being on their respective equilibrium steady-state growth paths; that is, $\dot{W}/W = \dot{C}/C = \tilde{\psi}$.

We turn now to the components of W, and in particular to the two types of capital. With p constant over time, q also is constant, so that traded capital grows at the steady rate

$$\frac{\dot{K}}{K} = \tilde{\phi} = \frac{\tilde{q}-1}{h}, \tag{5.72}$$

where $\tilde{q}$ is the solution to (5.64b). Comparing (5.70) and (5.72), we see that consumption and wealth, on the one hand, and traded capital, on the other, are always on their respective steady-state growth paths, growing at the rates $\tilde{\psi}$ and $\tilde{\phi}$, as in the one-good model having a perfect world bond market.

The market-clearing condition for nontraded capital is specified by $\dot{H} = Y_N - C_N$, which, using (5.67) and (5.56), can be written as

$$\dot{H} = \frac{1}{\tilde{p}}\left(\frac{1}{\delta - \alpha}\right)[\tilde{r}_k(1-\alpha)K - \tilde{r}_h\alpha H] - (1-\theta)\frac{C}{\tilde{p}}. \tag{5.73}$$

Substituting for $K(t) = K_0 e^{\tilde{\phi}t}$; $C(t) = C(0)e^{\tilde{\psi}t}$ into this equation, the solution for H, starting from the initial stock of nontraded capital H_0, is

$$H(t)$$
$$= \left[H_0 - \frac{(1-\alpha)\tilde{r}_k}{(\delta-\alpha)\tilde{p}[\tilde{\phi}+\alpha r/(\delta-\alpha)]}K_0 + \frac{(1-\theta)}{\tilde{p}[\tilde{\psi}+\alpha r/(\delta-\alpha)]}C(0)\right]e^{-(\alpha r/(\delta-\alpha))t}$$
$$+ \frac{(1-\alpha)\tilde{r}_k}{(\delta-\alpha)\tilde{p}[\tilde{\phi}+\alpha r/(\delta-\alpha)]}K_0 e^{\tilde{\phi}t} - \frac{(1-\theta)}{\tilde{p}[\tilde{\psi}+\alpha r/(\delta-\alpha)]}C(0)e^{\tilde{\psi}t}$$
$$\tag{5.74}$$

The transversality condition

$$\lim_{t \to \infty} \lambda p H e^{-\beta t} = 0$$

in (5.55d) now reduces to

$$\lim_{t \to \infty} H e^{-rt} = 0.$$

Applying this to the three exponential terms in (5.74), the following conditions must hold: (1) $(\alpha r/(\delta - \alpha)) + r > 0$; (2) $r > \tilde{\phi}$; (3) $r > \tilde{\psi}$. Condition (1) is assured under the capital intensity assumption $\delta > \alpha$; condition (2) is satisfied by the smaller root q_1 (see note 24); condition (3) has been imposed by the transversality conditions upon aggregate wealth, and is necessary and sufficient for the consumption:wealth ratio to be nonnegative; see (5.70) and (5.71).

The important observation is that the evolution of nontraded capital $H(t)$ involves a transitional adjustment path. It is restricted, however, by the requirement that the steady-rate K/H ratio must lie within the cone defined in (5.62); for this to occur, the growth rate of H must converge to that of K. If $\theta = 1$, so that the agent does not consume the nontraded good—a reasonable assumption if H is interpreted as being human capital —the convergence of the growth rate of nontraded capital $H(t)$ to the growth rate, $\tilde{\phi}$, of traded capital is assured. However, if $\theta < 1$, so that the agent consumes some of the nontraded good, the additional restriction $\tilde{\phi} > \tilde{\psi}$ must be imposed. This is because if $\tilde{\psi} > \tilde{\phi}$, so that consumption were to grow faster than traded capital, nontraded capital would ultimately need to grow at the rate of consumption in order to generate the nontraded output to satisfy the faster-growing nontraded consumption demand. The K/H ratio would therefore converge to zero, violating (5.62).

Thus, assuming either that $\theta = 1$ or that $\tilde{\phi} > \tilde{\psi}$, the ratio of traded to nontraded capital will converge to a balanced growth path along which[25]

$$\frac{\tilde{K}}{H} = \frac{[\tilde{\phi}(\delta - \alpha) + \alpha r]}{(1-\alpha)} \frac{\tilde{p}}{r_k(\tilde{p})}. \tag{5.75}$$

Using the fact that in steady state, $\tilde{r}_h = pr$, the steady-state K/H ratio (5.75) can be shown to satisfy the inequalities in (5.62) as long as the (common) equilibrium growth rate of capital $\tilde{\phi} \geq 0$.[26] If the growth rate is strictly positive, then $\widetilde{K/H}$ lies within the feasible cone. However, if $\tilde{\phi} = 0$, so that the economy is in fact stationary, then $\widetilde{K/H} \to \widetilde{K_T/H_T}$ and the equilibrium output of the nontraded good, Y_N, reduces to zero; see (5.67). The economy therefore is fully specialized in the production of the traded commodity. This is because with either no nontraded consumption ($\theta = 1$) or declining consumption ($\tilde{\phi} = 0 > \tilde{\psi}$) and a fixed stock of nontraded capital, asymptotically there is no demand for additional output of the nontraded good. All production needs can be met by allocating the existing fixed stocks of the two capital goods between the two sectors. The case where $\tilde{\phi} < 0$ so that the economy is declining, drives $\widetilde{K/H}$ beyond the boundary of the cone defined by K_T/H_T. This is because in a contracting economy $Y_N < 0$ in order for the market for the nontraded good to clear, that is for $\dot{H} = Y_N - C_N$ to hold. While this is unsatisfactory, it can be easily remedied, and a declining economy accommodated, by allowing nontraded capital to depreciate.

From these solutions for W, K, and H, we can derive the long-run implications for traded bonds. Rewriting (5.68) in the form

$$b = W - \tilde{q}K - \tilde{p}H,$$

it is evident that holdings of traded bonds are also subject to transitional dynamics, and the growth rate may converge to that either of wealth accumulation or of capital accumulation. Which it will be will depend in part upon whether or not the agent consumes nontraded output. In the event that he does not ($\theta = 1$), there is no restriction on the relative growth rates $\tilde{\phi}$ and $\tilde{\psi}$. In that case $\tilde{\psi} > \tilde{\phi}$ is possible, so that K and H both grow asymptotically slower than W; eventually the country will become a net creditor and continue to accumulate foreign assets. This condition characterizes a relatively patient country in which the agents choose to consume a small fraction of their wealth. This enables them to accumulate foreign assets, running up a current account surplus and generating a positively growing stock of foreign assets. It is the income from these assets that permits the small economy to sustain long-run growth rates of consumption and total wealth in excess of the growth rate of capital and productive capacity. However, as long as the agent consumes *some* nontraded output, the restriction $\tilde{\phi} > \tilde{\psi}$ must be imposed. In this case the country is relatively impatient. In the long run, the country consumes beyond its productive capacity and accumulates an increasing foreign debt.

$a > \delta$: Traded Sector Relatively Intensive in Traded Capital

Recall equation (5.58), the solution to which is

$$C(t) = C(0)e^{\int_0^t \psi(s)ds}.$$

Substituting this into the wealth accumulation equation (5.68), solving the equation, and invoking the transversality condition implies the aggregate consumption : wealth ratio:

$$\frac{C}{W} = \frac{1}{\int_t^\infty e^{\int_t^\tau [r-\psi(s)]ds} d\tau}, \tag{5.76}$$

where $\psi(t)$ is given in (5.58). In general, the consumption : wealth ratio is now time-varying. To the extent that the domestic agent consumes the foreign good ($\theta < 1$), movements in the relative price of the two consumption goods give rise to income and substitution effects, which are exactly offsetting when the utility function is logarithmic ($\gamma = 0$). Using (5.68) and the solution for $C(t)$, the equilibrium rate of growth of aggregate wealth may be expressed as

$$\frac{\dot{W}}{W} = \frac{\dot{C}}{C} + \left\{ (r - \psi) - \frac{C}{W} \right\}. \tag{5.77}$$

Thus both aggregate wealth and consumption have transitional dynamic time paths, reflecting the differential impacts of the relative price movements. As the price level converges to its steady-state level (i.e., as $\dot{p} \to 0$), C/W converges to its steady-state ratio (5.71), while $\dot{C}/C$ and $\dot{W}/W$ converge to their common constant growth rate (5.70).

The growth rate of traded capital is given by (5.4) and is also time-varying, reflecting the evolution of q along the stable locus. However, as q approaches its steady state, the growth rate of traded capital approaches the steady-state rate given in (5.72).

With the relative price of nontraded capital, $p(t)$, being time-varying, it is convenient to focus on the rate of accumulation of nontraded capital in value terms, which is given by

$$\frac{d}{dt}(pH) = \left[r + \frac{r_h(p)}{p}\left(\frac{\delta}{\alpha - \delta}\right)\right](pH) - r_k(p)\left(\frac{1-\alpha}{\alpha - \delta}\right)K - (1-\theta)C.$$

In the neighborhood of steady-state equilibrium, this equation can be approximated by

$$\frac{d}{dt}(pH) = r\left(\frac{\alpha}{\alpha - \delta}\right)(pH) - \tilde{r}_k\left(\frac{1-\alpha}{\alpha - \delta}\right)K - (1-\theta)C. \tag{5.73'}$$

A linear approximation to the solution for the time path of $p(t)H(t)$, valid in the neighborhood of the steady-state growth path, when the solutions for asset prices are near their respective steady-state levels, $\tilde{p}$ and $\tilde{q}$, is thus given by

$$p(t)H(t) = \left[p(0)H_0 - \frac{(1-\alpha)\tilde{r}_k}{(\delta-\alpha)[\tilde{\phi} + \alpha r/(\delta - \alpha)]} K_0 \right.$$
$$\left. + \frac{(1-\theta)}{[\tilde{\psi} + \alpha r/(\delta - \alpha)]} C(0)\right] e^{-(\alpha r/(\delta - \alpha))t}$$
$$+ \frac{(1-\alpha)\tilde{r}_k}{(\delta-\alpha)[\tilde{\phi} + \alpha r/(\delta - \alpha)]} K_0 e^{\tilde{\phi}t} - \frac{(1-\theta)}{[\tilde{\psi} + \alpha r/(\delta - \alpha)]} C(0)e^{\tilde{\psi}t}.$$
$$\tag{5.74'}$$

However, with the reversal of sectoral relative capital intensities (i.e., $\alpha > \delta$) condition (1), necessary for the transversality condition to hold, is no longer automatically met. This is because the partial effect of a higher pH is to increase its flow at the nonsustainable rate $\alpha r/(\alpha - \delta) > r$. Indeed, in order for the transversality condition to hold, we now require the term in the first parentheses in (5.74') to be zero. Noting that in the neighborhood of steady state

$$C(0) = (r - \tilde{\psi})W(0) = (r - \tilde{\psi})[q(0)K_0 + p(0)H_0 + b_0],$$

in order for the transversality condition to hold, we require

$$p(0)H_0 - \frac{(1-\alpha)\tilde{r}_k}{(\delta-\alpha)[\tilde{\phi} + \alpha r/(\delta - \alpha)]} K_0$$
$$+ \frac{(1-\theta)(r-\tilde{\psi})}{[\tilde{\psi} + \alpha r/(\delta - \alpha)]}[q(0)K_0 + p(0)H_0 + b_0] = 0. \tag{5.78}$$

While this transversality condition has been derived in terms of nontraded capital, it is in fact a recasting of the conventional national intertemporal budget constraint. This can be seen as follows. Conditions we have imposed have ensured that

$$\lim_{t\to\infty} \lambda W e^{-\beta t} = \lim_{t\to\infty} q' K e^{-\beta t} = 0$$

is met. It then follows from the definition of W in (5.67) that this implies

$$\lim_{t\to\infty} \lambda[pH + b]e^{-\beta t} = 0.$$

Thus the transversality condition on nontraded capital in (5.55d), together with the solution for

$$\lambda(t) = \lambda(0)e^{(\beta-r)t},$$

implies

$$\lim_{t\to\infty} b e^{-rt} = 0.$$

This latter condition is equivalent to the national intertemporal budget constraint. Thus (5.78) imposes conditions on the initial relative price of the two goods, $p(0)$, and on the initial price of installed capital, $q(0)$, that ensure that the resulting path of net exports is consistent with the intertemporal solvency of the economy. This equation, taken in conjunction with the stable saddlepath (5.66b), determines the initial values of the two price levels $p(0)$ and $q(0)$—both of which may respond instantaneously to new information—consistent with stable adjustment. The previous comments with respect to convergence of the aggregate K/H ratio and the behavior of traded bonds b continue to hold, at least locally.

5.8 Applications of the Two-Sector Model

We turn now to analyzing the effects of alternative types of disturbances on the equilibrium. Three types of shocks will be considered:

1. Domestic demand shock, taking the form of an increase in the rate of time preference

2. Domestic supply shocks, taking the form of proportional shifts in the production functions of the two sectors

3. An increase in the foreign interest rate.

Steady-State Responses

The effects of these disturbances upon the steady-state equilibria of key domestic variables are summarized in Table 5.1. Since the balanced growth equilibrium is characterized by only two growth rates, $\tilde{\psi}$ and $\tilde{\phi}$, these are

Table 5.1
Balanced growth effects

	Domestic demand shock	Domestic supply shocks		Foreign interest rate shocks
	$d\beta$	$\dfrac{da}{a}$	$\dfrac{dc}{c}$	$\dfrac{dr}{r}$
$\dfrac{d\tilde{p}}{\tilde{p}}$	0	1	$-\dfrac{\alpha}{\delta}$	$\dfrac{\alpha-\delta}{\delta}$
$\dfrac{d\tilde{\omega}}{\tilde{\omega}}$	0	0	$-\dfrac{1}{\delta}$	$\dfrac{1}{\delta}$
$\dfrac{d\tilde{r}_h}{\tilde{r}_h}$	0	1	$-\dfrac{\alpha}{\delta}$	$\dfrac{\alpha}{\delta}$
$\dfrac{d\tilde{r}_k}{\tilde{r}_k}$	0	1	$\dfrac{1-\alpha}{\delta}$	$-\dfrac{1-\alpha}{\delta}$
$d\tilde{q}$	0	$\dfrac{h(\tilde{r}_k/a)}{(1+hr)-\tilde{q}}$	$\dfrac{h\left(\dfrac{1-\alpha}{\delta}\right)\left(\dfrac{\tilde{r}_k}{c}\right)}{(1+hr)-\tilde{q}}$	$\dfrac{h\left(\dfrac{1-\alpha}{\delta}\right)\left(\dfrac{\tilde{r}_k}{r}\right)}{(1+hr)-\tilde{q}}$
$d\left(\dfrac{\tilde{C}}{W}\right)$	$\dfrac{1}{1-\gamma}$	0	0	$-\dfrac{\gamma}{1-\gamma}$
$d\tilde{\Psi}$	$-\dfrac{1}{1-\gamma}$	0	0	$\dfrac{1}{1-\gamma}$
$d\tilde{\phi}$	0	$\dfrac{(\tilde{r}_k/a)}{(1+hr)-\tilde{q}}$	$\dfrac{\left(\dfrac{1-\alpha}{\delta}\right)(\tilde{r}_k)}{(1+hr)-\tilde{q}}$	$-\dfrac{\left(\dfrac{1-\alpha}{\delta}\right)\left(\dfrac{\tilde{r}_k}{r}\right)}{(1+hr)-\tilde{q}}$

$1+hr-\tilde{q}>0$

the only two growth rates reported. We shall assume that $\theta = 1$, so that the growth rate of nontraded capital converges to that of traded capital. Thus $\tilde{\phi}$ can simply be referred to as the growth rate of capital. In the case where $\delta > \alpha$, the adjustments described in the table occur instantaneously; however, if $\alpha > \delta$, they represent long-run responses, following a transitional adjustment to be discussed below.

Increase in Rate of Time Preference

As noted, the steady-state relative price, the marginal physical products of capital, and sectoral capital intensities are determined by supply conditions and are independent of any domestic demand shock. Thus, $\tilde{p}$, $\tilde{\omega}$, $\tilde{r}_h$, $\tilde{r}_k$, and $\tilde{q}$ are independent of β. The equilibrium growth rate of traded capital, being determined by $\tilde{q}$, is therefore also independent of β. The same applies to nontraded capital. The only response to an increase in the rate of time preference is to induce domestic residents to increase the fraction of wealth that is consumed, leading to a reduction in the growth rate of consumption and wealth (see Table 5.1, Column 1).

Increase in Domestic Productivity

Column 2 of Table 5.1 summarizes the effects of a specified percentage increase in the efficiency in producing the traded commodity, as represented by the Hicks neutral technical change da/a. The key to understanding these relationships (as well as those in Column 3) is provided by considering the static efficiency conditions (5.54c) and (5.54d), the steady-state version of (5.55c), and (5.63b).

First, the increased efficiency in producing the traded good raises the relative price of the nontraded good; that is, $\tilde{p}$ must rise. In steady-state equilibrium, the real rate of return on nontraded capital measured in terms of the numeraire, $\tilde{r}_h/\tilde{p}$, must equal the foreign interest rate. With the latter remaining fixed, $\tilde{r}_h$ must therefore rise in proportion to the relative price $\tilde{p}$. But in order for the value of the marginal physical product of nontraded capital in terms of the numeraire (i.e., $\tilde{r}_h/\tilde{p}$) to remain constant, the relative capital intensity ratio in the nontraded sector K_N/H_N must remain constant. And since, further, capital is freely mobile across sectors, the relative capital intensity in the traded sector, K_T/H_T, remains constant as well; that is, ω remains unchanged. It then immediately follows that the marginal physical product of traded capital in the traded sector, $\tilde{r}_k$, increases in proportion to the productivity increase, implying that the increase in the relative price of the nontraded good is similarly proportionate. The higher marginal physical product of traded capital implies a higher rate of return to traded capital, thereby increasing the market price of installed capital, $\tilde{q}$. This in turn raises the growth rate of traded capital, and therefore that of nontraded capital as well. By contrast, the higher productivity of traded output has no effect either on the steady-state consumption:wealth ratio or on the equilibrium growth rates of consumption or wealth, all of which are determined by the difference between the rate of return on foreign bonds and the domestic rate of time preference.

From the results reported in Table 5.1, it is straightforward to determine the effect of the increase in da/a on the equilibrium aggregate traded:nontraded capital ratio, K/H, reported in (5.75). With $\tilde{r}_k/\tilde{p}$ remaining constant, the only effect is through the growth rate, with this depending upon the relative sectoral capital intensities. Thus, the increase in the growth rate, $\tilde{\phi}$, stemming from the productivity increase, will raise the ratio K/H if $\delta > \alpha$ and lower it otherwise. This is because during the transition H grows faster than K, converging to the growth rate of the latter from below. Thus, during the transition, relatively more traded than nontraded capital is accumulated, causing the K/H ratio to rise. If $\alpha > \delta$, the decline in p during the transition implies that H must grow at a faster rate than K, so that over time the K/H ratio will fall.

Column 3 summarizes the analogous effects of a specified percentage increase in the efficiency in producing the nontraded good, as represented by the change dc/c. Here the choice of numeraire plays a role leading to differences from the previous productivity shock. First, the increase in efficiency of producing the nontraded good will reduce its relative price; that is, $\tilde{p}$ will fall. With the world interest rate fixed, equilibrium in the world bond market requires that $\tilde{r}_h$ now decline in proportion to the decline in relative price $\tilde{p}$. Now in order for $\tilde{r}_h/\tilde{p}$ to remain constant in the face of an increase in the efficiency of the production of the nontraded good, (i.e., larger c), the relative capital intensity ratio in the nontraded sector, K_N/H_N, must decline, with an identical decline occurring in the traded sector. In other words, $\tilde{\omega}$ falls. The decline in K_T/H_T raises the marginal physical product of traded capital in terms of the numeraire; that is, $\tilde{r}_k$ rises. Thus, in contrast to the case of the productivity shock da, the two marginal physical products, $\tilde{r}_k$ and $\tilde{r}_h$, move in opposite directions. The higher marginal physical product of traded capital raises its installed price and the equilibrium growth rate of capital. The consumption:wealth ratio, as well as the equilibrium growth rates of consumption and total wealth, remain unaffected. The effect on the ratio of traded to nontraded capital is similar to that discussed in connection with the change in da/a, although in addition to the growth effect, which remains precisely as before, the increase in $\tilde{r}_k/\tilde{p}$ causes a decline in the K/H ratio.

Foreign Interest Rate Shocks

An increase in the foreign interest rate raises $\tilde{r}_h/\tilde{p}$. With the production function for the nontraded sector remaining constant, this raises the relative sectoral capital intensity in the nontraded sector, K_N/H_N (see (5.54d)), raising K_T/H_T proportionately; that is, $\tilde{\omega}$ rises. The rise in the K_T/H_T ratio reduces the marginal physical product of traded capital in the traded sector, so that $\tilde{r}_k$ falls. In order for the value of the marginal physical product of the two types of capital to be equated across the two sectors, the relative price of the nontraded good must move to offset the impact of the higher sectoral capital intensity $\tilde{\omega}$ on the marginal physical product of capital in that sector. Thus $\tilde{p}$ must rise or fall according to whether $\alpha \gtreqless \delta$. Whatever the response of the relative price, it is dominated by the direct effect of the foreign interest and $\tilde{r}_h$ rises unambiguously. The decline in the marginal physical product of traded capital reduces the market price of installed capital, thereby reducing the equilibrium growth rate of capital. Thus, in all these respects, the foreign interest rate operates like a negative shock on the productivity of nontraded output. Its effect on the equilibrium ratio of traded to nontraded capital is therefore the reverse of that in the previous case.

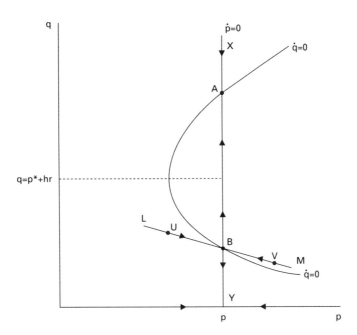

Figure 5.4
Increase in rate of time preference: $\alpha > \delta$

But it also has consumption effects. The higher interest rate has a positive income effect dr and a negative substitution effect $-dr/(1-\gamma)$, with the net effect being $-\gamma dr/(1-\gamma)$. Whatever the net effect on consumption, the higher income is more than offsetting, so that the net effect is to raise the growth rate of consumption and wealth.

Transitional Dynamics

We now consider the case where the traded sector is relatively more capital intensive in traded capital (i.e., $\alpha > \delta$), so that the adjustment to any shock involves a path of transitional dynamics. Two examples are illustrated in Figures 5.4 and 5.5.

Figure 5.4 illustrates the transitional adjustment in the case where the domestic economy becomes more impatient, and increases its rate of time preference. Suppose that the economy is initially in the steady-state equilibrium denoted by B. Since the steady-state values of $\tilde{p}$ and $\tilde{q}$ are independent of the rate of time preference, the stable saddlepath LM remains unchanged following this change in β, so that the system ultimately returns to B.

Upon impact, the higher rate of time preference will generate initial changes in both the relative price, $p(0)$, and the price of installed capital, $q(0)$. These initial jumps are required so as to (1) keep the economy on

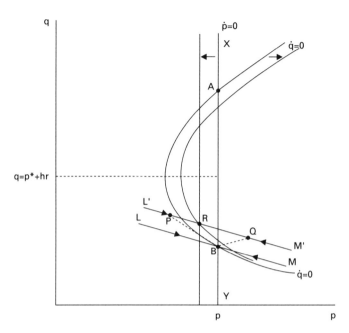

Figure 5.5
Increase in rate of productivity b: $\alpha > \delta$

the stable saddlepath, in this case LM; and (2) ensure that the transversality condition (5.78) for nontraded capital is satisfied. The movement is thus represented by a discrete jump from B to U or from B to V, at which point the economy reverses itself and proceeds continuously back to the equilibrium B.

The increase in the rate of time preference β raises the C/W ratio, thereby increasing the initial consumption demand for both goods. In order for (5.78) to be maintained, this increase needs to be offset by a decline in initial wealth; this is accomplished by initial jumps in the two prices $dp(0)$ and $dq(0)$. At the same time, these initial price changes are constrained by the requirement that they remain on the stable saddlepath LM. Denoting the negative slope of that line by $-\zeta$ (where $\zeta > 0$), we require $dq(0) = -\zeta \, dp(0)$, so that the two prices move in opposite directions. In general, we can establish a critical value of the ratio of nontraded to traded capital—$\bar{\kappa}$, say—such that the required initial reduction in wealth is accomplished by a reduction in the price of the relatively abundant form of capital, in terms of this critical ratio.

Thus, if the initial ratio of nontraded to traded capital $H_0/K_0 > \bar{\kappa}$, then the wealth reduction is brought about by a reduction in $p(0)$ together with a smaller increase in $q(0)$. This is represented by a jump from B to U and an initial increase in the growth rate of traded capital. The reduction in the relative price of nontraded output has immediate effects on the sectoral capital intensities and the rates of return on the two forms of capital, in accordance with (5.60). These effects are all transitory because the economy returns to B along UB. If the relative size of the two forms of capital is reversed, so that $H_0/K_0 < \bar{\kappa}$ holds, the reduction in wealth is accomplished by a reduction in $q(0)$, together with an increase in $p(0)$. The adjustment is a jump from B to V and involves a reduction in the growth rate of traded capital, which is only temporary, since the economy eventually returns to B along VB.

Figure 5.5 illustrates the dynamics in response to an increase in the productivity of the nontraded good, as represented by an increase in b. In this case the $\dot{p} = 0$ locus moves to the left and the $\dot{q} = 0$ locus shifts to the right. The new equilibrium is now at the point R, lying to the northwest of B, with the stable saddlepath shifting up from LM to $L'M'$. The transition to the new saddlepath occurs through jumps in $p(0)$ and $q(0)$ that may take place in the direction BP or along BQ, depending in part upon the initial relative sectoral intensities. But after the initial jump, the economy proceeds continuously along the new stable saddlepath to R.

5.9 Some Final Comments

This chapter has carried out an extensive treatment of growth in one- and two-sector AK models of a small open economy in which the source of growth is private investment. It is therefore useful to complete this discussion by providing an overview of our conclusions.

The one-good model has emphasized fiscal issues, and in so doing we have focused on two main aspects. First, we have considered pure tax effects, where the revenues resulting from some tax change are fully rebated. Second, we have discussed optimal tax policy in a situation where the tax revenues are used to finance some utility-augmenting government expenditure. Three taxes have been considered: taxes on bond and capital income, and a consumption tax. In order to ensure an equilibrium of ongoing growth, government expenditure must be tied to some index of growth; the rule $G = g_w W$, where the government indexes its expenditure to wealth, has been considered in detail. When government expenditure is determined by such a rule, it generates an externality in financial markets so that in general all three taxes are necessary to replicate the centrally planned economy. This is because the attainment of the first-best optimum involves three objectives. The first is to correct for the externality and its impact on private agents' decisions; the second is to attain the optimal portfolio growth; the third is to ensure that the government expenditure is financed. However, when government expenditure itself is optimally chosen in this latter case, this externality disappears. In that case, all rules converge to the same first-best equilibrium, in which government expenditure is fully financed by a consumption tax that, with fixed labor, operates like a lump-sum tax.

The two-sector endogenous growth model of a small open economy with traded and nontraded capital goods extends two important bodies of literature. The first is the dependent economy model, discussed in Chapter 4. Second, identifying traded capital with physical capital, and nontraded capital with human capital, the model is equivalent to the two-sector endogenous growth models that have recently been so prominent in the literature. The assumption that the small open economy faces a perfect bond market is crucial in enabling us to obtain a tractable closed-form solution.

The nature of the economy's growth path depends critically upon the relative sectoral capital intensities of the two domestic production functions. In the case where the *nontraded sector is relatively intensive in traded capital*, $(\delta > \alpha)$, neither the relative price of nontraded output nor the price of installed capital undergoes transitional dynamics; they are always at their respective steady-state levels. Thus traded capital and aggregate wealth are always on their respective steady-state growth paths, in general growing at different rates. Nontraded capital undergoes transitional dynamics, ultimately converging to the growth rate of traded capital and an equilibrium ratio of traded to nontraded capital.

In the case where the *traded sector is relatively intensive in traded capital*, $(\alpha > \delta)$, both asset prices will follow transitional paths before eventually converging to their respective steady-state equilibria, which remain the same as when $(\delta > \alpha)$. Corresponding to these transitional paths for prices are transitional growth paths for traded capital and wealth, which also converge to the same respective steady-state growth paths as before. Thus an important general implication of our framework is that the qualitative behavior of asset prices in a small economy depends crucially upon its underlying production structure, and specifically upon the relative intensities of the two sectors in the two types of capital.

The range of shocks we have considered has been purely illustrative. The two-sector model is versatile and lends itself to the analysis of a variety of issues and in particular to addressing the types of fiscal issues analyzed in the one-good context. In particular, Osang and Pereira (1996) analyze the role of tariffs in such a two-sector model, and in so doing extend some of the discussion in Section 3.5 to a growth context.

Finally, we should end with a reminder of the point made at the beginning. Growth theory is currently a burgeoning field, with both extensive theoretical research and empirical investigations receiving the attention of many economists. While this chapter has been long, our focus has been narrow, primarily on the role of fiscal policy and more generally on those aspects of recent growth models most closely akin to the policy issues discussed elsewhere in this book.

Notes

1. Mulligan and Sala-i-Martin (1993) note one exception to this. They show that endogenous growth is also possible is if there are increasing returns to scale in one sector that are precisely offset by decreasing returns in the other.

2. The logarithmic utility function emerges as $\lim_{\gamma \to 0}[(C^\gamma - 1)/\gamma]$. This differs from the objective function (5.1a) by the subtraction of the term -1 in the numerator and the two forms of utility function having identical implications.

3. Throughout we shall assume that all taxation is residence-based. Alternative modes of taxation will be discussed in Chapter 6.

4. As is typically assumed in small open economy models, foreign ownership of the domestic capital stock is excluded. This means that all of the burden of domestic capital taxes is borne by domestic residents. While we do not regard this as being particularly serious for a small economy, relaxing this assumption may be of interest, leading into questions of the nature of alternative tax regimes. See Razin and Yuen (1992, 1996) for a discussion of these issues in a two-country endogenous growth world.

5. There are some intermediate steps here that should be noted. If q were to converge to the larger (stable) root, q_2, it would do so along the stable adjustment path $q(s) = q_2 + (q(0) - q_2)e^{\mu t}$, where $\mu < 0$ is the corresponding stable eigenvalue. Along this path,

$$\int_0^t ([q(s) - 1]/h)\,ds = ([q_2 - 1]/h)t + ([q(0) - q_2]/\mu)(e^{\mu t} - 1).$$

Substituting this expression into (5.12), evaluating the expression, and letting $t \to \infty$, we verify that the transversality condition is indeed violated, as suggested in the text. In the case of the smaller (unstable) root there are no transitional dynamics; q is always at the unstable root, and the fact that it satisfies the transversality condition can be verified by substituting $q = q_1$ into (5.12) and evaluating the expression directly.

6. The result that a patient country is able to sustain a higher long-run consumption growth rate than an impatient country is analogous to the result of L. E. Jones and Manuelli (1990), who show that with identical rates of time preference, a country without taxes will grow at a faster rate than one with taxes. The parallel can be seen most directly from equation (5.6), where increasing patience (reducing β) is equivalent to reducing the tax rate. Jones and Manuelli also briefly discuss heterogeneous agents having different rates of time preference.

7. The only condition under which maintaining G/K will become feasible is if the central planner is able to control the initial stocks of capital and bonds, K_0 and b_0.

8. With all agents being identical, the individual can be identified with the aggregate.

9. This follows from the fact that $(\dot{W}/W) = (r - g_w) - (C/W)$.

10. There is a parallel here between our treatment of government expenditure as potentially generating externalities in utility, and models of economies of scale that are internal to an industry but external to individual firms. This kind of externality was central to the original work on endogenous growth models by Romer (1986). A further parallel exists between the present analysis and the externalities where government expenditure impacts directly on production, as in Barro (1990).

11. This decomposition of the return on an asset into an income effect and a substitution effect in the context of this type of model was first provided by Sandmo (1970).

12. This follows from the fact that (1) the product of the eigenvalues is negative and (2) the sum of the eigenvalues is positive.

13. Brock and Turnovsky (1994) identify the traded capital as equipment and the nontraded capital as structures.

14. One exception is Bond, Wang, and Yip (1996), who, using results from international economics, are able to characterize the transitional path of a two-sector model of a closed economy. Using a different approach, Caballé and Santos (1993) characterize the transitional dynamics in a two-sector generalization of the Lucas (1988) model.

15. In this respect, which is unimportant, the model differs from the corresponding two capital goods model developed in Section 4.6.

16. It would be straightforward to introduce adjustment costs on nontraded capital. But there is no need to do so, since their rate of adjustment is constrained by the endogenous adjustment in the relative price of nontraded goods; see the discussion in Chapter 4.

17. In the analysis carried out in Chapter 4, this is unnecessary because the production functions there are linearly homogeneous in the three factors of production: traded capital, nontraded capital, and the nonreproducible factor labor. The significance of this assumption will be noted in connection with equations (5.63a) and (5.63b).

18. These inequalities are sometimes referred to as the Lerner-Pearce conditions. They ensure that the economy is only incompletely specialized in the production of the two goods.

19. The specific constraints can be written most conveniently as

$$a(1-\alpha)m^\alpha p^{(\delta/(\alpha-\delta))} = r = a\alpha m^{\alpha-1} p^{((\alpha-1)/(\alpha-\delta))}.$$

Eliminating p from these two equations imposes a constraint on the exogenously given technological coefficients. This constraint is the analog to the standard arbitrage condition, $\alpha = r$, that applies in the one-sector, single-factor linear production function model.

20. Since there are only two factors of production, the statement that the traded sector is relatively intensive in traded (nontraded) capital is equivalent to the statement that the nontraded sector is relatively intensive in nontraded (traded) capital.

21. The argument is parallel to that set out in Section 5.2 for the one-good model. In particular, when assessing the stable root, one has to analyze the adjustment along the stable path, as discussed in note 5.

22. The comments made in note 21 apply here as well.

23. See, e.g., Fischer and Frenkel (1974) and Brock (1988).

24. The formal solution is

$$q_1 = [1 + hr] - \sqrt{[1 + hr]^2 - [1 + 2hr_k(\tilde{p})]}.$$

25. Using the expressions for $\tilde{\phi}$ and $\tilde{\psi}$, the restriction $\tilde{\phi} > \tilde{\psi}$ can be expressed in terms of underlying taste and technology parameters.

26. In showing that the solution for K/H given in (5.75) satisfies (5.62), use is also made of the transversality condition $r > \phi$.

II TWO-COUNTRY MODELS

6 Fiscal Policy in a Two-Country World Economy

Thus far, our discussion has focused on an open economy too small to influence what goes on in the rest of the world. While most of international macroeconomics deals with such economies, the fact is that larger economies cannot ignore the effects of their actions on the rest of the world. Chapters 6 through 8 extend the framework developed in Part I to analyze the dynamics of macroeconomic policy in a world economy, taking account of the interdependence between nations. These three chapters present a sequence of such economies dealing with different aspects of this interdependence. The models are real, and most of the thrust is on discussing fiscal policy and its international transmission. This chapter presents a basic one-good model, analogous to that presented in Chapter 3, and studies the transmission of both tax shocks and changes in government consumption expenditure. Chapter 7 extends the analysis in two directions. First, it relaxes the assumption made in Chapter 6 that while the aggregate stock of world capital is fixed instantaneously, in the short run it can be freely shuffled between the economies. Instead, it introduces costly adjustment of capital, thus reintroducing a role for the Tobin q, in the world economy. The second extension is to introduce a second good, thus permitting us to address issues relating to the determination of the real exchange rate in the world economy. This model further assumes that the agent does not have direct access to the ownership of capital in the foreign economy, but has only indirect access through the world bond market; that is, financial markets are incomplete. The international transmission of policy shocks introduces the potential for strategic interaction, and several models dealing with this issue are developed in Chapter 8. There we contrast the roles of government consumption expenditure and government production expenditure, with respect both to the transmission of shocks abroad and to their respective implications for strategic behavior.

Developing models of the world economy represents an exciting area in international macroeconomics. Most of the existing work assumes that the world consists of two economies. While this enables quantities that a small economy takes as given to be endogenously determined, the fact is that today, to a first approximation, the world can be reasonably viewed as consisting of three main trading blocs: North America, Europe, and East Asia. The extension from two to three countries is a major one, and opens up all kinds of interesting questions that are likely to become increasingly relevant in the modern world economy. These relate to issues such as the formation of coalitions of two trading partners and the impact of trading relationships between two countries on a third, and so on. Research on these topics is only beginning, but will surely increase in the future. In the meantime, Part II will exposit some existing aspects of the dynamic two-country model of the world, a necessary prerequisite for extending the dynamic framework in this direction.

6.1 Fiscal Policy Shocks

The transmission of fiscal disturbances and their repercussions abroad have long been central issues in international macroeconomics. This encompasses a broad area within which several aspects have been analyzed. The fiscal disturbance that has traditionally received most attention is the transmission of government consumption expenditure shocks. Early analyses examined this issue by using two-country variants of the static Mundell-Fleming model and static real trade models (see, e.g., Kemp 1966; Mussa 1979; Branson and Rotemberg 1980; Schmid 1982; and Corden and Turnovsky 1983). A comprehensive exposition of two-country Mundell-Fleming models is provided by Frenkel, Razin, and Yuen (1996). One of the issues emphasized in this early discussion concerns the potential for the *negative* transmission of fiscal shocks, the possibility that an expansion of activity in one country may lead to a contraction in another. This is in contrast to the "locomotive theory" advanced by the OECD, which suggested that major world economies should "pull up" the others through demand expansion.

With the emergence of large fiscal and current account deficits in the United States and other major Western economies during the 1980s, the analysis of expenditure shocks has continued to receive the attention of economists. But in contrast to the earlier work, this more recent literature typically employs some variant of the utility-maximizing representative agent framework adopted in this book. Among the earlier contributions to this literature, the work by Frenkel and Razin (1987) is particularly significant. This book, which incorporates a series of the authors' previous papers, provides a comprehensive treatment of the impact of fiscal deficits in a two-country world economy. For a large part their analysis abstracted from investment and output effects, and when these are included, they are restricted to a two-period analysis. Buiter (1987) introduces capital accumulation into a true intertemporal framework, although, like Frenkel and Razin, he assumes that employment remains fixed. The main question he addresses concerns the choice between borrowing and taxation to finance a given level of government expenditure. In order to obtain a nontrivial analysis of this issue, Ricardian equivalence must be broken; this is achieved by adopting the finite-life consumer model of Blanchard (1985).

Several other earlier papers have examined related issues, including Lipton and Sachs (1983), who adopt a large, infinite horizon two-country simulation model to study short-run and long- run effects of alternative forms of disturbances, and Frenkel and Razin (1985), who adopt simple two-period, two-country models to study the effects of government expenditure disturbances. The latter emphasize how the international transmission of an expansion in government expenditure depends upon whether the country is a net saver or a net dissaver in the world economy. In the specific case that (1) the world is stationary, (2) discount rates are equal across countries, and (3) labor supply is fixed, a permanent increase in government expenditure leads to full domestic crowding out, with no effects abroad. Lipton and Sachs (1983) similarly obtain full crowding out and no transmission in the case where labor supply is fixed, though in the variable labor supply case, they obtain transmission effects by considering a tax decrease coupled with an endogenous adjustment in government expenditures to balance the budget. More recently, Razin (1990) examines fiscal policy effects in a two-period, two-country world under alternative asset market structures and uncertainty. Devereux and Shi (1991) analyze fiscal shocks in a two-country framework, using the recursive preference structure of Epstein and Hynes (1983), discussed in Chapter 2. Bianconi and Turnovsky (1997) examine the transmission of government consumption shocks under alternative assumptions regarding their mode of financing. The latter part of this chapter exposits their model.

There is also a growing literature analyzing the transmission of fiscal and other shocks using the real business cycle approach. For example, Kollmann (1993) considers a model that incorporates variations in government purchases, distorting taxes, and technology shocks, and shows how the model's ability to track the U.S. trade balance depends upon the nature of the asset markets. Baxter (1993) uses a two-country, two-sector infinite horizon model to study government expenditure disturbances, and Backus, Kehoe, and Kydland (1994a) have applied two-country versions of the infinite horizon representative agent model to study the links between fiscal policy and trade deficits. Other contributions along these general lines include the theoretical analyzes of Cantor and Mark (1987, 1988), and the empirical studies of Gerlach (1988), Canova and Dellas (1993), and Yi (1993).

A more recent issue to receive attention pertains to tax policy, in particular to the viability of alternative tax regimes. The increasing integration of world financial markets has provided arbitrage opportunities to investors, thus imposing restrictions on the tax policies that the authorities in different jurisdictions may adopt. These restrictions depend upon the tax regime and have been discussed at length by a number of authors, including Slemrod (1988) and Frenkel, Razin, and Sadka (1991). They emerge naturally from the equilibrium to the intertemporal optimization problem that each agent is assumed to solve. The issue of viability in turn leads to questions of tax harmonization and tax competition, discussed by Razin and Sadka (1991a, 1991b), Giovannini, (1990), Sinn (1990), Bovenberg (1994), and Frenkel, Razin, and Yuen (1996), among others. Two principles of international capital income taxation represent two polar forms of tax regimes, elements of which are found in practice. These are (1) *source-based* taxation, where income is taxed according to its place of origin, and (2) *residence-based* taxation, where income is taxed on the basis of the residence of the taxpayer. Previous authors have shown how these two regimes are generally viable, though they lead to different allocations of the world capital stock. Residence-based taxation, by equating after-tax rates of return, leads to an efficient allocation of investment, but not of savings. Source-based taxation, by equating after-tax rates of return, leads to an efficient allocation of savings, but not of investment. Moreover, Razin and Sadka (1991b) have shown how the residence-based taxation scheme can emerge from tax competition as a Nash equilibrium, where authorities seek to maximize the welfare of their respective representative agents.

The international transmission of tax shocks has received relatively little attention in the literature, although that is beginning to change. The most comprehensive treatment of tax shocks in a world economy is that of Frenkel, Razin, and Sadka (1991), which is primarily based on a two-period model. Turnovsky and Bianconi (1992) examine the issue, using the intertemporal optimizing infinite-horizon representative agent model; the present discussion draws on that treatment. Their analysis is based on a fixed labor supply and is extended by Bianconi (1995) to include endogenous, but internationally immobile, labor. Nielsen and Sørensen (1991) analyze tax shocks in a small open economy, using a variable time discount rate. Christensen and Nielsen (1992) use a two-country infinite-horizon framework of overlapping families to study tax disturbances. Other recent contributions include Ihori (1991), who discusses issues of tax reform under alternative tax regimes in an overlapping generations framework, and Sibert (1990) and Nielsen (1992), who employ a similar framework to address issues in capital taxation.

This chapter focuses on two basic aspects of fiscal policy in a world economy: (1) the viability of alternative taxation and the international transmission of tax shocks, and (2) the transmission of government consumption expenditure shocks, dealing with them in that order. There are three good reasons for discussing them in this sequence. First, the viability of a tax regime is a basic requirement; unless the tax system is viable, there can be no interior equilibrium. Second, the effects of government expenditure shocks under alternative modes of tax financing can be broken down into two components: (1) a pure expenditure effect under lump-sum tax financing, and (2) the effects due to any accompanying change in a distortionary tax. The latter therefore serves as an input into the overall effects of expenditure shocks.

The third advantage of beginning with tax shocks is a pedagogic one, in that, being supply shocks, they yield dynamic effects even if the labor supply is fixed, thus enabling us to begin with a relatively simple model of the world economy. In order for government consumption expenditure (a demand shock) to generate corresponding dynamic effects, labor supply must be endogenous, and that complicates the model substantially.

6.2 Two-Country Macroeconomic Structure

Consider a two-country, one-good model of a decentralized world economy inhabited by households, firms, and their respective governments. Both countries accumulate capital gradually over time, and the world market for capital is perfectly integrated. Labor supply is fixed inelastically at unity and is assumed to be perfectly immobile across international borders. The analysis extends the basic infinite-horizon, representative agent framework of Part I to a two-country setting. In expositing the model, we shall focus primarily on the domestic economy. Variables pertaining to the domestic economy are unstarred, and the corresponding foreign economy variables are starred. The subscript d refers to the holdings of domestic residents, and f to the holdings of foreign agents.

Households

The economy is a real one, abstracting from money and other nominal assets, including bonds. The representative household has direct access to foreign capital markets, that is, to the ownership of foreign capital, and thus chooses its consumption level, c, and its holdings of domestic capital, k_d, and foreign capital, k_d^*, so as to

$$\text{Max} \int_0^\infty U(c)e^{-\beta t}dt, \tag{6.1a}$$

subject to the budget constraint

$$c + \dot{k}_d + \dot{k}_d^* = w + rk_d(1 - \tau_{rd}) + r^*k_d^*(1 - \tau_{nr}^* - \tau_{rf}) + T \tag{6.1b}$$

and given initial holdings of capital

$$k_{d,0} > 0, \quad k_{d,0}^* > 0, \tag{6.1c}$$

where $\beta > 0$ denotes the domestic rate of time preference, taken to be constant; w is the domestic (real) wage rate; r is the rental rate earned on domestic capital; and r^* is the rental rate earned on foreign capital.

Agents in both countries face a set of distortionary taxes defined as follows:

1. τ_{rd} is the tax rate levied on domestic residents on their domestic source income

2. τ_{rf} is the effective rate of additional tax levied on domestic residents on their foreign source income, over and above the tax paid abroad

3. τ_{nr} is the tax rate levied on nonresidents on their income earned in the other country.

Tax schedules are assumed to be linear, with the returns on foreign asset holdings being taxed by the domestic or by the foreign government, depending upon the regime. Since the main issue we want to focus on concerns capital income taxation in a world of capital mobility, labor income is untaxed. All tax revenues are rebated in lump-sum form T.

The first-order optimality conditions of this problem are

$$U_c(c) = \lambda \tag{6.2a}$$

$$(1 - \tau_{rd})r = \theta \tag{6.2b}$$

$$(1 - \tau_{rf} - \tau_{nr}^*)r^* = \theta \tag{6.2c}$$

$$\theta \equiv \beta - \dot{\lambda}/\lambda, \tag{6.2d}$$

together with the transversality conditions

$$\lim_{t \to \infty} \lambda k_d e^{-\beta t} = 0; \quad \lim_{t \to \infty} \lambda k_d^* e^{-\beta t} = 0, \tag{6.2e}$$

where λ is the Lagrange multiplier associated with the accumulation equation (6.1b), and is the marginal utility of wealth of the domestic resident. The optimality condition (6.2a) equates the marginal utility of consumption to the marginal utility of wealth. Equations (6.2b) and (6.2c) are arbitrage conditions equating the rates of return on domestic and foreign capital, net of all taxes paid, to the rate of return on consumption, defined in (6.2d).

The problem facing the foreign household is symmetric, with the corresponding optimality conditions being

$$U_c^*(c^*) = \lambda^* \tag{6.3a}$$

$$(1 - \tau_{rd}^*)r^* = \theta^* \tag{6.3b}$$

$$(1 - \tau_{rf}^* - \tau_{nr})r = \theta^* \tag{6.3c}$$

$$\theta^* \equiv \beta^* - \dot{\lambda}^*/\lambda^*, \tag{6.3d}$$

together with the transversality conditions

$$\lim_{t \to \infty} \lambda^* k_f e^{-\beta t} = 0; \quad \lim_{t \to \infty} \lambda^* k_f^* e^{-\beta t} = 0, \tag{6.3e}$$

where λ^* denotes the marginal utility of wealth of the foreign resident.

Firms

The domestic representative firm employs labor and capital to produce output, using a neoclassical production function having the usual neoclassical properties of positive, but diminishing, marginal physical products and constant returns to scale. In the absence of adjustment costs and corporate taxes, the optimality conditions for the domestic firm are the usual marginal productivity conditions:

$$F_k(k, 1) = r \tag{6.4a}$$

$$F_l(k, 1) = w, \tag{6.4b}$$

with the wage being determined so as to equate the demand for labor to the inelastically supplied quantity of unity. The foreign firm is symmetric, the optimality conditions being (for notational convenience the * is suppressed from the subscripts denoting partial derivatives):

$$F_k^*(k^*, 1) = r^* \tag{6.5a}$$

$$F_l^*(k^*, 1) = w^*. \tag{6.5b}$$

We should observe that k and k^* refer to the capital stock domiciled in the domestic and foreign economies, respectively. The fact that these capital stocks are owned either by domestic residents or by foreigners implies the relationships

$$k_d + k_f = k \tag{6.6a}$$

$$k_d^* + k_f^* = k^*. \tag{6.6b}$$

Governments

We assume that all revenues received by the government in each country are rebated to its own residents in lump-sum fashion, in accordance with the schemes[1]

$$T = \tau_{rd} r k_d + \tau_{rf} r^* k_d^* + \tau_{nr} r k_f \tag{6.7a}$$

$$T^* = \tau_{rd}^* r^* k_f^* + \tau_{rf}^* r k_f + \tau_{nr}^* r^* k_d^*. \tag{6.7b}$$

These depend upon the tax regimes. The two schemes most widely adopted and discussed in the literature, and that we shall consider, are (1) *source-based taxation* and (2) *residence-based taxation* (Giovannini 1990; Frenkel, Razin, and Sadka 1991). According to the source-based principle, income is taxed according to its origin and is therefore specified by

$$\tau_{nr} = \tau_{rd} = \tau, \ \tau_{rf} = 0; \quad \tau^*_{nr} = \tau^*_{rd} = \tau^*, \ \tau^*_{rf} = 0, \tag{6.8}$$

where τ and τ^* refer to the tax rates in the domestic and foreign countries, respectively. Under residence-based taxation, income is taxed on the basis of the residence of the taxpayer, regardless of the source of income:

$$\tau_{rd} = \tau_{rf} = \tau, \ \tau_{nr} = 0; \quad \tau^*_{rd} = \tau^*_{rf} = \tau^*, \ \tau^*_{nr} = 0. \tag{6.9}$$

These two regimes represent polar extremes; pure forms are not commonly found in practice. Nevertheless, they can capture the essential features of various more realistic international tax arrangements. For example, foreign tax credits can be accommodated in the following manner. Consider a domestic resident who is taxed abroad on his foreign capital income and who can credit the amount of tax paid abroad against his domestic tax liability. As long as the amount paid abroad is less than the domestic tax rate, his effective tax rate is residence-based. On the other hand, if the amount paid abroad exceeds the domestic tax rate, the domestic tax authorities will generally not refund the difference, and the individual's effective tax rate is source-based. However, the distribution of tax revenues across countries is indeed sensitive to the details of such arrangements. Finally, "tax haven" countries can be considered as operating source-based tax regimes.

World Goods Market Equilibrium

In a one-commodity world, goods market equilibrium is described by

$$F(k) + F^*(k^*) = c + c^* + \dot{k} + \dot{k}^*, \tag{6.10}$$

which states that the sum of private consumption and investment in the two economies must equal total world output. Henceforth, the labor argument (l) is dropped from the production function.

Wealth and Accumulation of Net Foreign Assets

Aggregate wealth in each country is defined to be

$$W = k_d + k_d^* \tag{6.11a}$$

$$W^* = k_f + k_f^*, \tag{6.11b}$$

so that aggregate world wealth is

$$W + W^* = k + k^*. \tag{6.12}$$

The net foreign asset position of the domestic economy—N, say—is defined as

$$N = k_d^* - k_f. \tag{6.13}$$

Domestic and foreign wealth can thus be expressed as $W = k + N$; $W^* = k^* - N$, and we shall say that the domestic economy has a positive or negative net asset position according to whether $N \gtreqless 0$. Taking the time derivative of (6.13) and using (1) the domestic household budget constraint; (2) the equilibrium conditions for firms; and (3) the government budget constraints, one obtains the following expression for the change in the net foreign asset position or the current account balance:

$$\dot{N} = F(k) - c - \dot{k} + (1 - \tau_{nr})F_k(k)N$$
$$+ \{(1 - \tau_{nr}^*)F_k^* - (1 - \tau_{nr})F_k\}k_d^*, \tag{6.14}$$

starting from initial N_0 and $k_0 > 0$. This equation asserts that the rate of accumulation of net foreign assets equals domestic output less domestic absorption, plus the net international flow of earnings on foreign assets. Observe that for an arbitrary tax structure, the rate of net foreign asset accumulation depends upon the international distribution of the capital stock, as reflected by k_d^*. In the absence of any distortionary taxation, (6.14) reduces to the familiar relationship

$$\dot{N} = F(k) - c - \dot{k} + F_k(k)N.$$

6.3 Viability of Alternative Tax Regimes

With integrated world capital markets and the arbitrage possibilities they offer, a key issue in any international taxation system concerns its viability. This issue was alluded to in the discussion of growth in Section 5.2. Central to this viability are the consumers' optimality conditions (6.2b) and (6.2c), and (6.3b) and (6.3c) in the two economies. Dividing (6.2b) by (6.3c) and (6.2c) by (6.3b) leads to the relationship

$$\frac{1 - \tau_{rd}}{1 - \tau_{rf}^* - \tau_{nr}} = \frac{1 - \tau_{rf} - \tau_{nr}^*}{1 - \tau_{rd}^*} = \frac{\theta}{\theta^*}. \tag{6.15}$$

The left-hand equality in (6.15) imposes an arbitrage relationship among the various tax rates set by the two tax authorities. The equilibrium conditions will thus be consistent and the tax system viable if and only if this relationship is met. This is the condition stressed by Frenkel, Razin, and Sadka (1991) and others.[2] Since the arbitrage condition pertains to the short run, we refer to (6.15) as a *short-run viability* condition.

In the short run, the rates of return, θ and θ^*, are endogenously determined by (6.2b) and (6.3b) and do not impose any additional constraints on the equilibrium tax system. However, θ and θ^*, being functions of k, evolve over time and, assuming that the system is stable, in the long run converge to the exogenously given rates of time preference, β and β^*, respectively; see (6.2d) and (6.3d). Thus, in order for the tax regime to be viable in the long run, the following *long-run viability* condition must hold:

$$\frac{1-\tau_{rd}}{1-\tau_{rf}^*-\tau_{nr}} = \frac{1-\tau_{rf}-\tau_{nr}^*}{1-\tau_{rd}^*} = \frac{\beta}{\beta^*}. \tag{6.16}$$

Long-run viability thus requires that the tax rates themselves must be appropriately related to the respective rates of time preference in the two economies.

Source-Based Taxation

In the case where taxation is source-based, equations (6.8) ensure that the short-run viability condition is met, thus implying further that $\theta = \theta^*$. The pairs of optimality conditions (6.2b) and (6.2c), and (6.3b) and (6.3c), together with (6.4a) and (6.5a), imply

$$(1-\tau)F_k(k) = (1-\tau^*)F_k^*(k^*). \tag{6.17}$$

Hence, equilibrium under source-based taxation requires that the after-tax marginal physical products of capital in the two economies be equated, so that the net returns to savers in different countries are equal. However, with differential tax rates this implies $F_k \neq F_k^*$; marginal products of capital are not equated, and thus the international allocation of the world capital stock is inefficient. In order for the source- based tax regime to be viable in the long run, we also require that $\beta = \beta^*$. That is, the representative agents in the two economies must have the same rates of time preference.

Residence-Based Taxation

This regime is more restrictive. Using (6.9), we find that (6.15) becomes

$$\frac{1-\tau}{1-\tau^*} = \frac{\theta}{\theta^*}.$$

The pairs of optimality conditions (6.2b) and (6.2c), and (6.3b) and (6.3c), together with (6.4a) and (6.5a), now imply

$$F_k(k) = F_k^*(k^*). \tag{6.17'}$$

Hence, equilibrium under residence-based taxation requires that the marginal physical product of capital be equated internationally; that is, the world capital stock is now allocated efficiently. But with differential tax rates, $(1-\tau)F_k \neq (1-\tau^*)F_k^*$, the net returns accruing to savers in different countries are no longer equal and thus the international allocation of world saving is now distorted. In order for the residence-based tax regime to be viable in the long run, the respective rates of time preference of the agents in the two economies must satisfy

$$\frac{1-\tau}{1-\tau^*} = \frac{\beta}{\beta^*}. \tag{6.18}$$

For given rates of time preference, this relationship thus imposes a constraint between domestic and foreign tax rates. It is evident that in general, a change in either one of the tax rates will require a compensating adjustment in the other, in order for (6.18) to be maintained. Thus, tax policy under the residence-based principle clearly involves serious problems of international coordination if it is to be viable in the long run.[3]

One less restrictive case in which (6.18) will hold is if one defines β' to be a "pure" rate of time preference and assumes that the agents in the two economies, recognizing that they are constrained by an integrated world financial system, adjust their rates of time preference to allow for their respective tax rates:

$$\beta = (1-\tau)\beta'; \quad \beta^* = (1-\tau^*)\beta'.$$

In this case, the long-run viability condition for residence-based taxation is met. This assumption is analogous to the standard procedure of setting the discount rate of a small open economy under perfect financial markets to the given world interest rate, with the latter being viewed as representing the "pure" rate of time preference in the world economy.

Mixed Regime

We now show that if the domestic economy taxes according to the residence principle and the foreign economy taxes in accordance with the source principle, then the viability condition (6.15) is not met. In this case, setting $\tau_{rd} = \tau_{rf} = \tau$, $\tau_{nr} = 0$; $\tau_{nr}^* = \tau_{rd}^* = \tau^*$, $\tau_{rf}^* = 0$, the viability condition becomes

$$1 - \tau = \frac{1 - \tau - \tau^*}{1 - \tau^*} = \frac{\theta}{\theta^*},$$

which is met only in the degenerate case if either $\tau = 0$ or $\tau^* = 0$. Hence, in general, the mixed tax regime is not viable. As long as the foreign country is taxing on a source basis and the domestic country is taxing on a residence basis, both domestic and foreign agents will want to hold only the assets of the domestic economy and thus escape the (additional) foreign tax.

6.4 Macroeconomic Equilibrium

Short-Run Equilibrium

The short-run macroeconomic equilibrium in the world economy can be characterized as follows:

Domestic Economy

$$U_c(c) = \lambda, \text{ i.e. } c = c(\lambda); \quad c_\lambda < 0 \tag{6.19a}$$

$$(1 - \tau_{rd})F_k(k) = \theta \tag{6.19b}$$

$$(1 - \tau_{rf} - \tau_{nr}^*)F_k^*(k^*) = \theta \tag{6.19c}$$

Foreign Economy

$$U_c^*(c^*) = \lambda^*, \text{ i.e. } c^* = c^*(\lambda^*); \quad c_{\lambda^*}^* < 0 \tag{6.20a}$$

$$(1 - \tau_{rd}^*)F_k^*(k^*) = \theta^* \tag{6.20b}$$

$$(1 - \tau_{rf}^* - \tau_{nr})F_k(k) = \theta^*, \tag{6.20c}$$

where the tax rates satisfy the short-run and long-run viability conditions discussed in Section 6.3. Equations (6.19a) and (6.20a) determine consumption levels in the two economies in terms of the respective marginal utilities of wealth. Because of (6.15) only one of the two pairs of optimality conditions (6.19b) and (6.19c), and (6.20b) and (6.20c) are independent. These equations express the rates of return on consumption, θ, θ^* in terms of the after-tax marginal physical product of the respective capital stocks.

Dynamics

The dynamic evolution of the world economy is represented by the set of equations

$$\frac{\dot{\lambda}}{\lambda} = \beta - \theta \tag{6.21a}$$

$$\frac{\dot{\lambda}^*}{\lambda^*} = \beta^* - \theta^* \tag{6.21b}$$

$$\dot{k} + \dot{k}^* = F(k) + F^*(k^*) - c(\lambda) - c^*(\lambda^*) \tag{6.21c}$$

$$\dot{N} = F(k) - c(\lambda) - \dot{k} + \theta'N, \tag{6.21d}$$

given k_0, k_0^*, N_0 and the intertemporal solvency condition

$$\lim_{t\to\infty} Ne^{-\int_0^t \theta' ds} = 0, \tag{6.21e}$$

where $\theta' \equiv (1-\tau)F_k(k)$ for the source-based regime and $\theta' \equiv F_k(k)$ for the residence-based regime. Equations (6.21a)–(6.21d) just restate (6.2d), (6.3d), (6.10), and (6.14), respectively, though with the perfectly integrated goods and capital markets, they are not all independent. Apart from possible initial jumps, λ^* mirrors λ, and likewise k^* reflects k. The intertemporal solvency condition (6.21e) prevents either economy from accumulating infinite net foreign assets.

The relationship between the marginal utilities of wealth in the two economies, obtained by solving the dynamic equations (6.21a) and (6.21b), depends upon the taxation regime. With source-based taxation, when viability implies $\theta = \theta^*$, $\beta = \beta^*$, they imply the relationship $\dot{\lambda}^*/\lambda^* = \dot{\lambda}/\lambda$. Solving this equation, we find that the two marginal utilities are proportional, being related by

$$\lambda^* = \bar{m}\lambda, \tag{6.22a}$$

where $\bar{m}$ is constant over time, being determined by the steady-state conditions. This equation implies that the ratio of the marginal utilities of consumption in the two economies, and therefore the distributions of consumption, remain fixed over time, being determined by $\bar{m}$.[4] It is equivalent to the constancy of the marginal utility of wealth that characterized the equilibrium in a small open economy under perfect capital mobility, discussed in Part I. With residence-based taxation, λ and λ^* are related by

$$\lambda^* = \bar{m}\lambda^{(1-\tau^*)/(1-\tau)}. \tag{6.22b}$$

In analyzing the dynamics, we assume that at any instant of time, each country's wealth, and therefore aggregate world wealth, is fixed by the total capital stock in existence,

$$W_0 + W_0^* = k_0 + k_0^*. \tag{6.23}$$

Wealth in the two economies is, respectively:

$$W_0 = k_0 + N_0, \quad W_0^* = k_0^* - N_0,$$

and either country can augment or diminish its capital stock instantaneously by entering the world capital market, in accordance with

$$dk_0 = -dk_0^* = -dN_0. \tag{6.24}$$

Thus the domestic economy can increase its initial stock of capital k_0 by repatriating capital, thereby reducing its net foreign asset position N_0.

The reverse occurs abroad. This assumption implies that even though the aggregate world supply of capital is given instantaneously, physical capital is fully mobile internationally. The capital stocks are interchangeable and respond instantaneously to exogenous disturbances. This assumption, which has been widely adopted in the static trade literature, abstracts from transportation costs and permits the possibility of the instantaneous reshuffling of physical capital between the two countries. It is the analog of the assumption of free sectoral capital mobility that was made in the two-sector models of Chapter 4. The alternative, and arguably more realistic, assumption, that capital is costly to move internationally, will be introduced in Chapter 7, where the instantaneous response to an exogenous shock occurs through the value of capital (the Tobin q) rather than through a shift in the quantity.

The general characteristics of the dynamic adjustment paths in the world economy are essentially the same under both forms of tax regimes. We shall derive the structure under source-based taxation as follows. Under this regime, the consumer arbitrage conditions are

$$(1 - \tau)F_k(k) = (1 - \tau^*)F_k^*(k^*). \quad (6.17)$$

Differentiating (6.17) with respect to t implies that along the transitional adjustment path,

$$(1 - \tau)F_{kk}(k)\dot{k} = (1 - \tau^*)F_{kk}^*(k^*)\dot{k}^*. \quad (6.25)$$

These two equations express k^* and $\dot{k}^*$ in terms of k and $\dot{k}$, respectively. Thus, note that following any initial jump, the capital stocks in the two economies evolve together. Linearizing the world product market equilibrium condition (6.21c) together with (6.21a), and taking account of (6.17) and (6.25), the linearized dynamics evolution of the world economy can be represented by

$$\begin{pmatrix} \dot{k} \\ \dot{\lambda} \end{pmatrix} = \begin{pmatrix} a_{11} & a_{12} \\ a_{21} & 0 \end{pmatrix} \begin{pmatrix} k - \tilde{k} \\ \lambda - \tilde{\lambda} \end{pmatrix}, \quad (6.26)$$

where

$$a_{11} = \frac{(1 - \tau^*)F_{kk}^* F_k + (1 - \tau)F_{kk} F_k^*}{(1 - \tau^*)F_{kk}^* + (1 - \tau)F_{kk}} > 0$$

$$a_{12} = -\frac{(c_\lambda + c_{\lambda^*}^* \bar{m})(1 - \tau^*)F_{kk}^*}{(1 - \tau^*)F_{kk}^* + (1 - \tau)F_{kk}} > 0; \quad a_{21} = -\tilde{\lambda}\theta_k$$

and tildes denote steady-state values.[5]

The dynamics described by (6.26) are a saddlepoint, with the stable eigenvalue being denoted by $\mu < 0$. Starting from an initial capital stock

k_0, the stable solution is

$$k(t) = \tilde{k} + (k_0 - \tilde{k})e^{\mu t} \tag{6.27a}$$

$$\lambda(t) = \tilde{\lambda} + \frac{a_{21}}{\mu}(k_0 - \tilde{k})e^{\mu t}. \tag{6.27b}$$

These two equations can be shown to define a negatively sloped stable locus in $k - \lambda$ space.

To determine the accumulation of net foreign assets, we consider (6.21d) and apply the procedure discussed in Chapter 3. This involves linearizing this equation about its steady state, substituting from (6.27a) and (6.27b), and invoking the intertemporal solvency condition (6.21e). Starting from an initial stock of net foreign assets, N_0, the stable adjustment, consistent with intertemporal solvency, is

$$N(t) = \tilde{N} + \frac{\Omega}{\mu - \beta}(k_0 - \tilde{k})e^{\mu t}, \tag{6.28a}$$

with

$$N_0 - \tilde{N} = \frac{\Omega}{\mu - \beta}(k_0 - \tilde{k}), \tag{6.28b}$$

and where

$$\Omega \equiv F_k - \mu + c_\lambda \lambda \theta_k/\mu + \theta'_k \tilde{N}.$$

The expression Ω describes the instantaneous effect of an increase in the domestic capital stock on the domestic current account. This operates through two channels. First, the expression

$$F_k - \mu + c_\lambda \lambda \theta_k/\mu \equiv \frac{\partial}{\partial k}(F - \dot{k} - c)$$

represents the impact of a change in the domestic capital stock on the trade balance. The increase in output and the decline in investment as k increases are both positive effects. The accompanying decline in λ and the increase in consumption that it generates is negative. The second factor represents the fact that as the capital stock increases, the rate of return declines. This leads to a declining current account balance if the country is a net creditor, and an increase otherwise. In the special case where the two economies have identical technologies, tax structures, and preferences, the trade balance effect is zero, and hence $\Omega = F_{kk}\tilde{N}$.[6] That is, if in equilibrium the economy is a net creditor, as it accumulates capital, it acquires foreign assets. The opposite holds for a debtor nation. The quantity $\Omega/(\mu - \beta)$ describes the extent to which the rate of foreign asset accumulation is tied to that of capital. While this relationship may be of either sign, we shall assume

$$\left|\frac{\partial \dot{N}}{\partial \dot{k}}\right| = \left|\frac{\Omega}{\mu - \beta}\right| < 1, \tag{6.29}$$

an assumption that is supported by numerical simulations carried out using the model and reported in notes 10–17.

The solutions (6.27a), (6.27b), and (6.28a) express the dynamics from the viewpoint of the domestic economy. The solution for the foreign capital stock is readily obtained from (6.25), and the foreign marginal utility of wealth from (6.21b)

Steady State

We shall focus on the case where the tax is source-based. In this case, the steady-state equilibrium, attained when $\dot{k} = \dot{k}^* = \dot{N} = \dot{\lambda} = \dot{\lambda}^* = 0$, includes the following relationships:

$$(1 - \tau)F_k(\tilde{k}) = \beta \tag{6.30a}$$

$$(1 - \tau^*)F_k^*(\tilde{k}^*) = \beta \tag{6.30a}$$

$$F(\tilde{k}) + F^*(\tilde{k}^*) = \tilde{c} + \tilde{c}^* \tag{6.30c}$$

$$\beta \tilde{N} = \tilde{c} - F(\tilde{k}) = F^*(\tilde{k}^*) - \tilde{c}^* \tag{6.30d}$$

$$N_0 - \tilde{N} = \frac{\Omega}{\mu - \beta}(k_0 - \tilde{k}). \tag{6.30e}$$

The first two equations are the steady-state arbitrage conditions, which in the long run involve equating the after-tax rates of return to the (common) given consumer rate of time preference. These equations determine the capital stocks in each of the two countries in terms of the tax rate prevailing in that country alone. Having determined the capital stocks, and hence national output, and therefore world output, the steady-state goods market equilibrium determines the long-run total world consumption. Observe that $\tilde{k}$, $\tilde{k}^*$ and $\tilde{c} + \tilde{c}^*$ are determined by production conditions alone.

Given $\tilde{k}$, (6.30e) determines the steady-state net asset position, $\tilde{N}$, of the domestic (and foreign) economy. This depends upon the initial stocks of the two assets, k_0 and N_0 and is a consequence of the integrated world capital market. As discussed in Chapter 3 in the context of the small open economy, it introduces hysteresis into the system. In this case, temporary shocks will have permanent effects on the international distribution of consumption and wealth, though not on the respective world aggregates.[7]

Having determined $\tilde{N}$, the first equality in (6.30d) determines domestic consumption. It equals domestic output plus net income (which may be positive or negative) on foreign assets. Foreign consumption is determined similarly. Having determined consumption, the marginal utilities are obtained from (6.19a) and (6.20a), with $\bar{m}$ being determined by the ratio between them.

Finally, the steady state is determined in a generally similar way in the case of residence-based taxation. The main difference is in the way that the income tax rates impact.

6.5 Transmission of Tax Shocks under a Source-Based Taxation Regime

Table 6.1 summarizes the short-run and long-run effects of an unanticipated permanent increase in the domestic tax rate under a source-based system of taxation. For expositional simplicity we assume that the economies have (1) identical tastes, (2) identical technologies, and (3) zero initial distortionary taxes. We shall also assume that in the neighborhood of the equilibrium we consider, the domestic economy is a net creditor nation; that is, $\tilde{N} > 0$ (or equivalently $\Omega < 0$).

Domestic Tax Increase

Suppose that the world economy is initially in steady-state equilibrium. The introduction of a distortionary tax in the domestic economy immediately reduces the after-tax marginal physical product of capital in the domestic economy below the corresponding rate of return abroad. As a consequence, this induces an instantaneous transfer of capital from the domestic to the foreign economy. Associated with this shift of the instantaneously given aggregate world capital stock is an increase in the net foreign asset holdings of domestic residents (with a corresponding reduction by foreigners) as they increase their holdings of foreign capital. The instantaneous move of capital from the domestic to the foreign economy lowers the marginal physical product of capital abroad, and hence the after-tax world rate of return on capital, θ.

In the long run, the after-tax return on capital in the two economies must equal the common, given world rate of time preference. In both economies, the after-tax marginal physical product of capital is therefore restored to its original level. With the tax rate abroad remaining unchanged, the capital stock in the foreign economy returns to its original level. Hence, following the initial purchase of capital from the domestic economy, the foreign economy decumulates capital. However, with the required return on capital being restored to its original level, the demand

Table 6.1
Increase in domestic tax rate

	A. Short run		B. Long run
k_0	$\dfrac{\beta}{2F_{kk}} < 0$	$\tilde{k}$	$\dfrac{\beta}{F_{kk}} < 0$
k_0^*	$-\dfrac{\beta}{2F_{kk}} > 0$	$\tilde{k}^*$	0
N_0	$-\dfrac{\beta}{2F_{kk}} > 0$	$\tilde{N}$	$-\dfrac{\beta}{2F_{kk}}\left[1 - \dfrac{\Omega}{\mu - \beta}\right]$
W_0	0	$\tilde{W}$	$\dfrac{\beta}{2F_{kk}}\left[1 + \dfrac{\Omega}{\mu - \beta}\right]$
W_0^*	0	$\tilde{W}^*$	$\dfrac{\beta}{2F_{kk}}\left[1 - \dfrac{\Omega}{\mu - \beta}\right]$
$W_0 + W_0^*$	0	$\tilde{W} + \tilde{W}^*$	$\dfrac{\beta}{F_{kk}} < 0$
θ_0	$-\dfrac{\beta}{2}$	$\tilde{\theta}$	0
$c(0)$	$\dfrac{\beta}{2(\mu - \beta)}\left[\dfrac{U_c}{U_{cc}} + \beta\tilde{N}\right]$	$\tilde{c}$	$\dfrac{\beta^2}{2F_{kk}}\left[1 + \dfrac{\Omega}{\mu - \beta}\right]$
$c^*(0)$	$\dfrac{\beta}{2(\mu - \beta)}\left[\dfrac{U_c}{U_{cc}} - \beta\tilde{N}\right]$	$\tilde{c}^*$	$\dfrac{\beta^2}{2F_{kk}}\left[1 - \dfrac{\Omega}{\mu - \beta}\right]$
$c(0) + c^*(0)$	$\dfrac{\beta}{2(\mu - \beta)}\dfrac{U_c}{U_{cc}} > 0$	$\tilde{c} + \tilde{c}^*$	$\dfrac{\beta^2}{F_{kk}} < 0$
$\lambda(0)$	$\dfrac{\beta U_{cc}}{2(\mu - \beta)}\left[\dfrac{U_c}{U_{cc}} + \beta\tilde{N}\right]$	$\tilde{\lambda}$	$\dfrac{\beta^2 U_{cc}}{2F_{kk}}\left[1 + \dfrac{\Omega}{\mu - \beta}\right]$
$\lambda^*(0)$	$\dfrac{\beta U_{cc}}{2(\mu - \beta)}\left[\dfrac{U_c}{U_{cc}} - \beta\tilde{N}\right]$	$\tilde{\lambda}^*$	$\dfrac{\beta^2 U_{cc}}{2F_{kk}}\left[1 - \dfrac{\Omega}{\mu - \beta}\right]$

These expressions assume: (i) identical preferences; (ii) identical technologies; (iii) zero initial distortionary taxes.

for capital in the domestic economy is reduced further, and capital decumulates over time in the domestic economy as well. For the case where the economies have identical preferences and production structures, the short-run reduction in the domestic capital stock is precisely equal to half its eventual steady-state decline. The time paths of the capital stocks in the two economies are illustrated in Figure 6.1A.

The effect on the long-run net asset position of the domestic economy is unclear. The initial sale of capital abroad raises the initial stock of net foreign assets, N_0. However, since the economy is assumed to be a net creditor nation, the subsequent decline in the domestic capital stock is associated with a current account deficit. Foreign assets are decumulated, and the net effect on the long-run net asset position depends upon whether the initial increase in foreign assets exceeds the subsequent

Fiscal Policy in a Two-Country World Economy

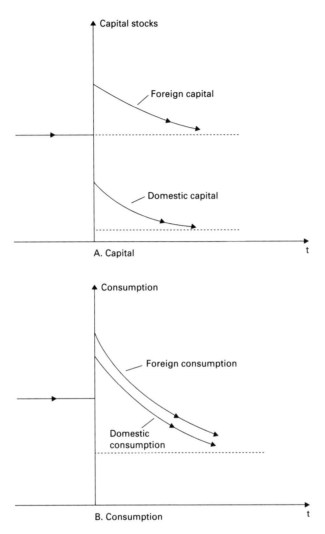

Figure 6.1
Adjustment time paths

decumulation through current account deficits. Provided (6.29) holds, the former effect dominates, so that $\tilde{N}$ rises.

The response of wealth is as follows. The initial trade of assets leaves wealth unchanged. But the decrease in the capital stock in the domestic economy over time, with the accompanying reduction in the economy's holdings of net foreign assets, leads to an unambiguous long-run decline in the wealth position of the domestic economy. With the long-run capital stock abroad returning to its original level, the response of wealth abroad depends solely upon the response in $\tilde{N}$. The initial increase in N_0 leads to a reduction in the holdings of foreign assets abroad, but the accumulation by the foreign economy leads to a positive effect, and the net effect on foreign wealth depends upon which dominates and (6.29) ensures that $\tilde{W}^*$ declines. With the net foreign asset position representing a transfer between the economies, aggregate world wealth, $\tilde{k} + \tilde{k}^*$, always declines in the long run.

In the absence of initial taxes, the response of consumption mirrors that of wealth. This can be seen by observing from (6.30d), together with the equilibrium condition $F_k = \beta$, that

$$\frac{d\tilde{c}}{d\tau} = \beta \left(\frac{d\tilde{N}}{d\tau} + \frac{d\tilde{k}}{d\tau} \right) = \beta \frac{d\tilde{W}}{d\tau}$$

$$\frac{d\tilde{c}^*}{d\tau} = -\beta \frac{d\tilde{N}}{d\tau} = \beta \frac{d\tilde{W}^*}{d\tau}.$$

Long-run consumption in the domestic economy therefore declines, foreign consumption may rise or fall (although it will fall if (6.29) holds) and, long-run world consumption always falls. These responses in wealth are reflected, as one would expect, in the corresponding marginal utilities, $\tilde{\lambda}$ and $\tilde{\lambda}^*$. Since wealth is more adversely affected in the domestic economy, the ratio of marginal utilities—rises.

Since agents are assumed to be forward-looking, short-run consumption and marginal utility are driven in part by the perfectly foreseen steady-state responses. The fact that it is known that it will be less desirable to accumulate capital in the future reduces the marginal utility of wealth today. At the same time, the knowledge that the reduction in steady-state wealth will raise the marginal utility of wealth in the long run tends to raise the short-run marginal utility as well. Which effect dominates depends upon tastes.

Consider the specific example in which the utility in both countries is represented by a logarithmic function. Then, using (6.30d), we can show that an increase in τ will lead to a decline in marginal utilities at home and abroad, and therefore to increases in the initial consumption levels.[8]

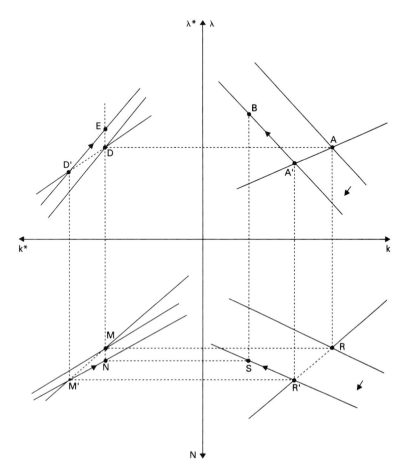

Figure 6.2
Phase diagram

With identical tastes, consumption rises less in the domestic economy if it is a net creditor nation ($\tilde{N} > 0$) than it does abroad. This is because of the expected decline in foreign earnings during the transition. For less restrictive utility functions, initial consumption in the domestic economy may rise or fall, although it will always rise abroad, as long as $\tilde{N} > 0$. However, initial aggregate consumption in the world economy, $c(0) + c^*(0)$, will always rise unambiguously. The time paths for consumption in the two economies are illustrated in Figure 6.1B.

A phase diagram representation of these adjustments is presented in Figure 6.2. The first (northeast) quadrant portrays the negatively sloped equilibrium relationship between the domestic capital stock, k, and the domestic marginal utility of wealth, λ. The second (northwest) quadrant depicts the corresponding relationship abroad. The lower two quadrants illustrate the relationships between the accumulation of the capital stock and foreign assets in the two economies. On the assumption that the two economies are identical and that the domestic economy is a net creditor ($\tilde{N} > 0$), these imply positive relationships between k and N, and between and k^* N, respectively.

The dynamics are as follows. The initial world equilibrium is represented by the points A, D, M, and R in the four quadrants. At time 0, say, when the tax τ is introduced, the short-run equilibrium jumps to A', D', M', and R', respectively. In the first quadrant, this represents the combination of (1) the initial decline in , accompanied by (2) the initial decline in $\lambda(0)$. The displacement of k_0^* in the second quadrant equals $-dk_0$, and, as we have noted, $\lambda^*(0)$ declines more than $\lambda(0)$, due to the anticipated transfer of wealth abroad. The jumps RR' and MM' represent the initial trades $dN_0 = dk_0^* = -dk_0$. The stable adjustment paths shift as indicated. Following the initial jump, the stocks of capital and foreign assets held by the domestic economy decline steadily, while the net foreign asset position abroad accumulates. These adjustments are represented by the movements $R'S$ and $M'N$ in the third and fourth quadrants. Likewise, the marginal utilities of wealth at home and abroad increase as the world capital stock declines. At all points $\lambda^*(t) < \lambda(t)$, reflecting the fact that domestic wealth is more adversely affected by the domestic tax.

Worldwide Tax Increase

The effects of a uniform worldwide tax increase can be readily obtained from Table 6.1. The main point to note is that equal tax increases imposed on identical economies lead to no initial trade in capital. The capital stocks in the two economies evolve gradually from their respective initial levels. In the long run, the fact that the tax increase is levied in both countries in effect leads to a doubling of the long-run adverse effects on wealth.

Welfare

The representative agent in each country derives utility from consumption. Thus the effects of a tax increase on his instantaneous level of welfare reflect what happens to consumption. A tax increase in the domestic economy will tend to raise welfare in the short run in the two economies, though with a more positive effect abroad than domestically. Over time, however, as consumption declines, the instantaneous level of welfare declines as well, declining more in the home country than abroad.

As in Chapter 4, an appropriate summary of welfare is provided by the intertemporal utility function (6.1a) of the representative agent. In the case of the domestic agent, the instantaneous level of utility at time t, as the economy follows the transitional dynamic adjustment path described in Section 6.5, may be approximated by the linear expression

$$U[c(t)] = U(\tilde{c}) + U_c[c(0) - \tilde{c}]e^{\mu t}.$$

Substituting this into (6.1a) and evaluating, the level of welfare of the representative agent along the optimized path is approximately

$$V \approx \frac{U(\tilde{c})}{\beta} + U_c\left(\frac{c(0) - \tilde{c}}{\beta - \mu}\right). \tag{6.31}$$

As in Chapter 4, the first term represents the agent's welfare if the steady state were attained instantaneously. The second term reflects the adjustment due to the fact that the steady state is reached only gradually along the transitional path.

Differentiating (6.31) with respect to τ yields

$$\frac{dV}{d\tau} = \frac{U_c(\tilde{c})}{\beta(\beta - \mu)}\left[\beta\frac{dc(0)}{d\tau} - \mu\frac{d\tilde{c}}{d\tau}\right].$$

Substituting for $dc(0)/d\tau$, $d\tilde{c}/d\tau$ from Table 6.1, we see that for identical economies, and in the absence of initial taxes, this expression and the corresponding effect abroad reduce to

$$\frac{dV}{d\tau} = -\frac{U_c}{2}\frac{\beta}{(\beta - \mu)}\tilde{N}; \quad \frac{dV^*}{d\tau} = \frac{U_c}{2}\frac{\beta}{(\beta - \mu)}\tilde{N}. \tag{6.32}$$

We thus conclude the following. If the two economies are identical and tax rates are initially zero, the introduction of a positive tax in the domestic economy will deteriorate domestic welfare if and only if the country is a net creditor. It will improve welfare abroad correspondingly, leaving total world welfare unchanged. The reverse applies if the country imposing the tax is a net debtor. It is well known that the imposition of a tax has no first-order welfare effect, starting from an initial zero tax situation. The intuition for the international redistribution of welfare that occurs reflects the fact that the decline in the return to capital during the transition results in a net transfer from the creditor nation to the debtor nation. One can also show that if the tax is initially positive, then a further increase in this rate will lower world welfare unambiguously.

6.6 Government Consumption Expenditure and Endogenous Labor Supply

We now extend the model developed in previous sections to examine the international transmission of shocks in government consumption expenditure. In order for such shocks to generate dynamics, for reasons discussed in Chapter 3 we need to endogenize the supply of labor. Our analysis emphasizes the importance of the method of government finance in the transmission process, both in the domestic economy and abroad. We analyze the dynamic transmission characteristics of an increase in government expenditure under three forms of tax financing (1) lump-sum taxes; (2) tax on capital income; (3) tax on labor income. The contrast between these forms of financing turns out to be striking. Since the model is one in which Ricardian equivalence holds, lump-sum tax financing is equivalent to bond financing. Taking the lump-sum tax as a benchmark, we show how in this intertemporal setting, an increase in domestic government expenditure will lead to a negative transmission of activity abroad, both in the short run and over time. However, a decline in activity abroad does not necessarily mean a decline in foreign welfare. On the contrary, we show how consumption, leisure, and ultimately welfare may actually be enhanced in the foreign economy.

An appealing aspect of the analysis is the ability to parameterize the various forms of financing, thereby enabling us to provide a very simple comparison of their effects. In contrast to lump-sum tax financing, distortionary tax financing has offsetting effects, which in the case of a capital tax will almost certainly outweigh the direct expenditure effects on activity; in the case of a labor tax they are less clear-cut. Thus, while an increase in government expenditure under lump-sum tax financing will stimulate domestic activity and reduce activity abroad, under plausible conditions these responses are reversed, if at the margin the additional expenditure is financed by a tax on capital. Accordingly, our analysis demonstrates, in an international context, the possibility of negative government expenditure multipliers, reflecting the existence of a "supply- side multiplier" (see Baxter and King 1993).

The modifications to the model required to incorporate government consumption expenditure and labor supply are modest. The representative household's optimization problem is modified to choose c, k_d, k_d^*, and now also its labor supply, l, so as to

$$\text{Max} \int_0^\infty U(c,l,g)e^{-\beta t}dt, \tag{6.1a'}$$

subject to the budget constraint

$$c + \dot{k}_d + \dot{k}_d^* = wl(1-\tau_w) + rk_d(1-\tau_k) + r^*k_d^*(1-\tau_k^*) - T \tag{6.1b'}$$

and given initial holdings of capital, $k_{d,0} > 0$, $k_{d,0}^* > 0$. The agent is subject to the following forms of taxation: τ_w is the tax paid on domestic labor income; τ_k is the tax paid on domestic capital income; τ_k^* is the tax paid on foreign capital income; and T is a lump-sum tax where the capital income taxes are *source-based*, so that τ_k is levied by the domestic government and τ_k^* is levied by the foreign government. In order to simplify the analysis, we shall assume that the utility function is additively separable in its three arguments: consumption; c; labor supply, l; government expenditure, g. That is, $U_{cl} = U_{cg} = U_{lg} = 0$. All other properties of the utility function and the production function remain unchanged.

The first-order optimality conditions to this modified optimization problem are

$$U_c(c) = \lambda \tag{6.2a}$$

$$U_l(l) = -\lambda w(1 - \tau_w) \tag{6.2a'}$$

$$(1 - \tau_k)r = \theta \tag{6.2b'}$$

$$(1 - \tau_k^*)r^* = \theta \tag{6.2c'}$$

$$\theta \equiv \beta - \dot{\lambda}/\lambda, \tag{6.2d}$$

together with the transversality conditions

$$\lim_{t \to \infty} \lambda k_d e^{-\beta t} = 0; \quad \lim_{t \to \infty} \lambda k_d^* e^{-\beta t} = 0, \tag{6.2e}$$

where is λ the Lagrange multiplier associated with the accumulation equation (6.1b') and is the marginal utility of wealth of the domestic resident. The optimality conditions for the foreign agent are analogous, and we shall assume that the rate of time discount of the foreign resident equals that of the domestic agent, an assumption that has been shown to be necessary for the source-based taxation scheme to be viable.

The optimality conditions for the domestic firm are the usual marginal productivity conditions:

$$F_k(k, l) = r \tag{6.4a'}$$

$$F_l(k, l) = w. \tag{6.4b'}$$

The foreign firm is symmetric. The ownership conditions (6.6a) and (6.6b) continue to hold, and national wealth, aggregate world wealth, and net foreign asset positions are still defined by (6.11)–(6.13). Goods market equilibrium (6.10) is modified to

$$F(k, l) + F^*(k^*, l^*) = c + c^* + \dot{k} + \dot{k}^* + g + g^*, \tag{6.10'}$$

while the current account balance is now

$$\dot{N} = F(k, l) - c - g - \dot{k} + (1 - \tau_k)F_k(k, l)N. \tag{6.14'}$$

We continue to abstract from government bonds so that each government maintains a continuously balanced budget in accordance with

$$g = wl\tau_w + rk\tau_k + T; \tag{6.33a}$$

$$g^* = w^*l^*\tau_w^* + r^*k^*\tau_k^* + T^*, \tag{6.33b}$$

where T now refers to lump-sum taxation (rather than rebate). The focus of subsequent analysis is to compare the effects of an increase in government expenditure under the following three alternative tax regimes:

1. The increase in government expenditure is financed entirely by a *lump-sum tax*.

2. The increase in government expenditure is financed in steady state entirely by an increase in the *tax on capital*.

3. The increase in government expenditure is financed in steady state entirely by an increase in the *tax on labor*.

As noted below, the two tax regimes (2) and (3) involve residual lump-sum tax financing along the transitional path to ensure that the government budget remains balanced at all times. See Cooley and Hansen (1992), who consider this form of financing in a closed economy context.[9]

6.7 Macroeconomic Equilibrium in Expanded Model

Short-Run Equilibrium

Combining the consumer optimality conditions, (6.2a) and (6.2a'), with the marginal productivity condition for labor, (6.3b'), enables one to solve for short-run consumption and employment in the form

$$c = c(\lambda); \quad c_\lambda < 0 \tag{6.34a}$$

$$l = l(\lambda, k, \tau_w); \quad l_\lambda > 0, l_k > 0, l_\tau < 0, \tag{6.34b}$$

where the partial derivatives and the form of the functions reflect the additive separability of the utility function. Combining the arbitrage conditions (6.2b) and (6.2c), together with the marginal productivity of capital condition (6.4a') for the domestic economy, and the corresponding relationships abroad implies

$$\theta = (1 - \tau_k)F_k(k, l) = (1 - \tau_k^*)F_k^*(k^*, l^*) = \theta^*. \tag{6.17''}$$

Dynamics

The dynamic evolution of the world economy is now represented by the set of equations

$$\frac{\dot{\lambda}}{\lambda} = \beta - (1 - \tau_k)F_k[k, l(\lambda, k, \tau_w)] \qquad (6.21a')$$

$$\frac{\dot{\lambda}^*}{\lambda^*} = \beta - (1 - \tau_k^*)F_k^*[k^*, l^*(\lambda^*, k^*, \tau_w^*)] \qquad (6.21b')$$

$$\dot{k} + \dot{k}^* = F[k, l(\lambda, k, \tau_w)] + F^*[k^*, l^*(\lambda^*, k^*, \tau_w^*)]$$
$$\qquad - c(\lambda) - c^*(\lambda^*) - g - g^* \qquad (6.21c')$$

$$\dot{N} = F[k, l(\lambda, k, \tau_w)] - c(\lambda) - \dot{k}$$
$$\qquad + (1 - \tau_k)F_k[k, l(\lambda, k, \tau_w)]N - g, \qquad (6.21d')$$

given k_0, k_0^*, N_0, and the intertemporal solvency condition

$$\lim_{t \to \infty} Ne^{-\int_0^t (1 - \tau_k)F_k \, ds} = 0, \qquad (6.21e')$$

The relationship (6.22a) continues to hold, and (6.24), describing the instantaneous mobility of capital, applies as well. However, the endogeneity of labor supply complicates the relationship between $\dot{k}$ and $\dot{k}^*$ along the transitional adjustment path. Differentiating (6.17″) with respect to t now implies

$$\phi_1 \dot{k} - \phi_1^* \dot{k}^* + (\phi_2 - \bar{m}\phi_2^*)\dot{\lambda} = 0, \qquad (6.35)$$

where $\phi_1 \equiv (1 - \tau_k)(F_{kk} + F_{kl}l_k) < 0$, $\phi_2 \equiv (1 - \tau_k)F_{kl}l_\lambda > 0$, and ϕ_1^* and ϕ_2^* are defined analogously. Thus equations (6.17″), (6.22a), and (6.35) enable us to express k^* and $\dot{k}^*$ in terms of k and $\dot{k}$, respectively. Linearizing the world product market equilibrium condition (6.21c′) around the steady state and taking account of (6.17′), (6.22a), and (6.35), the linearized dynamic evolution of the world economy can be represented by[10]

$$\begin{pmatrix} \dot{k} \\ \dot{\lambda} \end{pmatrix} = \begin{pmatrix} a_{11} & a_{12} \\ -\tilde{\lambda}\phi_1 & -\tilde{\lambda}\phi_2 \end{pmatrix} \begin{pmatrix} k - \tilde{k} \\ \lambda - \tilde{\lambda} \end{pmatrix}, \qquad (6.36)$$

where now

$$a_{11} = \frac{\tilde{\lambda}(\phi_1/\phi_1^*)(\phi_2 - \bar{m}\phi_2^*) + (F_k + F_l l_k) + (\phi_1/\phi_1^*)(F_k^* + F_l^* l_k^*)}{1 + (\phi_1/\phi_1^*)},$$

$$a_{12} = \frac{((\phi_2 - \bar{m}\phi_2^*)/\phi_1^*)(\tilde{\lambda}\phi_2 + F_k^* + F_l^* l_k^*) + (F_l l_\lambda - c_\lambda) + \bar{m}(F_l^* l_\lambda^* - c_\lambda^*)}{1 + (\phi_1/\phi_1^*)}.$$

The dynamics (6.36) are again a saddlepoint, with the stable solution now consisting of (6.27a), together with[11]

$$\lambda(t) = \tilde{\lambda} - \left(\frac{\tilde{\lambda}\phi_1}{\mu + \tilde{\lambda}\phi_2}\right)(k_0 - \tilde{k})e^{\mu t}. \tag{6.27b'}$$

The accumulation of foreign assets is given by (6.28a) and (6.28b) where Ω is modified to

$$\Omega \equiv F_k + F_l l_k - \mu - \frac{\tilde{\lambda}\phi_1(F_l l_\lambda - c_\lambda)}{\mu + \tilde{\lambda}\phi_2} + \frac{\tilde{\mu}\phi_1}{\tilde{\mu} + \tilde{\lambda}\phi_2}\tilde{N}$$

and all interpretations remain as before.[12]

Steady State

The steady state relationships now consist of

$$(1 - \tau_k)F_k[\tilde{k}, l(\tilde{\lambda}, \tilde{k}, \tau_w)] = (1 - \tau_k^*)F_k^*[\tilde{k}^*, l(\tilde{\lambda}^*, \tilde{k}^*, \tau_w^*)] = \beta \tag{6.37a}$$

$$F[\tilde{k}, l(\tilde{\lambda}, \tilde{k}, \tau_w)] + F^*[\tilde{k}^*, l(\tilde{\lambda}^*, \tilde{k}^*, \tau_w^*)] = c(\tilde{\lambda}) + c^*(\tilde{\lambda}^*) + g + g^* \tag{6.37b}$$

$$\beta\tilde{N} = c(\tilde{\lambda}) + g - F[\tilde{k}, l(\tilde{\lambda}, \tilde{k}, \tau_w)]$$
$$= F^*[\tilde{k}^*, l^*(\tilde{\lambda}^*, \tilde{k}^*, \tau_w^*)] - c^*(\tilde{\lambda}^*) - g^* \tag{6.37c}$$

$$N_0 - \tilde{N} = \frac{\Omega}{\mu - \beta}(k_0 - \tilde{k}). \tag{6.37d}$$

This system of equations jointly determines $\tilde{k}$, $\tilde{k}^*$, $\tilde{\lambda}$, $\tilde{\lambda}^*$, and $\tilde{N}$ in terms of the domestic and foreign government expenditures; domestic and foreign distortionary tax rates, and the initial stocks of assets k_0 and N_0. Having obtained this steady state, consumption levels, $\tilde{c}$ and $\tilde{c}^*$, and employment levels, $\tilde{l}$ and $\tilde{l}^*$, then follow from (6.34) and its foreign counterpart, while $\bar{m}$ is obtained from (6.22a). Finally, the steady-state government budget constraints in the two economies,

$$g = F_l[\tilde{k}, l(\tilde{\lambda}, \tilde{k}, \tau_w)]l(\tilde{\lambda}, \tilde{k}, \tau_w)\tau_w + F_k[\tilde{k}, l(\tilde{\lambda}, \tilde{k}, \tau_w)]\tilde{k}\tau_k + T \tag{6.37e}$$

$$g^* = F_l^*[\tilde{k}^*, l^*(\tilde{\lambda}^*, \tilde{k}^*, \tau_w^*)]l^*(\tilde{\lambda}^*, \tilde{k}^*, \tau_w^*)\tau_w^*$$
$$+ F_k^*[\tilde{k}^*, l^*(\tilde{\lambda}^*, \tilde{k}^*, \tau_w^*)]\tilde{k}^*\tau_k^* + T^*, \tag{6.37f}$$

determine one of the tax rates, (τ_w, τ_c, T) and $(\tau_w^*, \tau_c^*, T^*)$, in the domestic and foreign economy respectively, depending upon the chosen form of government expenditure financing.

Determination of Initial Distribution of World Capital Stock

As noted earlier, the steady state depends upon the initial stocks k_0 and N_0 (or equivalently k_0 and k_0^*). Formally, this is a consequence of the constancy of $\lambda^*/\lambda = \bar{m}$ over time. While the initial aggregate stock of capital $k_0 + k_0^*$ is predetermined as the sum of previously accumulated world wealth, the initial *allocation* of this aggregate capital stock is endogenously determined by the efficiency condition (6.17″). More specifically, k_0, k_0^*, and $\lambda(0)$ are jointly determined in terms of $\bar{m}$ and the distortionary tax rates by

$$(1 - \tau_k)F_k[k_0, l(\lambda(0), k_0, \tau_w)] = (1 - \tau_k^*)F_k^*[k_0^*, l^*(\lambda(0)\bar{m}, k_0^*, \tau_w^*)], \quad (6.17'')$$

together with (6.27b′) at time zero and the fact that $k_0 + k_0^*$ is fixed. An interesting aspect of the present model is that because of the dependence of the initial allocation of capital on $\bar{m}$, the short-run and long-run equilibria become simultaneously determined.

6.8 Government Expenditure under Alternative Forms of Tax Financing

Table 6.2 summarizes the expressions describing the effects of an unanticipated increase in domestic government expenditure $(dg > 0)$, financed under the alternative types of tax increase. The table consists of three parts describing the steady-state effects, the short-run effects, and the responses along the transitional adjustment paths. As before, these effects have been computed under the assumptions that (1) agents in the two economies have identical tastes; (2) the economies have identical technologies; (3) the initial equilibrium is one in which there are no distortionary taxes, so that any existing government expenditures are financed by lump-sum taxes. Under these conditions one can show that at the initial equilibrium, the consumption, employment, output, capital stocks, and so on in the two economies will be identical. The only source of an imbalance in asset holdings arises because of different sizes in the governments of the two economies. One can show under the present assumption that

$$\tilde{N} = \frac{1}{2\beta}(g - g^*).$$

Thus, the domestic economy will be a net exporter of capital in the initial steady state if $g > g^*$ and a net importer otherwise. This is because, with identical private consumption and production levels in the two economies, a higher level of expenditure by the domestic government, say, means that the domestic economy is running a trade balance deficit, which needs to be financed by positive earnings on its net holdings of foreign capital in order for the overall current account to remain in balance.

Under the assumption of zero initial distortionary taxes, the equilibrium is Pareto efficient. With the adjustments in the tax rates corresponding to

Table 6.2
Increase in domestic government expenditure

A. Steady-state effects

	Lump-sum tax T	Financed by Capital income tax τ_k	Wage income tax τ_w
$\tilde{k}$	$\dfrac{\psi - \dfrac{\beta}{2}\left(1 + \dfrac{\Omega}{\mu - \beta}\right)}{\psi(\psi - \beta)} > 0$	$(1-\delta_k)\dfrac{\psi - \dfrac{\beta}{2}\left(1 + \dfrac{\Omega}{\mu - \beta}\right)}{\psi(\psi - \beta)} < 0$	$(1-\delta_w)\dfrac{\psi - \dfrac{\beta}{2}\left(1 + \dfrac{\Omega}{\mu - \beta}\right)}{\psi(\psi - \beta)}$
$\tilde{k}^*$	$-\dfrac{\dfrac{\beta}{2}\left(1 - \dfrac{\Omega}{\mu - \beta}\right)}{\psi(\psi - \beta)} < 0$	$-(1-\delta_k)\dfrac{\dfrac{\beta}{2}\left(1 - \dfrac{\Omega}{\mu - \beta}\right)}{\psi(\psi - \beta)} > 0$	$-(1-\delta_w)\dfrac{\dfrac{\beta}{2}\left(1 - \dfrac{\Omega}{\mu - \beta}\right)}{\psi(\psi - \beta)}$
$\tilde{k} + \tilde{k}^*$	$\dfrac{1}{\psi} > 0$	$(1-\delta_k)\dfrac{1}{\psi} < 0$	$(1-\delta_w)\dfrac{1}{\psi}$
$\tilde{N}$	$-\dfrac{\left(1 - \dfrac{\Omega}{\mu - \beta}\right)}{2(\psi - \beta)} < 0$	$-(1-\delta_k)\dfrac{\left(1 - \dfrac{\Omega}{\mu - \beta}\right)}{2(\psi - \beta)} > 0$	$-(1-\delta_w)\dfrac{\left(1 - \dfrac{\Omega}{\mu - \beta}\right)}{2(\psi - \beta)}$
$\tilde{m}$	$-\dfrac{\phi_1}{\phi_2}\dfrac{\left(\psi - \dfrac{\beta\Omega}{\mu - \beta}\right)}{\alpha\psi(\psi - \beta)} < 0$	$(1-\delta_k)\dfrac{\phi_1}{\phi_2}\dfrac{\left(\psi - \dfrac{\beta\Omega}{\mu - \beta}\right)}{\alpha\psi(\psi - \beta)} - \dfrac{1}{\alpha\phi_2 k}$	$(1-\delta_w)\dfrac{\phi_1}{\phi_2}\dfrac{\left(\psi - \dfrac{\beta\Omega}{\mu - \beta}\right)}{\alpha\psi(\psi - \beta)} + \dfrac{1}{lF_l}$
$\tilde{l}$	$\left(\dfrac{\tilde{l}}{\tilde{k}}\right)\left(\dfrac{d\tilde{k}}{dg}\right)_T > 0$	$\left(\dfrac{\tilde{l}}{\tilde{k}}\right)\left(\dfrac{d\tilde{k}}{dg}\right)_{\tau_k} + \dfrac{1}{F_{kl}k}$	$\left(\dfrac{\tilde{l}}{\tilde{k}}\right)\left(\dfrac{d\tilde{k}}{dg}\right)_{\tau_w}$
$\tilde{l}^*$	$\left(\dfrac{\tilde{l}}{\tilde{k}}\right)\left(\dfrac{d\tilde{k}^*}{dg}\right)_T < 0$	$\left(\dfrac{\tilde{l}}{\tilde{k}}\right)\left(\dfrac{d\tilde{k}^*}{dg}\right)_{\tau_k} > 0$	$\left(\dfrac{\tilde{l}}{\tilde{k}}\right)\left(\dfrac{d\tilde{k}^*}{dg}\right)_{\tau_w}$
$\tilde{l} + \tilde{l}^*$	$\left(\dfrac{\tilde{l}}{\tilde{k}}\right)\dfrac{1}{\psi} > 0$	$(1-\delta_c)\left(\dfrac{\tilde{l}}{\tilde{k}}\right)\dfrac{1}{\psi} + \dfrac{1}{F_{kl}k}$	$(1-\delta_w)\left(\dfrac{\tilde{l}}{\tilde{k}}\right)\dfrac{1}{\psi}$

Fiscal Policy in a Two-Country World Economy

	Lump-sum tax T	Capital income tax τ_k	Wage income tax τ_w
$\tilde{\lambda}$	$-\left(\frac{\phi_1}{\phi_2}\right)\left(\frac{d\tilde{k}}{dg}\right)_T > 0$	$-\left(\frac{\phi_1}{\phi_2}\right)\left(\frac{d\tilde{k}}{dg}\right)_{\tau_k} + \frac{1}{\phi_2 k}$	$-\left(\frac{\phi_1}{\phi_2}\right)\left(\frac{d\tilde{k}}{dg}\right)_{\tau_w} + \frac{\tilde{\lambda}}{lF_l}$
$\tilde{\lambda}^*$	$-\left(\frac{\phi_1}{\phi_2}\right)\left(\frac{d\tilde{k}^*}{dg}\right)_T < 0$	$-\left(\frac{\phi_1}{\phi_2}\right)\left(\frac{d\tilde{k}^*}{dg}\right)_{\tau_k} > 0$	$-\left(\frac{\phi_1}{\phi_2}\right)\left(\frac{d\tilde{k}^*}{dg}\right)_{\tau_w}$
$\tilde{c}$	$-\frac{1}{U_{cc}}\left(\frac{\phi_1}{\phi_2}\right)\left(\frac{d\tilde{k}}{dg}\right)_T < 0$	$-\frac{1}{U_{cc}}\left(\left(\frac{\phi_1}{\phi_2}\right)\left(\frac{d\tilde{k}}{dg}\right)_{\tau_k} - \frac{1}{\phi_2 k}\right)$	$-\frac{1}{U_{cc}}\left(\left(\frac{\phi_1}{\phi_2}\right)\left(\frac{d\tilde{k}}{dg}\right)_{\tau_w} - \frac{\tilde{\lambda}}{lF_l}\right)$
$\tilde{c}^*$	$-\frac{1}{U_{cc}}\left(\frac{\phi_1}{\phi_2}\right)\left(\frac{d\tilde{k}^*}{dg}\right)_T > 0$	$-\frac{1}{U_{cc}}\left(\frac{\phi_1}{\phi_2}\right)\left(\frac{d\tilde{k}^*}{dg}\right)_{\tau_k} < 0$	$-\frac{1}{U_{cc}}\left(\frac{\phi_1}{\phi_2}\right)\left(\frac{d\tilde{k}^*}{dg}\right)_{\tau_w}$
$\tilde{c} + \tilde{c}^*$	$-\frac{1}{U_{cc}}\left(\frac{\phi_1}{\phi_2}\right)\frac{1}{\psi} < 0$	$-\frac{(1-\delta_k)}{U_{cc}}\left(\frac{\phi_1}{\phi_2}\right)\frac{1}{\psi} + \frac{1}{U_{cc}\phi_2 k}$	$-\frac{(1-\delta_w)}{U_{cc}}\left(\frac{\phi_1}{\phi_2}\right)\frac{1}{\psi} + \frac{\tilde{\lambda}}{U_{cc}lF_l}$

These expressions assume: (i) identical preferences; (ii) identical technologies; (iii) zero initial distortionary taxes.
$\psi \equiv \frac{F}{k} + \frac{U_{ll}}{U_{cc}}\frac{1}{kF_l} > \beta > 0$; $\delta_k \equiv \frac{F_l}{F_{kl}k} - \frac{1}{\phi_2 U_{cc}k}(>1)$ $\delta_w \equiv -\frac{\tilde{\lambda}}{U_{cc}F_l l} \gtrless 1$.

B. Short-run effects

Financed by

	Lump-sum tax T	Capital income tax τ_k	Wage income tax τ_w
k_0	$\frac{\left(\psi - \frac{\beta\Omega}{\mu-\beta}\right)}{2\psi(\psi-\beta)} > 0$	$(1-\delta_k)\frac{\left(\psi-\frac{\beta\Omega}{\mu-\beta}\right)}{2\psi(\psi-\beta)} < 0$	$(1-\delta_w)\frac{\left(\psi-\frac{\beta\Omega}{\mu-\beta}\right)}{2\psi(\psi-\beta)}$
k_0^*, N_0	$-\frac{\left(\psi-\frac{\beta\Omega}{\mu-\beta}\right)}{2\psi(\psi-\beta)} < 0$	$-(1-\delta_k)\frac{\left(\psi-\frac{\beta\Omega}{\mu-\beta}\right)}{2\psi(\psi-\beta)} > 0$	$-(1-\delta_w)\frac{\left(\psi-\frac{\beta\Omega}{\mu-\beta}\right)}{2\psi(\psi-\beta)}$
$\lambda(0)$	$\left(\frac{d\tilde{\lambda}}{dg}\right)_i - \frac{\tilde{\lambda}\phi_1}{\mu + \tilde{\lambda}\phi_2}\left(\frac{dk_0}{dg} - \frac{d\tilde{k}}{dg}\right)_i$ $i = T, \tau_k, \tau_w$; $\left(\frac{d\lambda(0)}{dg}\right)_T > 0$;		

Table 6.2 (continued)

	B. Short-run effects		
	Lump-sum tax T	Financed by Capital income tax τ_k	Wage income tax τ_w
$\tilde{\lambda}^*(0)$	$\left(\dfrac{d\tilde{\lambda}^*}{dg}\right)_i - \dfrac{\tilde{\lambda}\phi_1}{\mu+\tilde{\lambda}\phi_2}\left(\dfrac{dk_0^*}{dg} - \dfrac{d\tilde{k}^*}{dg}\right)_i$ $\quad i=T,\tau_k,\tau_w;$		$\left(\dfrac{d\lambda^*(0)}{dg}\right)_T > 0;$
$c(0)$	$\dfrac{1}{U_{cc}}\left(\dfrac{d\lambda(0)}{dg}\right)_T < 0$	$\dfrac{1}{U_{cc}}\left(\dfrac{d\lambda(0)}{dg}\right)_{\tau_k}$	$\dfrac{1}{U_{cc}}\left(\dfrac{d\lambda(0)}{dg}\right)_{\tau_w}$
$c^*(0)$	$\dfrac{1}{U_{cc}}\left(\dfrac{d\lambda^*(0)}{dg}\right)_T < 0$	$\dfrac{1}{U_{cc}}\left(\dfrac{d\lambda^*(0)}{dg}\right)_{\tau_k}$	$\dfrac{1}{U_{cc}}\left(\dfrac{d\lambda^*(0)}{dg}\right)_{\tau_w}$
$l(0)$	$\dfrac{\phi_2}{F_{kl}}\left(\dfrac{d\lambda(0)}{dg}\right)_T + \dfrac{\phi_2\tilde{\lambda}}{F_1}\left(\dfrac{dk_0}{dg}\right)_T > 0$	$\dfrac{\phi_2}{F_{kl}}\left(\dfrac{d\lambda(0)}{dg}\right)_i + \dfrac{\phi_2\tilde{\lambda}}{F_1}\left(\dfrac{dk_0^*}{dg}\right)_i$	$\dfrac{\phi_2}{F_{kl}}\left(\dfrac{d\lambda(0)}{dg}\right)_{\tau_w} + \dfrac{\phi_2\tilde{\lambda}}{F_1}\left(\dfrac{dk_0}{dg}\right)_{\tau_w} + \dfrac{\phi_2\tilde{\lambda}}{lF_l F_{kl}}$
$l^*(0)$		$\dfrac{\phi_2}{F_{kl}}\left(\dfrac{d\lambda^*(0)}{dg}\right)_i + \dfrac{\phi_2\tilde{\lambda}}{F_1}\left(\dfrac{dk_0}{dg}\right)_i$ $\quad i=T,\tau_k,\tau_w$	

	C. Transitional effects		
	Lump-sum tax T	Financed by Capital income tax τ_k	Wage income tax τ_w
$\tilde{k}-k_0$ $\tilde{k}^*-k_0^*$	$\dfrac{1}{2\psi} > 0$	$\dfrac{(1-\delta_k)}{2\psi} < 0$	$\dfrac{(1-\delta_w)}{2\psi}$
$\tilde{N}-N_0$	$\dfrac{\Omega}{2(\mu-\beta)\psi}$	$\dfrac{(1-\tau_k)\Omega}{2(\mu-\beta)\psi}$	$\dfrac{(1-\tau_w)\Omega}{2(\mu-\beta)\psi}$
$\tilde{\lambda}-\lambda(0)$ $\tilde{\lambda}^*-\lambda^*(0)$	$-\left(\dfrac{\tilde{\lambda}\phi_1}{\mu+\tilde{\lambda}\phi_2}\right)\dfrac{1}{2\psi} < 0$	$-\left(\dfrac{\tilde{\lambda}\phi_1}{\mu+\tilde{\lambda}\phi_2}\right)\dfrac{(1-\delta_k)}{2\psi} > 0$	$-\left(\dfrac{\tilde{\lambda}\phi_1}{\mu+\tilde{\lambda}\phi_2}\right)\dfrac{(1-\delta_w)}{2\psi}$
$\tilde{c}-c(0)$ $\tilde{c}^*-c^*(0)$	$-\left(\dfrac{\tilde{\lambda}\phi_1}{\mu+\tilde{\lambda}\phi_2}\right)\dfrac{1}{2U_{cc}\psi} > 0$	$-\left(\dfrac{\tilde{\lambda}\phi_1}{\mu+\tilde{\lambda}\phi_2}\right)\dfrac{(1-\delta_k)}{2U_{cc}\psi} < 0$	$-\left(\dfrac{\tilde{\lambda}\phi_1}{\mu+\tilde{\lambda}\phi_2}\right)\dfrac{(1-\delta_w)}{2U_{cc}\psi}$
$\tilde{l}-l(0)$ $\tilde{l}^*-l^*(0)$	$\dfrac{\tilde{\lambda}\phi_2[F_{lk}(\mu+\tilde{\lambda}\phi_2)-F_l\phi_1]}{F_l F_{kl}(\mu+\tilde{\lambda}\phi_2)2\psi}$	$\dfrac{\tilde{\lambda}\phi_2[F_{lk}(\mu+\tilde{\lambda}\phi_2)-F_l\phi_1]}{F_l F_{kl}(\mu+\tilde{\lambda}\phi_2)}\dfrac{(1-\delta_k)}{2\psi}$	$\dfrac{\tilde{\lambda}\phi_2[F_{lk}(\mu+\tilde{\lambda}\phi_2)-F_l\phi_1]}{F_l F_{kl}(\mu+\tilde{\lambda}\phi_2)}\dfrac{(1-\delta_w)}{2\psi}$

the various modes of financing requiring the budget to remain balanced across steady states, the corresponding changes in the tax rates (from zero in the case of the two distortionary taxes) under the three schemes being considered are as follows:

1. Lump-sum taxes; $dT = dg$
2. Taxes on capital income; $d\tau_k = dg/\tilde{k}\tilde{F}_k$
3. Taxes on wage income; $d\tau_w = dg/\tilde{l}\tilde{F}_l$.

Lump-sum tax financing ensures that the government budget remains balanced at all times during the transition. However, that is not the case with the other two tax schemes, since the income on which the distortionary tax is being levied during the transition does not correspond to the new steady-state level. In either case, we assume that any discrepancy in the expenditures and the revenues generated by the distortionary tax during the transition is financed by a (time-varying) lump-sum tax, thereby ensuring that the government budget remains in balance at all times.

Lump-Sum Tax Financing

The long-run, short-run, and transitional effects of an expansion in domestic government expenditure under the base case of lump-sum tax financing are summarized in the first column of the three parts of Table 6.2. We shall restrict ourselves to considering the effects of an increase in domestic government expenditure. By symmetry, the effects of an increase in foreign government expenditure on the domestic economy are similar and the effects of a worldwide increase in government expenditure can be readily obtained by aggregating the two country-specific effects. The intuition underlying these results can be understood most easily by discussing the case where $\Omega = 0$, so that the initial equilibrium is one in which both the trade account and the current account are in balance.

The initial effect of an increase in g financed by higher lump-sum taxes levied on domestic residents is to reduce the long-run permanent income. The fact that their long-run wealth is going to decline raises their initial marginal utility of wealth $\lambda(0)$, inducing them to increase their supply of labor and to reduce their consumption. The higher labor supply increases the productivity of domestic domiciled capital, inducing domestic investors to repatriate their capital and foreigners to invest in the domestic economy. In order for equilibrium in the capital market to prevail, the productivity of foreign domiciled capital must increase. In part, this occurs automatically through the initial outflow of the foreign capital stock, the reduced supply of which will raise the productivity of the capital that remains abroad. The fact that the tax increase associated with the higher government expenditure falls directly on domestic residents results in $\lambda(0)$ increasing more than $\lambda^*(0)$, so that $\bar{m}$ falls initially and remains constant throughout the transition.

With the world stock of capital fixed in the short run, the increase in k_0 is met by an equivalent reduction in k_0^*, that helps to restore the marginal productivity of foreign capital and maintain equilibrium in the capital market, without $\lambda^*(0)$ having to rise as much as $\lambda(0)$. The international movement of capital implies that the net foreign asset position of the domestic economy declines initially as a result of the initial exchange of assets. With identical individuals and $\Omega = 0$, there is no further accumulation of foreign assets during the transition.

The rise in the domestic marginal productivity of capital above its long-run equilibrium level causes capital to be accumulated until the capital:labor ratio is restored to its fixed long-run equilibrium level implied by (6.37a). Thus, in the domestic economy, the initial increase in the capital stock is accompanied by a further continuous increase as the new equilibrium is approached. In the foreign economy, the initial reduction in the capital stock is immediately offset by a continuing increase, in response to the higher rate of return to capital in that economy as well. Thus, the aggregate world capital stock rises over time as both countries accumulate capital, leading to a new steady-state equilibrium in which the world capital stock is increased. However, the capital stock abroad remains below its initial equilibrium (before the fiscal expansion), so that the long-run adjustment involves a reallocation of capital toward the domestic economy.

The initial increase in the domestic marginal utility of wealth, accompanied by the initial increase in domestic capital, induces an instantaneous increase in domestic employment. Over time, as capital is accumulated, the marginal utility of wealth declines. These two influences have offsetting effects on the supply of labor in the domestic economy. Under reasonable conditions, one can show that the wealth effect will dominate, and employment in the domestic economy will decline during the transition, though in the new long-run equilibrium it must increase in proportion to the domestic capital stock.[13] The initial response of the labor supply abroad is also ambiguous, though it will decline in the long run. Thus, during the transition, the capital stock and employment in both economies adjust in opposite directions over time, though in the long run, aggregate world employment rises in proportion to the rise in the aggregate world capital stock.

It is evident from this scenario that while the domestic fiscal expansion may stimulate the domestic economy, it has predominantly negative influences on activity abroad. Capital stock is always below its original level, and while it is possible for employment to rise in the short run, it too will decline overtime. This source of negative transmission occurs through the capital market and is very different from that discussed in the earlier literature by Branson and Rotemberg (1980), Corden and Turnovsky (1983), and others.[14]

What happens to consumption is of obvious importance. The initial increases in the marginal utility of wealth in the two economies, $\lambda(0)$ and $\lambda^*(0)$, cause initial reductions in consumption in the two economies as consumers substitute work for consumption. The greater increase in the marginal utility in the domestic economy implies a greater reduction of domestic consumption, which is a consequence of the crowding out generated by the additional domestic government expenditure. Over time, as capital is accumulated in both economies and the respective marginal utilities λ and λ^* decline, the consumption levels rise. While the new steady-state level of domestic consumption remains below its original level (crowded out by domestic government expenditure), the steady-state level of consumption abroad rises. However, this rise is dominated by the decline in domestic consumption, so that overall world consumption falls in the long run.

These effects are based on the assumption that $\Omega = 0$, so that the initial equilibrium is one in which both the trade account and the current account are in balance. In this circumstance, the fiscal shock generates a discrete initial *stock shift*, even though subsequent *net flows* are zero. The reason is that $\Omega = 0$ implies $dN = 0$, and hence $dk_d^* = dk_f$. Thus, as domestic capital varies, the cross hauling of assets allows for the efficient allocation of capital across countries. If $\Omega \neq 0$, then $dN \neq 0$ and the induced net flows offset some of the initial stock shift.

Suppose now that $\Omega < 0$, so that the domestic economy is a net exporter of capital in the initial equilibrium. Indeed, the initial equilibrium is one in which the domestic economy runs a trade deficit financed by positive earnings from capital abroad. In this case, both the expansionary effects in the domestic economy and the contractionary effects in the foreign economy, resulting from an increase in domestic government expenditure, are reduced. The reason for this is seen from (6.28a). As capital is accumulated by the domestic economy, foreign assets are accumulated, so that some of the domestic wealth is exported abroad. This is contractionary for the domestic economy and expansionary abroad, offsetting the effects we have been discussing. As long as (6.29) holds, these effects resulting from the induced capital flows are dominated by the adjustments described above, and the responses we have been discussing will continue to hold.

One final point worth observing is that the magnitudes of the transitional effects described in Table 6.2C are identical for the two economies. This is a consequence of the symmetry assumptions upon which this table is based. Under these conditions, the only difference in the responses of the two economies will result from the asymmetry of the initial shock (in this case an expenditure increase in the domestic economy) and the corresponding long-run adjustments that this induces.

Capital Income Tax Financing

This is described in Column 2 of Table 6.2. An increase in domestic government expenditure now has two components. The first is the direct expenditure effect, similar to that associated with lump-sum tax financing, which we have just been discussing. But, in addition, there is now an induced effect, resulting from the accompanying increase in the tax rate on capital, which is directly analogous to that discussed in Section 6.5 and generally offsets the direct expenditure effect.

From Table 6.2 it is seen that the net stimulative effect of an increase in government expenditure dg, financed by a tax on capital (starting with the initial tax on capital equal to zero), is

$$(1 - \delta_k) \, dg \equiv \left(1 - \left[\frac{F_l}{F_{kl}k} - \frac{1}{\phi_2 U_{cc}k}\right]\right) dg,$$

where the term in square brackets represents the total contractionary effect on the domestic economy. Letting $\sigma \equiv F_k F_l / F F_{kl}$ = elasticity of substitution; $s \equiv F_k k / F$ = share of output earned by capital; $\eta_c \equiv U_{cc} c / U_c < 0$ = elasticity of the marginal utility of consumption; $\eta_l \equiv U_{ll} l / U_l < 0$ = elasticity of the marginal utility of labor; and c/F = share of output devoted to consumption, we can establish

$$\delta_k \equiv \frac{\sigma}{s} - \frac{c/F}{(1-s)\eta_c} + \left(\frac{\eta_l}{\eta_c}\right) \frac{\sigma(c/F)}{s(1-s)}. \tag{6.38}$$

Under any plausible conditions (6.38) implies $\delta_k > 1$, so that the contractionary effect dominates. On the one hand, the lower permanent income resulting from the higher tax will raise the marginal utility of wealth, inducing more labor and raising the marginal product of domestic capital, as with the lump-sum tax. But the higher tax on capital induces firms to substitute labor for capital, and this tends to have the opposite effect. Indeed, (6.38) suggests that this latter effect will dominate, so that the long-run stock of domestic capital will fall under capital taxation. This will be so for the Cobb-Douglas production function ($\sigma = 1$); but it will hold under much weaker conditions as well. For example, it will still hold if $\sigma > s \approx 0.35$, and it may even hold if $\sigma = 0$ and the production function is one of fixed proportions. In our simulation, $\delta_k = 9.06$, well above unity, enabling us to maintain, for practical purposes, the assumption $\delta_k > 1$.

Assuming that the contractionary effects dominate, the adjustments described in the case of lump-sum tax financing are reversed. Thus, the net effect of an increase in domestic government expenditure is now an initial outflow of capital, leading to a contraction in the domestic capital stock and an expansion abroad. The accumulation of capital in the foreign country is mirrored by a long-run increase in employment abroad. The long-run response of employment in the domestic economy reflects two effects. While the reduction in capital will cause employment to fall, the substitution toward labor resulting from the higher tax on capital has a positive effect. On balance, the latter effect can be shown to dominate, so that overall, long-run employment in the domestic economy rises.[15]

The fact that the partial effect of a higher capital tax is contractionary is not surprising, but the fact that it is sufficiently large to dominate the expenditure effect, so that the overall effect of the increased government expenditure is negative, is rather striking. For example, a simulation yields impact and long-run multipliers on domestic output that are negative and greater than 1 in absolute value, the "supply-side multipliers" (see Baxter and King 1993).[16] This is a consequence of the burden imposed by distortionary capital income taxation on the accumulation of domestic capital, as measured by the parameter δ_k. The result stems, at least in part, from the assumption that the initial equilibrium is one of zero distortionary taxes, as a result of which the increase in capital taxes necessary to finance the additional expenditure is large. If instead the initial equilibrium was from one having preexisting distortionary taxes, the required marginal increase in the capital income tax rate would be smaller, because some of the additional revenues would be provided by higher activity at the initial rates. While this would likely reduce δ_k, it is still quite plausible that the contractionary effect would dominate, as Turnovsky (1992) showed for a closed economy.

Wage Income Tax Financing

This is reported in Column 3 of Table 6.2. As with capital taxation, government expenditure financed by a tax on labor income has a direct expenditure effect and an induced effect that operates through the accompanying increase in the tax rate on labor. This impinges on the economy through the labor supply decision, (6.2a'). An increase in the tax on wage income lowers the supply of labor, thereby reducing the marginal productivity of capital and generating a contractionary effect on the domestic economy.

From Table 6.2 it is seen that the net stimulative effect of an increase in government expenditure dg financed by a tax on wage income (starting with zero initial distortionary taxes) is

$$(1 - \delta_w) \, dg = \left(1 + \frac{\tilde{\lambda}}{U_{cc} F_l \tilde{l}}\right) dg,$$

where the second term represents the contractionary effect. This can be written as

$$\delta_w = -\frac{1}{\eta_c} \left(\frac{c/F}{1-s}\right). \tag{6.39}$$

In contrast to δ_k, there is much less presumption that $\delta_w > 1$ in an open economy. Assuming a logarithmic utility function, for example, and $s = 0.36$, in order for the contractionary effect to dominate, the ratio of consumption to output needs to be > 0.64, which need not necessarily hold. This contrasts with a closed economy, in which, since there is no trade in foreign assets, the condition $c/F = 1$ is automatically met in steady state, when capital accumulation ceases. Trade in foreign assets allows the country to be a net exporter of capital, and this may permit the economy to maintain the c/F ratio below 0.64. Thus, an increase in government expenditure financed by a wage tax may be either expansionary or contractionary from the standpoint of the domestic economy; for that reason we make no presumption about the likely signs of the expressions appearing in Column 3 of the Table 6.2.[17]

6.9 Welfare Effects

We now turn to analyzing the effects of government expenditure on the welfare of the representative agent in both the domestic and the foreign economies, as measured by their respective utility functions. We shall consider both the time path of instantaneous utility and the overall accumulated welfare over the agent's infinite planning horizon. We shall focus primarily on the case of expenditure financed by lump-sum taxation.

It suffices to spell out the details for the domestic economy. The instantaneous level of utility of the domestic representative agent at time t, $Z(t)$ say, is specified to be

$$Z(t) = U(c(t), l(t), g), \tag{6.40a}$$

where, it will be recalled, the utility function U is taken to be additively separable in its three arguments. Overall level of utility of the agent is thus

$$V = \int_0^\infty U(c, l, g) e^{-\beta t} dt = \int_0^\infty Z(t) e^{-\beta t} dt. \tag{6.40b}$$

The purpose is to consider the effects of government expenditure on both $Z(t)$ and V when c and l follow the equilibrium paths described by (6.34a) and (6.34b), and λ and k evolve along (6.27a) and (6.27b').

Differentiating (6.40a), the following impacts of an increase in domestic government expenditure on the time path of instantaneous welfare in the domestic economy can be derived:

$$\frac{dZ(0)}{dg} = U_g + U_c\left(\frac{dc(0)}{dg} - F_l\frac{dl(0)}{dg}\right) \tag{6.41a}$$

$$\dot{Z}(t) = U_c(\dot{c}(t) - F_l\dot{l}(t)) > 0 \tag{6.41b}$$

$$\frac{d\tilde{Z}}{dg} = U_g + U_c\left(\frac{d\tilde{c}}{dg} - F_l\frac{d\tilde{l}}{dg}\right). \tag{6.41c}$$

The initial reduction in consumption and increase in employment stemming from the increase in domestic government expenditure is welfare-reducing and offsets, at least in part, any direct benefits it yields. Over time, as consumption increases and employment falls (and leisure increases), welfare improves. Steady-state welfare (6.41c) is thus higher than initial short-run welfare (6.41a), though with steady-state consumption reduced and employment still below previous equilibrium levels, the changes in private behavior induced by the government expenditure lead to losses that need to be weighed against the direct benefits provided. The effects on the instantaneous welfare abroad are provided by analogous expressions, the only difference being that there is no direct impact effect corresponding to U_g.

A linear approximation to the overall level of domestic welfare, represented by (6.40b), is given by

$$V = \frac{\tilde{Z}}{\beta} + \frac{Z(0) - \tilde{Z}}{\beta - \mu}. \tag{6.31'}$$

Differentiating this expression with respect to g, after some algebraic manipulation, one can derive

$$\frac{dV}{dg} = \frac{U_g}{\beta} - \frac{U_c}{\beta}\left(1 - \frac{\beta}{2\psi}\left[1 + \frac{\Omega}{\mu - \beta}\right]\right) - \frac{U_c}{2\psi}, \tag{6.42a}$$

where $\psi(>\beta)$ is defined in Table 6.2. Written in this way, the response of the overall intertemporal measure of domestic welfare consists of three components. The first describes the positive marginal benefit of the additional government expenditure, which, being maintained indefinitely, is capitalized at the discount rate β. The second represents the steady-state losses resulting from (1) the private consumption being displaced by the

Table 6.3
Increase in domestic government expenditure

	Overall welfare effects		
Domestic economy		Foreign economy	World economy
$\dfrac{dW}{dg}$		$\dfrac{dW^*}{dg}$	$\dfrac{dW}{dg}+\dfrac{dW^*}{dg}$
	A. Financed by lump-sum tax		
$\dfrac{U_g}{\beta}-\dfrac{U_c}{\beta}\left(1-\left(\dfrac{\Omega}{\mu-\beta}\right)\dfrac{1}{2\psi}\right)$		$-\dfrac{U_c}{2\psi}\left(\dfrac{\Omega}{\mu-\beta}\right)$	$\dfrac{1}{\beta}(U_g-U_c)$
	B. Financed by capital income tax		
$\dfrac{U_g}{\beta}-\dfrac{(1-\delta_k)U_c}{\beta}\left(1-\left(\dfrac{\Omega}{\mu-\beta}\right)\dfrac{1}{2\phi}\right)-\delta_k\dfrac{U_c}{\beta}$		$-(1-\delta_k)\dfrac{U_c}{2\psi}\left(\dfrac{\Omega}{\mu-\beta}\right)$	$\dfrac{1}{\beta}(U_g-U_c)$
	C. Financed by wage income tax		
$\dfrac{U_g}{\beta}-\dfrac{(1-\delta_w)U_c}{\beta}\left(1-\left(\dfrac{\Omega}{\mu-\beta}\right)\dfrac{1}{2\psi}\right)-\delta_w\dfrac{U_c}{\beta}$		$-(1-\delta_w)\dfrac{U_c}{2\psi}\left(\dfrac{\Omega}{\mu-\beta}\right)$	$\dfrac{1}{\beta}(U_g-U_c)$

government expenditure and (2) the disutility resulting from the higher steady-state employment. The third term measures the discounted utility gains along the transitional path. These are subtracted because they are already contained in the second measure. The resulting expression is reported in Table 6.3.

The corresponding expression describing the effect on foreign welfare is given by

$$\frac{dV^*}{dg}=\frac{U_c}{2\psi}\left(1-\frac{\Omega}{\mu-\beta}\right)-\frac{U_c}{2\psi}, \qquad (6.42b)$$

which is similarly broken down into the steady-state effect, given by the first effect and the welfare along the transitional path. These are offsetting, and the net effect of an increase in domestic government expenditure on foreign welfare, reported in Table 6.3, depends simply upon $-(U_c/2\psi)(\Omega/(\mu-\beta))$. Ignoring this term, (6.42b) implies that the subsequent utility gains along the transitional path (as consumption and leisure increase abroad) exactly offset, in discounted utility terms, the losses incurred by the initial reduction in consumption and leisure.

The term $-(U_c/2\psi)(\Omega/(\mu-\beta))$ represents the transfer in welfare between the two economies that occurs as the net foreign asset position changes over time. Suppose that the equilibrium is one in which the domestic economy is a net supplier of capital, so that $\Omega<0$. As the domestic economy accumulates foreign assets over time, activity increases abroad, although, as we have seen, the reduction in leisure that it entails is welfare-deteriorating insofar as the foreign economy is concerned. The domestic economy thus confers a negative externality in terms of welfare on the foreign economy. We should acknowledge, however, that since this is a model of full employment, the negative externality (transmission) is associated with an expansion in foreign employment, and in this respect is fundamentally different from the negative transmission of the earlier models, which was associated with a decline in activity and employment.

Aggregating the welfare effects in the two economies, it is seen from Table 6.3 that the net effect of the domestic fiscal expansion on aggregate world welfare is simply

$$\frac{dV}{dg} + \frac{dV^*}{dg} = \frac{1}{\beta}(U_g - U_c). \tag{6.43}$$

Thus the net effect on world welfare is just equal to the capitalized difference of the direct utility of government expenditure and that of the private world consumption, which it is displacing.

Table 6.3 summarizes the expressions for welfare corresponding to all three forms of tax financing. We will not discuss these expressions in detail, other than to make two observations. The first is that the welfare spillovers in all cases depend upon Ω, though whether this confers a positive or a negative externality abroad depends upon the method of finance. Second, the aggregate effect on world welfare, reported in Column 3, is the same in all cases. This is a consequence of the fact that the initial equilibrium is one with no distortionary taxes. Starting from such an equilibrium, it is well known that the introduction of such a tax involves no welfare loss to the first order. It does, however, affect the intertemporal distribution of welfare gains along the welfare path, as well as the distribution of the gains internationally. These results are due to the fact that although the introduction of the tax affects incentives, being infinitesimally small its overall intertemporal welfare effects are negligible.

6.10 Conclusions

In this chapter we have developed our first two-country models and used them to address several issues pertaining to fiscal policy in an integrated world economy. One of the most basic issues concerns the viability of alternative tax regimes in such an environment, an issue that has attracted much attention in the literature. This has been shown to impose restrictions on the tax rates that the two authorities can set and still generate an interior equilibrium where the assets of both countries are held. These restrictions stem from a combination of (1) the long-run equality of after-tax rates of return and the rates of time preference and (2) the fact that the latter are taken to be fixed exogenously in the two economies. Since these conditions are both standard characteristics of intertemporal economics, this framework serves as a reasonable starting point.

However, it should be acknowledged that the combination of these two conditions could prove to be overly restrictive and that the conditions for long-run viability may be relaxed. There are several ways in which this may be accomplished. The first is to relax (2) through the introduction of variable discount rates. In this case the long-run rate of time preference becomes determined endogenously, rather than serving as a constraint. But the use of Uzawa preferences has its own problems, as we discussed in Chapter 2. Second, one can retain (2) but relax (1), by adopting the overlapping framework of Weil (1989). Alternatively, (1) can be relaxed in an equilibrium characterized by steady growth, as developed in Chapter 5. Finally, the introduction of risk in an intertemporal framework weakens the arbitrage conditions, thereby further relaxing (1). This aspect will be discussed in Part III.

Assuming that the tax regime is viable, we have gone on to analyze the transmission of tax shocks themselves, as well as government expenditure shocks financed under alternative forms of taxation. The general message to emerge from our analysis is that the form of financing dramatically alters the quantitative and qualitative characteristics of both the domestic impact of government expenditure and its transmission abroad. One of the appealing features of our analysis is the simple characterization of the alternative forms of financing in terms of the multiplicative tax factor $(1 - \delta_i, i = c, w)$, thus facilitating the comparison between them.

Although the results have been discussed at length, the following specific conclusions merit highlighting.

1. An expansion in government expenditure financed by a lump-sum tax has positive effects on employment and production in the domestic economy, and corresponding negative impacts abroad.

2. In the case where the government finances its expenditures through a tax on capital, these effects are almost certainly reversed; it has a contractionary effect on domestic activity and an expansionary effect abroad.

3. The case where the expenditure is financed by a tax on labor income is an intermediate one. While it also tends to have the opposite qualitative effects on the two economies, it is equally plausible for it to expand the domestic economy while having a negative impact abroad, or vice versa.

4. The impact of an expansion in domestic government expenditure on foreign welfare operates through the transfer of foreign assets over time, as the capital stock in the domestic economy changes in response to this fiscal shock. Negative transmission of activity does not necessarily mean

a decline in foreign welfare. Whether the domestic economy confers a positive or a negative externality in terms of welfare in the foreign country depends upon whether the domestic economy is a net supplier of capital and the mode of expenditure financing.

Several extensions of this basic model suggest themselves, and some of them are taken up in the next two chapters. Most important, the fact that government expenditure in one country generates externalities abroad raises the possibility of strategic behavior by the two governments vis-à-vis their respective expenditure policies. This issue, which has been analyzed by a number of authors in a range of contexts, will be taken up in Chapter 8, after we have extended the basic model to allow an enhanced role for relative price adjustments in the international transmission process.

Notes

1. In general, this assumption implies an international redistribution of tax revenues. An alternative assumption, which is almost identical, is to assume that tax revenues are rebated to the residents of the country that levied the original taxes.

2. See also Gordon (1986) for a discussion of this issue for a small open economy.

3. This may be easier to achieve when one of the countries is smaller and willing to adapt its tax policy to that of its larger trading partner, along the lines discussed by Feldstein and Hartman (1979). Turnovsky and Bianconi (1992) consider a model in which there is an explicit corporate sector and discuss how, given differential tax rates on dividends and capital gains, coordination of tax policy also requires coordination of dividend policy.

4. Note that in this model the distribution of consumption is endogenously obtained by explicitly taking into account the initial capital stocks and net asset position that satisfy the transversality condition (6.3e).

5. In the discussion of the transmission of the tax shock, we shall assume identical technologies, identical tastes, and identical tax structures—$a_{11} = F_k$, $a_{12} = -c_\lambda$—and the characteristic equation associated with (6.26) simplifies to $\mu^2 - F_k\mu + c_\lambda\tilde{\theta}_k = 0$.

6. Under these conditions, the trade balance effect is precisely the characteristic equation of the dynamic system: $F_k - \mu + c_\lambda\tilde{\theta}_k/\mu = 0$.

7. This is because long-run aggregate consumption and wealth depend upon production conditions alone, which in the steady state are unaffected by temporary tax changes. Temporary tax changes will have a permanent effect on capital stock, and therefore on aggregate world consumption, if labor is endogenous, as it is in sections 6.6–6.9.

8. This can be seen as follows for the logarithmic utility function, $\ln c$:

$$U_c/U_{cc} + \beta\tilde{N} = -\tilde{c} + \beta\tilde{N} = -F(\tilde{k}) < 0.$$

Thus, from Table 6.1 we see that initial consumption in the domestic economy increases; that is $c(0) > 0$. Likewise, for the identical foreign economy

$$U_c/U_{cc} - \beta\tilde{N} = -\tilde{c}^* - \beta\tilde{N} = -F^*(\tilde{k}^*) < 0,$$

implying that $c^*(0) > 0$ as well.

9. Turnovsky (1992) makes a slightly different assumption in that he assumes that the distortionary tax rate itself varies along the transitional path in order to maintain continuous budget balance. By contrast, Lipton and Sachs (1983) assume that it is government expenditure that adjusts.

10. Bianconi and Turnovsky (1997) supplement their formal analysis of this model with numerical simulations. They begin by parameterizing the model and solving it numerically under the assumption that both countries have identical preferences and production functions. Preferences are represented by $U = \ln c + \ln(1-l) + v[g - (1/2)g^2]$, with $v = 0.7$ (see Aschauer 1985). The rate of time preference, $\beta = 0.05$, implies a steady-state real interest rate of 5%. Production is Cobb-Douglas, $y = k^s l^{1-s}$, where $s = 0.36$. The only asymmetry is in the initial size of the government, where they assume $g = 0.15$, $g^* = 0.05$, as a result of which the domestic economy is a net exporter of capital in the initial equilibrium.

The procedure they follow is to evaluate a steady-state equilibrium and determine the quantitative magnitudes of the changes by computing the derivatives at this initial point. Lipton and Sachs (1983) follow a different strategy based on the "multiple shooting" approach proposed by Lipton, Poterba, Sachs, and Summers (1982).

11. μ is the negative root to the characteristic equation of the dynamic system (6.36) and is given by

$$\mu = \frac{\{(a_{11} - \tilde{\lambda}\phi_2) - \sqrt{(\tilde{\lambda}\phi_2 - a_{11})^2 - 4\tilde{\lambda}(a_{12}\phi_1 - a_{11}\phi_2)}\}}{2}.$$

Simulations based on the parameters in note 10 indicate a value of $\lambda = -0.0562$ with a half-life of about 5.4 periods (see, e.g., Barro and Sala-i-Martin 1992a). The stable locus defined in (6.27b′) will have a negative slope if and only if $\mu + \tilde{\lambda}\phi_2 < 0$. This can be shown to hold (at least as long as ϕ_2 and ϕ_2^* are not too different from one another) by considering the characteristic equation of (6.36). In our simulation, $\mu + \tilde{\lambda}\phi_2 = -0.0585$

12. The simulations suggest $(\Omega/(\mu - \beta)) \approx 0.04$, strongly supporting the restriction imposed in (6.29). Further support is provided by empirical evidence suggesting that the relationship between investment and the current account is weak (see, e.g., Feldstein and Horioka 1980). In any event, the restriction imposed in (6.29) has no influence on the stability properties of the model, since these are determined separately by the system (6.36).

13. A necessary and sufficient condition for employment to decrease uniformly during the transition is that $\sigma/s + (c/F)/\eta_c > 0$, where σ = elasticity of substitution in production; s = share of output earned by capital; c/F = share of output that is consumed; and η_c = the elasticity of the marginal utility of consumption. This condition is satisfied in the case of a Cobb-Douglas production function and a logarithmic utility function, as in our numerical simulations.

14. The impact and long-run multipliers of government expenditure on domestic and foreign output in our simulations are $dy(0)/dg|_{dT} = 0.4644$, $d\tilde{y}/dg|_{dT} = 0.5191$; $dy^*(0)/dg|_{dT} = -0.1012$, $d\tilde{y}^*/dg|_{dT} = -0.0464$. Thus, in this model, under plausible parameterization domestic government expenditure multipliers under lump-sum tax financing are well below unity. The negative transmission effects abroad are also implicit in the paper by Backus, Kehoe, and Kydland (1994a), where the model is along the same lines as the one being presented here.

15. The simulations support this assertion because the capital income tax necessary to finance the additional government expenditure is about 33.5%. This reduces the domestic capital stock by a little less than half, and since the elasticity of substitution of capital and labor is unity, the substitution effect clearly dominates.

16. Specifically, our simulations yields impact and long-run multipliers on domestic and foreign output: $dy(0)/dg|_{d\tau_k} = -1.0423$; $d\tilde{y}/dg|_{d\tau_k} = -1.7729$; $dy^*(0)/dg|_{d\tau_k} = 0.7425$; $d\tilde{y}^*/dg|_{d\tau_k} = 0.3746$.

17. In our simulations $c/F > 0.92$, implying $\delta_w = 1.37 > 1$. The impact and long-run government expenditure multipliers are $dy(0)/dg|_{d\tau_w} = -0.2036$; $d\tilde{y}(0)/dg|_{d\tau_w} = -0.2268$; $dy^*(0)/dg|_{d\tau_w} = 0.0435$; $d\tilde{y}^*/dg|_{d\tau_w} = 0.0203$. While the domestic multipliers are negative, they are well below unity, reflecting the fact that the distortionary effect of the wage income tax is moderate relative to that of the capital income tax.

7 Relative Price Adjustments in Two-Country Models

An important channel through which the international transmission of shocks takes place in a two country world economy is the adjustment of relative prices. Three relative prices can be identified. The first is the *intertemporal relative price*, or the interest rate. According to this mechanism, one country has an excess demand for future goods and is a lender, while the other has an excess demand for current goods and is a borrower. The adjustment takes place through the accumulation of net claims of the lending country against the assets of the borrowing country; it was the process underlying our discussion in Chapter 6. It will be recalled that that analysis was based on a one-good world, with physical capital being free to move instantaneously between the two economies in response to an unanticipated shock and changing rates of return.

The assumption made in Chapter 6 that capital is instantaneously mobile internationally, though convenient, is not particularly realistic. It is more appealing to assume, as in Chapter 3, that capital accumulation involves adjustment costs, with the Tobin q measuring the price of installed capital relative to that of new output. Thus a second form of adjustment by which disturbances are transmitted internationally is the *relative price of installed capital*, q. In this case, an unanticipated shock to the world economy will be accommodated initially by an adjustment in the price of capital, q, rather than through an instantaneous shifting of capital between the economies. Capital, in the form of new investment, will respond only gradually as a result of the change in q.

A third form of price adjustment is introduced if, as in the latter part of Chapter 3, each economy is specialized in the production of a distinct good. Even in the absence of adjustment costs, an unanticipated shock will now be reflected in an adjustment in the *relative price of the two goods* (the real exchange rate), rather than in an instantaneous shifting of capital. Again, capital will accumulate only gradually, now in response to the change in the real exchange rate.

This chapter presents two models focusing on the second and third forms of relative price adjustment. There are relatively few analytical models formulating the dynamics in a two-country world, and no careful treatment of the Tobin q formulation in a two-country framework. Frenkel and Razin (1985) consider relative commodities prices in a two-country model of fiscal policy. Similarly, relative price movements are the central mechanism of the two-period, two-country analysis of tariffs by Gardner and Kimbrough (1990), though like Frenkel and Razin, they abstract from the accumulation of physical capital. The adjustment of relative goods prices is the critical factor in the analysis of strategic tax policy by Devereux (1991), to be discussed in Chapter 8. Backus, Kehoe, and Kydland (1994b) provide a brief treatment of capital accumulation in two-country models in their discussion of relative price movements. Stockman and Tesar (1995) use a simple two-sector, two-country model to explain the comovements among key variables in a real business cycle setting.

7.1 Adjustment Costs in a Two-Country World

Our objective in this section is to bring out the role of adjustment costs in investment, so we shall keep the model as simple as possible in other dimensions. Specifically, we shall assume that labor is supplied inelastically at unity, and we shall abstract from the government. In other respects the model is analogous to that presented in Section 6.2, with the agent having access to the ownership of both domestic and foreign capital. In the absence of distortionary taxes, the perfect mobility of capital and the absence of risk ensure that the returns to capital around the world are equated. As before, variables pertaining to the domestic economy are unstarred, and the corresponding foreign variables are denoted by an asterisk.

Households

The representative household in the domestic economy is assumed to choose consumption, $c(t)$, and asset holdings so as to

$$\text{Max} \int_0^\infty U(c)e^{-\beta t}dt, \tag{7.1a}$$

subject to the wealth accumulation equation

$$\dot{a} = r(t)a + w(t) - c(t), \tag{7.1b}$$

where a denotes domestic wealth, $w(t)$ denotes the wage rate in the domestic economy, and $r(t)$ denotes the rate of return earned by domestic residents on their wealth, which, as in Section 6.2, may be held in the form of either domestic capital or foreign capital.

The domestic household's optimality conditions are

$$U_c(c) = \lambda \tag{7.2a}$$

$$r(t) = \beta - \frac{\dot{\lambda}}{\lambda}, \tag{7.2b}$$

where, as usual, λ is the shadow value of wealth, measured in terms of new output as numeraire. These equations are analogous to (6.2a) and (6.2d) and require no further discussion. In addition there is the transversality condition applicable to aggregate wealth:

$$\lim_{t \to \infty} \lambda a e^{-\beta t} = 0. \tag{7.2c}$$

The optimality conditions for foreign households are analogous:

$$U_c^*(c^*) = \lambda^* \tag{7.3a}$$

$$r^*(t) = \beta - \frac{\dot{\lambda}^*}{\lambda^*}, \tag{7.3b}$$

together with the corresponding transversality condition

$$\lim_{t \to \infty} \lambda^* a^* e^{-\beta t} = 0. \tag{7.3c}$$

In order for an interior equilibrium to obtain, the rate of time preference of foreign agents must equal that of domestic agents. In addition, the existence of a perfectly integrated world market for capital ensures that rates of return on capital are equalized around the world, so that

$$r(t) = r^*(t). \tag{7.4}$$

Firms

The domestic representative firm employs labor, l, and capital, k, to produce output by using a production function with the usual neoclassical properties of positive, but diminishing, marginal physical products and constant returns to scale. The accumulation of capital involves adjustment costs represented by the convex function $C(I)$, which has the properties set out in Section 3.2: $C(0) = 0$, $C'(0) = 1$. The firm's objective is to choose the rate of investment to

$$\text{Max} \int_0^\infty [F(k,l) - C(I) - wl] e^{-\int_0^t r(\tau)d\tau} dt, \tag{7.5a}$$

subject to the accumulation equation

$$\dot{k} = I. \tag{7.5b}$$

The optimality conditions are

$$C'(I) = q \tag{7.6a}$$

$$\frac{F_k(k,1)}{q} + \frac{\dot{q}}{q} = r(t), \tag{7.6b}$$

where q denotes the shadow price of capital in the domestic economy (the Tobin q), expressed in terms of the units of new output. For the choice of units in the adjustment cost function, zero investment is associated with a

Tobin q equal to unity. Equations (7.6a) and (7.6b) are identical to (3.4c) and (3.4d), with the real wage being set equal to the marginal physical product of labor that corresponds to its inelastically supplied quantity of unity; that is, w satisfies

$$F_l(k, 1) = w. \tag{7.6c}$$

Henceforth, the labor argument shall be suppressed from the production function.

The foreign firm is analogous, with the optimality conditions being

$$C^{*\prime}(I^*) = q^* \tag{7.7a}$$

$$\frac{F_k^*(k^*, 1)}{q^*} + \frac{\dot{q}^*}{q^*} = r^*(t), \tag{7.7b}$$

and the foreign wage w^* set by

$$F_l^*(k^*, 1) = w^*. \tag{7.7c}$$

Capital and Goods Market Equilibria

Capital market equilibrium requires that the rates of return on capital in the two economies must be equal, so that (7.4), in conjunction with (7.6b) and (7.7b), imply that

$$\frac{F_k^*(k^*)}{q^*} + \frac{\dot{q}^*}{q^*} = \frac{F_k(k)}{q} + \frac{\dot{q}}{q}. \tag{7.8a}$$

In a one-commodity world, goods market equilibrium is described by

$$F(k) + F^*(k^*) = c + c^* + C(I) + C^*(I^*). \tag{7.8b}$$

Accumulation of Net Foreign Assets

Analogous to Section 6.2, domestic wealth is expressed in the form

$$a = qk_d + q^*k_d^* = qk + q^*k_d^* - qk_f = qk + N, \tag{7.9}$$

where domestic and foreign capital are valued at their respective installed prices, q and q^*. The quantity qk is the value of capital domiciled domestically, of which qk_d is owned by domestic residents and qk_f is owned by foreign residents. Consequently, $N = q^*k_d^* - qk_f$ represents the net asset position of domestic residents. Foreign wealth can be expressed as

$$a^* = qk_f + q^*k_f^* = q^*k^* - q^*k_d^* + qk_f = q^*k^* - N, \tag{7.10}$$

so that aggregate world wealth is the value of capital

$$a + a^* = qk + q^*k^*. \tag{7.11}$$

Using the fact that $\dot{N} = \dot{a} - \dot{q}k - q\dot{k}$ and combining with (7.1b), we find that, analogous to (3.6), the rate of change of the net asset position of the domestic economy—its current account—can be written as

$$\dot{N} = rN + F - c - q\dot{k}. \tag{7.12}$$

The corresponding net asset position of the foreign economy is the mirror image of (7.12).

7.2 Macroeconomic Equilibrium

There are different ways to express the macroeconomic equilibrium and its dynamics. The most convenient is to express it in terms of four independently evolving variables: the two capital stocks, k and k^*; the marginal utility of wealth in one country, say the domestic, λ; and the relative price of capital in the two countries, $\theta \equiv q^*/q$.

To derive the equilibrium in this form, we proceed as follows. First, using (7.4) to equate (7.2b) and (7.3b), we find that, as in Chapter 6, the marginal utilities of wealth in the two economies are related by

$$\lambda^* = \bar{m}\lambda,$$

where $\bar{m}$ is constant, determined by steady-state equilibrium conditions. Using this relationship and the definition of θ, equations (7.2a), (7.3a), (7.6a), and (7.7a) can be solved in the form

$$c = c(\lambda); \quad c^* = c^*(\bar{m}\lambda) \quad c_\lambda < 0, c_\lambda^* < 0 \tag{7.13a}$$

$$I = I(q); \quad I^* = I^*(\theta q) \quad I_q > 0, I_q^* > 0 \tag{7.13b}$$

Substituting these expressions into the goods market clearing condition (7.8b),

$$F(k) + F^*(k^*) = c(\lambda) + c^*(\bar{m}\lambda) + C[I(q)] + C^*[I^*(\theta q)],$$

which determines the price of capital in the domestic economy in terms of the stocks of capital in the two economies, the marginal utilities of wealth, and θ:

$$q = q(k, k^*\lambda, \theta; \bar{m}), \quad q_k > 0, q_{k^*} > 0, \quad q_\lambda > 0, \quad q_\theta < 0. \tag{7.14}$$

An increase in the stock of either domestic capital or foreign capital raises world output, and for given consumption levels, this will require an increase in q in order to stimulate investment and thereby maintain product market equilibrium. An increase in the marginal utility of wealth lowers consumption, and for given capital stocks and output levels, this also requires an increase in q in order for product market equilibrium to continue. Finally, an increase in θ raises foreign investment and must be offset by a reduction in q in order for (7.8b) to hold.

The dynamics of the system are obtained as follows. First, substituting (7.14) into both (7.5b) and the analogous condition abroad yields

$$\dot{k} = I[q(k, k^*, \lambda, \theta; \bar{m})] \tag{7.15a}$$

$$\dot{k}^* = I^*[\theta q(k, k^*, \lambda, \theta; \bar{m})]. \tag{7.15b}$$

Next, differentiating θ with respect to t yields $\dot{\theta}/\theta = \dot{q}^*/q^* - \dot{q}/q$. Combining this with (7.8a), the definition of θ, and (7.14) implies

$$\dot{\theta} = \frac{1}{q(k, k^*, \lambda, \theta; \bar{m})}[\theta F_k(k) - F_k^*(k^*)]. \tag{7.15c}$$

Third, taking (7.2b) together with (7.6b), we obtain

$$\frac{\dot{\lambda}}{\lambda} = \beta - \frac{F_k(k)}{q(k, k^*, \lambda, \theta; \bar{m})} - \frac{\dot{q}}{q(k, k^*, \lambda, \theta; \bar{m})}. \tag{7.15d}$$

Fourth, differentiating (7.14) with respect to time leads to

$$\dot{q} = q_k \dot{k} + q_{k^*} \dot{k}^* + q_\theta \dot{\theta} + q_\lambda \dot{\lambda}. \tag{7.15e}$$

Finally, substituting (7.15a)–(7.15c) and (7.15e) into (7.15d), we obtain

$$\dot{\lambda} = \left(\frac{\lambda}{1 + \lambda q_\lambda/q}\right)\left[\beta - \frac{F_k(k)}{q} - \frac{q_k}{q}I - \frac{q_{k^*}}{q}I^* - \frac{q_\theta}{q^2}[\theta F_k(k) - F_k^*(k^*)]\right]. \tag{7.15d'}$$

Equations (7.15a), (7.15b), (7.15c), and (7.15d') comprise an autonomous system of four equations in the four variables k, k^*, θ, and λ.

The linearized dynamic system determining the evolution of the world economy is of the generic form

$$\begin{pmatrix} \dot{k} \\ \dot{k}^* \\ \dot{\theta} \\ \dot{\lambda} \end{pmatrix} = \begin{pmatrix} a_{11} & a_{12} & a_{13} & a_{14} \\ a_{21} & a_{22} & a_{23} & a_{24} \\ a_{31} & a_{32} & a_{33} & a_{34} \\ a_{41} & a_{42} & a_{43} & a_{44} \end{pmatrix} \begin{pmatrix} k - \tilde{k} \\ k^* - \tilde{k}^* \\ \theta - \tilde{\theta} \\ \lambda - \tilde{\lambda} \end{pmatrix}, \tag{7.16}$$

where the elements of the matrix $A \equiv (a_{ij})$ are obtained by taking appropriate partial derivatives of (7.15a)–(7.15c) and (7.15d'). In order for this system to have a unique stable adjustment in these variables, it must have two stable and two unstable eigenvalues, with the two capital stocks, k and k^*, evolving gradually and the shadow prices, θ and λ, jumping instantaneously to ensure that the economy is on the stable path.

Assuming that the system has this property, and denoting the two stable roots by $\mu_1 < 0$ and $\mu_2 < 0$, the stable solution is of the form

$$k(t) - \tilde{k} = B_1 e^{\mu_1 t} + B_2 e^{\mu_2 t} \tag{7.17a}$$

$$k^*(t) - \tilde{k}^* = B_1 v_{21} e^{\mu_1 t} + B_2 v_{22} e^{\mu_2 t} \tag{7.17b}$$

$$\theta(t) - \tilde{\theta} = B_1 v_{31} e^{\mu_1 t} + B_2 v_{32} e^{\mu_2 t} \tag{7.17c}$$

$$\lambda(t) - \tilde{\lambda} = B_1 v_{41} e^{\mu_1 t} + B_2 v_{42} e^{\mu_2 t}, \tag{7.17d}$$

where B_1 and B_2 are arbitrary constants and the vector $(1 \; v_{2i} \; v_{3i} \; v_{4i})'$ $i = 1, 2$ (where the prime denotes vector transpose) is the normalized eigenvector associated with the stable eigenvalue, μ_i. That is, $(1 \; v_{2i} \; v_{3i} \; v_{4i})'$ satisfies

$$\begin{pmatrix} a_{11} - \mu_i & a_{12} & a_{13} & a_{14} \\ a_{21} & a_{22} - \mu_i & a_{23} & a_{24} \\ a_{31} & a_{32} & a_{33} - \mu_i & a_{34} \\ a_{41} & a_{42} & a_{43} & a_{44} - \mu_i \end{pmatrix} \begin{pmatrix} 1 \\ v_{2i} \\ v_{3i} \\ v_{4i} \end{pmatrix} = 0. \tag{7.18}$$

The arbitrary constants, B_1 and B_2, appearing in the solution (7.17), are obtained from initial conditions, specifically that the world economy starts out with given initial stocks of capital, k_0 and K_0^*. Setting $t = 0$ in (7.17a) and (7.17b) and letting $d\tilde{k} \equiv \tilde{k} - k_0$, $d\tilde{k}^* \equiv \tilde{k}^* - k_0^*$, denote the changes from the initial stationary point, the constants B_1 and B_2 are obtained by solving the pair of equations

$$B_1 + B_2 = -d\tilde{k}$$

$$v_{21} B_1 + v_{22} B_2 = -d\tilde{k}^*. \tag{7.19}$$

Once these constants have been determined, the complete solution for the equilibrium evolution has been obtained. It is the two-dimensional analog to the conventional one-dimensional saddlepath applied in previous chapters. Because there are now two sluggish variables, the equilibrium system follows a two-dimensional stable path determined by the evolution of the capital stocks, (7.17a) and (7.17b).

The slope of the transitional path in $k^* - k$ is obtained by calculating the time derivatives of (7.17a) and (7.17b):

$$\frac{dk^*(t)}{dk(t)} = \frac{B_1 v_{21} \mu_1 e^{\mu_1 t} + B_2 v_{22} \mu_2 e^{\mu_2 t}}{B_1 \mu_1 e^{\mu_1 t} + B_2 \mu_2 e^{\mu_2 t}}.$$

This equation indicates that the slope of the transitional trajectory in $k^* - k$ space changes over time. It begins in the direction

$$\frac{dk^*(0)}{dk(0)} = \frac{B_1 v_{21} \mu_1 + B_2 v_{22} \mu_2}{B_1 \mu_1 + B_2 \mu_2}.$$

As $t \to \infty$, the path approaches the new equilibrium in the direction determined by

$$\frac{dk^*}{dk} \to v_{2i},$$

where v_{2i} corresponds to the larger of the stable eigenvalues $\mu_1 < 0$ and $\mu_2 < 0$ (see Calvo 1987). The initial endogenously determined values of the prices $\theta(0)$ and $\lambda(0)$ are obtained by substituting for the values of the arbitrary constants B_1 and B_2 from the solution to (7.19) into (7.17c) and (7.17d) at the initial time 0. The subsequent dynamics of these variables follows from these equations.

The accumulation of the net stock of foreign assets is obtained by substituting the stable solution for k and q into the current account relationship (7.12), solving this equation, and imposing the intertemporal national solvency condition, as in previous chapters. The resulting expression is also of the general form

$$\tilde{N} - N_0 = \Gamma_k(\tilde{k} - k_0) + \Gamma_{k^*}(\tilde{k}^* - k_0^*), \tag{7.20}$$

which is analogous to (6.30e), for example. Again, the difference is that the stable dynamics now depend upon the accumulation of domestic and foreign capital stocks, both of which are independent state variables of the stable transitional path. In general, the expressions Γ_k and Γ_{k^*} are rather complicated and we do not attempt to compute them, although that is not conceptually difficult to do. We may note that expressions analogous to (7.20) are obtained in the example of Section 7.3, where we allow for relative price effects rather than adjustment costs. We shall confine our discussion of current account dynamics to that case.

Steady-State Equilibrium

The steady-state equilibrium of this system is now obtained where $\dot{k} = \dot{k}^* = \dot{q} = \dot{q}^* = 0$. Given our choice of units, this implies the equilibrium price of capital $\tilde{q} = \tilde{q}^* = 1$; that is, $\tilde{\theta} = 1$. The remaining steady-state relationships are thus

$$F_k(\tilde{k}) = \beta = F_k^*(\tilde{k}^*) \tag{7.21a}$$

$$\beta\tilde{N} = c(\tilde{\lambda}) - F(\tilde{k}) = F^*(\tilde{k}^*) - c(\bar{m}\tilde{\lambda}) \tag{7.21b}$$

$$\tilde{N} - N_0 = \Gamma_k(\tilde{k} - k_0) + \Gamma_{k^*}(\tilde{k}^* - k_0^*). \tag{7.20}$$

The marginal productivity conditions determine the equilibrium stocks of capital, while the national solvency condition (7.20) determines the equilibrium net asset position of the two economies. Having determined $\tilde{k}$, $\tilde{k}^*$

and $\tilde{N}$, equations (7.21b) determine the long-run consumption levels in the two economies, and therefore their marginal utilities, $\tilde{\lambda}$, $\tilde{\lambda}^* = \bar{m}\tilde{\lambda}$.

Dynamic Response to Shock

The dynamics in response to a shock to the system operate as follows. Suppose the economy is initially in steady-state equilibrium and some disturbance to the system occurs. This will cause the steady-state equilibrium to respond so as to maintain the equilibrium relationships (7.20) and (7.21). Precisely how and what adjusts depends upon the nature of the shock. To the extent that it generates increases in the steady-state stocks of capital (either domestic or foreign), this will give rise to instantaneous jumps in q and θ, and thus in λ, in accordance with (7.17c) and (7.17d). These will then be transmitted to consumption and investment via the short-run equilibrium conditions (7.13a) and (7.13b). The fact that the fundamental dynamics are driven by two-state variables (domestic and foreign capital stocks) means that the stable dynamic path will be a two-dimensional version of that discussed in Chapter 3. This enriches the potential nature of the dynamic paths. For example, it now becomes possible for the two stable roots to be complex, in which case the transitional path will involve cyclical behavior.

7.3 A Two-Good, Two-Country World

The two-country model analyzed in Chapter 6 and the one outlined in Sections 7.1 and 7.2 both assume complete markets. That is, agents of both economies have direct access to the ownership of the physical capital in the other economy. This assumption is both polar and not particularly realistic. Even in a world of capital mobility, direct ownership of foreign assets may not be easy. Thus an alternative assumption is that agents, in addition to holding domestic capital, may hold traded bonds, through which they gain indirect ownership of foreign assets. This is a situation of incomplete markets; a similar kind of world economy is considered by Baxter and Crucini (1995).

In this section we discuss a two-country model in which both countries are specialized in the production of a single good, and in which agents in the two countries may consume two goods, the domestically produced good and an imported consumption good. In addition, the individual has access to a perfect world bond market, being able to borrow or lend as much as desired at a fixed interest rate, though in doing so he is constrained by his intertemporal solvency. In contrast to the small country model of Part I, the interest rate is now endogenously determined in the world bond market. The model is therefore a two-country extension of that presented in Chapter 3, where part of the adjustment now takes place through the relative price of foreign and domestic goods. To compensate for this extension to the model, we abstract from the adjustment costs associated with capital accumulation discussed in sections 7.1 and 7.2. Just as in the dependent economy model of Chapter 4, the adjustment of relative prices and the finiteness of the world economy ensure that nondegenerate dynamics exist, even in the absence of such adjustment costs. In many respects the model is similar to that of Section 7.1, with the relative price of the two outputs playing a role similar to that previously played by the relative price of installed capital. But since there is now only one such relative price, rather than the two relative prices of the two installed capital goods (domestic and foreign), the analysis turns out to be substantially simpler.

We will therefore explore the model in more detail and illustrate its dynamics more explicitly. The shock we shall consider is a change in a tariff, so in this respect our analysis will generalize the discussion of Section 3.5. The tariff is of particular interest because the international repercussions of tariffs is a subject with a long history. Most of the traditional analyses are static, but some work has been done in the context of simple two-period, two-country dynamic models (see, e.g., Gardner and Kimbrough 1990).

The Domestic and Foreign Economies

Since the tariff is a demand shock, for reasons discussed previously, the adjustment of labor supply is critical in order for it to give rise to nondegenerate dynamics. We therefore now endogenize labor supply as in Chapter 3, though we continue to assume that labor does not move internationally. Each country is specialized in the output of its own good, which it produces by means of a neoclassical production function using its labor and the capital domiciled in the economy. Domestic output is used in part for investment and in part for domestic consumption, x; the rest is exported for consumption abroad. The agent also consumes the quantity y of foreign output that it imports from abroad.

The domestic representative agent chooses his consumption levels, x and y; his labor supply, l; his rate of capital accumulation, $\dot{k}$; and his rate of accumulation of traded bonds, $\dot{n}$, so as to

$$\text{Max} \int_0^\infty U(x, y, l)e^{-\beta t}dt, \tag{7.22a}$$

subject to the accumulation equation

$$\dot{n} = F(k,l) - x - \dot{k} - \tau\sigma y + rn + T \qquad (7.22b)$$

and initial endowments

$$k(0) = k_0, n(0) = n_0, \qquad (7.22c)$$

where

- σ is the relative price of the foreign good in terms of the domestic good,
- n is the net stock of traded bonds (measured in terms of domestic output) held by the domestic agent,
- r is the real interest rate on the traded bond, measured in domestic units,
- τ is 1 plus the tariff rate,
- T is lump-sum transfers from the domestic government to its residents.

For simplicity, the utility function is assumed to be additively separable in its three arguments, x, y, and l, and the budget constraint is expressed in terms of the domestic good.

The domestic resident's optimality conditions are as follows:

$$U_x(x) = \lambda \qquad (7.23a)$$

$$U_y(y) = \lambda\sigma\tau \qquad (7.23b)$$

$$U_l(l) = -\lambda F_l(k,l) \qquad (7.24c)$$

$$r = \beta - \frac{\dot{\lambda}}{\lambda} \qquad (7.23d)$$

$$F_k(k,l) = r, \qquad (7.23e)$$

where λ is the marginal utility of wealth, expressed in terms of the domestic good. Equations (7.23a)–(7.23c) are virtually identical to (3.25a)–(3.25c), the only difference being the choice of numeraire and the separability in the two consumption goods. Equation (7.23d) is the analog to (7.2b), and in the absence of adjustment costs, (3.25e) and (3.26) reduce to (7.23e). The transversality conditions

$$\lim_{t\to\infty} \lambda n e^{-\beta t} = \lim_{t\to\infty} \lambda k e^{-\beta t} = 0 \qquad (7.23f)$$

are also standard.

We continue to abstract from the government, except to the extent that, as in the discussion of Section 3.5, its function is to collect tariff revenues from the public and to redistribute them in lump-sum fashion:

$$\sigma(\tau - 1)y = T. \qquad (7.24)$$

The foreign economy is analogous, with appropriate variables being denoted by asterisks. The optimization problem is

$$\text{Max} \int_0^\infty U^*(x^*, y^*, l^*) e^{-\beta t} dt, \qquad (7.22a')$$

subject to the accumulation equation, now expressed in terms of the foreign good,

$$\dot{n}^* = F^*(k^*, l^*) - \frac{\tau^* x^*}{\sigma} - \dot{k}^* - y^* + r^* n^* + T^*, \qquad (7.22b')$$

and initial endowments

$$k^*(0) = k_0^*, \quad n^*(0) = n_0^*. \qquad (7.22c')$$

The corresponding optimality conditions are

$$U_x^*(x^*) = \frac{\tau^* \lambda^*}{\sigma} \qquad (7.23a')$$

$$U_y^*(y^*) = \lambda^* \qquad (7.23b')$$

$$U_l^*(l^*) = -\lambda^* F_l^*(k^*, l^*) \qquad (7.23c')$$

$$r^* = \beta - \frac{\dot{\lambda}^*}{\lambda^*} \qquad (7.23d')$$

$$F_k^*(k^*, l^*) = r^*, \qquad (7.23e')$$

where the only differences from the domestic resident reflect the assumption that the foreign economy is specialized in the production of the foreign good. Observe that the marginal utility abroad is expressed in terms of the foreign good.

The corresponding transversality conditions are

$$\lim_{t \to \infty} \lambda^* n^* e^{-\beta t} = \lim_{t \to \infty} \lambda^* k^* e^{-\beta t} = 0 \qquad (7.23f')$$

and are also standard. The foreign government is assumed to redistribute its tariff revenues to its residents in accordance with

$$(\tau^* - 1) x^* = \sigma T^*. \qquad (7.24')$$

Equilibrium in the World Economy

Combining the optimality conditions for the two economies with market-clearing conditions in the two output markets enables us to describe equilibrium in the world economy. First, with a perfect world bond market, uncovered interest parity implies that the domestic and foreign interest rates are related by

$$r = r^* + \frac{\dot{\sigma}}{\sigma}. \tag{7.25}$$

Combining (7.23d), (7.23d'), and (7.24), as in Chapter 6 and in Section 7.1, the marginal utilities are related by

$$\lambda^* \equiv \bar{m}\sigma\lambda, \tag{7.26}$$

which differs from the previous relationship because λ and λ^* are measured in terms of domestic and foreign goods, respectively. Using this relationship, equilibrium in the two-good world economy can then be represented by the following sets of conditions.

Domestic Economy

$$U_x(x) = \lambda \tag{7.27a}$$

$$U_y(y) = \frac{\tau\lambda^*}{\bar{m}} \tag{7.27b}$$

$$U_l(l) = -\lambda F_l(k, l) \tag{7.27c}$$

$$F_k(k, l) = r \tag{7.27d}$$

Foreign Economy

$$U_x^*(x^*) = \tau^*\lambda\bar{m} \tag{7.27a'}$$

$$U_y^*(y^*) = \lambda^* \tag{7.27b'}$$

$$U_l^*(l^*) = -\lambda^* F_l^*(k^*, l^*) \tag{7.27c'}$$

$$F_k^*(k^*, l^*) = r^*, \tag{7.27d'}$$

with the relative price satisfying

$$\sigma = \frac{\lambda^*}{\lambda\bar{m}}.$$

Dynamic Equations

$$\dot{\lambda} = \lambda[\beta - r] \tag{7.28a}$$

$$\dot{k} = F(k, l) - x - x^* \tag{7.28b}$$

$$\dot{\lambda}^* = \lambda^*[\beta - r^*] \tag{7.28c}$$

$$\dot{k}^* = F^*(k^*, l^*) - y - y^* \tag{7.28d}$$

$$\dot{n} = x^* - \sigma y + rn \tag{7.28e}$$

Equations (7.27), (7.27'), (7.28a), and (7.28c) remain unchanged. Equation (7.28b) describes equilibrium in the domestic output market. The rate of accumulation of the domestic good as capital equals the excess of domestic production over domestic consumption, x, and exports, x^*. Equation (7.28d) is an analogous condition for the foreign goods market.

The final equation, (7.28e), describes the net accumulation of traded assets by the domestic economy, expressed in terms of units of domestic output. This equation is obtained by substituting the domestic government budget constraint, (7.24), and domestic goods market equilibrium, (7.28b), into the accumulation equation, (7.22b). The domestic economy's rate of accumulation of traded bonds is just equal to the trade balance, $x^* - \sigma y$, plus the interest earned on the traded asset. Equilibrium in the world bond market requires that the net stock of bonds, expressed in a common unit (e.g., the domestic good), must be zero:

$$n + \sigma n^* = 0, \tag{7.29}$$

from which it follows that

$$\dot{n} + \sigma \dot{n}^* + \dot{\sigma} n^* = 0. \tag{7.29'}$$

Combining (7.29) and (7.29') with (7.25), it is easy to show that one can express (7.28e) in the form

$$\dot{n}^* = y - x^*/\sigma + r^* n^*.$$

One can therefore choose to express the accumulation of traded bonds in terms of either the domestic good or the foreign good; they are equivalent.

The static equations (7.27) and (7.27') can be solved for consumption levels of the two goods in the two economies, foreign and domestic employment, and the domestic and foreign interest rates in the form

$$x = x(\lambda), x' < 0; \quad x^* = x^*(\tau^* \lambda \bar{m}), x^{*\prime} < 0 \tag{7.30a}$$

$$y = y\left(\frac{\tau \lambda^*}{\bar{m}}\right), y' < 0; \quad y^* = y^*(\lambda^*), y^{*\prime} < 0 \tag{7.30b}$$

$$l = l(\lambda, k), l_\lambda > 0, l_k > 0; \quad l^* = l^*(\lambda^*, k^*), l_\lambda^* > 0, l_k^* > 0 \tag{7.30c}$$

$$r = r(\lambda, k), r_\lambda > 0, r_k < 0; \quad r^* = r^*(\lambda^*, k^*), r_\lambda^* > 0, r_k^* < 0. \tag{7.30d}$$

An increase in the marginal utility of wealth measured in terms of domestic output will induce domestic workers to substitute labor for consumption, thereby reducing the consumption of the domestic good at home, increasing the marginal physical product of domestic capital, and driving up the domestic interest rate. It will also lower the relative price of foreign goods, thus reducing the amount of the domestic good consumed abroad. An interesting aspect of this short-run equilibrium is that the relative price, $\sigma = \lambda^*/(\lambda\bar{m})$, provides the mechanism whereby the domestic demand for foreign goods depends upon marginal utility abroad, and vice versa. Likewise, an increase in the domestic capital stock will raise the domestic real wage, again inducing domestic workers to increase their supply of labor. While this tends to raise the marginal product of capital, it is more than offset by the negative effect resulting from the higher capital stock; on balance, the marginal physical product of domestic capital, and therefore the domestic interest rate, decline. The effects of increases in the corresponding foreign variables, λ^* and k^*, are analogous.

7.4 Equilibrium Dynamics in the Two-Good, Two-Country World

Substituting (7.30) into the dynamic equations (7.28), the dynamics of the world economy can be represented by the system of equations

$$\dot{\lambda} = \lambda[\beta - r(\lambda, k)] \tag{7.31a}$$

$$\dot{k} = F[k, l(\lambda, k)] - x(\lambda) - x^*(\tau^*\lambda\bar{m}) \tag{7.31b}$$

$$\dot{\lambda}^* = \lambda^*[\beta - r^*(\lambda^*, k^*)] \tag{7.32a}$$

$$\dot{k}^* = F^*[k^*, l^*(\lambda^*, k^*)] - y\left(\frac{\tau\lambda^*}{\bar{m}}\right) - y^*(\lambda^*) \tag{7.32b}$$

$$\dot{n} = rn + x^*(\tau^*\lambda\bar{m}) - \frac{\lambda^*}{\lambda\bar{m}}y\left(\frac{\tau\lambda^*}{\bar{m}}\right). \tag{7.33}$$

The interesting feature of the dynamics is the decoupling of the intertemporal linkages between the two economies. Equations (7.31a) and (7.31b), for example, define a pair of dynamic equations in (λ, k), the marginal utility of wealth and the capital stock of the domestic economy, alone. Equations (7.32a) and (7.32b) define an analogous pair of equations for the foreign economy. The fact that the dynamics within each country is independent of the evolution within the other country means that the transmission of a shock from one country to another occurs solely through the induced jumps in the marginal utilities as reflected in $\bar{m}$. Once this has taken place, the dynamics are purely internally generated within the economy.

The separability of the dynamics is a consequence of the assumed additivity of the utility functions. If this assumption were dropped, the dynamics would become fully interdependent. For example, if the utility function of the domestic resident is nonseparable in just the two consumption goods, being of the form $U(x, y) + V(l)$, as assumed in Chapter 3, then the corresponding optimality conditions determine

$$x = x\left(\lambda, \frac{\tau\lambda^*}{m}\right); \quad y = y\left(\lambda, \frac{\tau\lambda^*}{m}\right),$$

which, when substituted into (7.32), clearly link the entire dynamic system. If, further, the utility function is nonseparable in labor supply, even more dynamic interdependence is introduced. In this case the equilibrium dynamics are of the generic form (7.18)–(7.20). One example where this would be so is if the utility function were of the constant elasticity form $U = (1/\gamma)(x^\theta y^{1-\theta})^\gamma$, which we have assumed elsewhere.

Linearizing (7.31a) and (7.31b) about their steady-state equilibrium values, these two equations may be represented by the following pair of linearized differential equations:

$$\begin{pmatrix} \dot{\lambda} \\ \dot{k} \end{pmatrix} = \begin{pmatrix} -\tilde{\lambda}r_\lambda & -\tilde{\lambda}r_k \\ F_l l_\lambda - x_\lambda - x_\lambda^* & F_k + F_l l_k \end{pmatrix} \begin{pmatrix} \lambda - \tilde{\lambda} \\ k - \tilde{k} \end{pmatrix}. \tag{7.34}$$

Evaluating the determinant appearing in (7.34), the dynamics can be seen to be a saddlepoint with the stable eigenvalue $\mu < 0$. As in previous models, while the capital stock always evolves continuously, the marginal utility may jump instantaneously in response to new information. Denoting the elements of the matrix appearing in (7.34) by b_{ij}, the stable locus evolving from the initial stock of capital, k_0, is described by

$$k(t) - \tilde{k} = (k_0 - \tilde{k})e^{\mu t} \tag{7.35a}$$

$$\lambda(t) - \tilde{\lambda} = \left(\frac{b_{12}}{\mu - b_{11}}\right)(k(t) - \tilde{k}) = \left(\frac{\mu - b_{22}}{b_{21}}\right)(k(t) - \tilde{k}), \tag{7.35b}$$

the latter yielding a negatively sloped saddlepath.

Analogously, λ^* and k^* are generated by

$$\begin{pmatrix} \dot{\lambda}^* \\ \dot{k}^* \end{pmatrix} = \begin{pmatrix} -\tilde{\lambda}^* r_\lambda^* & -\tilde{\lambda}^* r_k^* \\ F_l^* l_\lambda^* - y_\lambda^* - y_\lambda & F_k^* + F_l^* l_k^* \end{pmatrix} \begin{pmatrix} \lambda^* - \tilde{\lambda}^* \\ k^* - \tilde{k}^* \end{pmatrix}, \tag{7.34'}$$

with the stable saddlepath relating $\lambda^* - k^*$ also being negatively sloped:

$$k^*(t) - \tilde{k}^* = (k_0^* - \tilde{k}^*)e^{\mu^* t} \tag{7.35a'}$$

$$\lambda^*(t) - \tilde{\lambda}^* = \left(\frac{b_{12}^*}{\mu^* - b_{11}^*}\right)(k^*(t) - \tilde{k}^*)$$

$$= \left(\frac{\mu^* - b_{22}^*}{b_{21}^*}\right)(k^*(t) - \tilde{k}^*). \tag{7.35b'}$$

The dynamics of the current account are obtained by linearizing (7.33) around steady state to yield

$$\dot{n} = \beta(n - \tilde{n}) + \tilde{n}[r_\lambda(\lambda - \tilde{\lambda}) + r_k(k - \tilde{k})]$$

$$+ \left(\bar{m}\tau^* x^{*\prime} + \frac{\tilde{\lambda}^*}{\tilde{\lambda}^2 \bar{m}} y\right)(\lambda - \tilde{\lambda}) - \left(\frac{\tilde{\lambda}^* \tau}{\tilde{\lambda}\bar{m}^2} y' + \frac{1}{\tilde{\lambda}\bar{m}} y\right)(\lambda^* - \tilde{\lambda}^*).$$

From the domestic and foreign consumer optimality conditions and the definition of the relative price, we have the relationships

$$\frac{\partial x^*}{\partial \sigma} = -x^{*\prime} \frac{\tau^* \lambda^*}{\sigma^2} > 0, \quad \frac{\partial y}{\partial \sigma} = \tau y' \lambda < 0,$$

and imposing the steady-state conditions for (7.28) yields

$$\bar{m}\tau^* x^{*\prime} + \frac{\tilde{\lambda}^*}{\tilde{\lambda}^2 \bar{m}} y = \frac{x^*}{\tilde{\lambda}} \left(1 - \eta^* + \frac{\beta n}{x}\right),$$

where

$$\eta^* \equiv \frac{(\partial x^*/\partial \sigma)\sigma}{x^*} > 0$$

is the elasticity of foreign demand for the domestic good with respect to the relative price. Similarly, we may define

$$\frac{1}{\tilde{\lambda}\bar{m}} y + \frac{\tilde{\lambda}^* \tau}{\tilde{\lambda}\bar{m}^2} y' = \frac{\sigma y}{\tilde{\lambda}^*}(1 + \eta),$$

where

$$\eta \equiv \frac{(\partial y/\partial \sigma)\sigma}{y} < 0$$

is the elasticity of domestic demand for the foreign good with respect to the relative price.

Recalling the definitions of b_{11} and b_{12}, and using the fact that (7.35) and (7.35') hold along the stable adjustment path, the above expression for the current account can be expressed in the form

$$\dot{n} - \beta(n - \tilde{n}) = G_1\left(\frac{b_{12}}{\mu - b_{11}}\right)(k_0 - \tilde{k})e^{\mu t} - G_2\left(\frac{b_{12}^*}{\mu^* - b_{11}^*}\right)(k_0^* - \tilde{k}^*)e^{\mu^* t},$$

where

$$G_1 \equiv \frac{1}{\tilde{\lambda}}(x^*(1 - \eta^*) + (\beta - \mu)\tilde{n}),$$

$$G_2 \equiv \frac{\sigma y}{\tilde{\lambda}^*}(1 + \eta).$$

Assuming that the economy starts with an initial stock of traded bonds $n(0) = n_0$, the solution for $n(t)$ consistent with the intertemporal solvency of the domestic (and therefore the foreign) economy is

$$n(t) = \tilde{n} + G_1 \left(\frac{b_{12}}{\mu - b_{11}} \right) (k_0 - \tilde{k}) \frac{e^{\mu t}}{\mu - \beta}$$

$$- G_2 \left(\frac{b_{12}^*}{\mu^* - b_{11}^*} \right) (k_0^* - \tilde{k}^*) \frac{e^{\mu^* t}}{\mu^* - \beta}, \qquad (7.36a)$$

with the intertemporal budget constraint being

$$n_0 - \tilde{n} = G_1 \left(\frac{b_{12}}{\mu - b_{11}} \right) \frac{(k_0 - \tilde{k})}{\mu - \beta} - G_2 \left(\frac{b_{12}^*}{\mu^* - b_{11}^*} \right) \frac{(k_0^* - \tilde{k}^*)}{\mu^* - \beta}. \qquad (7.36b)$$

Equation (7.36b) specifies the relationship between the accumulation of bonds by the domestic economy and the accumulation of capital in the domestic and foreign economies. The direction of this relationship depends upon the price elasticities, η^* and η, incorporated in G_1 and G_2, respectively. This relationship is the two-country analog to (3.16) that has featured so prominently throughout earlier models. First consider domestic capital. If the domestic capital stock is increasing ($\dot{k} > 0$), it follows from (7.36a) that $\dot{n} \lessgtr 0$, according to whether $G_1 \lessgtr 0$; that is, whether $\eta^* \lessgtr \hat{\eta} \equiv 1 + (\beta - \mu)\tilde{n}/x^*$. Suppose that the domestic capital stock is initially k_0 and that some disturbance, say an expansion in government expenditure, increases its steady state to $\tilde{k} > k_0$. The capital stock starts to rise. At the same time this disturbance causes the marginal utility, λ, to increase immediately, implying, for given k^* and λ^*, a drop in the relative price, σ. This fall in σ has two offsetting effects on the current account. On the one hand, the value of exports, $x^*(\sigma)$, in terms of foreign goods rises. At the same time, the volume of exports declines. Which effect dominates and the net effect on the current account, and therefore on the rate of accumulation of traded bonds, depends upon whether the elasticity of demand $\eta^* \lessgtr \hat{\eta}$. The effect of foreign capital accumulation on n is analogous, though in this case the critical value of the relevant elasticity is unity. Note that the asymmetry in the critical values, G_1 and G_2, depends upon n being measured in terms of domestic units of output and the fact that if $\tilde{n} > 0$, the domestic economy is a net creditor If we choose to measure traded bonds in terms of foreign units of output, these expressions need to be modified appropriately. If the equilibrium is one with zero debt, then $\hat{\eta} = 1$.

The dynamics of the relative price are determined from (7.26), coupled with the subsequent adjustment in the relative marginal utilities. Specifically, the initial jump in the domestic and foreign marginal utilities, $\lambda(0)$

and $\lambda^*(0)$, obtained from (7.35b) and (7.35b'), respectively, at $t=0$, together with $\bar{m}$, determined from the steady state, will determine $\sigma(0)$. Thereafter, the relative price will evolve according to

$$\frac{\dot{\sigma}}{\sigma} = \frac{\dot{\lambda}}{\lambda} - \frac{\dot{\lambda}^*}{\lambda^*},$$

where the latter follow (7.35b) and (7.35b'). This change in the relative price determines the interest differential between the two economies, (7.25).

Steady-State Equilibrium

Steady-state equilibrium in the world economy is reached when all accumulation ceases; that is, when $\dot{k} = \dot{k}^* = \dot{n} = \dot{\lambda} = \dot{\lambda}^* = 0$, implying the following set of relationships:

$$F_k(\tilde{k}, \tilde{l}) = \tilde{r} = F_k^*(\tilde{k}^*, \tilde{l}^*) = \tilde{r}^* = \beta. \tag{7.37}$$

In the long run the returns to capital and interest rates are equalized at the exogenously given rate of time preference. It therefore follows that the capital:labor ratios in the two economies are fixed by β, as are the real wages. Thus, (7.37) enables us to express equilibrium employment in terms of the country's capital stock.

The steady state may be summarized by the following optimality conditions facing domestic and foreign residents.

Domestic Economy

$$U_x(\tilde{x}) = \tilde{\lambda} \tag{7.38a}$$

$$U_y(\tilde{y}) = \tau\tilde{\sigma}\tilde{\lambda} \tag{7.38b}$$

$$U_l(\tilde{k}, \beta) = -\tilde{\lambda}w(\beta) \tag{7.38c}$$

Foreign Economy

$$U_x^*(\tilde{x}^*) = \tau^*\tilde{\lambda}\bar{m} \tag{7.38a'}$$

$$U_y^*(\tilde{y}^*) = \tilde{\sigma}\bar{m}\tilde{\lambda} \tag{7.38b'}$$

$$U_l^*(\tilde{k}^*, \beta) = -\tilde{\sigma}\bar{m}\tilde{\lambda}w^*(\beta), \tag{7.38c'}$$

where $w(\beta)$ and $w^*(\beta)$ are the wage rates in the two economies, which in the long run are exogenously determined by the marginal physical product condition (7.37). In writing the marginal utility of labor condition, we have expressed the labor supply in terms of the capital stock, using the same condition.

Using these relationships, we can easily express equilibrium consumption levels, $\tilde{x}$, $\tilde{y}$, $\tilde{x}^*$, and $\tilde{y}^*$, in terms of equilibrium stocks of capital, $\tilde{k}$ and $\tilde{k}^*$:

$$\tilde{x} = x(\tilde{k}, \beta); \quad x_k < 0 \tag{7.39a}$$

$$\tilde{y} = y(\tilde{k}, \tilde{\sigma}, \tau, \beta); \quad y_k < 0, \; y_\sigma < 0, \; y_\tau < 0 \tag{7.39b}$$

$$\tilde{x}^* = x^*(\tilde{k}^*, \tilde{\sigma}, \tau^*, \beta); \quad x^*_{k^*} < 0, \; x^*_\sigma > 0, \; x^*_{\tau^*} < 0 \tag{7.39c}$$

$$\tilde{y}^* = y(\tilde{k}^*, \beta); \quad y_{k^*} < 0. \tag{7.39d}$$

An important element of these relationships is the negative relationship between long-run capital and long-run consumption, the intuition for which is as follows. An increase in the long-run stock of capital raises the productivity of labor, thereby raising the marginal utility of wealth and the inducement to work. Over time, workers choose to substitute work for consumption, which therefore declines.

To determine the equilibrium stocks of capital (and therefore employment), and the relative price, $\tilde{\sigma}$, we consider the steady-state versions of (7.32a), (7.32b), and (7.33). Substituting for $\tilde{x}$, $\tilde{y}$, $\tilde{x}^*$, and $\tilde{y}^*$, we obtain

$$f(\beta)\tilde{k} - x(\tilde{k}, \beta) - x^*(\tilde{k}^*, \tilde{\sigma}, \tau^*) = 0 \tag{7.40a}$$

$$f^*(\beta)\tilde{k}^* - y(\tilde{k}, \tilde{\sigma}, \tau, \beta) - y^*(\tilde{k}^*, \beta) = 0 \tag{7.40b}$$

$$x^*(\tilde{k}^*, \tilde{\sigma}, \tau^*, \beta) - \tilde{\sigma} y(\tilde{k}, \tilde{\sigma}, \tau, \beta) + \beta \tilde{n} = 0 \tag{7.40c}$$

$$\tilde{n} = n_0 - \Delta_1 (k_0 - \tilde{k}) + \Delta_2 (k_0^* - \tilde{k}^*), \tag{7.40d}$$

where

$$\Delta_1 \equiv G_1 \left(\frac{b_{12}}{\mu - b_{11}} \right) \frac{1}{\mu - \beta}; \quad \Delta_2 \equiv G_2 \left(\frac{b_{12}^*}{\mu^* - b_{11}^*} \right) \frac{1}{\mu^* - \beta}$$

$$f(\beta) = f(1/F_K^{-1}(\beta)); \quad f^*(\beta) = f^*(1/F_K^{*-1}(\beta)).$$

Equations (7.40a) and (7.40b) describe equilibrium in the domestic goods market and the foreign goods market, respectively. In the absence of capital accumulation, output must be consumed either domestically or abroad. Equation (7.40c) describes the long-run current account balance, expressed in terms of the domestic good. In steady-state equilibrium the domestic economy must run a net trade surplus or deficit equal to its net interest earnings or payments. Equation (7.40d) expresses the accumulated change in the traded bonds held by the domestic economy in terms of the accumulation of capital that takes place in the domestic and foreign economies; it restates (7.36b).

Table 7.1
Steady-state qualitative effects of increases in tariffs

Effect	τ	τ^*
$\tilde{k}/\tilde{l}$	0	0
$\tilde{k}$	−	$sgn(1+\eta)$
$\tilde{l}$	−	$sgn(1+\eta)$
$\tilde{x}$	+	$-sgn(1+\eta)$
$\tilde{y}$	$sgn(1-\eta^*)$	−
$\tilde{\lambda}$	−	$sgn(1+\eta)$
$\tilde{k}^*/\tilde{l}^*$	0	0
$\tilde{k}^*$	$sgn(1-\eta^*)$	−
$\tilde{l}^*$	$sgn(1-\eta^*)$	−
$\tilde{x}^*$	−	$sgn(1+\eta)$
$\tilde{y}^*$	$-sgn(1-\eta^*)$	+
$\tilde{\lambda}^*$	$sgn(1-\eta^*)$	−
$\tilde{\sigma}$	−	+
$\tilde{n}$	?	?

Equations (7.40a)–(7.40d) jointly determine the equilibrium levels of capital, traded bonds, and the relative price. Having determined these, the optimal consumption levels are derived from (7.39). The optimality conditions (7.38a) and (7.38a′) then determine the marginal utilities $\bar{\lambda}$ and $\bar{m}$. As in previous cases, the steady state depends upon initial conditions, reflecting the presence of the perfectly competitive traded bond market.

Increases in Tariffs

Table 7.1 summarizes the probable long-run qualitative effects of changes in the domestic and foreign tariff rates on the world equilibrium. These are obtained by taking the differentials of the equilibrium systems (7.39) and (7.40). For simplicity, these have been determined in the neighborhood of a balanced trade equilibrium in which $\tilde{n} = 0$. To some extent the results depend upon appropriate stability conditions being met. Among these, the most famous is the Marshall-Lerner condition, requiring that $|\eta| + \eta^* > 1$. Rather than dwelling on these technical details, we shall explain these results at a more intuitive level.

First, with the rate of time preference fixed, the marginal product conditions (7.37) imply that the long-run capital:labor ratios in both countries are independent of the two tariff rates, τ and τ^*. Capital and labor therefore change in the same proportions in the respective economies. We shall restrict our comments to the effects of a domestic tariff, with those of an increase in the foreign tariff being symmetric.

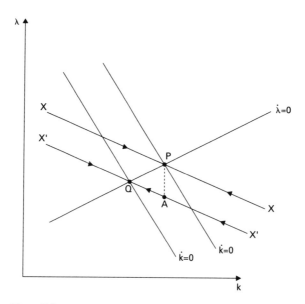

Figure 7.1
Increase in domestic tariff: dynamics of domestic economy

The direct effect of an increase in the domestic tariff rate is to raise the relative price of foreign goods to domestic residents, causing the domestic demand for imports to fall. This creates an incipient excess supply of foreign goods, thus generating a trade surplus for the domestic economy (trade deficit for the foreign economy). This trade surplus will tend to cause the relative price of domestic goods to rise; that is, $\tilde{\sigma}$ falls.

The net effect of the tariff and the rise in the relative price of domestic goods it generates is an overall contractionary one in the domestic economy, causing domestic employment, capital stock, and output to fall. By contrast, while the domestic protection yielded by the tariff is contractionary abroad, the increase in the relative price of domestic goods is expansionary. The net effect on foreign activity depends upon which effect dominates, and this depends upon the foreign price elasticity of demand, η^*, for the domestic good. If this elasticity is small (less than 1), the domestic tariff raises the marginal utility of foreign wealth measured in terms of foreign output. Foreigners substitute work for consumption, leading to an expansion in employment, capital, and output abroad. If the elasticity is large (greater than 1), the marginal utility of foreign wealth in terms of foreign goods declines. Foreigners substitute consumption for work, leading to an overall contractionary effect abroad.

The dynamic adjustments in the two-country world economy are illustrated in Figures 7.1 and 7.2. As already noted, the additive separability of

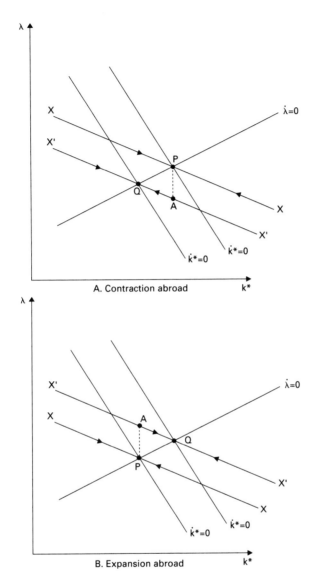

Figure 7.2
Increase in domestic tariff: dynamics of foreign economy

the utility function leads to a decoupling of the dynamics. The phase diagram for the domestic economy is illustrated in Figure 7.1. The economy begins in steady-state equilibrium at the point P on the original stable arm XX. The introduction of the tariff leads to an immediate reduction in the marginal utility, λ, causing the economy to jump from P to A on the new stable arm $X'X'$. This initial jump is associated with an increase in consumption together with a reduction in labor supply. The productivity of capital is thus reduced and the capital stock begins to decumulate. As the capital stock is reduced, the marginal utility of wealth increases, though only partially toward its original level, and is represented by the move AQ along $X'X'$. The dynamic response abroad depends critically upon whether the foreign elasticity of demand for domestic exports with respect to relative price is greater or less than unity. If it is relatively elastic (greater than 1), the contractionary effect of the tariff in the domestic economy will be mirrored abroad. If it is relatively inelastic (less than 1), the domestic tariff will have expansionary effects abroad. The adjustments in these two cases are illustrated in parts A and B of Figure 7.2.

Tariffs and the Balance of Trade

One of the traditional arguments supporting the introduction of a tariff was as a device to improve the balance of trade. Early supporters of this position included Robinson (1937) and Meade (1951). Central to the argument was the role of the relative price of importables to exportables and the associated within-period substitution in consumption this induced. Gardner and Kimbrough (1990) have developed a two-period, two-country model of a world economy that emphasizes the intertemporal elasticity of substitution. They show that in contrast to the conventional view, it is possible for both temporary and permanent tariffs to worsen the terms of trade of a large economy.

By focusing on the accumulation of capital, the present model is well suited for analyzing the intertemporal aspects of the adjustment of the trade balance in response to a tariff. Indeed, our analysis suggests that both the long-run and the short-run effects of a higher tariff on the trade balance are highly ambiguous, depending to a large degree upon the price elasticities of demand.

The long-run trade balance of the domestic economy, measured in terms of domestic output, is

$$\tilde{T} = \tilde{x}^* - \tilde{\sigma}\tilde{y} = -\beta\tilde{n}.$$

The effect of a higher tariff is thus given by

$$\frac{d\tilde{T}}{d\tau} = -\beta \frac{d\tilde{n}}{d\tau};$$

combining with (7.36b), we obtain

$$\frac{d\tilde{T}}{d\tau} = -\beta \frac{d\tilde{n}}{d\tau} = -\beta G_1 \left(\frac{b_{12}}{\mu - b_{11}}\right)\left(\frac{1}{\mu - \beta}\right)\frac{d\tilde{k}}{d\tau}$$
$$+ \beta G_2 \left(\frac{b_{12}^*}{\mu^* - b_{11}^*}\right)\left(\frac{1}{\mu^* - \beta}\right)\frac{d\tilde{k}^*}{d\tau}. \qquad (7.41)$$

The qualitative effect of a tariff on the long-run trade balance can be determined by noting the definitions of G_1 and G_2 and the effects summarized in Table 7.1. These depend critically upon the two price elasticities, η and η^*. For example, starting from a situation of balanced trade, we find that if $1 + \eta > 0$, then $sgn(d\tilde{T}/d\tau) = sgn(1 - \eta^*)$.

The short-run trade balance, measured in terms of domestic output, is

$$T = x^*(\tau^*\lambda\bar{m}) - \frac{\lambda^*}{\lambda\bar{m}} y\left(\frac{\tau\lambda^*}{\bar{m}}\right).$$

The short-run effect of the tariff is obtained by taking the differential of this expression and taking account of the jumps in the $\lambda(0)$ and $\lambda^*(0)$, $\bar{m}$. These, too, are dependent upon the price elasticities of import demand.

The Role of Relative Prices

A key element of these adjustments in response to a tariff, and in particular their transmission abroad, is the elasticity of demand for imports with respect to the relative price. This is so because the immediate effect of a country imposing a tariff is to improve its terms of trade, raising the price of imports abroad and decreasing foreigners' demand for domestic exports. To the extent that this response is large, it will dominate the expansionary effect of the tariff and the net effect on the foreign economy is contractionary. If the elasticity is relatively small, the direct expansionary effect will prevail and there will be an expansion abroad.

The role of the relative price adjustment can be shown to be important with respect to other sources of shocks. For example, it is straightforward to introduce government expenditures on both domestic goods and imports into the long-run equilibrium (7.40) and to analyze their effects on both the domestic and the foreign economies. Not surprisingly, one can show that an increase in the domestic government purchases of the domestic good raises the relative price of the domestic good, while a purchase of imports lowers this relative price. The transmission of this disturbance abroad then depends upon the elasticity of foreign import demand with respect to this induced change in the relative price. As a result, if this elasticity is small, an increase in domestic government expenditure on the domestic good will have an expansionary effect abroad, while an increase in government imports will generate a contraction in the foreign economy. These transmission effects are reversed if the relative price elasticity is large.

8 Strategic Behavior in the World Economy

8.1 Strategic Behavior in International Economics: Some Background

Once one allows government policy in one country to have spillovers abroad, the potential for strategic behavior on the part of policy makers arises. This has long been recognized in various contexts in international economics. Over half a century ago Joan Robinson (1937) introduced the notion of "beggar-thy-neighbor" policies as games played between nations, each one trying to increase employment at the expense of the others. A policy directed at increasing a country's employment by improving its trade balance deteriorates the trade balance of its trading partner, causing a contraction abroad. Robinson identified several ways that such improvements in the trade balance might be achieved: exchange depreciation, reductions in wages, subsidies to exports, and restrictions on imports by means of tariffs and quotas. Robinson recognized the role of strategic behavior and the potential for retaliatory actions by trading partners in response to adverse actions.

Of the four types of policies identified by Robinson, tariffs have received the most attention, leading to an extensive literature on optimal tariff policy and on commercial policy in general. The fact that an economy large enough to be able influence its terms of trade can exploit its monopoly power to the maximum by an appropriate choice of the tariff has been widely recognized. The notion of the optimum tariff was first introduced by Scitovsky (1942), and later by Johnson (1953). More recently it has been studied from a more formal game theoretic point of view by many authors, including Eaton and Grossman (1986), Jensen and Thursby (1990), Riezman (1991), and Young (1991). A comprehensive review of this literature is provided by Wong (1995, Chapter 12). Almost all this literature is set within the context of traditional pure trade models rather than within an intertemporal macroeconomic framework.

But macroeconomic policies also give rise to international spillovers, and two other areas where these spillovers have been extensively discussed should be mentioned. The first is in the area of the coordination of monetary policy and the choice of exchange rate regime. From early discussions of fixed versus flexible exchange rates, economists have recognized the externalities that monetary regimes impose, raising the question of the strategic aspects of monetary policy (see, e.g., Hamada 1974, 1976). This led to an extensive literature in the 1980s (see, e.g., Buiter and Marston 1985; and Canzoneri and Henderson 1991). Since this literature is not based on the intertemporal optimizing representative agent framework that is the central theme of this volume, we do not discuss it further. But it is important, and almost surely will become more so, as financial arrangements in Europe and other currency blocs evolve.

The second area of macroeconomic policy where the strategic aspects have received attention is that of fiscal policy. This approach is typically based on intertemporal utility maximization (though sometimes over only one or two periods), and is therefore close in spirit to the methods we have been developing. Like tariffs, fiscal instruments can generate relative price effects—either intertemporal or atemporal—giving rise to spillovers abroad, which the policy maker in each country may seek to exploit to his advantage. Early work by Hamada (1966) and Feldstein and Hartman (1979) examined strategic tax policy in simple static models of foreign investment. Turnovsky (1988) examines strategic government (consumption) expenditure in a static two-commodity real trade model, and Devereux (1991) has carried out the same type of analysis using a dynamic model, which with logarithmic utility preserves many of the properties of the static analysis. Both of these authors assume lump-sum taxation. Also, Hamada (1986) considers optimal strategic expenditure policy in a two-period, single-commodity framework. Kehoe (1987) and Chari and Kehoe (1990) examine the divergence between cooperative and noncooperative fiscal policies as the number of economies in the world increases. Ghosh (1991) addresses the same issue in an overlapping generations model in which taxes are distortionary. Buiter and Kletzer (1991) investigate the gains from cooperation in an overlapping generations model in which taxes are nondistortionary. Finally, Levine and Brociner (1994) apply dynamic game theory to the problem of fiscal policy coordination within the Economic Monetary Union.

This chapter discusses some of these strategic aspects of policy making in a two-country world, using basic methods of game theory. We shall restrict ourselves to fiscal policy making, beginning with the one-good model developed in Chapter 6. In focusing on the spillovers generated by fiscal policy and the strategic behavior to which they potentially give rise, it is important to realize that different types of government expenditure generate different types of externalities, both domestically and abroad, giving rise to different strategic actions. The discussion of government expenditure policy in Chapter 6 was restricted to government *consumption* expenditure and its effects under alternative modes of financing. It is important to realize that government expenditure directed toward productive activity—government *production* expenditure—has very different impacts, both at home and abroad. This is because it is a supply shock, akin to a subsidy to capital, rather than a demand shock. Thus, before conducting any strategic analysis of government expenditure policy, Section 8.2 begins by contrasting the effects of these two types of government expenditure policy, doing so under two forms of finance, lump-sum taxation and a general distortionary income tax. For a given level of a specific expenditure, each mode of finance leads to different levels of welfare domestically and to different spillovers abroad. In order to understand these, we find it convenient to contrast them against the benchmark of a central planner who, by controlling resources directly, is able to attain the first-best optimal outcome.

Strategic aspects of fiscal policy flowing from these international spillovers occupy the remainder of the chapter. Once one introduces strategic behavior, there are several issues that need to be addressed. First, what are the objectives of the individual policy makers? What are the rules of the game? What are the information sets upon which policy makers base their actions? Are the agents playing noncooperatively or cooperatively?

As far as objectives are concerned, we will maintain the assumption we have adopted in previous discussions of welfare: that the policy makers act benevolently, seeking to maximize the welfare of their respective representative residents. We therefore abstract entirely from political considerations, which may or may not be in conflict with this objective but nevertheless are important in any coordinated international policy making. For the most part we assume that policy makers act noncooperatively, as Nash players. That is, in making their respective decisions, they take the actions of their rival policy maker abroad as given. Section 8.3 derives such equilibria, doing so under a variety of assumptions regarding (1) the form of government expenditure (consumption or production) and (2) the mode of financing (lump-sum tax or distortionary tax).

This chapter emphasizes two particularly important aspects of the strategic interaction. First, by employing an intertemporal maximizing macroeconomic framework with capital accumulation, the spillovers focus on the allocation of saving and investment across countries, and their implications for the relative net asset positions of the economies. We show that the way countries interact strategically depends critically upon the international allocation of traded assets, which in turn dictates the allocation of gains and losses across nations, and upon the net wealth effects generated by government expenditure. Second, the foreign spillovers generated by domestic government production expenditure are very different from those associated with the more familiar government consumption expenditure. Thus conclusions regarding the gains from cooperation are sensitive to the nature of government expenditure and the externalities each form of expenditure generates.[1] Productive government expenditure introduces an externality in the production function of the private sector. Under the benchmark case of lump-sum tax financing, this leads to a non-Pareto optimal Nash equilibrium level of government expenditure as each policy maker seeks to take advantage of the spillovers it generates abroad. While this productive externality can be corrected by the introduction of a distortionary income tax, the latter also has the effect of distorting the country's capital allocation decision. Thus the choice between lump-sum tax financing and distortionary income tax financing involves trading off these two sources of distortions.

Suppose that policy makers are committed to some chosen form and level of government expenditure. The fact that each agent has a choice of financing, and that each form leads to different international distributions of welfare, raises the question of the optimal choice of taxation. A fruitful way to analyze this choice is in terms of a bimatrix game (see Basar and Olsder 1982), which is discussed in Section 8.4. To do this, we consider the welfares in the two economies under the various combinations of financing choices available to the policy makers. With each policy maker having the choice of two options (lump-sum taxation and distortionary income taxation), this gives rise to two 2×2 payoff matrices in welfares, one for each country. The optimal mode of tax financing for a given level of productive government expenditure is then determined as the Nash equilibrium to this bimatrix game; it is the policy choice from which neither policy maker has an incentive to deviate unilaterally.

As an alternative to noncooperative behavior, Section 8.5 assumes that the policy makers in the two economies cooperate, so as to maximize their joint welfare. Such an equilibrium is Pareto optimal, and the interesting issue here is the extent to which noncooperative behavior deviates from this outcome.

Section 8.6 applies strategic analysis to the two-commodity model similar to that developed in Chapter 7, which stressed the role of relative prices in the adjustment. The analysis is restricted to a static analysis of optimal government expenditure using the Heckscher-Ohlin technology. This same framework has been used for the traditional game theoretic analyses of the optimal tariff and has been extended in a straightforward way to a simple dynamic analysis of optimal taxation by Devereux (1991).

Our analysis of strategic behavior reduces it to a static problem, enabling it to be analyzed by employing basic concepts from static game theory. In an intertemporal setting, strategic behavior is a dynamic phenomenon, with governments continually intervening and responding to one another. Modeling this behavior requires the methods of dynamic game theory, which are in general difficult to apply. Section 8.7 provides a brief illustration of some of the basic equilibrium notions of dynamic game theory in the context of the dynamic model developed in the earlier parts of this chapter.

8.2 A Simple Two-Country Model with Two Types of Government Expenditure

The model developed in Chapter 6 assumes that government expenditure takes the form of a consumption good that increases the utility of the private agent in the economy.[2] One of the implications of this model is that an increase in domestic government expenditure leads to a reduction in domestic private consumption. That is, government consumption expenditure crowds out domestic private consumption. This implication is not strongly supported by the empirical evidence, which suggests that government expenditure is associated with the *crowding in*, rather than the crowding out of domestic private expenditure (see, e.g., Karras 1994).

For government consumption expenditure to generate the crowding in of private consumption, consistent with the empirical evidence, it is necessary to modify the utility function in some way. One form, suggested by Karras, is that the utility function be of the form $U = u(c + vg) + \phi(g)$, where $v < 0$ and $\phi' > 0$ and sufficiently large to ensure that $\partial U/\partial g > 0$. But there is nothing very compelling about this functional form. An alternative approach is to change the nature of the public good. In fact, if we assume that government expenditure impacts on the productive capacity of the economy, this leads to a very different story.

The role of government expenditure in enhancing the productive capacity of the economy has generated a growing literature, with respect to both its empirical relevance and its theoretical consequences. Most of this literature has focused on a closed economy, with much of the empirical research being stimulated by Aschauer's (1989a, 1989b) striking findings suggesting that public capital has a powerful impact on the productivity of private capital. Aschauer's results were controversial and have generated extensive research efforts directed at determining their robustness (see Gramlich 1994 for a review of this literature). Theoretical aspects of the role of government productive expenditure have been studied in Ramsey-type economies by various authors, beginning with Arrow and Kurz (1970), and more recently by Aschauer and Greenwood (1985), Aschauer (1988), Baxter and King (1993), and Turnovsky and Fisher (1995).

This literature is restricted to the closed economy. Yet the ramifications of productive government expenditure for the international economy are at least as important as those of the more traditional government consumption expenditure. Many important economies, such as France, Germany, and Japan, for which international trade is important also devote relatively large portions of government expenditure to infrastructure and productivity-enhancing activities. One of the few papers to consider productive government expenditure in an international setting is Lee (1995). His analysis is based on assumptions that minimize the interactions between the two economies so that his focus is primarily on the domestic economy and the effects of alternative fiscal policies on the terms of trade and trade balance.

But this literature is of interest for several other reasons, of both empirical and policy relevance. A change in productive government expenditure suffices to generate physical capital accumulation and capital flows among countries, irrespective of other aspects of the model, such as the nature of the labor supply or the mode of government financing. This is in contrast to government consumption expenditure, where with inelastic labor supply and lump-sum tax financing, the dynamics degenerate (see Section 3.2). Second, unless the level of government production expenditure is excessively large, it is likely to be associated with the *crowding in* of domestic consumption rather than its crowding out. In addition, the domestic capital stock unambiguously increases with an increase in government expenditure and the domestic economy experiences a capital outflow, both in the short run and in the long run. Finally, the short-run impact on the capital stock and production abroad is *negative*. Interest in the issue of the negative transmission of fiscal and other demand disturbances is a long-standing one, having been extensively analyzed in the early 1980s (see, e.g., Branson and Rotemberg 1980; Schmid 1982; Corden and Turnovsky 1983). However, the mechanism here, proceeding through the productive side of the economy, offers a perspective on that issue very different from that provided by the earlier literature.

To introduce government production expenditure, it is convenient to abstract from labor supply, and assume that labor is both inelastically supplied at unity, and perfectly immobile internationally. The fact that in that case government consumption generates no dynamics, leading to immediate and complete crowding out of private consumption, has the pedagogic advantage of sharpening the contrast between these two forms of government expenditure.

Government Consumption and Government Production Expenditures

The model is essentially a simplification of the one laid out in detail in Chapter 6. The main difference lies in the specification of production. Specifically, the domestic representative firm produces output by means of a production function $F(k, h)$ using capital (per inelastically supplied worker) and the flow of productive government expenditures h. The production function is assumed to have the usual neoclassical properties of positive, but diminishing, marginal physical products; that is, $F_k > 0$, $F_h > 0$; $F_{kk} < 0$, $F_{hh} < 0$. It is also assumed to be homogeneous of degree

1 in the private factors capital and inelastically supplied labor. To simplify formal expressions, it will be convenient on occasion to assume that the production function is multiplicatively separable in the private and public factors, enabling us to write it in the form $x(k)y(h)$, ($x' > 0, y' > 0$, $x'' < 0, y'' < 0$), so that the flow of public expenditure impacts in a Hicks neutral fashion on the productivity of both capital and labor. In this case $F_{kh} > 0$, so that the flow of public expenditure generates a positive externality on the economy.

Several aspects of our formulation of how government expenditure impacts on production merit comment. First, Aschauer (1988) does not restrict the sign of the marginal productivity of the public input, interpreting $F_h < 0$ as referring to government regulations that inhibit productivity. This contrasts with our focus on F_h as reflecting infrastructure, with its presumed positive effect on total output. Second, our assumption of linear homogeneity in the two private factors views infrastructure as providing economies of scale in production. An alternative assumption, discussed by Aschauer (1989b), is to assume that the production function is linearly homogeneous in all three factors of production.

Third, our specification assumes that it is the current *flows* of government infrastructure expenditure, rather than the services of the existing *stocks* of government infrastructure, that generate improvements in productivity. This specification is the prevalent one in the literature, almost all of which deals with a closed economy (see, e.g., Aschauer 1988; Barro 1989; Turnovsky and Fisher 1995). An alternative formulation would be to introduce government capital, since production-enhancing public goods, such as roads, are likely to impact on the economy through their accumulated stocks rather than their current flows.[3] However, this approach would substantially increase the dimensionality of the two-country dynamic system and considerably complicate the subsequent analysis, without yielding clear-cut advantages with respect to our discussion of strategic implications. Because of the additional sluggishness this would introduce into the system, some of the results pertaining to the short run would be affected by this alternative formulation. By contrast, since in the long run, expenditure flows consist of depreciation expenditures that tend to be proportional to stocks, our steady-state results are much less sensitive to this specification. Thus, on balance, we feel that the present formulation, which treats both types of government expenditures as flows, suffices to capture the salient distinctions between the two types of public goods.

In the absence of adjustment costs and corporate taxes, the optimality condition for the domestic firm is the usual marginal physical product of capital condition,

$$F_k(k, h) = r, \qquad (8.1)$$

with the real wage being determined by the marginal physical product of labor. The foreign firm is symmetric. Note that k and k^* (the analogous quantity abroad) refer to the capital stock domiciled in the domestic and foreign economies, respectively. Following a procedure identical to that of Chapter 6, we may summarize the macroeconomic equilibrium by the set of dynamic equations

$$\frac{\dot{\lambda}}{\lambda} = \beta - (1 - \tau)F_k(k, h) \qquad (8.2a)$$

$$\frac{\dot{\lambda}^*}{\lambda^*} = \beta - (1 - \tau^*)F_k^*(k^*, h^*) \qquad (8.2b)$$

$$\dot{k} + \dot{k}^* = F(k, h) + F^*(k^*, h^*) - c(\lambda, g)$$
$$\qquad - c^*(\lambda^*, g^*) - g - h - g^* - h^* \qquad (8.2c)$$

$$\dot{N} = F(k, h) - c(\lambda, g) - \dot{k} + (1 - \tau)F_k(k, h)N - g - h, \qquad (8.2d)$$

given k_0, k_0^*, N_0, and the intertemporal solvency condition

$$\lim_{t \to \infty} Ne^{-\int_0^t (1-\tau)F_k ds} = 0. \qquad (8.2e)$$

The parallels between (8.2) and (6.21) and (6.21′) are clear. The only differences from the previous models are (1) the introduction of the government production expenditure, h, in addition to the government consumption expenditure, g, and (2) the assumption that the distortionary tax rates τ and τ^* are uniform in the respective economies over both capital and the inelastic labor supply. The government budget constraints (6.33) are correspondingly modified to

$$g + h = (w + rk)\tau + T,$$

$$g^* + h^* = (w^* + r^*k^*)\tau^* + T^*.$$

This equilibrium provides the basis for the dynamic analysis of government expenditure shocks under alternative modes of tax financing. We shall analyze the effects of increases in government expenditure under the following two tax regimes:

1. The increase in government expenditure is financed entirely by a lump-sum tax.

2. The increase in government expenditure is financed entirely by an increase in the distortionary income tax.

As in Chapter 6, the marginal utilities are related by

$$\lambda^* = \bar{m}\lambda, \tag{8.3}$$

where $\bar{m}$ is constant over time. In addition, we assume that each country can augment or diminish its capital stock instantaneously by entering the world capital market, in accordance with

$$dk_0 = -dk_0^* = -dN_0. \tag{8.4}$$

For convenience, the steady state analogous to (6.30) is repeated here in the form

$$(1 - \tau)F_k(\tilde{k}, h) = \beta \tag{8.5a}$$

$$(1 - \tau^*)F_k^*(\tilde{k}^*, h^*) = \beta \tag{8.5b}$$

$$F(\tilde{k}, h) + F^*(\tilde{k}^*, h^*) = c(\tilde{\lambda}, g) + c^*(\tilde{\lambda}^*, g^*) + g + h + g^* + h^* \tag{8.5c}$$

$$\beta\tilde{N} = c(\tilde{\lambda}, g) + g + h - F(\tilde{k}, h)$$

$$= F^*(\tilde{k}^*, h^*) - c^*(\tilde{\lambda}^*, g^*) - g^* - h^* \tag{8.5d}$$

$$N_0 - \tilde{N} = \frac{\Omega}{\mu - \beta}(k_0 - \tilde{k}). \tag{8.5e}$$

Fiscal Expansions

Tables 8.1 and 8.2 summarize the expressions describing the effects of permanent increases in the two types of domestic government expenditure $(dg > 0, dh > 0)$, financed under the two alternative forms of taxation. In both cases the short-run and long-run responses are reported. For computational simplicity, these have been calculated under the assumptions that (1) agents in the two economies have identical tastes; (2) the economies have identical technologies; (3) the initial equilibrium is one in which there are no distortionary taxes, so that any existing government expenditures are financed by lump-sum taxes.

Increase in Government Consumption Expenditure

With the adjustments in the tax rates corresponding to the various modes of financing requiring the budget to remain balanced across steady states, the corresponding changes in the tax rates (from zero in the case of the two distortionary taxes) under the two schemes being considered are as follows:

Table 8.1
Increase in domestic government consumption expenditure

	A. Lump-sum tax finance			
	Short run			Long run
k_0	0	$\tilde{k}$	0
k_0^*	0	$\tilde{k}^*$	0
N_0	0	$\tilde{N}$	0
$c(0)$	-1	$\tilde{c}$	-1
$c^*(0)$	0	$\tilde{c}^*$	0

	B. Distortionary income tax finance			
	Short run			Long run
k_0	$\beta/2\tilde{F}F_{kk} < 0$	$\tilde{k}$	$\beta/\tilde{F}F_{kk} < 0$
k_0^*	$-\beta/2\tilde{F}F_{kk} > 0$	$\tilde{k}^*$	0
N_0	$-\dfrac{\beta}{2\tilde{F}F_{kk}} > 0$	$\tilde{N}$	$-\dfrac{\beta}{2\tilde{F}F_{kk}}\left[1 - \dfrac{\Omega}{\mu - \beta}\right]$
$c(0)$	$-1 + \dfrac{\beta}{2\tilde{F}(\mu - B)}\left[\dfrac{U_c}{U_{cc}} + \beta\tilde{N}\right]$	$\tilde{c}$	$-1 + \dfrac{\beta^2}{2\tilde{F}F_{kk}}\left[1 + \dfrac{\Omega}{\mu - \beta}\right]$
$c^*(0)$	$\dfrac{\beta}{2\tilde{F}(\mu - \beta)}\left[\dfrac{U_c^*}{U_{cc}^*} - \beta\tilde{N}\right]$	$\tilde{c}^*$	$\dfrac{\beta^2}{2\tilde{F}F_{kk}}\left[1 - \dfrac{\Omega}{\mu - \beta}\right]$

1. Lump-sum tax; $dT = dg$
2. Distortionary income tax; $d\tau = dg/\tilde{F}$.

Lump-sum tax financing ensures that the government budget remains balanced at all times during the transition. However, as noted in Chapter 6, that is not the case with scheme 2 above, since the income on which the distortionary income tax is being levied during the transition does not correspond to the new steady-state level. In either case, we assume that any discrepancy in the expenditures and the revenues generated by the distortionary tax during the transition is financed by a (time-varying) lump-sum tax, thereby ensuring that the government budget remains in balance at all times.

In Chapter 6 we presented a comprehensive discussion of the effects of an increase in government consumption expenditures in the more general case where labor is supplied elastically. Accordingly, our present discussion can be brief. With fixed employment and lump-sum tax financing, the only effect of an increase in domestic government consumption expenditure is to crowd out immediately and completely an equal amount of domestic private consumption expenditure. This is a consequence of the higher taxes required to finance the additional expenditure and reflects a

Table 8.2
Increase in domestic government production expenditure

	A. Lump-sum tax finance		
	Short run		Long run
k_0	$-F_{kh}/2F_{kk} > 0$	$\tilde{k}$	$-F_{kh}/F_{kk} > 0$
k_0^*	$F_{kh}/2F_{kk} < 0$	$\tilde{k}^*$	0
N_0	$\dfrac{F_{kh}}{2F_{kk}} < 0$	$\tilde{N}$	$\dfrac{F_{kh}}{2F_{kk}}\left[1 - \dfrac{\Omega}{\mu-\beta}\right]$
$c(0)$	$(F_h - 1) - \dfrac{F_{kh}}{2(\mu-\beta)}\left[\dfrac{U_c}{U_{cc}} + \beta\tilde{N}\right]$	$\tilde{c}$	$(F_h - 1) - \dfrac{\beta F_{kh}}{2F_{kk}}\left[1 + \dfrac{\Omega}{\mu-\beta}\right]$
$c^*(0)$	$-\dfrac{\beta F_{kh}}{2(\mu-\beta)}\left[\dfrac{U_c^*}{U_{cc}^*} - \beta\tilde{N}\right]$	$\tilde{c}^*$	$-\dfrac{\beta F_{kh}}{2F_{kk}}\left[1 - \dfrac{\Omega}{\mu-\beta}\right]$

	B. Distortionary income tax finance		
	Short run		Long run
k_0	$-(1-\delta)F_{kh}/2F_{kk}$	$\tilde{k}$	$-(1-\delta)F_{kh}/FF_{kk}$
k_0^*	$(1-\delta)F_{kh}/2F_{kk}$	$\tilde{k}^*$	0
N_0	$(1-\delta)\dfrac{F_{kh}}{2F_{kk}}$	$\tilde{N}$	$(1-\delta)\dfrac{F_{kh}}{2F_{kk}}\left[1 - \dfrac{\Omega}{\mu-\beta}\right]$
$c(0)$	$(F_h - 1) - \dfrac{(1-\delta)F_{kh}}{2(\mu-\beta)}\left[\dfrac{U_c}{U_{cc}} + \beta\tilde{N}\right]$	$\tilde{c}$	$(F_h - 1) - \dfrac{(1-\delta)\beta F_{kh}}{2F_{kk}}\left[1 + \dfrac{\Omega}{\mu-\beta}\right]$
$c^*(0)$	$-\dfrac{(1-\delta)\beta F_{kh}}{2(\mu-\beta)}\left[\dfrac{U_c^*}{U_{cc}^*} - \beta\tilde{N}\right]$	$\tilde{c}^*$	$-\dfrac{(1-\delta)\beta F_{kh}}{2F_{kk}}\left[1 - \dfrac{\Omega}{\mu-\beta}\right]$

where $\delta \equiv \beta/FF_{kh} = 1/F_h$

negative *wealth effect*. There are no other effects on domestic activity, and this form of fiscal expansion is not transmitted abroad.

If the expenditure is financed by introducing a distortionary income tax, this gives rise to a *substitution effect* (in addition to the crowding out just noted), which is very similar to that originally introduced by Turnovsky and Bianconi (1992) and discussed at length in Section 6.5. The argument presented there applies here as well, the only difference being that the higher income tax rate, taken as exogenous in that analysis, is now adjusted endogenously to meet the higher level of government consumption expenditure. In this case, the adjustment does not occur instantaneously. Indeed, the term involving $\Omega/(\mu - \beta)$ measures the intertemporal effects on consumption due to the international flow of assets during the transition.

The initial increase in the domestic income tax rate immediately reduces the after-tax marginal physical product of capital in the domestic economy below the rate of return abroad. This leads to an instantaneous transfer of capital from the domestic to the foreign economy, causing the marginal physical product of capital abroad to decline as well. The short-run reductions in the return to capital in both economies discourage the accumulation of capital. Over time, as the capital stock, and therefore output, in both economies decline, the marginal physical product of capital increases worldwide, and the after-tax rate of return on capital is gradually restored to its initial level. The higher tax rate on domestic capital tends to induce domestic agents to substitute consumption for savings in the short run, thus partly offsetting the direct crowding out of consumption in the domestic economy. Likewise, the reduction in the rate of return to capital abroad causes initial consumption abroad to increase. As the world capital stock, and therefore output, decline, world consumption declines unambiguously. In short, government consumption expenditure is associated with the intertemporal crowding out of private consumption in the world economy, with the allocation of these consumption losses being determined by the international allocation of traded assets.[4] To the extent that the domestic economy is a net creditor ($\tilde{N} > 0$), the decline in consumption falls more heavily on the domestic economy than it does on the foreign economy, where the initial increase is actually enhanced. This is because the reduction in the rate of return on capital during the transition favors the debtor nation at the expense of the creditor nation.

Increase in Government Production Expenditure

The corresponding changes in the tax rates under the two schemes being considered are now

1. Lump-sum taxes; $dT = dh$
2. Distortionary income taxes; $d\tau = dh/\tilde{F}$.

Since this form of government expenditure has not been analyzed previously, our discussion shall be more extensive.

Lump-Sum Tax Financing

The short-run and long-run effects of an expansion in domestic government production expenditure under lump-sum tax financing are summarized in Part A of Table 8.2. These depend critically upon the expression F_{kh}, which measures the impact of government expenditure on the productivity of private capital. Under the assumption that the production function is multiplicatively separable in public and private factors, $F_{kh} > 0$, so that the government expenditure enhances the productivity of private capital. However, we should note that if $F_{kh} = 0$, so that government expenditure has no impact on the productivity of capital, as in Aschauer (1988), the dynamics collapse, exactly as under lump-sum tax financing. The only response is the instantaneous and complete adjustment in domestic private consumption.

In the short run, an increase in domestic government production expenditure raises the marginal physical product of domestically domiciled capital, thereby inducing domestic investors to repatriate their capital and foreigners to invest in the domestic economy. With the world capital stock fixed instantaneously, the increase in k_0 is met by an equivalent reduction in k_0^* and an equivalent decrease in N_0. The international movement of capital immediately raises the marginal physical product of capital abroad while tending to offset, though only partially, the effects of government expenditure on the productivity of domestic capital. On balance, the marginal productivity of domestic capital therefore rises as well. Thus during the transition, both economies accumulate capital, restoring the marginal productivity of capital to its fixed long-run equilibrium level implied by (8.5a). In the long run, the domestic capital stock is increased further and the foreign capital stock is restored to its original level, so that the aggregate world capital stock is increased. The domestic fiscal expansion is thus associated with an increase in activity in the domestic economy. The level of activity abroad initially falls, though it reverts toward its initial level during the subsequent transition. Domestic government production expenditure therefore generates a recession abroad, albeit a transitory one. The source of this negative transmission through the allocation of the world capital stock is very different from that emphasized in the early literature, where the channels of operation emphasized included wage rigidity (Branson and Rotemberg 1980; Schmid 1982) and relative price adjustment (Corden and Turnovsky 1983).

We turn now to domestic private consumption, the response of which consists of two components. The first is $(F_h - 1)$. This reflects the fact that while the increase in government expenditure claims resources, thereby directly crowding out an equal amount of private consumption, it also contributes to the net production of output $(F_h > 0)$. The additional resources available for consumption are measured by the difference between these two quantities. The quantity $(F_h - 1)$ thus represents the net resource augmentation effect of the expansion in government expenditure, and can thus be interpreted as the net *wealth effect*. The second term reflects the consequence for consumption of the positive externality conferred by government expenditure on the productivity of capital. This can be identified as the *substitution effect*. By raising the marginal productivity of capital, in the short run this tends to attract resources toward investment and away from consumption. This is true in both the domestic and the foreign economies. Over time, however, as the world capital stock increases, consumption in both economies increases.

From Table 8.2 it is straightforward to observe that long-run aggregate world consumption is

$$\frac{\partial(\tilde{c}+\tilde{c}^*)}{\partial h} = (F_h - 1) + \beta \frac{\partial \tilde{k}}{\partial h},$$

which is unambiguously positive as long as the net wealth effect is nonnegative. In contrast to the case of government consumption expenditure, government production expenditure is associated with the intertemporal *crowding in* of world private consumption, with the international allocation of these consumption gains depending upon the net asset positions of the two economies. Indeed, the term involving $\Omega/(\mu - \beta)$ measures the intertemporal effects on consumption due to the international flow of assets during the transition. To the extent that the accumulation of capital in the domestic economy is associated with an accumulation of foreign assets by the domestic economy—$\Omega < 0$, in equation (8.5e)—this further enhances the level of consumption in the domestic economy while reducing it abroad. This is because the increase in the rate of return on capital during the transition favors the creditor nation at the expense of the debtor nation.

The parallel between an increase in government consumption expenditure under distortionary income tax financing and the effects of government production expenditure under lump-sum tax financing is clear. The wealth effect of the former is -1 and of the latter is $F_h - 1$. The substitution effects, given by the second terms, are in opposite directions. This is because the increase in domestic government production expenditure raises the marginal physical product of domestic capital, increasing its rate of return, and therefore operates like a subsidy (negative tax) to domestic capital.

Distortionary Income Tax Financing

This is described in Part B of Table 8.2. An increase in government production expenditure now has three effects. First, there is the wealth effect, which, as before, depends upon $F_h - 1$. Second is the substitution effect arising from the increase in government production expenditure and its positive impact on the productivity of private capital. Third is an additional effect resulting from the higher distortionary tax rate employed to finance the expansion in government expenditure. This reduces the after-tax return on capital, thus generating a contractionary substitution effect, which offsets that due to the higher expenditure itself. In general, the net effect of these two substitution effects is given by $(1 - \delta)$, where $\delta \equiv F_k/FF_{kh}$. In the case where the production function is multiplicatively separable in its two arguments, $\delta = 1/F_h$ and the net impact of the two substitution effects depends upon $F_h - 1$. In this case the entire qualitative effect of an increase in government production expenditure depends upon $F_h - 1$.

To see the significance of this, refer to Part B of Table 8.4, which summarizes the welfare effects of government production expenditure on domestic and foreign residents. Here it is seen that $F_h = 1$ corresponds to the welfare-maximizing level of government production expenditure under distortionary taxes.[5] Thus if the rate of domestic government production expenditure is initially at its welfare-maximizing level, an increase from this level will have no effect either domestically or abroad. The wealth effect is zero and the two components of the substitution effect are exactly offsetting.

To consider the international aspects of the transmission, suppose $F_h > 1$, so that the government production expenditure in the domestic economy is below its optimum, and also that the economy is a net creditor, $\tilde{N} > 0$. In this case, an increase in h will tend to raise the productivity of domestic capital relative to foreign capital, causing capital to relocate in the domestic economy. In this case the transmission operates very much as it does under lump-sum tax financing. On the other hand, if $F_h < 1$, so that government expenditure production is above its optimum, the negative effect of the distortionary tax dominates the positive expenditure externality, and a further increase in h will lower the net return to domestic capital and lead to a reversal of these transmission effects.

Welfare

In order to study the strategic interactions among nations, a welfare measure for that each country must be introduced. We shall assume that each country is run by a benevolent policy maker whose objective is to maximize the intertemporal utility of the representative agent as the world economy moves along its transitional equilibrium path. In the case of the domestic agent, the objective is

$$V \equiv \int_0^\infty U(c,g)e^{-\beta t}dt, \qquad (8.6)$$

a linear approximation to which is obtained by first substituting (8.2a) into $U(c,g)$ and linearizing to yield

$$U(c(t),g) \cong U(\tilde{c},g) + U_c c_\lambda [\lambda(0) - \lambda]e^{\mu t}$$

Table 8.3
Welfare effects of changes in government consumption expenditure

A. Lump-sum tax finance	
Domestic welfare	Foreign welfare
$\dfrac{\partial V}{\partial g} = \dfrac{1}{\beta}(U_g - U_c)$	$\dfrac{\partial V^*}{\partial g} = 0$
$\dfrac{\partial V}{\partial g^*} = 0$	$\dfrac{\partial V^*}{\partial g^*} = \dfrac{1}{\beta}(U_g^* - U_c^*)$

B. Distortionary income tax finance	
Domestic welfare	Foreign welfare
$\dfrac{\partial V}{\partial g} = \dfrac{1}{\beta}\left\{U_g - U_c\left(1 - \dfrac{\beta^2 \tilde{N}}{2F(\mu - \beta)}\right)\right\}$	$\dfrac{\partial V^*}{\partial g} = -\dfrac{U_c^* \beta \tilde{N}}{2F(\mu - \beta)}$
$\dfrac{\partial V}{\partial g^*} = \dfrac{U_c \beta \tilde{N}}{2F(\mu - \beta)}$	$\dfrac{\partial V^*}{\partial g^*} = \dfrac{1}{\beta}\left\{U_g^* - U_c^*\left(1 + \dfrac{\beta^2 \tilde{N}}{2F(\mu - \beta)}\right)\right\}$

for a given level of g. Substituting this expression into (8.6) and following the procedures of previous chapters, we obtain the following linear approximations for the expressions for the levels of intertemporal utility for the domestic and foreign residents:

$$V \cong \frac{U(\tilde{c}, g)}{\beta} - \frac{U_c^2 F_{kk}}{U_{cc} \mu(\beta - \mu)}(k_0 - \tilde{k}) \tag{8.7a}$$

$$V^* \cong \frac{U^*(\tilde{c}^*, g^*)}{\beta} - \frac{U_c^{*2} F_{kk}^*}{U_{cc}^* \mu(\beta - \mu)}(k_0 - \tilde{k}), \tag{8.7b}$$

where the coefficients of $(k_0 - \tilde{k})$ are evaluated at steady state. The first term is the capitalized value of steady-state utility and represents the agent's welfare if the steady state were attained instantaneously. The second term is the adjustment due to the fact that the steady state is attained only gradually along the transitional path. To the extent that the economy is accumulating capital during the transition ($k_0 < \tilde{k}$), this adjustment quantity is negative, reflecting the fact that this represents forgone consumption, and therefore a loss in utility.

Tables 8.3 and 8.4 summarize the partial derivatives of these welfare functions with respect to a change in each type of government expenditure under the two alternative modes of finance. These expressions are obtained by substituting the appropriate expressions from tables 8.1 and 8.2. The elements along the diagonal represent the effects on the own economy. These consist of (1) the capitalized wealth effects and (2) the accumulated substitution effects during the transition (which vary with the mode of

Table 8.4
Welfare effects of changes in government production expenditure

A. Lump-sum tax finance	
Domestic welfare	Foreign welfare
$\dfrac{\partial V}{\partial h} = U_c\left\{\left(\dfrac{F_h - 1}{\beta}\right) - \dfrac{F_{kh}\tilde{N}}{2(\mu - \beta)}\right\}$	$\dfrac{\partial V^*}{\partial h} = \dfrac{U_c^* F_{kh}\tilde{N}}{2(\mu - \beta)}$
$\dfrac{\partial V}{\partial h^*} = -\dfrac{U_c F_{kh}^* \tilde{N}}{2(\mu - \beta)}$	$\dfrac{\partial V^*}{\partial h^*} = U_c^*\left\{\left(\dfrac{F_h^* - 1}{\beta}\right) + \dfrac{F_{kh}^* \tilde{N}}{2(\mu - \beta)}\right\}$
B. Distortionary income tax finance	
Domestic welfare	Foreign welfare
$\dfrac{\partial V}{\partial h} = U_c(F_h - 1)\left\{\dfrac{1}{\beta} - \dfrac{F_{kh}\tilde{N}}{2F_h(\mu - \beta)}\right\}$	$\dfrac{\partial V^*}{\partial h} = \left(\dfrac{F_h - 1}{F_h}\right)\dfrac{U_c^* F_{kh}\tilde{N}}{2(\mu - \beta)}$
$\dfrac{\partial V}{\partial h^*} = -\left(\dfrac{F_h^* - 1}{F_h^*}\right)\dfrac{U_c F_{kh}^* \tilde{N}}{2(\mu - \beta)}$	$\dfrac{\partial V^*}{\partial h^*} = U_c^*(F_h^* - 1)\left\{\dfrac{1}{\beta} + \dfrac{F_{kh}^* \tilde{N}}{2F_h^*(\mu - \beta)}\right\}$

financing). The off-diagonal elements summarize the transmission of welfare effects abroad.

As a benchmark for our welfare analysis, it is useful to begin by considering a central planner who wishes to maximize the joint welfare, $V + V^*$, of the two representative agents and is able to do so by choosing all quantities directly, subject to the world resource constraint (8.2c). It is straightforward to establish that the steady-state equilibrium in such a distortion-free world is described by

$$F_k(\tilde{k}, \tilde{h}) = F_k^*(\tilde{k}^*, \tilde{h}^*) = \beta \tag{8.8a}$$

$$F_h(\tilde{k}, \tilde{h}) = F_h^*(\tilde{k}^*, \tilde{h}^*) = 1 \tag{8.8b}$$

$$U_c(\tilde{c}, \tilde{g}) = U_g(\tilde{c}, \tilde{g}) = U_c^*(\tilde{c}^*, \tilde{g}^*) = U_g^*(\tilde{c}^*, \tilde{g}^*). \tag{8.8c}$$

Three efficiency conditions thus characterize this long-run first-best optimum:

1. *Efficient production.* The marginal product of capital in the two economies should be equated to the common rate of time discount.

2. *Efficient government production expenditure.* The marginal product of government production expenditure in the two economies should equal its (unit) resource cost.[6]

3. *Efficient consumption.* The marginal utilities of private and public consumption should be equal to one another and equal across both economies.

The stock of capital and the flow of government production expenditure in each economy will thus be determined by production conditions in that economy alone; there are no spillovers abroad from either consumption or production.

It is apparent from tables 8.3 and 8.4 that the welfare effects in the decentralized economy depend critically upon three sets of factors. First, they depend upon the international allocation of traded assets, through the net asset position, $\tilde{N}$. Second, they depend upon the level of government production expenditure through the magnitude of the wealth effects, $F_h - 1$ and $F_h^* - 1$. Third, internal welfare depends upon differences between the marginal utility of private and public consumption.

These transmission effects can be summarized in the following proposition:

Proposition 8.1 (*International transmission of government expenditure*)
1. An expansion in government consumption expenditure by a creditor (debtor) nation has no effect abroad if it is financed by a lump-sum tax and a positive (negative) effect on foreign welfare if it is financed by a distortionary income tax.
2. An expansion in government production expenditure by a creditor (debtor) nation has a negative (positive) effect on foreign welfare if it is financed by a lump-sum tax or if it is financed by a distortionary tax and is initially set below its optimum ($F_h > 1$). If it is above its optimum, these latter effects are reversed.

The intuition for the welfare transmission effects revolves around the returns to capital as these affect creditor and debtor nations. An increase in the distortionary tax necessary to finance government consumption expenditure lowers the net after-tax return to capital. The creditor nation therefore earns less revenue from the debtor nation, and thus is able to enjoy less consumption and has a lower level of welfare. The intuition is reversed in the case of government production expenditure financed by lump-sum taxation. An increase in government production expenditure financed by a lump-sum tax increases the net after-tax return to capital during the transition. The creditor nation therefore earns more revenue from the debtor nation, and is able to enjoy more consumption and, hence, a higher level of welfare. The substitution effect therefore results in a transfer of wealth from the foreign economy to the domestic economy. If the production expenditure is financed by a distortionary tax, the higher tax rate has an offsetting negative effect on the return to capital. The net effect on foreign welfare thus depends upon whether the return to capital rises or falls, that is, upon whether $F_h \gtreqless 1$.

8.3 Noncooperative Strategic Behavior

In general, the objective functions for the representative agents in the two countries are functions of the fiscal instruments of both policy makers, that is,

$$V = V(g, h, g^*, h^*); \quad V^* = V^*(g, h, g^*, h^*).$$

Welfare of the domestic resident depends *directly* upon both the domestic policy instruments, g and h, insofar as they appear in the utility function and production function, respectively. It also depends upon these two policy instruments *indirectly*, through the effects these policy instruments have on the long-run stock of capital, $\tilde{k}$, and the consumption level, $\tilde{c}$. The foreign fiscal instruments g^* and h^* influence domestic welfare only indirectly, through $\tilde{k}$ and $\tilde{c}$. The value of the function also depends on the mode of finance, but since the taxes adjust endogenously to finance the given expenditures, the objectives are ultimately functions of the expenditure decisions, as indicated.

Two other aspects of this game theoretic formulation should be noted. First, each policy maker has at his disposal two independent fiscal instruments, and one could allow the strategic behavior to be over both simultaneously. However, we will not follow this approach; instead, we shall analyze strategic behavior with respect to the two types of government expenditure in turn. Second, since the steady state depends upon the initial stocks of capital and foreign assets, the optimal policy choices are potentially time inconsistent.[7] The problem of time inconsistency will arise in situations where the transition involves international capital movements leading to a change in these initial conditions through time. As these occur, the policy maker will have an incentive to reoptimize, and thus deviate from the previously optimal path. The issue of time inconsistency in the present strategic context is stressed by Devereux (1991).

As an introduction to the strategic aspects of international fiscal policy, consider a game in which the two policy makers act noncooperatively by choosing the level of government expenditure under a fixed financing method, taking the action of the rival policy maker as given. There are in fact four such games, corresponding to the two forms of expenditures and to the two forms of financing. These shall be considered in turn.

Government Consumption Expenditure under Lump-Sum Tax Finance

In this case, the domestic policy maker chooses g to optimize V, taking g^* as given, while the foreign policy maker chooses g^* to optimize V^*, taking g as given. The Nash equilibrium of this game is defined by the pairs (g, g^*), possibly multiple, determined by the conditions

$$\frac{\partial V(g, g^*)}{\partial g} = 0 \tag{8.9a}$$

$$\frac{\partial V^*(g, g^*)}{\partial g^*} = 0, \tag{8.9b}$$

where the arguments h and h^* are suppressed. Equation (8.9a) determines the optimal choice of g by the policy maker in the domestic economy, for a given level of g^* chosen by his foreign rival. Solving (8.9a) yields a relationship of the form $g = \phi(g^*)$. This is known as the domestic policy maker's reaction function, and its slope reflects the magnitude and direction of the international spillovers. Similarly, (8.9b) defines the reaction function, $g^* = \phi^*(g)$, for the foreign policy maker, given the choice of the domestic policy maker. The Nash equilibrium outcome is thus the intersection of these two reaction functions, $g = \phi(g^*)$ and $g^* = \phi^*(g)$.

From Table 8.3A we see that the reaction functions for lump-sum tax financing are

$$\frac{\partial V}{\partial g} \equiv \frac{1}{\beta}(U_g(c(g), g) - U_c(c(g), g)) = 0 \tag{8.9a'}$$

$$\frac{\partial V^*}{\partial g^*} \equiv \frac{1}{\beta}(U_g^*(c^*(g^*), g^*) - U_c^*(c^*(g^*), g^*)) = 0. \tag{8.9b'}$$

Since under this mode of financing domestic government expenditure has no effect on foreign consumption and vice versa, (8.9a') is independent of g^* and (8.9b') is independent of g. The reaction functions are thus parallel to the respective axes (in (g, g^*) space), reflecting the fact that there are no international spillovers. The Nash equilibrium once-and-for-all choice of government consumption expenditure under lump-sum tax financing is simply to equate the marginal utility of private consumption to that of government consumption in the two economies. Since aggregate (national) consumption remains unchanged, there are no effects on initial stocks, so that the Nash equilibrium is time consistent.

Government Consumption Expenditure under Distortionary Tax Finance

Suppose the game is played over government consumption expenditure financed by a distortionary income tax. Referring to Table 8.3B, the optimality conditions (8.9a) and (8.9b) are now, respectively,

$$U_g(\tilde{c}, g) = U_c(\tilde{c}, g)\{1 - \beta^2 \tilde{N}/2F(\mu - \beta)\} \tag{8.10a}$$

$$U_g^*(\tilde{c}^*, g^*) = U_c^*(\tilde{c}^*, g^*)\{1 + \beta^2 \tilde{N}/2F(\mu - \beta)\}. \tag{8.10b}$$

The intuition for the result is as follows. An increase in the distortionary-tax necessary to finance an increase in government expenditure lowers the after-tax return to capital. This hurts a creditor nation at the expense of a debtor nation, thus raising the relative shadow value of government expenditure in the former and reducing it in the latter. Accordingly, in equilibrium the marginal utility of public expenditure in a creditor economy must be raised above that of private consumption, in order to reflect this adverse effect on the rate of return.

Recognizing that with distortionary taxes, $\tilde{c} = c(g, g^*N_0)$, $\tilde{c}^* = c^*(g, g^*N_0)$, $\tilde{N} = N(g, g^*N_0)$, it can be seen that the slopes of the reaction functions defined by (8.10a) and (8.10b) now will depend upon the effects of government expenditure on the equilibrium stock of traded assets and consumption abroad. The fact that the steady-state consumption levels and stock of debt depend upon initial conditions renders this Nash equilibrium time inconsistent.

More important, note that the optimal size of government consumption expenditure under distortionary tax financing, relative to that under lump-sum tax financing, depends upon the relative net asset positions of the two economies. This can be seen as follows. Evaluating $\partial V/\partial g$ and $\partial V^*/\partial g^*$ at the optimum corresponding to lump-sum taxing, $U_g = U_c$; $U_g^* = U_c^*$, we find

$$\frac{\partial V}{\partial g} = \frac{U_c \beta \tilde{N}}{2F(\mu - \beta)}; \quad \frac{\partial V^*}{\partial g^*} = \frac{U_c^* \beta \tilde{N}}{2F(\mu - \beta)}.$$

This implies that for a creditor country $(\partial V/\partial g)_{lump\text{-}sum} < 0$, so that setting $g = g_L$, its optimum under lump-sum taxation exceeds the optimum, g_D, under distortionary taxation. The opposite holds for a debtor country. We thus can state the following:

Proposition 8.2 (*Optimal government consumption expenditure*) If the domestic economy is a net creditor, then its Nash equilibrium level of government consumption expenditure, g_L, under lump-sum tax financing is larger than that under distortionary tax financing, g_D. For the foreign economy, which is a debtor nation, the reverse applies: $g_L^* < g_D^*$. If the domestic economy is a net debtor, these relative magnitudes are reversed.

This result is important because it contradicts the presumption that since lump-sum tax finance is nondistortionary, it can support a larger level of government expenditure relative to a distortionary income tax, which induces capital to relocate abroad, thereby diminishing the domestic economy's tax base (see Devereux 1991; Ghosh 1991). We show, in effect, that the size of g depends ultimately on the net asset position of the economy relative to its trading partner, that is, on its saving:investment balance rather than on the method of finance per se.[8]

Government Production Expenditure

The case of government production expenditure under lump-sum tax finance is similar. The optimality conditions are now

$$F_h(\tilde{k}, h) = 1 + \beta F_{kh}(\tilde{k}, h)\tilde{N}/2(\mu - \beta) \qquad (8.11a)$$

$$F_h^*(\tilde{k}^*, h^*) = 1 - \beta F_{kh}^*(\tilde{k}^*, h^*)\tilde{N}/2(\mu - \beta). \qquad (8.11b)$$

Combining these relationships with the equilibrium conditions (8.5), one can eliminate $\tilde{k}$, $\tilde{k}^*$, and $\tilde{N}$, and thereby derive the reaction functions $h = \varphi(h^*)$ and $h^* = \varphi^*(h)$.

The case of government production expenditure under distortionary income tax finance is similar. In this case it is easy to note from Table 8.4 that the optimality conditions are now of the form

$$F_h(h, k(h)) = 1 \qquad (8.12a)$$

$$F_h^*(h^*, k^*(h^*)) = 1. \qquad (8.12b)$$

The reaction functions are therefore parallel to the respective axes (in (h, h^*) space), reflecting the fact that there are no international spillovers. The Nash equilibrium is time consistent. Analogous to Proposition 8.2, and using a similar argument, we obtain

Proposition 8.2′ (*Optimal government production expenditure*) If the domestic economy is a net creditor, then its Nash equilibrium level of government production expenditure, h_N, under lump-sum tax financing is larger than that under distortionary income tax financing, and the corresponding level of foreign government consumption expenditure, h_N^*, is smaller. If the domestic economy is a net debtor, these relative magnitudes are reversed.

The Nash equilibria in the decentralized market games represented by conditions (8.9)–(8.12) can be compared with the central planner allocation described by (8.8a) and (8.8b). First consider the government consumption game. Lump-sum tax financing ensures that the production efficiency condition, (8.8a), holds, while (8.9a′) and (8.9b′) ensure that consumption is allocated efficiently both across goods and internationally. This therefore represents a first-best optimum. Distortionary tax financing leads to a violation of both these conditions. A creditor country has an incentive to underexpand its level of government consumption expenditure, thereby lowering the distortionary tax rate and raising its capital income, at the expense of the debtor country. In addition, the introduction of the distortionary tax leads to a violation of the production efficiency condition (8.8a). Thus it can be only a second-best optimum.

In the case of government production expenditure, for both modes of financing only a second-best optimum is reached. While lump-sum tax financing ensures that the production efficiency condition (8.8a) holds, the externality due to government expenditure leads to a violation of the government expenditure efficiency condition (8.8b). That is, a creditor country now has an incentive to overexpand its level of government expenditure, and thus raise its capital income at the expense of the debtor country. By contrast, while the distortionary tax exactly neutralizes the externality due to government expenditure, thus ensuring that (8.8b) holds, the introduction of the distortionary tax also leads to a violation of the production efficiency condition (8.8a). Thus both are only second-best optima.

Other policy games are possible. For example, the government could choose to fix the amount of its tax revenues together with their mode of finance, and choose instead to behave strategically over its choice of expenditure.

8.4 Noncooperative Behavior and Bimatrix Games

One characteristic of the games described above is that the policies chosen are in some cases time inconsistent, so that policy makers will have an incentive to deviate from the optimal plan at some later date. This possibility gives rise to a more general bimatrix game defined over the mode of finance.

In general, a bimatrix game consists of two $(m \times n)$-dimensional payoff matrices, $A = (a_{ij})$, $B = (b_{ij})$, where each pair of entries (a_{ij}, b_{ij}) denotes the payoff (outcome) of the game corresponding to a particular pair of choices made by the decision makers. These alternatives are called strategies. Rows correspond to strategies by player 1 and columns to strategies by player 2. Thus if player 1 adopts the strategy of choosing row i, and player 2 adopts the strategy of column j, a_{ij} is the payoff to player 1, and b_{ij} is the payoff to player 2. Each agent seeks the outcome that provides him with the highest gain or smallest loss.

Assuming that there is no cooperation between the players, so that each agent makes his decision independently, the question is to determine the pair of strategies that defines an equilibrium to the bimatrix game. The property that is proposed is that a pair of strategies is an equilibrium to the bimatrix game if there is no incentive for any unilateral deviation by either of the players. Formally, we may state (see Basar and Olsder 1982):

A pair of strategies (row i^*, column j^*) is said to constitute a noncooperative (Nash) equilibrium solution to a bimatrix game $A = (a_{ij})$, $B = (b_{ij})$ if the following pair of inequalities is satisfied for all $i = 1,\ldots,m$, $j = 1,\ldots,n$: $a_{i^*j^*} \geq a_{ij^*}$, $b_{i^*j^*} \geq b_{i^*j}$. The payoff represented by the pair $(a_{i^*j^*}, b_{i^*j^*})$ represents the noncooperative Nash equilibrium outcome of the bimatrix game.

It is possible that the game can admit more than one Nash equilibrium outcome, in which case it may be possible to rank them. In such cases a Nash equilibrium is said to be admissible if it is not dominated by some other equilibrium that yields equal or higher payoffs to both agents and a strictly higher payoff to at least one. (For an excellent discussion of bimatrix games, see Basar and Olsder 1982.)

We shall describe the game with respect to government consumption expenditure, and note below the analogous game with respect to government production expenditure. Specifically, assume that domestic and foreign economies have set their government consumption expenditure levels at g and g^*, respectively. Suppose the domestic government agrees to change its level of expenditure by the fixed amount $dg \equiv a \gtrless 0$, and the foreign government agrees to change its level of expenditure by $dg^* \equiv a^* \gtrless 0$. Both countries have the choice of lump-sum or distortionary income taxation and each country makes its choice independently. This gives rise to a 2×2 bimatrix game, with payoff matrices, A and B, as set out in tables 8.5 and 8.6. These payoffs include the externalities imposed abroad by choosing one's own policy instrument independently, fully taking into account the international transmission of fiscal policies discussed in Section 8.2.

The domestic and foreign payoffs for each type of government expenditure follow from the definitions above:

$$\left. \begin{array}{l} dV = a\partial V/\partial x + a^*\partial V/\partial x^* \\ dV^* = a\partial V^*/\partial x + a^*\partial V^*/\partial x^* \end{array} \right\} \quad x = g, h.$$

Each element of the payoff matrices presented in tables 8.5 and 8.6 corresponds to a well-defined strategy. Thus, if both the domestic and the foreign economy adopt the strategy of financing their respective marginal consumption expenditures with lump-sum taxation, the payoffs (incentives) associated with the changes from the initial equilibrium are $a\omega_1$ and $a^*\omega_1^*$, respectively. We define a particular choice of tax instruments (strategies) to be a Nash equilibrium to the bimatrix game if neither policy maker has an incentive to switch unilaterally from this point.

Table 8.5
Bimatrix game: Government consumption expenditure

	A. Domestic economy payoff matrix	
	T^*	τ^*
T	$a\omega_1$	$a\omega_1 + a^* \dfrac{U_c \beta \tilde{N}}{2F(\mu - \beta)}$
τ	$a\omega_1 + a \dfrac{U_c \beta \tilde{N}}{2F(\mu - \beta)}$	$a\omega_1 + (a + a^*) \dfrac{U_c \beta \tilde{N}}{2F(\mu - \beta)}$
where $\omega_1 \equiv (1/\beta)(U_g - U_c)$		
	B. Foreign economy payoff matrix	
	T^*	τ^*
T	$a^* \omega_1^*$	$a^* \omega_1^* - a^* \dfrac{U_c^* \beta \tilde{N}}{2F(\mu - \beta)}$
τ	$a^* \omega_1^* - a \dfrac{U_c \beta \tilde{N}}{2F(\mu - \beta)}$	$a^* \omega_1^* - (a + a^*) \dfrac{U_c^* \beta \tilde{N}}{2F(\mu - \beta)}$
where $\omega_1^* \equiv (1/\beta)(U_g^* - U_c^*)$		

Bimatrix Game over Government Consumption Expenditure

Table 8.5 presents this case. We use the notation (x, y^*) $x, y = T, \tau$ to denote the fact that the domestic economy is using tax instrument x and the foreign economy is employing tax instrument y. Table 8.5 implies the following result:

Proposition 8.3 (*Bimatrix game over government consumption expenditure*) Assume, without loss of generality, that the domestic economy is a net creditor ($\tilde{N} > 0$).

1. The pair (T, T^*) is a noncooperative Nash equilibrium if and only if $a > 0$, $a^* < 0$.

2. The pair (T, τ^*) is a noncooperative Nash equilibrium if and only if $a > 0$, $a^* > 0$.

3. The pair (τ, T^*) is a noncooperative Nash equilibrium if and only if $a < 0$, $a^* < 0$.

4. The pair (τ, τ^*) is a noncooperative Nash equilibrium if and only if $a < 0$, $a^* > 0$.

If the domestic economy is a net debtor, these results are reversed.

The intuition behind these results is as follows. Suppose both countries agree to expand their government consumption expenditure and both initially employ lump-sum tax financing; that is, $a > 0$, $a^* > 0$, and (T, T^*). Inspecting Table 8.5 indicates that this is not a Nash equilibrium. In Part

304   Chapter 8

Table 8.6
Bimatrix game: Government production expenditure

	A. Domestic economy payoff matrix	
	T^*	τ^*
T	$a\omega_2 - (aF_{kh} + a^*F_{kh}^*)\dfrac{U_c\tilde{N}}{2(\mu-\beta)}$	$a\omega_2 - aF_{kh}\dfrac{U_c\tilde{N}}{2(\mu-\beta)} - a^*F_{kh}^*\dfrac{(F_h^*-1)U_c\tilde{N}}{2F_h^*(\mu-\beta)}$
τ	$a\omega_2 - aF_{kh}\dfrac{U_c\tilde{N}(F_h-1)}{2F_h(\mu-\beta)} - a^*F_{kh}^*\dfrac{U_c\tilde{N}}{2(\mu-\beta)}$	$a\omega_2 - aF_{kh}\dfrac{U_c\tilde{N}(F_h-1)}{2F_h(\mu-\beta)} - a^*F_{kh}^*\dfrac{U_c\tilde{N}(F_h^*-1)}{2F_h^*(\mu-\beta)}$

where $\omega_2 \equiv (1/\beta)U_c(F_h - 1)$

	B. Foreign economy payoff matrix	
	T^*	τ^*
T	$a^*\omega_2^* + (aF_{kh} + a^*F_{kh}^*)\dfrac{U_c\tilde{N}}{2(\mu-\beta)}$	$a^*\omega_2^* + aF_{kh}\dfrac{U_c^*\tilde{N}}{2(\mu-\beta)} + a^*F_{kh}^*\dfrac{(F_h^*-1)U_c^*\tilde{N}}{2F_h^*(\mu-\beta)}$
τ	$a^*\omega_2^* + aF_{kh}\dfrac{U_c^*\tilde{N}(F_h-1)}{2F_h(\mu-\beta)} + a^*F_{kh}^*\dfrac{U_c\tilde{N}}{2(\mu-\beta)}$	$a^*\omega_2^* + aF_{kh}\dfrac{U_c^*\tilde{N}(F_h-1)}{2F_h(\mu-\beta)} + a^*F_{kh}^*\dfrac{U_c^*\tilde{N}(F_h^*-1)}{2F_h^*(\mu-\beta)}$

where $\omega_2^* \equiv (1/\beta)U_c^*(F_h^* - 1)$

A we note that when $a > 0$, the domestic economy is always better off choosing T, whether the foreign economy chooses T^* or τ^*. This can be seen by comparing elements as one moves down the two columns of the matrix and observing that

$$a\omega_1 > a\omega_1 + a\frac{U_c\beta\tilde{N}}{2F(\mu-\beta)};$$

$$a\omega_1 + a^*\frac{U_c\beta\tilde{N}}{2F(\mu-\beta)} > a\omega_1 + (a+a^*)\frac{U_c\beta\tilde{N}}{2F(\mu-\beta)}.$$

In short, the domestic economy has no incentive to switch to distortionary taxes because that will lower the after-tax return and the net income it earns being a creditor nation. However, the foreign economy, being a debtor nation, will be better off switching to a distortionary tax τ^*. This can be seen by noting that along both rows in Part B of Table 8.5,

$$a^*\omega_1^* < a^*\omega_1^* - a^*\frac{U_c^*\beta\tilde{N}}{2F(\mu-\beta)};$$

$$a^*\omega_1^* - a\frac{U_c^*\beta\tilde{N}}{2F(\mu-\beta)} < a\omega_1 - (a+a^*)\frac{U_c^*\beta\tilde{N}}{2F(\mu-\beta)}.$$

By switching to distortionary taxes, and thus reducing the after-tax rate of return on capital, the foreign economy reduces the amount of debt service owed to the domestic economy, thereby enabling it to increase its consumption and thus enjoy a higher level of welfare. The strategic pair (T, τ^*) is therefore a Nash equilibrium in this case. The other cases can be discussed analogously.

Bimatrix Game over Government Production Expenditure

This case is analogous and is reported in Table 8.6, which implies the following result:

Proposition 8.3′ (*Bimatrix game over government production expenditure*) Assume, without loss of generality, that the domestic economy is a net creditor ($\tilde{N} > 0$) and that $F_h > 1$.

1. The pair (T, T^*) is a noncooperative Nash equilibrium if and only if $a < 0$, $a^* > 0$.

2. The pair (T, τ^*) is a noncooperative Nash equilibrium if and only if $a < 0$, $a^* < 0$.

3. The pair (τ, T^*) is a noncooperative Nash equilibrium if and only if $a > 0$, $a^* > 0$.

4. The pair (τ, τ^*) is a noncooperative Nash equilibrium if and only if $a > 0$, $a^* < 0$.

If the domestic economy is a net debtor or $F_h < 1$, these results are reversed.

To see the intuition in this case, suppose both countries agree to expand their respective government production expenditures and both initially employ lump-sum tax financing (T, T^*). Table 8.6 indicates that this is not a Nash equilibrium. While the foreign economy will now have no incentive to switch, the domestic economy, being a creditor nation, will be better off introducing a distortionary tax, as long as $F_h > 1$. By switching to such a tax, it raises the after-tax rate of return on capital, thereby increasing the amount of capital income it earns from abroad, and enabling it to increase its consumption and enjoy a higher level of welfare. The strategic pair (τ, T^*) is therefore a Nash equilibrium. The other cases can be discussed analogously.

8.5 Cooperative Equilibrium

An issue discussed by several authors concerns the gains from cooperation (see Hamada 1986; Turnovsky 1988; Chari and Kehoe 1990; Devereux 1991). To address this issue in the context of the present model, suppose that the two countries act to maximize their aggregate welfare cooperatively:

$$\Psi \equiv V(.) + V^*(.), \tag{8.13}$$

where $V(.)$ and $V^*(.)$ are given by (8.6a) and (8.6b), respectively.[9] Differentiating the joint welfare function (8.13) with respect to each government's expenditure instrument for the two types of expenditure and for the different modes of finance leads to the cooperative equilibria:

$$\frac{\partial \Psi}{\partial x} \equiv \frac{\partial V(.)}{\partial x} + \frac{\partial V^*(.)}{\partial x} = 0 \tag{8.14a}$$

$$\frac{\partial \Psi}{\partial x^*} \equiv \frac{\partial V(.)}{\partial x^*} + \frac{\partial V^*(.)}{\partial x^*} = 0 \qquad x = g, h. \tag{8.14b}$$

In the cases of (1) government consumption expenditure with lump-sum tax finance and (2) government production expenditure with income tax finance, we have seen that there are no international spillovers in the neighborhood of the Nash equilibrium. In case (1), $\partial V^*/\partial g = \partial V/\partial g^* = 0$, so that the cooperative equilibrium coincides with the Nash equilibrium and, accordingly, there are no gains from cooperation.

Government Consumption Expenditure with Income Tax Finance

From Table 8.3B and equations (8.14) we note that because there are international transmission effects, the cooperative and noncooperative outcomes diverge. In particular, evaluating cooperative welfare at the Nash equilibrium yields the expressions

$$\left.\frac{\partial \Psi}{\partial g}\right|_{Nash} = -\frac{U_c^* \beta \tilde{N}}{2F(\mu - \beta)} \tag{8.15a}$$

$$\left.\frac{\partial \Psi}{\partial g^*}\right|_{Nash} = \frac{U_c \beta \tilde{N}}{2F(\mu - \beta)}. \tag{8.15b}$$

These expressions demonstrate the well-known property that when agents act noncooperatively, they fail to take into account the externality their own action generates abroad. Thus, if the domestic economy is a net creditor, aggregate welfare will be raised if it increases its government consumption expenditure above that forthcoming in the Nash equilibrium. Assuming that government consumption expenditure is financed by a distortionary income tax, we may thus state:

Proposition 8.4 (*Cooperative verse noncooperative government consumption levels*) A noncooperative equilibrium leads to an *undersupply* (*oversupply*) of government *consumption* expenditure in a net creditor (debtor) economy relative to the cooperative equilibrium where joint welfare is being maximized.

Government Production Expenditure with Lump-Sum Tax Finance

From Table 8.4A and equations (8.14), we again observe the presence of international transmission effects, causing the cooperative and noncooperative outcomes to diverge. Evaluating cooperative welfare at the Nash equilibrium yields the expressions

$$\left.\frac{\partial \Psi}{\partial h}\right|_{Nash} = \frac{U_c^* F_{kh} \tilde{N}}{2F(\mu - \beta)} \tag{8.16a}$$

$$\left.\frac{\partial \Psi}{\partial h^*}\right|_{Nash} = -\frac{F_{kh}^* \beta \tilde{N}}{2F(\mu - \beta)}. \tag{8.16b}$$

In this case, if the domestic economy is a net creditor, aggregate welfare will be raised if it decreases its government production expenditure below that forthcoming in the Nash equilibrium. Thus, if productive government expenditure is financed by a lump-sum tax, we may state:

Proposition 8.4' (*Cooperative versus noncooperative government production levels*) A noncooperative equilibrium leads to an *oversupply* (*undersupply*) of government *production* expenditure in a net creditor (debtor) economy relative to the cooperative equilibrium where joint welfare is being maximized.

8.6 Strategic Behavior in a Two-Good Model

In the analysis of sections 8.3–8.5, the key source of strategic behavior has been the distribution of net foreign assets and its asymmetric payoffs to creditor and debtor nations. In this section we consider strategic behavior in a two-good model, with the source of strategic behavior being the terms of trade, as emphasized in the traditional discussions of commercial policy. We shall illustrate the strategic role of fiscal policy in such a model by considering a simplified version of the model developed by Turnovsky (1988).

The model is static, based on the following assumptions (1) the two countries are each specialized in the production of a single good; (2) each government spends only on the domestic good, with the expenditure being in the nature of a consumption good; (3) government expenditure is financed by lump-sum taxation; and (4) the respective utility functions are logarithmic:

$$U^i = \alpha_x^i \ln C_x^i + \alpha_y^i \ln C_y^i + \beta^i \ln G^i, \quad i = A, B, \tag{8.17}$$

where $i = A, B$ indexes the countries and the elasticities $\alpha_x^i + \alpha_y^i = 1$. We assume that good x is produced by country A and good y by country B. We assume that output is fixed in each economy at the levels $\bar{Q}^A$ and $\bar{Q}^B$, respectively. This is consistent with the dynamic models developed in earlier chapters if we assume that the supply of labor is inelastic. In this case, as we have seen, the capital stock remains at the level where the marginal physical product of capital equals the fixed rate of time discount, with the output levels being fixed at $\bar{Q}^A$ and $\bar{Q}^B$, respectively. The budget constraints for the two economies are

$$C_x^A + \sigma C_y^A = \bar{Q}^A - G^A \tag{8.18a}$$

$$\frac{1}{\sigma} C_x^B + C_y^B = \bar{Q}^B - G^B, \tag{8.18b}$$

where σ denotes the relative price of the two goods, and good x is the numeraire good.

The logarithmic utility function has the advantage that explicit solutions are easily obtained. Maximizing the utility functions subject to the respective national budget constraints leads to the following demand functions for the two goods in the two economies:

$$C_x^A = \alpha_x^A(\bar{Q}^A - G^A); \quad C_y^A = \frac{\alpha_y^A}{\sigma}(\bar{Q}^A - G^A) \tag{8.19a}$$

$$C_x^B = \alpha_x^B \sigma(\bar{Q}^B - G^B); \quad C_y^B = \alpha_y^B(\bar{Q}^B - G^B). \tag{8.19b}$$

There are no bonds, so that the relative price, σ, is obtained from the balance of trade equilibrium condition,

$$C_x^B = \sigma C_y^A,$$

and substituting from (8.19a) and (8.19b),

$$\sigma = \left(\frac{\alpha_y^A}{\alpha_x^B}\right)\left(\frac{\bar{Q}^A - G^A}{\bar{Q}^B - G^B}\right). \tag{8.20}$$

The relative price is therefore inversely proportional to the ratio of disposable income in the two economies. Furthermore, substituting (8.20) into (8.19) leads to the following solutions for consumption levels in the two economies:

$$C_x^A = \alpha_x^A(\bar{Q}^A - G^A); \quad C_y^A = \alpha_x^B(\bar{Q}^B - G^B) \tag{8.21a}$$

$$C_x^B = \alpha_y^A(\bar{Q}^A - G^A); \quad C_y^B = \alpha_y^B(\bar{Q}^B - G^B). \tag{8.21b}$$

The interesting feature is that through the adjustment in the relative price, the equilibrium quantities of the imported good in each case depend upon the other country's disposable income. This terms of trade effect gives rise to large spillover effects of fiscal policy in one country to the other.

The next step is to substitute (8.21a) and (8.21b) into the respective utility functions; this yields

$$U^i(G^A, G^B) = K^i + \alpha_x^i \ln(\bar{Q}^A - G^A) + \alpha_y^i \ln(\bar{Q}^B - G^B) + \beta^i \ln G^i,$$
$$i = A, B, \tag{8.22}$$

where the constants K^i are functions of the parameters α_j^i. The noncooperative Nash equilibrium is obtained by setting

$$\frac{\partial U^A}{\partial G^A} \equiv -\frac{\alpha_x^A}{\bar{Q}^A - G^A} + \frac{\beta^A}{G^A} = 0 \tag{8.23a}$$

$$\frac{\partial U^B}{\partial G^B} \equiv -\frac{\alpha_y^B}{\bar{Q}^B - G^B} + \frac{\beta^B}{G^B} = 0. \tag{8.23b}$$

Equations (8.23a) and (8.23b) are the respective reaction functions in the two economies. They are plotted in Figure 8.1 as horizontal and vertical lines, respectively, intersecting at the noncooperative Nash equilibrium point A, where

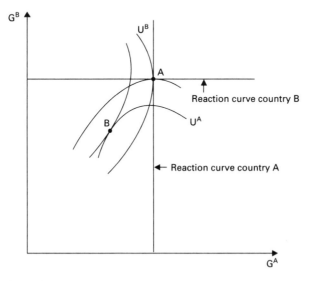

Figure 8.1
Noncooperative and cooperative equilibria

$$G^A = \left(\frac{\beta^A}{\alpha_x^A + \beta^A}\right)\bar{Q}^A; \quad G^B = \left(\frac{\beta^B}{\alpha_y^B + \beta^B}\right)\bar{Q}^B. \qquad (8.24)$$

The corresponding levels of private consumption in the two economies are obtained by substituting (8.24) into (8.21a) and (8.21b):

$$C_x^A = \left(\frac{(\alpha_x^A)^2}{\alpha_x^A + \beta^A}\right)\bar{Q}^A; \quad C_y^A = \left(\frac{(\alpha_x^B)^2}{\alpha_x^B + \beta^B}\right)\bar{Q}^B \qquad (8.21a')$$

$$C_x^B = \left(\frac{\alpha_x^A \alpha_y^A}{\alpha_x^A + \beta^A}\right)\bar{Q}^A; \quad C_y^B = \left(\frac{\alpha_x^B \alpha_y^B}{\alpha_x^B + \beta^B}\right)\bar{Q}^B. \qquad (8.21b')$$

The implied levels of utility in the two countries are obtained by substituting these two solutions into the indirect utility function (8.22).

By substitution one can verify that the optimal relationship between private and government consumption in country A, for example, satisfies the general relationship (see Turnovsky 1988)

$$\frac{\partial U^A}{\partial G^A} = \frac{\partial U^A}{\partial C_x^A}\left(1 + E_y^A \frac{\partial \sigma}{\partial G^A}\right), \qquad (8.25)$$

where E_y^A denotes the excess demand for good y in country A. Under the assumption that the domestic economy is specialized in the production of good x and that the government purchases only the domestic good, $E_y^A = C_y^A > 0$.

The advantage of expressing the optimum in this way is that it highlights the parallels between the present static two-good analysis, in which the spillovers occur through the relative price, and the analysis of Section 8.3, where the spillovers occurred through the net foreign debt position. This is seen most clearly by comparing (8.25) with (8.9') and (8.10). In the absence of a relative price effect, as in a static one-commodity world, (8.25) would imply that the optimal level of government expenditure would be to equate the marginal utility of government expenditure to the marginal utility of private expenditure, as in (8.9'a) and (8.9'b). However, in the present two-commodity world, an increase in government expenditure on good x raises its relative price (reduces σ) in accordance with (8.20). This causes the private agent to substitute away from that good, so that the marginal utility of the public good should be equated to something less than the marginal utility of the private good x. But it is clear that an improvement in the terms of trade in the current static two-good model (that is, the decline in σ) plays precisely the same role as being a debtor (negative N) in the intertemporal one-good model.

Suppose now that the two policy makers act cooperatively, and maximize their joint utility functions:

$$U^A + U^B = K^A + K^B + (\alpha_x^A + \alpha_x^B)\ln(\bar{Q}^A - G^A)$$
$$+ (\alpha_y^A + \alpha_y^B)\ln(\bar{Q}^B - G^B) + \beta^A \ln G^A + \beta^B \ln G^B.$$

The optimality conditions are

$$\frac{\partial(U^A + U^B)}{\partial G^A} \equiv -\frac{(\alpha_x^A + \alpha_x^B)}{\bar{Q}^A - G^A} + \frac{\beta^A}{G^A} = 0 \tag{8.26a}$$

$$\frac{\partial(U^A + U^B)}{\partial G^B} \equiv -\frac{(\alpha_y^A + \alpha_y^B)}{\bar{Q}^B - G^B} + \frac{\beta^B}{G^B} = 0, \tag{8.26b}$$

the solutions to which are

$$G^A = \left(\frac{\beta^A}{\alpha_x^A + \alpha_x^B + \beta^A}\right)\bar{Q}^A; \quad G^B = \left(\frac{\beta^B}{\alpha_y^A + \alpha_y^B \beta^B}\right)\bar{Q}^B. \tag{8.27}$$

This is illustrated by the point B in Figure 8.1, which lies at the tangency points between the two indifference curves. Comparing (8.24) with (8.27) (or point A with point B), we see that cooperation leads to a reduction in the levels of government expenditure.

An interesting issue concerns the magnitudes of the difference between the two equilibria. One conclusion prevalent among macroeconomic models analyzing the gains from monetary cooperation is that the noncooperative and cooperative equilibria typically are closely clustered, rendering the numerical gains from cooperation small (see, e.g., Oudiz and Sachs 1985; Taylor 1985). In the present example we find the respective percentage changes in the levels of G^A and G^B (measured from the non-cooperative equilibria as bases) to be

$$\frac{\Delta G^A}{G^A} = \frac{\alpha_x^B}{\alpha_x^A + \alpha_x^B + \beta^A}; \quad \frac{\Delta G^B}{G^B} = \frac{\alpha_y^A}{\alpha_y^A + \alpha_y^B + \beta^B}.$$

Suppose, for example, one takes $\alpha_x^A = \alpha_y^B = 0.6$, $\alpha_y^A = \alpha_x^B = 0.6$, $\beta^A = \beta^B = 0.3$, suggesting that each economy has a preference for its own good. Then from (8.24) the ratios of government expenditure to output in the two economies are $G^A/\bar{Q}^A = G^B/\bar{Q}^B = 0.333$. Moving to a cooperative equilibrium reduces these shares to around 0.231 (see (8.27)), which is a relative reduction in government expenditure of nearly 31 percent. While the ratios of consumption levels to disposable income remain fixed (set by α_j^i), the absolute levels increase correspondingly by around 15 percent. Although these parameter values are arbitrary, they are certainly plausible insofar as the implied shares of government expenditure in output and consumption patterns are concerned. Furthermore, these differences in the equilibria are substantially larger than those obtained from macroeconomic models.

Effects of a Coalition

Most of the formal literature analyzing strategic behavior deals with the gains from cooperation in a two-country world. But in reality, cooperative arrangements are formed among groups of countries, with some countries being excluded from such coalitions. This raises interesting issues, such as how the gains from cooperation between two countries—A and B, say—impact on a third country, C, which produces a third good, say z. This type of issue can be readily addressed by using the logarithmic model of this section.

Augmented to three countries, the model contains the following relationships. The utility functions for country i are

$$U^i = \alpha^i_x \ln C^i_x + \alpha^i_y \ln C^i_y + \alpha^i_z \ln C^i_z + \beta^i \ln G^i,$$

$$\alpha^i_x + \alpha^i_y + \alpha^i_z = 1, \quad i = A, B, C, \tag{8.28}$$

and the corresponding budget constraints are

$$C^A_x + \sigma_y C^A_y + \sigma_z C^A_z = \bar{Q}^A - G^A \tag{8.29a}$$

$$(1/\sigma_y) C^B_x + C^B_y + C^B_z (\sigma_z/\sigma_y) = \bar{Q}^B - G^B \tag{8.29b}$$

$$(1/\sigma_z) C^C_x + (\sigma_y/\sigma_z) C^C_y + C^C_z = \bar{Q}^C - G^C, \tag{8.29c}$$

where σ_y is the relative price of good y to good x, and σ_z is the relative price of good z to good x.

There are two bilateral balance of trade conditions,

$$\sigma_y C^A_y + \sigma_z C^A_z = C^B_x + C^C_x \tag{8.30a}$$

$$(1/\sigma_y) C^B_x + (\sigma_z/\sigma_y) C^B_y = C^A_y + C^C_y, \tag{8.30b}$$

together with three market-clearing conditions:

$$C^A_j + C^B_j + C^C_j + G^i = \bar{Q}^i; \quad i = A, B, C, \quad j = x, y, z, \tag{8.31}$$

only two of which are independent.

Solving the system as before leads to

$$\sigma_y = \psi_y \left(\frac{\bar{Q}^A - G^A}{\bar{Q}^B - G^B} \right); \quad \sigma_z = \psi_z \left(\frac{\bar{Q}^A - G^A}{\bar{Q}^C - G^C} \right),$$

where

$$\psi_y = \frac{\alpha_y^C(1-\alpha_x^A) + \alpha_x^C\alpha_y^A}{\alpha_x^B\alpha_y^C + \alpha_x^C(1-\alpha_y^B)}; \quad \psi_z = \frac{\alpha_z^A(1-\alpha_y^B) + \alpha_z^B\alpha_y^A}{\alpha_x^B\alpha_y^C + \alpha_x^C(1-\alpha_y^B)}$$

and

$$C_x^A = \alpha_x^A(\bar{Q}^A - G^A); \quad C_y^A = (\alpha_y^A/\psi_y)(\bar{Q}^B - G^B);$$
$$C_z^A = (\alpha_z^A/\psi_z)(\bar{Q}^C - G^C)$$
$$C_x^B = (\alpha_x^B/\psi_y)(\bar{Q}^A - G^A); \quad C_y^B = \alpha_y^B(\bar{Q}^B - G^B);$$
$$C_z^A = (\alpha_z^B\psi_y/\psi_z)(\bar{Q}^C - G^C)$$
$$C_x^C = (\alpha_x^C/\psi_z)(\bar{Q}^A - G^A); \quad C_y^C = (\alpha_y^C\psi_z/\psi_y)(\bar{Q}^B - G^B);$$
$$C_z^C = \alpha_z^C(\bar{Q}^C - G^C).$$

The corresponding levels of utility are therefore of the form

$$U^i(G^A, G^B, G^C) = K^i + \alpha_x^i \ln(\bar{Q}^A - G^A) + \alpha_y^i \ln(\bar{Q}^B - G^B)$$
$$+ \alpha_z^i \ln(\bar{Q}^C - G^C) + \beta^i \ln G^i, \quad i = A, B, C.$$

Suppose that initially all three countries act noncooperatively. The optimal levels of government expenditure for the three countries are of the form

$$G^A = \left(\frac{\beta^A}{\alpha_x^A + \beta^A}\right)\bar{Q}^A; \quad G^B = \left(\frac{\beta^B}{\alpha_y^B + \beta^B}\right)\bar{Q}^B; \quad G^C = \left(\frac{\beta^C}{\alpha_y^C + \beta^C}\right)\bar{Q}^C, \tag{8.32}$$

analogous to (8.24).

Now assume that countries A and B form a coalition and cooperate to maximize their joint welfare $U^A + U^B$. The optimality conditions are as in (8.27),

$$G^A = \left(\frac{\beta^A}{\alpha_x^A + \alpha_x^B + \beta^A}\right)\bar{Q}^A; \quad G^B = \left(\frac{\beta^B}{\alpha_y^A + \alpha_y^B + \beta^B}\right)\bar{Q}^B,$$

with both G_A and G_B being reduced from their respective noncooperative equilibrium levels. Denoting these reductions by dG^A and dG^B, the net welfare gains for countries A and B are

$$dU^A = -\frac{\alpha_y^A}{(\bar{Q}^B - G^B)} dG^B; \quad dU^B = -\frac{\alpha_x^B}{(\bar{Q}^A - G^A)} dG^A, \tag{8.33}$$

where G^A and G^B are evaluated at their respective noncooperative levels.

How does the formation of this coalition affect the welfare of the excluded country C? The answer is given by the expression

$$dU^C = -\frac{\alpha_x^C}{(\bar{Q}^A - G^A)} dG^A - \frac{\alpha_y^C}{(\bar{Q}^B - G^B)} dG^B,$$

which, with dG^A and dG^B both being negative, implies an unambiguous welfare improvement. In fact, the welfare gain to country C may quite plausibly exceed those accruing to either of the partners in the coalition. This is so, for example, if all countries have identical tastes and the coefficients α_j^i are equal. The reason is that the coalition reduces both G^A and G^B, and this has a favorable effect on the terms of trade for country C with respect to both of its trading partners.

8.7 A Simple Dynamic Game Theory Formulation

Our analysis has reduced the strategic decision to a single static decision. That is, the government has been assumed to choose the level of its policy variable only once, taking into account the responses of the private agents in both economies and the impact of their decisions on their respective welfares over the subsequent dynamics. Once chosen, the fiscal instruments have been held fixed over time. This is of course a serious simplification, but it has the advantage of having enabled us to formulate the model in simple static game theoretic terms, and to apply basic concepts from static game theory.

An important step toward making this analysis more relevant and realistic is to extend the strategic decision-making to a dynamic setting, permitting policy makers to react continually over time, as the economies evolve. Analyzing this requires the methods of dynamic game theory (see Basar and Olsder 1982). Once we advance to a dynamic setting, the role of information, to which we referred at the beginning of this chapter, becomes crucial. In particular, the concepts of *open-loop* and *closed-loop* solutions assume central importance, because they distinguish between two different information structures relevant in dynamic games. Under an open-loop information structure, the decisions are expressed as functions of calendar time. The dynamics of the capital stock and other variables we have discussed in previous chapters have been expressed in open-loop form. These equilibria have the characteristic that the policy maker, having announced a policy, may have an incentive to renege. The solutions may therefore be *time inconsistent*. Under a closed-loop information structure, on the other hand, policies at time t, say, are expressed in terms of the state of the economy untill that time. These are often expressed in terms of feedback rules, with each policy maker taking account of the response of the other to the change in the state. They are solved by using dynamic programming methods, which by their construction are *time consistent*. In this section, we illustrate these two solution concepts by considering a canonical version of the two-country world economy that we have been discussing in this chapter.

Open-Loop Nash Equilibrium

The strategic problem facing each policy maker can be expressed in terms of the following system. The models we have developed in this chapter express the reduced-form dynamics of the world economy in terms of

$$\dot{k} = H(k, x, x^*) \qquad k(0) = k_0, \tag{8.34}$$

where k is the stock of capital in the domestic economy, and x and x^* are the domestic and foreign government policy instruments, respectively. For present purposes it is not necessary to identify them as consumption or production expenditures. Equation (8.34) can be thought of as being the stable reduced-form representation of the dynamic system described by (8.2). All other dynamic variables, including k^* and N, can be expressed in terms of the evolution of k.

The indirect instantaneous utility functions of domestic and foreign residents are $V(k, x, x^*)$ and $V^*(k, x, x^*)$, respectively. These are obtained by solving for consumption in terms of the state variable, k, and the two policy variables, x and x^*.

At any point of time, t, the domestic policy maker's strategic problem is to choose his policy, $x(t)$, given the chosen policy of the foreign policy maker, $x^*(t)$, to

$$\text{Max} \int_0^\infty V(k, x, x^*)e^{-\beta t}dt, \tag{8.35}$$

subject to the dynamic system (8.34). Similarly, the foreign policy maker's problem is to choose $x^*(t)$, given the level of policy of the domestic policy maker, $x(t)$, to

$$\text{Max} \int_0^\infty V^*(k, x, x^*)e^{-\beta t}dt. \tag{8.35'}$$

The optimality conditions for the domestic policy maker are thus given by

$$V_x(k, x, x^*) + vH_x(k, x, x^*) = 0 \tag{8.36a}$$

$$V_k(k, x, x^*) + vH_k(k, x, x^*) = -\dot{v} + \beta v, \tag{8.36b}$$

where v is the costate variable associated with the accumulation equation (8.34). Similarly, the optimality conditions for the foreign policy maker are

$$V^*_{x^*}(k, x, x^*) + v^* H_{x^*}(k, x, x^*) = 0 \tag{8.36a'}$$

$$V^*_k(k, x, x^*) + v^* H_k(k, x, x^*) = -\dot{v}^* + \beta v^*. \tag{8.36b'}$$

As usual, v and v^* measure the marginal utility of *domestic* capital, though now from the viewpoint of the two policy makers. For this reason they should not confused with λ and λ^*, which measured marginal utility from the standpoint of the representative agents and are subsumed in the stable accumulation process described in (8.34).

Solving (8.36a) and (8.36a') simultaneously, we obtain the solutions for the joint decision variables at time t, as functions of the state of the world economy at that time, as described by k and the two marginal utilities, v and v^*:

$$x = x(k, v, v^*) \tag{8.37}$$

$$x^* = x^*(k, v, v^*). \tag{8.37'}$$

Substituting (8.37) and (8.37') into (8.34), (8.36b), and (8.36b') leads to the equilibrium dynamic system in capital, k, and the two costate variables, v and v^*:

$$\dot{k} = H[k, x(k, v, v^*), x^*(k, v, v^*)] \tag{8.38a}$$

$$\dot{v} = \beta v - V_k[k, x(k, v, v^*), x^*(k, v, v^*)]$$
$$\quad - v H_k[k, x(k, v, v^*), x^*(k, v, v^*)] \tag{8.38b}$$

$$\dot{v}^* = \beta v^* - V^*_k[k, x(k, v, v^*), x^*(k, v, v^*)]$$
$$\quad - v^* H_k[k, x(k, v, v^*), x^*(k, v, v^*)]. \tag{8.38c}$$

Assuming the system is well behaved, the linearized approximation to (8.38) will have two unstable roots, one corresponding to each of the jump variables, v and v^*, and one stable root, $\mu_{OL} < 0$, corresponding to the sluggish capital stock (the subscript OL denotes "open loop"). Linearizing (8.38) about the steady state, the open-loop Nash equilibrium is approximated by the dynamic system

$$k = \tilde{k} + (k_0 - \tilde{k}) e^{\mu_{OL} t} \tag{8.39a}$$

$$v(t) - \tilde{v} = \theta_{OL}[k(t) - \tilde{k}] \tag{8.39b}$$

$$v^*(t) - \tilde{v}^* = \theta^*_{OL}[k(t) - \tilde{k}], \tag{8.39c}$$

where θ_{OL} and θ_{OL}^* denote the slopes of the stable saddlepaths in $v-k$ and v^*-k space, respectively. The time paths for the respective government policy variables are obtained by substituting (8.39) into (8.37) and (8.37′). The potential for time inconsistency comes from the possibility that the government may be able to choose the initial capital stock in the domestic country, k_0, as we permitted earlier in this chapter; see (8.4).

Closed-Loop (Feedback) Nash Equilibrium

The closed-loop Nash equilibrium assumes that each agent observes and reacts to the current state of the economy, as represented by k. That is, each agent operates in accordance with a *feedback rule* that we denote by $x = \psi(k)$ and $x^* = \psi^*(k)$, respectively. In the closed-loop Nash equilibrium, each agent takes the feedback rule of the other as given. Thus, when calculating the effect of a change in the state on each agent's welfare, account must be taken of the response of the other agent to the change in the state, in accordance with his given feedback rule.

To determine the optimal strategy for the domestic policy maker, we substitute the feedback of the foreign agent into his objective function, as well as into the dynamics of the world economy. Thus, the domestic policy maker's strategic problem can now be stated as being to choose the time path of expenditure, $x(t)$, to

$$\text{Max} \int_0^\infty V[k, x, \psi^*(k)] e^{-\beta t} dt, \qquad (8.40)$$

subject to

$$\dot{k} = H[k, x, \psi^*(k)] \qquad k(0) = k_0. \qquad (8.41)$$

The optimality conditions for the domestic agent are now

$$V_x[k, x, \psi^*(k)] + v H_x[k, x, \psi^*(k)] = 0 \qquad (8.42a)$$

$$V_k[k, x, \psi^*(k)] + V_{x^*}[k, x, \psi^*(k)] \cdot \psi^{*'}(k)$$
$$+ v\{H_k[k, x, \psi^*(k)] + H_{x^*}[k, x, \psi^*(k)] \cdot \psi^{*'}(k)\} = -\dot{v} + \beta v. \qquad (8.42b)$$

Analogously, the optimality conditions for the foreign policy maker are

$$V_{x^*}^*[k, \psi(k), x^*] + v^* H_{x^*}^*[k, \psi(k), x^*] = 0 \qquad (8.42a')$$

$$V_k^*[k, \psi(k), x^*] + V_x^*[k, \psi(k), x^*] \cdot \psi'(k)$$
$$+ v^*\{H_k[k, \psi(k), x^*] + H_x[k, \psi(k), x^*] \cdot \psi'(k)\} = -\dot{v}^* + \beta v^*. \qquad (8.42b')$$

Solving (8.42a) and (8.42a′) yields expressions for the policy decisions of the form

$$x = x[k, \psi^*(k), v] \tag{8.43}$$

$$x^* = x^*[k, \psi(k), v^*]. \tag{8.43'}$$

Substituting (8.43) and (8.43′) into (8.41), (8.42b), and (8.42b′) yields a third-order dynamic system in the three variables k, v, and v^*, analogous to (8.38). The difference is that it, and therefore the eigenvalues of the associated linearized system, depend upon the assumed form of the feedback functions $\psi(.)$ and $\psi^*(.)$.

Again assuming a well-behaved saddlepath solution, the stable linearized equilibrium path is of the form

$$k = \tilde{k} + (k_0 - \tilde{k})e^{\mu_{CL}t} \tag{8.44a}$$

$$v(t) - \tilde{v} = \theta_{CL}[k(t) - \tilde{k}] \tag{8.44b}$$

$$v^*(t) - \tilde{v}^* = \theta^*_{CL}[k(t) - \tilde{k}], \tag{8.44c}$$

where the subscript CL denotes "closed loop." The final stage is to substitute (8.44b) into (8.43) and (8.44c) into (8.43′), and use the resulting relationships to calculate the solutions for the assumed feedback rules, ψ and ψ^*, that are in fact consistent with the policy rules actually implemented. The result is a closed-loop Nash equilibrium.

The practical application of these solution methods is extremely difficult. Analytical solutions are almost impossible to obtain, and numerical solution almost certainly becomes necessary. A definitive exposition of the methods and algorithms is provided by Basar and Olsder (1982). Examples of both open-loop and closed-loop solutions applied to the problem of monetary coordination have been obtained by Miller and Salmon (1985).

8.8 Some Final Remarks

The fact that fiscal policy generates spillovers abroad introduces strategic aspects into international fiscal policy. In this respect two main aspects of our results should be highlighted. First, the existence of international spillovers in the cases where (1) government consumption expenditure is financed with a distortionary income tax and, (2) government production expenditure is financed by a lump-sum tax indicates the potential gains from cooperation in those cases. Second, we have characterized the noncooperative Nash equilibrium in the case where each country is committed to some specified change in its level of government expenditure(s) and is choosing between a lump-sum tax and a distortionary tax.

This leads to a bimatrix game, the equilibrium to which can be given the following general characterization. The preferred choice between lump-sum tax financing and distortionary tax financing depends upon whether the country wishes to expand or to contract its expenditures and whether it is a creditor or a debtor. In general, a creditor country wishing to expand its government consumption expenditure is better off using lump-sum taxation; if it wishes to contract, it should employ distortionary taxation. The same nation wishing to expand its government production expenditure should use distortionary income taxation and employ lump-sum taxation if it wishes to contract. These choices are reversed for a debtor economy.

Our discussion of strategic behavior in the world economy does little more than scratch the surface. There is a huge literature, the bulk of it focusing on the strategic aspects of trade policy rather than macroeconomic policy. But there are several papers related to the approach discussed here.

First, the two-good, one-period model, considered in Section 8.6, is almost identical to the one-good, two-period model used by Hamada (1986) to study strategic fiscal policy. The present model can be translated to his by reinterpreting the subscripts x and y as two periods (the present and the future, say) so that the utility function applies intertemporally. Furthermore, combining (8.18a), (8.18b), and the balance of trade condition yields

$$C_x^i + \sigma C_y^i = (\bar{Q}_x^i - G_x^i) + \sigma(\bar{Q}_y^i - G_y^i),$$

which can now be reinterpreted as being a two-period intertemporal budget constraint in which σ denotes the intertemporal price (the interest rate) rather than the intratemporal terms of trade. Formally, everything else applies as before. The assumption that $E_y^A > 0$, which appeared in (8.25), can now be interpreted that country A has an excess demand for future goods and is a lender, while country B is a borrower.

Devereux (1991) has analyzed strategic fiscal policy in terms of a dynamic two-good model capital accumulation, analogous to that developed in Chapter 7. He emphasizes the two sources of international spillovers giving rise to strategic behavior. The first is the static linkage through the terms of trade, which we emphasized in Section 8.6, and which, as Devereux notes, leads to a strategic outcome analogous to the traditional optimal tariff argument. The second is the dynamic linkage through the effect on the capital stock, which was the source of international transmission in sections 8.3–8.5. He analyzes the gains from cooperation and finds them to be substantial. However, as he notes, the fact that his analysis is based on logarithmic preferences tends to rule out problems of time inconsistency and associated issues of credibility.

Previous authors have shown that with problems of time inconsistency, international cooperation may not be welfare-improving. On the contrary, all countries may be made worse off. Rogoff (1985) and Kehoe (1987) have presented examples where cooperation between two governments can exacerbate the distortion caused by the lack of credibility between governments and their own private sectors.

Finally, we mention two issues that are relevant to studying strategic behavior and that should not be ignored. The first is that of tax smoothing. The discussion of sections 8.4 and 8.5 proposed using the tax rate as a strategic policy variable. To the extent that is done, strategic tax policy will involve frequent adjustment in the tax rate, as each policy maker responds to the decision of the other. This runs counter to the notion of tax smoothing. In a seminal paper, Barro (1979) introduced the idea that the government should spread the burden associated with tax increases over time. Thus, for example, when faced with a temporary increase in its expenditure, the government should issue debt in order to spread the increase in taxes over a longer period and thus reduce the welfare costs of higher tax rates. This has led to the proposition that taxes should be adjusted only gradually, and to the prediction that tax rates should follow a random walk, analogous to the prediction of the Hall (1978) model that consumption should follow a random walk. Empirical work by Ghosh (1995) provides some support for tax smoothing, and clearly the costs associated with frequent tax changes should be taken into account.

The final issue that we have not considered, but that a serious analysis of international policy coordination needs to take into account, is the role of political considerations. Our analysis has been a narrow strategic one, expressed in terms of limited economic payoffs. But there are all kinds of important political constraints, both within economies and between countries, that limit the abilities of governments to implement what might otherwise be their preferred economic policies. In addition, economic policy making within an economy is not in the hands of a single policy maker. Fiscal decisions are typically in the hands of one set of agents, the treasury, while monetary decisions are in the hands of another set of agents, the central bank. Both of these agencies have possibly conflicting objectives that may, or may not, coincide with the benign objective of maximizing the intertemporal welfare of the representative agent. This leads into questions of political economy that are beginning to receive attention in economics (see, e.g., Persson and Tabellini 1990). These are clearly important issues, and are bound to become more so in the future, as economists begin to recognize the reality and significance of political constraints.

Notes

1. Authors such as Aizenman (1992) and Casella (1992) present related analyses in the context of monetary policy and monetary integration, respectively.

2. The material for sections 8.2–8.5 is adapted from Bianconi and Turnovsky (1996).

3. For example, Arrow and Kurz (1970, Chapter 4) and Baxter and King (1993) introduce the stock of government capital into the production function.

4. As discussed in Chapter 6, lump-sum tax financing with an elastic labor supply generates real dynamic effects in both the domestic and the foreign economies. Generally, these can be summarized by saying that in this case an increase in government consumption expenditure will tend to be expansionary domestically and contractionary abroad. Consumption tends to get crowded out in both economies.

5. The same condition determines the optimal government production expenditure in a closed economy (see Turnovsky and Fisher 1995).

6. The difference between the efficiency conditions (1) and (2) reflects the fact that private capital is a stock and government expenditure is a flow. If one were to introduce government expenditure as a stock, then in the absence of congestion, the long-run efficiency condition for the provision of public capital in the two countries would be $F_h(\bar{k},\bar{h}) = F_h^*(\bar{k}^*,\bar{h}^*) = \beta$.

7. The notion of time inconsistency was introduced by Kydland and Prescottt (1977). An introduction to the topic of time consistency is provided by Turnovsky (1995, Chapter 11).

8. In Devereux (1991) the size of g is given by the effect of the optimum time-consistent tax on the terms of trade and the net asset position is zero. In Ghosh (1991) the size of g is determined by the conflicting interests of wage earners and capital owners for a fixed level of world savings.

9. The welfare weights in the world welfare function are assumed to be identically equal to 1. Relaxing this assumption does not alter the results of this section, as shown in the model of Turnovsky (1988). (See, e.g., Chari and Kehoe 1990 for a discussion of the welfare weights in this context.)

III STOCHASTIC GROWTH MODELS

9 Stochastic Growth in a Small Open Economy

9.1 Introduction

All of the models developed thus far have assumed complete certainty so that agents are endowed with perfect foresight. The three chapters of Part III extend the analysis to introduce uncertainty. This is important for several reasons. First, international trading is by nature risky, so that to ignore this aspect is a serious shortcoming. Second, insofar as we are interested in analyzing the international aspects of tax policy, it is important to do so in a stochastic environment. It will be recalled from earlier chapters that in the presence of perfect financial markets, the viability of alternative tax regimes is limited by the presence of arbitrage possibilities (see, e.g., Chapter 6). However, as Slemrod (1988) has suggested, these stringent conditions are essentially an artifact of the absence of risk and the corner solutions this yields with respect to portfolio decisions. The viability issue ceases to be important in the presence of risk and risk-averse agents. Third, the presence of risk highlights the important role played by the portfolio adjustment in determining the response of the growth rate to a tax shock.

As with any dynamic model, the introduction of stochastic elements involves a choice as to whether the model should be formulated using discrete or continuous time. We choose to formulate and solve the problem using continuous-time intertemporal optimizing methods, rather than adopting the more familiar discrete-time approach. Our main reason for this choice is that although continuous-time stochastic problems are tractable only under restrictive conditions, when these conditions are met, the solutions they yield are highly transparent, providing substantial insights into the characteristics of the equilibrium. The present chapter outlines the analytical techniques we shall employ and applies them to a simple real model of a small open economy.[1]

As a historical matter, continuous-time stochastic optimization methods have been more readily adopted by finance theorists than by economists. It is generally agreed that the use of such methods in finance and economics was pioneered by Robert Merton. A collection of his seminal contributions has been brought together in Merton (1990), which contains an extensive bibliography. A review of many of the examples in both finance and economics is provided by Malliaris and Brock (1982). As far as the specific applications to macroeconomics are concerned, these are relatively sparse. Bourguignon (1974), Eaton (1981), Gertler and Grinols (1982), Stulz (1986), Corsetti (1991), Grinols and Turnovsky (1993), Benavie, Grinols, and Turnovsky (1996), and Smith (1996) provide examples of general equilibrium models of closed economies. Applications of these methods to general equilibrium models of open economies include Stulz (1981), Turnovsky (1993), Grinols and Turnovsky (1994), Obstfeld (1994), and Asea and Turnovsky (1997).[2]

The specification of the economy is simple. Production takes place by means of a linear technology in which capital is the only factor of production. With the production function thus exhibiting constant returns to scale in the input being accumulated, the equilibrium is one of ongoing, endogenously determined growth. The economy is subject to various stochastic disturbances of both domestic and foreign origin, all of which are taken to be Brownian motion processes. Accordingly, the model can be characterized as a "stochastic endogenous growth model." In this respect, it can be viewed as an extension of the deterministic one-sector endogenous growth model developed in Sections 5.2–5.4.

Chapter 10 extends this model to introduce a monetary sector along the lines of Grinols and Turnovsky (1994) and Turnovsky and Grinols (1996), and uses it to analyze issues relating to monetary policy in an open economy, such as the choice of exchange rate regime. These are clearly important issues that the present stochastic approach is well suited to address. The final chapter goes on to construct a stochastic two-country model to analyze the role of savings and investment in a stochastically growing world economy. It also generalizes some of the discussion of taxes carried out in Chapter 6 to a stochastic environment.

The present chapter is structured as follows. Since the methods of continuous-time stochastic optimization are not so familiar to economists, Section 9.2 introduces the necessary results from stochastic calculus. The key observation here is that under reasonable assumptions, variances are of the first order of magnitude in time and therefore interact with the first moments (the means) in the dynamic evolution of the system. Section 9.3 sets out a stochastic version of the one-sector growth model discussed in Chapter 5, deriving a closed-form solution for its equilibrium, which is presented in Sections 9.4 and 9.5. The model is then applied to discuss two main issues: terms of trade shocks and tax policy. In Section 9.6 we extend the discussion of the Laursen-Metzler effect, introduced in Section 3.4, to a stochastic situation. As we will note, once the analysis is extended to a stochastic environment, the range of shocks one can address increases. For example, one can consider the effects of structural changes, such as changes in the means and variances of terms of trade shocks, on the economy, as well as the shocks themselves. These issues are taken up in Sections 9.7–9.9. Section 9.10 focuses on taxes and the transmission of tax shocks, while Sections 9.11 and 9.12 consider optimal tax policy and a more general optimal integrated fiscal policy, respectively.

One critical assumption necessary to sustain an equilibrium of steady stochastic growth is that all stochastic disturbances are proportional to the current state of the economy, as represented by the capital stock or wealth. This is not an unreasonable assumption; in fact, the idea of the magnitude of stochastic shocks being linked to the size of the economy is more plausible than the alternative, where they are taken to be purely additive. Assuming a constant relative risk-averse utility function, this leads to an equilibrium having ongoing stochastic growth, in which means and variances of relevant endogenous variables are jointly and consistently determined. Such an equilibrium, which we term a *mean-variance equilibrium*, is analogous to that familiar from finance theory, the elements of which may thereby be incorporated into a complete macroeconomic framework in a more satisfactory way.

It is also useful to think of this approach from the perspective of the rational expectations methodology. There the objective is the development of an internally consistent stochastic system to examine the economy, under the assumption that the underlying relationships depend only upon the *means* (first moments) of the relevant variables and not on any higher moments. That approach might therefore be said to provide a *certainty equivalent* macroeconomic framework. By contrast, the objective here is to develop a model that is internally consistent in both the *means* and the *variances*, thereby enabling us to address important tradeoffs that in general exist between the *level* of macroeconomic performance and the associated *risk*. We view this as an important step forward in the construction of a comprehensive macroeconomic model.

One characteristic of the equilibrium we shall derive in all our models is that portfolio shares remain constant over time. Given the stationarity of the structure of the model and that it yields a recurring ongoing equilibrium, this is not an unreasonable property for it to have. But while the derivation of such a consistent equilibrium is tractable, it involves a certain amount of detail. Again, the analogy here with the rational expectations methodology is useful. The general strategy we adopt for determining the macroeconomic equilibrium is to posit specific forms for the stochastic processes facing the agents in the economy, and then to determine restrictions on these processes that make them consistent with optimizing behavior and market clearance. This procedure will be recognized as an application of the method of undetermined coefficients, which serves as one of the standard solution procedures for solving linear rational expectations equilibria.

9.2 Some Basic Results from Continuous-Time Stochastic Calculus

We begin by presenting a brief summary of the main results from continuous-time stochastic calculus to be used in Chapters 9–11. More detailed but nontechnical treatments accessible to economists are provided by

Chow (1979), Malliaris and Brock (1982), and, more recently, Dixit and Pindyck (1994). For our purposes, Chow provides a compact review of the relevant techniques, and to some extent we shall draw upon his exposition. Before proceeding, a word about notation is in order. We shall follow convention and let E denote expected value, except in the few places where it is used in conjunction with the nominal exchange rate, also denoted by E; there, to avoid confusion, we shall denote expected value by E; see (9.34). Also, cov denotes covariance.

Linear Stochastic Differential Equations

The starting point is a system of linear stochastic difference equations, expressed over the period t to $t+h$,

$$y(t+h) - y(t) = [A(t)y(t) + B(t)]h + v(t+h) - v(t), \qquad (9.1)$$

where $A(t)$ and $B(t)$ are matrices, and h is arbitrary and not necessarily an integer. We assume that the stochastic residual term $v(t+h) - v(t)$ has the following properties: (1) it is a Markov process, meaning that its probability distribution is independent of anything prior to time t; (2) it has mean zero and is independently distributed over time. We shall consider the continuous limit of this system as the time interval h approaches zero. In the absence of the residual, one could derive this limit by dividing through by h, letting $h \to 0$, and obtain the usual system of deterministic ordinary differential equations. However, this process is complicated by the presence of the stochastic term, which needs to be considered further.

In the case of a unit time interval $h = 1$, we have the usual system of first-order linear stochastic difference equations. Let us assume that the covariance matrix of the residuals is Σ. Suppose we divide the unit period $(t, t+1)$ into n segments of length $h = 1/n$ units. By the assumption that each successive increment $v(t+h) - v(t)$ is statistically independent and identically distributed, the covariance matrix Σ of their sum equals n times the covariance matrix of each increment, implying

$$\operatorname{cov}[v(t+h) - v(t)] = h\Sigma = (1/n)\Sigma. \qquad (9.2)$$

Thus the variance-covariance matrix increases linearly with h. If one further assumes that the successive increments are normally distributed, the process is called a *Wiener process* or *Brownian motion*. This is the assumption upon which almost all of continuous-time stochastic calculus is based, and is the assumption that we shall invoke. As will become apparent in the course of this chapter, a great advantage of this formulation is that variances are introduced into the dynamics in a most natural way.

The key observation about (9.2) is that the covariance matrix of the increment $v(t+h) - v(t)$ is proportional to the time interval h, implying that the standard deviation of each component of the vector $v(t+h) - v(t)$ is proportional to $\sqrt{h}$. This is an important property because it means that terms involving squares of elements of $v(t+h) - v(t)$ are of order h and not h^2. In other words, the variances are of the first order, and do not vanish as the time interval $h \to 0$. This is what makes the methods of continuous-time stochastic calculus so attractive; the means and variances are interdependent. As $h \to 0$, we denote h by dt, rewriting (9.1) as

$$dy = [A(t)y + B(t)]dt + dv, \qquad (9.3)$$

where $E(dv) = 0$ and $\text{cov}(dv) = \Sigma(t)dt$. Thus (9.3) is a system of linear stochastic differential equations. The covariance matrix Σ may or may not be a function of t. That depends upon how the stochastic disturbances impact on the system. Since dv is of order $\sqrt{dt}$, the derivative dv/dt does not exist and we must write the stochastic differential equation as in (9.3). It is a fundamental property of the Wiener process that while it is continuous everywhere, it is differential nowhere. On the other hand, since $E(dv) = 0$, $E(dy)/dt = A(t)y + B(t)$ and is well defined.

In the case that $A(t)$ is constant, one can show by a formal argument that the solution to (9.3), starting from y_0 at time t_0, is

$$y(t) = e^{A(t-t_0)}y_0 + \int_{t_0}^{t} e^{A(t-s)}[B(s)ds + dv(s)]. \qquad (9.4)$$

Such an integral is called a *stochastic integral* (see, e.g., Arnold 1974). Economists are often interested in forward-looking solutions. With independent increments, and provided appropriate convergence conditions are met, the forward-looking solution to (9.3) is

$$y(t) = e^{At}E_t \int_{t}^{\infty} e^{-A(s-t)}B(s)ds. \qquad (9.5)$$

Itô's Lemma

The fact that the variances are of order dt means that we have to be careful in taking differentials of stochastic functions. We essentially have to take second-order expansions of the relevant Taylor series, in order to be sure that we have retained all the appropriate first-order terms. This is the central aspect of Itô's rule for stochastic differentiation.

Suppose dy is generated by the nonlinear system of stochastic differential equations

$$\begin{aligned} dy &= f(y,t)dt + dv \\ &= f(y,t)dt + S(y,t)dz, \end{aligned} \qquad (9.6)$$

where f and the variance-covariance matrix of $dv \equiv \Sigma(y,t)dt$ may be functions of y. If z is a Wiener process and the variance-covariance matrix of the increment dz is Rdt, we can write $dv = S(y,t)dz$, where $SRS' = \Sigma$. Here the prime denotes the vector transpose.

In the course of solving continuous-time stochastic optimization problems, we are required to study functions of stochastic processes. Let $G(y,t)$ be a function that is twice differentiable in y and continuously differentiable in t. We seek to derive its stochastic differential. To do so, expand

$$dG = G(y(t+dt), t+dt) - G(y(t), t)$$
$$= \frac{\partial G}{\partial t} dt + \left(\frac{\partial G}{\partial y}\right)' dy + \frac{1}{2}(dy)' \frac{\partial^2 G}{\partial y \partial y'} dy + o(dt), \tag{9.7}$$

where $o(dt)$ denotes terms of order smaller than dt. Denoting the matrix of second partial derivatives of G with respect to y by G_{yy}, and substituting (9.6) for dy, dy' while noting that dv is of order $\sqrt{dt}$, we show that to $o(dt)$

$$(dy)' G_{yy} dy = (dv)' G_{yy} dv + o(dt) = tr(G_{yy} dv\, dv') + o(dt), \tag{9.8}$$

where tr denotes the trace of the matrix. Substituting (9.6) and (9.8) into (9.7) leads to

$$dG = \left[\frac{\partial G}{\partial t} + \left(\frac{\partial G}{\partial y}\right)' f\right] dt + \frac{1}{2} tr(G_{yy} dv\, dv') + \left(\frac{\partial G}{\partial y}\right)' dv + o(dt).$$

Since $E(dv\, dv') = \Sigma dt$, and dropping the term $o(dt)$, we can write the stochastic differential dG as

$$dG = \left[\frac{\partial G}{\partial t} + \left(\frac{\partial G}{\partial y}\right)' f + \frac{1}{2} tr(G_{yy}\Sigma)\right] dt + \left(\frac{\partial G}{\partial y}\right)' dv. \tag{9.9}$$

The coefficient of dt is thus $E(dG)$, and

$$\text{var}(dG) = \left(\frac{\partial G}{\partial y}\right)' \Sigma \left(\frac{\partial G}{\partial y}\right) dt.$$

In our applications we will be dealing with scalar systems (i.e., G is a scalar function), in which case (9.9) becomes

$$dG = \left[\frac{\partial G}{\partial t} + \frac{\partial G}{\partial y} f + \frac{1}{2} G_{yy}\sigma_v^2\right] dt + \frac{\partial G}{\partial y} dv, \tag{9.9'}$$

where in the scalar case $E(dv)^2 = \sigma_v^2 dt$.

Differential Generator

An important operator that emerges as part of the optimization of a stochastic system is the differential generator of a function $G(y,t)$. This measures the expected rate of change over time dt of the function $G(y,t)$, resulting from the evolution of the underlying stochastic process $y(t)$. Formally, it is defined as

$$L_y[G(y,t)] \equiv \lim_{dt \to 0} E_t\left[\frac{dG}{dt}\right], \tag{9.10}$$

and from (9.9) it is given by the expression

$$L_y[G(y,t)] \equiv \frac{\partial G}{\partial t} + \left(\frac{\partial G}{\partial y}\right)' f + \frac{1}{2} tr(G_{yy}\Sigma). \tag{9.11}$$

Stochastic Control and the Stochastic Bellman Equation

The stochastic optimal control problems we shall consider are of the following generic form.

Maximize: $\quad V(y(0),0) = E_0 \int_0^\infty U(y(s),x(s),s)ds, \tag{9.12a}$

subject to

$$dy(t) = Q[y(t),x(t)]dt + T[y(t),x(t)]dv, \tag{9.12b}$$

where $y(t)$ is a vector of state variables and $x(t)$ is a vector of control variables. Define

$$V(y(t),t) = \max_{x(s)} E_t \int_t^\infty U(y(s),x(s),s)ds, \tag{9.13}$$

to be the optimized value of (9.12a) starting from time t. Splitting up the integral appearing in (9.13), we have

$$V(y(t),t) = \max_{x(s)} E_t \int_t^\infty U(y(s),x(s),s)ds$$

$$= \max_{x(s)} E_t \int_t^{t+\Delta t} U(y,x,s)ds + \max_{x(s)} E_{t+\Delta t} \int_{t+\Delta t}^\infty U(y,x,s)ds$$

$$= \max_{x(s)} E_t \left\{ \int_t^{t+\Delta t} U(y,x,s)ds + V[y(t+\Delta t), t+\Delta t] \right\}$$

$$= \max_{x(s)} \{U(y(t),x(t),t)\Delta t + E_t[V[y(t+\Delta t), t+\Delta t]]\},$$

implying that

$$V(y(t),t) = \max_{x(s)}\{U(y(t),x(t),t)\Delta t + V(y(t),t) + E_t dV\}, \qquad (9.14)$$

where $E_t dV$ is as defined in (9.9). Subtracting $V(y(t),t)$ from both sides of (9.14); dividing by Δt, denoted in the limit by dt; and recognizing the definition of the differential generator given in (9.10), the optimality condition (9.14) can be written as

$$0 = \max_{x(s)}\{U(y(t),x(t),t) + L_y[V(y(t),t)]\}. \qquad (9.15)$$

This is the stochastic Bellman equation that the optimum has to satisfy. In deriving this condition, the control variables $x(t)$ are taken to be optimally chosen in accordance with their corresponding first-order optimality conditions. As we will see in the applications to be developed below, (9.15) introduces a partial differential equation that the value function must satisfy.

In all of our examples, the utility function will assume a constant rate of time discount and will therefore be of the form $Ue^{-\beta t}$. In this case, it is possible to rewrite the Bellman equation (9.15) in a more intuitive and familiar form. For a time-separable utility function, the corresponding value function will be of an analogous form, $V(y)e^{-\beta t}$, say. Now recall the definition of the differential generator function given in (9.10) and (9.11). In particular, observe that the expectation defined in $L_y[V(y(t),t)]$ also takes into account the effect on the value due to the expected change in t, as measured by the term $\partial V/\partial t$. For the constant discount function, this is $-\beta V(y)e^{-\beta t}$. Subtracting this term from $L_y[V(y(t),t)]$, moving it to the left-hand side of (9.15), and dividing by $e^{-\beta t}$, the Bellman equation can be written in the equivalent form

$$\beta V(t) = \max_x \left\{ U(y(t),x(t),t) + E'_t\left[\frac{dV}{dt}\right] \right\}, \qquad (9.15')$$

where the expectation operator E'_t takes account of the fact that we have netted out the term $-\beta V(y)e^{-\beta t}$.

This form of the Bellman function is written in familiar asset pricing terms. The left-hand side describes the required return on holding an asset, where the agent discounts at his rate of time preference. The right-hand side consists of the payout (in terms of utility) from holding the asset, plus its expected rate of capital gain or loss over the next instant of time, with the maximization ensuring that current decisions are made optimally. This equation is just a stochastic version of the standard arbitrage conditions encountered throughout earlier chapters.

9.3 Stochastic Small Open Economy

We now apply these methods to the development of a simple stochastic model of a small open economy. This section describes the analytical framework and the behavior of the relevant agents in the economy. The economy we study is specialized in the production of a single good. It is, however, sufficiently small in the world production of this good that it has no impact on its market price.

Prices and Asset Returns

The economy is inhabited by a representative agent who consumes both the domestically produced good and a second good that it imports from abroad. Since it is small in the markets for both goods, the relative price E of the imported good, in terms of the domestically produced good taken as numeraire, is given exogenously and is assumed to be generated by the geometric Brownian motion process:

$$\frac{dE}{E} = \varepsilon\,dt + de, \tag{9.16a}$$

where ε is the instantaneous expected rate of change in the relative price and de is a temporally independent, normally distributed, random variable with mean zero and variance $\sigma_e^2 dt$.

In addition, the representative agent holds three securities in his portfolio: traded bonds, B^*; domestic government bonds, B, which are nontraded; and equity claims (which may be traded) on physical capital, K. There is no money, so the model is real. Traded bonds are assumed to be denominated in terms of foreign output, so that their price in terms of the numeraire also follows (9.16a). Capital is measured in terms of the numeraire. The domestic bonds are assumed to be consols paying one unit of output over the instant dt. The relative price of these domestic bonds (in terms of the numeraire) is assumed to evolve according to the stochastic process:

$$\frac{dQ}{Q} = \eta\,dt + dq, \tag{9.16b}$$

where η is the instantaneous expected rate of change and dq is a temporally independent, normally distributed random variable with mean zero and variance $\sigma_q^2 dt$. Although the representative agent perceives the stochastic process (9.16b) as being parametrically given, it will ultimately be determined as part of the macroeconomic equilibrium. In contrast to ε, which by assumption is constant, η may be time-varying, as will be shown below.

There are two reasons, both practical, for requiring the domestic bonds nontraded. The first is that if they were traded, the risk parity conditions between the foreign and domestic bonds would become exogenously determined by risk conditions and preferences in the rest of the world because the domestic economy is small. Rather than impose such a condition arbitrarily, or attempt to model the entire world economy, we assume that domestic bonds are nontraded, thereby determining the risk parity condition between the two assets endogenously in the market of the small open economy. The second reason is that if we assume that the government issues the traded bonds, then these bonds will follow a transitional dynamic path, just as they did in Chapter 5; see equation (5.19). This means that the domestic agent will not in general hold a constant portfolio share of his wealth in such bonds, thus invalidating this assumption. The alternative of allowing portfolio shares to be time-varying requires the introduction of an additional state variable into the analysis, severely complicating the analytical solution.

In general, the stochastic rate of return, dR, on a bond the price of which is P, paying a coupon of dZ/Z units of output per period, is

$$dR \equiv \frac{d(PZ)}{PZ} = \frac{dP}{P} + \frac{dZ}{Z} + \left(\frac{dP}{P}\right)\left(\frac{dZ}{Z}\right).$$

With domestic and foreign bonds paying deterministic coupons of $(1/Q)dt$ and i^*dt, respectively, and with their respective prices following (9.16b) and (9.16a), the real rates of return on domestic and foreign bonds, expressed in terms of the domestic good as numeraire, are

$$dR_B = r_B dt + du_B; \quad r_B \equiv \frac{1}{Q} + \eta; \quad du_B \equiv dq \qquad (9.17a)$$

$$dR_F = r_F dt + du_F; \quad r_F \equiv i^* + \varepsilon; \quad du_F \equiv de, \qquad (9.17b)$$

where the foreign interest rate, i^*, is exogenously given. In deriving these expressions, only terms of order dt have been retained.

Domestic output Y is produced by using domestic capital K, through the simple stochastic constant returns technology:

$$dY = \alpha K\, dt + \alpha K\, dy, \qquad (9.18)$$

where α is the (constant) marginal physical product of capital and dy is a temporally independent, normally distributed random variable with zero mean and variance $\sigma_y^2 dt$. In order to obtain a tractable, closed-form solution, all real variables must grow at the same stochastic rate. This requires the technology to be linear, as specified in (9.18). Note that with dy

being normally distributed, the possibility of negative instantaneous flows of net output is not precluded. The same comment applies to the flow of government expenditure specified in (9.24b). Equity investment is the real investment opportunity represented by this technology. Hence, in the absence of adjustment costs to investment, the before-tax real rate of return on equity (capital) is

$$dR_K = r_K dt + du_K; \quad r_K \equiv \alpha; \quad du_K \equiv \alpha \, dy. \tag{9.17c}$$

Consumer Optimization

The representative consumer's asset holdings are subject to the wealth constraint

$$W = K + QB + EB^*, \tag{9.19}$$

where W denotes real wealth, expressed in terms of the domestic good as numeraire. In addition, over the instant dt he is assumed to purchase output of the two commodities at the nonstochastic rates $C_D(t)dt$ and $C_M(t)dt$, respectively.

The agent's objective is to select these rates of consumption, together with his portfolio of assets, to maximize the expected value of discounted utility

$$E_0 \int_0^\infty \frac{1}{\gamma}(C_D^\theta C_M^{1-\theta})^\gamma e^{-\beta t} dt \quad -\infty < \gamma < 1; \quad 0 \leq \theta \leq 1, \tag{9.20a}$$

subject to the wealth constraint (9.19) and the stochastic wealth accumulation equation, expressed in real terms as

$$dW = W[n_K dR_K + n_B dR_B + n_F dR_F] - (C_D + EC_M)dt - dT, \tag{9.20b}$$

where

$n_K \equiv \dfrac{K}{W}$ = share of portfolio held in the form of capital

$n_B \equiv \dfrac{QB}{W}$ = share of portfolio held in the form of domestic bonds

$n_F \equiv \dfrac{EB^*}{W}$ = share of portfolio held in the form of traded bonds

dT = taxes paid (described below).

With utility being represented by the constant elasticity function, $r \equiv 1 - \gamma$ measures the constant coefficient of relative risk aversion. The value $\gamma = 0$ corresponds to the logarithmic utility function.

The government is assumed to tax the various sources of income in accordance with

$$dT = \tau_K K(r_K dt + du_K) + \tau_B QB(r_B dt + du_B) + \tau_F EB^*(r_F dt + du_F)$$
$$+ \tau_D C_D dt + \tau_M EC_M dt, \qquad (9.21)$$

where τ_K, τ_B, and τ_F denote the rates at which the three sources of income are taxed.[3] In addition, the domestic consumption good is taxed at the rate τ_D, and τ_M is the tariff on the imported consumption good.

Substituting for the portfolio shares n_i into (9.19), and for (9.17a)–(9.17c) and (9.21) into (9.20b), the stochastic optimization problem can be expressed as choosing the consumption:wealth ratios C_D/W and C_M/W, and portfolio shares n_i to maximize (9.20a), subject to

$$\frac{dW}{W} = \psi\, dt + dw \qquad (9.22a)$$

$$n_K + n_B + n_F = 1, \qquad (9.22b)$$

together with (9.16a), where, for convenience, we denote the deterministic and stochastic components of the rate of asset accumulation, dW/W, by

$$\psi \equiv n_K(1-\tau_K)r_K + n_B(1-\tau_B)r_B + n_F(1-\tau_F)r_F$$
$$- \frac{(1+\tau_D)C_D}{W} - \frac{(1+\tau_M)EC_M}{W} \qquad (9.22c)$$

$$dw \equiv n_K(1-\tau_K)du_K + n_B(1-\tau_B)du_B + n_F(1-\tau_F)du_F. \qquad (9.22d)$$

In performing the optimization, the representative agent takes the rates of return on the assets and the relevant variances and covariances as given. However, these will ultimately be determined in the equilibrium to be derived.

The details of the solution to this optimization problem are presented in the Appendix to this chapter. Defining aggregate consumption, inclusive of consumption taxes and expressed in terms of domestic output, by

$$C \equiv (1+\tau_D)C_D + (1+\tau_M)EC_M,$$

the first-order optimality conditions can be expressed in the form

$$(1+\tau_D)C_D = \theta C \qquad (9.23a)$$

$$(1+\tau_M)EC_M = (1-\theta)C \qquad (9.23b)$$

$$\frac{C}{W} = \frac{1}{1-\gamma}\left\{\beta + \varepsilon\gamma(1-\theta) - \gamma\rho - \frac{1}{2}\gamma(\gamma-1)\sigma_w^2\right.$$
$$\left. - \frac{1}{2}\gamma(1-\theta)[\gamma(1-\theta) + 1]\sigma_e^2 + \gamma^2(1-\theta)\sigma_{ew}\right\} \quad (9.23c)$$

$$[(1-\tau_B)r_B - (1-\tau_K)r_K]dt = (1-\gamma)\text{cov}[dw, (1-\tau_B)du_B - (1-\tau_K)du_K]$$
$$+ \gamma(1-\theta)\text{cov}[de, (1-\tau_B)du_B - (1-\tau_K)du_K] \quad (9.23d)$$

$$[(1-\tau_F)r_F - (1-\tau_K)r_K]dt = (1-\gamma)\text{cov}[dw, (1-\tau_F)du_F - (1-\tau_K)du_K]$$
$$+ \gamma(1-\theta)\text{cov}[de, (1-\tau_F)du_F - (1-\tau_K)du_K], \quad (9.23e)$$

where

$$\rho \equiv n_K(1-\tau_K)r_K + n_B(1-\tau_B)r_B + n_F(1-\tau_F)r_F$$

and the expressions for σ_w^2, σ_e^2, and σ_{ew}, which appear in (9.23c), are computed from equations (9.16a) and (9.22d).

Equations (9.23a) and (9.23b) describe the tax-included consumptions of the two goods as fixed fractions of overall consumption expenditure, expressed in terms of domestic output. Equation (9.23c) is the solution for the aggregate consumption:wealth ratio. In the case of the logarithmic utility function $\gamma = 0$, (9.23c) reduces to the familiar relationship $C/W = \beta$. If $\gamma \neq 0$, an increase in the expected net of tax return ρ will raise the consumption:wealth ratio if $\gamma < 0$ and lower it otherwise. As discussed in Chapter 5, this is because an increase in expected income can be broken down into a positive income effect, $d\rho$, inducing more consumption, and a negative substitution effect, $-d\rho/(1-\gamma)$, encouraging a switch away from consumption; the net effect on the consumption:wealth ratio is $-\gamma d\rho/(1-\gamma)$. The terms involving the variances, σ_w^2 and σ_e^2, and the covariance, σ_{ew}, reflect the effects of risk on consumption and can be decomposed in an analogous (but opposite) way.[4] As long as the agent is risk averse $(1 > \gamma)$, a higher risk is equivalent to a reduction in income and therefore leads to a reduction in the consumption:wealth ratio. At the same time, the higher variance raises the risk associated with savings, thereby inducing more consumption. These two effects are exactly offsetting in the case of the logarithmic function.

Equations (9.23d) and (9.23e) are asset pricing relationships familiar from finance theory. In the absence of risk, these two equations imply the equality of all after-tax rates of return; that is, $(1-\tau_B)r_B = (1-\tau_K)r_K = (1-\tau_F)r_F$. Otherwise, equation (9.23d) expresses the differential after-tax real rates of return on domestic bonds and capital in terms of their relative risk differentials, as measured by the covariance of their returns with the return on the overall portfolio. Equation (9.23e) is an analogous relationship between the differential after-tax real rates of return on traded bonds and capital. Solving (9.23d) and (9.23e) in conjunction with the normalized wealth constraint (9.22b), one can determine the agent's portfolio demands n_i.

Government Policy

Government policy is described by the choice of government expenditure, the issuing of debt (assumed to be nontraded), and the collection of taxes, all of which must be specified subject to its budget constraint. This may be expressed in real flow terms as

$$d(QB) = dG + (QB)dR_B - dT, \qquad (9.24a)$$

where dG denotes the stochastic rate of real government expenditure.

Government expenditure policy is specified by

$$dG = g\alpha K\, dt + \alpha K\, dz, \qquad (9.24b)$$

where dz is an intertemporally independent, normally distributed random variable with zero mean and variance $\sigma_z^2 dt$. According to this specification, the mean level of public expenditure is assumed to be a fraction, g, of the mean level of output, with a proportional stochastic disturbance.[5] The stochastic term reflects the possibility that policy makers may not be able to set government expenditures with certainty. For example, program needs may not be foreknown exactly, because real resources to meet a policy objective are known only imperfectly. As is evident from the discussion of the consumer described above, this government expenditure has no direct impact on the behavior of the private sector. It can be interpreted as being either a real drain on the economy or, alternatively, as some public good that does not affect the marginal utility of private consumption or the productivity of private capital. As discussed in Chapter 5, this serves as a reasonable benchmark case that enables us to isolate the effects of distortionary taxation from government expenditure (see Rebelo 1991).

Having specified expenditures in (9.24b) and tax collection in (9.21), the government finances its deficit by issuing long bonds (consols) paying a unit return over the instant dt. Such bonds have a market price Q, which is endogenously determined in the market. Thus, in this economy, the government sets expenditure levels and tax rates independently, floating as many bonds as needed to finance the budget. Substituting (9.24b) and (9.21) into (9.24a) and dividing by W, the rate of accumulation of government bonds is given by

$$\frac{d(QB)}{QB} = \frac{1}{n_B}\{[(g-\tau_K)\alpha n_K + (1-\tau_B)r_B n_B - \tau_F r_F n_F - \tau_D C_D - \tau_M C_M]dt$$

$$+ \alpha n_K dz - \tau_K n_K du_K + (1-\tau_B)n_B du_B - \tau_F n_F du_F\}. \qquad (9.25)$$

The Goods Market and the Current Account

Net exports are determined by the excess of production over domestic uses, $dY - dC - dK - dG$. Balance of payments equilibrium, in turn, requires the transfer of new foreign bonds (in excess of interest on earlier issues) to finance net exports of the domestic economy. This is expressed in real terms by the relationship

$$d(EB^*) = [dY - dC - dK - dG] + (EB^*)dR_F. \qquad (9.26)$$

Dividing by W, this can be expressed in the form

$$n_F \frac{d(EB^*)}{EB^*} + n_K \frac{dK}{K}$$

$$= \left[\alpha(1-g)n_K + n_F r_F - \frac{C}{W}\right]dt + \alpha n_K(dy - dz) + n_F du_F. \qquad (9.27)$$

We should note, however, that the accumulation equations (9.22a), (9.25), and (9.27) are not independent; any two imply the third, just as they have done in earlier models.

9.4 Macroeconomic Equilibrium

We now combine the elements introduced in Section 9.3 to determine the overall stochastic equilibrium of the small open economy. This equilibrium determines the rates of consumption and savings; the value and rates of return on all assets; the portfolio allocation; the economy's investment and growth rate together with its current account; and the risk characteristics of each asset. The exogenous factors include the initial stocks of assets, K_0, B_0, B_0^*, and the initial exchange rate E_0; the stochastic process generating the exchange rate (ε, de); the stochastic process describing government expenditure (g, dz); the tax rates (τ_K, τ_B, τ_F); the stochastic process characterizing technology (α, dy); and the preference parameters (γ, β). Processes (de, dy, dz) are assumed to be mutually uncorrelated. This assumption is made for convenience only, and nonzero patterns of correlation could be introduced if desired. The remaining stochastic disturbances for prices and wealth, dq and dw, are endogenously determined and can be expressed as functions of the exogenous shocks. The endogenous variances and covariances can then be determined, and an overall mean-variance equilibrium derived.

Our objective is to reduce the components of Section 9.3 to a set of core relationships that jointly determine the deterministic and stochastic components of the macroeconomic equilibrium. From the relationships in (9.23) it is reasonable to posit that if assets have the same stochastic characteristics through time, they will generate the same allocation of portfolio holdings and the same consumption:wealth ratio.[6] Our strategy, therefore, is to look for an equilibrium in which portfolio shares, n_i, and the C/W ratio are constant functions through time of the underlying parameters of the model, and to observe that the restrictions thus implied are in fact consistent with this assumption.

The derivation of this equilibrium takes place in two interrelated steps. Step 1 solves for the stochastic relations implied by the equilibrium. Using these, one then solves for the deterministic conditions that describe the economy. These relationships themselves imply relations among the stochastic components. Thus, in a consistent equilibrium one must check that the constraints implied by the deterministic dynamics are met by the stochastic relations, and vice versa.

Stochastic Adjustments

The key observation is that the intertemporal constancy of portfolio shares implies

$$\frac{dK}{K} = \frac{d(QB)}{QB} = \frac{d(EB^*)}{EB^*} = \frac{dW}{W} = \psi\, dt + dw. \tag{9.28}$$

Focusing on the stochastic components of equations (9.22a), (9.25), and (9.27) and equating in accordance with (9.28), while recalling the definitions of du_K, du_B, and du_F appearing in (9.17), enables us to solve for dw and dq as follows:

$$dw = \alpha\omega(dy - dz) + (1 - \omega)de \tag{9.29a}$$

$$dq = \frac{\alpha[\omega - n_K(1 - \tau_K)]dy - \alpha\omega\, dz + [(1 - \omega) - n_F(1 - \tau_F)]de}{n_B(1 - \tau_B)}, \tag{9.29b}$$

where for notational convenience we define

$$\omega \equiv \frac{n_K}{n_K + n_F}$$

to be the share of capital in the traded portion of the agent's portfolio.

The solutions (9.29a) and (9.29b) enable us to compute all the necessary variances and covariances. In particular, we note the following expressions, which appear in the consumer optimality conditions (9.23c)–(9.23e):

$$\sigma_w^2 = \alpha^2\omega^2(\sigma_y^2 + \sigma_z^2) + (1-\omega)^2\sigma_e^2 \qquad \sigma_{ew} = (1-\omega)\sigma_e^2 \qquad (9.30a)$$

$$\text{cov}[dw, (1-\tau_B)du_B - (1-\tau_K)du_K]$$
$$= \left\{\alpha^2\omega\left[-(1-\omega) + \left(\frac{n_B + n_K}{n_B}\right)\tau_K\right]\sigma_y^2 \right.$$
$$\left. + \frac{\alpha^2\omega^2}{n_B}\sigma_z^2 + (1-\omega)\left[(1-\omega) + \frac{n_F}{n_B}\tau_F\right]\sigma_e^2\right\}dt \qquad (9.30b)$$

$$\text{cov}[de, (1-\tau_B)du_B - (1-\tau_K)du_K] = \left[(1-\omega) + \frac{n_F}{n_B}\tau_F\right]\sigma_e^2 dt \qquad (9.30c)$$

$$\text{cov}[dw, (1-\tau_F)du_F - (1-\tau_K)du_K]$$
$$= \{-\alpha^2\omega(1-\tau_K)\sigma_y^2 + (1-\omega)(1-\tau_F)\sigma_e^2\}dt \qquad (9.30d)$$

$$\text{cov}[de, (1-\tau_F)du_F - (1-\tau_K)du_K] = (1-\tau_F)\sigma_e^2 dt. \qquad (9.30e)$$

Note that these expressions are not complete solutions; they are expressed in terms of the portfolio shares that are yet to be determined. Once this has been done, they become reduced-form solutions.

Equilibrium System

We may now collect the equations of the complete system. First, substituting (9.30d) and (9.30e) into the consumer optimality condition (9.23e), while recalling the definitions for r_K and r_F given in (9.17), leads to the following solution for ω, the share of capital in the traded portion of the investor's portfolio:

$$\omega = \frac{\alpha(1-\tau_K) - (i^* + \varepsilon)(1-\tau_F)}{(1-\gamma)[\alpha^2(1-\tau_K)\sigma_y^2 + (1-\tau_F)\sigma_e^2]}$$
$$+ \left(\frac{1-\gamma\theta}{1-\gamma}\right)\frac{(1-\tau_F)\sigma_e^2}{[\alpha^2(1-\tau_K)\sigma_y^2 + (1-\tau_F)\sigma_e^2]}. \qquad (9.31a)$$

Choosing ω in accordance with (9.31a) ensures the equality of the risk-adjusted after-tax rates of return on the two traded assets. The optimal relative portfolio share ω is determined by two sets of factors. The first is the speculative component, which is proportional to the expected differential after-tax real rate of return on the two assets, and inversely related to its variance. The second reflects the hedging behavior of the investor. This depends upon the covariance of the after-tax asset return with wealth. Under the assumption that dy, dz, and de are mutually uncorrelated, these expressions are completely independent of the stochastic properties of dz. Fiscal shocks will impact on this component of the portfolio decision only to the extent that they are correlated with either the productivity shock or the real exchange rate.

Equation (9.31a) also brings out the importance of risk in the analysis of taxation in a small open economy. In the absence of risk, $\sigma_e^2 = \sigma_y^2 = 0$, and this relationship reduces to the arbitrage condition

$$\alpha(1 - \tau_K) = (i^* + \varepsilon)(1 - \tau_F). \tag{9.31a'}$$

With the before-tax rates of return α and $i^* + \varepsilon$ being parametrically given to the small open economy, the constraint on the tax rates imposed by the arbitrage condition (9.31a') becomes clear; a change in τ_K requires a compensating change in τ_F in order for (9.31a') to hold. In the presence of risk, the representative agent is able to adjust his portfolio share in accordance with his risk tolerance, thus permitting the two tax rates to be set independently. In this respect the presence of risk plays a role analogous to adjustment costs in the linear deterministic growth model developed in Chapter 5.

Next, substituting (9.30b) and (9.30c) into the consumer optimality condition (9.23d) implies the following expression for the after-tax rate of return on domestic bonds:

$$r_B(1 - \tau_B)$$

$$= \alpha(1 - \tau_K) + (1 - \gamma)\omega\alpha^2 \left(\left[-(1 - \omega) + \left(\frac{n_K + n_B}{n_B} \right) \tau_K \right] \sigma_y^2 + \frac{\omega}{n_B} \sigma_z^2 \right)$$

$$+ [(1 - \gamma)(1 - \omega) + \gamma(1 - \theta)] \left[(1 - \omega) + \frac{n_F}{n_B} \tau_F \right] \sigma_e^2. \tag{9.31b}$$

This equation describes the real risk premium on domestic bonds relative to domestic capital. It depends linearly upon the variances of the three exogenous shocks, σ_y^2, σ_z^2, σ_e^2. The magnitude and the direction of the sensitivity to these shocks depend upon the endogenously determined portfolio shares n_i. Third, combining (9.28) with the deterministic component of (9.27) implies the following expression for the equilibrium growth rate ψ:

$$\psi = \omega \left(\alpha(1 - g) - \frac{C/W}{n_K} \right) + (1 - \omega)(i^* + \varepsilon). \tag{9.31c}$$

Equation (9.31c) expresses the equilibrium mean growth rate of the domestic economy as a weighted average of the domestic and foreign sources of growth. The former consists of net domestic output less the amount used for private and public consumption, and the latter is the growth attributable to interest earnings from abroad, with the weights being the relative portfolio shares, ω and $(1-\omega)$, respectively.

Equations (9.31a), (9.31b), and (9.31c), together with the consumer equilibrium conditions (9.23a), (9.23b), and (9.23c); expressions for σ_w^2 and σ_{ew} in (9.30a); the portfolio shares "adding up" condition (9.22b); and the consumer accumulation equation (9.22c), form a complete system determining the equilibrium values of $(1+\tau_D)C_D/W$, $(1+\tau_M)EC_M/W$, and C/W; the portfolio shares n_K, n_B, and n_F; the real rate of return on domestic bonds, r_B; and the equilibrium growth rate, ψ. In addition, the instantaneous attainment of portfolio equilibrium involves an initial price of domestic bonds, $Q(0)$, and corresponding initial wealth, $W(0)$, determined by

$$Q(0) = \left(\frac{n_B}{n_K + n_F}\right)\left(\frac{K_0 + E_0 B_0^*}{B_0}\right); \quad W(0) = \frac{K_0 + E_0 B_0^*}{n_K + n_F}. \quad (9.32)$$

Finally, combining (9.31b) with (9.17a) enables one to determine η. With r_B as given in (9.31b) being stationary through time, it follows that η is time-varying as the price Q evolves through time; see (9.16b).

9.5 Equilibrium Solutions

Eliminating the real rate of return on domestic bonds, r_B, and substituting yields the following closed-form solution for the key economic variables:

$$\omega = \frac{\alpha(1-\tau_K) - (i^* + \varepsilon)(1-\tau_F) + (1-\gamma\theta)(1-\tau_F)\sigma_e^2}{(1-\gamma)[\alpha^2(1-\tau_K)\sigma_y^2 + (1-\tau_F)\sigma_e^2]} \quad (9.33a)$$

$$\psi = \frac{1}{1-\gamma}\Big\{\alpha(1-\tau_K) - \beta - \gamma\varepsilon(1-\theta)$$

$$+ \frac{1}{2}(\gamma-1)\alpha^2\omega[2(1-\tau_K) + \omega(\gamma-2)]\sigma_y^2$$

$$+ \frac{1}{2}\alpha^2\omega^2(\gamma-1)(\gamma-2)\sigma_z^2$$

$$+ \left([1+\gamma(\omega-\theta)]\left[1-\omega+\frac{1}{2}\gamma(\omega-\theta)\right] + \frac{1}{2}\omega(1-\omega)(\gamma-2)\right)\sigma_e^2\Big\} \quad (9.33b)$$

$$\frac{C}{W} = \beta + \gamma[\varepsilon(1-\theta) - \psi] - \frac{1}{2}\gamma(\gamma-1)\alpha^2\omega^2(\sigma_y^2 + \sigma_z^2)$$

$$- \frac{1}{2}\gamma[(\omega-\theta)[1 + \gamma(\omega-\theta)] + \omega(1-\omega)]\sigma_e^2 \qquad (9.33c)$$

$$\frac{n_K}{\omega} = n_k + n_F = \frac{(C/W)}{\alpha\omega(1-g) + (1-\omega)(i^* + \varepsilon) - \psi} \qquad (9.33d)$$

Equations (9.33) determine the equilibrium in a simple recursive manner. First, (9.33a), which simply repeats (9.31a), expresses ω in terms of the relevant tax rates and the relative risks of the two traded assets, enabling us to write $\omega = (\tau_K, \tau_F, \sigma_y^2, \sigma_e^2)$. Given ω, (9.33b) then determines the equilibrium growth rate ψ in the form $\psi = \psi(\tau_K, \omega, \sigma_y^2, \sigma_z^2, \sigma_e^2)$. Having obtained both ω and ψ, (9.33c) determines the C/W ratio as

$$\frac{C}{W} = \frac{C}{W}(\omega, \psi; \sigma_y^2, \sigma_z^2, \sigma_e^2).$$

Finally, (9.33d) implies the total share of traded assets,

$$\frac{n_K}{\omega} \equiv n_K + n_F,$$

in the form

$$\frac{n_K}{\omega} = \frac{n_K}{\omega}(\omega, \psi; \sigma_y^2, \sigma_z^2, \sigma_e^2).$$

From these "core" solutions, other equilibrium solutions can be derived. From (9.33) we observe that the equilibrium is indeed one having a constant consumption: wealth ratio and constant portfolio shares, thereby validating these initial assumptions.

Looking at these equilibria, a number of observations can be made. First, the equilibrium is completely independent of the tax rate on domestic interest income, (τ_B). Though the government offers a unit return on its bonds, the after-tax real return to bondholders depends upon the market equilibrium, and adjusts as needed to produce the required after-tax return, regardless of the magnitude of the before-tax return taxed by the government.

Second, the tax rates on capital (τ_K) and on foreign bonds (τ_F) impact on the C/W ratio and on the total portfolio share of traded assets, n_K/ω, only through their effects on ω and ψ. The effects of tax rates on growth can be obtained from (9.33b) and will be discussed in Section 9.10.

Third, the equilibrium, in particular the equilibrium growth rate, is independent of the two consumption taxes. An increase in either τ_D or τ_M simply leads to an offsetting reduction in the quantity of that good consumed. Thus, in this economy a tariff imposed on the foreign consumption good has no substantive effect on the equilibrium. This finding is in contrast to much of the recent literature analyzing tariffs in an intertemporal optimizing context, as well of the analysis carried out in Section 3.5, where we found that a tariff has an adverse effect on the long-run capital stock (see, e.g., Sen and Turnovsky 1989b). There are two critical differences in the present model that account for this difference in results. The first is that in the tariff models, one channel of adjustment to the tariff is through the supply of labor; second, these models typically also allow for endogenous terms of trade. Both of these sources of adjustment are absent in the present analysis.

Fourth, the equilibrium growth rate ψ is independent of mean government expenditure g. While an increase in g reduces the real growth rate directly (see (9.31c)), this is offset by the fact that with the expenditure financed by additional debt, the price of government bonds is reduced. This leads to a decline in financial wealth, thereby reducing private consumption by an amount exactly equal to the increase in government expenditure. In short, private consumption is fully crowded out, leaving the net rate of capital accumulation (i.e., the growth rate) unchanged. By contrast, the growth rate does depend (positively) upon the variance of government expenditure. This is because an increase in this variance raises the relative riskiness of domestic bonds, causing the agents to shift their portfolios in favor of capital and foreign bonds, thus increasing the expected growth rate.

Finally, the equilibrium must satisfy certain feasibility conditions. First is the transversality condition, which for the constant elasticity utility function is given by

$$\lim_{t \to \infty} \mathrm{E}[W^\gamma E^{-\gamma(1-\theta)} e^{-\beta t}] = 0, \tag{9.34}$$

where E denotes expected value, in order to avoid confusion with our designated use of E for the nominal exchange rate. To evaluate (9.34), we begin by expressing the accumulation of wealth by the equation

$$dW = \psi W dt + W dw, \tag{9.28'}$$

the solution to which, starting from initial wealth $W(0)$ at time 0, is (see, e.g., Arnold 1974)

$$W(t) = W(0) e^{(\psi - (1/2)\sigma_w^2)t + w(t) - w(0)}.$$

Similarly, solving (9.16a) for the exchange rate at time t yields

$$E(t) = E_0 e^{(\varepsilon - (1/2)\sigma_e^2)t + e(t) - e(0)}.$$

Using the fact that $w(t) - w(0)$ and $e(t) - e(0)$ are lognormal, we have

$$\begin{aligned}\mathrm{E}[W^\gamma E^{-\gamma(1-\theta)}e^{-\beta t}] &= \mathrm{E}[W(0)^\gamma E_0^{-\gamma(1-\theta)}\exp\{\gamma[\psi - (1/2)\sigma_w^2]t \\
&\quad - \gamma(1-\theta)[\varepsilon - (1/2)\sigma_e^2]t + \gamma[w(t) - w(0)] \\
&\quad - \gamma(1-\theta)[e(t) - e(0)] - \beta t\}] \\
&= W(0)^\gamma E_0^{-\gamma(1-\theta)}\exp\{\gamma[\psi - (1/2)(1-\gamma)\sigma_w^2] \\
&\quad - \gamma(1-\theta)\varepsilon + (\gamma(1-\theta)/2)[1 + \gamma(1-\theta)]\sigma_e^2 \\
&\quad - \gamma^2(1-\theta)\sigma_{we} - \beta\}t.\end{aligned}$$

The transversality condition (9.34) will be met if and only if

$$\gamma[\psi - (1/2)(1-\gamma)\sigma_w^2] - \gamma(1-\theta)\varepsilon + (\gamma(1-\theta)/2)[1 + \gamma(1-\theta)]\sigma_e^2 \\ - \gamma^2(1-\theta)\sigma_{we} - \beta < 0.$$

Combining with (9.22c), and (9.23c), this condition is equivalent to

$$\frac{C}{W} > 0, \tag{9.35}$$

as originally shown by Merton (1969).

With the equilibrium being one of balanced real growth, in which all real assets grow at the same rate, (9.34) also implies that the *intertemporal* government budget constraint is met, so that the equilibrium is intertemporally viable. Using (9.33a)–(9.33c), the condition (9.35) can be shown to imply a constraint on the tax rates and other parameters, though this constraint is automatically met in the case of the logarithmic utility function ($\gamma = 0$).

Second, economic viability requires that the initially determined price of domestic bonds $Q(0) > 0$. Assuming that nonnegative stocks of domestic bonds are always held, (9.32) implies that this condition will be met if and only if $0 \le n_K/\omega \equiv n_K + n_F \le 1$; that is, the share of traded assets in the agent's portfolio is positive. The behavior of bond prices is unimportant and will depend upon the specific nature of the bonds. Grinols and Turnovsky (1997) show how, in a closed economy, it is possible for the government to choose a particular coupon for the bond so that it is consistent with attaining the balanced growth path and its price remains positive throughout the transition. Their argument extends to the present context.

Welfare

In sections 9.9 and 9.10 we shall analyze the effects of various structural changes on economic welfare, and to do so a welfare criterion must be introduced. For this purpose, we consider the welfare of the representative agent, as specified by the intertemporal utility function (9.20a) evaluated along the optimal path. By definition, this equals the value function used to solve the intertemporal optimization problem.

As shown in the Appendix, for the constant elasticity utility function, the optimized level of utility starting from an initial stock of wealth $W(0)$ is

$$V(W(0), E_0) = \delta W(0)^\gamma E_0^{-\gamma(1-\theta)}, \tag{9.36}$$

where

$$\delta = \frac{1}{\gamma} \left(\frac{\theta}{1+\tau_D} \right)^{\gamma\theta} \left(\frac{1-\theta}{1+\tau_M} \right)^{-\gamma(1-\theta)} \left(\frac{\widehat{C}}{W} \right)^{\gamma-1},$$

where $\widehat{C/W}$ is the equilibrium value given in (9.33c). Using the relationship (9.32), the welfare criterion can be expressed as

$$V(K_0, B_0^*, E_0) = \frac{1}{\gamma} \left(\frac{\theta}{1+\tau_D} \right)^{\gamma\theta} \left(\frac{1-\theta}{1+\tau_M} \right)^{-\gamma(1-\theta)} \left(\frac{\widehat{C}}{W} \right)^{\gamma-1}$$

$$\times \left(\frac{\omega}{n_K} \right)^\gamma (K_0 + E_0 B_0^*)^\gamma E_0^{-\gamma(1-\theta)}. \tag{9.37}$$

Assuming that C/W and ω/n_K are positive ensures that $\gamma V(K_0, B_0^*, E_0) > 0$.

Taking the differential of (9.37) yields

$$\frac{dV}{V} = (\gamma - 1) \frac{d(C/W)}{C/W} + \gamma \frac{d(\omega/n_K)}{\omega/n_K} - \gamma\theta \frac{d\tau_D}{(1+\tau_D)}$$

$$- \gamma(1-\theta) \frac{d\tau_M}{(1+\tau_M)}. \tag{9.37'}$$

The key point to observe is the contrast between how terms of trade shocks and income taxes, on the one hand, and consumption taxes, on the other, impact on economic welfare. The former do so only through the growth rate ψ and the portfolio share ω. The latter have no effect on these variables, but instead operate directly through the consumptions of the corresponding goods.

9.6 Stochastic Terms of Trade Shocks

A natural question to apply to this model is the effects of a terms of trade shock in a stochastic context. In Section 3.4, we reviewed some of the vast literature that has studied the Laursen-Metzler effect, in particular that based on intertemporal optimization methods. All of that literature was based on deterministic models. More recently, Stulz (1988) and Turnovsky (1993) have analyzed terms of trade shocks by using a continuous-time stochastic approach. This section is devoted to a discussion of these models.

Stulz considers the relationship between unanticipated changes in the terms of trade, on the one hand, and consumption expenditure, together with the current account balance, on the other. His main result is to show how the effect of an unanticipated change in the terms of trade on consumption depends upon the differential between the expected real rates of return on foreign and domestic bonds. In the absence of such a differential, the agent will choose a portfolio of assets such that an unanticipated change in the terms of trade has no effect through consumption on the current account.

Turnovsky employs the model developed by Stulz, though with a somewhat different emphasis, and focuses on a broader range of issues pertaining to the terms of trade shocks on real activity and growth. In addition to considering unanticipated shocks, he analyzes the effects of changes in the expected terms of trade, and in the variances of the terms of trade, on the expected rates of change of consumption, savings, growth, and the current account, all of which are closely tied in equilibrium. Paradoxically, he shows how an increased variance in the terms of trade may quite plausibly have a stabilizing effect on the growth path, in the sense of reducing its variance.

A Simplified Equilibrium Model

The stochastic models employed by Stulz and Turnovsky to analyze terms of trade shocks are simpler than that developed in sections 9.3 and 9.4, in that they abstract from the government. In order to focus on these shocks, we, too, shall specialize the model to that case. It is obtained by setting all parameters pertaining to government activity to zero:

$$\tau_K = \tau_B = \tau_F = 0; \quad g = dz = 0; \quad n_B = 0.$$

In addition, to simplify things further, we shall assume that $\sigma_y^2 = 0$, so that the only source of stochastic shocks is fluctuations in the terms of trade. Although we lose the interaction between terms of trade shocks and both government shocks and domestic productivity shocks, the simplification has the advantage of sharpening the analysis.

With these simplifications, the equilibrium (9.33) reduces drastically to

$$n_F = \frac{i^* + \varepsilon - \alpha}{(1-\gamma)\sigma_e^2} - \frac{\gamma(1-\theta)}{1-\gamma} \qquad (9.38a)$$

$$\frac{C}{W} = \frac{1}{1-\gamma}\left\{\beta + \gamma[\varepsilon(1-\theta) - \alpha] - \frac{1}{2}\gamma(1-\gamma)n_F^2\sigma_e^2 \right.$$

$$\left. - \frac{1}{2}\gamma\sigma_e^2(1-\theta)[1+\gamma(1-\theta)]\right\} \qquad (9.38b)$$

$$\frac{dX}{X} \equiv \frac{dW}{W} = \frac{dC}{C} = \frac{dK}{K} = \frac{d(EB^*)}{EB^*} = \left[\alpha + (i^* + e - \alpha)n_F - \frac{C}{W}\right]dt + n_F de, \qquad (9.38c)$$

where the portfolio shares $n_F + n_K = 1$.[7] In principle, the domestic economy may be either a net creditor $(n_F > 0)$ or a net debtor $(n_F < 0)$; it is also possible for $n_K < 0$. However, we rule out this last case, assuming that the returns are such that domestic residents always hold some positive fraction of domestic capital in their portfolios.[8] Given the equilibrium portfolio share n_F as determined by (9.38a), the equilibrium consumption:wealth ratio follows from (9.38b). Having determined both, the common equilibrium growth rate is seen to equal the rate of earnings on assets less the consumption:wealth ratio.

To this point, everything has been expressed in terms of units of domestic output. In fact, the impact of terms of trade shocks on real behavior is sensitive to the units in which the real activity is being measured; previous discussions have varied in this regard. The original discussion measured everything in terms of the exportable good, and this was the unit of measurement adopted by Obstfeld (1982), Sen and Turnovsky (1989a), and the discussion of Section 3.4. By contrast, Stulz (1988), Svensson and Razin (1983), Persson and Svensson (1985), and Bean (1986) evaluate the real effects of terms of trade shocks in terms of a general price index.

For the constant elasticity utility function (9.20a) it is straightforward to go from one unit of measurement to the other, since it implies an exact price index—P, say—of the form

$$P = NE^{1-\theta},$$

where N is a constant. Deflating expenditures by P yields real quantities expressed in terms of the domestic consumption bundle. Stochastic differentiation of P implies

$$\frac{dP}{P} = (1-\theta)\frac{dE}{E} - \frac{1}{2}\theta(1-\theta)\left(\frac{dE}{E}\right)^2,$$

and substituting from (9.16a) and retaining terms to order dt yields

$$\frac{dP}{P} = \left[(1-\theta)\frac{dE}{E} - \frac{1}{2}\theta(1-\theta)\sigma_e^2\right]dt + (1-\theta)de. \tag{9.39}$$

The real rates of return expressed in terms of the domestic consumption bundle (rather than the domestic good) are

$$dR'_K = \left[\alpha - (1-\theta)\varepsilon + \frac{1}{2}(1-\theta)(2-\theta)\sigma_e^2\right]dt - (1-\theta)de$$

$$\equiv r'_K dt - (1-\theta)de \tag{9.40a}$$

$$dR'_F = \left[i^* + \theta\varepsilon - \frac{1}{2}\theta(1-\theta)\sigma_e^2\right]dt + \theta\, de \equiv r'_F dt + \theta\, de. \tag{9.40b}$$

Observe that if $\theta = 1$, these reduce to $dR'_K = \alpha\, dt$ and $dR'_F = (i^* + \varepsilon)dt + de$, respectively.

Using these measures of expected returns, the equilibrium portfolio shares of the two assets can be written in the convenient form[9]

$$n_F = \frac{r'_F - r'_K}{(1-\gamma)\sigma_e^2} + (1-\theta); \quad n_K = \frac{r'_K - r'_F}{(1-\gamma)\sigma_e^2} + \theta, \tag{9.41}$$

with the hedging components now being simply the fractions $1 - \theta$ and θ of the corresponding commodity in the overall consumption bundle.

We now define real consumption, capital, stock of bonds, and wealth in terms of the domestic consumption bundle by

$$c \equiv \frac{C}{P}; \quad k \equiv \frac{K}{P}; \quad b^* \equiv \frac{EB^*}{P}; \quad w \equiv \frac{W}{P}.$$

Stochastically differentiating these quantities and noting the definitions of r'_K and r'_F, the common growth rate expressed in terms of the domestic consumption bundle is

$$\frac{dx}{x} \equiv \frac{dw}{w} = \frac{dc}{c} = \frac{dk}{k} = \frac{d(b^*)}{b^*} = \left[r'_K + (r'_F - r'_K)n_F - \frac{C}{W}\right]dt$$

$$+ [n_F - (1-\theta)]de. \tag{9.42}$$

The parallels between the two expressions for the growth rates, (9.38c) and (9.42), are immediate.

9.7 Terms of Trade Shocks and Growth

Equations (9.38c) and (9.42) provide the information pertaining to how changes in the terms of trade impact on the real growth of the economy.

Stochastic Growth in a Small Open Economy

A comparison of these two relationships indicates the importance of the choice of units, and both shall be discussed. Critical elements in understanding the behavior of the growth rates are the response of the portfolio share, n_F, and the consumption:wealth ratio, C/W. We therefore begin with a consideration of these.

Differentiating (9.38a) and (9.38b), we can establish

$$\frac{\partial n_F}{\partial \varepsilon} = \frac{1}{(1-\gamma)\sigma_e^2} > 0; \quad \frac{\partial n_F}{\partial \sigma_e^2} = -\frac{(i^* + \varepsilon - \alpha)}{(1-\gamma)\sigma_e^4},$$

$$\frac{\partial [C/W]}{\partial \varepsilon} = \frac{\gamma}{1-\gamma}[(1-\theta) - n_F] = \frac{\gamma}{(1-\gamma)^2}\left(\frac{r'_K - r'_F}{\sigma_e^2}\right),$$

$$\frac{\partial [C/W]}{\partial \sigma_e^2} = \frac{\gamma}{2(1-\gamma)^2}\left[\frac{(i^* + \varepsilon - \alpha)^2}{\sigma_e^4} - (1-\theta)(1-\gamma\theta)\right].$$

These effects are essentially modifications of the early results by Levhari and Srinivasan (1969) and Sandmo (1970), analyzing the effects of uncertainty and rates of return on savings and consumption. An increase in ε will raise the expected return on foreign bonds, leading to an increase in n_F. It also increases the rate at which the relative price of the imported good is expected to rise. Whether an increase in ε results in an overall positive or negative net real return to the domestic agent depends upon whether $n_F \gtrless (1-\theta)$. Suppose, for example, the net return is positive. Then the substitution effect will dominate and the consumption:wealth ratio will fall if $\gamma > 0$, and rise otherwise.

An increase in the variance, σ_e^2, will lead the agent to reduce his speculative position in the foreign bond; that is, to decrease n_F if $i^* + \varepsilon > \alpha$, and to increase n_F otherwise. The substitution away from the more risky bonds reduces the risk in the returns. At the same time, the higher variance will raise the uncertainty associated with future changes in the terms of trade, and this raises the risk. Suppose that the former effect dominates so that there is a net reduction in risk. If $\gamma > 0$, the substitution effect dominates and the consumption:wealth ratio rises.

Growth in Terms of Domestic Output

From equation (9.38c), the following responses can be derived between the terms of trade shocks and the common growth rate:

$$\text{cov}\left(\frac{dX}{X}, de\right) = n_F \sigma_e^2 dt \tag{9.43a}$$

$$\frac{\partial}{\partial \varepsilon}\left(\frac{E(dX)}{X}\right) = \left[(i^* + \varepsilon - \alpha)\frac{\partial n_F}{\partial \varepsilon} + n_F - \frac{\partial [C/W]}{\partial \varepsilon}\right]dt = \left(\frac{2-\gamma}{1-\gamma}\right)n_F dt \tag{9.43b}$$

$$\frac{\partial}{\partial \sigma_e^2}\left(\frac{E(dX)}{X}\right) = \left[(i^* + \varepsilon - \alpha)\frac{\partial n_F}{\partial \sigma_e^2} - \frac{\partial [C/W]}{\partial \sigma_e^2}\right]dt$$

$$= -\frac{1}{2(1-\gamma)^2}\left[\frac{(2-\gamma)(i^* + \varepsilon - \alpha)^2}{\sigma_e^4} - \gamma(1-\theta)(1-\gamma\theta)\right]dt$$

(9.43c)

$$\frac{\partial}{\partial \sigma_e^2}\left(\text{var}\left(\frac{dX}{X}\right)\right) = \left(n_F^2 + 2n_F\sigma_e^2\frac{\partial n_F}{\partial \sigma_e^2}\right)dt = -n_F\left(n_F + \frac{2\gamma(1-\theta)}{1-\gamma}\right)dt.$$

(9.43d)

Equation (9.43a) indicates the effect of an unanticipated deterioration in the terms of trade; that is, a positive shock de on the current rate of growth depends upon the sign of n_F (i.e., whether the economy is a net creditor or a net debtor). In the former case, when $n_F > 0$, a stochastic deterioration in the terms of trade raises the real rate of return on traded bonds, expressed in terms of domestic output, leading to an increase in the rate of accumulation of wealth, dW/W, and therefore in the ratio of savings to wealth. With the equilibrium consumption: wealth ratio and the portfolio shares being constant over time, it immediately follows that the growth rates of real consumption, capital, and domestic output, and the rate of accumulation of traded bonds, all expressed in terms of domestic output, also increase at the same rate as wealth. The additional savings are therefore distributed across the assets in proportion to their respective portfolio shares. These effects are reversed—in which case the Laursen-Metzler effect holds—if and only if the country is a net debtor.

The effect of an increase in the anticipated rate of appreciation of the relative price, ε, is reported in (9.43b). It is equal to the difference between its impact on the total expected rate of earnings and the consumption: wealth ratio. This net effect depends upon n_F in much the same way, and for much the same reason, as does the effect of an unanticipated shock, de.

In general, the effect of an increased variance in the terms of trade on the expected growth rate depends to an important degree upon the elasticity γ. To consider this, it is convenient to begin with the benchmark logarithmic case, $\gamma = 0$, when the higher variance is seen from (9.43c) to have an unambiguously adverse effect on the expected growth rate. To see why, consider the case where $n_F > 0$, so that the expected return on foreign bonds exceeds that on capital. The increase in σ_e^2 will cause a substitution from the higher-earning to the lower-earning asset, causing a decline in the overall expected rate of return, and therefore in the expected rate of growth. If $n_F < 0$, then $\alpha > i^* + \varepsilon$. The increase in σ_e^2 reduces the net indebtedness of the country and the net stock of capital, and hence the rate of growth. If $\gamma < 0$, so that the coefficient of relative risk aversion $r > 1$, an increase in σ_e^2 continues to have an adverse effect on growth. This is because the reduction in earnings more than offsets any possible rise in C/W. However, when $\gamma > 0$, it is possible for an increase in σ_e^2 to be growth-enhancing. For example, this will be so if $\alpha = i^* + \varepsilon$, when the only effect of the higher variance is to reduce the C/W ratio, thereby increasing the growth rate.

Equation (9.43d) describes the impact of an increased variance in the terms of trade on the variance along the real growth path. This consists of two offsetting effects. On the one hand, for a given portfolio share, n_F, an increase in σ_e^2 will increase the variance along the growth path. But at the same time, the higher σ_e^2 will induce a reduction in the country's position in traded bonds, thereby reducing the impact of a given variance, σ_e^2, on the variance of the growth path. Which effect prevails depends upon n_F and γ. For the logarithmic utility function, the portfolio adjustment effect is the dominant effect, so that on balance, and paradoxically, more variability in the terms of trade will actually stabilize the real growth rate.

Growth in Terms of Domestic Consumption Bundle

Analogous kinds of propositions can be derived from a consideration of equation (9.42), which expresses the rate of growth in terms of the consumption bundle. Parallel to (9.43), we can establish the following:

$$\text{cov}\left(\frac{dx}{x}, de\right) = [n_F - (1-\theta)]\sigma_e^2 dt \tag{9.44a}$$

$$\frac{\partial}{\partial \varepsilon}\left(\frac{E(dx)}{x}\right) = \left[\frac{\partial r'_K}{\partial \varepsilon} + (r'_F - r'_K)\frac{\partial n_F}{\partial \varepsilon} + \left(\frac{\partial r'_F}{\partial \varepsilon} - \frac{\partial r'_K}{\partial \varepsilon}\right)n_F - \frac{\partial[C/W]}{\partial \varepsilon}\right]dt$$

$$= \left(\frac{2-\gamma}{1-\gamma}\right)[n_F - (1-\theta)]dt \tag{9.44b}$$

$$\frac{\partial}{\partial \sigma_e^2}\left(\frac{E(dx)}{x}\right) = \left[\frac{\partial r'_K}{\partial \sigma_e^2} + (r'_F - r'_K)\frac{\partial n_F}{\partial \sigma_e^2} + \left(\frac{\partial r'_F}{\partial \sigma_e^2} - \frac{\partial r'_K}{\partial \sigma_e^2}\right)n_F - \frac{\partial[C/W]}{\partial \sigma_e^2}\right]dt$$

$$= -\frac{1}{2(1-\gamma)^2}\left[\frac{(2-\gamma)(i^* + \varepsilon - \alpha)^2}{\sigma_e^4} - (1-\theta)[(1-\theta) + (1-\gamma)]\right]dt \tag{9.44c}$$

$$\frac{\partial}{\partial \sigma_e^2}\left(\text{var}\left(\frac{dx}{x}\right)\right) = [n_F - (1-\theta)]\left(n_F - (1-\theta) + 2\sigma_e^2 \frac{\partial n_F}{\partial \sigma_e^2}\right)dt$$

$$= -[n_F - (1-\theta)]\left(n_F + (1-\theta)\frac{1+\gamma}{1-\gamma}\right)dt. \tag{9.44d}$$

We do not discuss these expressions in detail except to note that the critical role previously played by n_F is now played by $n_F - (1 - \theta)$. While a positive disturbance, de, will raise the rate of return and the accumulation of wealth to the extent that $n_F > 0$, the effect on real wealth, now measured in terms of the consumption bundle, is offset by the higher price of the proportion of goods imported, $(1 - \theta)$. Thus an adverse terms of trade shock will raise the growth rates of real consumption, capital, and output, and the real accumulation of foreign bonds, all measured in terms of the consumption bundle, if and only if $n_F > (1 - \theta)$. Alternatively, the Laursen-Metzler effect will hold, in the sense of an adverse terms of trade shock being associated with a decline in savings and the real accumulation of traded assets if and only if $n_F < (1 - \theta)$; that is, if and only if the share of traded bonds in the portfolio of domestic investors is less than the share of foreign goods in the overall consumption bundle.[10]

We should note that there are some differences between the present stochastic analysis and much of the existing literature as reviewed in Chapter 3. First, the equilibrium is one of steady stochastic growth, so that our discussion of the terms of trade shocks pertains to the effects on growth rates. While this is natural here, it does contrast with most of the literature, which focuses on levels. Second, the counterpart to the price shock considered in the deterministic literature is E itself. In the present case a non-stochastic increase in E would have no effect on the equilibrium. It would lead to only a corresponding reduction in C_M, leaving the expenditure share, EC_M/C, and everything else, unchanged. This is perfectly consistent with the discussion in Section 3.4, which is a close deterministic analog to the present analysis. A change in E has an effect in that model through the endogeneity of labor. If labor were fixed, as it is here, the capital stock that is the driving force of the dynamics would no longer respond to a change in E, and the adjustment would degenerate, as it does here.

9.8 Terms of Trade Shocks and the External Account

The two measures pertaining to external activity considered in Section 9.6, $d(EB^*)/(EB^*)$ and db^*/b^*, describe the real growth rates of foreign bond holdings expressed in terms of domestic output and the domestic consumption bundle, respectively. While each represents a perfectly valid measure of the external account, neither corresponds to the usual measure of the current account. Nor does it exactly reflect the balance of trade, which was the concern of the original Harberger (1950) paper.

The balance of trade, expressed in terms of the domestic good, is defined by

$$dZ = dY - C\,dt - dK. \tag{9.45}$$

The conventional definition of the current account balance, expressed in terms of the domestic good, is thus

$$(E + dE)dB^* = dZ + i^*EB^*dt. \tag{9.46}$$

Observe that we are assuming that bonds are purchased at the price $E + dE$, rather than E. The difference between these two prices involves second-order terms that are unimportant in a world of certainty. But with the variances of the stochastic terms being of the first order, this pricing can be shown to be necessary if the consistency of ex ante and ex post wealth accumulation is to be preserved. The left-hand side of (9.46) may be written as

$$EB^*\left[\frac{d(EB^*)}{EB^*} - \frac{dE}{E}\right],$$

which differs from the real growth rate dX/X by the netting out of the capital gains component dE/E.

Substituting for $d(EB^*)/EB^*$ from (9.38c) and for dE/E from (9.16a), we obtain the following expressions for the current account and trade balance:

$$(E+dE)dB^* = EB^*\left[\left(\alpha - \varepsilon + (i^* + \varepsilon - \alpha)n_F - \frac{C}{W}\right)dt - n_K de\right] \tag{9.47a}$$

$$dZ = -EB^*\left[\left((i^* + \varepsilon - \alpha)n_K + \frac{C}{W}\right)dt + n_K de\right]. \tag{9.47b}$$

From these two relationships, we obtain

$$\text{cov}[(E+dE)dB^*, de] = \text{cov}[dZ, de] = -Kn_F\sigma_e^2 dt. \tag{9.48}$$

Thus we see that a positive shock in the relative price of the import good (i.e., an unanticipated deterioration in the terms of trade) will lead to a deterioration in both the current account balance, as measured by (9.46) and the trade balance if and only if the country is a net creditor ($n_F > 0$). In this case the Laursen-Metzler effect holds. This is in direct contrast to the effect on the savings rate and the real growth rate of foreign assets, which were both shown to respond negatively to an adverse shock in the terms of trade if and only if the country is a net debtor ($n_F < 0$). The difference is accounted for by the exclusion of the capital gains, dE/E, which contributed positively to the rate of growth as defined in terms of domestic output.[11]

One can show that the qualitative result in (9.48) continues to apply to the current account and trade balance when they are measured in terms of the domestic consumption bundle. This is in contrast to the measures of the real growth rate discussed in Section 9.7.

9.9 Terms of Trade Shocks and Welfare

The results discussed so far have described the effects of the terms of trade disturbance, and the characteristics of the probability distribution generating it, on various measures of economic performance pertaining to growth, real expenditures, and external balance. As we have commented at several stages, what is ultimately of concern, and what these measures are presumably attempting to proxy, is economic welfare. We now address this question directly, by considering the welfare of the representative agent, as measured by (9.36).

An unanticipated permanent terms of trade shock, de, which occurs at time 0, say, will impact on both the initial level of real wealth, W_0, and the relative price, E_0. The effect on welfare is thus

$$\frac{dV(W_0, E_0)}{de} = \gamma V \left[\frac{dW_0/de}{W_0} - (1-\theta)\frac{dE_0/de}{E_0} \right].$$

Substituting for the percentage changes in wealth and price from (9.38c) and (9.16), respectively, yields

$$\frac{dV(W_0, E_0)}{de} = \gamma V [n_F - (1-\theta)] = \gamma V \frac{dx/de}{x}. \tag{9.49a}$$

Thus it is seen that the effect on welfare of an unanticipated positive shock in the terms of trade is proportional to its effect on the real growth rate, dx/x, measured in terms of the consumption bundle. While the positive shock will increase welfare through the higher return, this is offset by the adverse effect on the cost of living.

The effect on welfare of an increase in the mean and the variance can be shown to be

$$\frac{dV/d\varepsilon}{V} = (\gamma - 1)\frac{d(C/W)/d\varepsilon}{C/W} = \frac{\gamma}{C/W}[n_F - (1-\theta)] \tag{9.49b}$$

$$\frac{dV/d\sigma_e^2}{V} = (\gamma - 1)\frac{d(C/W)/d\sigma_e^2}{C/W}$$

$$= \frac{\gamma}{2(1-\gamma)C/W}\left[(1-\theta)(1-\gamma\theta) - \frac{(i+\varepsilon-\alpha)^2}{\sigma_e^2}\right]. \tag{9.49c}$$

Of these, the latter is of greater interest. It is seen to have two effects. On the one hand, the higher variance in the relative price will, for a given portfolio, raise welfare. This is because the value function is convex in E. At the same time, the higher variance will reduce the rate of wealth accumulation. The net effect thus depends upon which of these two effects dominates.

The result that a risk-averse country may be better off with an increase in the variability of its terms of trade is not new, although the present intertemporal framework within which it is established is significantly different. This result was first obtained in the case of an individual consumer facing stochastic prices by Waugh (1944), using an analysis based on consumer surplus welfare measures. It was found to hold in more general cases for risk-averse consumers by several authors, including Hanoch (1977). The finding is also a manifestation of the results obtained in the 1970s, that the gains from trade may increase when there is uncertainty (see, e.g., Turnovsky 1974; Anderson and Riley 1976). But in contrast to the present approach, these analyses were based on static welfare measures.

9.10 Effects of Income Taxes

We now return to the complete equilibrium model set out in (9.33) and investigate the effects of change in income taxes on four key economic variables: equilibrium portfolio shares, the mean growth rate, the variance of the growth rate, and welfare. It is clear that any residual change in government revenue resulting from these tax changes is financed by an appropriate accommodating adjustment in the stock of bonds.

Equilibrium Portfolio Shares

Differentiating equation (9.33a) implies the following:

$$\frac{\partial \omega}{\partial \tau_K} = -\frac{\alpha}{(1-\gamma)[\alpha^2(1-\tau_K)\sigma_y^2 + (1-\tau_F)\sigma_e^2]}[1 - \alpha(1-\gamma)\omega\sigma_y^2] < 0 \quad (9.50a)$$

$$\frac{\partial \omega}{\partial \tau_F} = \frac{\alpha}{(1-\gamma)[\alpha^2(1-\tau_K)\sigma_y^2 + (1-\tau_F)\sigma_e^2]}\left[\frac{1-\tau_K}{1-\tau_F}\right][1 - \alpha(1-\gamma)\omega\sigma_y^2] > 0. \quad (9.50b)$$

The signs in (9.50a) and (9.50b) are predicated on the assumption that $1 > \alpha(1-\gamma)\omega\sigma_y^2$, which will be met as long as the variance of the productivity shocks is not too large. The interpretation of this condition is as follows. On the one hand, an increase in τ_K reduces the after-tax mean return to capital, thereby inducing investors to shift away from capital in their portfolios. At the same time, it reduces the associated risk, which investors "price" at $1 - \gamma$, and this encourages the holding of capital. The restriction we have imposed assumes that the former effect dominates, and in this case an increase in the tax rate on capital will reduce the share of capital in the traded portion of the agent's portfolio. An increase in the tax on foreign bonds, τ_F, has precisely the opposite effect.

Mean Growth Rate

The effect of increases in the tax rate on the mean equilibrium growth rate can be written as

$$\frac{\partial \psi}{\partial \tau_K} = -\frac{\alpha}{(1-\gamma)}[1 - \alpha\omega(1-\gamma)\sigma_y^2] + \frac{\partial \psi}{\partial \omega}\frac{\partial \omega}{\partial \tau_K}$$

$$= \left[\frac{\partial \psi}{\partial \omega} + \alpha^2(1-\tau_K)\sigma_y^2 + (1-\tau_F)\sigma_e^2\right]\frac{\partial \omega}{\partial \tau_K} \quad (9.51a)$$

$$\frac{\partial \psi}{\partial \tau_F} = \frac{\partial \psi}{\partial \omega}\frac{\partial \omega}{\partial \tau_F}. \quad (9.51b)$$

An increase in either tax has two effects on the growth rate. Consider τ_K. First, given ω, it reduces the risk-adjusted after-tax return to capital, thereby reducing the growth rate. Second, it causes a portfolio shift from domestic capital to traded bonds, thus reducing ω. Whether such a shift in the traded portion of the portfolio raises or lowers the mean growth rate depends upon the sign of $\partial \psi/\partial \omega$, which in turn depends upon the predominant sources of risk. This can be seen from (9.33b), where we find

$$\frac{\partial \psi}{\partial \omega} = -\alpha^2[(1-\tau_K) + \omega(\gamma-2)]\sigma_y^2 - \alpha^2(\gamma-2)\sigma_z^2$$
$$- [\omega(\gamma-2) + (2-\gamma\theta)]\sigma_e^2.$$

For example, if the only source of risk is domestic, domestic assets will tend to have higher rates of return than do foreign assets, in order to compensate. In that case an increase in the portfolio share of foreign assets will tend to reduce the growth rate (i.e., $\partial \psi/\partial \omega > 0$), thereby accentuating the reduction in the growth rate due to the first effect. On the other hand, if the primary sources of risk are foreign, foreign assets will tend to have higher rates of return, so that a portfolio shift toward foreign assets will raise the growth rate (i.e., $\partial \psi/\partial \omega < 0$). This will tend to offset the reduction in the growth rate due to the first effect. Indeed, it is possible for the portfolio shift to be of sufficient magnitude for this second effect to dominate, so that a higher tax on domestic capital income is actually growth-enhancing, in contrast to its known adverse effect on growth under certainty.

The effect of an increase in the tax rate on foreign assets depends upon the response of ω. Accepting the sign of (9.50b), we see that $sgn(\partial\psi/\partial\tau_F) = sgn(\partial\psi/\partial\omega)$. In this case it is possible for the growth rate to be more adversely affected by a rise in the tax on foreign assets than it is by a rise in the tax rate on domestic capital. But if $\partial\psi/\partial\omega > 0$, we also see that a rise in the foreign tax rate by inducing a switch to higher yielding domestic capital will be growth-enhancing. It will be observed that there is a slight asymmetry in the response of the growth rate to the two tax rates. This is because the growth rate is being measured in terms of the domestic good.

Finally, it is immediately apparent that a uniform tax increase ($d\tau_K = d\tau_F > 0$) leaves the optimal portfolio share ω unchanged, so that the net effect on the growth rate depends only upon $-1 + (1-\gamma)\alpha^2\omega\sigma_y^2$ and, provided (9.50a) applies, will be unambiguously growth-reducing.

Variance of Growth Rate

The effects of a higher tax rate on the variance of the growth rate are given by

$$\frac{\partial \sigma_w^2}{\partial \tau_i} = 2([\alpha^2(\sigma_y^2 + \sigma_z^2) + \sigma_e^2]\omega - \sigma_e^2)\frac{\partial \omega}{\partial \tau_i} \qquad i = K, F. \tag{9.52}$$

Thus, assuming the signs of (9.50), an increase in the tax on domestic capital income, τ_K, will stabilize the growth rate (i.e., reduce σ_w^2) if $\omega > \overline{\omega} \equiv (\sigma_e^2/[\alpha^2(\sigma_y^2 + \sigma_z^2) + \sigma_e^2])$ and destabilize it otherwise. An increase in τ_F will have precisely the opposite effect. This is because $\overline{\omega}$ is the variance minimizing portfolio and any tax change that shifts the portfolio toward $\overline{\omega}$ is stabilizing.

Welfare

The welfare effects of taxation are obtained from (9.37). From this relationship it is immediately seen that an increase in either consumption tax imposes direct welfare losses of the magnitudes

$$\frac{\partial V}{\partial \tau_D} = -\frac{(\gamma V)\theta}{1+\tau_D} < 0; \quad \frac{\partial V}{\partial \tau_M} = -\frac{(\gamma V)\theta}{1+\tau_M} < 0. \tag{9.53}$$

The effects on welfare of changes in the income tax rates operate through ψ and ω and are somewhat more complicated to determine. A convenient expression can be obtained by the following steps. First, from

(9.37′) we have

$$\frac{\partial V/\partial \tau_i}{V} = (\gamma - 1)\frac{\partial (C/W)/\partial \tau_i}{C/W} + \gamma \frac{\partial (\omega/n_K)/\partial \tau_i}{\omega/n_K} \qquad i = K, F. \qquad (9.54)$$

Second, differentiating (9.33c) and (9.33d) with respect to the tax rate yields

$$\frac{\partial (C/W)}{\partial \tau_i} = -\gamma \frac{\partial \psi}{\partial \tau_i} + \gamma(1-\gamma)[\alpha^2(\sigma_y^2 + \sigma_z^2) + \sigma_e^2]\omega \frac{\partial \omega}{\partial \tau_i} - \gamma(1-\gamma\theta)\sigma_e^2 \frac{\partial \omega}{\partial \tau_i} \qquad (9.55a)$$

$$\frac{\partial (\omega/n_K)/\partial \tau_i}{\omega/n_K} = \frac{[\alpha(1-g) - (i^* + \varepsilon)](\partial \omega/\partial \tau_i) - (\partial \psi/\partial \tau_i)}{(\omega/n_K)(C/W)} - \frac{\partial (C/W)/\partial \tau_i}{C/W}. \qquad (9.55b)$$

Third, consider the portfolio share

$$\tilde{\omega} \equiv \frac{\alpha(1-g) - (i^* + \varepsilon) + (1-\gamma\theta)\sigma_e^2}{(1-\gamma)[\alpha^2(\sigma_y^2 + \sigma_z^2) + \sigma_e^2]}. \qquad (9.55c)$$

This can be shown to be the portfolio share that results in the first-best equilibrium where the government, acting as a central planner, controls resources directly. That is, it is the solution to the following stochastic optimization problem: Maximize expected utility (9.20a), subject to the national budget constraint (9.27), with the portfolio shares $n_F + n_K = 1$.

Combining equations (9.54) and (9.55a)–(9.55c), the effects of income tax on welfare can be stated in the following equivalent ways (recalling that $\gamma V > 0$; see (9.37)):

$$\frac{\partial V/\partial \tau_i}{V}$$
$$= \frac{1}{C/W}\left\{\gamma(1-\gamma)(n_K + n_F)[\alpha^2(\sigma_y^2 + \sigma_z^2) + \sigma_e^2](\tilde{\omega} - \omega)\frac{\partial \omega}{\partial \tau_i} - n_B \frac{\partial (C/W)}{\partial \tau_i}\right\} \qquad (9.56a)$$

$$\frac{\partial V/\partial \tau_i}{V} = \frac{\gamma}{C/W}\left\{n_B \frac{\partial \psi}{\partial \tau_i} + (1-\gamma)[\alpha^2(\sigma_y^2 + \sigma_z^2) + \sigma_e^2](\tilde{\omega} - \omega)\frac{\partial \omega}{\partial \tau_i}\right\}$$
$$+ \frac{\gamma}{C/W}\left\{[(i^* + \varepsilon) - \alpha(1-g)]n_B \frac{\partial \omega}{\partial \tau_i}\right\}. \qquad (9.56b)$$

A higher income tax rate thus has two effects on welfare: a growth effect and a portfolio effect. To the extent that an increase in a particular tax rate reduces the growth rate, it will be welfare-reducing. However, the portfolio effect may either decrease or improve welfare, depending upon the size of the existing portfolio share, ω, relative to the first-best optimum, $\tilde{\omega}$. In the absence of risk, only the first effect exists, so that a higher tax is unambiguously welfare-deteriorating. In the presence of risk, and starting from a second-best optimum, it is possible for a further increase in the tax rate to be actually welfare-improving. This may be the case if the higher tax shifts the portfolio in the direction of $\tilde{\omega}$ and an example can easily be constructed.

9.11 Optimal Tax Policy

The fact that the first-best optimal portfolio, (9.55c), depends upon the share of government expenditure implies that in general it will be optimal to levy some taxes. Whether it is possible to attain this first-best optimal outcome through taxation in a decentralized economy depends upon the range of tax instruments at the disposal of the policy maker. In the present example, in which government expenditure has no utility benefits, it is indeed possible, through the appropriate choice of income tax rates, to get arbitrarily close to the first-best equilibrium of the central planner. If government expenditure yields some externality, the attainment of the first-best equilibrium is not in general possible with income taxes alone; some other tax instrument is necessary. A consumption tax, which in the absence of a labor-leisure choice acts as a lump-sum tax, can achieve this and an example of this is provided in Section 9.12.

The optimal structure can be obtained by optimizing the welfare function, (9.36), directly with respect to the tax rates. Alternatively, and less tediously, it can be obtained by seeking the combination of tax rates that will replicate the first-best equilibrium of the central planner. Either way, we find that the optimal income tax rates are

$$\hat{\tau}_K = \frac{g + \alpha(1-\gamma)\tilde{\omega}\sigma_z^2}{1 - \alpha(1-\gamma)\tilde{\omega}\sigma_y^2}; \quad \hat{\tau}_F = 0, \tag{9.57}$$

while the optimal consumption taxes are obviously $\tau_D = \tau_M = 0$. Setting the income tax rates as in (9.57) ensures that $\omega = \tilde{\omega}$, in which case (9.56) implies that $n_B = 0$; that is, the equilibrium stock of government bonds is zero.

Further understanding of this relationship is obtained by considering the government budget constraint when the government ceases to issue additional debt (when $\tau_F = 0$). Focusing on the deterministic component of (9.25) and supposing that $\tau_F = \tau_D = \tau_M = 0$, this leads to

$$\alpha n_K g + (1 - \tau_B) r_B n_B = \alpha n_K \tau_K. \tag{9.25'}$$

This equation asserts that capital income tax revenues must suffice to finance total government expenditures plus the net of tax interest owing on its outstanding debt. Now let $n_B \to 0$, as the optimal tax policy requires. In the absence of risk, (9.25′) reduces to $\tau_K = g$.

As long as the economy starts with a strictly positive stock of government bonds, the share n_B is reduced to zero by driving the price of bonds to zero. But in the present stochastic environment, as this occurs, the risk premium on these bonds implied by (9.31b) tends to infinity. Thus, in the presence of risk, these bonds, though negligible as a fraction of wealth, in the limit actually generate nonzero interest income:

$$\lim_{n_B \to 0} (1 - \tau_B) r_B n_B = (1 - \gamma) \alpha^2 \omega^2 [\tau_K \sigma_y^2 + \sigma_z^2]. \tag{9.31b′}$$

Substituting (9.31b′) and (9.57) yields (9.25′), so that the government's budget is met.

But this optimal equilibrium can hold only as a limit. If, instead, the economy sets the actual quantity of bonds to zero, thereby attaining the equilibrium $n_B = 0$ exactly, then the government's budget would need to balance at all times; that is, $dG = dT$ in (9.25). Equating the deterministic and stochastic components in this case (assuming $\tau_F = \tau_D = \tau_M = 0$) implies $\tau_K = g$ and $dz = \tau_K dy$. In order for this to be sustainable, the government can no longer set its stochastic expenditures independently, but instead must adjust them in response to the stochastic component of tax receipts. An example of how this may be achieved through a tax rebate scheme is provided in Section 9.12. Another possibility may be to introduce a state-dependent tax rate.

Interest in the question of the optimal taxation of capital was stimulated by Chamley (1986), who showed that asymptotically the optimal tax on capital should converge to zero. This result was obtained in a standard deterministic Ramsey model of a closed economy in which the government sets the *level* of its expenditure exogenously. As noted in Chapter 3, that result has been extended to an open economy Ramsey model by Correia (1996). The framework employed in the present chapter differs from that analysis in one key respect that accounts for the difference in the nature of the optimal taxation of capital. By specifying government expenditure to be a fixed fraction of output, its level is no longer exogenous but instead is proportional to the size of the growing capital stock. The private sector's decision to accumulate capital enlarges the economy and leads to an increase in the supply of public goods in the future. Since the private sector treats government expenditure as being independent of its own capital accumulation decision—when in fact it is not—a tax on capital is necessary to correct this distortion and thereby internalize the externality. In the absence of risk, the optimal tax on capital reduces to $\tau_K = g$. Income from domestic capital should be taxed at a rate that precisely corrects for the externality generated. In effect, agents are charged a "user fee" for accumulating capital. The optimal tax (9.57) is essentially a "risk-adjusted" version of this taxing scheme, adjusting for the risk associated with government expenditure, on the one hand, and the risk associated with uncertain tax revenues, on the other.

Since the context is one of ongoing growth, the optimal tax structure is much more closely related to that derived in Chapter 5, of which the present analysis can be viewed as a stochastic analog. At this point it is useful to recall equations (5.37a) and (5.37b). Those results expressed optimal tax rates in terms of the deviation between an arbitrarily set ratio of government expenditure to wealth and the optimal. Since in the present analysis government expenditure is useless, to compare (9.57) with (5.37a,b) we should set $\eta = \tilde{g}_w = 0$ in the latter, when they reduce to $\hat{\tau}_b = g_w/r$ and $\hat{\tau}_k = qg_w/\alpha$. The other differences are accounted for by noting that in the present analysis (1) government expenditure is tied to domestic output, rather than wealth; (2) there are no costs of adjustment to investment; and, of course, (3) risk is present.

Since the policy rule determining the growth of government expenditure links it to domestic output, and therefore to the domestic capital stock, this externality applies only to domestic capital. Accordingly, there is no such externality with respect to the economy's holdings of foreign bonds. On the other hand, if instead of being determined by (9.24b), government expenditure were tied to the growth of overall GNP, including foreign-source income growth, then the accumulation of foreign bonds would generate an analogous externality and foreign-source income would need to be taxed correspondingly, just as it was in (5.37a).

The fact that at the optimum $n_B \to 0$ implies that in the limit the government must run a balanced budget, financing its expenditures with a capital income tax. Bonds therefore have no welfare-enhancing role in this economy, a fact that is neither surprising nor new. This result has been established in a variety of endogenous growth models, both deterministic and stochastic (see, e.g., Corsetti 1991; Saint-Paul 1992; Turnovsky 1995, Chapter 13). With identical agents, there is no scope for welfare-enhancing risk-sharing through trade in government bonds, with their associated stochastic return.

9.12 Optimal Integrated Fiscal Policy

The optimal tax structure is sensitive to the assumption we have made that the expenditure has no impact on the agent's decisions. The discussion in

Section 5.4 emphasized the nature of government expenditure in the determination of the optimal tax structure and its relationship to the socially optimal level. We shall conclude this chapter by briefly considering an optimal integrated fiscal policy in the present stochastic context, basing our discussion on the following simple example.

Second-Best Fiscal Policy

There is now only a single consumption good, no nontraded bond, and no consumption tax. The government chooses a deterministic rate of government consumption $dG = G(t)dt$, which is analogous to the rate of private consumption $dC = C(t)dt$ and, along with the latter, yields utility to the representative agent, described by the logarithmic function

$$E_0 \int_0^\infty [\ln C + \eta \ln G] e^{-\beta t} dt \qquad \eta > 0. \tag{9.58}$$

The agent maximizes (9.58) subject to the stochastic wealth accumulation equation specified by (9.22a)–(9.22d), with $C_D = C$, $C_M = 0$, $n_B = 0$, $\tau_D = \tau_F = 0$. In so doing, he takes the level of government expenditure G to be given.

The government finances its deterministic rate of expenditure in accordance with the budget constraint:

$$\frac{G}{W} = \tau_K \alpha n_K + \tau_F(i^* + \varepsilon) n_F. \tag{9.59a}$$

Taxes, however, are levied uniformly on all income, and all tax revenues collected on the stochastic component of capital income are rebated in accordance with

$$dv = \tau_K \alpha n_K dy + \tau_F(i^* + \varepsilon) n_F de. \tag{9.59b}$$

The macroeconomic equilibrium in this simplified economy is described as follows[12]

$$n_K = \frac{\alpha(1 - \tau_K) - (i^* + \varepsilon)(1 - \tau_F)}{[\alpha^2(1 - \tau_K)\sigma_y^2 + (1 - \tau_F)\sigma_e^2]} + \frac{(1 - \tau_F)\sigma_e^2}{[\alpha^2(1 - \tau_K)\sigma_y^2 + (1 - \tau_F)\sigma_e^2]}$$

$$n_F = 1 - n_K \tag{9.60a}$$

$$\frac{C}{W} = \beta \tag{9.60b}$$

$$\psi = \alpha n_K + (i^* + \varepsilon) n_F - \frac{C}{W} - \frac{G}{W} \tag{9.60c}$$

$$\sigma_w^2 = \alpha^2 n_K^2 \sigma_y^2 + n_F^2 \sigma_e^2. \tag{9.60d}$$

Stochastic Growth in a Small Open Economy

The optimal fiscal policy problem confronting the policy maker is to choose the two tax rates, τ_K and τ_F, together with government expenditure, G, to maximize the agent's utility (9.58), subject to the equilibrium conditions (9.60) and its balanced budget condition (9.59). Omitting details, the following optimality conditions obtain:

$$\frac{G}{W} = \eta\beta \tag{9.61a}$$

$$\tau_K = \left(\frac{\eta\beta}{\alpha}\right) \frac{[1 - (i^* + \varepsilon)n_F \sigma_e^2]}{[1 - n_K n_F (\alpha \sigma_y^2 + (i^* + \varepsilon)\sigma_e^2)]} \tag{9.61b}$$

$$\tau_F = \left(\frac{\eta\beta}{i^* + \varepsilon}\right) \frac{[1 - \alpha n_K \sigma_y^2]}{[1 - n_K n_F (\alpha \sigma_y^2 + (i^* + \varepsilon)\sigma_e^2)]}, \tag{9.61c}$$

where n_K and n_F are given by (9.60a) and (9.60b) Substituting for these expressions into (9.61a)–(9.61c), one can obtain explicit solutions determining the optimal income tax rates, τ_K and τ_F.

The following inferences can be drawn. As in Section 5.4, the optimal ratio of public to private consumption equals η, the (percentage) marginal rate of substitution between the two goods in the utility function. But in contrast to the deterministic analysis, the tax rates on the two sources of resident's income, τ_K and τ_F are *not* in general equal. Instead, they reflect differences in the risk characteristics of the underlying assets.

First-Best Fiscal Policy

The optimum set in (9.61) is only second-best. Because of the externality generated by government expenditure, capital income taxes alone are incapable of achieving the first-best outcome of the central planner. Some additional tax is necessary to correct for the externality generated by the growing level of government consumption expenditure. To see the issue, we begin by solving the command optimum.

The central planner's problem is to choose C, G, n_K, and n_F directly to maximize the discounted utility function (9.58), subject to the economy-wide stochastic wealth accumulation equation:

$$\frac{dW}{W} = \left(\alpha n_K + (i^* + \varepsilon)n_F - \frac{C}{W} - \frac{G}{W}\right)dt + \alpha n_K dy + n_F de. \tag{9.62}$$

Performing the optimization leads to the following first-best equilibrium outcome for the domestic economy

$$n_K = \frac{\alpha - (i^* + \varepsilon)}{\alpha^2 \sigma_y^2 + \sigma_e^2} + \frac{\sigma_e^2}{\alpha^2 \sigma_y^2 + \sigma_e^2}; \quad n_F = 1 - n_K \tag{9.63a}$$

$$\frac{C}{W} = \frac{\beta}{1+\eta} \tag{9.63b}$$

$$\frac{G}{W} = \eta \frac{C}{W} \tag{9.63c}$$

$$\psi = \alpha n_K + (i^* + \varepsilon) n_F - (1+\eta)\frac{C}{W} \tag{9.63d}$$

$$\sigma_w^2 = \alpha^2 n_K^2 \sigma_y^2 + n_F^2 \sigma_e^2. \tag{9.63e}$$

The main difference between this optimal centralized equilibrium and the corresponding decentralized equilibrium summarized in equations (9.60a)–(9.60d) and (9.61a) is that the central planner internalizes the externality generated by G in his choice of the optimal private consumption ratio C/W. Comparing the two equilibria, it is clearly impossible to replicate the command optimum by setting only the two tax rates, τ_K and τ_F, in the decentralized system. By failing to recognize the positive externality generated by government expenditure on private consumption, and the fact that the government is choosing G (along with taxes on capital) optimally, private agents choose to overconsume, relative to the command optimum, resulting in too slow a growth rate. An additional tax is necessary to correct for the distortion, and it turns out that this can be accomplished most easily by introducing a general consumption tax.

It is a straightforward exercise to re-solve the decentralized equilibrium in the case where, in addition to the two tax rates on capital, the representative agent is subject to a tax on consumption—τ_C, say. The macroeconomic equilibrium now consists of (9.60a) and (9.60d), together with

$$\frac{C}{W} = \frac{\beta}{(1+\omega)} \tag{9.60b'}$$

$$\psi = \alpha n_K + (i^* + \varepsilon) n_F - (1+\eta)\frac{C}{W} \tag{9.60c'}$$

and the government budget constraint

$$\tau_K \alpha n_K + \tau_F (i^* + \varepsilon) n_F = (\eta - \tau_C)\frac{C}{W}. \tag{9.59a'}$$

Comparing this equilibrium with the command optimum (9.63a)–(9.63e), it is evident that the addition of the third tax rate enables the latter to be replicated. Specifically, if the tax rates on capital are both set to zero, $(\tau_K = \tau_F = 0)$, so that government expenditure is fully financed by the consumption tax, $(\tau_C = \eta)$, the decentralized economy will replicate the first-best optimum of the centrally planned economy. This optimal fiscal structure is thus seen to be identical to the overall optimal fiscal structure obtained in Section 5.4, where government expenditure was set optimally along with tax rates. When government expenditure is set arbitrarily, however, capital will need to be taxed to correct for the distortion created by government's not being at its socially optimal level. Unlike the deterministic case, the size of this distortion, and therefore the appropriate tax, will depend upon the risk in the economy.

Appendix

The consumer's stochastic optimization problem is to choose his consumption: wealth ratio and portfolio shares to

$$\text{Max } E_0 \int_0^\infty \frac{1}{\gamma}(C_D^\theta C_M^{1-\theta})^\gamma e^{-\beta t} dt \quad -\infty < \gamma < 1; \quad 0 \leq \theta \leq 1, \quad (9.A.1a)$$

subject to the stochastic wealth accumulation and the evolution of the real exchange rate,

$$\frac{dW}{W} = \psi \, dt + dw \quad (9.A.1b)$$

$$\frac{dE}{E} = \varepsilon \, dt + de, \quad (9.A.1c)$$

and the portfolio adding-up condition

$$n_K + n_B + n_F = 1, \quad (9.A.1d)$$

where for notational convenience

$$\psi \equiv n_K(1 - \tau_K)r_K + n_B(1 - \tau_B)r_B + n_F(1 - \tau_F)r_F$$

$$-\frac{(1+\tau_D)C_D}{W} - \frac{(1+\tau_M)EC_M}{W} \quad (9.A.1e)$$

$$dw \equiv n_K(1 - \tau_K)du_K + n_B(1 - \tau_B)du_B + n_F(1 - \tau_F)du_F. \quad (9.A.1f)$$

We define the differential generator of the value function $V(W, E, t)$ by

$$L[V(W, E, t)] \equiv \frac{\partial V}{\partial t} + \psi W \frac{\partial V}{\partial W} + \varepsilon E \frac{\partial V}{\partial E}$$

$$+ \frac{1}{2}\sigma_w^2 W^2 \frac{\partial^2 V}{\partial W^2} + \frac{1}{2}\sigma_e^2 E^2 \frac{\partial^2 V}{\partial E^2} + \sigma_{we} WE \frac{\partial^2 V}{\partial W \partial E}. \quad (9.A.2)$$

Given the exponential time discounting, V can be assumed to be of the time-separable form

$$V(W, E, t) = e^{-\beta t} X(W, E).$$

The formal optimization problem is now to choose C_D, C_M, n_K, n_B, and n_F to maximize the Lagrangian expression

$$e^{-\beta t}\frac{1}{\gamma}(C_D^\theta C_M^{1-\theta})^\gamma + L[e^{-\beta t}X(W,E)] + e^{-\beta t}\frac{\lambda}{\beta}[1 - n_K - n_B - n_F]. \quad (9.A.3)$$

Taking partial derivatives of this expression and canceling $e^{-\beta t}$ yields

$$\theta(C_D^\theta C_M^{1-\theta})^{\gamma-1} C_D^{\theta-1} C_M^{1-\theta} = X_W(1 + \tau_D) \quad (9.A.4a)$$

$$(1-\theta)(C_D^\theta C_M^{1-\theta})^{\gamma-1} C_D^\theta C_M^{-\theta} = EX_W(1 + \tau_M) \quad (9.A.4b)$$

$$(1-\tau_K)r_K W X_W dt + \text{cov}(dw, (1-\tau_K)du_K)X_{WW}W^2$$
$$+ WEX_{WE}\text{cov}(de, (1-\tau_K)du_K) = \frac{\lambda}{\beta}dt \quad (9.A.4c)$$

$$(1-\tau_B)r_B W X_W dt + \text{cov}(dw, (1-\tau_B)du_B)X_{WW}W^2$$
$$+ WEX_{WE}\text{cov}(de, (1-\tau_B)du_B) = \frac{\lambda}{\beta}dt \quad (9.A.4d)$$

$$(1-\tau_F)r_F W X_W dt + \text{cov}(dw, (1-\tau_F)du_F)X_{WW}W^2$$
$$+ WEX_{WE}\text{cov}(de, (1-\tau_F)du_F) = \frac{\lambda}{\beta}dt \quad (9.A.4e)$$

$$n_K + n_B + n_F = 1. \quad (9.A.4f)$$

These equations determine the optimal values for C_D, C_M, n_K, n_B, n_F, and λ, as functions of X_W, X_{WW}, and X_{EW} of the value function. In addition, the value function must satisfy the Bellman equation

$$\max_{C_D, C_M, n_K, n_B, n_F}\left\{\frac{1}{\gamma}(C_D^\theta C_M^{1-\theta})^\gamma e^{-\beta t} + L[e^{-\beta t}X(W,E)]\right\} = 0. \quad (9.A.5)$$

This involves substituting for the optimized values obtained from (9.A.4) and solving the resulting differential equation for $X(W, E)$:

$$\frac{1}{\gamma}(\hat{C}_D^\theta \hat{C}_M^{1-\theta})^\gamma - \beta X(W,E) + \hat{\psi}WX_W + \varepsilon EX_E$$
$$+ \frac{1}{2}\sigma_w^2 W^2 X_{WW} + \frac{1}{2}\sigma_e^2 E^2 X_{EE} + \sigma_{we}WEX_{WE} = 0, \quad (9.A.6)$$

where the circumflex denotes optimized value.

The solution is by trial and error, finding a function $X(W, E)$ that satisfies both the optimality condition and the Bellman equation. We postulate a solution of the form

$$X(W, E) = \delta W^\gamma E^x, \quad (9.A.7)$$

where the coefficients δ and x are to be determined. This equation immediately implies

$$X_W = \delta\gamma W^{\gamma-1}E^x; \quad X_E = \delta x W^\gamma E^{x-1}; \quad X_{WW} = \delta\gamma(\gamma-1)W^{\gamma-2}E^x$$

$$X_{EE} = \delta x(x-1)W^\gamma E^{x-2}; \quad X_{WE} = \delta\gamma x W^{\gamma-1}E^{x-1}. \quad (9.A.8)$$

To solve, we begin by dividing (9.A.4a) by (9.A.4b). Combining the resulting expression with the definition of expenditure, $C \equiv (1+\tau_D)C_D + (1+\tau_M)EC_M$, yields the expenditure shares

$$(1+\tau_D)C_D = \theta C; \quad (1+\tau_M)EC_M = (1-\theta)C,$$

so that

$$C_D^\theta C_M^{1-\theta} = \left(\frac{\theta}{1+\tau_D}\right)^\theta \left(\frac{1-\theta}{1+\tau_M}\right)^{1-\theta} CE^{-(1-\theta)}. \quad (9.A.9)$$

Substituting the expressions for C_D, C_M, and X_W back into (9.A.4a) yields

$$C = \left(\delta\gamma\left(\frac{\theta}{1+\tau_D}\right)^{-\gamma\theta}\left(\frac{1-\theta}{1+\tau_M}\right)^{-\gamma(1-\theta)}E^{x+\gamma(1-\theta)}\right)^{1/(\gamma-1)} W. \quad (9.A.10)$$

Next, substituting from (9.A.8), (9.A.9), and (9.A.10) into the Bellman equation (9.A.6), we obtain

$$\frac{1}{\gamma}\left(\frac{\theta}{1+\tau_D}\right)^{-\gamma\theta/(\gamma-1)}\left(\frac{1-\theta}{1+\tau_M}\right)^{-\gamma(1-\theta)/(\gamma-1)}(\delta\gamma)^{\gamma/(\gamma-1)}W^\gamma E^{[x+(1-\theta)]\gamma/(\gamma-1)}$$

$$-\beta\delta W^\gamma E^x + \hat\psi\delta\gamma W^\gamma E^x + \varepsilon\delta x W^\gamma E^x$$

$$+\frac{1}{2}\sigma_w^2\delta\gamma(\gamma-1)W^\gamma E^x$$

$$+\frac{1}{2}\sigma_e^2\delta x(x-1)W^\gamma E^x + \delta\gamma x\sigma_{we}W^\gamma E^x = 0. \quad (9.A.11)$$

This equation consists of terms involving W and E raised to constant powers.

The function (9.A.7) will be a viable solution if and only if

$$x = -\gamma(1-\theta),$$

in which case (9.A.10) reduces to

$$C = \left(\delta\gamma\left(\frac{\theta}{1+\tau_D}\right)^{-\gamma\theta}\left(\frac{1-\theta}{1+\tau_M}\right)^{-\gamma(1-\theta)}\right)^{1/(\gamma-1)} W. \quad (9.A.10')$$

Canceling the terms $W^\gamma E^x$ (recalling $x = -\gamma(1-\theta)$) in (9.A.11), and noting the definition of $\hat\psi$, we find that the optimal solution for C/W and the undetermined coefficient δ are given by

$$\frac{C}{W} = \left(\delta\gamma\left(\frac{\theta}{1+\tau_D}\right)^{-\gamma\theta}\left(\frac{1-\theta}{1+\tau_M}\right)^{-\gamma(1-\theta)}\right)^{1/(\gamma-1)}$$

$$= \frac{1}{1-\gamma}\left\{\beta + \varepsilon\gamma(1-\theta) - \gamma\rho - \frac{1}{2}\gamma(\gamma-1)\sigma_w^2\right.$$

$$\left. - \frac{1}{2}\gamma(1-\theta)[\gamma(1-\theta)+1]\sigma_e^2 + \gamma^2(1-\theta)\sigma_{we}\right\}. \qquad (9.A.12)$$

The solution for the value function is therefore

$$X(W, E) = \delta W^\gamma E^{-\gamma(1-\theta)}, \qquad (9.A.13)$$

where δ, obtained from the first equation in (9.A.12), can be written as

$$\delta = \frac{1}{\gamma}\left(\frac{\theta}{1+\tau_D}\right)^{\gamma\theta}\left(\frac{1-\theta}{1+\tau_M}\right)^{\gamma(1-\theta)}\left(\frac{\widehat{C}}{W}\right)^{\gamma-1} \qquad (9.A.14)$$

and the optimal consumption: wealth ratio is obtained from the second equation in (9.A.12). This is equation (9.23c) of the text. Note that the equilibrium $C/W > 0$ implies $\delta\gamma > 0$. Equation (9.36) in the text corresponds to welfare starting from initial values Finally, substituting for X_W, X_{WW}, and X_{WE} into (9.A.4c)–(9.A.4e) and subtracting, yields the optimality conditions (9.23d) and (9.23e).

Notes

1. Examples of dynamic stochastic models of open economies formulated by using discrete time can be found throughout Obstfeld and Rogoff (1996) and Frenkel, Razin, and Yuen (1996).

2. Two further areas of international macroeconomics in which continuous-time optimization methods have been successfully applied include (1) international finance (see, e.g., Stulz 1981, 1983, 1984, 1987; Adler and Dumas 1983) and (2) target zone models (see, e.g., Krugmann 1991; Krugman and Miller 1992; and Bertola 1994).

3. Essentially we are assuming that all taxation is residence-based.

4. For early discussions of the effects of uncertainty on consumption for this type of utility function, see Levhari and Srinivasan (1969) and Sandmo (1970), who showed how the effects could be decomposed into income and substitution effects.

5. In order for the equilibrium to be one of ongoing endogenous growth, government expenditure must grow with the economy. If that were not so, such an equilibrium would eventually become unsustainable. The notion that the government seeks to claim a share of domestic output is a natural one and feasible under present assumptions, in contrast with the deterministic growth model of Chapter 5.

6. For a general utility function the optimal portfolio shares and consumption: wealth ratio will be functions of time. The constancy is a consequence of the constant elasticity utility function, the linear production function, and the assumption that the means and variances of the underlying stochastic processes are constant through time.

7. In the absence of domestic bonds, $\omega = n_K$ and $1 - \omega = n_F$.
8. The restriction $n_K > 0$ is equivalent to $\alpha - i^* - \varepsilon + (1-\gamma)\sigma_e^2 > 0$.
9. Equations (9.41) imply $r'_F - r'_K = i^* + \varepsilon - \alpha - (1-\theta)\sigma_e^2$.
10. In the case where these two shares are equal, the growth of the real domestic economy, so defined, is independent of the foreign price disturbance. As Stulz (1988) has noted, by investing in the portfolio shares $n_K = \theta$ and $n_F = 1 - \theta$, the agent can create a perfectly safe asset in terms of the domestic consumption bundle.
11. Formally, the relationship is as follows:

$$\text{cov}\left(\frac{d(EB^*)}{EB^*}, de\right) = \frac{1}{EB^*}\text{cov}[(E+dE)dB^*, de] + \text{cov}\left(\frac{dE}{E}, de\right)$$

$$= (-n_K + 1)\sigma_e^2 dt = n_F \sigma_e^2 dt.$$

12. These equations correspond to (9.33a), (9.33c), (9.33d), and (9.30a), respectively.

10 A Stochastic Monetary Growth Model and Financial Policy

10.1 Introduction

This chapter extends the stochastic growth model developed in Chapter 9 to include money and government financial policy. As in the previous chapter, the objective is to develop a stochastic macroeconomic general equilibrium system in which both the means and variances of the endogenous variables are simultaneously determined. By introducing monetary factors, the distinction between real and nominal quantities is made explicit.

Among the variables to be determined, the endogenous process describing the nominal exchange rate is particularly relevant, and the equilibrium will determine both its deterministic and its stochastic components. This approach builds on work of the early 1980s, in which asset demands were determined, with exchange rate dynamics, returns on traded and domestic bonds, and stochastic movements in prices all being specified as exogenous Brownian motion processes.[1] This chapter also describes the relationship between the investor's choices in the same way, although we shall endogenize the stochastic processes describing the domestic price level, the exchange rate, and the real rates of return on assets. International finance has provided a fruitful area for the application of continuous-time stochastic methods; the important contributions of Stulz (1981, 1983, 1984, 1987) and Adler and Dumas (1983) should be mentioned in this regard. A comprehensive survey of this literature is provided by Stulz (1994). The primary focus in these papers is on establishing equilibrium portfolio relationships, determining asset demands, and the equilibrating pricing of assets. By contrast, the emphasis of the present chapter is to embed these considerations into a complete macroeconomic framework and to investigate the effects of macroeconomic policy shocks (and other changes) on this stochastic equilibrium (see also Grinols and Turnovsky 1994; Obstfeld 1994).

After the model is developed, it is used to address three general issues that have been studied in the international macroeconomic literature from varying standpoints: (1) analysis of the stochastic equilibrium and its responsiveness to policy shocks and structural changes; (2) applications to issues in international finance, including the foreign exchange risk premium and capital asset pricing relationships; (3) applications to exchange rate management.

The first topic is taken up in Sections 10.4 and 10.5. We begin by considering the effects of both domestic monetary and fiscal policy on the economy, contrasting the effects of changes in the levels (means) of these instruments with changes in their associated risks (variances). Next, we analyze the effects of changes in the foreign inflation rate and its variance on the domestic economy. The extent to which flexible exchange rates insulate an economy against foreign price shocks was discussed at some length in the 1970s following the worldwide move toward flexible exchange rates. These analyses were based on the portfolio balance models of the time. The present stochastic model is a useful vehicle for revisiting this issue and, turns out, confirming some of the previous propositions.

Substantial attention is devoted to analyzing the determinants of the equilibrium growth rate of the economy. This is determined by a stochastic differential equation, the deterministic and stochastic components of which are investigated. This aspect was also addressed in Chapter 9, where we analyzed the effects of terms of trade shocks and taxes on the equilibrium growth rate. The discussion in this chapter focuses more broadly on the effects of various sources of risk on the equilibrium growth rate. The short-run covariation between the stochastic shocks to growth and other key macroeconomic variables is discussed, along the lines of the real business cycle literature. The effects of increased risk, arising from policy as well as exogenous sources, on both the mean growth rate and its variance are also considered.

It is important to emphasize that the implications of this type of mean-variance equilibrium model, in which risks are endogenously determined, can sometimes overturn those obtained in more conventional models where the endogeneity of some aspects of the structure is ignored. To give one result, simple ad hoc stochastic models, in which the structural parameters are assumed to be independent of the stochastic structure, typically predict that an increase in the variance of the foreign price shocks will increase the variance of the nominal exchange rate. In the present model, the reverse may turn out to be true. An increase in the variance of foreign price shocks may bring about a readjustment of the equilibrium portfolio sufficient to mitigate the effects of foreign price shocks on the exchange rate, thereby reducing the variance of the latter. In effect, the structural changes induced by the change—the key element of the Lucas Critique—are the dominant influence.

This type of mean-variance optimization framework has formed the basis for much important empirical work pertaining to interest rate parity relationships and the determination of the exchange rate risk premium; see, e.g., Frankel 1986; Giovannini and Jorion 1987; Hodrick and Srivastava 1986; Lewis 1988; Engel and Rodrigues 1993; and Hakkio and Sibert 1995. This literature has been extensively surveyed by Engel (1996). By incorporating this financial subsector into a general equilibrium macroeconomic framework, the present model provides a convenient vehicle for analyzing the determinants of the foreign exchange risk premium within a general equilibrium setting and for examining its responsiveness to the exogenous risks impinging on the economy. This issue, and other related questions pertaining to capital asset pricing, are discussed in Section 10.6 from the perspective of the present stochastic general equilibrium model.

The third major issue to which the model is applied, discussed in Sections 10.7–10.10, is that of monetary policy and, in particular, optimal exchange rate management. This question is a fundamental one in international macroeconomics and has occupied the attention of economists over a long period of time. Early discussions centered on the choice of fixed versus flexible exchange rates. Recognizing that these represent polar regimes, economists began analyzing systems of managed floats and addressing the question of the optimal exchange rate regime.[2]

During the 1980s an extensive literature analyzing optimal exchange market intervention evolved.[3] Although this literature has served to place the earlier debate of fixed versus flexible rates in a more general context, it suffers from several limitations. First, the underlying behavioral relationships of these models are usually some variant of the static *IS-LM* model and are not grounded in any intertemporal optimizing behavior. Second, the optimality criterion used to evaluate the alternative regimes is typically some measure of the variance of output (often taken in conjunction with the variance of inflation) about some appropriately chosen benchmark level. While this is analytically convenient within the linear mean-variance framework that these studies usually adopt, this objective is at best of limited welfare significance.[4] Further, even for this minimum variance criterion, the guidance for optimal policy is modest. The optimal exchange rate regime, attained by an optimal monetary intervention rule, is critically dependent upon the nature, the sources, and the relative sizes of the stochastic disturbances affecting the economy. Optimal policy is generally a managed float, with the authorities continuously intervening in response to stochastic fluctuations in the exchange rate. The implementation of such a policy may require the authorities either to lean *against* the wind—contract the money supply in response to a depreciating exchange rate—or to lean *with* the wind, depending upon the stochastic environment. Both alternatives are plausible, even for the simplest model.

The derivation of optimal exchange rate policy within the present stochastic intertemporal optimizing framework offers both substantial advantages over, and different perspectives from, those of the more traditional literature. First, the intertemporal optimization takes account of the response of private agents to regime changes—the Lucas Critique—an aspect that almost the entire exchange market intervention literature ignores.[5] Two exceptions to this are Helpman and Razin (1979, 1987).

The former is a three-period model, and the latter is based on an overlapping generations model. Lapan and Enders (1980) and Eaton (1985) also analyze the choice of exchange rate regime, using a stochastic overlapping generations framework.

This approach leads to a very different measure for assessing exchange rate regimes. The central feature of the present analysis is to characterize optimal policy in terms of attaining an appropriately determined target interest rate, thus suggesting that the focus on optimal monetary intervention rules may be misdirected. Our analysis shows that the monetary authorities should lean neither against nor with the wind. Instead, they should direct their stabilization efforts at attaining an internal interest rate target. Because optimal policy is characterized by a single target and there is more than one policy tool, the target can be reached in any one of an infinite number of ways. In particular, it can always be attained by setting an appropriate deterministic monetary growth rate. But any exchange rate regime consistent with the optimal interest rate target is equally satisfactory. Furthermore, while an independent exchange market intervention policy may (or may not) succeed in reaching the objective, it is redundant once the appropriate rate of monetary growth has been set.

Although we find the approach adopted to be attractive, it has its own limitations that should be borne in mind. For example, the model abstracts from any nominal rigidities. These are typically important aspects of short-run stabilization policy and central to the typical model of exchange market intervention noted earlier. In this respect our approach can be viewed as focusing on the optimal choice of exchange rate regime from a longer-run perspective, and in this sense it complements, rather than supersedes, these earlier contributions. Moreover, as will become apparent, the specific results highlighting the role of interest rate targeting are consequences of specific features of the model. In this regard the assumption that the residual form of government finance is a distortionary tax on wealth is important. In contrast to the case of lump-sum tax financing, when monetary growth is superneutral and the optimal monetary growth rate is the Friedman (1969) satiation rule, the distortionary aspect of the wealth tax has to be traded off against the rate of monetary decline necessary to attain the Friedman rule. This trade-off is analogous to that between income tax and inflation tax introduced by Phelps (1973) and discussed in Chapter 2.

10.2 The Analytical Framework

As in the previous chapter, the economy is small, being a price taker in all its international trading activities. There are, however, a number of

A Stochastic Monetary Growth Model and Financial Policy

differences in the model, the most important of which is the introduction of money. The other, minor difference is that there is now only a single consumption good. We begin by describing the stochastic environment, financial assets, and choices of consumers and the government.

Prices and Asset Returns

At each instant of time the domestic representative agent chooses the consumption of a single traded good and the allocation of his wealth between four assets. The assets are domestic money, M, and domestic government bonds, B, both of which are denominated in terms of domestic currency and are assumed to be internationally nontraded; tradable foreign bonds, B^*, which are denominated in terms of foreign currency; and equity claims on capital, denominated in terms of domestic output and also assumed to be internationally traded.

The assumption that domestic bonds are nontraded, and the (implicit) assumption that domestic residents may not hold foreign equity, introduce a form of incomplete markets into the model. This turns out to be inessential to the main results pertaining to the targeting of monetary policy to the domestic interest rate, since these are driven by the specification of tax and debt policies and the trade-off that these induce between domestic growth and liquidity. As in the previous chapter, since the domestic economy is small, if domestic bonds were internationally traded, the risk parity conditions between the foreign and domestic bonds would become exogenously determined by risk conditions and preferences in the rest of world. This would affect the equilibrium portfolio mix, but not the nature of the trade-off determining the interest rate target.

There are three prices in the model: P, the domestic price of the traded good; Q, the foreign price level of the traded good; and E, the nominal exchange rate, measured in terms of domestic currency per unit of foreign currency.[6] With this convention an increase in E corresponds to a depreciation of the domestic currency. While Q is assumed to be exogenous, P and E are to be endogenously determined. These prices evolve in accordance with the geometric Brownian motion processes:

$$\frac{dP}{P} = \pi\, dt + dp \qquad (10.1a)$$

$$\frac{dQ}{Q} = \eta\, dt + dq \qquad (10.1b)$$

$$\frac{dE}{E} = \varepsilon\, dt + de, \qquad (10.1c)$$

where π, η, and ε are the respective expected instantaneous rates of change. The terms dp, dq, and de are temporally independent, normally distributed random variables with zero means and instantaneous variances $\sigma_p^2 dt$, $\sigma_q^2 dt$, and $\sigma_e^2 dt$. The assumption of Brownian motion, as specified by these stochastic processes, is convenient in that it leads to a mean-variance equilibrium in a natural way. As discussed by Grinols and Turnovsky (1994), we will allow the nominal exchange rate, E, and therefore the domestic price level, P, to undergo discrete jumps where once-and-for-all unanticipated discrete changes, such as policy changes, occur. Elsewhere, they will follow the continuous (but nondifferentiable) processes specified in (10.1). Assuming free trade and a single traded good, the price level in the domestic economy must be related to that in the rest of the world by the purchasing power parity (*PPP*) relationship

$$P = QE. \tag{10.2}$$

Taking the stochastic derivative of this relationship implies

$$\frac{dP}{P} = \frac{dQ}{Q} + \frac{dE}{E} + \frac{dQ}{Q}\frac{dE}{E}. \tag{10.3}$$

Substituting for (10.1a)–(10.1c) into this relationship and retaining terms to order dt implies

$$\pi = \eta + \varepsilon + \sigma_{qe} \tag{10.4a}$$

$$dp = dq + de, \tag{10.4b}$$

where $\sigma_{qe} dt$ is the instantaneous covariance between dq and de.

Equation (10.4a) portrays an important difference from the conventional specification of inflation in a small open economy under conditions of *PPP*. Under these conditions it is standard to assert that the domestic inflation rate is the sum of the world inflation rate plus the rate of exchange depreciation of the domestic currency (see Section 2.1). In a stochastic world, account also needs to be taken of the covariance between the world inflation rate and the domestic exchange rate. As we will see in due course, the latter term tends to be negative, in which case the conventional *PPP* relationship would overstate the rate of domestic inflation. Equation (10.4b) describes the stochastic component of the *PPP* relationship. A positive random shock in the foreign price level or a stochastic depreciation of the domestic currency leads to a proportionate stochastic increase in the domestic price level.

While the foreign price level, Q, is always assumed to be exogenous to the small open economy, the determination of P and E depends upon the policy of the monetary authority. For example, if monetary policy is to target the exchange rate, E can be viewed as being exogenously determined by the stochastic process (10.1c). In this case, ε is the target rate of exchange depreciation, with the stochastic component de reflecting random deviations about the target. Under this regime P is endogenously determined by the *PPP* condition. Monetary growth also has to accommodate to sustain the target. By contrast, if monetary policy targets the monetary growth rate, P and E become endogenously determined, with their respective stochastic components, dp and de, responding to the various stochastic disturbances impinging on the economy.

Domestic and foreign bonds are assumed to be short bonds, paying nonstochastic nominal interest rates i and i^* respectively, over the period dt. Using the Itô calculus, the real rates of return to domestic residents on their holdings of money, the domestic bond, and the foreign bond are, respectively:

$$dR_M = r_M dt - dp; \quad r_M \equiv -\pi + \sigma_p^2 \qquad (10.5a)$$

$$dR_B = r_B dt - dp; \quad r_B \equiv i - \pi + \sigma_p^2 \qquad (10.5b)$$

$$dR_F = r_F dt - dq; \quad r_F \equiv i^* - \eta + \sigma_q^2. \qquad (10.5c)$$

Again, it will be observed that these rates of return differ from the corresponding standard deterministic quantities by two terms, the stochastic component and the variances. Consider the rate of return on money. In general, this is defined by the quantity

$$dR_M \equiv \frac{d(1/P)}{(1/P)}.$$

Taking the second-order differential of the right-hand side of this expression yields

$$dR_M \cong -\left(\frac{dP}{P}\right) + \left(\frac{dP}{P}\right)^2.$$

Under deterministic conditions, the second term is negligible, so that this expression is simply $-dP/P$, which per unit of time is simply $-\pi$. Under stochastic conditions, however, $(dP/P)^2 = \sigma_p^2 dt$, in which case we obtain

$$dR_M \equiv [-\pi + \sigma_p^2]dt - dp,$$

which is (10.5a). The important point to observe is that because of the convexity of $1/P$ in P, the variance of the stochastic component of P contributes positively to the expected rate of return. The same procedures can be used to derive the returns on the bonds, the only point to note being the plausible assumption that the nominal interest rate over the period $(t, t+dt)$ is nonstochastic.

The production technology remains similar to that of Chapter 9. The flow of domestic output, dY, is produced from capital, K, by means of the stochastic constant returns technology

$$dY = \alpha K(dt + dy), \qquad (10.6)$$

where α is the (constant) marginal physical product of capital and dy is a temporally independent, normally distributed stochastic process with mean zero and variance $\sigma_y^2 dt$. Hence, in the absence of adjustment costs to investment, the real rate of return on capital (equity) is

$$dR_K = \frac{dY}{K} = r_K dt + dk \equiv \alpha\, dt + \alpha\, dy. \qquad (10.5d)$$

Consumer Optimization

The representative consumer's asset holdings are subject to the wealth constraint

$$W \equiv \frac{M}{P} + \frac{B}{P} + \frac{EB^*}{P} + K, \qquad (10.7)$$

where W denotes real wealth. In addition, he is assumed to consume output over the period $(t, t+dt)$ at the nonstochastic rate $C(t)dt$ generated by these asset holdings.

The objective of the representative agent is to select his rate of consumption and his portfolio of assets to maximize the expected value of lifetime utility:

$$E_0 \int_0^\infty \frac{1}{\gamma}\left(C(t)^\theta \left(\frac{M(t)}{P(t)}\right)^{1-\theta}\right)^\gamma e^{-\beta t} dt \qquad 0 \le \theta \le 1; -\infty \le \gamma \le 1, \qquad (10.8a)$$

subject to the wealth constraint (10.7) and the stochastic wealth accumulation equation, expressed in real terms as

$$dW = W[n_M dR_M + n_B dR_B + n_K dR_K + n_F dR_F] - C(t)dt - dT, \qquad (10.8b)$$

where

$$n_M \equiv \frac{M/P}{W} = \text{share of portfolio held in money}$$

$$n_B \equiv \frac{B/P}{W} = \text{share of portfolio held in domestic government bonds}$$

$$n_K \equiv \frac{K}{W} = \text{share of portfolio held in terms of capital}$$

$$n_F \equiv \frac{EB^*/P}{W} = \frac{B^*/Q}{W} = \text{share of portfolio held in foreign bonds}$$

dT = taxes paid to the domestic government.

The consumer's objective function reflects utility from the holding of real money balances, as well as from current consumption. As in Chapter 9, the specification of the constant elasticity utility function is convenient, with θ measuring the relative importance of money in utility. In Chapter 2 we commented on the procedure of introducing money into the utility function, noting that Feenstra (1986) had shown how, under certain regularity conditions, this is equivalent to introducing a demand for money through a transactions technology. The constant elasticity utility function, defined over the positive orthant but omitting a neighborhood of the origin, satisfies the necessary regularity conditions discussed by Feenstra. We should also note that government expenditure yields no utility, though this, too, can be introduced along the lines of Chapter 5 and Section 9.12.

In the present analysis, taxes will be endogenously determined to satisfy the government budget constraint, specified in equation (10.12), and will therefore include a stochastic component reflecting the changing need for taxes. Since in a growing economy, taxes and other real variables grow with the size of the economy, measured here by real wealth, we relate total taxes to wealth according to

$$dT = \tau W dt + W dv, \qquad (10.9)$$

where dv is a temporally independent, normally distributed random variable with zero mean and variance $\sigma_v^2 dt$. As we will see below, the parameters τ and dv must be set to ensure that the government's budget constraint is met. It will also become evident that in a steadily growing economy, the tax rate τ on the deterministic component of total wealth is nondistortionary; it operates essentially as a lump-sum tax. This is not true, however, of the stochastic component, which will have real effects through the portfolio decision. We assume that the agent is fully rational in the sense of correctly perceiving τ and the relevant variances and covariances involving the stochastic component dv. This treatment of the wealth tax as the residual balancing item is an important aspect of the model and accounts for some of the specific results we attain.

Substituting for n_i into (10.7), for n_M into (10.8a), and for (10.5a)–(10.5d) and (10.9) into (10.8b), the stochastic optimization problem can be expressed as being to choose the consumption: wealth ratio, C/W and the portfolio shares, n_i, to maximize (10.8a), subject to

$$dW/W = \left[n_M r_M + n_B r_B + n_K r_K + n_F r_F - \frac{C}{W} - \tau\right]dt + dw \qquad (10.10a)$$

$$n_M + n_B + n_K + n_F = 1, \qquad (10.10b)$$

where for convenience, we denote the stochastic component of dW/W by

$$dw \equiv -(n_M + n_B)dp + n_K \alpha\, dy - n_F dq - dv. \qquad (10.10c)$$

In performing this optimization, the representative agent takes the real rates of return, the tax rate τ, and the relevant first and second moments of all stochastic processes (including those involving dv) as given. However, these will ultimately be determined in the stochastic equilibrium to be derived.

The details of the optimization parallel those of Chapter 9, and it can be solved following a procedure identical to that presented in the Appendix to that chapter.[7] The resulting optimality conditions can be expressed as follows:

Consumption: $\quad \dfrac{C}{W} = \dfrac{\theta}{1-\gamma\theta}\left(\beta - \rho\gamma - \tfrac{1}{2}\gamma(\gamma-1)\sigma_w^2\right) \qquad (10.11a)$

Money balances: $\quad n_M = \left(\dfrac{1-\theta}{\theta}\right)\dfrac{C/W}{i} \qquad (10.11b)$

Equities and bonds: $\quad (r_K - r_B)dt = (1-\gamma)\mathrm{cov}(dw, \alpha\,dy + dp) \qquad (10.11c)$

$$(r_F - r_B)dt = (1-\gamma)\mathrm{cov}(dw, -dq + dp), \qquad (10.11d)$$

where

$$\rho \equiv n_M r_M + n_B r_B + n_K r_K + n_F r_F - \tau$$

$$\sigma_w^2 = \lim_{dt\to 0} E\frac{(dw)^2}{dt}$$

$$= (n_M+n_B)^2\sigma_p^2 + n_K^2\alpha^2\sigma_y^2 + n_F^2\sigma_q^2 + \sigma_v^2 - 2(n_M+n_B)n_K\alpha\sigma_{py}$$

$$- 2(n_M+n_B)n_F\sigma_{pq} + 2(n_M+n_B)\sigma_{pv} + 2n_K n_F\alpha\sigma_{yq} - 2n_K\alpha\sigma_{yv} - 2n_F\sigma_{qv}.$$

The form of consumption : wealth ratio is analogous to that derived in Chapter 9, so that the comments we made previously continue to apply. The only change is in the parameter θ, which represents the relative importance of consumption in utility. Equation (10.11b) determines the demand for real money balances. With domestic bonds and money belonging to the same risk class, (10.11b) is in effect the equality between the real rate of return on domestic money and on bonds, the former including its utility return measured by

$$\left(\frac{1-\theta}{\theta}\right)\left(\frac{C/W}{n_M}\right).$$

To see this, we may observe that the optimality condition determining the demand for money, analogous to (10.11c) and (10.11d), is

$$\left(r_M + \left(\frac{1-\theta}{\theta}\right)\left(\frac{C/W}{n_M}\right) - r_B\right)dt$$
$$= (1-\gamma)\text{cov}(dw, dp - dp) = 0. \qquad (10.11b')$$

Noting from (10.5a) and (10.5b) that $r_B - r_M = i$, this equation immediately implies (10.11b). The implied demand for money obtained from this latter equation can be written as

$$\frac{M}{P} = \left(\frac{1-\theta}{\theta}\right)\frac{C}{i},$$

which can be seen to be an interest-elastic cash-in-advance constraint.

Equations (10.11c) and (10.11d) describe the differential real rates of return on the assets, in terms of their respective risk differentials, as measured by the covariance with the overall market return. Observe that if the investor is risk-neutral (i.e., $\gamma \to 1$), all expected real rates of return have to be equal. Solving equations (10.11b)–(10.11d), in conjunction with the normalized wealth constraint (10.10b), one can determine the agent's portfolio demands n_M, n_B, n_K, and n_F.

Government Policy

Government policy is characterized by the choice of government expenditures, the issuing of money and bonds, and the collection of taxes, all of which must be specified subject to the government budget constraint. This is expressed in real terms as

$$d\left(\frac{M}{P}\right) + d\left(\frac{B}{P}\right) = dG + \left(\frac{M}{P}\right)dR_M + \left(\frac{B}{P}\right)dR_B - dT, \qquad (10.12)$$

where dG denotes the stochastic rate of real government expenditure. Like the analogous equation for the representative agent (10.8b), this can be derived from the basic nominal budget constraint, as in Merton (1971).

Government expenditure policy is specified by the process

$$dG = g\alpha K\, dt + \alpha K\, dz, \qquad (10.13a)$$

where dz is an intertemporally independent, normally distributed random variable with zero mean and variance $\sigma_z^2 dt$. As in Section 9.3, government expenditure is specified to be a stochastic share of output.

Having introduced money, we need to introduce monetary policy, which we specify by the stochastic growth rule:

$$\frac{dM}{M} = \phi\, dt + dx, \tag{10.13b}$$

where ϕ is the mean monetary growth rate and dx is an independently distributed random variable with zero mean and variance $\sigma_x^2 dt$. This equation reflects how monetary policy is chosen and encompasses a potentially rich set of policies. To be concrete, we shall assume that the monetary authority sets the growth rate, ϕ, directly. The stochastic component, dx, may reflect exogenous stochastic failures to meet this target, in which case it will be uncorrelated with other stochastic variables. Alternatively, it may reflect stochastic adjustments in the money supply as the authorities respond to exogenous stochastic movements in intermediate targets, such as the exchange rate or price level; in this case it will be correlated with stochastic movements in these targets. As we will show, optimal monetary policy is independent of the precise process determining dx. We shall also note how, if monetary policy is chosen to target some other variable, ϕ will have to be adjusted appropriately.

Debt policy is formulated in terms of maintaining a chosen ratio of domestic government (nontraded) bonds to money

$$\frac{B}{M} = \lambda, \tag{10.13c}$$

where λ is a policy parameter set by the government. This specification can be thought of as a stochastic version of a balanced growth equilibrium assumption, which has a well established tradition in the monetary growth literature (see, e.g., Foley and Sidrauski 1971). In the present international context, the choice of λ also reflects sterilization policy.

There are several aspects of both a practical and an empirical nature motivating the specification of debt policy by (10.13c). If we were to assume (1) that debt is determined residually, so as to finance the government budget constraint, and (2) that government bonds are long bonds (perpetuities), then monetary policy turns out to be superneutral. If we want to assign a more central role to monetary policy, either or both of these assumptions must be modified. Suppose we were to continue to adopt what may seem to be the most natural assumption, that government bonds are determined residually by the needs to finance the government budget. We would then find that the ratio of money to short government bonds would evolve stochastically over time as bonds were issued as necessary to meet the stochastic borrowing requirements of the government. This would mean that it would be impossible to have an equilibrium in which portfolio shares remain constant over time, as we assumed previously. On the contrary, they would have to change stochastically through time, and this leads to a substantial complication in the derivation of the portfolio equilibrium. In effect, it becomes impossible to represent the stochastic dynamics in terms of only one state variable, wealth, as we have been doing. Instead, we would need to include a second state variable, such as the stochastic ratio of bonds to money. This converts the optimization into a two-state variable problem, which in general becomes much more difficult, and frequently intractable, to solve.[8]

While the assumption that deficits are bond-financed is the prevalent one in the analytical modeling of macroeconomic equilibria, it is not clear that it is necessarily the appropriate description of actual debt policy. In fact, historically, there have been substantial swings in U.S. debt policy, with the specification (10.13c) providing a reasonable characterization of debt policy over substantial periods of time. For example, over the period 1967–85, the ratio of publicly held debt to M3 in the United States averaged 0.24 with a standard deviation of only 0.055, while the ratio of maturities less than one year to M3 averaged 0.11 with a standard deviation of only 0.018.[9] In this case, the constancy of bonds to money in the long run is also dictated by the fact that assuming differential growth rates for B and M would imply that the asset with the smaller growth rate would ultimately become vanishingly small in the portfolio of the representative investor. In any event, when the ratio of bonds to money is held fixed, it is more appropriate to refer to the common growth rate of money and bonds (ϕ) and its stochastic component (dx) as being a more general characterization of *government finance* policy, rather than a pure monetary policy. It is also the reason the superneutrality of money no longer obtains in this case. The issue of the optimal composition of the government's liabilities—the ratio of debt to money—is then addressed by the optimal choice of λ.

Given the policy specification (10.13a)–(10.13c), both the mean and the stochastic component of taxes dT must be set in order to meet the government budget constraint (10.12). While the treatment of taxes as the residual budget item is a little unusual, it is a consequence of the restrictions imposed on the specification of debt policy. We should add, however, that once the optimal debt ratio is chosen, this is essentially equivalent to choosing the tax rate, so that the choice of residual budget item becomes much less significant.

Product Market Equilibrium and Balance of Payments

As in Chapter 9, balance of payments equilibrium is expressed in real terms by the relationship

$$d\left(\frac{B^*}{Q}\right) = [dY - dC - dK - dG] + \left(\frac{B^*}{Q}\right)dR_F. \tag{10.14}$$

Rearranging (10.14) and using equations (10.5c), (10.6), and (10.13a) leads to the following equation describing the real rate of accumulation of traded assets in the economy:

$$d\left(\frac{B^*}{Q}\right) + dK = \left[\alpha K(1-g) - C + \left(\frac{B^*}{Q}\right)(i^* - \eta + \sigma_q^2)\right]dt$$

$$+ \alpha K(dy - dz) - \left(\frac{B^*}{Q}\right)dq. \tag{10.15}$$

10.3 Macroeconomic Equilibrium

The elements described in the previous section are now combined to yield the overall equilibrium of the small open economy. Our solution procedures will parallel those of Section 9.4, though with stochastic prices and additional assets, the equilibrium is more complicated to derive. The exogenous factors are (1) the specification of monetary policy, ϕ; (2) the mean rate of government expenditure, g; (3) debt policy, λ; (4) the mean foreign inflation rate, η; and (5) the preference and technology parameters, γ, β, and α. There are three exogenous stochastic processes impinging on the economy: (1) government expenditure shocks, dz; (2) productivity shocks, dy; and (3) foreign inflation shocks, dq. These are assumed to be mutually uncorrelated.[10] The stochastic rate of return on equities is defined in (10.5d), and the stochastic components of taxes dv and real wealth dw are determined endogenously. At least two of the three purely monetary shocks, dx, dp, and de, are endogenous, depending upon the specification of government financial policy. For example, if the monetary growth rate is targeted independently, then dx is exogenous and de and dp reflect the effects of the exogenous stochastic influences on the exchange rate and price level. However, if government finance policy targets the exchange rate, then dx will also adjust endogenously, in response to the stochastic movements in the latter. To allow for this possibility, we permit dx to be correlated with the other exogenous stochastic shocks.

The Price Level

As argued in Chapter 9, the optimality conditions imply that if assets have the same stochastic characteristics through time, then in equilibrium, portfolio shares will remain constant. We shall therefore look for an equilibrium in which portfolio shares have this property, and verify that the equilibrium is consistent with this assumption.

Assuming constant portfolio shares implies that

$$\frac{M/P}{K+B^*/Q} = \frac{n_M}{n_K + n_F}$$

is constant over time. The price level can then be written as

$$P = \left(\frac{n_K + n_F}{n_M}\right)\left(\frac{M}{B^*/Q + K}\right). \tag{10.16}$$

Taking the stochastic differential of (10.16) (noting that portfolio shares are constant through time), leads to

$$\begin{aligned}\frac{dP}{P} &\equiv \pi\, dt + dp \\ &= \frac{dM}{M} - \frac{d[(B^*/Q) + K]}{(B^*/Q) + K} - \left(\frac{dM}{M}\right)\left(\frac{d[(B^*/Q) + K]}{(B^*/Q) + K}\right) \\ &\quad + \left(\frac{d[(B^*/Q) + K]}{(B^*/Q) + K}\right)^2. \end{aligned} \tag{10.17}$$

Using (10.13b) and (10.15), and noting that the variances are of order dt, the right-hand side of this equation can be expressed as

$$\begin{aligned}&\left\{\phi - \left(\omega\left[\alpha(1-g) - \frac{1}{n_K}\frac{C}{W}\right] + (1-\omega)[i^* - \eta + \sigma_q^2]\right) + \alpha^2\omega^2(\sigma_y^2 + \sigma_z^2)\right. \\ &\quad \left. + (1-\omega)^2\sigma_q^2 - \alpha\omega(\sigma_{xy} - \sigma_{xz}) + (1-\omega)\sigma_{xq}\right\}dt \\ &\quad + dx - \alpha\omega(dy - dz) + (1-\omega)dq,\end{aligned}$$

where, as in Chapter 9, we define $\omega \equiv n_K/(n_K + n_F)$ to be the share of capital in the traded portion of the consumer's portfolio. Equating the deterministic and stochastic components of (10.17) implies

$$\begin{aligned}\pi = \phi &- \left(\omega\left[\alpha(1-g) - \frac{1}{n_K}\frac{C}{W}\right] + (1-\omega)[i^* - \eta + \sigma_q^2]\right) \\ &+ \alpha^2\omega^2(\sigma_y^2 + \sigma_z^2) + (1-\omega)^2\sigma_q^2 \\ &- \alpha\omega(\sigma_{xy} - \sigma_{xz}) + (1-\omega)\sigma_{xq}\end{aligned} \tag{10.18a}$$

$$dp = dx - \alpha\omega(dy - dz) + (1-\omega)dq. \tag{10.18b}$$

Equation (10.18a) specifies the expected rate of domestic inflation that is consistent with maintaining unchanging portfolio balance. It varies positively with the expected rate of monetary growth and inversely with the expected rate of growth of traded assets. In addition, it increases with the variance of the growth of traded assets (through the last term on the right-hand side of (10.17) and decreases with the covariance of the monetary growth rate and the growth of traded assets. The second equation determines the endogenous stochastic component of the domestic inflation rate in terms of the stochastic components of financial asset growth, the fiscal and productivity shocks, and the foreign inflation rate. The share of domestic capital in the traded portion of the portfolio, ω, is an important determinant of how these shocks affect domestic inflation. For example, the influence of foreign price disturbances increases with the share of foreign bonds in the portfolio of traded assets.

Determination of Tax Adjustments

To determine the tax adjustments, recall the government budget constraint (10.12). Dividing both sides by W, we may rewrite this equation as

$$n_M \frac{d(M/P)}{M/P} + n_B \frac{d(B/P)}{B/P} = \frac{dG - dT}{W} + n_M dR_M + n_B dR_B. \tag{10.12'}$$

Substituting for government expenditure policy (10.13a), monetary policy (10.13b), debt policy (10.13c), tax collection (10.9), and the price evolution (10.1a) into (10.12'), while noting the stochastic derivatives of $d(M/P)$ and $d(B/P)$, this equation becomes

$$(n_M + n_B)(\phi - \pi - \sigma_{xp} + \sigma_p^2)dt + (n_M + n_B)(dx - dp)$$

$$= [\alpha n_K g - \tau + n_M(-\pi + \sigma_p^2) + n_B(i - \pi + \sigma_p^2)]dt$$

$$- (n_M + n_B)dp + \alpha n_K dz - dv. \tag{10.12''}$$

Equating deterministic and stochastic parts of this equation leads to the relationships

$$\tau = \alpha n_K g - (n_M + n_B)\phi + n_B i + (n_M + n_B)\sigma_{xp} \tag{10.19a}$$

$$dv = \alpha n_K dz - (n_M + n_B)dx. \tag{10.19b}$$

These equations determine the endogenous adjustments in the mean and stochastic components of taxes necessary to finance the government budget. Observe that while τ need be set only once to maintain equilibrium, dv must adjust continuously to offset the stochastic shocks in monetary and fiscal policy as they occur. Equation (10.19a) asserts that an increase in government expenditure will, ceteris paribus, require a higher mean tax rate, as will higher interest payments. However, a higher monetary growth rate will generate higher inflation tax revenues, permitting a reduction in the mean rate of tax. A positive covariance between the monetary growth rate and the price level reduces the growth rates of the real stocks of money and bonds, and thus requires a higher tax rate to finance the government's expenditures. Equation (10.19b) has an analogous interpretation with respect to the stochastic components.

Summary of Stochastic Adjustments

The stochastic adjustments in the economy include (1) the *PPP* relationship (10.4b); (2) the definition of the stochastic component of wealth (10.10c); (3) the stochastic adjustment in the domestic price level, (10.18b); and (4) the stochastic adjustment in taxes (10.19b). Combining (2)–(4) leads to the following expression for the stochastic adjustment in real wealth, dw:

$$dw = \alpha\omega(dy - dz) - (1 - \omega)dq, \qquad (10.20a)$$

which is seen to be *independent* of the specification of financial policy. The remaining stochastic expressions can be summarized as

$$dp = dx - \alpha\omega(dy - dz) + (1 - \omega)dq \qquad (10.20b)$$

$$de = dx - \alpha\omega(dy - dz) - \omega\, dq \qquad (10.20c)$$

$$dv = \alpha n_K dz - (n_M + n_B)dx. \qquad (10.20d)$$

These three independent equations involve the stochastic adjustments in the quantities dp, de, dv, and dx. Once the stochastic component of government finance policy is specified, the remaining three stochastic components are determined. As written, these equations are conditioned on dx, and this suffices for the present. Observe also that these expressions involve the portfolio shares n_i, which have yet to be determined

Core Equilibrium Relationships

Using equations (10.20a)–(10.20d), together with (10.5d), one can calculate the endogenous variances and covariances that appear in the optimality conditions (10.11a), (10.11c), (10.11d), and elsewhere. The calculations are straightforward, and here we record the key expressions only:

$$\sigma_w^2 = \alpha^2\omega^2(\sigma_y^2 + \sigma_z^2) + (1-\omega)^2\sigma_q^2 \qquad (10.21a)$$

$\text{cov}(dw, \alpha\, dy + dp)$
$$= [\alpha^2\omega(1-\omega)\sigma_y^2 - \alpha^2\omega^2\sigma_z^2 - (1-\omega)^2\sigma_q^2 + \sigma_{xw}]dt \qquad (10.21b)$$

$$\text{cov}(dw, -dq + dp) = [-\alpha^2\omega^2(\sigma_y^2 + \sigma_z^2) + \omega(1-\omega)\sigma_q^2 + \sigma_{xw}]dt. \qquad (10.21c)$$

The variance of the domestic real wealth is essentially a weighted average of the domestic and foreign sources of variances, the weights being the squares of the relative portfolio shares of the two traded assets.

Substituting (10.21b) into (10.11c), the latter may be written as

$r_K - r_B$
$$= (1-\gamma)[\alpha^2\omega(1-\omega)\sigma_y^2 - \alpha^2\omega^2\sigma_z^2 - (1-\omega)^2\sigma_q^2 + \sigma_{xw}]. \qquad (10.22a)$$

This equation expresses the differential expected rate of return between domestic bonds and domestic capital. The right-hand side of (10.22a) thus represents the real risk premium on domestic capital over domestic bonds, with risk being "priced" at $(1-\gamma)$. As long as $0 < \omega < 1$, this differential may be either positive or negative. Substituting for r_K and r_B into (10.22a), this relationship may be expressed in the equivalent form:

$$\alpha - (i - \pi) = (1-\gamma)[\alpha^2\omega(1-\omega)\sigma_y^2 - \alpha^2\omega^2\sigma_z^2$$
$$- (1-\omega)^2\sigma_q^2 + \sigma_{xw}] + \sigma_p^2. \qquad (10.23a)$$

Likewise, substituting (10.21c) into (10.11d) yields

$$r_F - r_B = (1-\gamma)[-\alpha^2\omega^2(\sigma_y^2 + \sigma_z^2) + \omega(1-\omega)\sigma_q^2 + \sigma_{xw}], \qquad (10.22b)$$

expressing the differential between the expected real rate of return on domestic and traded bonds. The right-hand side is the real risk premium on foreign bonds. Substituting for r_B and r_F from (10.5b) and (10.5c), this can be written as

$$(i^* - \eta) - (i - \pi) = (1-\gamma)[-\alpha^2\omega^2(\sigma_y^2 + \sigma_z^2) + \omega(1-\omega)\sigma_q^2 + \sigma_{xw}]$$
$$+ \sigma_p^2 - \sigma_q^2. \qquad (10.23b)$$

Next, subtracting (10.23b) from (10.23a) yields the following solution for ω:

$$\omega = \frac{\alpha - (i^* - \eta + \sigma_q^2)}{(1-\gamma)(\alpha^2\sigma_y^2 + \sigma_q^2)} + \frac{\sigma_q^2}{\alpha^2\sigma_y^2 + \sigma_q^2}. \qquad (10.24)$$

Equation (10.24) expresses the relative share of capital in the traded portion of the representative agent's portfolio. The expression is seen to be analogous to the solution (9.31a), and like that equation has been decomposed into a speculative and a hedging component. It is determined by *real* quantities and is therefore *independent* of the domestic government's finance policy. It thus obtains whether the authority is targeting the monetary growth rate or the exchange rate, or following some accommodating policy. This observation is important in our subsequent discussion.

Having determined ω, the remainder of the equilibrium can now be summarized by the following sets of relationships.

Consumption, Growth, and Portfolio Shares

With portfolio shares remaining constant over time, all real components of wealth must grow at the same stochastic rate. That is,

$$\frac{d(M/P)}{M/P} = \frac{d(B/P)}{B/P} = \frac{d(B^*/Q)}{B^*/Q} = \frac{dK}{K} = \frac{dW}{W} \equiv \psi \, dt + dw. \tag{10.25}$$

Taking expectations of the accumulation equation (10.15), using (10.25) and the definition of ω, the mean real rate of growth is given by the expression

$$\psi = \omega \left(\alpha(1-g) - \frac{1}{n_K} \frac{C}{W} \right) + (1-\omega)(i^* - \eta + \sigma_q^2) \tag{10.26a}$$

and is a weighted average of the domestic and foreign sources of growth.

Next, substituting for σ_w^2 into the consumer optimality condition (10.11a), the equilibrium consumption-wealth ratio is

$$\frac{C}{W} = \frac{\theta}{1-\gamma\theta} \left(\beta - \rho\gamma - \frac{1}{2}\gamma(\gamma-1)[\alpha^2\omega^2(\sigma_y^2 + \sigma_z^2) + (1-\omega)^2\sigma_q^2] \right), \tag{10.26b}$$

where by combining (10.10a) and (10.25) with the definition of return ρ, defined in (10.11), the latter can be expressed as

$$\rho = \psi + \frac{C}{W}. \tag{10.26c}$$

The real part of the equilibrium is completed by recalling (10.11b),

$$n_M = \left(\frac{1-\theta}{\theta} \right) \frac{(C/W)}{i}, \tag{10.26d}$$

and the normalized wealth constraint (10.10b), which, recalling (10.13c), can be written as

$$(1+\lambda)n_M + \frac{n_K}{\omega} = 1. \tag{10.26e}$$

Having determined the partial portfolio share ω, equations (10.26a)–(10.26e) can be viewed as determining the equilibrium solutions for the consumption:wealth ratio, C/W; the total net rate of return, ρ; the mean growth rate, ψ; the portfolio shares of money and capital n_M and n_K; in terms of the domestic nominal interest rate, i; debt policy, λ; and other exogenous real parameters such as the exogenous *real* sources of risk, $\sigma_y^2, \sigma_z^2, \sigma_q^2$; preference parameters, θ and β; the technology parameter, α; and the target share of government expenditure, g.

The remaining portfolio shares, n_F and n_B, follow immediately from combining ω with n_K, and from the debt policy specification (10.13c), respectively. Furthermore, having obtained this "core" set of relationships, the real returns, and with r_F and r_K being exogenously given from (10.5c) and (10.5d), respectively, the real rate of return on domestic bonds and money can be obtained from (10.22a) and (10.11b′), respectively.

Nominal Quantities

Once the real part of the equilibrium is determined, the nominal quantities can be derived from the following relationships:

$$\pi = \eta + \varepsilon - \omega\sigma_q^2 + \sigma_{xq} \tag{10.27a}$$

$$\pi = \phi - \psi(i, \lambda, g, \sigma_y^2, \sigma_z^2, \sigma_q^2) + \sigma_w^2 - \sigma_{xw} \tag{10.27b}$$

$$i = \alpha + \pi - \sigma_x^2 - (1-\gamma)\alpha^2\omega\sigma_y^2 - \gamma\sigma_w^2 + (1+\gamma)\sigma_{xw}. \tag{10.27c}$$

Equation (10.27a) is the "risk-adjusted" *PPP* equation (10.4a). Assuming that the agent holds a positive stock of capital, and domestic monetary policy is not strongly positively correlated with the world inflation rate, then the sum of the world inflation rate plus the expected rate of exchange depreciation overstates the expected rate of domestic inflation. Equation (10.27b) describes the rate of inflation necessary to maintain portfolio balance (10.18a). It asserts that for portfolio balance to be maintained, the risk-adjusted rate of real monetary growth rate, $\phi - \pi + \sigma_w^2 - \sigma_{xw}$, must equal the real equilibrium growth rate in the economy, ψ.[11] Equation (10.27c) is obtained by using (10.20a) and (10.20b) to evaluate σ_p^2 and σ_w^2, and substituting into the risk premium relationship (10.23a). These equations are expressed in terms of the variances of the exogenous variables and the covariance of these variables with the monetary growth rate. Given the specification of monetary policy, these three equations jointly determine the equilibrium solutions for (1) the domestic rate of inflation, π; (2) the rate of exchange depreciation, ε; and (3) the domestic nominal interest rate, i. In particular, the stochastic process generating the equilibrium exchange rate can be expressed as

$$\frac{dE}{E} = \tilde{e}\,dt + dx - \tilde{\omega}[\alpha(dy - dz) + dq],$$

where $\tilde{\omega}$ is determined from (10.24) and $\tilde{\varepsilon}$ is the equilibrium obtained from (10.27a)–(10.27c).

Substituting (10.27a) into (10.23b) and using (10.20a) and (10.20b) to simplify, we may also solve for i in the form

$$i = i^* + \varepsilon - \sigma_x^2 - \gamma[\sigma_w^2 - (1-\omega)\sigma_q^2] + \sigma_{xq} + (1+\gamma)\sigma_{xw}. \qquad (10.27c')$$

Equation (10.27c') is a "risk-adjusted" statement of nominal interest parity. It is clear that in general, uncovered nominal interest parity $i = i^* + \varepsilon$ does not hold, which is hardly surprising. More surprising is that in the absence of domestic monetary risk ($\sigma_x^2 = 0$), and if the utility function is logarithmic ($\gamma = 0$), uncovered interest parity does obtain, even when agents are risk-averse, as they are assumed to be here. The fact that uncovered interest parity may hold even for risk-averse agents has been emphasized by Engel (1992), and our analysis provides a simple confirmation of that result.

Alternative Financial Closures

Target values for π, ε, or i can be attained by the appropriate choice of monetary instrument, and in general this can be accomplished in a multiplicity of ways.

Financial Growth Rate

Combining equations (10.27b) and (10.27c), the monetary authorities can attain the target rate of interest, $\hat{\iota}$, say, by directly setting the common growth rate of its financial assets in accordance with

$$\hat{\phi} = \hat{\iota} + \psi(\hat{\iota}, \lambda) - \alpha + \sigma_x^2 + (1-\gamma)\alpha^2\omega\sigma_y^2 - (1-\gamma)\sigma_w^2 - \gamma\sigma_{xw}. \qquad (10.28a)$$

Exchange Rate Depreciation

The monetary authorities can target the rate of exchange depreciation and allow their financial liabilities to adjust as appropriate. Rewriting (10.27c'), the implied rate of exchange depreciation can be expressed by the risk-adjusted nominal interest differential:

$$\hat{\varepsilon} = \hat{\iota} - i^* + \sigma_x^2 + \gamma[\sigma_w^2 - (1-\omega)\sigma_q^2] - [\sigma_{xq} + (1+\gamma)\sigma_{xw}]. \qquad (10.28b)$$

Under certainty, these policies are equivalent in all respects.

Stochastic Intervention

The above policies are expressed in terms of the deterministic component of monetary policy. It may also be possible to attain the target value of the interest rate by adjusting the money supply in response to stochastic shocks, thereby selecting the appropriate variance, σ_x^2, and covariances, σ_{xq} and σ_{xw}. However, intervention in this form is redundant. Also, by changing the covariance structure, each such form of stochastic policy will have a different impact on the other variables, in particular on the risk premia. Stochastic intervention also may not be feasible, as a result of the simple fact that the variance required to attain the target, σ_x^2, may turn out to be negative.

The key point to observe in these examples is that government policy affects the real economy only through the domestic interest rate i. A natural question to ask is whether any other variable, in particular the real interest rate, could also be the target variable through which the economy is affected. In fact the real interest rate and the nominal interest rate move monotonically with respect to one another, enabling us to express the target equivalently in terms of the real interest rate, r_B. This leads to the following proposition:

Proposition 10.1 Government finance policy affects the consumption: wealth ratio and growth entirely through its impact on the domestic interest rates i and r_B. Different forms of monetary policy that give rise to the same nominal or real interest rate will have the same effect on these variables.

Henceforth we shall focus on i as the target variable. Any changes in the conduct of government finance policy that leave the nominal interest rate fixed are reflected in changes in the mean-variance structure of assets returns, such that equilibrium portfolio choices and the intertemporal allocation of real resources remain unchanged.

Initial Exchange Rate and Initial Wealth

The equilibrium growth path defined by (10.24) and (10.26) describes a stable rational expectations equilibrium. As in any rational expectations macroeconomic system, the attainment of such an equilibrium, or the shift from one equilibrium to another resulting from a structural change, is brought about by an appropriate initial jump, in this case through the initial exchange rate $E(0)$, and thus the price of output $P(0)$. To the extent that the representative agent holds domestic money and bonds in his equilibrium portfolio, these jumps impose initial capital gains or losses, thereby affecting initial wealth.

With asset supplies and the foreign price level assumed to follow continuous-time Brownian motion processes, at any initial time M_0, B_0, B_0^*, K_0, and Q_0 are predetermined. Given constant portfolio shares, the corresponding initial exchange rate is determined by

$$E(0) = \left(\frac{n_K + n_F}{n_M + n_B}\right)\left(\frac{M_0 + B_0}{Q_0 K_0 + B_0^*}\right) = \frac{n_K}{\omega(1+\lambda)n_M}\left(\frac{M_0 + B_0}{Q_0 K_0 + B_0^*}\right). \tag{10.29a}$$

Thus, given M_0, B_0, B_0^*, K_0, and Q_0, any policy that generates a change in the relative portfolio share of traded to nontraded assets, $(n_K + n_F)/(n_M + n_B)$, will lead to a jump in the initial exchange rate, $E(0)$. The corresponding endogenously determined initial value of wealth, $W(0)$, is

$$W(0) = \frac{K_0 + (B_0^*/Q_0)}{n_K + n_F} = \left(K_0 + \frac{B_0^*}{Q_0}\right)\frac{\omega}{n_K}. \tag{10.29b}$$

Taking the differential of this expression for given initial stocks, the change in initial wealth generated by the capital gains or losses resulting from the change in the exchange rate is

$$\frac{dW(0)}{W(0)} = -\frac{d(n_K + n_F)}{n_K + n_F}, \tag{10.29b'}$$

and is inversely proportional to the induced percentage change in the fraction of traded asset held in the agent's portfolio. This initial wealth effect must be taken into account in assessing the effects of any structural or policy change on economic welfare. Indeed, this is precisely the significance of the term ω/n_K in the expression for welfare given in Section 9.5.

Feasibility of Equilibrium

Finally, the equilibrium must satisfy certain feasibility conditions. First is the transversality condition, which, as in Chapter 9, is

$$\lim_{t \to \infty} E[W^\gamma e^{-\beta t}] = 0. \tag{10.30}$$

As shown in Section 9.5, this is equivalent to the condition $C/W > 0$. For a balanced growth equilibrium in which all real assets grow at the same rate, (10.30) also implies that the intertemporal government budget constraint is met. Second, economic viability of this equilibrium requires that $E(0) > 0$. Assuming that positive stocks of domestic money and bonds, and capital are always held, this condition will be met if and only if $0 < n_K/\omega \equiv n_K + n_F < 1$; that is, the share of traded assets in the agent's portfolio is positive.

10.4 Equilibrium Properties

We are now in a position to analyze the properties of the equilibrium. To do so, it is convenient to understand the structure of the equilibrium in more detail. First, the solution for the *real* quantities, determined by the system (10.26), are of the form

$$\frac{C}{W} = \frac{C}{W}(i, i^* - \eta, \lambda, g, \sigma_y^2, \sigma_z^2, \sigma_q^2) \tag{10.31a}$$

$$\psi = \psi(i, i^* - \eta, \lambda, g, \sigma_y^2, \sigma_z^2, \sigma_q^2) \tag{10.31b}$$

$$n_K = n_K(i, i^* - \eta, \lambda, g, \sigma_y^2, \sigma_z^2, \sigma_q^2) \tag{10.31c}$$

$$n_M = n_M(i, i^* - \eta, \lambda, g, \sigma_y^2, \sigma_z^2, \sigma_q^2). \tag{10.31d}$$

In the case of the logarithmic utility function, which serves as a useful benchmark, these solutions simplify to the following:

$$\frac{C}{W} = \theta\beta \tag{10.31a'}$$

$$\psi = \omega\left[\alpha(1-g) - \frac{i\theta\beta}{\omega[i - (1-\theta)(1+\lambda)\beta]}\right] + (1-\omega)[i^* - \eta + \sigma_q^2]$$

$$\equiv \psi(i, i^* - \eta, \lambda, g, \sigma_y^2, \sigma_q^2) \tag{10.31b'}$$

$$\frac{n_K}{\omega} = 1 - \frac{(1-\theta)(1+\lambda)\beta}{i} \equiv n_K(i, \lambda) \tag{10.31c'}$$

$$n_M = \frac{(1-\theta)\beta}{i} \equiv n_M(i). \tag{10.31d'}$$

In either case, these are only partial solutions, in that they involve the equilibrium domestic nominal interest rate, i, which has yet to be determined.

The *nominal* variables may be conveniently solved as follows. Equation (10.27b) may be combined with (10.27c) to yield the following expression for the equilibrium nominal interest rate:

$$i = \alpha + \phi - \psi(i, i^* - \eta, \lambda, g, \sigma_y^2, \sigma_z^2, \sigma_q^2)$$
$$- \sigma_x^2 + (1-\gamma)(\sigma_w^2 - \alpha^2\omega\sigma_y^2) + \gamma\sigma_{xw}, \tag{10.32}$$

where the solution for σ_w^2 is given in (10.21a) and the covariance, σ_{xw}, can be computed by combining (10.20a) with the assumptions about dx. This equation, together with the expression for the growth rate contained in

(10.31b), provides a complete reduced-form solution for the domestic nominal interest rate of the form

$$i = \psi(\phi, i^* - \eta, \lambda, g, \sigma_x^2, \sigma_y^2, \sigma_z^2, \sigma_q^2, \sigma_{xw}). \tag{10.33}$$

Once i is thus determined, the rest of the real equilibrium, summarized in (10.32), follows. Furthermore, given i, the expected rate of exchange depreciation and the domestic equilibrium rate of inflation π follow from (10.27b) and (10.27c), respectively. Henceforth, for simplicity we shall assume that the stochastic component of the monetary growth rate is exogenous, so that $\sigma_{xw} = 0$.

The key point to observe is that *monetary* policy, as reflected in the mean rate of monetary growth ϕ and its variance σ_x^2, impacts on the real part of the system only through the domestic nominal interest rate i. Monetary policy may be characterized as being "partially" superneutral. Any form of nominal monetary policy that delivers the same domestic nominal interest rate will, given the bond to money ratio λ, yield the same equilibrium level of real activity in the domestic economy. The reason why nominal monetary policy is now able to have some real effects is due to the form of debt policy and the fact that any nominal monetary growth is accompanied by a corresponding growth of government debt, in order for the money-debt ratio to remain constant. Debt policy, as reflected by a change in λ, will also have an independent effect on the real equilibrium.

Changing the Domestic Interest Rate

To understand the transmission of policy further, it is necessary to consider the impact of changes in the domestic nominal interest rate (which may result from a change in policy) on the equilibrium consumption-wealth ratio, growth rate, and portfolio shares. Differentiating the equilibrium set of relationships (10.26), the following expressions can be derived:

$$\frac{\partial(C/W)/(C/W)}{\partial i/i} = -\frac{(1+\lambda)n_M \gamma \theta \omega}{n_K^2/\omega - \gamma \theta \omega} \tag{10.34a}$$

$$\frac{\partial \psi}{\partial i} = \frac{(1+\lambda)n_M \omega (C/W)}{i[n_K^2/\omega - \gamma \theta \omega]} > 0 \tag{10.34b}$$

$$\frac{\partial n_K/n_K}{\partial i/i} = -\frac{(1+\lambda)n_M(n_K - \gamma \theta \omega)}{n_K^2/\omega - \gamma \theta \omega}$$

$$= (1+\lambda)n_M \left(1 + \frac{(1+\lambda)n_M n_K}{n_K^2/\omega - \gamma \theta \omega}\right) > 0 \tag{10.34c}$$

$$\frac{\partial n_M/n_M}{\partial i/i} = -\frac{(n_K/\omega)(n_K - \gamma\theta\omega)}{n_K^2/\omega - \gamma\theta\omega}$$

$$= -\left(\frac{n_K}{\omega}\right)\left(1 + \frac{(1+\lambda)n_M n_K}{n_K^2/\omega - \gamma\theta\omega}\right) < 0, \qquad (10.34d)$$

where we assume that $(n_K^2/\omega) > \gamma\theta\omega$, a condition that is clearly met for the logarithmic utility function. From (10.27b) and (10.5b) we see that $dr_B/di = 1 - d\pi/di = 1 + d\psi/di > 0$, so that the equilibrium real and nominal interest rates move together.[12]

The effects reported in (10.34) are seen to depend upon the elasticity of the utility function γ. In the case of the logarithmic utility function, the consumption-wealth ratio remains unchanged. The higher interest rate reduces the demand for money, and thus for domestic bonds (which are tied to money via debt policy λ), while the shares of foreign bonds and equities are correspondingly increased. The ratio of consumption to capital is thus reduced. With output being proportional to the capital stock, the consumption-output ratio declines as well, thereby increasing the equilibrium real growth rate ψ.

In the more general case, where the elasticity $\gamma \neq 0$, these effects are compounded by the impact of the increase in i on the consumption-wealth ratio. In general, an increase in i will increase net income, ρ, giving rise to the usual income and substitution effects in consumption. The latter will dominate if $\gamma > 0$, thereby reducing the consumption-wealth ratio. In this case, the decline in C/W will reduce the equilibrium share of money and domestic bonds even further. If the income effect prevails, the rise in the C/W ratio will tend to offset, though only partially, the direct effect of the increase in i, and the portfolio shares of money and domestic bonds will still decline. The portfolio shares of traded bonds and capital rise correspondingly, as does the equilibrium growth rate.

The fact that the equilibrium real growth rate depends upon the monetary growth rate (inflation) through the interest rate is a dynamic manifestation of the familiar Mundell-Tobin effect.[13] It means that the superneutrality of money associated with the traditional Sidrauski (1967a, 1967b) model does not apply in the present context, even though it has been shown to extend to other stochastic growth models in which the residual financing of the government budget is through lump-sum taxation or, equivalently, debt issuance.[14]

The breakdown of superneutrality in the present analysis is primarily due to the treatment of the wealth tax as the residual mode of government finance. Thus, a higher monetary growth rate and a higher associated inflation tax lead to a lower equilibrium tax rate on wealth. This raises the after-tax rate of return on savings to the consumer, thereby causing an increase in the equilibrium savings and growth rate. To the extent that the government maintains a constant bonds:money ratio $B/M = \lambda$, as specified in (10.13c), this effect is accentuated. This can be seen directly from (10.34b), where the positive effect of the nominal interest rate on growth, $d\psi/di$, increases directly with λ. Intuitively, $\lambda > 0$ implies that the amount of nontax financing of the deficit is higher, since every new unit of money being printed is accompanied by λ units of new bonds. This reinforces the basic effect of the monetary growth rate by creating even more opportunity for the wealth tax rate to be endogenously reduced as the monetary growth rate is increased. Crucial to this argument is our assumption that consumers are fully rational, in that they know their taxes will increase with their wealth. Were we to assume that consumers believe the size of their taxes is unrelated to the size of their wealth (i.e., taxes are lump-sum), this connection would break down.

Domestic Policy and Policy Risk

We now analyze the effects of domestic monetary and government expenditure policies, and their associated risks, on the equilibrium.

Domestic Monetary Policy

We have already observed that monetary growth influences the real equilibrium only through the domestic nominal interest rate. Differentiating (10.32) with respect to the mean and variance of the monetary growth rate, while noting (10.27b) and (10.27c′), we find

$$\frac{\partial i}{\partial \phi} = \frac{\partial \pi}{\partial \phi} = \frac{\partial \varepsilon}{\partial \phi} = \frac{1}{1 + \partial \psi/\partial i} > 0 \tag{10.35a}$$

$$\frac{\partial \psi}{\partial \phi} = \frac{\partial \psi/\partial i}{1 + \partial \psi/\partial i} > 0 \tag{10.35b}$$

$$\frac{\partial i}{\partial \sigma_x^2} = -\frac{1}{1 + \partial \psi/\partial i} < 0; \quad \frac{\partial \pi}{\partial \sigma_x^2} = \frac{\partial \varepsilon}{\partial \sigma_x^2} = \frac{\partial \psi/\partial i}{1 + \partial \psi/\partial i} > 0 \tag{10.36a}$$

$$\frac{\partial \psi}{\partial \sigma_x^2} = -\frac{\partial \psi/\partial i}{1 + \partial \psi/\partial i} < 0. \tag{10.36b}$$

A one percentage point increase in the rate of monetary growth rate will lead to equiproportionate increases in the domestic nominal interest rate, rate of inflation, and expected rate of exchange depreciation, although in all cases by a lesser amount than the monetary expansion. This is because the higher nominal interest rate stimulates growth in the economy, thereby reducing the pressure on nominal quantities.

By contrast, an increase in domestic monetary uncertainty will reduce the domestic nominal interest rate, thereby reducing the equilibrium growth rate. The following intuitive explanation for this effect may be given. A higher variance in the monetary growth rate increases the variance in the domestic price level, which ceteris paribus will raise the real rate of return on bonds; see (10.5b). However, with the rate of return on domestic capital and the real risk premium on domestic bonds both unchanged by the increased variance of this nominal quantity, r_B must be restored to its original level in order for the equilibrium asset pricing condition (10.22a) to continue to hold. This equilibration is accomplished by a combination of a higher domestic inflation rate and a lower domestic nominal interest rate.

Domestic Fiscal Policy

Fiscal policy impacts on the real equilibrium both directly and through the domestic interest rate. Differentiating (10.32) with respect to g and noting (10.27b) and (10.27c'), we obtain

$$\frac{\partial i}{\partial g} = \frac{\partial \pi}{\partial g} = \frac{\partial \varepsilon}{\partial g} = -\frac{\partial \psi/\partial g}{1 + \partial \psi/\partial i} > 0 \tag{10.37a}$$

$$\frac{d\psi}{dg} = \frac{\partial \psi}{\partial g} + \frac{\partial \psi}{\partial i}\frac{\partial i}{\partial g} = -\frac{\partial \pi}{\partial g} < 0. \tag{10.37b}$$

The immediate effect of an increase in the share of government expenditure g is to leave less output available for investment, thereby reducing the growth rate; that is, $\partial \psi/\partial g < 0$. With the nominal growth of the money supply fixed at ϕ, the rate of inflation must increase in order to reduce the real monetary growth correspondingly and thereby maintain portfolio balance in accordance with (10.27b). The higher domestic inflation rate will in turn increase the rate of exchange depreciation and raise the domestic nominal interest rate. The latter will in turn tend to stimulate the real growth rate, partly but not completely offsetting the initial reduction in the growth rate.

In discussing the effect of a higher variance in domestic fiscal policy, we shall restrict our attention to the case of the logarithmic utility function, where it has only an indirect effect on growth, through the nominal interest rate. Differentiating the equilibrium, we obtain

$$\frac{\partial i}{\partial \sigma_z^2} = \frac{\partial \pi}{\partial \sigma_z^2} = \frac{\partial \varepsilon}{\partial \sigma_z^2} = \frac{\alpha^2 \omega^2}{1 + \partial \psi/\partial i} > 0 \tag{10.38a}$$

$$\frac{d\psi}{d\sigma_z^2} = \frac{\partial \psi}{\partial i}\frac{\partial i}{\partial \sigma_z^2} = \frac{(\partial \psi/\partial i)\alpha^2 \omega^2}{1 + \partial \psi/\partial i} > 0. \tag{10.38b}$$

Intuitively, the partial effect of an increase σ_z^2 in is to raise σ_p^2, thereby raising the real return on domestic bonds. It also raises the risk premium on these assets relative to both domestic capital and foreign bonds. In order for equilibrium to be maintained in the asset market, the rate of return on domestic bonds must rise, forcing up the domestic interest rate. The higher interest rate raises the rate of exchange depreciation, thereby increasing the domestic inflation rate but also inducing a higher equilibrium growth rate. In the case of the more general utility function, these effects would also need to take into account the impact of the higher fiscal risk on the consumption-wealth ratio and its resulting impact on the equilibrium growth rate.

It is important to recall from (10.29a) that any of these policy changes (or other policy shocks) are associated with a concurrent one-time discrete jump in the level of the exchange rate $E(0)$. Consider an increase in the monetary growth rate. By raising the nominal interest rate, it lowers the portfolio share of money and raises the share of domestic capital, thereby increasing the ratio (n_K/n_M). Given that M_0, B_0, K_0, B_0^*, and Q_0 are predetermined, this requires a one-time depreciation of the exchange rate in order for portfolio balance to be maintained. Thereafter, the nominal exchange rate evolves continuously in accordance with the equilibrium stochastic process. Furthermore, the initial depreciation of the exchange rate has an adverse effect on the initial level of wealth $W(0)$. An increase in the variance of the monetary growth rate has the directly opposite effect. By lowering i, it lowers the ratio (n_K/n_M), inducing a discrete appreciation of the exchange rate, the effect of which is to increase the initial level of wealth.

Foreign Inflation and Inflation Risk

Early discussions of flexible exchange rates focused on the extent to which such a regime insulates the domestic economy against foreign price disturbances.[15] Using a portfolio balance model, Turnovsky (1977) showed that a necessary and sufficient condition for a flexible exchange rate regime to provide perfect insulation against changes in the foreign inflation rate is that the rest of the world be "Fisherian," in the sense that the foreign nominal interest rate fully adjusts to changes in the foreign inflation rate; that is, $di^*/d\eta = 1$. If this condition holds, then $d\varepsilon/d\eta = -1$ and the higher inflation rate leads to an equivalent decrease in the rate of exchange depreciation of the domestic currency, thereby fully insulating the domestic economy from the foreign inflationary shock. This same condition was later shown to provide perfect insulation in a deterministic intertemporal utility maximizing model (see Turnovsky 1985).

Examining the solution for the real part of the system summarized by (10.31), it follows that the Fisherian condition $di^*/d\eta = 1$ is also a necessary and sufficient condition to ensure perfect insulation against changes in the foreign mean inflation rate, in the present stochastic setting. If this condition is met, then the increase in η is matched by an equal reduction in the rate of exchange depreciation ε, leaving the domestic inflation rate and interest rate unchanged.

By contrast, an increase in the variance of the foreign inflation rate σ_q^2 will generate real effects on the domestic economy. In general, holding i^* and η fixed, an increase in σ_q^2 will increase the rate of return on foreign bonds. This leads to adjustments in the representative agent's portfolio, and thus to real effects in the economy.

10.5 Risk and the Equilibrium Growth Rate

Constancy of equilibrium portfolio shares implies that the equilibrium rates of growth of all real assets are equal. Recalling (10.25) and (10.26a), this common stochastic rate of growth is

$$\frac{dK}{K} = \left\{ \omega\left(\alpha(1-g) - \frac{1}{n_K}\frac{C}{W}\right) + (1-\omega)(i^* - \eta + \sigma_q^2) \right\} dt$$
$$+ [\alpha\omega(dy - dz) - (1-\omega)dq]. \tag{10.39}$$

As noted, the mean growth rate has two components. The first, $\omega[\alpha(1-g) - (1/n_K)(C/W)]$, is associated with the growth of domestic output; the second, $(1-\omega)[i^* - \eta + \sigma_q^2]$, is the growth generated by foreign income earnings. In general, the equilibrium we are considering is one in which capital is steadily accumulating or decumulating, though at a sufficiently slow rate to be sustainable in the sense of being consistent with the intertemporal budget constraint facing the economy.

This section discusses three aspects of the equilibrium growth rate in further detail: (1) short-run stochastic components of growth; (2) further comments on the determinants of the mean growth rate; (3) variance of the growth rate.

Short-Run Stochastic Behavior of Growth

The recent business cycle literature focuses on the covariation of contemporaneous stochastic movements of various key macroeconomic variables. While that literature was originally formulated in terms of a closed economy, it has been focusing increasingly on international correlations and covariances.[16] Among the variables that have received particular attention are those pertaining to growth and the accumulation of assets. We shall restrict our observations to these aspects.

Consider the stochastic component of the real growth rate: $dw = \alpha\omega(dy - dz) - (1 - \omega)dq$. It is evident that this responds positively to productivity shocks and negatively to fiscal shocks. Its response to foreign price shocks is negative as long as the nation is a creditor, but positive otherwise. These stochastic responses are summarized by the covariance expressions

$$\text{cov}(dw, dy) = \alpha\omega\sigma_y^2 dt; \quad \text{cov}(dw, dz) = -\alpha\omega\sigma_z^2 dt;$$

$$\text{cov}(dw, dq) = \alpha(1 - \omega)\sigma_q^2 dt. \tag{10.40}$$

The magnitudes of these responses depend upon the relative proportion of traded bonds in the economy's portfolio of traded assets. The smaller the fraction of traded bonds (i.e., the closer ω is to 1), the more sensitive are the fluctuations in growth to the domestic shocks and the less sensitive to the foreign shocks. The fact that government expenditure is negatively correlated with growth (investment) is consistent with results from the real business literature investigating this aspect.

One issue that has received a good deal of attention is the correlation between domestic savings and investment. This phenomenon was originally investigated empirically by Feldstein and Horioka (1980), who argued that the high correlations they obtained between the savings to *GDP* ratio and investment to *GDP* ratio were inconsistent with the assumption of perfect capital markets. An immediate consequence of the fixed portfolio shares equilibrium is that the real growth rate of capital dK/K and the real savings rate dW/W are perfectly correlated, at least in the present model. This is more or less consistent with the empirical findings of Feldstein and Horioka, and provides an example of how, in an environment of ongoing growth, their results are in fact compatible with a high degree of capital mobility.

The relationship between the current account and the rate of domestic investment has been investigated analytically by Stockman and Svensson (1987) and empirically by Glick and Rogoff (1995), who found an almost unambiguous negative relationship between these two variables. The precise definition is of some importance, and the choice is not an unambiguous one. One natural definition is the quantity dB^*/Q, which nets out the capital gains or losses associated with changes in the foreign price level. From the balanced growth condition (10.25), the stochastic component of this expression, denoted by $d\tilde{N}$, is given by $d\tilde{N} = (B^*/Q)[dw + dq]$. Recalling (10.20a) and the definition of ω, this can be written as

$$d\tilde{N} = (1 - \omega)K[\alpha(dy - dz) + dq].$$

Taking this in conjunction with the stochastic component of (10.39) (and denoting the stochastic component of dK by $d\tilde{K}$) implies

$$\text{cov}(d\tilde{N}, d\tilde{K}) = (1 - \omega)K^2[\alpha\omega(\sigma_y^2 + \sigma_z^2) - (1 - \omega)\sigma_q^2]dt. \quad (10.41)$$

To the extent that the sources of stochastic disturbances are of domestic origin, the current account surplus and the rate of capital accumulation will be positively correlated if the country is a creditor nation and negatively correlated otherwise. The two quantities will be unambiguously negatively correlated if the shocks are in the form of foreign price disturbances.

Finally, considering (10.20c) in conjunction with (10.39), we find that the covariance between the nominal exchange rate and the rate of growth is

$$\text{cov}(de, dw) = [-\alpha^2\omega^2(\sigma_y^2 + \sigma_z^2) + \omega(1 - \omega)\sigma_q^2 + \sigma_{xw}]dt. \quad (10.42)$$

Thus an appreciation of the domestic currency resulting from either an increase in domestic output or a decline in government expenditure will be accompanied by a higher growth rate. If the source of the appreciation is a foreign price increase, then whether this is accompanied by a lower or a higher growth rate depends upon whether the country is a net creditor or net debtor. Recalling (10.22b), we see that

$$sgn\{\text{cov}(de, dw)\} = sgn(r_F - r_B).$$

That is, the covariance between the nominal exchange rate and the growth rate is positive if and only if the real foreign exchange rate premium is positive.

Mean Growth Rate

We have already considered the mean growth rate partially in the course of discussing the impact of domestic monetary and fiscal policy on the macroeconomic equilibrium. There we showed that an increase in the mean monetary growth rate raises the real growth rate, while an increase in its variance has an adverse effect. Fiscal policy tends to be the reverse. An increase in the target share of output claimed by the government lowers the growth rate, whereas an increase in its variance will be growth-enhancing, at least for the logarithmic utility function. The key channel through which these influences operate is the nominal interest rate, a consequence of the specified form of debt policy.

The effects of an increase in the variance of the productivity shock, σ_y^2, or of the foreign price shock, σ_q^2, are more complicated to determine because each has a portfolio adjustment effect as well as an impact through the nominal interest rate and consumption. Higher production risk will induce a shift from capital toward traded bonds; that is, ω will decline. Whether this is in itself growth-enhancing depends upon whether or not this portfolio switch is toward the higher yielding asset. Moreover, while the higher productivity variance will impact on the share of output claimed by consumption, through the nominal interest rate, the net impact is not an unambiguous one. Much the same comments apply to the effects of a higher variance in foreign prices. In fact, their impact on the portfolio adjustment is even less clear. This is because an increase in σ_q^2 raises both the mean return on the foreign asset and its associated risk, with the net effect on the portfolio depending upon both its preexisting composition and the agent's degree of risk aversion.

Variance of the Equilibrium Growth Rate

The variance of the equilibrium growth rate is given by the expression (10.21a):

$$\sigma_w^2 = \alpha^2 \omega^2 (\sigma_y^2 + \sigma_z^2) + (1-\omega)^2 \sigma_q^2.$$

The behavior of this expression is of interest not only in its own right but also insofar as it impacts on the equilibrium consumption:wealth ratio and the equilibrium growth rate itself. With the portfolio share being independent of both σ_x^2 and σ_z^2, it is immediate that the variance of the growth path (1) is independent of the variance of the monetary growth rate and (2) increases directly with the variance of fiscal policy. The latter effect has an adverse effect on the welfare of a risk-averse agent and offsets any welfare gains resulting from any higher mean growth rate it may generate.

Increases in the remaining variances σ_y^2 and σ_q^2 involve two effects. First, for given portfolio shares ω and $(1-\omega)$ they will both directly increase the variance of the growth rate. Second, an increase in either will involve a portfolio adjustment. To see the net effects most clearly, we focus on the logarithmic utility function, when we obtain

$$\frac{d\sigma_w^2}{d\sigma_y^2} = \frac{\alpha^2 \omega}{\alpha^2 \sigma_y^2 + \sigma_q^2}[-\alpha^2\omega^2(\sigma_y^2 + 2\sigma_z^2) + (2-\omega)\sigma_q^2] \quad (10.43a)$$

$$\frac{d\sigma_w^2}{d\sigma_q^2} = \frac{1}{\alpha^2 \sigma_y^2 + \sigma_q^2}[-\alpha^2(1 - 2\omega - \omega^2)\sigma_y^2 - 2\alpha^2\omega^2\sigma_z^2 + (1-\omega^2)\sigma_q^2].$$

(10.43b)

The interesting aspect of these expressions is that an increase in either of these variances may quite plausibly reduce the variance of the growth path. Paradoxically, increased exogenous risk may be stabilizing. This occurs if the portfolio adjustment in favor of the more stable asset more than offsets the direct destabilizing effect of the increased exogenous risk. In the case of the productivity shock, for example, this arises if $\sigma_q^2 = 0$, when traded bonds become a riskless asset.

10.6 Applications to Issues in International Finance

The stochastic equilibrium we have derived offers important insights into a number of questions that have received attention in international finance. In this section we address three such issues: (1) the foreign exchange risk premium; (2) the equity premium puzzle; and (3) implications for capital asset pricing.

Foreign Exchange Risk Premium

An important concept in international finance is the foreign exchange risk premium. The present stochastic general equilibrium model offers a convenient vehicle for examining its determinants. The literature frequently distinguishes between real and nominal measures, and we shall focus on the former. Adapting a measure used by Engel (1992) and others,[17] we shall define the real risk premium over the period (t, T) by

$$\Omega(t, T) \equiv 1 - \frac{F(t, T)}{\Phi(t, T)},$$

where

$$\Phi(t, T) = \frac{E_t[E(T)/P(T)]}{E_t[1/P(T)]}, \tag{10.44}$$

the conditional expectation formed at time t, and $F(t, T)$ is the forward exchange rate at time t, for the future time T. If agents are risk-neutral and markets are efficient, then $\Phi(t, T) = F(t, T)$ and the foreign exchange risk premium $\Omega(t, T) = 0$. As defined, a positive real risk premium on the foreign exchange risk implies an expected value of the real exchange rate in excess of the forward rate, so that $\Omega > 0$.

We shall derive the expression for $\Omega(t, T)$ under the assumption that *covered interest parity* (*CIP*) prevails. This condition, which is much less restrictive and receives much more empirical support than does uncovered interest parity, requires that the real rate of return on an investment in a foreign bond, with the exchange risk covered by a corresponding position in the forward exchange market, must equal the rate of return on the domestic bond. Formally, this equality is described by the relationship

$$\frac{F(t,T)}{E(t)} \exp[i^*(T-t)] = \exp[i(T-t)]. \tag{10.45}$$

To determine $E_t[E(T)/P(T)]$, we consider the stochastic process followed by the real exchange rate $E(t)/P(t)$. Taking the stochastic differential of this quantity yields

$$\frac{d(E(t)/P(t))}{E(t)/P(t)} = \frac{dE(t)}{E(t)} - \frac{dP(t)}{P(t)} - \left(\frac{dE(t)}{E(t)}\right)\left(\frac{dP(t)}{P(t)}\right) + \left(\frac{dP(t)}{P(t)}\right)^2.$$

Substituting the stochastic processes for $P(t)$ and $E(t)$ from (10.1a) and (10.1c), and retaining terms to the order dt, implies

$$\frac{d(E(t)/P(t))}{E(t)/P(t)} = [\varepsilon - \pi - \sigma_{ep} + \sigma_p^2]dt + de - dp.$$

The expected value of this expression is

$$\frac{E\{d(E(t)/P(t))\}}{E(t)/P(t)} = [\varepsilon - \pi - \sigma_{ep} + \sigma_p^2]dt,$$

which may be solved to yield

$$E_t(E(T)/P(T)) = [E(t)/P(t)]\exp[(\varepsilon - \pi - \sigma_{ep} + \sigma_p^2)(T-t)]. \tag{10.46a}$$

Similarly,

$$E_t[1/P(T)] = [1/P(t)]\exp[(-\pi + \sigma_p^2)(T-t)], \tag{10.46b}$$

and substituting (10.46a) and (10.46b) into (10.44) and dividing leads to the expression

$$\Phi(t,T) = E(t)\exp[(\varepsilon - \sigma_{ep})(T-t)]. \tag{10.47}$$

Substituting for $F(t,T)$ from (10.45) and $\Phi(t,T)$ from (10.47) into $\Omega(t,T)$ implies

$$\Omega(t,T) = 1 - \exp[(i - i^* - \varepsilon + \sigma_{ep})(T-t)].$$

Using (10.27c'), and computing σ_{ep} from (10.20b) and (10.20c), we obtain

$$\Omega(t,T) = 1 - \exp[(1-\gamma)(\alpha^2\omega^2(\sigma_y^2 + \sigma_z^2) - \omega(1-\omega)\sigma_q^2 - \sigma_{xw})(T-t)]$$
$$= 1 - \exp[(r_B - r_F)(T-t)]. \tag{10.48}$$

Thus, under conditions of *CIP*, the real risk premium as measured by $\Omega(t, T)$ is an increasing function of the differential expected real return on foreign and domestic bonds.

Equation (10.48) expresses the real foreign exchange risk premium in terms of exogenous sources of risk. It can be seen to be either positive or negative, depending upon the relative magnitudes of the domestic and foreign sources of risk. It is immediate that an increase in both domestic sources of risk, σ_y^2 and σ_z^2, lower the risk premium on foreign bonds, as one would expect. The risk premium on foreign bonds declines with the expected rate of foreign inflation if $1 > \omega > 1/2$; that is, if the domestic economy holds more traded capital than traded bonds. Since from (10.24) ω is a function of $i^* - \eta$, it is independent of any change in η that is accompanied by an equal change in the foreign interest rate. An increase in foreign price risk σ_q^2 directly raises the risk premium on foreign bonds. It also induces a shift in the traded portion of the investor's portfolio in their favor, thereby serving to reduce the equilibrium risk premium. The net effect depends upon ω, and under the reasonable condition $1 > \omega > 1/2$, the risk premium will rise.

Equity Premium Puzzle

One issue that has attracted the attention of applied researchers in finance is the large observed differential in the average rates of return between equities and bonds. This fact was first documented by Mehra and Prescott (1985), using long-term data for the United States, but it is characteristic of other economies as well. Being riskier, one would expect stocks to earn a higher return, but the size of the differential is surprising and has become known as the *equity premium puzzle*.

The issue can be seen in the present model by focusing on the relationship (10.22a). The question is whether the differential real rate of return, given by the left-hand side, is compatible with the risk premium, given by the right-hand side, for plausible values of the degree of risk aversion, as measured by γ. Mankiw and Zeldes (1991) and Kandel and Stambaugh (1991) have suggested that values of γ somewhere between 30 and 100 are required to reconcile the differential returns with the risk premia! Most economists, used to working with the logarithmic utility function ($\gamma = 0$) as a benchmark, find such values to be implausible.

Looking at (10.22a), the present model does not appear to yield such dire predictions. For example, supposing $\sigma_y^2 = \sigma_x^2 = 0$, we find that $r_K < r_B$; that is, a negative risk premium on domestic capital. While this is not plausible, clearly, by introducing sufficient domestic production risk, one can generate a positive risk premium for capital.

In addition, the risk premium to equities involves the magnitude of the traded portfolio share ω, given in (10.24), which therefore gives an international dimension to the equity premium puzzle. This can be seen from the solution for ω, given in (10.24). As we discussed in Chapter 9, this is important in the analysis of risk on growth. The difficulty is that the variances of the returns that appear in the denominator are empirically very small, given the differential rates of return, as in the numerator. Plausible values of the equilibrium portfolio can be obtained only for high values of the degree of risk aversion, σ (see Obstfeld 1994; Eicher and Turnovsky 1997). The potential for implausible values of ω then translates into the magnitude of the equity premium in (10.22a).

Most empirical studies of rates of return measure the return on bonds by $r'_B \equiv i - \pi$, rather than by $r_B \equiv i - \pi + \sigma_p^2$. In this case the differential rate of return is measured by (10.23a). In fact, for economies like the United States, where inflation is relatively stable, adjusting the rate of return on bonds by adding σ_p^2 has little effect on the magnitudes involved (see, e.g., Frankel 1988). By contrast, for economies such as Mexico, which over periods of time have experienced high and variable inflation, the difference between r_B and r'_B can be substantial (see Eicher and Turnovsky 1997).

Capital Asset Pricing Relationships

One of the fundamental issues in finance concerns the pricing of assets. One way this is expressed is in terms of the consumption-based capital asset pricing relationship, the consumption-based CAPM. This asserts that the excess return an asset must yield over the riskless rate of return depends negatively upon the covariance of the asset's return with the rate of growth of the marginal utility of consumption. This relationship is implicit in our equilibrium pricing conditions. To see this, return to the consumer optimality conditions (10.11). The return on asset i, say $i = K$, B, F, is of the form

$$(r_i - \eta)dt = (1 - \gamma)\text{cov}(dw, du_i), \tag{10.49}$$

where η is the expected return on an asset that is uncorrelated with dw, a riskless asset. Recall the optimality condition (9.A.4a) for consumption. In the present case of only one consumption good, this condition reduces to

$$C^{\gamma-1} = X_w, \tag{10.50}$$

where X_W is the marginal utility of wealth, which in equilibrium equals the marginal utility of consumption. Taking the stochastic differential of this relationship and focusing on the stochastic component, noted by tildes, yields

$$d\tilde{X}_W/X_W = (\gamma - 1)d\tilde{C}/C = (\gamma - 1)dw. \tag{10.51}$$

Substituting this relationship into (10.49) leads to

$$(r_i - \eta)dt = \text{cov}(-d\tilde{X}_W/X_W, du_i), \tag{10.52}$$

which is precisely the consumption-based CAPM relationship.

It is also possible to express the equilibrium rates of return in terms of the assets' beta coefficients. To do this, return to the general asset return relationship, (10.49). Define the market portfolio, $Q \equiv n_M W + n_B W + n_K W + n_F W$. The stochastic return on this portfolio is

$$dR_Q = r_Q dt + du_Q,$$

$$r_Q \equiv n_M r_M + n_B r_B + n_K r_K + n_F r_F;$$

$$du_Q \equiv n_M du_M + n_B du_B + n_K du_K + n_F du_F = dw. \tag{10.53}$$

Applying (10.49), we thus have

$$(r_Q - \eta)dt = (1 - \gamma)\text{cov}(dw, dw) = (1 - \gamma)\sigma_w^2 dt. \tag{10.54}$$

The beta coefficient of asset i, β, is defined by

$$\beta_i = \frac{\text{cov}(dw, du_i)}{\text{var}(dw)} = \frac{\text{cov}(dw, du_i)}{\sigma_w^2 dt}. \tag{10.55}$$

Thus,

$$(r_i - \eta)dt = (1 - \gamma)\text{cov}(dw, du_i) = (1 - \gamma)\beta_i \text{var}(dw)$$

and, combined with (10.54), implies

$$r_i - \eta = \beta_i (r_Q - \eta). \tag{10.56}$$

Thus equation (10.56) sets out the well-known equilibrium capital asset pricing relationship, in the form originally due to Sharpe (1964), Lintner (1965), and Mossin (1966). While this relationship is equivalent to (10.52), being expressed in terms of market returns renders it more practical for empirical work, since β_i is essentially a regression coefficient.

Equation (10.56) states that the expected return on a given asset in excess of the return on the riskless asset is proportional to the expected return on the market portfolio in excess of the riskless return. The coefficient of proportionality is the beta coefficient and reflects the degree of risk associated with the asset. The asset is more risky or less risky than the overall market according to whether its beta coefficient is greater or less than unity. Equation (10.56) implies that an asset with a large variance of returns may or may not require a positive risk premium. That depends upon the covariance of the asset's returns with that of the overall market. If the covariance is positive, then its beta is positive and it will require a positive risk premium. If the covariance is zero, then its risk can be diversified away and the equilibrium rate of return will equal the riskless rate. If the covariance is negative, the asset provides a hedge against the overall market risk and it will be willingly held at a rate below the riskless rate.

In the present example, the beta coefficients for the four assets in the model are

$$\beta_M = \beta_B = 1 - \frac{\sigma_{xw}}{\sigma_w^2} \tag{10.57a}$$

$$\beta_K = \frac{\alpha^2 \omega \sigma_y^2}{\sigma_w^2} \tag{10.57b}$$

$$\beta_F = \frac{(1-\omega)\sigma_q^2}{\sigma_w^2}. \tag{10.57c}$$

In general, all assets have positive betas, indicating that they require a risk premium. The real risk associated with money and bonds arises from the stochastic movements in prices. Whether these assets are riskier than the overall market depends upon whether the monetary growth rate is negatively or positively correlated with wealth. Equation (10.57c) implies that if the economy is a debtor ($\omega > 1$), then foreign bonds provide a hedge against overall market risk.[18]

10.7 Government Financial Policy and Welfare

To assess the consequences of changes in government finance policy on economic welfare, an appropriate criterion must be introduced. As in Chapter 9, we consider the welfare of the representative agent, as specified by the intertemporal utility function (10.8a), evaluated along the optimal balanced growth path (10.25).

Following the procedure set out in the Appendix to Chapter 9, the optimized level of utility starting from an initial stock of wealth, $W(0)$, is given by

$$V(W(0)) = \frac{\theta}{\gamma} n_M^{\gamma(1-\theta)} \left(\frac{C}{W}\right)^{\theta\gamma-1} W(0)^\gamma, \tag{10.58}$$

where n_M and C/W, are obtained from the equilibrium values determined by (10.24) and (10.26). Using the relationship (10.29b), the optimized welfare criterion can be expressed as

$$V\left(K_0 + \frac{B_0^*}{Q_0}\right) = \frac{\theta}{\gamma} n_M^{\gamma(1-\theta)} \left(\frac{C}{W}\right)^{\theta\gamma-1} \left(\frac{\omega}{n_K}\right)^{\gamma} \left(K_0 + \frac{B_0^*}{Q_0}\right)^{\gamma}, \quad (10.59)$$

where ω is given by (10.24) and n_K is obtained from the equilibrium relationships (10.26). Assuming that C/W, n_M, and $E(0)$ are all positive ensures $\gamma V(K_0 + B_0^*/Q_0) > 0$. The similarity with (9.36) and (9.37) should be apparent.

The expression for $V(K_0 + B_0^*/Q_0)$ becomes more transparent in the case of the logarithmic utility function $(\gamma \to 0)$ when (10.59) can be shown to simplify to

$$V\left(K_0 + \frac{B_0^*}{Q_0}\right) = \frac{\theta}{\beta} \ln(\theta\beta) + \frac{1-\theta}{\beta} \ln n_M + \frac{\psi}{\beta^2} + \frac{1}{\beta} \ln\left(\frac{\omega}{n_K}\right)$$

$$+ \frac{1}{\beta} \ln\left(K_0 + \frac{B_0^*}{Q_0}\right) - \frac{1}{2\beta^2} \sigma_w^2. \quad (10.59')$$

Apart from exogenous constants and the initial stock of traded assets, intertemporal welfare depends upon four elements. The first is the utility from holding real money balances, $((1-\theta)/\beta)\ln n_M$. The second term, ψ/β^2, is the utility resulting from the growth of wealth, insofar as this increases future consumption possibilities. The third, represented by the term $(1/\beta)\ln(\omega/n_K)$, results from wealth effects due to initial jumps in the exchange rate. The final term, $-(1/2\beta^2)\sigma_w^2$, represents the welfare losses due to the exogenous sources of real risk to the economy.

Government financial policy, however conducted, affects welfare only through the first three channels, by means of its impact on the nominal interest rate i. We can thus state:

Proposition 10.2 The welfare consequences of government finance policy operate through their effect on the domestic nominal interest rate, i, and its impact on (1) the equilibrium portfolio of money balances; (2) the growth rate of the economy; (3) initial jumps in the exchange rate.

This result, together with Proposition 10.1, implies that the domestic nominal interest serves as an intermediate target for both growth and welfare.

Differentiating (10.59) with respect to i, yields

$$\frac{dV/V}{di/i} = \gamma(1-\theta)\frac{dn_M/n_M}{di/i} + (\theta\gamma - 1)\frac{d(C/W)/C/W}{di/i} - \gamma\frac{dn_K/n_K}{di/i}.$$

$$(10.60)$$

This equation highlights the three effects of a change in the domestic nominal interest rate on welfare. First, any policy that raises the interest rate lowers the demand for money, and therefore real money balances; this is *welfare-deteriorating*. Second, the higher nominal interest rate reduces the mean rate of consumption (expressed as a share of mean output, not wealth), which with g fixed, increases the proportion of output devoted to capital accumulation and growth. This increases expected future consumption and is *welfare-improving*. Third, an increase in the domestic nominal interest rate causes an initial depreciation of the exchange rate, generating a reduction in initial real wealth; this is *welfare-deteriorating*.

10.8 The Optimal Target Interest Rate

Optimal government finance policy requires choosing the nominal interest rate to balance the three conflicting effects in (10.60). This obtains when $(dV/V)/(di/i) = 0$. Substituting for dn_M/n_M, $d(C/W)/(C/W)$, and dn_K/n_K from (10.34) into (10.60), and setting the resulting expression to zero, the optimality condition can be shown to lead to an equation in the nominal interest rate i, the solution to which determines the optimal interest rate target, say $\hat{i}$. We thus obtain the following:

Proposition 10.3 Optimal government finance policy is characterized by an interest rate target, $\hat{i}$, that is the same for all policy specifications. As long as the policy achieves this target, it does not matter how it is conducted. In particular, since $\hat{i}$ can be attained by setting parameters in accordance with (10.28a), there is no advantage in trying to "fine-tune" monetary policy in the sense of continuously responding to stochastic influences as they impinge on the economy. Exchange market intervention to accommodate current disturbances is therefore redundant.

In general, the solution of (10.60) for $\hat{i}$ is cumbersome. From the relevant expressions appearing in (10.34), it is clear that the target rate of interest depends upon the variances of the exogenous disturbances impacting on the economy; taste and technological parameters; the share of government expenditure; and debt policy. It does not depend on anything involving domestic monetary risk.

The solution simplifies substantially in the case of the logarithmic utility function ($\gamma = 0$), on which we shall focus in greater detail. In this case, (10.60) can be shown to reduce to the following quadratic equation in i (provided $i \neq 0$):[19]

$$i^2 - \beta(1+\lambda)(1-\theta)i - \beta^2(1+\lambda)^2\theta(1-\theta) = 0. \tag{10.61}$$

The positive root to this equation,

$$\hat{i} = \frac{\beta(1+\lambda)(1-\theta)}{2}\left[1 + \sqrt{1 + \frac{4\theta}{1-\theta}}\right] \geq \beta(1+\lambda)(1-\theta), \tag{10.62}$$

is the optimal domestic nominal interest rate.[20] This optimal solution is positive, satisfies the second-order conditions for maximizing welfare, and ensures equilibrium portfolio shares, n_i, that satisfy the conditions $0 < n_M < 1/(1+\lambda)$; $0 < n_B < \lambda/(1+\lambda)$; $0 < n_K + n_F < 1$ and are therefore economically viable.[21] Thus we can establish the following:

Proposition 10.4 Assume that the representative agent has a logarithmic utility function. For $0 < \theta < 1$, the welfare of the representative agent is maximized by the attainment of the nominal interest rate $\hat{i}$ defined in equation (10.62). This optimal interest rate depends only upon the preference parameters, θ and β, and debt policy, as specified by λ. It is independent of all sources of risk in the economy.

Proposition 10.4 implies that money and bond financing of government expenditure policy should be directed at attaining this target level of the domestic interest rate, $\hat{i}$, at which the marginal welfare gains from a higher interest rate on increased growth just equal the marginal losses from a higher interest rate on reduced money balance holdings and capital losses. The implied values of $\hat{i}$ appear to be perfectly plausible. For example, taking $\beta = .03$, $\theta = .8$, and $\lambda = 2$, we find $\hat{i} = 4.6$ percent. The fact that $\hat{i}$ is independent of the various sources of risk is a consequence of the fact that for the logarithmic utility function the consumption: wealth ratio is independent of risk. The corresponding portfolio shares $n_M = 0.16$, $n_B = 0.33$, and $n_K = 0.51$ are reasonable. We may also observe that the optimal interest rate $\hat{i}$ may be associated with either positive or negative equilibrium real growth.

One of the most celebrated propositions in monetary policy is the Friedman (1969) rule, discussed in Chapter 2. This characterizes optimal monetary policy as being to drive the nominal interest rate to zero, and is obtained in an economy where bond financing and/or lump-sum tax financing is available. Money is therefore superneutral, in which case monetary policy influences welfare only through real money balances. The optimal monetary policy is thus to drive money to its satiation level, and this is achieved by setting the nominal interest rate to zero. We can relate the optimal interest rate target identified in propositions 10.3 and 10.4 to this Friedman full liquidity rule.

To do this, we observe that with the utility function being logarithmic and with $B/M = \lambda$, a decline in i raises the portfolio share of domestic assets, $n_M + n_B$, and lowers the share of traded assets, $n_K + n_F$, in the portfolio. From (10.26d) we see that if i is reduced to $\beta(1+\lambda)(1-\theta)$, then $n_M = 1/(1+\lambda)$, $n_B = \lambda/(1+\lambda)$, and $n_K + n_F = 0$. It then follows from (10.29a) that this interest rate sets $E(0) = 0$, so that in real terms equilibrium holdings of domestic money and bonds become infinite, thereby driving the share of traded assets in the portfolio to zero. This is clearly the minimum feasible interest rate, and accordingly we identify $\beta(1+\lambda)(1-\theta) \equiv i_{\min}$. Driving the interest rate down to this level yields a form of the Friedman satiation rule, the difference being that with money and bonds growing in accordance with the debt policy (10.13c), satiation is in terms of total domestic government assets rather than in terms of real money balances alone.

As long as $\theta > 0$, so that some utility is attached to consumption, the optimal interest target $\hat{i}$ in (10.62) *exceeds* $i_{\min}$. The intuition behind this result runs as follows. The Friedman rule is associated with a constant rate of monetary contraction, yielding an inflation subsidy. In the absence of lump-sum taxation, the revenue required to finance this optimum must be raised through a tax on wealth. But this tax will reduce the amount of saving, investment, and growth, thereby increasing the distortions caused by this form of taxation. Hence the objective of a zero nominal interest rate must be balanced against the objective of a zero wealth tax. Put another way, in the absence of the superneutrality of money, there is a trade-off between having a higher nominal interest rate leading to a higher growth rate and greater future consumption benefits, and the lower utility resulting from the corresponding reduction in real money balances. This trade-off is directly analogous to the trade-off between an income tax and an inflation tax originally introduced by Phelps (1973) and discussed in Chapter 2.

If $\theta = 0$, so that only money balances yield utility, this trade-off disappears; the optimal interest rate target $\hat{i} = i_{\min}$; and the above version of the Friedman rule is obtained. Driving $\hat{i}$ to zero, as in the original Friedman rule, is ruled out for two reasons. First, to induce private agents to hold the positive quantity of government bonds implied by this equilibrium, the corresponding interest rate, $i_{\min}$, must be strictly positive rather than zero. Second, the constant elasticity utility function does not contain an interior satiation level of real money balances at which their marginal utility is reduced to zero, as the pure Friedman rule requires.

Optimal monetary policy in open economies is often characterized in terms of the implied rate of exchange depreciation (crawling peg).[22] This can easily be done here. In particular, we can state the following formal proposition:

Proposition 10.5 The optimal exchange rate target should be set so that at the target nominal interest rate, $\hat{i}$, the expected rate of exchange depreciation is determined by (10.28b). This depreciation rate implies that the expected real rate of return on domestic bonds differs from the rate of return on foreign bonds by the risk premium specified by the right-hand side of (10.22b). The induced portfolio share held in real capital (n_K) balances the advantages of greater growth that depends upon n_K against the benefits of faster money creation.

In the case that the government asset (money and bonds) growth rate is set nonstochastically ($dx \equiv 0$) and the utility function is logarithmic, the implied optimal rate of exchange depreciation reduces to the difference between the target interest rate, $\hat{i}$, and the world nominal interest rate, i^*.

10.9 Alternative Financial Rules

The analysis has been based on monetary rules of the form specified in (10.13b). We have emphasized that what is critical is the determination of the mean monetary growth rate ϕ and how the stochastic component can be set arbitrarily. Precisely the same optimal target interest rate, $\hat{i}$, emerges if the monetary authorities follow a rule of (1) targeting the *inflation rate*, as has been the explicit policy of the Reserve Bank of New Zealand; (2) targeting the *rate of exchange depreciation*, as is the case in many developing economies;[23] (3) or an intervention rule of the form

$$\frac{dM}{M} = \frac{dB}{B} = v_1 \varepsilon \, dt + v_2 \, de, \tag{10.63}$$

in which policy responds to current movements in the exchange rate, as in the exchange market intervention literature.[24] It makes little difference how monetary policy is formulated, as long as the parameters under control (in this case v_1 and v_2) are optimally chosen. There may, however, be limitations to the feasibility of a rule such as (10.63), if the monetary authorities do not set an appropriate underlying nominal growth rate and instead intervene only in response to current shocks.

The issues can be illustrated conveniently in the case where the underlying utility function is logarithmic ($\gamma = 0$), an assumption we shall henceforth maintain. Suppose that the authorities follow a deterministic policy $dM/M = \phi \, dt \, (= v_1 \varepsilon \, dt)$. In this case, the optimal financial growth rate (10.28a) can be shown to reduce to[25]

$$\hat{\phi} = \hat{i} - \alpha \omega [g + c(\hat{i})] - \alpha^2 \omega^2 \sigma_z^2, \tag{10.64}$$

where

$$c(\hat{i}) \equiv \frac{C/W}{\alpha n_K} = \frac{\theta\beta}{\alpha\omega[1 - (1+\lambda)\beta(1-\theta)/\hat{i}]}.$$

The fact that in general $\hat{\phi}$ may be either positive or negative can be seen most simply in the absence of fiscal policy ($g = \sigma_z^2 = 0$). In this case, the right-hand side of (10.64) reduces to $\hat{i} - \alpha\omega c(\hat{i})$, where $\hat{i}$ is the welfare-maximizing interest rate determined by (10.62). Using this solution, one can show

$$sgn(\hat{\phi}) = sgn\left[\frac{\lambda(1+\lambda)}{\lambda(1+\lambda)+1} - \theta\right]. \tag{10.65}$$

For a sufficiently small value of λ, the optimal policy is one of negative nominal growth. A low ratio of bonds to money implies a low optimal interest rate $\hat{i}$, which in turn implies an optimal rate of inflation that not only is negative but also dominates the real growth rate so that the optimal growth rate is negative. We observe that as the ratio of bonds to money, λ, rises, $\hat{i}$ increases and the optimal financial growth rate eventually becomes positive.

In general, (10.64) shows how the optimal growth rate of government financial assets depends upon the mean and variance of fiscal policy, as well as upon the risk terms contained in ω. An increase in either g or σ_z^2 was shown in Section 10.4 to raise the equilibrium interest rate, i. If i is initially at its optimum, $\hat{i}$, it will now become too high. Accordingly, the optimal growth policy requires ϕ to be reduced so as to offset these effects and to restore i to its optimum.

In the case where financial asset policy is conducted solely by responding to current stochastic movements in the exchange rate (i.e., setting $v_1 = 0$ in (10.63)), (10.28a) can be shown to reduce to[26]

$$\frac{1 - 2v_2}{(1 - v_2)^2} \omega^2[\alpha^2(\sigma_y^2 + \sigma_z^2) + \sigma_q^2]$$
$$= \hat{i} + \alpha\omega[1 - g - c(\hat{i})] - (i^* - q)\omega. \tag{10.66}$$

Since equation (10.66) is quadratic in v_2, this gives rise to possible problems of nonexistence and nonuniqueness of solutions for the optimal $\hat{v}_2$. The potential nonexistence of a solution can be seen to arise in the absence of fiscal policy ($g = \sigma_z^2 = 0$), when, using (10.24), (10.66) reduces to

$$-\left(\frac{v_2}{1 - v_2}\right)^2 \omega^2[\alpha^2\sigma_y^2 + \sigma_q^2] = \hat{i} - \alpha\omega c(\hat{i}). \tag{10.66'}$$

If the right-hand side of (10.65) is positive, so that $\hat{i} - \alpha\omega c(\hat{i}) > 0$, there is *no* real value for v_2 that will satisfy this equation. Choosing a positive rate of growth ϕ is the only feasible way of conducting government finance policy to attain the target nominal interest rate.

In this case the target interest rate $\hat{i}$ cannot be attained without financial asset growth is because in the absence of such an expansionary policy, the equilibrium nominal interest rate will always be too low. This can be seen by going back to the core equilibrium equations (10.26) and (10.27), which in the absence of any financial asset intervention ($\phi = dx = 0$) or fiscal policy ($g = \sigma_z^2 = 0$) can be readily solved explicitly for the nominal interest rate as follows:

$$i_f = (1 + \lambda)\beta(1 - \theta) + \theta\beta. \qquad (10.67)$$

The condition that $\hat{i} - \alpha\omega c(\hat{i}) > 0$ is equivalent to $\hat{i} > i_f$, and in order to maximize welfare, i_f needs to be raised. But the problem with intervening in response to current shocks in the exchange rate de (whether positively or negatively) is that this introduces variances into the money supply process; this tends to *reduce* the interest rate, taking it further from its target level $\hat{i}$; see (10.36a). The reason for this is that monetary uncertainty raises the variance of the domestic price level, thereby increasing the expected return on domestic bonds relative to those on capital and traded bonds. In order for these latter two assets to continue to be held, the return on domestic bonds must decline; this is accomplished in part by a reduction in the nominal interest rate.

On the other hand, suppose the growth of government financial assets is set exogenously at $\phi > 0$ and/or there is positive government expenditure ($g > 0$) with its associated risk ($\sigma_z^2 > 0$). Each of these influences can be shown to raise the equilibrium nominal interest rate, i; see (10.37a) and (10.38a). For sufficiently large values of these policy parameters, i can easily be raised *above* its optimal level, $\hat{i}$. In this case, v_2 may now be chosen to generate sufficient monetary risk to reduce i back to its target level $\hat{i}$. Formally, the required v_2 is obtained as the solution to the quadratic equation (10.66), the roots of which in this case are now both real. This implies that there are now two values of the intervention parameter v_2 that will permit the optimal interest rate $\hat{i}$ to be attained.

10.10 Optimal Debt Policy

The ratio λ, determining the degree of monetization of debt, is a key government policy instrument that directly affects economic welfare. A natural question, therefore, is how a benevolent government will seek to choose λ, in conjunction with the optimal overall growth rate of financial assets. In general, the welfare function is of the form $X(i(\lambda,\ldots),\lambda)$, with debt policy affecting welfare both directly, and indirectly through the interest rate. The total effect of a change in debt on economic welfare is given by the expression

$$\frac{dV}{d\lambda} = \frac{\partial V}{\partial i}\frac{\partial i}{\partial \lambda} + \frac{\partial V}{\partial \lambda}.$$

With the optimal choice of government finance policy ensuring that the first term of this expression is zero, the total effect of a change in debt on welfare, is just the partial effect, given by the latter term.

To consider this issue further, it suffices to restrict attention to the logarithmic utility function, in which case

$$\frac{\partial V}{\partial \lambda} = \left[\frac{\theta\omega}{n_K} - 1\right]\frac{\partial n_K/\partial \lambda}{n_K \beta}.$$

Raising the debt ratio has two (partial) effects on welfare. First, it raises the consumption:mean output ratio, thereby reducing the growth rate; this is welfare-deteriorating. It also reduces the initial depreciation of the exchange rate, which is offsetting. When evaluated at the optimal interest rate determined by (10.62), the first effect dominates and the overall welfare effect is negative. That is, increasing the debt ratio is welfare-deteriorating, and assuming that the government cannot lend to the public, the optimal debt policy is to set $\hat{\lambda} = 0$. This no-borrowing constraint in turn implies the corresponding optimal target interest rate

$$\hat{i} = \frac{\beta(1-\theta)}{2}\left[1 + \sqrt{1 + \frac{4\theta}{1-\theta}}\right] \tag{10.62'}$$

and the optimal portfolio shares

$$\hat{n}_M = \frac{2}{[1 + \sqrt{1 + (4\theta/(1-\theta))}]}; \quad \hat{n}_B = 0;$$

$$\hat{n}_K + \hat{n}_F = \frac{\sqrt{1 + (4\theta/(1-\theta))} - 1}{[1 + \sqrt{1 + (4\theta/(1-\theta))}]}. \tag{10.68}$$

Evaluating (10.68), we see further that the optimal rate of monetary growth is negative. These results may thus be summarized as follows:

Proposition 10.6 The jointly optimal monetary-debt policy is to eliminate domestic government bonds, setting the optimal interest rate target in accordance with (10.62'); the corresponding optimal monetary growth rate is negative.

To understand this overall optimal monetary-debt policy further, it is useful to combine it with (10.19a), the implied optimal tax rate. Assuming that the domestic monetary growth rate can be set nonstochastically, with zero debt, this reduces to

$$\hat{\tau} = \alpha \hat{n}_K g - \hat{n}_M \hat{\phi}. \tag{10.69}$$

This result will be recognized as similar to that obtained in (9.57). A similar externality generated by the ongoing growth accounts for the need to tax wealth. There are three differences. First, as long as money is held in positive quantities, the required tax rate must finance not only the share of government expenditure but also the inflation subsidy generated by the negative monetary growth rate. Second, the solution is only a second-best one, since it is not set to replicate the centrally planned equilibrium. Third, the tax is applied to aggregate wealth rather than to consumption. By combining (10.69) with (10.64) and the no-debt condition, $\lambda = 0$, explicit solutions for both the optimal monetary growth rate, $\hat{\phi}$, and the optimal tax rate, $\hat{\tau}$, can be derived.[27] If $\theta = 1$, so that money has no utility, $n_M = 0$ and the optimal tax reduces to $\hat{\tau} = \alpha n_K g$. Recalling that τ is a wealth tax (rather then an income tax), this simply describes a balanced budget.

10.11 Some Final Comments

In the latter part of this chapter we have analyzed the choice of optimal monetary policy and exchange rate system in a stochastic model of a small open economy, based on the intertemporal optimizing behavior of a risk-averse representative agent. The nature of the optimal monetary policy derived in such an economy is in sharp contrast with that obtained in previous literature based on objectives related to the stabilization of output. In the present framework, the choice of monetary policy is evaluated in terms of the marginal impact of changes in the domestic interest rate on the intertemporal welfare of the representative agent. Optimal monetary policy, which determines the optimal exchange rate regime, should be directed at trying to attain an optimal target nominal interest rate. This rate, which maximizes the intertemporal utility of the representative agent, is determined by balancing the marginal gains of a higher interest rate on increased growth and the future consumption it generates, against the marginal losses stemming from a reduction in the holdings of real money balances. This optimal interest rate can always be achieved by an appropriately set mean monetary growth rate, which may be either positive or negative, depending upon how fiscal instruments are set.

Under certain conditions the target may also be attained by continuously adjusting the current rate of monetary growth in response to stochastic fluctuations in the current exchange rate. However, this latter form of intervention may not always be feasible. In other circumstances, it may be associated with multiple equilibria. But in any event, an appropriately set monetary growth rate eliminates the need for continuous intervention in the exchange market.

The intertemporal welfare criterion at the center of this analysis may also be used to carry out comparisons such as the relative merits of fixed versus flexible exchange rates. Because of the smoothness of the value function $V(i, W(0))$ as a function of i, it can be shown that the relative merits of fixed versus flexible exchange rates can be ranked in terms of the relative closeness of the corresponding equilibrium domestic interest rate to the optimal target level. This focus on the comparison of the nominal interest rates delivered by alternative exchange rate regimes is very different from the earlier criterion based on relative variances of output (and other variables).

Notes

1. Branson and Henderson (1985) review the earlier literature and discuss asset demands in a three-asset partial equilibrium stochastic model.

2. Early contributions to this literature include Boyer (1978) and Henderson (1979).

3. See, e.g., Bhandari (1985) and the papers cited therein.

4. For example, Gray (1976), Flood and Marion (1982), and Aizenman and Frenkel (1985) measure the variance of output around the equilibrium level in a frictionless economy. Under appropriate conditions this can be identified with the welfare losses resulting from the existence of rigidities, such as contracts, in the economy.

5. In most cases the traditional models of optimal exchange rate determination are based on the assumption of risk neutrality, in which the treatment of certain parameters, such as the degree of speculation, as being invariant with respect to policy regime is reasonable. One paper that attempts to allow for this in the framework of the traditional model is Black (1985).

6. Note that Q now refers to the nominal price of foreign output, in contrast to Chapter 9, where it denoted the price of foreign bonds, expressed in terms of foreign output.

7. In some ways the stochastic optimization problem is easier than in Chapter 9, since the dynamics involve only a single state variable, wealth. However, offsetting that is the additional asset and stochastic returns.

8. We should note that although the stochastic optimization problem of Chapter 9 involved two-state variables, the problem had a particularly simple structure and certainly was not representative of typical two-state stochastic optimization problems.

9. These figures are computed from tables B-65 and B-84 for the years 1967–85, *Economic Report of the President* (Washington, DC: Government Printing Office, January 1993).

10. The stochastic terms dz and dy are errors (unplanned deviations) from planned policy and production choices. There is no reason to believe that these should be related to one another or to stochastic fluctuations in the foreign inflation rate, dq. Thus we assume that they are uncorrelated. Alternatively, if one believes there is a common mechanism explaining the errors, then one can easily introduce the desired pattern of correlation.

11. Stochastic differentiation yields $d(M/P)/(M/P) = dM/M - dP/P + (dP/P)^2 - (dM/M)(dP/P)$, the deterministic component of which equals $(\phi - \pi + \sigma_p^2 - \sigma_{xp})dt$. From equations (10.20a) and (10.20b), $dp = dx - dw$, from which we obtain $\sigma_p^2 = \sigma_x^2 - 2\sigma_{xw} + \sigma_w^2$; $\sigma_{px} = \sigma_x^2 - \sigma_{xw}$. Substituting yields the expression in the text.

12. In deriving the expressions in (10.34), use is made of the normalized wealth constraint (10.10b).

13. See Mundell (1965) and Tobin (1965). Gertler and Grinols (1982) and Grinols and Turnovsky (1993) discuss the Mundell-Tobin effect in a stochastic growth model of a closed economy and examine the first two moments. They show how an increase in the monetary growth rate will increase the growth rate of capital, while an increase in its variance will have the opposite effect.

14. Grinols and Turnovsky (1997) develop a stochastic growth model of a closed economy in which money is superneutral with respect to its mean as well as its variance. The super-neutrality of money was also shown to obtain under appropriate conditions in an earlier stochastic model by Stulz (1986).

15. This issue was discussed at some length in the 1970s, using the portfolio balance framework (see, e.g., Floyd 1978; Laidler 1977; and Turnovsky 1977). In this discussion, the distinction was drawn between once-and-for-all increases in the foreign price level, and increases in the steady foreign rate of inflation. Our discussion considers only the latter.

16. Some of this literature will be discussed in Section 11.8.

17. See also Stockman (1978), Frankel (1979), and Sibert (1989) for discussion of the risk premium. A comprehensive review of the literaure is provided by Engel (1996).

18. In general,

$$\sum_i n_i \beta_i = 1.$$

This is not the case here, because the market portfolio as defined in (10.53) does not take account of the taxation of asset returns. It is easy to amend the definition of β_i to take this into account. For an example of this using a similar continuous-time model for a closed economy, see Grinols and Turnovsky (1993).

19. The most direct way to establish (10.61) is to take the differential of the value function corresponding to logarithmic utility, (10.59'),

$$\frac{\partial V}{\partial i} = \frac{1-\theta}{\beta} \frac{\partial n_M/\partial i}{n_M} + \frac{1}{\beta^2} \frac{\partial \psi}{\partial i} - \frac{1}{\beta} \frac{\partial n_K/\partial i}{n_K},$$

and then substitute for the partial derivatives $\partial n_M/\partial i$, $\partial \psi/\partial i$, and $\partial n_K/\partial i$, from (10.34b)–(10.34d), evaluated for the logarithmic utility function (i.e., setting $\gamma = 0$).

20. The positive root to (10.61) can be shown to satisfy the second-order condition for the optimization. The negative root to (10.61) yields a negative value for i and can be shown to be welfare-minimizing.

21. That is, the conditions $E(0) > 0$ and $W(0) > 0$ are met.

22. For discussions of the optimal crawling peg in deterministic models, see, e.g., Mathieson (1976); Clarke and Kingston (1979); Turnovsky (1987).

23. For example, since 1965, when it was first adopted by Chile, some form of crawling peg has become a standard regime for Latin American countries.

24. This type of rule has been adopted by the literature cited in Bhandari (1985).

25. Equation (10.64) can be derived from (10.28a) by following steps:

(1) Substitute (10.26a) into (10.28a), recognizing that for the logarithmic utility function, $C/n_3 W = c(\hat{i})$

(2) Substitute for σ_w^2 obtained from (10.21a), and utilize the solution for ω given in (10.24)

(3) Note that for the deterministic monetary policy rule, $\sigma_x^2 = 0$.

26. Equation (10.66) can be derived from (10.28a) by following steps (1) and (2) outlined in note 25 and in addition noting that for the monetary intervention rule $dM/M = v_2 de$,

(10.20c) implies

$$\sigma_x^2 = [v_2/(1-v_2)]^2 \omega^2 [\alpha^2(\sigma_y^2 + \sigma_z^2) + \sigma_q^2]$$

27. These solutions are as follows:

$$\hat{\phi} = \alpha\omega g + \frac{\hat{i}(\hat{i}-\beta)}{\hat{i}-\beta(1-\theta)} - \alpha^2\omega^2\sigma_z^2; \quad \hat{\tau} = \alpha\omega g + \frac{\beta(1-\theta)(\beta-\hat{i})}{\hat{i}-\beta(1-\theta)} + \frac{\beta(1-\theta)\alpha^2\omega^2\sigma_z^2}{\hat{i}}.$$

Using (10.24) and (10.62), these can be expressed in terms of the underlying parameters of the economy.

11 Stochastic Growth in the World Economy

11.1 Introduction

Risk plays a critical role in the international allocation of capital. Previous analyses of this issue based on continuous-time stochastic models include the important contributions of Solnik (1974), Stulz (1981, 1986, 1987), and Adler and Dumas (1983), and focus on the implications of risk for international portfolio allocation.[1] In this final chapter we embed this aspect into a stochastic macroeconomic model of a world economy. The basic structure is a linear model in which the returns to capital in the two economies are described by linear technologies, subject to stochastic disturbances, which we take to be described by Brownian motion processes. In addition, stochastic movements in fiscal expenditure generate demand shocks, which also are described by Brownian motion processes. This framework is generally similar to the approach pioneered by Stulz (1981, 1987) to study international asset pricing and exchange rate determination, and used more recently by Obstfeld (1994) to analyze the effect of risk-taking on the rate of economic growth in the world economy. As a stochastic two-country model, the analysis can be viewed as combining the deterministic model of Chapter 6 with the stochastic model of Chapter 9.

Using this framework, several important questions are addressed. First, we discuss the issue addressed by Obstfeld: showing how the introduction of risky investment abroad in general both enhances the growth rate over what it would otherwise be in a closed economy and improves welfare

The second issue is an analysis of the stochastic equilibrium in the world economy and its responses to the stochastic structure. We are particularly concerned with the effects of productivity risk on the macroeconomic equilibrium of the world economy and various aspects of macroeconomic performance. These include an analysis of portfolio adjustment; its effects on various output measures and consumption; its effect on growth (and its variance), as measured both by the rate of accumulation of assets *owned* by representative agents, and by the rate of capital accumulation *domiciled* in the respective economies; its effects on external accounts; and finally and most important, its impact on economic welfare. One of the characteristics of this type of model is that it is essentially "nationless." How risk impacts on the representative agents depends upon their differences in risk attitudes rather than on where they happen to be domiciled. The same kind of analysis is applied to fiscal policy, both to its mean and to its associated risk.

A third application of the model is to address an issue that has occupied the attention of economists for some period of time. This concerns the relationship between export instability and growth. This relationship has been subject to a substantial amount of empirical investigation, with a variety of conflicting results. By analyzing it within a formal stochastic general equilibrium structure, we are able to understand the potential reasons for the range of empirical results obtained.

The small analytical framework developed in this chapter is very similar in scope and in character to that adopted in the real business cycle theory literature. However, instead of focusing on the effects of risk on the macroeconomic equilibrium, as we do here, that literature analyzes the comovements in various key variables in response to contemporaneous (or lagged) stochastic shocks as they impinge on the economy. Thus a fourth application of our model is to undertake this kind of analysis. Without performing the extensive numerical calibration analysis characteristic of the real business methodology, our formal analytical model is still able to provide substantial insight into several of the issues studied by that literature.

The latter part of the chapter indicates how the model may be extended in two key directions. Most of the analysis is based on a one-good model, as developed in Chapter 6. It therefore cannot address important issues relating to the real exchange rate. One extension therefore is to introduce the real exchange rate, albeit in a very simple manner. The other extension is to indicate the complications associated with introducing distortionary taxes. As we will note, these introduce interdependencies in the economies that are absent in the simpler model and make its analytical solution much more difficult.

11.2 Two-Country Stochastic World Economy

The model is essentially a stochastic analog to that developed in Chapter 6. Consider a two-country, one-good model of a decentralized world economy inhabited by representative agents and their respective governments. The world is a real one, abstracting from money and other nominal assets. In outlining the model, we shall focus primarily on the domestic economy. Variables pertaining to the domestic economy are unstarred; the corresponding foreign economy variables are starred. The subscript d refers to the holdings of domestic residents, and f refers to the corresponding holdings of foreign agents.

Both countries produce a single traded good that can be consumed or accumulated gradually over time as capital and traded in a perfectly integrated world capital market. We assume that domestic output, Y, is produced using domestic domiciled capital, K (interpreted broadly to include human as well as nonhuman capital), by means of the simple stochastic linear production function

$$dY = \alpha K(dt + dy), \tag{11.1a}$$

where $\alpha > 0$ is the constant marginal physical product of capital and dy represents a proportional productivity shock, which is assumed to be temporally independent and normally distributed, with mean zero and variance $\sigma_y^2 dt$. Similarly, foreign output is produced using foreign domiciled capital, K^*, with the analogous stochastic linear production function

$$dY^* = \alpha^* K^*(dt + dy^*), \tag{11.1b}$$

where $\alpha^* > 0$ and dy^* is a temporally independent and normally distributed productivity shock, with mean zero and variance $\sigma_{y^*}^2 dt$. The two productivity disturbances may or may not be correlated, depending upon whether the shocks are worldwide or country-specific. Assuming that the domestic and foreign capital stocks can be adjusted instantaneously, the real rates of return on domestic and foreign capital are, respectively,

$$dR = \frac{dY}{K} = \alpha(dt + dy) \tag{11.2a}$$

$$dR^* = \frac{dY^*}{K^*} = \alpha^*(dt + dy^*). \tag{11.2b}$$

With capital being perfectly mobile internationally, it may be owned either by domestic residents or by foreigners. Accordingly, the following relationships must hold:

$$K = K_d + K_f \qquad K^* = K_d^* + K_f^*,$$

where K_d refers to the domestic holdings of domestic domiciled capital and K_f denotes foreign ownership of domestic domiciled capital. The wealth of the domestic and foreign representative agents, W and W^*, respectively, are thus given by

$$W = K_d + K_d^* \tag{11.3a}$$

$$W^* = K_f + K_f^*. \tag{11.3b}$$

The net foreign asset position of the domestic economy, N say, is thus defined as

$$N \equiv K_d^* - K_f = W - K = K^* - W^*. \tag{11.4}$$

We shall identify the domestic economy as having a positive or negative net asset position according to whether $N \gtreqless 0$, with that of the foreign economy being the mirror image.

Domestic Economy

In addition to holding domestic and foreign capital, the representative agent in the domestic economy consumes output, at the nonstochastic rate $dC = C(t)dt$, out of the income generated by his holdings of domestic and foreign capital. He is also subject to a tax on wealth, specified by

$$dT = \tau W \, dt + W \, dv, \tag{11.5}$$

where τ denotes a deterministic mean tax rate and dv is the stochastic tax rate. For simplicity there is no labor income. His objective is to select this rate of consumption, as well as his portfolio of assets, so as to maximize the expected value of the discounted constant elasticity utility function

$$E_0 \int_0^\infty \frac{1}{\gamma} C^\gamma e^{-\beta t} dt \qquad -\infty < \gamma < 1, \tag{11.6a}$$

subject to his wealth constraint (11.3a) and the stochastic wealth accumulation equation

$$dW = W[n_d dR + n_d^* dR^*] - C \, dt - dT, \tag{11.6b}$$

where

$n_d = K_d/W =$ share of domestic capital in the portfolio of domestic agents

$n_d^* = K_d^*/W =$ share of foreign capital in the porfollio of domestic agents.

The maximization of (11.6a), subject to (11.2a), (11.2b), and (11.6b), is now a familiar one. Substituting for (11.2a), (11.2b), and (11.5) into (11.6b), we can write the stochastic wealth accumulation equation in the more convenient form

$$\frac{dW}{W} = \psi \, dt + dw, \tag{11.7a}$$

where

$$\psi \equiv \alpha n_d + \alpha^* n_d^* - \tau - \frac{C}{W} \equiv \rho - \frac{C}{W} \tag{11.7b}$$

$$dw \equiv \alpha n_d \, dy + \alpha^* n_d^* dy^* - dv.$$

The following optimality conditions obtain:

$$(\alpha - \alpha^*)dt = (1 - \gamma)\text{cov}(dw, \alpha \, dy - \alpha^* dy^*) \tag{11.8a}$$

$$\frac{C}{W} = \frac{1}{1-\gamma}\left(\beta - \gamma\rho - \frac{1}{2}\gamma(\gamma - 1)\sigma_w^2\right) \tag{11.8b}$$

$$\psi = \frac{1}{1-\gamma}\left(\rho - \beta + \frac{1}{2}\gamma(\gamma-1)\sigma_w^2\right), \tag{11.8c}$$

where ρ is defined in (11.7b) to be the ratio of net-of-tax income to wealth, so that ρW measures disposable income, and the variance of wealth is $\mathrm{var}(dw) = \sigma_w^2 \, dt$. Equation (11.8a) equates the differential rate of return on the two assets, given by the left-hand side, to the differential risk premium, given by the right-hand side, where risk is "priced at" $(1-\gamma)$. Using the fact that portfolio shares sum to 1, $n_d + n_d^* = 1$, this equation can be solved to determine the equilibrium portfolio shares, from which ρ and σ_w^2 then follow. Equations (11.8b) and (11.8c) then determine the agent's C/W ratio and his rate of asset accumulation, ψ.

The domestic government engages in stochastic expenditure that increases with the growth of the domestic economy, as specified by its wealth, in accordance with

$$dG = gW\,dt + W\,dz, \tag{11.9}$$

where g is the mean proportion of current wealth devoted to government expenditure and dz is the stochastic component assumed to be temporally independently and normally distributed with mean zero and variance $\sigma_z^2 dt$, where g and dz are assumed to be exogenously determined. For simplicity, government expenditure is assumed to yield no direct utility. In addition, we assume that the stochastic component of government expenditure is uncorrelated with the output shocks in the domestic and foreign economies, and that the government continually balances its budget so that expenditures specified by (11.9) just equal revenues specified by (11.5); that is, $dT = dG$, implying

$$\tau = g, \qquad dv = dz.$$

Foreign Economy

The situation facing the foreign economy is symmetric. Defining

$$\rho^* \equiv \alpha n_f + \alpha^* n_f^* - \tau^*$$

$$dw^* \equiv \alpha n_f dy + \alpha^* n_f^* dy^* - dv^*,$$

the corresponding optimality conditions for the foreign representative agent are

$$(\alpha - \alpha^*)dt = (1 - \gamma^*)\mathrm{cov}(dw^*, \alpha\,dy - \alpha^*dy^*) \tag{11.10a}$$

$$\left(\frac{C}{W}\right)^* = \frac{1}{1-\gamma^*}\left(\beta^* - \gamma^*\rho^* - \frac{1}{2}\gamma^*(\gamma^*-1)\sigma_{w^*}^2\right) \tag{11.10b}$$

$$\psi^* = \frac{1}{1-\gamma^*}\left(\rho^* - \beta^* + \frac{1}{2}\gamma^*(\gamma^* - 1)\sigma_{w^*}^2\right). \tag{11.10c}$$

Using the foreign portfolio shares adding-up condition, $n_f + n_f^* = 1$, (11.10a) solves for the equilibrium foreign portfolio shares, from which the rest of the foreign equilibrium variables follow. Analogous to (11.9), the foreign government sets its expenditure levels in accordance with

$$dG^* = g^* W^* dt + W^* dz^*, \tag{11.11}$$

which, as in the domestic economy, is financed solely by taxes. Analogously, dz^* is uncorrelated with the two productivity shocks.

11.3 Equilibrium in the World Economy

Using (11.8) and (11.10), and the assumptions about the correlation of the various stochastic shocks, the macroeconomic equilibrium in the two economies can be expressed as shown below.

Domestic Economy

Equilibrium portfolio shares and the ratio of consumption to wealth in the domestic economy are

$$n_d = \frac{\alpha - \alpha^*}{(1-\gamma)[\alpha^2 \sigma_y^2 - 2\alpha\alpha^* \sigma_{yy^*} + \alpha^{*2} \sigma_{y^*}^2]} + \frac{\alpha^{*2}\sigma_{y^*}^2 - \alpha\alpha^* \sigma_{yy^*}}{\alpha^2 \sigma_y^2 - 2\alpha\alpha^* \sigma_{yy^*} + \alpha^{*2}\sigma_{y^*}^2};$$

$$n_d^* = 1 - n_d \tag{11.12a}$$

$$\frac{C}{W} = \frac{1}{1-\gamma}\left(\beta - \gamma(\alpha n_d + \alpha^* n_d^* - g) - \frac{1}{2}\gamma(\gamma-1)\sigma_w^2\right), \tag{11.12b}$$

where

$$\sigma_w^2 = \alpha^2 n_d^2 \sigma_y^2 + \alpha^{*2} n_d^{*2} \sigma_{y^*}^2 + 2\alpha\alpha^* n_d n_d^* \sigma_{yy^*} + \sigma_z^2. \tag{11.12c}$$

These equations are familiar from Chapters 9 and 10. The only difference is that the productivity shocks may be correlated, and this is reflected in the variance of the growth rate, σ_w^2, and in the hedging component in (11.12a). Observe further that the equilibrium portfolio is independent of the mean rate of government expenditure g. This is a consequence of the assumption that G is proportional to W rather than to the various components of income. If, instead, G were set in proportion to the different components of income in accordance with $dG = (g\alpha n_d + g^*\alpha^* n_d^*)W\,dt$, say, then g and g^* would affect the portfolio shares in precisely the same way as did the distortionary taxes in Chapter 9.

The equilibrium rate of wealth accumulation in the domestic economy follows the stochastic process:

$$\frac{dW}{W} = \psi\, dt + dw, \tag{11.12d}$$

where the mean and stochastic components of the growth rate of real wealth are

$$\psi = \frac{1}{1-\gamma}\left((\alpha n_d + \alpha^* n_d^* - g) - \beta + \frac{1}{2}\gamma(\gamma-1)\sigma_w^2\right) \tag{11.12e}$$

$$dw = \alpha n_d dy + \alpha^* n_d^* dy^* - dz. \tag{11.12f}$$

Since portfolio shares and the consumption: wealth ratio remain constant over time, it follows that consumption and savings also follow the growth process (11.12d). Finally, equilibrium requires that the transversality condition $\lim_{t\to\infty} E[W^\gamma e^{-\beta t}] = 0$ be met.

Foreign Economy

Portfolio shares and consumption abroad are, respectively,

$$n_f = \frac{\alpha - \alpha^*}{(1-\gamma^*)[\alpha^2\sigma_y^2 - 2\alpha\alpha^*\sigma_{yy^*} + \alpha^{*2}\sigma_{y^*}^2]} + \frac{\alpha^{*2}\sigma_{y^*}^2 - \alpha\alpha^*\sigma_{yy^*}}{\alpha^2\sigma_y^2 - 2\alpha\alpha^*\sigma_{yy^*} + \alpha^{*2}\sigma_{y^*}^2}$$

$$n_f^* = 1 - n_f \tag{11.13a}$$

$$\left(\frac{C}{W}\right)^* = \frac{1}{1-\gamma^*}\left(\beta^* - \gamma^*(\alpha n_f + \alpha^* n_f^* - g^*) - \frac{1}{2}\gamma^*(\gamma^*-1)\sigma_{w^*}^2\right) \tag{11.13b}$$

$$\sigma_{w^*}^2 = \alpha^2 n_f^2 \sigma_y^2 + \alpha^{*2} n_f^{*2} \sigma_{y^*}^2 + 2\alpha\alpha^* n_f n_f^* \sigma_{yy^*} + \sigma_{z^*}^2. \tag{11.13c}$$

Equilibrium real wealth accumulation abroad follows the stochastic process

$$\frac{dW^*}{W^*} = \psi^* dt + dw^*, \tag{11.13d}$$

where

$$\psi^* = \frac{1}{1-\gamma^*}\left(\alpha n_f + \alpha^* n_f^* - g^* - \beta^* + \frac{1}{2}\gamma^*(\gamma^*-1)\sigma_{w^*}^2\right) \tag{11.13e}$$

$$dw^* = \alpha n_f dy + \alpha^* n_f^* dy^* - dz^*. \tag{11.13f}$$

Analogously, consumption abroad grows at the same rate as foreign real wealth, and a corresponding transversality condition applies. As each economy accumulates wealth, the net asset position of the domestic economy, say, is $N = n_d^* W - n_f W^*$. The satisfaction of the two transversality conditions ensures that each economy remains internationally solvent.

Comparing (11.12) and (11.13), the following characteristics of the equilibrium can be observed. First, the equilibrium portfolios held by residents of the two economies differ only through differences in their degrees of risk aversion and how these impact on their speculative demand for assets. If the agents in the two economies have identical degrees of risk aversion (e.g., if they both have logarithmic utility functions), then the chosen portfolio shares in the two economies will be identical ($n_d = n_f; n_d^* = n_f^*$) and a perfectly pooled equilibrium will obtain. This characteristic was first pointed out by Stulz (1981) and Adler and Dumas (1983). In short, the equilibrium is essentially "nationless" in that any differences in portfolio shares are determined by differentials in risk attitudes rather than by where the agent is domiciled.

With identical preferences and portfolios, differences in the international growth rates of wealth and therefore of consumption are due entirely to differences in the respective size of government, $g - g^*$, in the two economies. If the size of government is uniform, then the equilibrium growth rates, ψ and ψ^*, will be identical. There is, however, strong empirical evidence against equalization of growth rates (see, e.g., Madison 1987), and the cross correlations of consumption, mentioned in Section 11.8, are far from unity (see Backus, Kehoe, and Kydland 1992). Furthermore, empirical studies by French and Poterba (1991) and Tesar and Werner (1995) point to a home bias in the allocation of portfolios, suggesting that the assumption of complete capital markets being made in the present model is open to question.[2]

Devereux and Saito (1997) develop a continuous-time stochastic model very similar to this, except that markets are incomplete. That is, agents may invest either in risky domestic capital or in a risk-free traded bond; they may not hold foreign capital. Thus their model is essentially a stochastic analog to the two-country model developed in Chapter 7. The same assumption is made by Baxter and Crucini (1995) in their two-country real business cycle model. In such an environment, each economy will grow at a different stochastic rate; Devereux and Saito focus on the stochastic distribution of world wealth, determining simple conditions under which this will converge to a nondegenerate stationary probability distribution.

The second feature of the equilibrium is that wealth accumulation processes of the two economies completely decouple. Despite the perfectly integrated capital markets, each economy can accumulate wealth at an independently determined growth rate, as discussed by L. E. Jones and Manuelli (1990) and Rebelo (1991).[3] Once the equilibrium portfolio shares are determined, the consumption: wealth ratio, the variance of wealth, and the mean and stochastic components of the respective growth rates follow. Insofar as they impact on portfolio shares, differences in risk attitude are therefore also determinants of differential national growth rates, as well as of their variances. But in addition, the mean national rate of wealth accumulation also reflects the national rate of time preference, the mean rate of national government expenditure, and the variance of the latter in all cases except for the logarithmic utility function.

The fact that the equilibrium stocks of capital, K and K^*, in the two economies are strictly positive imposes restrictions on the underlying stochastic processes if an interior equilibrium is to obtain. Equilibrium requires that the following relations hold:

$$n_d W + n_f W^* = K \qquad (11.14a)$$

$$n_d^* W + n_f^* W^* = K^*. \qquad (11.14b)$$

In the event that the two countries have identical degrees of risk aversion, and therefore hold identical portfolio shares $(n_d = n_f; n_d^* = n_f^*)$, (11.14a) and (11.14b) imply that these common portfolio shares must be strictly positive. Equations (11.12a) and (11.13a) thus immediately impose restrictions on the underlying risk parameters in the world economy. In the case of a logarithmic utility function, for example, the following restrictions will be required:

$$\alpha^* > \alpha(1 - \alpha\sigma_y^2 + \alpha^*\sigma_{yy^*}); \quad \alpha > \alpha^*(1 - \alpha^*\sigma_{y^*}^2 + \alpha\sigma_{yy^*}).$$

In the cases where the two economies have different degrees of risk aversion, it is possible for one of the portfolio shares to be negative. However, for expositional purposes we shall rule out such a possibility and assume that all equilibrium portfolio shares are strictly positive.

Other Relationships

The equilibrium relationships summarized above describe what we characterize as the "core" relationships. In considering the response of the world economy to various disturbances, there are many other aspects that one might want to consider and that can be derived from these equilibrium conditions.

In particular, the growth rates reported in (11.12d) and (11.13d) describe the (percentage) rates of accumulation of assets *owned* by the respective representative agents in the two economies; that is, the growth rate of their wealth, a measure of the national rate of *savings*. In discussing growth, however, one may be equally concerned with the rate of growth of assets *domiciled* in the respective economies; that is, the national rate of *investment*. Taking the differentials of (11.14a) and (11.14b) yields

$$\frac{dK}{K} = \left(\frac{n_d W}{n_d W + n_f W^*}\right)\frac{dW}{W} + \left(\frac{n_f W^*}{n_d W + n_f W^*}\right)\frac{dW^*}{W^*} \qquad (11.15a)$$

$$\frac{dK^*}{K^*} = \left(\frac{n_d^* W}{n_d^* W + n_f^* W^*}\right)\frac{dW}{W} + \left(\frac{n_f^* W^*}{n_d^* W + n_f^* W^*}\right)\frac{dW^*}{W^*}. \qquad (11.15b)$$

Substituting from (11.12d) and (11.13d) enables us to express the rate of growth of capital in the two economies as

$$\frac{dK}{K} = \left(\frac{n_d W \psi + n_f W^* \psi^*}{n_d W + n_f W^*}\right) dt + \frac{n_d W\, dw + n_f W^*\, dw^*}{n_d W + n_f W^*} \qquad (11.15a')$$

$$\frac{dK^*}{K^*} = \left(\frac{n_d^* W \psi + n_f^* W^* \psi^*}{n_d^* W + n_f^* W^*}\right) dt + \frac{n_d^* W\, dw + n_f^* W^*\, dw^*}{n_d^* W + n_f^* W^*}. \qquad (11.15b')$$

From (11.15a) and (11.15b) it is seen that the percentage growth rate of the capital stock domiciled in the domestic economy is a weighted average of the rates of wealth accumulation by the two economies, the weights being the proportions of domestic domiciled capital owned by domestic and foreign residents, respectively. The same applies with respect to the growth of capital abroad. In either case, the mean growth varies over time as the relative wealth of the two economies changes, as a consequence of their differential equilibrium rates of asset accumulation.

Subtracting (11.15b) from (11.15a) and using (11.14a, 11.14b), we can write

$$\left(\frac{dK}{K}\right) - \left(\frac{dK^*}{K^*}\right) = \left(\frac{n_d W}{n_d W + n_f W^*} - \frac{n_d^* W}{n_d^* W + n_f^* W^*}\right)\left(\frac{dW}{W} - \frac{dW^*}{W^*}\right),$$

from which we see that the difference between the respective growth rates of domiciled capital is just a fraction of the differential rate of asset accumulation by the two economies. In other words, there is substantially more scope for each economy to enjoy an independent national rate of wealth accumulation than there is for each economy to set an independent rate of growth of domiciled capital. Note further that in the particular case where risk attitudes are the same in the two countries, so that their portfolio shares are identical, the stochastic growth rates of capital in the two economies become identical, with the relative weights in (11.15a) and (11.15b) now reducing to the fractions of worldwide wealth owned by the two economies.

An important distinction concerns *GNP* and *GDP*. Since we are abstracting from labor income, we are of course omitting the major component of both these income measures. However, since we are concerned with investigating adjustments at the margin—a margin along which labor supply is likely to remain largely unaffected—we do not regard this simplification as being too serious for our purposes. In any event, focusing on the domestic economy, the *GNP*, which is based on assets owned by domestic residents, evolves in accordance with the stochastic process

$$d(GNP) = (\alpha n_d + \alpha^* n_d^*) W \, dt + W(\alpha n_d dy + \alpha^* n_d^* dy^*), \tag{11.16a}$$

while the *GDP*, described by (11.1a) and based on income generated within the domestic economy, can be expressed as

$$d(GDP) = \alpha(n_d W + n_f W^*) dt + \alpha(n_d W + n_f W^*) dy. \tag{11.16b}$$

As we will note at the appropriate place below, these measures respond very differently to the various disturbances. We may also observe that while the core solutions are expressed in terms of the ratios of consumption or savings to wealth, discussions of the behavior of consumption or savings are usually in terms of its ratio to various measures of income or output. These can be derived in a very straightforward way from the results thus far obtained. Thus, for example, taking the stochastic differential

$$\frac{d(C/GNP)}{(C/GNP)} = \frac{dC}{C} - \frac{d(GNP)}{GNP} - \left(\frac{dC}{C}\right)\left(\frac{d(GNP)}{GNP}\right) + \left(\frac{d(GNP)}{GNP}\right)^2$$

and substituting for dC/C from (11.12d) and for $d(GNP)$ from (11.16a), one can derive the evolution of the consumption: *GNP* ratio.

Net Asset Position, Current Account, and Trade Balance

In assessing the effects of various disturbances on the world economy, it is important to consider their relative impacts on the two nations. There are many ways this may be measured, and we shall consider three—(1) the net asset position, (2) the current account, and (3) the trade balance—as being important.

Substituting the expressions for portfolio shares into the definition of the net asset position for the domestic economy, N, defined in (11.4), we may write

$$N = n_d^* W - n_f W^*. \tag{11.17}$$

In the short run, the stocks of wealth in the two economies, W and W^*, are predetermined. Thus any change that gives rise to portfolio adjustments has instantaneous effects on the net asset positions of the two economies.

The current account, defined as dN, the change in the net asset position of the domestic economy, is obtained by taking the differential of (11.17). This can be written as

$$dN = n_d^* W \left(\frac{dW}{W}\right) - n_f W^* \left(\frac{dW^*}{W^*}\right).$$

The domestic economy thus has a current account surplus if it is accumulating foreign assets faster than its assets are being purchased abroad. Substituting for (dW/W) and (dW^*/W^*) from (11.7) and the corresponding equation abroad, and using the balanced budget condition $dT = dG$, the current account can be expressed in the form

$$dN = \left\{ n_d^* \left[(\alpha n_d + \alpha^* n_d^*) - \frac{C}{W} - g \right] W \right.$$
$$\left. - n_f \left[(\alpha n_f + \alpha^* n_f^*) - \left(\frac{C}{W}\right)^* - g^* \right] W^* \right\} dt$$
$$+ \alpha(n_d n_d^* W - n_f^2 W^*) dy + \alpha^* (n_d^{*2} W - n_f n_f^* W^*) dy^*$$
$$+ (n_f W^* dz^* - n_d^* W \, dz) \tag{11.18}$$

where again W and W^* are predetermined in the short run. In general, since wealth in the two economies grows at different constant rates, the equilibrium growth rate of the current account dN/N cannot be constant.

Third, the trade balance (net exports), dX say, of the domestic economy is defined as

$$dX = \alpha K(dt + dy) - C \, dt - dG - dK,$$

being in surplus if and only if $dX > 0$. Upon substitution, this can be expressed as[4]

$$dX = \left\{ (n_d n_d^* W + n_f n_f^* W^*)(\alpha - \alpha^*) - \left(\frac{C}{W} + g\right) n_d^* W \right.$$
$$\left. + \left(\left(\frac{C}{W}\right)^* + g^* \right) n_f W^* \right\} dt$$
$$+ \{ (n_d n_d^* W + n_f n_f^* W^*)(\alpha \, dy - \alpha^* dy^*)$$
$$+ (n_f W^* dz^* - n_d^* W \, dz) \}. \tag{11.19}$$

This expression forms the basis for the analysis of issues pertaining to the trade balance to be discussed in later sections.

Welfare

As in previous chapters, we will be concerned with analyzing the effects of various shocks on economic welfare. To address this issue, as we have been doing, we consider the welfare of the representative agent, as specified by the intertemporal utility function (11.6a), evaluated along the optimal path. As shown in Chapter 9, this is equal to

$$V(W_0) = \frac{1}{\gamma} \left(\frac{C}{W}\right)^{\gamma-1} W_0^\gamma, \tag{11.20}$$

where W_0 *denotes* initial wealth and C/W is the equilibrium domestic consumption: wealth ratio given in (11.12b). Assuming that this is positive, as is required for the transversality condition to hold, implies that $\gamma V(W_0) > 0$ as well. It is also convenient to focus on the case of the logarithmic utility function, when (11.20) simplifies to

$$V(W_0) = \frac{1}{\beta} \ln \beta + \frac{1}{\beta^2}\left(\psi - \frac{1}{2}\sigma_w^2\right) + \frac{1}{\beta} \ln W_0. \tag{11.20'}$$

11.4 Effects of Risky Investment on Growth and Welfare

The first issue we consider is that addressed by Obstfeld (1994). Using a model similar to the present one, he showed how international risk-sharing, by inducing a portfolio shift from safe, but low yield assets into riskier, high yield assets, can raise growth and welfare. We shall consider this problem by comparing the growth rate and welfare of an economy under autarky with those of an economy whose equilibrium has been described in Section 11.3.

Suppose that the domestic economy is closed to international trade and that the only asset available to it is riskless domestic capital, the marginal physical product of which is α. With no portfolio choice and no risk, the equilibrium growth rate in such a closed economy, ψ_c, will be

$$\psi_c = \frac{1}{1-\gamma}(\alpha - \beta), \tag{11.21}$$

where for convenience we abstract from the government.

Suppose now that the economy is open to trade in international assets. In addition to the domestic asset, which remains riskless, it can now invest abroad in a risky asset. With the domestic asset being riskless, the portfolio share, the equilibrium risk, and the mean growth rate are now given by

$$n_d = \frac{\alpha - \alpha^*}{(1-\gamma)\alpha^{*2}\sigma_{y^*}^2} + 1; \quad n_d^* = \frac{\alpha^* - \alpha}{(1-\gamma)\alpha^{*2}\sigma_{y^*}^2};\quad (11.12a')$$

$$\sigma_w^2 = \alpha^{*2} n_d^{*2} \sigma_{y^*}^2 \quad (11.12c')$$

$$\psi_o = \frac{1}{1-\gamma}\left((\alpha n_d + \alpha^* n_d^*) - \beta + \frac{1}{2}\gamma(\gamma - 1)\sigma_w^2\right). \quad (11.12e')$$

where the subscript "o" refers to "open."

Subtracting (11.21) from (11.12e') and substituting from (11.12a'), we find that

$$\psi_o - \psi_c = \frac{(\alpha^* - \alpha)^2}{(1-\gamma)^2 \alpha^{*2}\sigma_{y^*}^2}\left[1 - \frac{\gamma}{2}\right] > 0. \quad (11.22)$$

Thus the introduction of the opportunity to trade in a risky foreign asset is growth-enhancing. Being risky, it must yield a higher expected return than domestic capital (i.e., $\alpha^* > \alpha$) in order to induce investors to take a positive position in the asset, thus raising the domestic equilibrium growth rate of domestic wealth (consumption) and its variance.

The effect on the growth rate of capital domiciled in the domestic economy is less clear. This is because it depends in part upon the growth rate of foreign wealth (see (11.15a')). Subtracting (11.21) from (11.15a'), we find

$$E\left(\frac{dK}{K}\right)_o - E\left(\frac{dK}{K}\right)_c = \left(\frac{n_d W(\psi_o - \psi_c) + n_f W^*(\psi^* - \psi_c)}{n_d W + n_f W^*}\right) dt. \quad (11.23)$$

In (11.23) we are using the fact that in a closed economy the growth rates of wealth and domestic domiciled capital coincide. While the increase in the growth rate of domestic wealth will tend to raise the growth rate of domestic domiciled capital, the effect on the latter of opening up trade in assets will also depend upon whether the autarkic growth rate of domestic wealth exceeds that of foreign wealth. If it does, then it is possible for the availability of the foreign asset to have an adverse effect on domestic domiciled capital.

To assess the effects of the availability of the foreign risky asset on domestic welfare, we shall restrict ourselves to the logarithmic utility function (11.20'). The effect on welfare is given by

$$V_o - V_c = \frac{1}{\beta^2}\left[\psi_o - \psi_c - \frac{1}{2}\sigma_w^2\right].$$

Substituting from (11.21), (11.12a'), (11.12c'), and (11.12e') into this expression reduces it to

$$V_o - V_c = \frac{(\alpha^* - \alpha)^2}{2\beta^2 \alpha^{*2} \sigma_{y^*}^2} > 0. \tag{11.24}$$

Thus, at least for the logarithmic utility function, the higher growth rate more than offsets the additional risk, and the opportunity to invest in a higher return, higher risk foreign asset improves welfare.

Obstfeld (1994) pursues the issue in greater detail and generality, numerically evaluating the magnitude of the welfare gains and finding that they may be quite substantial. Other authors examine this question, using a variety of approaches and frameworks. Most closely related to Obstfeld are Devereux and Smith (1994), who consider a multicountry model of diversification and growth, and show how the risk reduction implied by diversification may either increase or decrease growth, depending upon the intertemporal consumption substitutability and the nature of risk.

11.5 Effects of Production Risk on the World Economy

An important focal point of the model is the role of production risk; this section analyzes the effects of production risk on the equilibrium in the world economy. For convenience, we shall consider the variance associated with the domestic productivity disturbance, σ_y^2. We shall assume that domestic and foreign production shocks are uncorrelated, $\sigma_{yy^*} = 0$, so that the risk being considered is purely *country-specific*. We shall also focus primarily on the domestic economy, with most of the responses abroad being parallel.

Portfolio Adjustment

Much of the response in the world economy to changes in risk and other exogenous parameters is driven by adjustments in portfolios. Differentiating (11.12a) with respect to σ_y^2, we obtain

$$\frac{\partial n_d}{\partial \sigma_y^2} = -\frac{\alpha^2 n_d}{\alpha^2 \sigma_y^2 + \alpha^{*2} \sigma_{y^*}^2} < 0; \qquad \frac{\partial n_d^*}{\partial \sigma_y^2} = -\frac{\partial n_d}{\partial \sigma_y^2} > 0. \tag{11.25}$$

That is, an increase in the variance of the domestic productivity shock will lead to a portfolio shift away from domestic and toward foreign capital, with the shift being less than proportionate (i.e., the elasticity $0 > (\partial n_d/\partial \sigma_y^2)/(n_d/\sigma_y^2) \equiv \eta > -1$). Interestingly, the elasticity η is *independent* of the degree of risk aversion γ in the domestic economy. Since the only way in which the portfolios held in the two economies may differ is through possible differences in risk aversion, the corresponding elasticity abroad is identical; that is, $0 > (\partial n_f/\partial \sigma_y^2)/(n_f/\sigma_y^2) \equiv \eta > -1$, implying identical proportionate adjustments in the portfolios of foreign agents.

Output Measures

The effect of an increase in domestic risk on domestic disposable income per unit of wealth, ρ, is given by the expression

$$\frac{\partial \rho}{\partial \sigma_y^2} = (\alpha - \alpha^*) \frac{\partial n_d}{\partial \sigma_y^2} \qquad (11.26)$$

and depends upon whether $\alpha \lessgtr \alpha^*$. If the foreign asset, the portfolio share of which is increased, is higher yielding, then domestic disposable income is raised and vice versa.

With W being fixed instantaneously, the effect of the higher risk on the domestic mean GNP is similar to (11.26), except that it is proportional to W. By contrast, the fact that the increased risk associated with domestic capital causes a reduction in the share of domestic capital in the portfolios of *both* domestic and foreign investors, so that with W and W^* fixed instantaneously, the amount of capital domiciled in the domestic economy declines unambiguously, implies an unambiguous decline in the expected domestic GDP; see (11.16b).

Variance of the Growth of Wealth

What happens to consumption and to the rate of asset accumulation depends in part upon the impact on the variance of the growth rate, σ_w^2. This is given by the expression

$$\frac{\partial \sigma_w^2}{\partial \sigma_y^2} = \alpha^2 n_d \left(\frac{2\alpha^{*2} \sigma_{y^*}^2}{\alpha^2 \sigma_y^2 + \alpha^{*2} \sigma_{y^*}^2} - n_d \right). \qquad (11.27)$$

The response of σ_w^2 to an increase in the domestic productivity variance reflects two effects. On the one hand, an increase in σ_y^2 will raise the variance of the return associated with the fraction of the portfolio allocated to domestic capital, n_d. At the same time, it will induce a shift in the portfolio away from the domestic asset toward foreign capital, thereby stabilizing the overall portfolio return. The net effect depends upon which effect dominates; under most conditions it will be the former. However, it can be seen from (11.27) that it is possible for the latter effect to dominate, in which case an increase in σ_y^2 will actually *stabilize* the variance along the growth path. This will be so if

$$n_d > \frac{2\alpha^{*2} \sigma_{y^*}^2}{\alpha^2 \sigma_y^2 + \alpha^{*2} \sigma_{y^*}^2}, \qquad (11.28)$$

with $\alpha^2 \sigma_y^2 > \alpha^{*2} \sigma_{y^*}^2$ required to hold in order to ensure viability (i.e, $n_d < 1$). Notice that if this inequality condition holds, it can then be shown that the portfolio share of foreign capital n_d^* is sufficiently large to ensure that an increase in the variance of foreign productivity $\sigma_{y^*}^2$ will increase σ_w^2. In short, while it is likely that an increase in either σ_y^2 or $\sigma_{y^*}^2$ will raise the variance along the growth path, it is possible for an increase in one, but not both, to be stabilizing.

Consumption Behavior

The effect of an increase in the variance of domestic productivity on the consumption:wealth ratio depends critically upon the elasticity γ. In the case of the logarithmic utility function ($\gamma = 0$), the C/W ratio equals the rate of time preference β and is invariant with respect to risk or any other parameter. Otherwise, we can establish

$$\frac{\partial(C/W)}{\partial \sigma_y^2} = -\frac{\gamma}{1-\gamma}\left(\frac{\partial \rho}{\partial \sigma_y^2} + \frac{1}{2}(\gamma-1)\frac{\partial \sigma_w^2}{\partial \sigma_y^2}\right), \quad (11.29)$$

which upon substitution from (11.25)–(11.27) can be reduced to the expression

$$\frac{\partial(C/W)}{\partial \sigma_y^2} = \frac{1}{2}\gamma\alpha^2 n_d^2. \quad (11.30)$$

From (11.30), we see that the consumption:wealth ratio increases with the variance if $\gamma > 0$ and decreases otherwise. We commented in Chapter 9 how higher risk can be broken down into a positive substitution effect and a negative income effect with respect to consumption, the net effect of which depends upon $sgn(\gamma)$.

Other relative measures of consumption may respond very differently. This can be illustrated most conveniently in the case of a logarithmic utility function, when the consumption:wealth ratio reduces to β. In this case, the ratio of consumption to the deterministic component of GNP, for example is given by the expression

$$\frac{\beta}{\alpha n_d + \alpha^* n_d^*}$$

and depends upon the expression in (11.26) and whether the portfolio shift induces a rise or fall in GNP. By contrast, the consumption:GDP ratio is given by

$$\frac{\beta}{\alpha(n_d + n_f(W/W^*))}.$$

This time the decline in both n_d and n_f, and therefore in GDP, implies an unambiguous increase in this ratio.

Growth

The effect of an increase in σ_y^2 on the mean rate of growth of domestic wealth ψ is given by the expression

$$\frac{\partial \psi}{\partial \sigma_y^2} = \frac{\partial \rho}{\partial \sigma_y^2} - \frac{\partial(C/W)}{\partial \sigma_y^2}, \qquad (11.31)$$

which is the difference between the effect on disposable income and the effect on the consumption:wealth ratio. In the case of the logarithmic utility function, this depends solely on the first term and the portfolio adjustment it reflects. In this case, an increase in σ_y^2 will be growth-enhancing if $\alpha^* > \alpha$ and growth-reducing if $\alpha^* < \alpha$. In the more general case the impact on the consumption:wealth ratio needs to be taken into account as well. Thus, the tendency for an increase in σ_y^2 to be growth-enhancing if $\alpha^* > \alpha$ is strengthened if $\gamma < 0$, so that the consumption:wealth ratio declines as well. In general, the following criterion can be derived:

$$sgn\left(\frac{\partial \psi}{\partial \sigma_y^2}\right) = sgn\left[\left(\frac{\gamma}{2} - 1\right)(\alpha - \alpha^*) + \frac{1}{2}\gamma(\gamma - 1)\sigma_{y^*}^2\right]. \qquad (11.32)$$

Observe that if $\sigma_{y^*}^2 = 0$, so that foreign capital is riskless, the condition that $n_d > 0$ implies $\alpha > \alpha^*$, so that the growth rate is reduced.

It is of interest to compare this last result with that discussed in Section 11.4, where we gave an example in which the introduction of a risky asset is growth-enhancing. For this purpose it suffices to assume a logarithmic utility function (i.e., $\gamma = 0$) when (11.32) implies

$$sgn\left(\frac{\partial \psi}{\partial \sigma_y^2}\right) = sgn(\alpha^* - \alpha).$$

Suppose initially there is only riskless foreign capital. The domestic economy's equilibrium growth rate will thus be $\alpha^* - \rho$. Suppose now that risky domestic capital also becomes available as an investment. Being risky, it must yield a higher expected return than foreign capital (i.e., $\alpha > \alpha^*$) in order to induce investors to take a positive position in the asset. Equilibrium growth rate in the domestic economy is now $n_d\alpha + (1 - n_d)\alpha^* - \rho > \alpha^* - \rho$, so that the additional risky asset is growth-enhancing, as previously shown. Our result (11.32) says that while this is certainly the case, the *marginal* gains to growth decline with increasing domestic risk.

Since the effect of risk on the rate of asset accumulation is largely independent of the agent's place of residence (except insofar as agents in different economies may have different degrees of risk aversion), the effect of σ_y^2 on the foreign rate of asset accumulation ψ^* is essentially the same. Moreover, since the elasticities of portfolio adjustment with respect to σ_y^2 are the same in both economies, the fractions $n_d W/(n_d W + n_f W^*)$, etc. appearing in (11.15a) and (11.15b) are independent of σ_y^2. Thus, differentiating the deterministic components of (11.15a) and (11.15b) with respect to σ_y^2 yields

$$\frac{\partial (E(dK)/K)}{\partial \sigma_y^2} = \left(\frac{n_d W}{n_d W + n_f W^*}\right) \frac{\partial \psi}{\partial \sigma_y^2} + \left(\frac{n_f W^*}{n_d + n_f W^*}\right) \frac{\partial \psi^*}{\partial \sigma_y^2} \quad (11.33a)$$

$$\frac{\partial (E(dK^*)/K^*)}{\partial \sigma_y^2} = \left(\frac{n_d^* W}{n_d^* W + n_f^* W^*}\right) \frac{\partial \psi}{\partial \sigma_y^2} + \left(\frac{n_f^* W^*}{n_d^* + n_f^* W^*}\right) \frac{\partial \psi^*}{\partial \sigma_y^2}. \quad (11.33b)$$

From these two equations we see that the effect of an increase in domestic production risk, σ_y^2, on the rate of capital accumulation domiciled in either the domestic or the foreign economy is equal to a weighted average of its effects on the rates of wealth accumulation by the two economies. In the event that agents in the world economy have identical degrees of risk aversion, so that $\partial \psi/\partial \sigma_y^2$ and $\partial \psi^*/\partial \sigma_y^2$ are identical, the effects on the national rates of capital accumulation are also the same and equal to the effect on this common rate of wealth accumulation.[5]

International Accounts

The fact that an increase in domestic risk σ_y^2 leads to a portfolio shift from domestic to foreign assets immediately implies an instantaneous increase in the net asset position N of the domestic economy; see (11.17). These portfolio adjustments, together with the impact on the growth rates, in turn impact on the current account dN and the balance of trade dX. These effects can be obtained from (11.18) and (11.19) but are not pursued further. It is worth noting, however, that in the case where the domestic and foreign economies accumulate capital at the same rate, $(dW/W = dW^*/W^*)$, the growth rate of net asset accumulation dN/N is also equal to this common growth rate, and thus responds in a similar manner to increases in risk as noted in (11.31).

Welfare

Thus far, we have been discussing the effects of increased domestic risk on various specific aspects of macroeconomic performance. While an increase in such risk may increase or decrease the rate of consumption and the growth rate in the economy, what is ultimately of interest is the effect on economic welfare. To address this issue, we take the differential of the welfare function (11.20) to obtain

$$\frac{\partial V/\partial \sigma_y^2}{V} = (\gamma - 1)\frac{\partial (C/W)/\partial \sigma_y^2}{C/W}. \tag{11.34}$$

Substituting for $\partial(C/W)/\partial \sigma_y^2$ into (11.34), we see that

$$\frac{\partial V/\partial \sigma_y^2}{V\gamma} = \frac{1}{2}(\gamma - 1)\alpha^2 n_d^2 < 0. \tag{11.35a}$$

Thus an increase in the risk associated with domestic capital will lower the welfare of the domestic representative agent unambiguously. The amount by which welfare is reduced increases with the fraction of domestic capital in the portfolio of domestic residents.

It is straightforward to show that the effect of an increase in the risk of domestic capital on the welfare of the foreign representative agent is analogous:

$$\frac{\partial V^*/\partial \sigma_y^2}{V^*\gamma^*} = \frac{1}{2}(\gamma^* - 1)\alpha^2 n_f^2 < 0. \tag{11.35b}$$

And the same applies to the impact of foreign risk on the welfares of the two agents. Thus even if risk is growth-enhancing, overall it still results in a welfare loss for all agents. Clearly, eliminating all sources of productivity risk is a Pareto optimal situation.

The case of a common worldwide productivity risk corresponds to setting $\sigma_y^2 = \sigma_{yy^*} = \sigma_{y^*}^2 \equiv \sigma_u^2$, say, and can be treated analogously. In many respects the conclusions are qualitatively quite similar to those we have been discussing. There are, however, some differences worth noting. For example, an increase in the common risk will now cause both ρ and σ_w^2 to decrease unambiguously, though the effect on the consumption-wealth ratio remains dependent upon the elasticity γ, precisely as it did before. Furthermore, the decline ρ more than offsets the adjustment in C/W so that the growth rate ψ declines unambiguously as well, as does welfare.

11.6 Effects of Government Expenditure

We now turn to the effects of changes in the mean rate of government expenditure g, and its variance σ_z^2, on the macroeconomic equilibrium. Again, we shall focus primarily on the effects of domestic policy, with foreign government expenditure policy effects being analogous. The impacts are significantly simpler than those arising from production risk, due to the fact that the portfolio shares, which, as we have noted, are the driving force behind most of the economywide responses to production risk, are unaffected by fiscal policy.

With both domestic and foreign portfolio shares remaining fixed, both *GNP* and *GDP* remain unaffected. Disposable income ρ declines one-for-one in response to g, although it is unaffected by any change in its variance. The variance of wealth accumulation σ_w^2 increases one-for-one with the change in σ_z^2. The effects on the consumption-wealth ratio and the growth of assets are as follows:

$$\frac{\partial (C/W)}{\partial g} = \frac{\gamma}{1-\gamma}; \quad \frac{\partial (C/W)}{\partial \sigma_z^2} = \frac{\gamma}{2} \tag{11.36a}$$

$$\frac{\partial \psi}{\partial g} = -\frac{1}{1-\gamma} \quad \frac{\partial \psi}{\partial \sigma_z^2} = -\frac{\gamma}{2}. \tag{11.36b}$$

Analogous to the effect of an increase in productivity risk, the dependence of the response of the C/W ratio on γ reflects the net impact of a positive substitution effect and a negative income effect of changes in g and σ_z^2 on consumption. The reduction in disposable income resulting from an increase in g leads to a proportionate reduction in the growth rate, while the impact of the variance on the growth rate is the mirror image of its effect on the consumption-wealth ratio.

It can be seen from the equilibrium summarized in (11.12) and (11.13) that there is no transmission of changes in g and σ_z^2 to the consumption-wealth ratio and the mean rate of wealth accumulation abroad. By contrast, the rate of capital accumulation domiciled in one economy will be impacted by both domestic fiscal policy and fiscal policy abroad. This can be seen from the capital accumulation equations (11.15a′) and (11.15b′) and the fact that they respond to the growth rates ψ and ψ^* in both the domestic and the foreign economies. Thus, for example, insofar as an increase in the mean rate of domestic government expenditure reduces the domestic rate of asset accumulation, it reduces the domestic residents' holdings of foreign capital, thereby reducing the growth rate of physical capital domiciled abroad.

With portfolio shares being independent of government expenditure policy (either domestic or foreign), the effects of g and σ_z^2 on the various international accounts are straightforward to determine. The net effect of an increase in g is to reduce both the current account and the trade balance of the domestic economy. An increase in σ_z^2 will have similar effects, insofar as they lead to reductions in C/W. The effects of changes in the corresponding foreign government expenditure parameters are analogous.

Finally, turning to welfare, we find

$$\frac{\partial V/\partial g}{V\gamma} = \frac{(\gamma-1)}{\gamma}\frac{\partial(C/W)/\partial g}{C/W} = -\frac{1}{C/W} < 0 \qquad (11.37\text{a})$$

$$\frac{\partial V/\partial \sigma_z^2}{V\gamma} = \frac{(\gamma-1)}{\gamma}\frac{\partial(C/W)/\partial \sigma_z^2}{C/W} = \frac{\gamma-1}{2C/W} < 0. \qquad (11.37\text{b})$$

With government expenditure not yielding any direct utility, not surprisingly any increase in its mean level of expenditure is welfare-reducing, for the simple reason that it drains resources from the private sector. Also, to the extent that agents are risk-averse (i.e., $\gamma < 1$), any risk generated by government expenditure is also welfare-reducing. With the consumption-wealth ratio in each economy being independent of fiscal policies abroad, government expenditure policies adopted by one economy have no impact on the welfare of the other.

In observing these welfare propositions, the assumptions upon which they are based should be borne in mind. Two are critical. The first is the assumption of a single traded good, so that there is no transmission of terms of trade shocks. Second, government expenditure in either economy has no impact on the decisions of the private agents in that economy. Both of these are restrictions, and a more complete analysis of the welfare effects of expenditure policy would involve relaxing them.

11.7 Export Instability, Growth, and Investment

A widely discussed issue concerns the effects of export instability on investment and growth. Several authors have studied correlations between measures of export instability and growth, with a variety of conflicting results.[6] For example, Kenen and Voidodas (1972) find the investment-*GNP* ratio to be negatively correlated with export instability. By contrast, Yotopoulos and Nugent (1976) find a positive correlation. Other studies focusing on the growth of GNP and export instability also get conflicting results. Voivodas (1974) and Özler and Harrigan (1988) find a negative correlation between instability and growth rates of *GNP*. By contrast, Yotopoulos and Nugent (1976) obtain a positive correlation, while Kenen and Voivodas find no correlation. The present framework is able to offer a conciliation of these findings.

From (11.19), the variance of net exports, which we shall take as our measure of export instability, is given by

$$E(dX)^2 = (n_d n_d^* W + n_f n_f^* W^*)^2(\alpha^2 \sigma_y^2 - 2\alpha\alpha^* \sigma_{yy^*} + \alpha^{*2}\sigma_{y^*}^2)$$
$$+ (n_d^{*2} W^2 \sigma_z^2 - 2n_d^* n_f \sigma_{zz^*} WW^* + n_f^2 W^{*2} \sigma_{z^*}^2). \qquad (11.38)$$

The issue of the effects of export instability on growth thus centers around the relationship between (11.38) and the deterministic component of the relevant growth rate. In the present analysis, export instability is endogenous and reflects the exogenous sources of risk in the world economy, σ_y^2, $\sigma_{y^*}^2$, σ_z^2, and $\sigma_{z^*}^2$.

Consider first an increase in the variance of domestic fiscal policy, σ_z^2. This has no effect on portfolio shares and, assuming $\sigma_{zz^*} = 0$, will raise the instability of net exports by an amount $n_d^{*2} W^2 d\sigma_z^2$. The effect on the rate of asset accumulation in the domestic economy operates through the associated increase in σ_w^2 and the effect this has on the C/W ratio. This depends upon the elasticity γ, and we find that export stability will be positively or negatively associated with the rate of asset accumulation by domestic residents ψ, according to whether $\gamma \lessgtr 0$. This source of export instability has no effect on the domestic GNP, nor does it affect the rate of asset accumulation by foreign residents. To the extent that it increases or decreases ψ, it will have a similar, though lesser, effect on the rate of capital accumulation domiciled in both economies; see (11.15a) and (11.15b). In short, export instability arising from domestic fiscal instability may be either positively or negatively associated with growth, depending upon precisely what is being considered as well as the nature of the underlying utility function. Parallel remarks apply to an increase in the degree of export instability arising from an increase in foreign fiscal instability.

An increase in domestic production instability is more complicated, and for simplicity we shall focus on the case where both countries have the same degree of risk aversion, so that they hold identical portfolio shares: $n_d = n_f \equiv n$, $n_d^* = n_f^* \equiv 1 - n$. From (11.19) it can be shown that an increase in σ_y^2 (with uncorrelated production shocks) will raise the variance of net exports unambiguously. What this does to the growth path is far from clear. As we have seen, in the case of a logarithmic utility function it will be associated with a positive or a negative effect on domestic GNP, and therefore on the rate of asset accumulation, according to whether $\alpha \lessgtr \alpha^*$. The response in the growth rate is more complicated in the case of the more general utility function, when the response of the C/W ratio needs to be taken into account as well. Parallel effects on the rate of asset accumulation by foreign residents will apply. Furthermore, as is apparent from (11.15a) and (11.15b), the relationship between this source of export instability and the rate of capital accumulation is an average of the effects on the respective rates of wealth accumulation by the residents of the two economies.

In summary, our model is consistent with all patterns of correlation between export instability and growth. To some degree a critical element is the origin of the export instability. But it also depends upon structural properties of the particular economies.

11.8 Contemporaneous Responses to Current Shocks and Real Business Cycle Models

One of the influential contemporary approaches to macroeconomics is the theory of real business cycles (RBC). The fundamental view of modern business cycle theorists is that long-run growth and short-run fluctuations should emerge from a common analytical framework, arising as the equilibrium outcome of fully rational intertemporal optimizing economic agents. In many respects, the type of model we have developed in Part III is similar both in its analytical framework and in its dimension to that employed in the RBC literature, which typically employs small stochastic models like those we have been constructing. Our analysis differs from the RBC approach in two respects. The first, and unimportant, difference is that we have chosen to use continuous time, whereas the RBC models are typically formulated in discrete time.

The second, and substantive, difference is in the focus. After developing the model, the analysis has followed in the tradition of the international portfolio literature of Adler and Dumas (1983), Stulz (1981, 1987), and, more recently, Obstfeld (1994), Turnovsky (1993), and Grinols and Turnovsky (1994), and has examined the effects of risk—in this case production risk and fiscal risk—on various aspects of the behavior of the world economy. We have carried out what one might call a *structural* comparative static analysis of the equilibrium. That is, our concern has been on examining the effects of structural changes, specifically increases in risk as measured by variances, on the equilibrium behavior of the economy, focusing on aspects such as the growth rate, consumption, and welfare.

By contrast, the RBC literature is concerned with studying the short-run comovements of certain key variables. The emphasis is on analyzing the relative and absolute magnitudes of the various disturbances, as measured by their variances, as well as the correlation of various key economic variables, both nationally and across countries (see, e.g., Backus, Kehoe and Kydland 1992; Baxter 1993; Baxter and Crucini 1995; Danthine and Donaldson 1993; Glick and Rogoff 1995; and Kollmann 1993). In doing this, it is particularly interested in seeing how well the model is able to mimic the pattern of variances and covariances characteristic of the real world economies. This is often then used as a test of the model (see Cooley 1994).

Much of this literature, although using a model of about the same dimensionality as that developed in sections 11.2 and 11.3, proceeds numerically. While we do not engage in the numerical calibration methods that the RBC literature adopts, our approach nevertheless provides a useful framework for examining the same kinds of issues. Since this approach focuses on the comovement of the stochastic components of the solutions, it is convenient to summarize some of the relevant components at this point. We shall use $\sim$ to denote the stochastic component only. In order to maintain simplicity, we shall focus on the case where all agents have the same degree of risk aversion, so that the same proportion of assets is held in the portfolios of domestic and foreign investors; that is, $n_d = n_f \equiv n$; $n_d^* = n_f^* \equiv n^*$. We also shall summarize the stochastic components for the domestic economy only, with those for the foreign economy being analogous and obtainable from the solutions given previously. The relevant stochastic components (denoted by $\sim$) can be grouped as follows:

1. *Stochastic Components of Growth and Capital Accumulation*

$$\left(\frac{d\tilde{C}}{C}\right) = \left(\frac{d\tilde{W}}{W}\right) = \alpha n\, dy + \alpha^* n^* dy^* - dz \tag{11.39a}$$

$$\frac{d\tilde{K}}{K} = \alpha n\, dy + \alpha^* n^* dy^* - \left(\frac{W}{W+W^*}\right) dz - \left(\frac{W^*}{W+W^*}\right) dz^* \tag{11.39b}$$

2. *Stochastic Components of Income*

$$\frac{d(\tilde{GNP})}{E(GNP)} = \left(\frac{1}{\alpha n + \alpha^* n^*}\right)(\alpha n\, dy + \alpha^* n^* dy^*) \tag{11.39c}$$

$$\frac{d(\tilde{GDP})}{E(GDP)} = dy \tag{11.39d}$$

3. *Current Account and Trade Balance*

$$d\tilde{N} = (n^* W - nW^*)(\alpha n\, dy + \alpha^* n^* dy^*) + (nW^* dz^* - n^* W\, dz) \tag{11.39e}$$

$$d\tilde{X} = nn^*(W + W^*)(\alpha\, dy - \alpha^* dy^*) + (nW^* dz^* - n^* W\, dz) \tag{11.39f}$$

These stochastic relationships, and those that can be derived from them, help provide insight into the various short-run correlations, both those characterizing the empirical data and those discussed by real business cycle theorists. We shall now consider some of these.

Some Stylized Measures Characterizing National Measures of Variability

Hansen (1985) has presented a small table summarizing stylized facts pertaining to the stochastic structure of the U.S. economy that has served as a benchmark for the calibration analysis of real business cycle theorists (see, e.g., Backus, Kehoe, and Kydland 1992; Baxter and Crucini 1995; and Danthine and Donaldson 1993). The comparisons include the following:

$$\sigma_I = 8.60 > \sigma_Y = 1.76 > \sigma_C = 1.29 > \sigma_K = 0.63,$$

$$\rho_{IY} = 0.92 > \rho_{CY} = 0.85 > \rho_{KY} = 0.04,$$

where σ_i is the standard deviation of variable i in percentage form, where $i = I$ (investment), Y (output), C (consumption), and K (capital). The terms ρ_{ij} refer to corresponding correlations.[7] Thus, the stylized data suggest that investment is substantially more volatile than output, consumption is less so, and the capital stock much less so. Output is most highly correlated with investment, less so but still substantially with consumption, and only slightly with the capital stock. This pattern is generally confirmed for other countries, though the conformity is more robust for investment than for consumption, where for several economies the variability of consumption exceeds that of output (see Danthine and Donaldson 1993).[8]

The question is the extent to which this pattern of stochastic characteristics can be replicated by the model. To consider this, we shall calculate the variances of the expressions in (11.39) on the simplifying assumption that all stochastic disturbances are uncorrelated. This yields the following:

$$\sigma_{GDP}^2 = \sigma_y^2 \tag{11.40a}$$

$$\sigma_{GNP}^2 = \left(\frac{1}{\alpha n + \alpha^* n^*}\right)^2 (\alpha^2 n^2 \sigma_y^2 + \alpha^{*2} n^{*2} \sigma_{y^*}^2) \tag{11.40b}$$

$$\sigma_C^2 = \alpha^2 n^2 \sigma_y^2 + \alpha^{*2} n^{*2} \sigma_{y^*}^2 + \sigma_z^2 \tag{11.40c}$$

$$\sigma_K^2 = \alpha^2 n^2 \sigma_y^2 + \alpha^{*2} n^{*2} \sigma_{y^*}^2 + \left(\frac{W}{W+W^*}\right)^2 \sigma_z^2 + \left(\frac{W^*}{W+W^*}\right)^2 \sigma_{z^*}^2. \tag{11.40d}$$

In principle, and with appropriate interpretation, these expressions can be reconciled with the stylized facts, at least to the extent that one can reasonably expect this to be accomplished using such a simple model.

The following observations can be made. In general, the variance of *GNP* is less than that of *GDP*, due to the fact that the former, by including capital income from abroad, incorporates the diversification of risk accomplished by the worldwide capital market. In the absence of any stochastic disturbances in fiscal expenditure, the variances of consumption and capital are the same, while the variance of *GNP* is strictly a multiple (greater than unity) of their common variance. Indeed, with α and α^* representing rates of return, this multiple is unrealistically large. There are two mitigating factors to this, however. The first is that these measures of national output ignore labor income, which in practice is the largest component of national income and is likely to be much more stable. Second, the variance of consumption is increased by the variability of fiscal policy. The empirical evidence suggests that the variance of government expenditure is of the same order as the variance of output, implying $\sigma_z^2 \approx \alpha^2 \sigma_y^2$ (see Danthine and Donaldson 1993, Table 3). Taking these two factors into account suggests that the expressions in (11.40a) and (11.40b) grossly overstate the relative variability of output, leading to the conclusion that output is indeed likely to be somewhat more variable than consumption, as implied by the data. Once one allows for the variablility of fiscal policy, it is seen that the variance of capital is likely to be reduced below that of consumption, at least as long as σ_z^2 and $\sigma_{z^*}^2$ are not too different. At the same time, its variability is still likely to be overstated. This is because the model abstracts from adjustment costs, so that our expression for the variance of capital represents a mixture of the volatility of investment and the gradual adjustment of capital.

Turning to the consumption-output correlation, we see that in the absence of fiscal shocks, *GNP* and consumption are perfectly correlated. This is because both variables reflect the diversification associated with the international diversification of capital. On the one hand, consumption is proportional to wealth, which reflects the international diversification of capital, while *GNP* reflects the international sources of income. In the presence of domestic fiscal shocks, the correlation with income declines, though it may still remain quite high, consistent with the data. By contrast, the correlation between consumption and *GDP* is much lower, due to the fact that the latter reflects only domestic stochastic disturbances. The consumption-output correlation is unrealistically high for *GNP*, though much more reasonable in the case of *GDP*.[9]

Recent contributions to RBC literature have considered the role of fiscal shocks in more detail (see, e.g., Kollmann 1993; Baxter 1993). The consensus is that government expenditure is negatively correlated with both domestic private consumption and domestic investment, an implication consistent with our model; see (11.39a) and (11.39b).

Savings and Investment

One of the issues that has received a good deal of attention is correlation between domestic savings and investment. This phenomenon was originally investigated empirically by Feldstein and Horioka (1980), who argued that the high correlations they obtained between the savings: *GDP* ratio and the investment: GDP ratio were inconsistent with the assumption of perfect capital markets.

Defining savings to be the accumulation of wealth, the stochastic component of domestic savings is given by the right-hand side of (11.39a), and domestic investment is represented by (11.39b). In the absence of fiscal disturbances $(dz = dz^* \equiv 0)$, these two quantities are identical, so that domestic investment will be perfectly correlated with the domestic savings rate. Moreover, under these conditions, savings and investment abroad are also identical, so that these domestic quantities are perfectly correlated with their foreign counterparts. To the extent that there are fiscal shocks, the correlation will be reduced somewhat. It will be reduced further by the extent to which domestic and foreign agents have different degrees of risk aversion and hold different portfolio shares. Intuitively, any shock that increases the domestic savings rate will tend to have a similar effect abroad, and therefore impact on foreign savings. With constant portfolio shares, this will in turn tend to have proportional effects on the rates of investment in the two economies. The fact that the equilibrium is one of constant portfolio shares and steady growth is the reason for these correlations. For such an equilibrium the empirical findings of Feldstein and Horioka are indeed consistent with high (perfect) capital mobility. Other authors obtain lower correlations between these variables (see, e.g., Backus, Kehoe, and Kydland 1992). The savings-investment correlation has received increased attention recently. Tesar (1991) provides a survey of the theoretical and empirical literature, and shows how the positive saving-investment correlation is robust across an extensive sample range of OECD countries. Baxter and Crucini (1993) show how the observed positive correlation between savings and investment arises naturally within a quantitatively restricted equilibrium model with perfect mobility of financial and physical capital. Using data from the United States and Canada, Grinols (1996) shows how the stochastic growth model developed in Chapter 10 accounts quite well for the observed investment-savings correlation, even in the presence of perfect capital mobility.

Correlations between Internal and External Variables

The recent applications of RBC models to the international economy present numerous correlations between internal and external variables, to which we now turn.

Net Exports and Output

The stylized data indicate that net exports are uniformly negatively correlated with domestic output (see, e.g., Backus, Kehoe, and Kydland

1992; Danthine and Donaldson 1993). From equations (11.39f), (11.39d), and (11.39c) we can see

$$\text{cov}(d\tilde{X}, dG\tilde{D}P) > 0 \tag{11.41a}$$

$$sgn(\text{cov}(d\tilde{X}, dG\tilde{N}P)) = sgn(\alpha^2 n \sigma_y^2 - \alpha^{*2} n^* \sigma_{y*}^2). \tag{11.41b}$$

The difficulty is that in the one-good model, a domestic productivity (output) shock raises output more than it does domestic absorption, leading to an increase in net exports, thereby accounting for the positive correlation noted in (11.41a). This is offset by a similar correlation with respect to foreign productivity shocks, so that the correlation between net exports and *GNP* depends upon which effect dominates. The failure to replicate this aspect of the data uniformly is characteristic of other real business cycle models.

Net Exports and Fiscal Policy

A positive domestic fiscal shock reduces the net exports of the domestic economy (raises net exports abroad) and reduces the net asset position (current account) of the domestic economy; see equations (11.39e) and (11.39f). This result is supported by the empirical evidence provided by Baxter (1993) and Kollmann (1993).

Current Account and Output

From (11.39c)–(11.39e) one can establish the following covariances between *GDP*, *GNP*, and the current account:

$$\text{cov}\left(d\tilde{N}, \frac{dG\tilde{D}P}{E(GDP)}\right) = (n^*W - nW^*)\alpha n \sigma_y^2 dt \tag{11.42a}$$

$$\text{cov}\left(d\tilde{N}, \frac{dG\tilde{N}P}{E(GNP)}\right) = \left(\frac{n^*W - nW^*}{\alpha n + \alpha^* n^*}\right) \text{var}(\alpha n\, dy + \alpha^* n^*\, dy^*). \tag{11.42b}$$

In both cases, this depends upon $n^*W - nW^*$, which is precisely the net foreign asset position of the domestic economy. If the domestic economy has a positive net asset position, then the covariance between output and the current account will be positive; the increase in foreign asset holdings by domestic residents resulting from a domestic productivity shock exceeds the increase in domestic asset holdings going to foreigners. This result is significantly different from that obtained by Stockman and Svensson (1987), who, using a two-commodity model, find the response to depend critically upon the magnitude of the marginal utility of consumption of the domestic good.

Current Account and Domestic Investment

Stockman and Svensson also analyze the relationship between the current account and domestic investment, and again find the elasticity of the marginal utility of consumption of the domestic good to be the critical determinant. In our model, (11.39b) and (11.39e) imply the covariance relationship:

$$\text{cov}\left(\frac{d\tilde{K}}{K}, d\tilde{N}\right) = (n^*W - nW^*)\text{var}(\alpha n\, dy + \alpha^* n^* dy^*)$$

$$+ \left(\frac{1}{W + W^*}\right)(n^*W^2\sigma_z^2 - nW^{*2}\sigma_{z^*}^2)dt. \qquad (11.43)$$

In the absence of fiscal shocks (as in Stockman and Svensson), the covariance between these two variables depends upon the net asset position. However, these effects are modified in the presence of fiscal shocks. Empirical evidence on the covariance between the current account and domestic investment is provided by Glick and Rogoff (1995), who find an almost unambiguously negative relationship between these two variables.

Cross-Country Correlations

One issue that has attracted attention concerns the relative magnitudes of the cross-country correlations between respective outputs and consumptions. The empirical evidence is that output fluctuations generally are positively correlated, with the correlation in some cases being quite large (see Danthine and Donaldson 1993, Table 7). One puzzle, however, is that while cross-country consumption correlations are generally positive, they are generally less so than output. This tends to contradict the one-good model, where international risk-sharing leads consumption to be highly correlated across countries.[10]

The implied international correlations can be seen from (11.39) and the corresponding expressions abroad. The expressions exhibit a sharp contrast between the output measures *GDP* and *GNP*. The covariance between domestic and foreign *GDP* equals σ_{yy^*} and depends upon the correlation between the productivity shocks in the two countries. If these are uncorrelated, as we have been assuming, then *GDP* will be uncorrelated. By contrast, with identical portfolio shares being held, national *GNP*s will be perfectly correlated, though this will be diminished once one allows for different degrees of national risk aversion and the relative stability of labor income. The international correlation of consumption depends upon government expenditure in the respective economies. If there are no expenditure shocks, consumption will be perfectly correlated internationally. In the presence of national fiscal shocks, the international consumption correlations decline, and are now less than those of *GNP*, consistent with the stylized empirical data.

Overview

Although this model does not fare particularly well in terms of the RBC criterion of replicating the relevant moments, we do not view this as particularly discouraging. Our objective was a different one, to understand policy and to yield insights into policy making in a stochastic intertemporal environment. In this respect, we have found the simple model to be quite helpful.

The failure of simple models like the one just discussed to replicate the stochastic characteristics of real world economies is common, and hardly unexpected. In fact, the opposite would be surprising, since the stochastic movement of aggregate real variables reflects the random behavior of many thousands of variables. Is it reasonable to expect that this will be closely matched by a small analytical model having at most a handful of random shocks? One response is to introduce additional shocks into the model, thereby weakening the stochastic relationships between the variables. One difficulty with this approach is that while one adjustment to the model may succeed in doing a better job in matching up one set of correlations, in the process it may worsen the ability of the model to replicate other statistics. Also, why focus on the second moment? Why not the third or higher moments? Still, the RBC model has introduced an interesting methodology that presents serious challenges for the construction of stochastic intertemporal models.[11]

11.9 Nontraded Consumption and the Real Exchange Rate

The analysis, thus far, has focused on a single-good world economy, and thus has not addressed issues pertaining to the real exchange rate. While these are obviously critical, a general introduction of a second good and corresponding treatment of the real exchange rate become quite intractable. In order to get some idea of the behavior of the real exchange rate, we shall adapt the setup introduced by Stulz (1987).

Specifically, in addition to the traded capital we have been considering, we shall assume that each economy is endowed with a fixed stock of nontraded capital, which may be used to generate an exogenously given, steady deterministic flow of a nontraded consumption good. We shall denote the price of the nontraded consumption good (in terms of the traded good) produced in the domestic economy by P, and the corresponding nontraded consumption good produced abroad by P^*. The derivation of the macroeconomic equilibrium is analogous to that described in sections 11.2 and 11.3, and accordingly our treatment will be brief.

The representative agent in the domestic economy now chooses his consumption of both the traded good C_T and the nontraded good C_N, as well as his portfolio shares, to maximize

$$E_0 \int_0^\infty \frac{1}{\gamma}(C_T^\theta C_N^{1-\theta})^\gamma dt \qquad 0 < \theta < 1, \ -\infty < \gamma < 1, \tag{11.44a}$$

subject to the wealth accumulation equation

$$dW = W[n_d\, dR + n_d^*\, dR^*] + PY_N\, dt - (C_T + PC_N)dt - dT, \tag{11.44b}$$

where Y_N denotes the exogenously given fixed output flow of the nontraded consumption good. The representative agent in the foreign economy solves an analogous problem.

Following the usual procedure leads to the following "core" equilibrium relationships in the domestic and foreign economies.

Domestic Economy

The solutions for the portfolio shares n_d and n_d^*; the stochastic component of the rate of wealth accumulation, dw; and its variance, σ_w^2, remain as specified by equations (11.12a), (11.12f), and (11.12c), respectively. Defining total consumption C, expressed in terms of the traded good as numeraire by $C \equiv C_T + PC_N$, the solutions for the consumption to wealth ratio and mean growth rate of assets are modified to

$$\frac{C}{W} = \frac{1}{1-\gamma\theta}\left(\beta - \gamma(\alpha n_d + \alpha^* n_d^* - g) - \frac{1}{2}\gamma(\gamma-1)\sigma_w^2\right) \tag{11.12b'}$$

$$\psi = \frac{1}{1-\gamma\theta}\left([1+\gamma(1-\theta)](\alpha n_d + \alpha^* n_d^* - g) - \beta + \frac{1}{2}\gamma(\gamma-1)\sigma_w^2\right). \tag{11.12e'}$$

Foreign Economy

The modifications to the foreign economy are analogous. Equations (11.13a), (11.13f), and (11.13c) remain unchanged. Defining foreign total consumption C^* to be $C^* \equiv C_T^* + P^* C_N^*$, the solutions for the foreign consumption to wealth ratio and foreign mean growth rate of assets become

$$\left(\frac{C}{W}\right)^* = \frac{1}{1-\gamma^*\theta^*}\left(\beta^* - \gamma^*(\alpha n_f + \alpha^* n_f^* - g^*) - \frac{1}{2}\gamma^*(\gamma^*-1)\sigma_{w^*}^2\right)$$

$$\tag{11.13b'}$$

$$\psi^* = \frac{1}{1-\gamma^*\theta^*}\left([1+\gamma^*(1-\theta^*)](\alpha n_f + \alpha^* n_f^* - g^*) - \beta^* + \frac{1}{2}\gamma^*(\gamma^*-1)\sigma_{w^*}^2\right). \tag{11.13e'}$$

From these relationships we see that the structure of the basic equilibrium remains essentially unchanged from that discussed in Section 11.3. Thus the analyses of the various issues considered in sections 11.4–11.8 remain unaltered.

The new aspect, the real exchange rate, can be determined as follows. Given the Cobb-Douglas nature of the subutility function, the equilibrium shares of total consumption devoted to the traded and nontraded goods in the domestic economy are, respectively,

$$C_T = \theta C; \quad PC_N = (1-\theta)C.$$

Equilibrium in the nontraded consumption good sector is thus described by

$$PY_N = (1-\theta)C. \tag{11.45}$$

Denoting, for notational convenience, the consumption-wealth ratio by ϕ, the relative price of the nontraded to the traded good in the domestic economy is determined by

$$P = \left(\frac{1-\theta}{Y_N}\right)\phi W. \tag{11.46}$$

For the domestic utility function of the form (11.44a), the domestic *CPI*, Q say, is of the form

$$Q = NP^{1-\theta} = MW^{1-\theta}, \tag{11.47}$$

where M and N are constants. Analogously, the foreign *CPI*, Q^* say, is of the form

$$Q^* = N^* P^{*(1-\theta^*)} = M^* W^{*(1-\theta^*)}, \tag{11.48}$$

where M^* and N^* are constants pertaining to the foreign economy.

The real exchange rate, measured in terms of the ratio of the foreign *CPI* to the domestic *CPI*, is defined as

$$E \equiv \frac{Q^*}{Q} = \left(\frac{N^*}{N}\right)\left(\frac{P^{*(1-\theta^*)}}{P^{1-\theta}}\right) = \left(\frac{M^*}{M}\right)\left(\frac{W^{*(1-\theta^*)}}{W^{1-\theta}}\right). \tag{11.49}$$

Thus an increase in the stock of foreign wealth leads to an increase in the foreign *CPI*, resulting in an increase in the real exchange rate, E.

Taking the stochastic differential of (11.49), the real exchange rate can be shown to follow the stochastic process:

$$\frac{dE}{E} = \left\{ (1-\theta^*)\psi^* - (1-\theta)\psi - \frac{1}{2}\theta^*(1-\theta^*)\sigma_{w^*}^2 \right.$$
$$\left. + \frac{1}{2}(1-\theta)(2-\theta)\sigma_w^2 - (1-\theta)(1-\theta^*)\sigma_{ww^*} \right\} dt$$
$$+ (1-\theta^*)dw^* - (1-\theta)dw. \qquad (11.50)$$

The mean rate of real exchange depreciation depends upon the relative movements of the *CPI* in the two economies, which in turn depend upon the relative changes in wealth weighted by the nontraded good in the consumption bundle of the respective economies. To explore the properties of (11.50) further, we shall restrict ourselves to the case of the logarithmic utility function ($\gamma = 0$), when the equilibrium portfolio shares held in the two economies are identical.

Differentiating (11.50) with respect to σ_y^2 and assuming for further simplicity the absence of fiscal shocks, we have $\sigma_w^2 = \sigma_{w^*}^2 = \sigma_{ww^*}$, and hence

$$\frac{\partial [E(dE)/E]}{\partial \sigma_y^2} = (\theta - \theta^*)\left[\frac{\partial \psi}{\partial \sigma_y^2} - \frac{1}{2}(1-\theta+\theta^*)\frac{\partial \sigma_w^2}{\partial \sigma_y^2}\right], \qquad (11.51)$$

The response of the expected real exchange rate to risk thus depends upon several sets of factors. First, it depends upon what happens to the (common) growth rate of wealth in the two economies. Second, it depends upon what it does to the (common) second moments of domestic and foreign wealth, which in turn reflect the portfolio adjustment; see (11.27). Whatever the net effect of these responses, the overall response of the real exchange rate depends upon the relative weights of the traded good in the respective utility functions of the two agents.

The effects of fiscal policy on the exchange rate are much more straightforward. An increase in the domestic rate of government expenditure g will reduce the rate of growth of asset accumulation by domestic residents, leading to a depreciation of the domestic real exchange rate. Likewise, an increase in domestic fiscal risk will raise the variance of the rate of domestic asset accumulation; this, too, will cause the domestic real exchange rate to depreciate.

Finally, by considering the stochastic component of (11.50) with the various stochastic relationships reported in (11.39), one can determine the covariance of the real exchange rate with the various stochastic influences. While we do not pursue this in detail, we may note the following. First, a stochastic increase in domestic *GDP* will be accompanied by a real depreciation of the domestic exchange rate if and only if the share of the nontraded good in foreign consumption exceeds that of the nontraded good in domestic consumption. Second, a stochastic increase in domestic government expenditure reduces wealth and will thus be accompanied by a depreciation of the real exchange rate. Stockman and Svensson (1987) discuss the covariance between capital flows and the real exchange rate; this, too, can be analyzed in the present model by considering (11.50) in conjunction with (11.39e).

11.10 Distortionary Taxes and Growth

The stochastic framework developed in this chapter provides a suitable vehicle for analyzing the effects of distortionary taxes on economic growth as well as issues pertaining to the viability of alternative tax regimes. As we have demonstrated for the small economy model of Chapter 9, the introduction of risk introduces flexibility into the choice of tax regime, so that the viability discussed in Chapter 6 ceases to be an issue. There are, however, other technical problems that render such an analysis difficult.

First, the standard analysis of distortionary taxes assumes that the tax revenues received by a government are redistributed to its own residents. To the extent that nonresidents are being taxed, through taxation at source, this involves an international redistribution of the tax revenues, with the amount of the transfer being proportional to the wealth of the other country. A consequence of this is that the stochastic rates of wealth accumulation in the two countries become interdependent, and this complicates the formal solution enormously. With stochastic shocks it is no longer the case that an equilibrium with constant portfolio shares exists. Instead, they will evolve stochastically over time, as wealth is redistributed stochastically between the two economies.

A second technical difficulty concerns the perception that agents may be assumed to have regarding the rebate they will receive on the income tax they have paid. Traditional tax theory assumes that the agent takes them as exogenously given. How the agent perceives the rebate scheme when making his private consumption and portfolio allocation decisions is important. Various schemes can be considered, and have different implications for the nature of the equilibrium. For the conventional framework in which the long-run equilibrium is stationary, this is of course natural. But in a context of ongoing, steady stochastic growth, it is less evident that this is the most appropriate benchmark. For example, consider a situation where the government maintains a balanced budget, continuously rebating the tax revenues as they are received. Since in equilibrium, tax revenues increase steadily in proportion to the growth of wealth, it does not seem unreasonable to assume that the agent perceives the nature of this linkage in making his private decisions. If, further, the agent has rational expectations and perceives this link exactly, then the income tax will operate as a lump-sum tax and have no effect on the growth rate. This is essentially why the mean tax rate had no effect on the growth rate in the model of Chapter 10.

An alternative assumption would be that the agent perceives the stochastic rebate, $dZ(t)$, as following some purely exogenous stochastic process, $dZ(t) = s(t)dt + dv$, say. As long as the actual rebate is proportional to wealth, as in the deterministic growth model of Chapter 5, this will still generate an equilibrium with steady stochastic growth and constant portfolio shares, though the growth rate will now respond negatively to the tax rate. A third possibility is that the agent perceives the tax rate as growing with aggregate wealth, which he treats as exogenous but which, with identical agents, in equilibrium equals the average of the endogenously determined wealth of the agent.

11.11 Some Final Comments

This completes our analysis of the macroeconomic dynamics of an international economy. The models we have presented are based on the intertemporal optimization of rational agents and are more or less the standard paradigm at the present time. They are clearly much more sophisticated than the early dynamic models, in which the dynamics arose either through assumed sluggish adjustment of prices or the gradual accumulation of assets. Despite the relatively tight focus of our analysis, we have covered a lot of ground, progressing through a sequence of small, open economy models, multicountry models, and stochastic models. We have also dealt with economies that converge to a steady-state level, as well as those that may experience ongoing growth.

One of the strengths of the representative agent framework that we have employed is that it emphasizes the intertemporal dimensions of fiscal policy and the restrictions imposed on the agents in the economy—the private individuals and the government—and therefore the overall economy itself, in order for it to remain intertemporally viable. That is perhaps the single most important insight of the representative agent model.

Over time things will change. International economics, and particularly international macroeconomics, is exciting, and new problems and issues are always arising. The representative agent model, which has served as a useful vehicle for addressing many important problems, may or may not prove to be useful in the future. No doubt it will be superseded by other models, such as heterogeneous agent models, and other analytical developments. Currently the stochastic calculus models that we have used in Part III present a promising avenue for future research. Although these methods are hardly new, they have been used only sparsely in studying macroeconomic dynamics. One reason, no doubt, is that the class of models for which they are analytically tractable is limited. As these methods are applied to more complex formulations, numerical solutions will become necessary, but with computing capabilities increasing as they are, richer and more relevant models will surely become solvable and help in our understanding of more complex and realistic macroeconomic systems.

Notes

1. For a discussion of stochastic portfolio models using discrete time, see Obstfeld and Rogoff (1996, Chapter 5).

2. This observation is related to the work of Gordon and Varian (1989), who analyze tax policy in a model where governments have market power in the international market for financial securities. They show how such governments have an incentive to set tax rates such that investors are induced to specialize in domestic securities.

3. See also King and Rebelo (1990). An extensive survey of the literature attempting to explain the international differences in growth rates is provided by Rebelo (1992).

4. Equation (11.19) is established as follows. Using (11.14), together with its differential, we may write

$$dX = \alpha(n_d W + n_f W^*)(dt + dy) - \left(\frac{C}{W} + g\right) W \, dt - W \, dz - n_d W \left(\frac{dW}{W}\right) - n_f W^* \left(\frac{dW^*}{W^*}\right).$$

Noting (11.7) with $\tau = g$, $dv = dz$ and the corresponding relationships abroad, we obtain

$$dX = \left\{ \alpha(n_d W + n_f W^*) - \left(\frac{C}{W} + g\right) W - n_d W \left(\alpha n_d + \alpha^* n_d^* - \left(\frac{C}{W} + g\right)\right) \right.$$
$$\left. - n_f W^* \left(\alpha n_f + \alpha^* n_f^* - \left(\left(\frac{C}{W}\right)^* + g^*\right)\right) \right\} dt + \alpha(n_d W + n_f W^*) dy - W \, dz$$
$$- n_d W [\alpha n_d \, dy + \alpha^* n_d^* \, dy^* - dz] - n_f W^* [\alpha n_f \, dy + \alpha^* n_f^* \, dy^* - dz^*].$$

Rearranging terms and noting the adding-up conditions in (11.12a) and (11.13a) leads to (11.19).

5. It is straightforward to consider the effect of domestic productivity risk on the variance of the rate of capital accumulation. In the case where portfolio shares held by domestic and foreign agents are identical,

$$\text{var}\left(\frac{dK}{K}\right) = \left(\frac{W}{W + W^*}\right)^2 \sigma_w^2 + 2\left(\frac{W}{W + W^*}\right)\left(\frac{W^*}{W + W^*}\right) \sigma_{ww^*} + \left(\frac{W^*}{W + W^*}\right)^2 \sigma_{w^*}^2.$$

and the effects of risk are obtained by taking the derivative of this expression.

6. This issue is also examined analytically by Brock (1991).

7. These comparisons are taken from Danthine and Donaldson (1993, Table 1). Backus, Kehoe, and Kydland (1992) and Baxter and Crucini (1995) report slightly different benchmark statistics.

8. Most notably this is true for France.

9. These magnitudes also tend to be supported by the data. Consumption tends to be more highly correlated with output for those countries using *GNP* measures (e.g., Canada, Germany, Japan, and the U.S.) rather than those using *GDP* (see Danthine and Donaldson 1993, Table 2).

10. This has been analyzed at length (see, e.g., Backus, Kehoe, and Kydland 1992; Devereux, Gregory, and Smith 1992; Stockman and Tesar 1995).

11. For recent evaluations of the real business cycle approach, see Hansen and Heckman (1996), Kydland and Prescott (1996), and Sims (1996).

References

Abel, A. 1982. "Dynamic Effects of Permanent and Temporary Tax Policies in a q Model of Investment." *Journal of Monetary Economics* 9:353–373.

Abel, A. 1987. "Optimal Monetary Growth." *Journal of Monetary Economics* 19:437–450.

Abel, A., and O. J. Blanchard. 1983. "An Intertemporal Model of Saving and Investment." *Econometrica* 51:675–692.

Adler, M., and B. Dumas. 1983. "International Portfolio Choice and Corporation Finance: A Synthesis." *Journal of Finance* 38:925–984.

Agénor, P. R., and P. J. Montiel. 1996. *Development Macroeconomics*. Princeton, N.J.: Princeton University Press.

Aghion, P., and P. Howitt. 1992. "A Model of Growth Through Creative Destruction." *Econometrica* 60:323–351.

Aizenman, J. 1992. "Competitive Externalities and the Optimal Seignorage." *Journal of Money, Credit, and Banking* 24:61–71.

Aizenman, J., and J. A. Frenkel. 1985. "Optimal Wage Indexation, Foreign Exchange Market Intervention, and Monetary Policy." *American Economic Review* 75:402–423.

Anderson, J., and J. Riley. 1976. "International Trade with Fluctuating Prices." *International Economic Review* 17:79–97.

Arnold, L. 1974. *Stochastic Differential Equations: Theory and Applications*. New York: Wiley.

Arrow, K. J., and M. Kurz. 1970. *Public Investment, the Rate of Return, and Optimal Fiscal Policy*. Baltimore: Johns Hopkins University Press.

Aschauer, D. A. 1985. "Fiscal Policy and Aggregate Demand." *American Economic Review* 75:117–127.

Aschauer, D. A. 1988. "The Equilibrium Approach to Fiscal Policy." *Journal of Money, Credit, and Banking* 20:41–62.

Aschauer, D. A. 1989a. "Is Public Expenditure Productive?" *Journal of Monetary Economics* 23:177–200.

Aschauer, D. A. 1989b. "Does Public Capital Crowd Out Private Capital?" *Journal of Monetary Economics* 24:171–188.

Aschauer, D. A., and J. Greenwood. 1985. "Macroeconomic Effects of Fiscal Policy," in *The "New Monetary Economics": Fiscal Issues and Unemployment*, K. Brunner and A. H. Meltzer, eds. Carnegie-Rochester Conference Series on Public Policy Vol. 23. Amsterdam: North-Holland.

Asea, P. K., and W. M. Corden, eds. 1994. "Thirty Years of the Balassa-Samuelson Model." *Review of International Economics* 2.

Asea, P. K., and E. G. Mendoza. 1994. "The Balassa-Samuelson Model: General Equilibrium Appraisal." *Review of International Economics* 2:244–267.

Asea, P. K., and S. J. Turnovsky. 1997. "Capital Income and Risk-Taking in a Small Open Economy." *Journal of Public Economics*.

Auerbach, A. J., and J. A. Hines. 1987. "Anticipated Tax Changes and the Timing of Investment," in *The Effects of Taxation on Capital Accumulation*, M. Feldstein, ed. Chicago: University of Chicago Press.

Aukrust, O. 1977. "Inflation in the Open Economy: A Norwegian Model," in *Worldwide Inflation*, L. B. Krause and W. S. Salant, eds. Washington, D.C.: Brookings Institution.

Backus, D. K. 1993. "Interpreting Comovements in the Trade Balance and Terms of Trade." *Journal of International Economics* 34:375–387.

Backus, D. K., P. Kehoe, and T. Kehoe. 1992. "In Search of Scale Effects in Trade and Growth." *Journal of Economic Theory* 58:377–409.

Backus, D. K., P. J. Kehoe, and F. E. Kydland. 1992. "International Real Business Cycles." *Journal of Political Economy* 100:745–775.

Backus, D. K., P. Kehoe, and F. E. Kydland. 1994a. "Dynamics of the Trade Balance and the Terms of Trade: The J-Curve?" *American Economic Review* 84:84–103.

Backus, D. K., P. Kehoe, and F. E. Kydland. 1994b. "Relative Price Movements in Dynamic General Equilibrium Models of International Trade," in *Handbook of International Macroeconomics*, F. van der Ploeg, ed. Oxford: Blackwell.

Bailey, M. J. 1956. "The Welfare Cost of Inflationary Finance." *Journal of Political Economy* 64:93–110.

Balassa, B. 1964. "The Purchasing Power Parity Doctrine: A Reappraisal." *Journal of Political Economy* 72:584–596.

Bardhan, P. K. 1967. "Optimum Foreign Borrowing," in *Essays on the Theory of Optimal Economic Growth*, K. Shell, ed. Cambridge, MA: MIT Press.

Barro, R. J. 1979. "On the Determination of the Public Debt." *Journal of Political Economy* 87:940–971.

Barro, R. J. 1989. "The Neoclassical Approach to Fiscal Policy," in *Modern Business Cycle Theory*, R. J. Barro, ed. Cambridge, MA: Harvard University Press.

Barro, R. J. 1990. "Government Spending in a Simple Model of Endogenous Growth." *Journal of Political Economy* 98:S103–S125.

Barro, R. J. 1991. "Economic Growth in a Cross Section of Countries." *Quarterly Journal of Economics* 106:407–443.

Barro, R. J., and J. W. Lee. 1994. "Sources of Economic Growth," in A. H. Meltzer and C. I. Plosser, eds. Carnegie-Rochester Conference Series on Public Policy, Vol. 40. Amsterdam: North-Holland.

Barro, R. J., and X. Sala-i-Martin. 1992a. "Convergence." *Journal of Political Economy* 100:223–251.

Barro, R. J., and X. Sala-i-Martin. 1992b. "Public Finance in Models of Economic Growth." *Review of Economic Studies* 59:645–661.

Barro, R., and X. Sala-i-Martin. 1995. *Economic Growth*. New York: McGraw-Hill.

Basar, T., and G. J. Olsder. 1982. *Dynamic Noncooperative Game Theory*. New York: Academic Press.

Baxter, M. 1993. "Financial Market Linkages and the International Transmission of Fiscal Policy." Rochester Center for Economic Research Working Paper No. 336.

Baxter, M., and M. J. Crucini. 1993. "Explaining Saving-Investment Correlations." *American Economic Review* 83:416–436.

Baxter, M., and M. J. Crucini. 1995. "Business Cycles and the Asset Structure of Foreign Trade." *International Economic Review* 36:821–854.

Baxter, M., and R. G. King. 1993. "Fiscal Policy in General Equilibrium." *American Economic Review* 83:315–334.

Bazdarich, B. 1978. "Optimal Growth and Stages in the Balance of Payments." *Journal of International Economics* 8:425–443.

Bean, C. R. 1986. "The Terms of Trade, Labour Supply, and the Current Account." *Economic Journal Supplement* 98:38–47.

Benavie, A., E. L. Grinols, and S. J. Turnovsky. 1996. "Adjustment Costs and Investment in a Stochastic Endogenous Growth Model." *Journal of Monetary Economics* 38:77–100.

Bertola, G. 1994. "Continuous-Time Models of Exchange Rates and Intervention," in *Handbook of International Macroeconomics*, F. van der Ploeg, ed. Oxford: Blackwell.

Bhandari, J. S., ed. 1985. *Exchange Rate Management under Uncertainty*. Cambridge, MA: MIT Press.

Bhandari, J. S., N. U. Haque, and S. J. Turnovsky. 1990. "Growth, External Debt, and Sovereign Risk in a Small Open Economy." *IMF Staff Papers* 37:388–417.

Bianconi, M. 1995. "Fiscal Policy in a Simple Two-Country Dynamic Model." *Journal of Economic Dynamics and Control* 19:395–419.

Bianconi, M., and S. J. Turnovsky. 1996. "Fiscal Policy in the World Economy: Transmission and Implications for Strategic Behavior." Manuscript, Tufts University and University of Washington.

Bianconi, M., and S. J. Turnovsky. 1997. "International Effects of Government Expenditure in Interdependent Economies." *Canadian Journal of Economics* 30:57–84.

Black, S. W. 1985. "The Effect of Alternative Policies on the Variability of Exchange Rates: The Harrod Effect," in *Exchange Rate Management under Uncertainty*, J. S. Bhandari, ed. Cambridge, MA: MIT Press.

Blanchard, O. J. 1985. "Debt, Deficits, and Finite Horizons." *Journal of Political Economy* 93:223–247.

Blanchard, O. J., and S. Fischer. 1989. *Lectures on Macroeconomics*. Cambridge, MA: MIT Press.

Blanchard, O. J., and C. M. Kahn. 1980. "The Solution of Linear Difference Models under Rational Expectations." *Econometrica* 48:1305–1311.

Blanchard, O. J., and L. Summers. 1986. "Hysteresis and the European Unemployment Problem," in *NBER Macroeconomics Annual 1986*, S. Fischer, ed. Cambridge, MA: MIT Press.

Bond, E. W., P. Wang, and C. K. Yip. 1996. "A General Two-Sector Model of Endogenous Growth with Human and Physical Capital." *Journal of Economic Theory* 68:149–173.

Bourguignon, F. 1974. "A Particular Class of Continuous-Time Stochastic Growth Models." *Journal of Economic Theory* 9:141–158.

Bovenberg, A. L. 1986. "Capital Income Taxation in Growing Open Economies." *Journal of Public Economics* 31:347–376.

Bovenberg, A. L. 1994. "Capital Taxation in the World Economy," in *Handbook of International Macroeconomics*, F. van der Ploeg, ed. Oxford: Blackwell.

Boyer, R. 1978. "Optimal Exchange Market Intervention." *Journal of Political Economy* 86:1045–1056.

Branson, W. H., and D. W. Henderson. 1985. "The Specification and Influence of Asset Markets," in *Handbook in International Economics*, R. W. Jones and P. B. Kenen, eds. Amsterdam: North-Holland.

Branson, W. H., and J. J. Rotemberg. 1980. "International Adjustment with Wage Rigidity." *European Economic Review* 13:309–332.

Brock, P. L. 1988. "Investment, the Current Account and the Relative Price of Nontraded Goods in a Small Open Economy." *Journal of International Economics* 24:235–253.

Brock, P. L. 1991. "Export Instability and the Economic Performance of Developing Countries." *Journal of Economic Dynamics and Control* 15:129–147.

Brock, P. L. 1996. "International Transfers, the Relative Price of Nontraded Goods and the Current Account." *Canadian Journal of Economics* 29:163–180.

Brock, P. L., and S. J. Turnovsky. 1993. "The Growth and Welfare Consequences of Differential Tariffs." *International Economic Review* 34:765–794.

Brock, P. L., and S. J. Turnovsky. 1994. "The Dependent Economy Model with Both Traded and Nontraded Capital Goods." *Review of International Economics* 2:306–325.

Bruno, M. 1976. "The Two-Sector Open Economy and the Real Exchange Rate." *American Economic Review* 66:566–577.

Bruno, M. 1982. "Adjustment and Structural Change under Supply Shocks." *Scandinavian Journal of Economics* 84:199–221.

Bruno, M., and J. Sachs. 1982. "Energy and Resource Allocation in a Small Open Economy." *Review of Economic Studies* 49:845–859.

Buiter, W. H. 1981. "Time Preference and International Lending and Borrowing in an Overlapping Generations Model." *Journal of Political Economy* 89:769–797.

Buiter, W. H. 1984. "Saddlepoint Problems in Continuous Time Rational Expectations Models: A General Method and Some Macroeconomic Examples." *Econometrica* 52:665–680.

Buiter, W. H. 1987. "Fiscal Policy in Open Interdependent Economies," in *Economic Policy in Theory and in Practice*, A. Razin and E. Sadka, eds. New York: St. Martin's Press.

Buiter, W. H., and K. M. Kletzer. 1991. "The Welfare Economics of Cooperative and Noncooperative Fiscal Policy." *Journal of Economic Dynamics and Control* 15:215–244.

Buiter, W. H., and R. C. Marston, eds. 1985. *International Economic Policy Coordination.* Cambridge, U.K.: Cambridge University Press.

Caballé, J., and M. S. Santos. 1993. "On Endogenous Growth with Physical and Human Capital." *Journal of Political Economy* 101:1042–1067.

Cairnes, J. E. 1859. "The Australian Episode." *Frazier's Magazine* (September). Reprinted in J. E. Cairnes, *Essays in Political Economy.* London: Macmillan, 1873.

Calvo, G. A. 1987. "Real Exchange Rate Dynamics with Nominal Parities: Structural Change and Overshooting." *Journal of International Economics* 22:141–155.

Canova, F., and H. Dellas 1993. "Trade Interdependence and the International Business Cycle." *Journal of International Economics* 34:23–47.

Cantor, R., and N. C. Mark. 1987. "International Debt and World Business Fluctuations." *Journal of International Money and Finance* 6:153–166.

Cantor, R., and N. C. Mark. 1988. "The International Transmission of Real Business Cycles." *International Economic Review* 29:493–507.

Canzoneri, M. B., and D. W. Henderson. 1991. *Monetary Policy in Interdependent Economies.* Cambridge, MA: MIT Press.

Casella, A. 1992. "Participation in a Currency Union." *American Economic Review* 82:847–863.

Chamley, C. 1986. "Optimal Taxation of Capital Income in General Equilibrium with Infinite Lives." *Econometrica* 54:607–622.

Chan, K. S. 1978. "The Employment Effects of Tariffs under a Free Exchange Rate Regime." *Journal of International Economics* 8:414–424.

Chari, V. V., and P. J. Kehoe. 1990. "International Fiscal Policy Coordination in Limiting Economies." *Journal of Political Economy* 98:617–636.

Chow, G. C. 1979. "Optimum Control of Stochastic Differential Equation Systems." *Journal of Economic Dynamics and Control* 1:143–175.

Christensen, T. A., and S. B. Nielsen. 1992. "International Repercussions of Capital Income Taxation in Large Economies: The Source versus Residence Principle." Manuscript, Copenhagen Business School.

Clarke, H. R., and G. H. Kingston. 1979. "The Optimal Crawl: A Comment." *Journal of International Economics* 9:131–136.

Clower, R. 1967. "A Reconsideration of the Microfoundations of Monetary Theory." *Western Economic Journal* 6:1–8.

Cohen, D. 1994. "Growth and External Debt," in *Handbook of International Macroeconomics*, F. van der Ploeg, ed. Oxford: Blackwell.

Cooley, T. F., ed. 1994. *Frontiers of Business Cycle Research.* Princeton, N.J.: Princeton University Press.

Cooley, T. F., and G. D. Hansen. 1992. "Tax Distortions in a Neoclassical Monetary Economy." *Journal of Economic Theory* 58:290–316.

Cooper, R. N., and J. Sachs. 1985. "Borrowing Abroad: The Debtor's Perspective," in *International Debt and Developing Countries*, G. W. Smith and J. T. Cuddington, eds. Washington, D.C.: World Bank.

Corden, W. M. 1960. "The Geometric Representation of Policies to Attain Internal and External Balance." *Review of Economic Studies* 28:1–19.

Corden, W. M., and S. J. Turnovsky. 1983. "Negative Transmission of Economic Expansion." *European Economic Review* 20:289–310.

Correia, I. 1996. "Dynamic Optimal Taxation in Small Open Economies." *Journal of Economic Dynamics and Control* 20:691–708.

Correia, I., and P. Teles. 1996. "Is the Friedman Rule Optimal When Money Is an Intermediate Good?" *Journal of Monetary Economics* 38:223–244.

Corsetti, G. 1991. "Fiscal Policy and Endogenous Growth: A Mean-Variance Approach." Working paper, Yale University.

Danthine, J. P., and J. B. Donaldson. 1993. "Methodological and Empirical Issues in Real Business Cycle Theory." *European Economic Review* 37:1–35.

De Gregorio, J., A. Giovannini, and T. Krueger. 1994. "The Behavior of Nontradable Goods Prices in Europe: Evidence and Interpretation." *Review of International Economics* 2:284–305.

De Long, J. B., and L. H. Summers. 1991. "Equipment Investment and Economic Growth." *Quarterly Journal of Economics* 106:445–502.

Devereux, M. B. 1991. "The Terms of Trade and the International Coordination of Fiscal Policy." *Economic Inquiry* 29:720–736.

Devereux, M. B., A. Gregory, and G. W. Smith. 1992. "Realistic Cross-Country Consumption Correlations in a Two-Country, Equilibrium, Business-Cycle Model." *Journal of International Money and Finance* 11:3–16.

Devereux, M. B., and D. R. Love. 1994. "The Effects of Factor Taxation in a Two-Sector Model of Endogenous Growth." *Canadian Journal of Economics* 27:509–536.

Devereux, M. B., and M. Saito. 1997. "Growth, Convergence, and Risk-Sharing with Incomplete International Asset Markets." *Journal of International Economics* 42:453–481.

Devereux, M. B., and S. Shi. 1991. "Capital Accumulation and the Current Account in a Two Country Model." *Journal of International Economics* 30:1–25.

Devereux, M. B., and G. Smith. 1994. "International Risk-Sharing and Economic Growth." *International Economic Review* 35:535–550.

Diamond, P. A. 1965. "National Debt in a Neoclassical Growth Model." *American Economic Review* 55:1126–1150.

Diaz Alejandro, C. F. 1965. *Exchange-Rate Devaluation in a Semi-Industrialized Country: The Experience of Argentina 1955–1961*. Cambridge, MA: MIT Press.

Dixit, A. K., and R. S. Pindyck. 1994. *Investment under Uncertainty*. Princeton, N.J.: Princeton University Press.

Dornbusch, R. 1976. "Expectations and Exchange Rate Dynamics." *Journal of Political Economy* 84:1161–1176.

Dornbusch, R. 1980. "Home Goods and Traded Goods: The Dependent Economy Model," in R. Dornbusch, *Open Economy Macroeconomics*. New York: Basic Books.

Dornbusch, R. 1983. "Real Interest Rates, Home Goods, and Optimal External Borrowing." *Journal of Political Economy* 91:141–153.

Dornbusch, R. 1985. "Intergenerational and International Trade." *Journal of International Economics* 18:123–139.

Dornbusch, R., and S. Fischer. 1980. "Exchange Rate and the Current Account." *American Economic Review* 70:960–971.

Driskill, R., and S. A. McCafferty. 1980. "Exchange Rate Variability, Real and Monetary Shocks, and the Degree of Capital Mobility under Rational Expectations." *Quarterly Journal of Economics* 95:577–586.

Easterly, W., and S. Rebelo. 1993. "Fiscal Policy and Growth: An Empirical Investigation." *Journal of Monetary Economics* 32:417–458.

Eaton, J. 1981. "Fiscal Policy, Inflation, and the Accumulation of Risky Capital." *Review of Economic Studies* 48:435–445.

Eaton, J. 1985. "Optimal and Time Consistent Exchange-Rate Management in an Overlapping Generations Economy." *Journal of International Money and Finance* 4:83–100.

Eaton, J. 1987. "A Dynamic Specific-Factors Model of International Trade." *Review of Economic Studies* 54:325–338.

Eaton, J., and M. Gersovitz. 1980. "LDC Participation in the International Financial Markets: Debt and Reserves." *Journal of Development Economics* 7:3–21.

Eaton, J., and M. Gersovitz. 1981. "Debt with Potential Repudiation: Theoretical and Empirical Analysis." *Review of Economic Studies* 48:289–309.

Eaton, J., and G. Grossman. 1986. "Optimal Trade and Industrial Policy under Oligopoly." *Quarterly Journal of Economics* 101:383–406.

Edwards, J. H. Y. 1990. "Congestion Function Specification and the 'Publicness' of Local Public Goods." *Journal of Urban Economics* 27:80–96.

Edwards, S. 1987. "Tariffs, Terms of Trade, and the Real Exchange Rate in an Intertemporal Optimizing Model of the Current Account." Working Paper No. 2175, National Bureau of Economic Research.

Eichengreen, B. J. 1981. "A Dynamic Model of Tariffs, Output, and Employment under Flexible Exchange Rates." *Journal of International Economics* 11:341–359.

Eicher, T. 1996. "Interaction between Endogenous Human Capital and Technological Change." *Review of Economic Studies* 63:127–144.

Eicher, T., and S. J. Turnovsky. 1997. "Risk and Financial Development: A Comparative Case Study of Mexico and Indonesia," in *Managing Capital Flows and Exchange Rates: Lessons from the Pacific Basin*, R. Glick, ed. Cambridge, U.K.: Cambridge University Press.

Eisner, R., and R. H. Strotz. 1963. "Determinants of Business Investment," in *Commission on Money and Credit: Impacts of Monetary Policy*. Englewood Cliffs, N.J.: Prentice-Hall.

Engel, C. M. 1992. "On the Foreign Exchange Risk Premium in a General Equilibrium Model." *Journal of International Economics* 32:305–319.

Engel, C. M. 1996. "The Forward Discount Anomaly and the Risk Premium: A Survey of Recent Evidence." *Journal of Empirical Finance* 3:123–192.

Engel, C. M. and K. Kletzer. 1989. "Saving and Investment in an Open Economy with Nontraded Goods." *International Economic Review* 30:735–752.

Engel, C. M. and K. Kletzer. 1990. "Tariffs and Saving in a Model with New Generations." *Journal of International Economics* 28:71–91.

Engel, C. M., and A. P. Rodrigues. 1993. "Tests of Mean-Variance Efficiency of International Equity Markets." *Oxford Economic Papers* 45:403–421.

Epstein, L. G., and J. A. Hynes. 1983. "The Rate of Time Preference and Dynamic Economic Analysis." *Journal of Political Economy* 91:611–625.

Feenstra, R. 1986. "Functional Equivalence between Liquidity Costs and the Utility of Money." *Journal of Monetary Economics* 17:271–291.

Feldstein, M., and D. Hartman. 1979. "The Optimal Taxation of Foreign Source Investment Income." *Quarterly Journal of Economics* 93:613–629.

Feldstein, M., and C. Horioka. 1980. "Domestic Saving and International Capital Flows." *Economic Journal* 90:314–329.

Fender, J., and C. K. Yip. 1989. "Tariffs and Employment: An Intertemporal Approach." *Economic Journal* 99:806–817.

Fischer, S., and J. A. Frenkel. 1972. "Investment, the Two-Sector Model and Trade in Debt and Capital Goods." *Journal of International Economics* 2:211–233.

Fischer, S., and J. A. Frenkel. 1974. "Economic Growth and Stages of the Balance of Payments," in *Trade, Stability and Macroeconomics: Essays in Honor of Lloyd A. Metzler*, G. Horwich and P. A. Samuelson, eds. New York: Academic Press.

Fisher, W. 1995. "An Optimizing Analysis of the Effects of World Interest Rate Disturbances on the Open Economy Term Structure of Interest Rates." *Journal of International Money and Finance* 14:105–126.

Fleming, J. M. 1962. "Domestic Financial Policies under Fixed and Floating Exchange Rates." *IMF Staff Papers* 9:369–379.

Flemming, J. S. 1982. "Comment on J. P. Neary and D. D. Purvis, 'Sectoral Shocks in a Dependent Economy: Long-Run Adjustment and Short-Run Accommodation.'" *Scandinavian Journal of Economics* 84:255–257.

Flood, R. P., and N. P. Marion. 1982. "The Transmission of Disturbances under Alternative Exchange Rate Regimes with Optimal Indexing." *Quarterly Journal of Economics* 97:43–66.

Floyd, J. E. 1978. "The Asset Market Theory of the Exchange Rate: A Comment." *Scandinavian Journal of Economics* 80:100–103.

Foley, D. K., and M. Sidrauski. 1971. *Monetary and Fiscal Policy in a Growing Economy*. New York: Macmillan.

Frankel, J. A. 1979. "The Diversifiability of Exchange Risk." *Journal of International Economics* 9:379–393.

Frankel, J. A. 1986. "The Implications of Mean-Variance Optimization for Four Questions in International Macroeconomics." *Journal of International Money and Finance* 5:S53–S75.

Frankel, J. A. 1988. "Recent Estimates of Time-Variation in the Conditional Variance and in the Exchange-Rate Risk Premium." *Journal of International Money and Finance* 7:115–125.

French, K. R., and J. Poterba. 1991. "Investor Diversification and International Equity Markets." *American Economic Review* 81:222–226.

Frenkel, J. A., and A. Razin. 1985. "Government Spending, Debt, and International Economic Interdependence." *Economic Journal* 95:619–636.

Frenkel, J. A., and A. Razin. 1987, *Fiscal Policies and the World Economy*. Cambridge, MA: MIT Press.

Frenkel, J. A., A. Razin, and E. Sadka. 1991. *International Taxation in an Integrated World*. Cambridge, MA: MIT Press.

Frenkel, J. A., A. Razin, and C. W. Yuen. 1996. *Fiscal Policies and Growth in the World Economy*. Cambridge, MA: MIT Press.

Friedman, M. 1969. "The Optimum Quantity of Money," in *The Optimum Quantity of Money and Other Essays*, M. Friedman, ed. Chicago: Aldine.

Friedman, M. 1971. "The Revenue from Inflation." *Journal of Political Economy* 79:846–856.

Frisch, H. 1983. *Theories of Inflation*. Cambridge, U.K.: Cambridge University Press.

Froot, K., and K. Rogoff. 1995. "Perspectives on PPP and Long-Run Real Exchange Rates," in *Handbook of International Economics*, Vol. 3, G. Grossman and K. Rogoff, eds. Amsterdam: North-Holland.

Futagami, K., Y. Morita, and A. Shibata. 1993. "Dynamic Analysis of an Endogenous Growth Model with Public Capital." *Scandinavian Journal of Economics* 95:607–625.

Galor, O. 1996. "Convergence? Inferences from Theoretical Models." *Economic Journal* 106:1056–1069.

Gardner, G. W., and K. P. Kimbrough. 1990. "The Effects of Trade-Balance-Triggered Tariffs." *International Economic Review* 31:117–129.

Gavin, M. 1990. "Structural Adjustment to a Terms of Trade Disturbance: The Role of Relative Prices." *Journal of International Economics* 28:217–243.

Gavin, M. 1991. "Tariffs and the Current Account: On the Macroeconomics of Commercial Policy." *Journal of Economic Dynamics and Control* 15:27–52.

Gerlach, H. M. S. 1988. "World Business Cycles under Fixed and Flexible Exchange Rates." *Journal of Money, Credit, and Banking* 20:621–632.

Gertler, M., and E. Grinols. 1982. "Monetary Randomness and Investment." *Journal of Monetary Economics* 10:239–258.

Ghosh, A. 1991. "Strategic Aspects of Public Finance in a World with High Capital Mobility." *Journal of International Economics* 30:229–247.

Ghosh, A. 1995. "Intertemporal Tax Smoothing and the Government Budget Surplus: Canada and the United States." *Journal of Money, Credit, and Banking* 27:1033–1045.

Giavazzi, F., and C. Wyplosz. 1984. "The Real Exchange Rate, the Current Account, and the Speed of Adjustment," in *Exchange Rate Theory and Practice*, J. Bilson and R. Marston, eds. Chicago: University of Chicago Press.

Giovannini, A. 1990. "International Capital Mobility and Capital Income Taxation: Theory and Policy." *European Economic Review* 34:480–488.

Giovannini, A., and P. Jorion. 1987. "Interest Rates and Risk Premia in the Stock Market and in the Foreign Exchange Market." *Journal of International Money and Finance* 6:107–123.

Glick, R., and K. Rogoff. 1995. "Global versus Country-Specific Productivity Shocks and the Current Account." *Journal of Monetary Economics* 35:159–192.

Gordon, R. H. 1986. "Taxation of Investment and Savings in a World Economy." *American Economic Review* 76:1086–1102.

Gordon, R. H., and H. Varian. 1989. "Taxation of Asset Income in the Presence of a World Securities Market." *Journal of International Economics* 26:205–226.

Gould, J. P. 1968. "Adjustment Costs in the Theory of Investment of the Firm." *Review of Economic Studies* 35:47–56.

Graham, F. D. 1922. "International Trade under Depreciated Paper: The United States, 1862–79." *Quarterly Journal of Economics* 36:220–273.

Gramlich, E. M. 1994. "Infrastructure Investment: A Review Essay." *Journal of Economic Literature* 32:1176–1196.

Gray, J. A. 1976. "Wage Indexation: A Macroeconomic Approach." *Journal of Monetary Economics* 2:221–235.

Grier, K. B., and G. Tullock. 1989. "An Empirical Analysis of Cross-National Economic Growth, 1950–1980." *Journal of Monetary Economics* 24:259–276.

Grinols, E. L. 1996. "The Link between Domestic Investment and Domestic Savings in Open Economics: Evidence from Balanced Stochastic Growth." *Review of International Economics* 4:119–140.

Grinols, E. L., and S. J. Turnovsky. 1993. "Risk, the Financial Market, and Macroeconomic Equilibrium." *Journal of Economic Dynamics and Control* 17:1–36.

Grinols, E. L., and S. J. Turnovsky. 1994. "Exchange Rate Determination and Asset Prices in a Stochastic Small Open Economy." *Journal of International Economics* 36:75–97.

Grinols, E. L., and S. J. Turnovsky. 1997. "Risk, Optimal Government Finance, and Monetary Policies in a Growing Economy." *Economica*.

Grossman, G. M., and E. Helpman. 1991. *Innovation and Growth in the Global Economy*. Cambridge, MA: MIT Press.

Guidotti, P. E., and C. A. Vegh. 1993. "The Optimal Inflation Tax When Money Reduces Transactions Costs." *Journal of Monetary Economics* 31:189–205.

Hakkio, C. S., and A. Sibert. 1995. "The Foreign Exchange Risk Premium: Is It Real?" *Journal of Money, Credit, and Banking* 27:301–317.

Hall, R. E. 1978. "Stochastic Implications of the Life Cycle-Permanent Income Hypothesis: Theories and Evidence." *Journal of Political Economy* 86:971–987.

Hamada, K. 1966. "Strategic Aspects of Taxation of Foreign Investment Income." *Quarterly Journal of Economics* 80:361–375.

Hamada, K., 1974. "Alternative Exchange Rate Systems and the Interdependence of Monetary Policies," in *National Monetary Policies and the International Financial System*, R. Z. Aliber, ed. Chicago: University of Chicago Press.

Hamada, K. 1976. "A Strategic Analysis of Monetary Interdependence." *Journal of Political Economy* 84:677–700.

Hamada, K. 1986. "Strategic Aspects of Fiscal Interdependence." *Economic Studies Quarterly* 37:165–180.

Hanoch, G. 1977. "Risk Aversion and Consumer Preferences." *Econometrica* 45:413–426.

Hansen, G. D. 1985. "Indivisible Labor and the Business Cycle." *Journal of Monetary Economics* 16:309–327.

Hansen, L. P., and J. J. Heckman. 1996. "The Empirical Foundations of Calibration." *Journal of Economic Perspectives* 10:87–104.

Harberger, A. C. 1950. "Currency Depreciation, Income and the Balance of Trade." *Journal of Political Economy* 58:47–60.

Harrod, R. F. 1939. "An Essay in Dynamic Theory." *Economic Journal* 49:14–33.

Hayashi, F. 1982. "Tobin's Marginal *q*, Average *q*: A Neoclassical Interpretation." *Econometrica* 50:213–224.

Helpman, E., and A. Razin. 1979. "Towards a Consistent Comparison of Alternative Exchange Rate Regimes." *Canadian Journal of Economics* 12:394–409.

Helpman, E., and A. Razin. 1987. "Exchange Rate Management: Intertemporal Tradeoffs." *American Economic Review* 77:107–123.

Henderson, D. W. 1979. "Financial Policies in Open Economies." *American Economic Review, Papers and Proceedings* 69:232–239.

Hodrick, R. J. 1982. "On the Effects of Macroeconomic Policy in a Maximizing Model of a Small Open Economy." *Journal of Macroeconomics* 4:195–213.

Hodrick, R. J., and S. Srivastava. 1986. "The Covariation of Risk Premiums and Expected Future Spot Exchange Rates." *Journal of International Money and Finance* 5:5–21.

Ihori, T. 1991. "Capital Income Taxation in a World Economy: A Territorial System versus a Residence System." *Economic Journal* 101:958–965.

Jensen, R., and M. Thursby. 1990. "Tariffs with Private Information and Reputation." *Journal of International Economics* 29:43–67.

Johnson, H. G. 1953. "Optimum Tariffs and Retaliation." *Review of Economic Studies* 21:142–153.

Jones, C. 1995a. "Time Series Tests of Endogenous Growth Models." *Quarterly Journal of Economics* 110:495–527.

Jones, C. 1995b. "R&D Based Models of Economic Growth." *Journal of Political Economy* 103:759–784.

Jones, L. E., and R. E. Manuelli. 1990. "A Convex Model of Equilibrium Growth: Theory and Implications." *Journal of Political Economy* 98:1008–1038.

Jones, L. E., R. E. Manuelli, and P. E. Rossi. 1993. "Optimal Taxation in Models of Endogenous Growth." *Journal of Political Economy* 101:485–517.

Jones, R. W. 1971. "A Three Factor Model in Theory, Trade and History," in *Trade, Balance of Payments and Growth*, J. Bhagwati, R. W. Jones, R. A. Mundell, and J. Vanek, eds. Amsterdam: North-Holland.

Jones, R. W., and S. T. Easton. 1983. "Factor Intensities and Factor Substitution in General Equilibrium." *Journal of International Economics* 15:65–99.

Judd, K. L. 1985. "Redistributive Taxation in a Simple Perfect Foresight Model." *Journal of Public Economics* 28:59–83.

Kandel, S., and R. F. Staumbaugh. 1991. "Asset Returns and Intertemporal Preferences." *Journal of Monetary Economics* 27:39–71.

Karayalcin, C. 1995. "Heterogeneous Households, the Distribution of Wealth, and the Laursen-Metzler Effect." *Review of International Economics* 3:86–103.

Karras, G. 1994. "Government Spending and Private Consumption: Some International Evidence." *Journal of Money, Credit, and Banking* 26:9–22.

Kehoe, P. J. 1987. "Coordination of Fiscal Policies in a World Economy." *Journal of Monetary Economics* 19:349–376.

Kemp, M. C. 1966. "Monetary and Fiscal Policy under Alternative Assumptions about International Capital Mobility." *Economic Record* 42:598–607.

Kenen, P. B., and C. S. Voidodas. 1972. "Export Instability and Economic Growth." *Kyklos* 25:791–804.

Kharas, H. J. 1984. "The Long-Run Creditworthiness of Developing Countries: Theory and Practice." *Quarterly Journal of Economics* 99:415–439.

Kharas, H. J., and H. Shishido. 1987. "Foreign Borrowing and Macroeconomic Adjustment to External Shocks." *Journal of Development Economics* 25:125–148.

Kimbrough, K. P. 1986. "The Optimum Quantity of Money Rule in the Theory of Public Finance." *Journal of Monetary Economics* 18:277–284.

Kimbrough, K. P. 1991. "Optimal Taxation and Inflation in an Open Economy." *Journal of Economic Dynamics and Control* 15:179–196.

King, R. G., and S. Rebelo. 1990. "Public Policy and Economic Growth: Developing Neoclassical Implications." *Journal of Political Economy* 98:S126–S150.

Kirman, A. P. 1992. "Whom or What Does the Representative Individual Represent?" *Journal of Economic Perspectives* 6:117–136.

Kletzer, K. M. 1984. "Asymmetries of Information and LDC Borrowing with Sovereign Risk." *Economic Journal* 94:287–307.

Kletzer, K. M. 1987. "External Borrowing by LDCs: A Survey of Some Theoretical Issues," in *The State of Development Economics: Progress and Perspectives*, G. Ranis and T. P. Schultz, eds. Oxford: Blackwell.

Kletzer, K. M. 1994. "Sovereign Immunity and International Lending," in *Handbook of International Macroeconomics*, F. van der Ploeg, ed. Oxford: Blackwell.

Klundert, T. van de, and F. van der Ploeg. 1989. "Wage Rigidity and Capital Mobility in an Optimizing Model of a Small Open Economy." *De Economist* 137:47–75.

Kollmann, R. 1993. "Fiscal Policy, Technology Shocks and the U.S. Trade Balance Deficit." Manuscript, University of Montreal.

Krugman, P. 1982. "The Macroeconomics of Protection with a Floating Exchange Rate," in *Monetary Regimes and Protectionism*, K. Brunner and A. H. Meltzer, eds. Carnegie-Rochester Conference Series on Public Policy, Vol. 6. Amsterdam: North-Holland.

Krugman, P. 1991. "Target Zones and Exchange Rate Dynamics." *Quarterly Journal of Economics* 106:669–682.

Krugman, P., and M. H. Miller, eds. 1992. *Exchange Rate Targets and Currency Bands*. Cambridge, U.K.: Cambridge University Press.

Kydland, F. E., and E. C. Prescott. 1977. "Rules Rather Than Discretion: The Inconsistency of Optimal Plans." *Journal of Political Economy* 85:473–491.

Kydland, F. E., and E. C. Prescott. 1982. "Time to Build and Aggregate Fluctuations." *Econometrica* 50:1345–1370.

Kydland, F. E., and E. C. Prescott. 1996. "The Computational Experiment: An Econometric Tool." *Journal of Economic Perspectives* 10:69–86.

Laidler, D. E. W. 1977. "Expectations and the Behaviour of Price and Output under Flexible Exchange Rates." *Economica* 44:327–336.

Lapan, H. E., and W. Enders. 1980. "Random Disturbances and the Choice of Exchange Regimes in an Intergenerational Model." *Journal of International Economics* 10:263–283.

Laursen, S., and L. A. Metzler. 1950. "Flexible Exchange Rates and the Theory of Employment." *Review of Economics and Statistics* 32:281–299.

Lee, Y. 1995. "The Effects of Fiscal Policy in a Two-Country World Economy: An Intertemporal Analysis." *Journal of Money, Credit, and Banking* 27:135–159.

Levich, R. 1985. "Empirical Studies of Exchange Rates: Price Behavior, Rate Determination, and Market Efficiency," in *Handbook of International Economics*, Vol. 2, R. Jones and P. Kenen, eds. Amsterdam: North-Holland.

Levhari, D., and T. N. Srinivasan. 1969. "Optimal Savings under Uncertainty." *Review of Economic Studies* 36:153–163.

Levine, P., and A. Brociner. 1994. "Fiscal Policy Coordination and EMU: A Dynamic Game Theory Approach." *Journal of Economic Dynamics and Control* 18:699–729.

Lewbel, A. 1989. "Exact Aggregation and a Representative Consumer." *Quarterly Journal of Economics* 104:622–633.

Lewis, K. K. 1988. "Inflation Risk and Asset Market Disturbances: The Mean-Variance Model Revisited." *Journal of International Money and Finance* 7:273–288.

Lewis, K. K. 1995. "Puzzles in International Financial Markets," in *Handbook of International Economics*, Vol. 3, G. Grossman and K. Rogoff, eds. Amsterdam: North-Holland.

Lindbeck, A., and D. J. Snower. 1987. "Union Activity, Unemployment Persistence, and Wage-Unemployment Ratchets." *European Economic Review* 31:157–167.

Lintner, J. 1965. "The Valuation of Risky Assets and the Selection of Risky Investments in Stock Portfolios and Capital Budgets." *Review of Economics and Statistics* 47:13–37.

Lippi, M. 1988. "On the Dynamic Shape of Aggregate Error Correction Models." *Journal of Economic Dynamics and Control* 12:561–585.

Lipton, D., J. Poterba, J. Sachs, and L. Summers. 1982. "Multiple Shooting in Rational Expectations Models." *Econometrica* 50:1329–1333.

Lipton, D., and J. Sachs. 1983. "Accumulation and Growth in a Two-Country Model: A Simulation Approach." *Journal of International Economics* 15:135–159.

Lucas, R. E. 1967. "Adjustment Costs and the Theory of Supply." *Journal of Political Economy* 75:321–334.

Lucas, R. E. 1988. "On the Mechanics of Economic Development." *Journal of Monetary Economics* 22:3–42.

Madison, A. 1987. "Growth and Slowdown in Advanced Capitalist Economies: Techniques of Quantitative Assessment." *Journal of Economic Literature* 25:649–698.

Malliaris, A. G., and W. A. Brock. 1982. *Stochastic Methods in Economics and Finance*. Amsterdam: North-Holland.

Mankiw, N. G., D. Romer, and D. N. Weil. 1992. "A Contribution to the Empirics of Economic Growth." *Quarterly Journal of Economics* 107:407–437.

Mankiw, N. G., and S. P. Zeldes. 1991. "The Consumption of Stockholders and Nonstockholders." *Journal of Financial Economics* 29:97–112.

Mansoorian, A. 1993. "Habit Persistence and the Harberger-Laursen-Metzler Effect in an Infinite Horizon Model." *Journal of International Economics* 34:153–166.

Mantel, R., and A. M. Martirena-Mantel. 1982. "Exchange Rate Policies in a Small Economy: The Active Crawling Peg." *Journal of International Economics* 13:301–320.

Marion, N. P. 1984. "Nontraded Goods, Oil Price Increases and the Current Account." *Journal of International Economics* 16:29–44.

Mathieson, D. J. 1976. "Is There an Optimal Crawl?" *Journal of International Economics* 6:183–202.

Matsuyama, K. 1987. "Current Account Dynamics in a Finite Horizon Model." *Journal of International Economics* 23:299–313.

Matsuyama, K. 1988. "Terms of Trade, Factor Intensities, and the Current Account in a Life-Cycle Model." *Review of Economic Studies* 55:247–262.

McDougall, I. A. 1965. "Non-Traded Goods and the Transfer Problem." *Review of Economic Studies* 32:67–84.

McKenzie, I. M. 1982. *Essays on the Real Exchange Rate, Investment, and the Current Account*. Ph.D. Dissertation, MIT.

McKibbin, W. 1991. "A Multi-Sector Growth Model of the World Economy Focussing on the Linkages between OECD and Non-OECD Economies." Prepared for International Economic Conditions and Prospects Section, World Bank.

Meade, J. 1951. *The Theory of International Economic Policy*, Vol. 1, *The Balance of Payments*. London: Oxford University Press.

Mehra, R., and E. C. Prescott. 1985. "The Equity Premium: A Puzzle." *Journal of Monetary Economics* 15:145–161.

Merton, R. C. 1969. "Lifetime Portfolio Selection under Uncertainty: The Continuous-Time Case." *Review of Economics and Statistics* 51:247–257.

Merton, R. C. 1971. "Optimum Consumption and Portfolio Rules in a Continuous-Time Model." *Journal of Economic Theory* 3:373–413.

Merton, R. C. 1990. *Continuous-Time Finance*. Oxford: Blackwell.

Miller, M. H., and M. Salmon. 1985. "Policy Coordination and Dynamic Games," in *International Economic Policy Coordination*, W. H. Buiter and R. C. Marston, eds. Cambridge, U.K.: Cambridge University Press.

Mino, K. 1996. "Analysis of a Two-Sector Model of Endogenous Growth with Capital Income Taxation." *International Economic Review* 37:227–251.

Mossin, J. 1966. "Equilibrium in a Capital Asset Pricing Model."*Econometrica* 34:768–783.

Mulligan, C. B., and X. Sala-i-Martin. 1993. "Transitional Dynamics in Two-Sector Models of Endogenous Growth." *Quarterly Journal of Economics* 108:739–773.

Mundell, R. A. 1961. "Flexible Exchange Rates and Employment Policy." *Canadian Journal of Economics and Political Science* 27:509–517.

Mundell, R. A. 1962. "The Appropriate Use of Monetary and Fiscal Policy for Internal and External Stability." *IMF Staff Papers* 9:70–79.

Mundell, R. A. 1965. "Growth, Stability, and Inflationary Finance." *Journal of Political Economy* 73:97–109.

Murphy, R. G. 1986. "Productivity Shocks, Non-Traded Goods and Optimal Capital Accumulation." *European Economic Review* 30:1081–1095.

Murphy, R. G. 1989. "Stock Prices, Real Exchange Rates, and Optimal Capital Accumulation." *IMF Staff Papers* 36:102–129.

Mussa, M. 1978. "Dynamic Adjustment in the Heckscher-Ohlin-Samuelson Model." *Journal of Political Economy* 82:1191–1203.

Mussa, M. 1979. "Macroeconomic Interdependence and Exchange Rate Regime," in *International Economic Policy: Theory and Evidence*, R. Dornbusch and J. A. Frenkel, eds. Baltimore: Johns Hopkins University Press.

Muth, J. F. 1961. "Rational Expectations and the Theory of Price Movements." *Econometrica* 29:315–335.

Neary, J. P. 1978. "Short-Run Capital Specificity and the Pure Theory of International Trade." *Economic Journal* 86:488–510.

Neary, J. P., and D. Purvis. 1982. "Sectoral Shocks in a Dependent Economy: Long-Run Adjustment and Short-Run Adjustment." *Scandinavian Journal of Economics* 84:229–253.

Nielsen, S. B. 1992. "Capital Income Taxation in a Growing World Economy." *Zeitschrift für Nationalökonomie* 55:77–99.

Nielsen, S. B., and P. B. Sørensen. 1991. "Capital Income Taxation in a Growing Open Economy." *European Economic Review* 34:179–197.

Obstfeld, M. 1981. "Macroeconomic Policy, Exchange Rate Dynamics and Optimal Asset Accumulation." *Journal of Political Economy* 89:1142–1161.

Obstfeld, M. 1982. "Aggregate Spending and the Terms of Trade: Is There a Laursen-Metzler Effect?" *Quarterly Journal of Economics* 97:251–270.

Obstfeld, M. 1983. "Intertemporal Price Speculation and the Optimal Current Account Deficit." *Journal of International Money and Finance* 2:135–145.

Obstfeld, M. 1989. "Fiscal Deficits and Relative Prices in a Growing World Economy." *Journal of Monetary Economics* 23:461–484.

Obstfeld, M. 1994. "Risk-Taking, Global Diversification, and Growth." *American Economic Review* 84:1310–1329.

Obstfeld, M., and K. Rogoff. 1996. *Foundations of International Macroeconomics*. Cambridge, MA: MIT Press.

Obstfeld, M., and A. Stockman. 1985. "Exchange Rate Dynamics," in *Handbook of International Economics*, R. W. Jones and P. B. Kenen, eds. Amsterdam: North-Holland.

Ohlin, B. 1929. "The Reparation Problem: A Discussion. I. Transfer Difficulties, Real and Imagined." *Economic Journal* 39:172–178.

Osang, T., and A. Pereira. 1996. "Import Tariffs and Growth in a Small Open Economy." *Journal of Public Economics* 60:45–71.

Ostry, J. D. 1991. "Trade Liberalization in Developing Countries." *IMF Staff Papers* 38:447–479.

Oudiz, G., and J. Sachs. 1985. "International Policy Coordination in Dynamic Macroeconomic Models," in *International Economic Policy Coordination*, W. H. Buiter and R. C. Marston, eds. Cambridge, U.K.: Cambridge University Press.

Özler, S., and J. Harrigan. 1988. "Export Instability and Growth." Working Paper No. 486, UCLA.

Pearce, I. F. 1961. "The Problem of the Balance of Payments." *International Economic Review* 2:1–28.

Pecorino, P. 1993. "Tax Structure and Growth in a Model with Human Capital." *Journal of Public Economics* 52:251–271.

Persson, T. 1985. "Deficits and Intergenerational Welfare in Open Economies." *Journal of International Economics* 19:67–84.

Persson, T., and L. E. O. Svensson. 1985. "Current Account Dynamics and the Terms of Trade: Harberger-Laursen-Metzler Two Generations Later." *Journal of Political Economy* 93:43–65.

Persson, T., and G. Tabellini. 1990. *Macroeconomic Policy, Credibility, and Politics.* Chur, Switzerland: Harwood Academic.

Phelps, E. S. 1973. "Inflation in the Theory of Public Finance." *Swedish Journal of Economics* 75:67–82.

Ploeg, F. van der. 1996. "Budgetary Policies, Foreign Indebtedness, the Stock Market, and Economic Growth." *Oxford Economic Papers* 48:382–396.

Quah, D. 1996. "Convergence Empirics Across Economies with (Some) Capital Mobility." *Journal of Economic Growth* 1:95–124.

Razin, A. 1984. "Capital Movements, Intersectoral Resource Shifts and the Trade Balance." *European Economic Review* 26:135–152.

Razin, A. 1990. "Fiscal Policies and the Integrated World Stock Market." *Journal of International Economics* 29:109–122.

Razin, A., and E. Sadka. 1991a. "International Fiscal Policy Coordination and Competition: An Exposition." NBER Working Paper No. 3779.

Razin, A., and E. Sadka. 1991b. "International Tax Competition and Gains from Tax Harmonization." *Economic Letters* 37:69–76.

Razin, A., and C. W. Yuen. 1992. "Convergence in Growth Rates: The Role of Capital Mobility and International Taxation." NBER Working Paper No. 4214.

Razin, A., and C. W. Yuen. 1996. "Capital Income Taxation and Long-Run Growth: New Perspectives." *Journal of Public Economics* 59:239–263.

Rebelo, S. 1991. "Long-Run Policy Analysis and Long-Run Growth." *Journal of Political Economy* 99:500–521.

Rebelo, S. 1992. "Growth in Open Economies," in A. H. Meltzer and C. I. Plosser, eds. Carnegie-Rochester Conference Series on Public Policy, Vol. 36. Amsterdam: North-Holland.

Riezman, R. 1991. "Dynamic Tariffs with Asymmetric Information." *Journal of International Economics* 30:267–283.

Robinson, J. 1937. *Essays on the Theory of Employment.* Oxford: Blackwell.

Rogoff, K. 1985. "Can International Monetary Policy Cooperation Be Counterproductive?" *Journal of International Economics* 18:199–217.

Romer, P. M. 1986. "Increasing Returns and Long-Run Growth." *Journal of Political Economy* 94:1002–1037.

Romer, P. M. 1990. "Endogenous Technological Change." *Journal of Political Economy* 98:S71–S103.

Romer, P. M. 1994. "The Origins of Endogenous Growth." *Journal of Economic Perspectives* 8:3–22.

Ryder, H. E., and G. M Heal. 1973. "Optimal Growth with Temporally Dependent Preferences." *Review of Economic Studies* 40:1–31.

Sachs, J. 1984. "Theoretical Issues in International Borrowing." *Princeton Studies in International Finance* 54.

Sachs, J., and D. Cohen. 1982. "LDC Borrowing with Default Risk." NBER Working Paper No. 925.

Saint-Paul, G. 1992. "Fiscal Policy in an Endogenous Growth Model." *Quarterly Journal of Economics* 107:1243–1259.

Salter, W. E. G. 1959. "Internal and External Balance: The Role of Price and Expenditure Effects." *Economic Record* 35:226–238.

Samuelson, P. A. 1958. "An Exact Consumption Loan Model of Interest with or without the Social Contrivance of Money." *Journal of Political Economy* 66:467–482.

Samuelson, P. A. 1964. "Theoretical Notes on Trade Problems." *Review of Economics and Statistics* 46:145–154.

Sandmo, A. 1970. "The Effect of Uncertainty on Savings Decisions." *Review of Economic Studies* 37:353–360.

Schmid, M. 1982. "Devaluation: Keynesian and Trade Models and the Monetary Approach: The Role of Nominal and Real Wage Rigidity." *European Economic Review* 17:27–50.

Scitovsky, T. 1942. "A Reconsideration of the Theory of Tariffs." *Review of Economic Studies* 9:89–110.

Sen, P. 1994. "Savings, Investment, and the Current Account," in *Handbook of International Macroeconomics*, F. van der Ploeg, ed. Oxford: Blackwell.

Sen, P., and S. J. Turnovsky. 1989a. "Deterioration of the Terms of Trade and Capital Accumulation: A Re-examination of the Laursen-Metzler Effect." *Journal of International Economics* 26:227–250.

Sen, P., and S. J. Turnovsky. 1989b. "Tariffs, Capital Accumulation and the Current Account in a Small Open Economy." *International Economic Review* 30:811–831.

Sen, P., and S. J. Turnovsky. 1990. "Investment Tax Credit in an Open Economy." *Journal of Public Economics* 42:277–309.

Sharpe, W. F. 1964. "Capital Asset Prices: A Theory of Market Equilibrium under Conditions of Risk." *Journal of Finance* 19:425–442.

Sibert, A. 1989. "The Risk Premium in the Foreign Exchange Market." *Journal of Money, Credit, and Banking* 21:49–65.

Sibert, A. 1990. "Taxing Capital in a Large Open Economy." *Journal of Public Economics* 41:297–317.

Sidrauski, M. 1967a. "Inflation and Economic Growth." *Journal of Political Economy* 75:796–810.

Sidrauski, M. 1967b. "Rational Choice and Patterns of Growth in a Monetary Economy." *American Economic Review* 57:534–544.

Sims, C. A. 1996. "Macroeconomics and Methodology." *Journal of Economic Perspectives* 10:105–120.

Sinn, H. W. 1987. *Capital Income Taxation and Resource Allocation*. Amsterdam: North-Holland.

Sinn, H. W. 1990. "Tax Harmonization and Tax Competition in Europe." *European Economic Review* 34:489–504.

Slemrod, J. 1988. "Effects of Taxation with International Capital Mobility," in *Uneasy Compromise: Problems of a Hybrid Income-Consumption Tax*, H. Aaron, H. Galper, and J. A. Pechman, eds. Washington, D.C.: Brookings Institution.

Smith, W. T. 1996. "Taxes, Uncertainty, and Long-Term Growth." *European Economic Review* 40:1647–1664.

Solnik, B. H. 1974. "An Equilibrium Model of the International Capital Market." *Journal of Economic Theory* 8:500–524.

Solow, R. M. 1956. "A Contribution to the Theory of Economic Growth." *Quarterly Journal of Economics* 70:65–94.

Solow, R. M. 1994. "Perspectives on Economic Growth." *Journal of Economic Perspectives* 8:45–54.

Sørensen, P. B. 1990. "Optimal Capital Taxation in a Small Capital-Importing Economy," in *Public Finance, Trade, and Development*, V. Tanzi, ed. Detroit: Wayne State University Press.

Stockman, A. 1978. "Risk, Information, and Forward Exchange Rates," in *The Economics of Exchange Rates*, J. A. Frenkel and H. G. Johnson, eds. Reading, MA: Addison-Wesley.

Stockman, A., and L. Svensson. 1987. "Capital Flows, Investment, and Exchange Rates." *Journal of Monetary Economics* 19:171–201.

Stockman, A., and L. Tesar. 1995. "Tastes and Technology in a Two-Country Model of the Business Cycle: Explaining International Comovements." *American Economic Review* 85:168–185.

Stokey, N. L., and S. Rebelo. 1995. "Growth Effects of Flat-Rate Taxes." *Journal of Political Economy* 103:519–550.

Stulz, R. M. 1981. "A Model of International Asset Pricing." *Journal of Financial Economics* 9:383–406.

Stulz, R. M. 1983. "The Demand for Foreign Bonds." *Journal of International Economics* 15:225–238.

Stulz, R. M. 1984. "Currency Preferences, Purchasing Power Risks, and the Determination of Exchange Rates in an Optimizing Model." *Journal of Money, Credit, and Banking* 16:302–316.

Stulz, R. M. 1986. "Interest Rates and Monetary Policy Uncertainty." *Journal of Monetary Economics* 17:331–347.

Stulz, R. M. 1987. "An Equilibrium Model of Exchange Rate Determination and Asset Pricing with Nontraded Goods and Imperfect Information." *Journal of Political Economy* 95:1024–1040.

Stulz, R. M. 1988. "Capital Mobility and the Current Account." *Journal of International Money and Finance* 7:167–180.

Stulz, R. M. 1994. "International Portfolio Choice and Asset Pricing." NBER Working Paper No. 4645.

Summers, L. H. 1991. "The Scientific Illusion in Empirical Macroeconomics." *Scandinavian Journal of Economics* 93:129–148.

Svensson, L. E. O. 1982. "Comment on M. Bruno, 'Adjustment and Structural Change under Supply Shocks.'" *Scandinavian Journal of Economics* 84:223–227.

Svensson, L. E. O., and A. Razin. 1983. "The Terms of Trade and the Current Account: The Harberger-Laursen-Metzler Effect." *Journal of Political Economy* 91:97–125.

Swan, T. W. 1956. "Economic Growth and Capital Accumulation." *Economic Record* 32:334–361.

Swan, T. W. 1960. "Economic Control in a Dependent Economy." *Economic Record* 36:51–66.

Taussig, F. W. 1917. "International Trade under Depreciated Paper. A Contribution to Theory." *Quarterly Journal of Economics* 31:380–403.

Taussig, F. W. 1920. "Germany's Reparation Payments." *American Economic Review* 10:31–49.

Taylor, J. B. 1985. "International Coordination in the Design of Macroeconomic Policy Rules." *European Economic Review* 28:53–82.

Tesar, L. 1991. "Savings, Investment, and International Capital Flows." *Journal of International Economics* 31:55–78.

Tesar, L., and I. Werner. 1995. "Home Bias and High Turnover." *Journal of International Money and Finance* 14:467–492.

Tobin, J. 1965. "Money and Economic Growth." *Econometrica* 33:671–684.

Tobin, J. 1968. "Notes on Optimal Monetary Growth." *Journal of Political Economy* 76:833–859.

Turnovsky, S. J. 1974. "Technological and Price Uncertainty in a Ricardian Model of International Trade." *Review of Economic Studies* 47:201–217.

Turnovsky, S. J. 1977. *Macroeconomic Analysis and Stabilization Policy*. Cambridge, U.K.: Cambridge University Press.

Turnovsky, S. J. 1985. "Domestic and Foreign Disturbances in an Optimizing Model of Exchange Rate Determination." *Journal of International Money and Finance* 4:151–171.

Turnovsky, S. J. 1987. "Optimal Monetary Growth with Accommodating Fiscal Policy in a Small Open Economy." *Journal of International Money and Finance* 6:179–193.

Turnovsky, S. J. 1988. "The Gains from Fiscal Cooperation in the Two-Commodity Real Trade Model." *Journal of International Economics* 25:111–127.

Turnovsky, S. J. 1991. "Tariffs and Sectoral Adjustments in an Open Economy." *Journal of Economic Dynamics and Control* 15:53–89.

Turnovsky, S. J. 1992. "Alternative Forms of Government Expenditure Financing: A Comparative Welfare Analysis." *Economica* 59:235–252.

Turnovsky, S. J. 1993. "The Impact of Terms of Trade Shocks on a Small Open Economy: A Stochastic Analysis." *Journal of International Money and Finance* 12:278–297.

Turnovsky, S. J. 1995. *Methods of Macroeconomic Dynamics*. Cambridge, MA: MIT Press.

Turnovsky, S. J. 1996a. "Fiscal Policy, Growth, and Macroeconomic Performance in a Small Open Economy." *Journal of International Economics* 40:41–66.

Turnovsky, S. J. 1996b. "Endogenous Growth in a Dependent Economy with Traded and Nontraded Capital." *Review of International Economics* 4:300–321.

Turnovsky, S. J. 1996c. "Fiscal Policy, Adjustment Costs, and Endogenous Growth." *Oxford Economic Papers* 48:361–381.

Turnovsky, S. J. 1996d. "Optimal Tax, Debt, and Expenditure Policies in a Growing Economy." *Journal of Public Economics* 60:21–44.

Turnovsky, S. J. 1997. "Public and Private Capital in an Endogenously Growing Open Economy." in *Dynamics, Economic Growth, and International Trade*, B. S. Jensen and K. Y. Wong, eds. Ann Arbor, MI: University of Michigan Press.

Turnovsky, S. J., and M. Bianconi. 1992. "The International Transmission of Tax Policies in a Dynamic World Economy." *Review of International Economics* 1:49–72.

Turnovsky, S. J., and W. A. Brock. 1980. "Time Consistency and Optimal Government Policies in Perfect Foresight Equilibrium." *Journal of Public Economics* 13:183–212.

Turnovsky, S. J., and W. H. Fisher. 1995. "The Composition of Government Expenditure and Its Consequences for Macroeconomic Performance." *Journal of Economic Dynamics and Control* 19:747–786.

Turnovsky, S. J., and E. L. Grinols. 1996. "Optimal Government Finance Policy and Exchange Rate Management in a Stochastically Growing Open Economy." *Journal of International Money and Finance* 15:687–716.

Turnovsky, S. J., and P. Sen. 1991. "Fiscal Policy, Capital Accumulation, and Debt in an Open Economy." *Oxford Economic Papers* 43:1–24.

Turnovsky, S. J., and P. Sen. 1995. "Investment in a Two-Sector Dependent Economy." *Journal of Japanese and International Economies* 9:29–55.

Uzawa, H. 1968. "Time Preference, the Consumption Function and Optimum Asset Holdings," in *Value, Capital and Growth: Papers in Honour of Sir John Hicks*, J. N. Wolfe, ed. Chicago: Aldine.

Voidodas, C. S. 1974. "The Effect of Foreign Exchange Instability on Growth." *Review of Economics and Statistics* 56:410–412.

Waugh, F. V. 1944. "Does the Consumer Benefit from Price Instability?" *Quarterly Journal of Economics* 58:602–614.

Weil, P. 1989. "Overlapping Families of Infinitely-Lived Agents." *Journal of Public Economics* 38:183–198.

Wijnbergen, S. van. 1985. "Optimal Capital Accumulation and the Allocation of Investment between Traded and Nontraded Sectors in Oil-Producing Countries." *Scandinavian Journal of Economics* 87:89–101.

Wijnbergen, S. van. 1987. "Tariffs, Employment, and the Current Account: Real Wage Resistance and the Macroeconomics of Protection." *International Economic Review* 28:691–706.

Wincoop, E. van. 1993. "Structural Adjustment and the Construction Sector." *European Economic Review* 17:177–201.

Wong, K. Y. 1995. *International Trade in Goods and Factor Mobility*. Cambridge, MA: MIT Press.

Yi, K. M. 1993. "Can Government Purchases Explain the Recent U.S. Net Export Deficits?" *Journal of International Economics* 35:201–225.

Yotopoulos, P. A., and J. B. Nugent. 1976. *Economics of Development: Empirical Investigations*. New York: Harper & Row.

Young, L. 1991. "Optimal Tariffs: A Generalization." *International Economic Review* 32:341–372.

Author Index

Abel, A., 54, 76, 98
Adler, M., 370, 373, 425, 432, 448
Agénor, P. R., 5
Aghion, P., 154
Aizenman, J., 321, 421
Anderson, J., 357
Arnold, L., 329
Arrow, K. J., 283, 321
Aschauer, D. A., 252, 283, 285, 291
Asea, P. K., 149, 326
Auerbach, A. J., 141
Aukrust, O., 149

Backus, D. K., 84, 154, 211, 252, 253, 432, 448, 450, 452, 461, 462
Bailey, M. J., 31
Balassa, B., 102
Bardhan, P. K., 43
Barro, R. J., 10, 151, 154, 155, 156, 165, 177, 178, 179, 205, 206, 252, 285, 320
Basar, T., 282, 302, 314, 318
Baxter, M., 211, 232, 245, 261, 283, 321, 432, 448, 450, 451, 452, 453, 461
Bazdarich, B., 103
Bean, C. R., 84, 349
Benavie, A., 325
Bertola, G., 370
Bhandari, J. S., 43, 93, 421, 422
Bianconi, M., 157, 211, 212, 251, 252, 289, 321
Black, S. W., 421
Blanchard, O. J., 3, 23, 42, 54, 56, 98, 210
Bond, E. W., 153, 206
Bourguignon, F., 325
Bovenberg, A., 76, 212
Boyer, R., 421
Branson, W. H., 210, 243, 284, 291, 421
Brociner, A., 280
Brock, P. L., 29, 32, 33, 55, 87, 98, 103, 104, 115, 124, 144, 145, 149, 167, 191, 205, 206, 461
Brock, W. A., 4, 325, 328
Bruno, M., 102, 123, 124, 150
Buiter, W. H., 3, 41, 55, 98, 210, 279, 280

Caballé, J., 206
Cairnes, J. E., 102, 149
Calvo, G. A., 93, 260
Canova, F., 211
Cantor, R., 211
Canzoneri, M. B., 279
Casella, A., 321
Chamley, C., 77, 362
Chan, K. S., 87
Chari, V. V., 280, 305, 321
Chow, G. C., 328
Christensen, T. A., 212
Clarke, H. R., 54, 422
Clower, R., 20
Cohen, D., 43, 54
Cooley, T. F., 234, 448

Cooper, R. N., 43, 54
Corden, W. M., 102, 149, 210, 243, 284, 291
Correia, I., 54, 77, 362
Corsetti, G., 325, 363
Crucini, M. J., 261, 432, 448, 450, 452, 461

Danthine, J. P., 448, 450, 451, 453, 454, 461, 462
De Gregorio, J., 149
De Long, J. B., 141
Dellas, H., 211
Devereux, M. B., 39, 183, 211, 253, 280, 282, 297, 299, 305, 319, 321, 432, 439, 462
Diamond, P. A., 41
Diaz Alejandro, C. F., 102
Dixit, A. K., 328
Donaldson, J. B., 448, 450, 451, 453, 454, 461, 462
Dornbusch, R., 2, 8, 18, 41, 124, 150
Driskill, R., 40
Dumas, B., 370, 373, 425, 432, 448

Easterly, W., 155
Easton, S. T., 144
Eaton, J., 43, 54, 150, 279, 325, 376
Edwards, J. H. Y., 179
Edwards, S., 57, 93
Eichengreen, B. J., 87, 89, 93
Eicher, T., 154, 409
Eisner, R., 58
Enders, W., 376
Engel, C. M., 55, 57, 87, 123, 374, 393, 406, 422
Epstein, L. G., 39, 211

Feenstra, R., 20, 381
Feldstein, M., 66, 251, 252, 280, 403, 451, 452
Fender, J., 57
Fischer, S., 2, 8, 18, 23, 102, 103, 124, 149, 206
Fisher, W., 43, 46, 283, 285, 321
Flemming, J. M., 1, 124
Flood, R. P., 421
Floyd, J. E., 422
Foley, D. K., 384
Frankel, J. A., 374, 409, 422
French, K. R., 432
Frenkel, J. A., 5, 10, 41, 48, 55, 76, 77, 102, 103, 124, 149, 157, 206, 210, 211, 212, 216, 218, 253, 370, 421
Friedman, M., 8, 19, 31, 376, 414
Frisch, H., 149
Froot, K., 53
Futagami, K., 177

Galor, O., 152, 165
Gardner, G. W., 253, 262, 276
Gavin, M., 55, 57, 87, 143
Gerlach, H. M. S., 211

Gersovitz, M., 43, 54
Gertler, M., 325, 422
Ghosh, A., 280, 299, 320, 321
Giavazzi, F., 56
Giovannini, A., 149, 212, 216, 374
Glick, R., 403, 448, 454
Gordon, R. H., 251, 461
Gould, J. P., 58
Graham, F. D., 102, 149
Gramlich, E. M., 283
Gray, J. A., 421
Greenwood, J., 283
Gregory, A., 462
Grier, K. B., 155
Grinols, E. L., 67, 325, 326, 346, 373, 378, 422, 448, 452
Grossman, G. M., 10, 152, 154, 279
Guidotti, P. E., 54

Hakkio, C. S., 374
Hall, R. E., 320
Hamada, K., 279, 280, 305, 319
Hanoch, G., 357
Hansen, G. D., 234, 449
Hansen, L. P., 462
Haque, N. U., 43, 93
Harberger, A. C., 83, 354
Harrigan, J., 446
Harrod, R. F., 153
Hartman, D., 251, 280
Hayashi, F., 58, 98
Heckman, J. J., 462
Heal, G. M., 54
Helpman, E., 10, 152, 154, 375
Henderson, D. W., 279, 421
Hines, J. A., 141
Hodrick, R. J., 54, 374
Horioka, C., 66, 252, 403, 451, 452
Howitt, P., 154
Hynes, J. A., 39, 211

Ihori, T., 212

Jensen, R., 279
Johnson, H. J., 279
Jones, C., 154, 155
Jones, L. E., 155, 205, 432
Jones, R. W., 143, 144
Jorion, P., 374
Judd, K. L., 77

Kandel, S., 408
Kahn, C. M., 3, 54
Karayalcin, C., 84
Karras, G., 283
Kehoe, P., 154, 211, 252, 253, 280, 305, 320, 321, 432, 448, 450, 452, 461, 462
Kehoe, T., 154
Kemp, M. C., 210
Kenen, P. B., 446
Kharas, H. J., 42

Kimbrough, K. P., 54, 253, 262, 276
King, R. G., 155, 232, 245, 283, 321, 461
Kingston, G. H., 54, 422
Kirman, A. P., 7
Kletzer, K. M., 43, 54, 55, 57, 87, 123, 280
Klundert, T. van de, 54
Kollmann, R., 211, 448, 451, 453
Krueger, T., 149
Krugman, P., 87, 370
Kurz, M., 283, 321
Kydland, F. E., 58, 211, 252, 253, 321, 432, 448, 450, 452, 461, 462

Laidler, D. E. W., 422
Lapan, H. E., 376
Laursen, S., 83
Lee, J. W., 155
Lee, Y., 284
Levhari, D., 351, 370
Levich, R., 53
Levine, P., 280
Lewbel, A., 7
Lewis, K. K., 53, 54, 374
Lindbeck, A., 56
Lintner, J., 410
Lippi, M., 7
Lipton, D., 210, 211, 251, 252
Love, D. R., 183
Lucas, R. E., 58, 153, 182, 183, 206

Madison, A., 432
Malliaris, A. G., 4, 325, 328
Mankiw, N. G., 152, 165, 408
Mansoorian, A., 54
Mantel, R., 54
Manuelli, R. E., 155, 205, 432
Martirena-Mantel, A. M., 54
Marion, N. P., 103, 124, 421
Mark, N. C., 211
Marston, R. C., 279
Mathieson, D. J., 31, 422
Matsuyama, K., 57, 98, 103
McCafferty, S. A., 40
McDougall, I. A., 102, 149
McKenzie, I. M., 123
McKibbin, W., 8
Meade, J., 276
Mehra, R., 408
Mendoza, E. G., 149
Merton, R. C., 325, 346
Metzler, L. A., 83
Miller, M. H., 318, 370
Mino, K., 155
Montiel, P. J., 5
Morita, Y., 177
Mossin, J., 410
Mulligan, C. B., 153, 183, 205
Mundell, R. A., 1, 87, 422
Murphy, R. G., 103, 124, 150
Mussa, M., 143, 210
Muth, J. F., 6

Neary, J. P., 124, 143, 149
Nielsen, S. B., 76, 212
Nugent, J. B., 446

Obstfeld, M., 5, 13, 23, 24, 37, 40, 43, 48, 65, 67, 84, 85, 103, 123, 124, 326, 349, 370, 373, 409, 425, 437, 439, 448, 461
Ohlin, B., 102, 149
Olsder, G. J., 282, 302, 314, 318
Osang, T., 204
Ostry, J. D., 123
Oudiz, G., 311
Özler, S., 446

Pearce, I. F., 102
Pecorino, P., 183
Pereira, A., 204
Persson, T., 41, 57, 84, 85, 320, 349
Phelps, E. S., 8, 34, 376, 415
Pindyck, R. S., 328
Ploeg, F. van der, 43, 54, 155
Poterba, J., 252, 432
Prescott, E. C., 58, 321, 408, 462
Purvis, D., 124, 149

Quah, D., 152, 165

Razin, A., 5, 10, 41, 48, 55, 57, 76, 77, 84, 85, 102, 123, 155, 157, 165, 205, 210, 211, 212, 216, 218, 253, 349, 370, 375
Rebelo, S., 153, 155, 156, 167, 170, 338, 432, 461
Riezman, R., 279
Riley, J., 357
Robinson, J., 92, 276, 279
Rodrigues, A. P., 374
Rogoff, K., 5, 48, 53, 65, 67, 320, 370, 403, 448, 454, 461
Romer, D., 152, 165
Romer, P. M., 152, 153, 154, 205
Rossi, P. E., 155
Rotemberg, J. J., 210, 243, 284, 291
Ryder, H. E., 54

Sachs, J., 43, 54, 124, 210, 211, 251, 252, 311
Sadka, J., 10, 76, 157, 211, 212, 216, 218
Saint-Paul, G., 363
Saito, M., 432
Sala-i-Martin, X., 10, 151, 153, 154, 165, 178, 179, 183, 205, 252
Salmon, M., 318
Salter, W. E. G., 102
Samuelson, P. A., 41, 102
Sandmo, A., 205, 351, 370
Santos, M. S., 206
Schmid, M., 210, 284, 291
Scitovsky, T., 279
Sen, P., 55, 56, 57, 76, 84, 85, 86, 87, 88, 92, 98, 103, 149, 345, 349

Sharpe, W. F., 410
Shi, S., 39, 211
Shibata, A., 177
Shishido, H., 42
Sibert, A., 212, 374, 422
Sidrauski, M., 20, 28, 384, 398
Sims, C. A., 462
Sinn, H. W., 76, 212
Slemrod, J., 157, 211, 325
Smith, G., 439, 462
Smith, W. T., 325
Snower, D. J., 56
Solnik, B. H., 425
Solow, R. M., 151, 153
Sørenson, P. B., 76, 77, 212
Srinivasan, T. N., 351, 370
Srivastava, S., 374
Stambaugh, R. F., 408
Stockman, A., 84, 124, 254, 403, 422, 453, 454, 459, 462
Stokey, N. L., 155
Strotz, R. H., 58
Stulz, R. M., 84, 325, 326, 348, 349, 370, 371, 373, 422, 425, 432, 448, 455
Summers, L. H., 7, 56, 141, 252
Svensson, L. E. O., 41, 57, 84, 85, 123, 124, 349, 403, 453, 454, 459
Swan, T. W., 102, 151

Tabellini, G., 320
Taylor, J. B., 311
Taussig, F. W., 102, 149
Teles, P., 54
Tcsar, L., 254, 432, 452, 462
Thursby, M., 279
Tobin, J., 31, 422
Tullock, G., 155
Turnovsky, S. J., 2, 4, 5, 6, 24, 29, 31, 32, 33, 39, 40, 43, 49, 54, 55, 56, 57, 65, 66, 69, 76, 84, 85, 86, 87, 88, 92, 93, 98, 103, 104, 124, 144, 145, 149, 155, 157, 167, 170, 174, 177, 178, 179, 191, 206, 210, 211, 212, 243, 245, 251, 252, 280, 283, 284, 285, 289, 291, 305, 307, 310, 321, 325, 326, 345, 346, 348, 349, 357, 363, 373, 378, 401, 409, 422, 448

Uzawa, H., 24, 37

Varion, H., 461
Vegh, C. A., 54
Voidodas, C. S., 446

Wang, P., 153, 206
Waugh, F. V., 357
Weil, P., 42, 152, 165, 250
Werner, I., 432
Wijnbergen, S. van, 87, 124
Wincoop, E. van, 103, 124, 145
Wong, K. Y., 279
Wyplosz, C., 56

Yi, K. M., 211
Yip, C. K., 57, 153, 206
Yotopoulos, P. A., 446
Young, L., 279
Yuen, C. W., 5, 41, 48, 55, 76, 77, 155, 165, 205, 210, 212, 370

Zeldes, S. P., 408

Subject Index

Arbitrage condition, 22, 23, 60, 79, 91, 107, 112, 122, 127, 161, 170, 173, 180, 183–184, 192, 222, 224, 234, 250, 332, 342

Assets
  accumulation of, 2, 38, 59, 64, 78, 109, 116, 123, 151, 156, 166, 171, 194, 217, 221, 223–224, 230, 242–243, 248, 256, 260, 266, 292, 336, 354, 403, 425, 429, 433–434, 447, 458
  beta coefficients, 410–411
  consumption-CAPM, 409–411
  costs of holding foreign assets, 8
  dynamics of, 191–197
  mean growth rate of, 388
  net asset position, 435–436
  prices of, 190–191, 196, 333, 337, 373, 375, 377
  return on, 21, 156, 332, 341, 373, 377, 383, 405
  tradable assets, 103
  variance of growth rate, 388

Balance of payments, 67, 102, 134, 339, 386
Balance of trade, 17, 25, 27, 64, 87, 89, 92–93, 211, 223, 237, 243, 272–277, 279, 284, 312, 354–355, 435–436, 444, 449
"Beggar-thy-neighbor" policies, 279
Bimatrix game, 12, 282, 301–305, 318
  equilibrium in, 301, 303
  over government consumption expenditure, 303
  over government production expenditure, 305
  and noncooperative behavior, 301–305
Blanchard model, 42
Bonds
  accumulation of, 25–27, 58, 64–66, 68, 73–75, 84, 92–93, 105–106, 108, 112, 114, 116–117, 122, 126–127, 131, 137, 158, 163–164, 171, 183, 262, 266, 270, 338, 352, 363
  bond-money ratio, 385, 399
  cost of holding, 40
  demand for, 40
  imperfect bond market, 157
  imperfect substitutability between domestic and foreign bonds, 40
  nontraded bonds, 40, 333–334, 377
  perfect bond market, 183, 193, 261, 264
  rate of return on, 20, 22, 25, 60, 69, 107, 128, 159–161, 165, 170, 175–176, 199, 337–338, 342, 373, 379, 382–383, 390, 400, 402, 407, 409, 418
  risk parity between domestic and foreign bonds, 334
  social rate of return on, 176
  traded bonds, 18, 20–21, 25, 40, 64, 74, 89, 106, 113, 121, 123, 157, 163–165, 184, 194, 261, 263, 270, 272–273, 333, 352, 358, 377, 403, 405–406, 408, 418
  transitional dynamics of, 165

Brownian motion (Wiener process), 4, 326, 328–330, 373, 377–378, 395, 425

Capital
  capital gain, 60, 107, 160, 332, 394, 403
  capital-consumption ratio, 398
  capital-labor ratio, 67–69, 73, 88, 107, 117–120, 242, 271, 273
  equilibrium dynamics of, 109–112
  growth rate of, 161, 165–166, 168–169, 172, 174, 182, 187–188, 192, 195, 198, 200, 438
  human capital, 182–183
  imperfect mobility of, 29, 40, 142–143, 284
  initial distribution of world capital stock, 236–237
  marginal physical product of, 67–69, 74, 86, 91, 105, 107, 112, 114, 118, 121, 144–145, 157, 159–161, 165, 184–186, 191, 199–200, 215, 218–220, 225, 234, 242, 244, 255, 266–267, 285–286, 289, 290–292, 308, 334, 437
  nontraded capital, 9–10, 104–106, 109–112, 114, 123–126, 128–129, 132, 142, 177, 182–183, 187–188, 193–205
  perfect capital markets, 24, 42, 56, 62, 76, 78, 156, 179, 182
  perfect mobility of, 9, 60, 103, 107, 144, 183, 213, 221–222, 253–254, 261, 403, 426
  perfectly integrated capital markets, 213, 221, 255, 403, 426
  private vs. public capital, 177
  rate of return on, 60, 112, 114, 170, 182, 199, 213–214, 225, 242, 254–256, 290, 292, 296, 299, 304–305, 334, 337–338, 390, 400, 418, 427
  relative price of installed capital, 253–254
  sectoral capital intensity, 104, 109–110, 112–121, 123–125, 128–133, 135, 137–138, 140, 142, 145–146, 185–205
  shadow price of, 59, 61–62, 64, 71, 81, 90–91
  tax-adjusted price of, 167
  traded capital, 9–10, 104–106, 109–114, 123–124, 126, 127, 142, 156–157, 177, 182–183, 187–188, 190, 192–196, 199, 202–205, 408, 455
  traded-nontraded capital ratio, 186, 199–202
  transitional dynamics of, 187–191

Capital accumulation, 9–10, 39, 48, 55–57, 59, 64–66, 68, 73–75, 81, 84–85, 93, 101, 103–104, 111, 113–114, 116, 121, 125–126, 131, 137, 142, 145, 153, 158, 170–171, 179, 183–184, 225, 230, 243, 244, 246, 253, 255, 272, 276, 281, 290–291, 193–294, 319, 362, 404, 425, 444, 447, 449
  and long-run growth, 151–157
  one-good model of, 57–77
  two-good model of, 77–83

Subject Index

Cash-in-advance constraint, 20
  interest elastic cash-in-advance constraint, 383
Centralized vs. decentralized economy
  in one-sector endogenous growth model, 173–176, 203–204
  in model with noncooperative strategic behavior, 300
  in stochastic endogenous growth model, 360–361, 365–366
Coalitions, 312–314
Commercial policy, 279
Complete markets, 261, 432
Constant elasticity utility function, 23
Consumption
  consumption-capital ratio, 169, 181
  consumption function, 65
  consumption-leisure choice, 33, 61
  consumption maximizing rate of monetary growth, 31
  consumption-output ratio, 398
  consumption real interest rate, 114
  consumption smoothing, 23, 26, 64–65, 84, 92
  consumption-wealth ratio, 166, 168, 170–175, 192–193, 195, 199–200, 202, 336–337, 340, 343–344, 349, 351–353, 366, 381–382, 392, 394, 397–398, 401, 405, 414–415, 429–431, 433, 441, 444, 456
  efficient level of, 295
  elasticity of the marginal utility of, 23, 244
  growth rate of, 160, 165–169, 171–174, 182, 185, 198, 201
  instantaneous elasticity of substitution of, 23, 119
  intertemporal elasticity of substitution of, 158
  marginal rate of substitution of consumption for leisure, 28, 33, 36
  marginal utility of, 19, 21–22, 33, 35, 44, 59, 86, 89, 107–108, 159, 169, 184, 221, 225, 228, 243, 296, 298, 338, 381, 409
  of nontraded goods, 105–109, 115–116, 119, 122, 128, 130, 135, 137–139, 145, 184–185, 194, 455–459
  random walk behavior of, 320
  rate of return on, 22, 170, 214
  of traded goods, 105–109, 115–116, 119, 126, 128, 135, 137–139, 145, 184–185, 377, 455, 457
Continuous-time vs. discrete time modeling, 5–6, 325
Cooperative behavior, 305–307
Covered interest rate parity, 406, 408
Country-specific risk, 439
Current account, 25–26, 39, 46, 55, 63–65, 67, 75, 83–87, 92–93, 101, 103–104, 108, 113, 127, 132–133, 137, 141, 163, 166, 171, 180, 194, 210, 217, 223, 226, 233, 237, 243, 257, 270, 272, 339, 348, 354–355, 403–404

Debt-capital ratio, 180
Demand shocks, 9, 24, 46, 101, 123, 145, 191, 262, 280, 425
  domestic demand shocks, 197
Dependent economy, 102–105
  endogenous growth model of, 182
  traded and nontraded capital in, 123–134
  traded vs. nontraded goods, 102–105
  two-sector model, 105–115
Dividend yield, 60
Domestic output market clearing condition, 79
Dornbusch overshooting model, 2–4
Dutch disease, 101, 145
Dynamic game theory
  closed-loop solutions, 314, 317–318
  feedback rule, 307–308
  open-loop solutions, 314–316, 318
Dynamic systems
  autonomous systems, 39, 61
  backward-looking dynamics, 2, 3
  basic monetary model, 36–42
  degenerate dynamics, 17, 26–27, 31
  external dynamics, 9
  forward-looking dynamics, 3, 65
  internal dynamics, 9
  intrinsic dynamics, 2
  "jump" variables, 3, 39, 52–53, 93
  linearization of, 39
  saddlepoint dynamics, 3, 38–42, 46, 62, 69–70, 93, 104, 110, 112, 123, 129, 132, 222, 235
  "sluggish" variables, 3, 52–53, 93, 259
  sources of sluggishness, 28, 37
  stability of, 39
  transitional dynamics, 69, 69–71, 81–83, 109–114, 129–133, 187–197, 220–224, 234–236, 267–271

Economic growth
  determinants of, 374
  effects of policy on, 151–152, 155
  endogenous growth models, 10, 152–154
  exogenous growth models, 151
  and export instability, 426, 446–448
  and government expenditure, 169–176
  knife-edge property, 153
  mean growth rate, 402, 404–405
  in neoclassical model, 151–154
  and risk, 402–406
  Solow-Swan model, 151–152, 154–155
  and taxes, 325, 359, 459–460
  variance of growth rate, 402, 404–405, 429
Economic Monetary Union, 280
Edgeworth complementary, 78, 80–81
Endogenous growth models
  accumulation of private capital as the source of growth in, 153
  adjustment cost of capital accumulation in, 156, 158, 160–161, 165
  "AK" models, 153–157, 203
  balanced growth path in, 10, 161, 346, 403

club convergence, 152
conditional convergence, 152
constant returns to scale in the factors
  being accumulated, 153, 157, 183
convergence hypothesis, 151–152, 165
and domestic productivity, 199–200
endogenous development of knowledge as
  the source of growth in, 153–154
and foreign interest rate shocks, 200–201
human capital in, 153
nonhuman capital in, 153
nonscale models of, 154–155
one-sector model of, 10, 158–164
rate of time preference in, 198
relative sector intensities in, 192–197
scale effects in, 154
stochastic growth model of, 326
transitional dynamics in, 10, 156, 163, 165,
  171, 201–204
two-sector model of, 10, 153, 157, 182–185
upward-sloping supply curve of debt in
  one-sector model, 179–182
Equipment, 123, 125, 127–128, 130, 132–
  133, 135, 137–138, 140
equilibrium dynamics of, 130–131
Equity premium puzzle, 408–409
Exchange rates, 253
  deterministic component, 373
  dynamics of, 373
  exchange market intervention, 375–376,
    413
  exchange rate management, 373, 375
  exchange rate risk, 4, 12, 40, 373–374, 404,
    406–408
  fixed vs. flexible, 279, 374–375, 421
  managed float, 375
  and nontraded consumption goods, 455–
    459
  optimal exchange rate crawl, 31, 33
  optimal regime, 375, 420
  overshooting, 2
  rate of exchange rate crawl, 31
  rate of exchange rate depreciation, 18, 26,
    31, 279, 378–379, 392–393, 399–400, 406,
    415–416
  regime, 369, 375–376
  stochastic component, 373
  target, 377–378, 386, 391, 416
  variance of, 374
Expectations
  backward-looking, 2
  forward-looking, 2–3
  rational, 2, 327
External accounts, 354–356, 425

Feldstein-Horioka puzzle, 67
Fiscal policy, 17, 28–29, 68, 177
  effects on growth, 155
  and the exchange rate, 458
  first best, 365–367
  fiscal accommodation, 29, 31, 35, 47

fiscal expansion, 287–296
fiscal instability, 447
fiscal rule, 448
fiscal shocks, 56, 69, 210–213
  international spillovers of, 280–282, 298,
    300, 309–310, 318
  international transmission of, 209–210,
    212, 231–234, 249–251, 253, 261, 267,
    284, 291, 293, 296, 306
  long-run effects of, 68–69
  mean of, 425
  and net exports, 458
  optimal integrated policy, 326, 363–367
  optimality of, 10, 17, 32, 35–36
  risk associated with, 425
  second best, 364–365
  shocks to, 388, 403
  strategic aspects of, 280–281
  wealth effects of, 56
Fisher hypothesis, 401–402
Foreign exchange risk premium, 4, 12, 373–
  374, 404, 406–408
Friedman rule, 8, 31–36, 376, 414–415
  "distorted" Friedman rule, 33

Goods market equilibrium, 216, 233, 235,
  339, 386
Golden rule, 31
Government budget constraint
  flow constraint, 25, 34, 60, 79, 217, 286,
    338, 361, 366, 381, 383–385, 388
  intertemporal constraint, 24–25, 28, 60–63,
    68, 79, 82–83, 346, 395
  steady-state constraint, 34, 236
Government budget deficit 28, 216
  balanced budget, 45, 116, 163, 173, 211,
    234, 241, 287–288, 429
  bond-financed, 25, 414
  debt-capital ratio, 180
  method of financing, 25, 399
  money-financed, 25
  optimal debt ratio, 385
Government expenditure
  as the accommodating variable, 29
  anticipated permanent change in, 55, 71
  bond financing of, 210, 338, 357, 385
  consumption expenditure, 209–210, 280–
    281, 283–306, 318–319, 365
  congestion of, 178–179
  crowding in of, 283–284, 291
  crowding out of, 211, 243, 283–284, 288–
    291
  on domestic consumption good, 77, 80, 277
  effects on growth, 155, 157
  efficient government production expendi-
    ture, 295
  externalities associated with, 172, 174, 176,
    204, 247, 280–282, 285, 301, 361–363,
    365–366
  as a fixed proportion of consumption, 169–
    170, 174

Government expenditure (cont.)
as a fixed proportion of output, 169, 362
as a fixed proportion of wealth, 169–170, 172, 203, 363, 429–430
on foreign consumption good, 77
international transmission of shocks, 231–234, 277–278
marginal utility of, 35, 169, 247, 310
maximization of government revenue, 31
mean growth rate of, 373–374, 386, 417, 430, 446
method of financing, 10–11, 204, 211, 232, 241, 280–281, 284, 300–301, 318, 362–363, 365, 388–389, 398, 414, 420
national debt, 93
negative spillover to asset markets of, 176
on nontraded goods, 107, 115–118
optimality of, 36, 47, 171, 174, 282, 299, 313
production expenditure, 209, 280–281, 283–296, 307
productivity of, 69, 177
proportional congestion of, 178
shocks to, 101, 210–213, 250, 286, 386
substitution effects of, 289, 291, 293–294, 296
tax-financed, 169, 172, 174, 176, 210
on traded goods, 56, 73, 107, 115–117
unanticipated permanent change in, 71–73, 115, 237–241
unanticipated temporary change in, 55, 73–75
utility enhancing, 157, 169–176
variance of, 373–374, 400, 417
wealth effects of, 69, 76, 115, 171, 281, 288, 291–294, 296
welfare effects of, 246–249, 293–296, 405, 411–413, 446
welfare-maximizing level of production expenditure, 293
Government policy
debt policy, 377, 384–386, 388, 392, 397, 404, 413–414
expenditure policy, 388
financial growth rule, 393
finance policy, 385–386, 389, 394, 411–413, 418
international spillovers of, 279
optimal debt policy, 418–420
optimality of, 25, 29–32
policy shocks, 101
sterilization policy, 384
stochastic intervention, 394
time invariance of, 25

Heckscher-Ohlin model, 86, 101, 142–144, 282
Hicks-neutral technological change, 118, 199, 285
Hysteresis, 56, 224

Incomplete markets, 261, 209, 377
Inflation
foreign inflation, 373, 388, 401–402
foreign inflation risk, 401–402
foreign inflation shocks, 386
mean rate of foreign inflation, 386
optimal rate of, 417
in a small open economy, 17
subsidy, 35
tax, 27, 31, 34–35, 376, 389, 398
variance of foreign inflation, 373–374
Interest parity, 374
risk-adjusted interest parity, 393
International risk sharing, 437, 454
Intertemporal envelope conditions, 184
Intertemporal relative price, 253
Intertemporal solvency condition, 63, 113–115, 131, 221, 223, 235, 260–261, 270, 286
Investment, 64–67
cost of adjustment, 55, 57–59, 61–62, 66, 78, 101, 103–104, 123, 177, 183, 187, 209, 253–255, 262, 285
criticisms of the cost of adjustment function, 58
and the current account, 454
in equipment, 123, 125, 127–128, 130, 132–133, 135, 137–138, 140
and export instability, 446–448
intersectoral adjustment costs, 9, 142–143
investment output ratio, 66, 403, 452
linear homogeneity of the adjustment cost function, 58
nontraded investment, 101, 103–105, 124, 129–131, 138, 140, 145, 182
shadow price of, 91
in structures, 123, 125, 127–130, 132–133, 135, 137, 140–141
tradability of investment goods, 101, 121, 123–124
traded investment, 101, 103–104, 121, 123–124, 126, 129, 133, 140–141, 182
IS-LM model, 87, 375

Keynes-Ramsey rule, 23, 159

Labor
average labor productivity, 130
inelastic supply of, 22–23, 37, 72, 105, 117, 158, 166, 204, 211–213, 215, 254, 256, 284–286, 288, 308, 354
labor-leisure choice, 36, 166
labor shift from traded to nontraded sector, 118–121, 128, 135, 137, 146
marginal product of, 24, 105, 127, 144, 234, 285
marginal utility of, 19, 244, 271
mobility of, 142–144, 212–213
supply of, 33, 46–47, 80, 211–212, 231–235, 242, 245, 262, 268, 271, 276, 284, 345

Laursen-Metzler effect, 12, 56, 77, 83–86, 92, 326, 348, 352, 354–355
  validity of, 84
Leisure
  consumption-leisure choice, 33, 61
  marginal utility of, 19, 21
Life-cycle income hypothesis, 65
Locomotive theory, 210
Lucas critique, 374–375

Markov processes, 328
Marshall-Lerner condition, 273
Mean-variance equilibrium, 327, 374, 378
Monetary policy, 17, 28–29
  exchange rate targeting, 377–378, 386, 391, 416
  externalities of, 279
  inflation target, 416
  interest rate target, 376, 394, 418
  monetary target, 377, 391
  open market operations, 29
  optimal, 17, 31–36, 384, 415, 419–420
  optimal interest rate rule, 375–376, 413–416, 420
  stochastic growth rule, 384
  strategic monetary policy, 279
  target rate of exchange depreciation, 416
Money
  consumption maximizing growth rate of, 31
  in the utility function, 20, 381
  interest elasticity of demand for, 31
  marginal utility of, 19, 20
  mean growth rate of, 373–374, 384, 397, 399, 406, 420
  monetary risk, 418
  monetary shocks, 386
  money-debt ratio, 397
  optimal growth rate of, 17, 29, 31–36, 47, 376, 419
  partial superneutrality of, 397
  rate of return on, 22, 379, 382
  risk-adjusted monetary growth rate, 392
  superneutrality of, 28, 376, 384–385, 398, 414
  variance of, 373–374, 399–401, 405
Mundell-Flemming model, 1, 4, 210
Mundell-Tobin effect, 398

Nash equilibrium, 12, 212, 282, 297–300, 302–303, 305–307, 309
  admissibility of, 302
  closed-loop, 317–318
  open-loop, 315–317
National budget constraint
  flow constraint, 17, 32, 36, 60, 79, 179
  intertemporal constraint, 62–64, 68, 79, 82, 196–197, 402
Noncooperative games, 11
Nontraded goods, 102–112, 114–115, 118–119, 122, 143–144, 182–184, 191, 194

Nontraded market equilibrium condition, 122, 127

One-good monetary model, 17–29
Open market operations, 29
Overlapping generations models, 8, 17, 41–42, 48, 212, 280, 376
  bequest motive, 48

Pareto optimality, 237, 281–282, 444
Perfect capital mobility, 29
Perfect financial markets, 219, 325
Perfect foresight, 6, 18, 26, 68, 146, 325
Perfect foresight equilibrium, 6, 25, 27, 29, 47
Permanent income hypothesis, 65
Portfolio analysis
  adding up condition, 343, 429–430
  constancy of shares, 327, 334, 340, 344, 385, 387, 391, 395, 402, 452, 459
  equilibrium portfolio shares, 350, 357–358, 373, 385, 429
  and fiscal shocks, 342
  home bias, 432
  international portfolio allocation, 425
  portfolio balance 87, 102, 392, 400
  share of capital, 381, 383, 387–388, 391–392, 398, 401, 416, 428, 441
  share of domestic bonds, 380, 383, 392, 398
  share of foreign bonds, 354,. 381, 383, 388, 392, 398
  share of money, 380, 383, 392, 398, 401
Productivity shocks, 24, 67, 101, 103, 211, 348, 386, 388, 403, 405–406, 426, 430, 439
Purchasing power parity, 18, 20, 31, 47, 378–379, 389
  risk-adjusted purchasing power parity, 392
Pure rate of time preference, 219

Quotas, 279

Ramsey model, 10, 283, 362
Random walk behavior, 56, 320
Rational expectations hypothesis, 6
Rational expectations models, 2–3, 327
  caveats, 3
  equilibrium in, 327
  linear stochastic models, 3
  method of undetermined coefficients, 327
  perfect foresight in, 6
Real business cycle models, 211, 253, 426, 432, 448–455
Reaction function, 298–300
Recursive preferences, 39–40
Relative price of domestic and foreign goods, 253, 262–263, 266–267, 269–270, 272, 274–278, 333
  elasticity of domestic demand, 269–270, 276–278
  elasticity of foreign demand, 269–270, 276–278

Relative price of nontraded goods, 102, 105, 109–114, 116–121, 123, 126, 128–130, 132–133, 135, 137–138, 140–142, 144–145, 183, 186, 195, 199, 201–203
  equilibrium dynamics of, 109–112, 129–130
  transitional dynamics of, 187–191
Representative agent model, 3, 6–8, 29, 48
  caveats, 7, 48
  flow budget constraint, 58, 77, 126, 158, 163, 184, 217
  intertemporal budget constraint, 6–7, 24, 27, 60, 65, 127
Ricardian equivalence, 29, 210, 232
Risk, 325–327, 334–335, 353, 373–376
  and fiscal policy, 400–401
  and foreign inflation, 401–402
  and growth, 402–406
  inflation, 401–402
  and investment, 437–439
  and monetary policy, 399–400
  and production, 439–444
Risk adjusted interest parity, 43
Risk aversion, 40, 325, 405, 409, 432–433, 439, 452
  relative risk aversion, 327, 335, 353
  risk neutrality, 383
Risk premium
  on bonds, 42–43, 390, 392, 400–401, 416
  country-specific risk premium, 43
  on foreign exchange, 4, 12, 373–374, 404, 406–408
  differential risk premium, 429

Saddlepoint behavior, 3, 38–42, 46, 62, 69–70, 93, 104, 110, 112, 123, 129, 132, 222, 235
  formal solution procedure, 49–53
  transitional dynamics, 69
  transversality conditions, 52
Savings, 66–67, 80, 83, 114, 281, 351, 433, 451–452
  private returns to, 175–176
  savings-investment balance, 300–301
  savings-output ratio, 66, 403, 451–452
  savings-wealth ratio, 352
  social returns to, 175–176
Sector-specific factors of production, 9, 55, 101–102, 142
Semi-small open economy, 77–83
Small open economy monetary model, 8
Sources of sluggishness, 28, 37
  adjustment costs of capital accumulation, 9
  costs of holding foreign assets, 8, 40–41
  overlapping generations, 8, 41–42
  recursive preferences, 39–40
  upward-sloping supply curve of debt, 9, 37, 42–47
  variable rate of time preference, 8, 17, 37–39
Stability of steady-state equilibrium, 39

Stochastic Bellman equation, 331–332
Stochastic calculus, 4, 12, 326–333
  differential generator, 331–332
  interdependency of means and variances, 329, 373
  Itô's lemma, 329–330, 379
  stochastic residual, 328
  variances being of order dt, 329
  Wiener process, 4, 326, 328–330, 373, 377–378, 395, 425
Stochastic differential equations, 328–329, 374
Stochastic growth
  mean rate of, 358–359
  small open economy of, 333–339
  and taxes, 357–363
  and terms of trade shocks, 347–357
  variance of, 359
  and welfare, 346–347, 359–361
Stochastic integrals, 329
Strategic behavior, 209, 279–283
  cooperative, 305–307
  noncooperative, 297–301
  in a two-good model, 307–314
Structures
  equilibrium dynamics of, 129–130
  structures-labor ratio, 137
Structural shocks, 101, 115–121
  demand shocks, 115–119, 123
  long-run relative price adjustment, 140–142
  permanent increase in foreign transfers, 134–138, 141, 149
  relative intensity in structures, 138–140
  supply shocks, 115, 118–121
  with two types of capital, 134–142
  welfare effects, 138
Stylized facts about the stochastic structure of the U.S. economy, 449–451
Supply shocks, 9, 101, 115, 213, 280
  domestic, 197
  multiplicative, 118
Supply-side multiplier, 232, 245

Tariffs, 9, 77–79, 86–93, 101, 145, 253, 262–264, 336, 345
  effects on the balance of trade, 276–277, 279
  effects on the capital-labor ratio, 89
  effects on consumption, 89
  effects on the current account balance, 92–93
  effects on employment, 91
  effects on imported consumption good, 77
  effects on output, 88–89
  effects on relative prices, 273–276
  effects on savings, 87, 93
  effects on the terms of trade, 87–92
  effects on the trade balance, 92–93
  expected future tariff increase, 92–93
  implementation effects, 91

news effects, 91
optimal tariff policy, 279, 282
sectoral impacts, 103
uniform tariff, 145, 167
Taxes
 on bond income, 158, 166–168, 176, 182, 203, 344
 on capital income, 76–77, 158, 166–168, 176, 182, 203, 212–213, 216, 232–233, 245, 359, 365
 capital income tax financing, 232, 234, 241, 244–245, 250, 290, 362–363
 on consumption, 158, 166, 168, 174–176, 203–204, 344, 347, 361, 366
 consumption tax financing, 365
 corporate tax, 285
 differential tax, 141, 218–219.
 distortionary tax, 29, 33–36, 157, 211–212, 225, 236, 245, 280, 282, 286–289, 290, 296, 298–302, 304–305, 318–319, 338, 415, 426
 on foreign bond income, 160–161, 168
 foreign tax credits, 216
 and growth, 155, 166–168, 325, 359
 growth-maximizing rate, 155
 on income, 25, 29, 33–36, 175, 179, 225, 289, 347, 361, 376
 on inflation, 27, 31, 34–35, 376, 389, 398
 international transmission of shocks, 209, 212
 investment tax credit, 76
 on labor income, 232
 labor income tax financing, 232, 234, 241, 245–246, 250
 long-run viability condition, 218–220
 lump sum tax, 21, 25, 27, 29, 32–33, 35, 44, 58, 63, 107, 166, 204, 212, 232, 234, 241–246, 250, 280–282, 284, 286–288, 290–292, 296–300, 302, 304–305, 318–319, 361, 376, 398–399, 414–415, 460
 mean rate of, 389, 426, 460
 optimal tax on bond income, 174
 optimal tax on capital, 77, 362–363
 optimal tax on consumption, 174
 optimal tax policy, 36, 76–77, 170, 172, 174–176, 178–179, 282, 326, 361–363, 420
 random walk behavior of, 320
 rebates, 157–158, 163, 166–168, 172, 214–245, 362, 459
 residence-based taxation, 212, 216, 218–221, 225
 source-based taxation, 212, 216, 218–222, 224–225, 233
 state-dependent, 362
 strategic tax policy, 253, 280, 320
 tax competition, 212
 tax harmonization, 212
 tax haven, 216
 tax neutrality, 173–174, 179
 tax smoothing, 325
 unanticipated permanent increase in domestic tax rate, 225–230
 viability of tax regimes, 212, 217–220, 249–250, 325, 346, 459
 and wealth, 376, 398–399, 478
 and welfare, 166–168, 230–232, 249
 welfare-maximizing rate, 155
 worldwide tax increase, 230
Terms of trade, 56, 77, 83–85, 101, 104, 134, 284, 309–310, 309, 345
 expected value, 348
 variance, 348
Terms of trade shocks, 9, 83–85, 347–379, 351, 354
 effects on the external account, 354–356
 effects on growth, 350–354, 374
 effects on taxes, 374
 effects on welfare, 347, 356–357
Three-sector models, 145–146
Time consistency, 297, 299–301, 314–315, 319–320
Tobin's q, 55–56, 59, 61–62, 65–67, 69, 157, 209, 222, 253, 255–256
Traded goods, 9–10, 105–109, 115–116, 116, 126, 128, 135, 137–139, 145, 184–185, 377, 426, 455, 457
Transitional dynamics
 in a one-good model of capital accumulation, 69–71
Transversality conditions
 in basic monetary model, 24
 in dependent economy with traded and nontraded capital, 127
 in dependent economy with traded and nontraded investment, 123
 in government consumption expenditure model with endogenous labor supply, 233
 in one-good model of capital accumulation, 60
 in one-sector endogenous growth model, 160, 162–164
 in small open economy endogenous growth model, 346
 in stochastic growth model of the world economy, 431–432
 in stochastic monetary growth model, 395
 in two-country model of adjustment costs, 254–255
 in two-country model of fiscal policy, 214–215
 in two-good model of capital accumulation, 79
 in two-good two-country model, 263–264
 in two-sector endogenous growth model, 185, 193, 196–197
 in two-sector models, 112
 with upward-sloping supply curve of debt, 44
Two-country models, 13, 41, 209–210, 249, 251–257, 326, 426–430
Two-sector models, 102–105, 182–185

Uncovered interest parity, 18, 20, 31, 79, 264, 393, 406
Uncovered interest risk differential, 40–41
Upward-sloping supply curve of debt, 5, 9, 17, 37, 42–47, 93, 157, 160, 169, 179–182
Uzawa preferences, 24, 37, 250

Variable rate of time preference, 8, 17, 37–39, 250

Wage rate
 real wage, 20–21, 24, 61, 69, 80, 214, 280
 wage rigidity, 291
 wage-rental ratio, 118
Wealth
 accumulation of, 2, 56, 66, 156, 172–173, 191, 216–217, 335, 345, 352, 354, 380, 428, 430, 432–433, 444, 452, 456, 459
 growth rate of, 168, 171–174, 195, 198, 201, 442, 438, 440–443
 marginal utility of, 21, 23, 26, 37, 45–47, 59, 61, 65–66, 69, 71, 74, 78, 80–81, 86, 89, 91, 93, 106–107, 116, 119, 133–134, 159, 184, 214–215, 220–221, 228–230, 233, 241–244, 254, 257, 263, 266–267, 272, 274, 276, 409
 national nonhuman wealth, 66, 68, 191
 response to tax changes, 228
 tax-adjusted wealth, 164, 166–167
 variance of, 429, 433, 438, 440–441, 456